# THE LAW AND THE KNOWLEDGE OF GOOD & EVIL

The Law and the Knowledge of
# GOOD & EVIL

*The Edenic Background
of the Catalytic Operation
of the Law in Paul*

Chris A. Vlachos

☙PICKWICK *Publications* • Eugene, Oregon

THE LAW AND THE KNOWLEDGE OF GOOD AND EVIL
The Edenic Background of the Catalytic Operation of the Law in Paul

Copyright © 2009 Chris A. Vlachos. All rights reserved. Except for brief quotations in critical publications or reviews, no part of this book may be reproduced in any manner without prior written permission from the publisher. Write: Permissions, Wipf & Stock, 199 W. 8th Ave., Suite 3, Eugene, OR 97401.

Pickwick Publications
A Division of Wipf and Stock Publishers
199 W. 8th Ave., Suite 3
Eugene, OR 97401

ISBN 13: 978-1-59752-864-1

*Cataloging-in-Publication data:*

Vlachos, Chris A.
    The law and the knowledge of good and evil : the edenic background of the catalytic operation of the law in Paul / Chris A. Vlachos.

    xxii + 290 p. ; 23 cm. Includes bibliographical references.

    ISBN 13: 978-1-59752-864-1

    1. Paul, the Apostle, Saint—Theology. 2. Law (Theology)—Biblical teaching. 3. Fall of man. 4. Genesis II-III—Criticism, interpretation, etc. I. Title.

BS2655 L35 .V6 2009

Manufactured in the U.S.A.

*To Doug and Jenny Moo*

# Contents

*Abbreviations* ix

1  The Power of Sin Is the Law  1

2  Interpretations of 1 Corinthians 15:56  13

3  1 Corinthians 15:56 and Its Context  45

4  The Power of Sin Is the Law: An Edenic Axiom  87

5  The Genesis Fall Narrative Revisited  131

6  A Catalytic Operation of the Law in Eden  175

7  Reflections: The Axiomatic Nature
   of the Catalytic Operation of the Law  200

8  Reflections: The Catalytic Operation
   of the Law and Paul's Assessment of the Law  222

9  Reflections: The Catalytic Operation
   of the Law and Freedom from Sin  237

*Bibliography*  255

# Abbreviations

| | |
|---|---|
| AB | Anchor Bible |
| *ABD* | *Anchor Bible Dictionary*. 6 vols. Edited by David Noel Freedman. New York: Doubleday, 1992 |
| ʾ*Abot R. Nat.* | ʾ*Abot de Rabbi Nathan* |
| ABR | Australian Biblical Review |
| ABRL | Anchor Bible Reference Library |
| ACNT | Augsburg Commentaries on the New Testament |
| AGJU | Arbeiten zur Geschichte des antiken Judentums und des Urchristentums |
| ALBO | Analecta Lovaniensia Biblica et Orientalia |
| *Alleg. Interp.* | *Allegorical Interpretation* |
| *Am.* | *Amores* |
| AnBib | Analecta biblica |
| *ANET* | *Ancient Near Eastern Texts Relating to the Old Testament*. Edited by James B. Pritchard. 3rd ed. Princeton, 1969 |
| *Ant.* | *Jewish Antiquities* |
| ANTC | Abingdon New Testament Commentaries |
| *Aph.* | *Aphorisms* |
| *Apoc. Ab.* | *Apocalypse of Abraham* |
| *Apoc. Adam* | *Apocalypse of Adam* |
| *Apoc. Mos.* | *Apocalypse of Moses* |
| *Apoc. Sedr.* | *Apocalypse of Sedrach* |
| APOT | *The Apocrypha and Pseudepigrapha of the Old Testament*. Edited by R. H. Charles. 2 vols. Oxford, 1913 |
| *ArBib* | *The Aramaic Bible: The Targums*. Edited by Kevin Cathcart, et al. 19 vols. Collegeville, MN, 1987–2003 |

| | |
|---|---|
| AUSDDS | Andrews University Seminary Doctoral Dissertation Series |
| *AUSS* | *Andrews University Seminary Studies* |
| AusSch | Ausgewählte Schriften |
| AusVerk | Auslegung und Verkündigung |
| AV | Authorized Version |
| *b. ʿAbod. Zar.* | *Babylonian (Talmud) ʿAbodah Zarah* |
| *b. Bat.* | *Babylonian (Talmud) Baba Batra* |
| *b. Ber.* | *Babylonian (Talmud) Berakot* |
| *b. ʿErub.* | *Babylonian (Talmud) ʿErubin* |
| *b. Moʿed Qaṭ.* | *Babylonian (Talmud) Moʿed Qaṭan* |
| *b. Ned.* | *Babylonian (Talmud) Nedarim* |
| *b. Qidd.* | *Babylonian (Talmud) Qiddušin* |
| *b. Šabb.* | *Babylonian (Talmud) Šabbat* |
| *b. Sanh.* | *Babylonian (Talmud) Sanhedrin* |
| *b. Sukkah* | *Babylonian (Talmud) Sukkah* |
| *b. Taʿan.* | *Babylonian (Talmud) Taʿanit* |
| *b. Tem.* | *Babylonian (Talmud) Temurah* |
| *Bar.* | *Baruch* |
| BCBC | Believers Church Bible Commentary |
| BDAG | Frederick W. Danker, et al. *Greek-English Lexicon of the New Testament and Other Early Christian Literature*. 3rd ed. Chicago: University of Chicago Press, 2000 |
| BDB | Francis S. Brown, et al. *A Hebrew and English Lexicon of the Old Testament*. Oxford: Clarendon, 1977 |
| BDR | Blass, F. A., et al. *A Greek Grammar of the New Testament and Other Early Christian Literature*. Chicago: University of Chicago Press, 1961 |
| BET | Biblical Exegesis and Theology |
| BEvT | Beiträge zur evangelischen Theologie |
| BFCT | Beiträge zur christlicher Theologie |
| *BHS* | *Biblia Hebraica Stuttgartensia*. Edited by Karl Elliger and Wilhelm Rudolph. Stuttgart: Württembergische Bibelanstalt, 1983 |
| BHT | Beiträge zu historischen Theologie |
| *Bib* | *Biblica* |
| *BibInt* | *Biblical Interpretation* |

| | |
|---|---|
| BibS(N) | Biblische Studien |
| BIS | Biblical Interpretation Series |
| BJRL | *Bulletin of the John Rylands University Library of Manchester* |
| BKNT | Bibel-Kommentar zum Neuen Testament |
| BNTC | Black's New Testament Commentaries |
| BRev | *Bible Review* |
| BRS | Bible Resource Series |
| Bsr | Bibliothèque de sciences religieuses |
| BTal. | *The Babylonian Talmud*. 35 vols. Edited and translated by I. Epstein. London: Soncino, 1935–1952 |
| BU | Biblische Untersuchungen |
| BWANT | Beiträge zur Wissenschaft vom Alten und Neuen Testament |
| BZAW | Beihefte zur Zeitschrift für die alttestamentliche Wissenschaft |
| BZNW | Beihefte zur Zeitschrift für die neutestamentliche Wissenschaft |
| CB | The Century Bible |
| CBC | Cambridge Bible Commentary |
| CBQ | *Catholic Biblical Quarterly* |
| CC | Continental Commentaries |
| CD | Collection Didaskalia |
| C. du ep. Pelag. | *Against the Two Letters of the Pelagians* |
| CEB | Commentaire Évangélique de la Bible |
| CFTL | Clark's Foreign Theological Library |
| CGTC | Cambridge Greek Testament Commentary |
| CGTSC | Cambridge Greek Testament for Schools and Colleges |
| CNT | Commentaire du Nouveau Testament |
| ConC | Concordia Commentary |
| Cont. | *On Continence* |
| CPS | Clarendon Plato Series |
| CQ | *Covenant Quarterly* |
| CR | *Classical Review* |
| CSEL | Corpus scriptorum ecclesiasticorum latinorum |
| CSJH | Chicago Studies in the History of Judaism |
| CTJ | *Calvin Theological Journal* |

| | |
|---|---|
| *CurTM* | *Currents in Theology and Mission* |
| DBS | Daily Bible Studies |
| *Decal.* | *On the Decalogue* |
| *Demon.* | *Demonax* |
| *Deut. Rab.* | *Deuteronomy Rabah* |
| *Diatr.* | *Diatribai (Discourses)* |
| diss. | dissertation |
| *Diss.* | *Dissertationes* |
| *Div. Quaest.* | *Eighty Three Different Questions* |
| *Div. Quaest. Simpl.* | *To Simplician on Various Questions* |
| DPL | *Dictionary of Paul and His Letters*. Edited by Gerald F. Hawthorne and Ralph P. Martin. Downers Grove, IL: InterVarsity, 1933 |
| DSSSE | *The Dead Sea Scrolls Study Edition*. Edited and translated by Florentino García Martínez et al. 2 vols. Leiden: Brill, 1997–1998 |
| EBC | *Expositor's Bible Commentary*. Edited by Frank E. Gaebelein. 12 vols. Grand Rapids: Zondervan, 1990 |
| EBib | Études bibliques |
| EC | Epworth Commentaries |
| ECNT | Baker Exegetical Commentary of the New Testament |
| EDNT | *Exegetical Dictionary of the New Testament*. Edited by Horst Balz and Gerhard Schneider. Grand Rapids, 1990–1993 |
| EGT | *The Expositor's Greek New Testament*. Edited by W. R. Nicoll. 5 vols. London: Hodder & Stoughton, 1900; reprint, Grand Rapids, 1970 |
| *EgT* | *Église et Théologie* |
| EKKNT | Evangelisch-katholischer Kommentar zum Neuen Testament |
| *En.* | *Enoch* |
| *Ep.* | *Epistles* |
| *epist. ad Cor.* | *epistulas ad Corinthios* |
| *epist. ad Rom.* | *epistulam ad Romanos.* |
| *epistolae ad Cor.* | *epistolae ad Corinthios* |
| EQ | *Evangelical Quarterly* |
| ESV | English Standard Version |
| ETL | *Ephemerides theologicae lovanienses* |

| | |
|---|---|
| *ETR* | *Etudes théologiques et religieuses* |
| ETSM | Evangelical Theological Society Monograph |
| *EvT* | *Evangelische Theologie* |
| *ExAud* | *Ex auditu* |
| *Exod. Rab.* | *Exodus Rabah* |
| *Exp. Quaest. Rom.* | *Expositio Quarundam Propositionum ex Epistula ad Romanos* |
| *ExpTim* | *Expository Times* |
| FB | Forschung zur Bibel |
| FC | Fathers of the Church |
| FRLANT | Forschungen zur Religion and Literatur des Alten und Neuen Testaments |
| GBS | Grove Biblical Series |
| *Gen. Rab.* | *Genesis Rabah* |
| *Geogr.* | *Geography* |
| Ggs. | Gegensatz |
| *Gk. Apoc. Ezra* | *Greek Apocalypse Ezra* |
| GKC | *Gesenius' Hebrew Grammar*. Edited by E. Kautzsch. Translated by A. E. Cowley. Oxford: Clarendon, 1910 |
| *Gos. Phil.* | *Gospel of Philip* |
| *Grat.* | *On Grace and Free Will* |
| *Greg* | *Gregorianum* |
| GTA | Göttinger theologischer Arbeiten |
| *HALOT* | Koehler, L., et al. *The Hebrew and Aramaic Lexicon of the Old Testament*. 5 vols. Edited by Ludwig Koehler, Walter Baumgartner, and J. J. Stamm. Leiden: Brill, 1994–2000 |
| *Hel. Syn. Pr.* | *Hellenistic Synagogal Prayers* |
| Herm. *Sim.* | Shepherd of Hermas, *Similitude* |
| *HeyJ* | *Heythrop Journal* |
| *Hist. Rech.* | *History of the Rechabites* |
| HNT | Handbuch zum Neuen Testament |
| *Hom. 1 Cor.* | *Homilies on the Epistles of Paul to the Corinthians* |
| HSAT | Die Heilige Schrift des Alten Testaments |
| HSM | Harvard Semitic Monographs |
| HSMP | Harvard Semitic Museum Publications |
| HTKNT | Herder's theologischer Kommentar zum Neuen Testament |

| | |
|---|---|
| HTS | Harvard Theological Studies |
| *HUCA* | *Hebrew Union College Annual* |
| HUT | Hermeneutische Untersuchung zur Theologie |
| IBC | Interpretation: A Bible Commentary for Teaching and Preaching |
| *IBHS* | *An Introduction to Biblical Hebrew Syntax.* B. Waltke and M. O'Connor. Winona Lake, IN: Eisenbrauns, 1990 |
| *IBS* | *Irish Biblical Studies* |
| ICC | International Critical Commentary |
| *Int* | *Interpretation* |
| ITC | International Theological Commentary |
| *ITQ* | *Irish Theological Quarterly* |
| IVPNTCS | The IVP New Testament Commentary Series |
| JB | Jerusalem Bible |
| *JBQ* | *Jewish Biblical Quarterly* |
| *JBL* | *Journal of Biblical Literature* |
| *JETS* | *Journal of the Evangelical Theological Society* |
| JPS | Jewish Publication Society |
| JPSTC | Jewish Publication Society Torah Commentary |
| *JSNT* | *Journal for the Study of the New Testament* |
| JSNTSup | Journal for the Study of the New Testament: Supplement Series |
| *JSOT* | *Journal for the Study of the Old Testament* |
| JSOTSup | Journal for the Study of the Old Testament: Supplement Series |
| JSPSup | Journal for the Study of the Pseudepigrapha: Supplement Series |
| *JSS* | *Journal of Semitic Studies* |
| JTal. | Jacob Neusner, editor, *The Talmud of the Land of Israel: A Preliminary Translation and Explanation.* 35 vols. Translated by Zahary Tzvee et al. CSJH. Chicago: University of Chicago Press, 1982–1994 |
| JTS | *Journal of Theological Studies* |
| Jub. | *Jubilees* |
| KB | *Keilinschriftliche Bibliothek.* Edited by Eberhard Schrader. 6 vols. Berlin: Rauther & Richard, 1889–1915 |

| | |
|---|---|
| KEHNT | Kurzgefasstes exegetisches Handbuch zum Neuen Testament |
| KEK | Kritisch-exegetischer Kommentar über das Neue Testament (Meyer-Kommentar) |
| KNT | Kommentar zum Neuen Testament |
| L.A.B. | *Liber antiquitatum biblicarum* (Pseudo Philo) |
| L.A.E. | *Life of Adam and Eve* |
| LB | *Linguistica Biblica* |
| LCC | Library of Christian Classics |
| LCL | Loeb Classical Library |
| LD | Lectio divina |
| *Leg.* | *Allegorical Interpretation* |
| *Lev. Rab.* | *Leviticus Rabah* |
| LPS | Library of Pauline Studies |
| LS | *Louvain Studies* |
| LSJ | H. G. Liddell, et al. *A Greek-English Lexicon*. 9th ed. with revised supplement. Oxford: Clarendon, 1996 |
| LTPM | Louvain Theological and Pastoral Monographs |
| *Lucil.* | *Ad Lucilium* |
| LW | *Luther's Works*. Edited by Jaraslov Pelikan. 55 vols. Translated by George Schick et al. Saint Louis; Philadelphia, 1955–1976 |
| LXX | Septuagint |
| LXXR | *Septuaginta*. Edited by Alfred Rahlfs. Stuttgart: Württembergische Bibelanstalt, 1979 |
| *m. Pirqe ʾAbot* | *Mishnah Pirqe ʾAbot* |
| *Mek.* | *Mekhilta* |
| *Mek. Exod.* | *Mekilta Exodus* |
| *Mem.* | *Memorabilia* |
| *Mctam.* | *Metamorphoses* |
| *Midr. Deut.* | *Midrash Deuteronomy* |
| *Midr. Eccl.* | *Midrash Ecclesiastes* |
| *Midr. Prov.* | *Midrash Proverbs* |
| *Midr. Pss.* | *Midrash Psalms* |
| *Midr. Song* | *Midrash Song of Solomon* |

| | |
|---|---|
| *Mish. Tor.* | Moses Maimonides, *The Code of Maimonides (Mishneh Torah)*. 14 vols. Translated by Jacob J. Rabinowitz et al. New Haven: Yale University Press, 1949 |
| MIT | Massachusetts Institute of Technology |
| MM | James Hope Moulton and George Milligan. *The Vocabulary of the Greek Testament: Illustrated from the Papyri and Other Non-Literary Sources.* London, 1930. Reprint, Grand Rapids: Eerdmans, 1982 |
| MNTC | Moffatt New Testament Commentary |
| *Mor.* | *Moralia* |
| *Mor. Eccl.* | *On the Morals of the Catholic Church* |
| MT | Masoretic Text |
| *MTS* | *Marburger Theologische Studien* |
| NA$^{27}$ | *Novum Testamentum Graece*. Edited by Barbara Aland et al. 27th rev. ed. Stuttgart: Stuttgart: Württembergische Bibelanstalt, 2001 |
| NAB | New American Bible |
| NAC | New American Commentary |
| NASB | New American Standard Bible |
| NCB | New Century Bible |
| NEB | New English Bible |
| NEchtB | Neue Echter Bibel |
| NET | New English Translation |
| *NewDocs* | *New Documents Illustrating Early Christianity.* 9 vols. Edited by G. R. S. Horsley and S. Llewelyn. North Ryde, N. S. W.: Macquarie University: Ancient History Documentary Research Center, 1981– |
| *NHL* | *Nag Hammadi Library in English*. Edited by James M. Robinson. 3rd ed. Leiden: Brill, 1988 |
| *NIB* | *The New Interpreter's Bible: General Articles and Introduction, Commentary, and Reflections for Each Book of the Bible, Including the Apocryphal/Deuterocanonical Books.* 12 vols. Edited by Leander E. Keck. Nashville: Abingdon, 1994–2002 |
| NIBC | New International Biblical Commentary |

| | |
|---|---|
| NICNT | New International Commentary on the New Testament |
| NICOT | New International Commentary on the Old Testament |
| *NIDNTT* | *New International Dictionary of New Testament Theology*. Edited by Colin Brown. 4 vols. Grand Rapids, 1975–1985 |
| *NIDOTTE* | *The New International Dictionary of Old Testament Theology and Exegesis*. 5 vols. Edited by W. A. VanGemeren. Grand Rapids: Zondervan, 1997 |
| NIGTC | New International Greek Testament Commentary |
| NIV | New International Version |
| NJB | New Jerusalem Bible |
| *NovT* | *Novum Testamentum* |
| NovTSup | Novum Testamentum Supplements |
| *NPNF*[1] | *Nicene and Post-Nicene Fathers*, Series 1 |
| NRSV | New Revised Standard Version |
| NSBT | New Studies in Biblical Theology |
| NTAbh | Neutestamentliche Abhandlungen |
| NTC | New Testament Commentary |
| NTD | Das Neue Testament Deutsch |
| NTG | New Testament Guides |
| NTL | New Testament Library |
| NTOA | Novum Testamentum et Orbis Antiquus |
| NTR | New Testament Readings |
| *NTS* | *New Testament Studies* |
| NTTh | New Testament Theology |
| *Num. Rab.* | *Numbers Rabah* |
| NZSTR | Neue Zeitschrift für systematicshe Theologie und Religions-philosophie |
| OTD | Oxford Theological Documents |
| OTL | Old Testament Library |
| *OTP* | *Old Testament Pseudepigrapha*. 2 vols. Edited by James H. Charlesworth. New York: Doubleday, 1983–1985 |
| *Pan.* | *Panarion* (*Adversus haereses*) |
| PBTM | Paternoster Biblical and Theological Monographs |
| *Pesiq. Rab.* | *Pesiqta Rabbati* |

| | |
|---|---|
| *Pesiq. Rab. Kah.* | *Pesiqta de Rab Kahana* |
| PFES | Publications of the Finnish Exegetical Society |
| *PG* | *Patrologia graeca [= Patrologiae cursus completus: Series graeca]*. 162 vols. Edited by J.-P. Migne. Paris: Migne, 1857–1886 |
| *Pirqe R. El.* | *Pirqe Rabbi Eliezer* |
| PNit | De prediking van het Nieuwe Testament |
| PNT | Pillar New Testament |
| *Prot.* | *Protagoras* |
| *PRSt* | *Perspectives in Religious Studies* |
| *Pss. Sol.* | *Psalms of Solomon* |
| PVTG | Pseudepigrapha Veteris Testameanti Graeca |
| *PWCJS* | *Proceedings of the World Congress of Jewish Studies* |
| QD | Quaestiones disputatae |
| QG | Questions and Answers on Genesis |
| RB | Revue biblique |
| REB | Revised English Bible |
| *Resp.* | *De republica* |
| ResQ | Restoration Quarterly |
| RevExp | Review and Expositor |
| RevScRel | *Revue des sciences religieuses* |
| *Rhet. Her.* | *Rhetorica ad Herennium* |
| RL | Revidierte Lutherbibel |
| RL | *Religion and Life* |
| RNTS | Reading the New Testament Series |
| RSR | *Revue des sciences religieuses* |
| RSV | Revised Standard Version |
| *RTR* | *Reformed Theological Review* |
| SBEC | Studies in the Bible and Early Christianity |
| SBL | Society of Biblical Literature |
| SBLDS | Society of Biblical Literature Dissertation Series |
| SBLEJL | Society of Biblical Literature Early Judaism and Its Literature |
| SBLSBS | Society of Biblical Literature Source for Biblical Study |
| *SBLSP* | *Society of Biblical Literature Seminar Papers* |
| SBLSymS | Society of Biblical Literature Symposium Series |
| SBM | Stuttgarter biblische Monographien |
| SBT | Studies in Biblical Theology |

| | |
|---|---|
| SBTE | Studien zur Bedeutung der Thora für die pauline Ethik |
| SchNT | Die Schriften des Neuen Testaments |
| *SEÅ* | *Svensk exegetisk årsbok* |
| SFSHJ | South Florida Studies in the History of Judaism |
| SHBC | Smyth and Helwys Bible Commentary |
| *Sifr. d'be Rab.* | *Siphre d'be Rab. Fasciculus primus: Siphre ad Numeros adjecto* Siphre zutta. Edited by H. S. Horovitz. Jerusalem, 1976 |
| *Sifr. Deut.* | *Sifre Deuteronomy* |
| *Sifr. Lev.* | *Sifre Leviticus* |
| *Sifr. Num.* | *Sifre Numbers* |
| SJT | Scottish Journal of Theology |
| SKKNT | Stuttgarter kleiner Kommentar. Neues Testament |
| SMBen | Série monographique de Benedictina: Section paulinienne |
| SNT | Studien zum Neuen Testament |
| SNTSMS | Society for New Testament Studies Monograph Series |
| SNTW | Studies of the New Testament and Its World |
| *Sol.* | *Solon* |
| SP | Sacra Pagina |
| SPCIC | *Studiorum Paulinorum Congressus Internationalis Catholicus* |
| *Spec.* | *On the Special Laws* |
| SPhilo | *Studia philonica* |
| *Spir. et Litt.* | *On the Spirit and the Letter* |
| SR | *Studies in Religion* |
| SSN | Studia Semitica Neerlandica |
| ST | *Studia Theologica* |
| Str-B | H. L. Strack and P. Billerbeck. *Kommentar zum Neuen Testament aus Talmud und Midrasch*. 6 vols. Munich: Beck, 1922–1961 |
| *SubBi* | *Subsidia Biblica* |
| *SumT* | Thomas Aquinas. *Summa Theologiae: Latin Text and English Translation, Introductions, Notes, Appendices and Glossaries*. 61 vols. Edited by Thomas Gilbey. New York: McGraw-Hill, 1964–1981 |

| | |
|---|---|
| *Syb. Or.* | *Sibylline Oracles* |
| *T. Ab.* | *Testament of Abraham* |
| *T. Ash.* | *Testament of Asher* |
| *Tanh. Gen.* | *TanHuma Genesis* |
| *Tanh. Lev.* | *TanHuma Leviticus* |
| *Tarbiz* | *Tarbiz* |
| TB | Theologische Bücherei: Neudrucke und Berichte aus dem 20. Jahrhundert |
| TBC | Torch Bible Commentaries |
| *TBib.* | *Theologika Biblia* |
| TDNT | *Theological Dictionary of the New Testament.* 10 vols. Edited by Gerhard Kittel and Gerhard Friedrich. Translated by Geoffrey W. Bromiley. Grand Rapids: Eerdmans, 1964–1976 |
| TDOT | *Theological Dictionary of the Old Testament.* 14 vols. Edited by G. J. Botterweck and Helmer Ringgren. Translated by J. T. Willis, et al. Grand Rapids: Eerdmans, 1964–2004 |
| TDTRSECJ | The Third Durham-Tübingen Research Symposium on Earliest Christianity and Judaism (Durham, September, 1994) |
| TEV | Today's English Version |
| *Tg.* | *Targum* |
| *Tg. Neb.* | *Targum of the Prophets* |
| *Tg. Neof.* | *Targum Neofiti* |
| *Tg. Onq.* | *Targum Onqelos* |
| *Tg. Ps.-J.* | *Targum Pseudo-Jonathan* |
| TEH | Theologische Existenz Heute |
| TEV | Today's English Version |
| TG | *Theologie und Glaube* |
| *Them* | *Themelios* |
| THKNT | Theologischer Handkommentar zum Neuen Testament |
| *ThLZ* | *Theologische Literaturzeitung* |
| *ThT* | *Theologisch Tijdschrift* |
| TI | Text and Interpretation |
| TJ | *Trinity Journal* |

| | |
|---|---|
| TLNT | Ceslas Spicq. *Theological Lexicon of the New Testament*. 3 vols. Translated and edited by James D. Ernest. Peabody, MA: Hendrickson, 1994 |
| TLOT | *Theological Lexicon of the Old Testament*. 3 vols. Edited by Ernst Jenni and Claus Westermann. Translated by M. E. Biddle. Peabody, MA: Hendrickson, 1997 |
| TNIV | Today's New International Version |
| TNTC | Tyndale New Testament Commentaries |
| Tosef. | *The Tosefta: Translated from the Hebrew*. 6 vols. Edited by Jacob Neusner and Richard S. Sarason. Hoboken, NJ: Ktav, 1986 |
| TOTC | Tyndale Old Testament Commentaries |
| TPINTC | *TPI New Testament Commentaries* |
| TRE | *Theologische Realenzyklopädie*. 36 vols. Edited by Gerhard Krause and Gerhard Müller. Berlin: de Gruyter, 1976–2004 |
| TSAJ | Texte und Studien zum antiken Judentum |
| TSF | Theological Students Fellowship |
| TTZ | *Trierer Theologische Zeitschrift* |
| TUMSR | Trinity University Monograph Series in Religion |
| TVM | Theologische Verlagsgemeinschaft: Monographien |
| TWNT | *Theologische Wörterbuch zum Neues Testament*. 10 vols. Edited by Gerhard Kittel and Gerhard Friedrich. Stuttgart. Grand Rapids, 1933– |
| TynBul | *Tyndale Bulletin* |
| TZ | *Theologische Zeitschrift* |
| UBSHS | UBS Handbook Series |
| UCPNES | University of California Publications: Near Eastern Studies |
| VD | *Verbum domini* |
| vg. | *Vulgate* |
| VSOD | *Veröffentlichungen der Stiftung Oratio Dominica* |
| VT | *Vetus Testamentum* |
| VTSup | Vetus Testamentum Supplement |
| WBC | Word Bible Commentary |
| WBComp | Westminster Bible Companion |
| WC | Westminster Commentaries |

| | | |
|---|---|---|
| WMANT | | Wissenschaftliche Monographien zum Alten und Neuen Testament |
| *WTJ* | | *Westminster Theological Journal* |
| WUNT | | Wissenschaftliche Untersuchungen zum Neuen Testament |
| *y. Qidd* | | *Jerusalem (Talmud) Qiddušin* |
| *y. Yoma* | | *Jerusalem (Talmud) Yoma* |
| ZBK | | Zürcher Bibelkommentare |
| *ZNW* | | *Zeitschrift für die neutestamentliche Wissenschaft und die Kunde der älteren Kirche* |
| *ZTK* | | *Zeitschrift für Theologie und Kirche* |
| *ZWB* | | *Zürcher Werkkommentare zur Bibel* |

# 1

## The Power of Sin Is the Law

ONE OUGHT NOT BE surprised that Friedrich Horn, in his examination of 1 Cor 15:56, titled his article, "1 Korinther 15,56—ein exegetischer Stachel," or that Ulrich Wilckens in his study of Paul and the law expressed what has become a classic statement regarding the passage, "Im dortigen Kontext ist dieser Satz in seiner gedrängten, sentenzhaften Kürze rätselhaft."[1] The verse appears at the conclusion of Paul's carefully argued apologetic for the resurrection of Christ and the believer. After two Old Testament quotations triumphantly and poetically exulting in the eschatological defeat of death (vv. 54–55) and before an emotional outburst of gratitude for this victory (v. 57), Paul makes an unexpected, unexplained, and, what would appear to be a spontaneously generated remark concerning the relation between law, sin, and death: "The sting of death is sin, and the power of sin is the law" (v. 56).[2]

To virtually every commentator, and indeed to most every reader who pauses to ponder it,[3] the verse gives the impression of being abrupt and oddly situated.[4] Rather than providing a logical and meaningful punch-line to the step-by-step argument that led up to it, which would be expected of a statement occupying such a climactic position,[5] the verse

---

1. Horn, "Stachel," 88; Wilckens, "Entwicklung," 161.

2. English Bible and Old Testament Apocrypha quotations are taken from the NRSV unless otherwise noted.

3. It is not just exegetes who are caught up short by 1 Cor 15:56. Fee aptly notes, "Anyone who has heard this paragraph read at a Christian funeral senses the dissonance these words seem to bring to the argument" (*First Corinthians*, 805).

4. The unexpected reference to the law, Schnelle notes, leaves the interpreter with the feeling that "the verse is out of place here" (*Paul*, 231).

5. Söding remarks that vv. 50–58 signal "einen Höhepunkt des Gedankengangs"

2  THE LAW AND THE KNOWLEDGE OF GOOD AND EVIL

seems "gratuitous,"[6] "utterly out of place,"[7] and "semble n'avoir aucun lien logique avec ce qui précède."[8] Indeed, except for the difficulty itself that the verse poses, nothing, it might seem, would be lost were v. 56 to be eliminated from the chapter.[9] Its omission would appear to give a far smoother and more logical reading with the thanksgiving for victory in v. 57 following immediately after the declaration of victory in vv. 54–55. As it is, however, the verse "bulges awkwardly out of its context and is uncomfortably anticlimactic,"[10] and compared to the lyrical expressions of vv. 54–55 and the exuberant doxological celebration of v. 57, the verse seems bland.[11]

## THE RIDDLE OF 1 CORINTHIANS 15:56

1 Corinthians 15:56 thus is puzzling,[12] or, to use Horn's metaphor, it is like a scorpion or thorn that pricks the hand of the approaching exegete. The difficulty resides not only in understanding the verse, though the interpreter can turn to Romans 5–7, where the triad of law, sin, and death recurs and interpret the passage with the help of the parallel thoughts found there. The challenge lies in explaining its appearance and significance in 1 Corinthians 15. While 15:21–22 might prepare for the sin-death nexus in v. 56a,[13] there appears to be no precursor to *law* in the

---

("Kraft," 77).

6. Sampley, "First Corinthians," 989.

7. Horsley, *1 Corinthians*, 215. Weiss considers the verse to be "eine fremde Exegese" (*Korintherbrief*, 380). Schick deems it "losgelöst" (*Allen*, 307).

8. Matand Bulembat, *Noyau et enjeux*, 124. Schrage senses "eine gewisse Beziehungslosigkeit" (*Korinther*, 4:366). Räisänen agrees: "It has no connection with the main thrust of the section" (*Paul and the Law*, 143). Likewise Horn: "Eine Beziehung zum Kontext kann nur mühevoll hergestellt werden" ("Stachel," 103).

9. See García Pérez, "1 Co 15,56," 405.

10. Thielman, "Coherence," 249. Elsewhere Thielman notes that the verse "is as anticlimactic as it is unexpected" (*Paul and the Law*, 107). Indeed, at surface level, the verse appears to Orr and Walther as an "amazing anticlimax" (*1 Corinthians*, 352).

11. Compared to the enthusiastic and rhetorical tone of the surrounding verses, v. 56, according to Weiß, falls with a theological thud (*Korintherbrief*, 380). Lietzmann dubs the verse "nüchterne" (*Korinther*, 88).

12. Klauck dubs it a "Chiffre" (*Korintherbrief*, 122).

13. Of the key terms in v. 56 only νόμος lacks precedent in the chapter. The terms θάνατος (vv. 21, 26, 55, 56), κεςντρον (vv. 55, 56), and δυςναμι (vv. 24, 43, 56) belong

context leading up to v. 56b,[14] nor to (what we will argue is) a reference to the *catalytic* operation of the law.[15] It comes as a "surprise,"[16] or worse, appears to be a virtual "non sequitur."[17] This is the real "puzzler," according to Fee, "especially since in this Gentile community the relationship of sin to the law has not seemed to emerge as a problem.

Nowhere do the issues that have arisen, either between him and them or between them internally reflect concern over the law."[18] Indeed,

---

to the chapter's lexical stock. The closest antecedent of νόμος is in 1 Cor 9:20.

14. "That the sting of death is sin is very easy to understand," notes Elias. "It is not so easy at first sight to understand the introduction here of St. Paul's favorite doctrine that the strength of sin is the law" (*First Corinthians*, 185; see also Sellin, *Streit*, 227; Díaz Rodelas, *Pablo*, 27; Matand Bulembat, "Noyau et enjeux," 124 n. 117; Horn, "Stachel," 93-94).

15. By "catalytic" we mean *that which sets in motion*. Although the term "causative" is often used to refer to the sin-simulating operation of the law (see, e.g., Räisänen, *Paul and the Law*, 143), the term "catalytic" will be the term used throughout the present study since, as will be noted, the law is not the *cause* of sin, but the *catalyst* by which serpent/sin sets transgression in motion (see Weima, "Function," 231 n. 35). The term "catalytic" will safeguard Paul's concern that sin, not law, is the villain, as Lagrange carefully notes: "Le mal qui en est résulté ne provient pas de la loi elle-même; mais du péché, qui est le vrai coupable" (*Romains*, 164; note also Martin's corrective: "It is . . . incorrect to say that the law causes men to sin; . . . *sin uses the law to cause men to sin*" [*Christ and the Law*, 97; italics mine]).

16. Conzelmann, *1 Corinthians*, 293. Söding remarks, "Dass die gesetzeskritische Sentenz in 1 Kor 15 überraschend kommt, läßt sich nicht leugnen" ("Kraft," 76). For Müller the verse enters "abrupt und ohne eigentliche inhaltliche Vorbereitung durch den Kontext" ("Leiblichkeit," 240).

17. Hays, *First Corinthians*, 277. Gertner observes that "the sequence of his argument is, on the face of it, lacking in logical sequence" ("Midrashim," 282). For Sampley, the verse "appears to have nothing to do with any controversy the Corinthians seem to be having" ("First Corinthians," 989).

18. *First Corinthians*, 806. Spörlein notes that vv. 55-58 "zeigen keine polemische Absicht und tragen auch sonst nichts bei für eine Näherbestimmung der korinthischen Auferstehungsleugnung und deren Urheber" (*Leugnung*, 107-8). Wilckens likewise observes that "in den Thessalonicher- und Korintherbriefen sehen wir vielmehr, daß innerhalb der konstituierten Gemeinden selbst die Gesetzesfrage kein Thema gewesen ist, das gezielter und ausführlicher Behandlung bedurft hätte. Offenbar war die Gesetzesfreiheit hier die mehr oder weniger selbstverständliche Basis" ("Entwicklung," 158; see also idem, "Statements," 18-20; Schlatter, 446; Thurén, *Derhetorizing*, 104-5). This appears to have been the case even though there was clearly a Jewish presence among the Christian community in Corinth (as evidenced by 1 Cor 7:18; 10:32; 12:13; see Horrell, *Social Ethos*, 91-92; Verburg, *Endzeit*, 246-47). In addition, though Paul appears to have had opponents in Corinth (see, e.g., 2 Corinthians 10-12) it would be difficult at best, based on the scarcity of references in 1 Corinthians, to identify them as legalists (as is

elsewhere in the letter the law appears to be cast in a favorable light.[19] Here, however, "law" is associated with "sin" and "death," entities belonging to the present evil age that are destined to pass away.

How, then, do these words relate to its chapter or to the letter as a whole, and what explains their appearance in a chapter in which sin had hardly figured,[20] and law not at all?[21] Would such a theological aside even have been intelligible to the Corinthians, who, unlike readers today, would have been unable to turn back a few pages to Romans where the relationship between law and sin is explicated at much greater length?[22] And what significance could this enigmatic verse have had for Paul's readers? Indeed, what significance can it have for readers today, especially in light of the recent perspectives of Paul and the law and the current interest in law as a topic of biblical theology?

## THE NEGLECT OF 1 CORINTHIANS 15:56

Considering that 1 Cor 15:56 is regarded as among "the most problematic in the Pauline corpus,"[23] it might be expected that it has been the focus of considerable exegetical and theological investigation. This has not

---

attempted, for example, by Manson, *Studies*, 194; Barrett, *First Corinthians*, 87–88; idem, *Essays*, 32–33; Lüdemann, *Opposition*, 76–78). The fact that one must squint to read law issues between the lines of 1 Corinthians indicates that the law was probably not a significant issue in Corinth at the time of Paul's letter.

19. See 1 Cor (7:19); 9:8–9, 20–21; 14:21, 34. Wilckens observes in 1 Corinthians "daß ... die Bewahrung der Toragebote auch für Heidenchristen von positiver Bedeutung ist" ("Entwicklung," 158; see also Stanley, *Arguing*, 111).

20. Besides v. 56, ἁμαρτία occurs in 15:3, 17 (in the plural). The verb ἁμαρτάνω occurs in 6:18 (2x); 7:28 (2x), 36; 8:12 (2x); 15:34. The noun ἁμάρτημα appears in 6:18.

21. This is Söding's question: "Dann aber ergibt sich das Problem, wie die offenkundig massive Gesetzeskritik von 1 Kor 15,56 zustandekommt und wie sie aus ihrem genuinen, nicht unmittelbar durch nomistische Kontroversen bestimmten Kontext heraus verstanden werden kann" ("Kraft," 76). Gertner finds this to be the Gordian knot: "What this, his opinion about the law,' has to do with his immediately preceding theme of 'death' has as yet remained an unsolved problem" ("Midrashim," 283). Matand Bulembat laconically asks, "D'où provient cette intuition paulinienne?" *(Noyau et enjeu.x,* 124 n. 117).

22. See Carter, *Power*, 75. Nuanced differently, might Paul have failed to make his point to the Corinthians? Both Söding and Hollander and Holleman pose this question to set up their respective studies (Söding, "Kraft," 74; Hollander and Holleman, "Relationship," 272).

23. Hollander and Holleman, "Relationship," 270.

been the case.[24] Although the commentaries (to lesser or greater degrees) dutifully address it,[25] it has not received the overall consideration that it deserves. It is found, for instance, in the Scripture indexes of most studies of Pauline theology, but it rarely receives the attention that Paul's remarks in Romans or Galatians enjoy. Most often it is merely cited as a parallel to Rom 5:20; 7:5, 7–11, which similarly concern the relationship of law to sin.[26] Likewise, only a few scholarly journal articles have targeted the verse,[27] though this academic genre offers an ideal forum to grapple with the questions that such a verse raises. And no monograph exists with 1 Cor 15:56 in its title or as its main subject, though its themes of law, sin, and death would provide stimulating theological plot lines, especially at a time when the study of Paul and the law "has stepped again into the focal point of the discussion."[28]

Why a verse that offers such a challenge has attracted so little attention is actually not as puzzling as the verse itself. Since the verse contains in embryo notions that appear fully developed in Romans, it is often viewed as a brief seconding motion to these other explicit statements.

24. As Morissette notes (see "Midrash," 161).

25. As it is, many commentators confine themselves primarily to interpreting the verse rather than attempting to explain how the statement functions in its context (see, e.g., Orr and Walther, *I Corinthians*, 352–53; Robertson and Plummer, *First Corinthians*, 378–79; Hodge, *First Corinthians*, 358–59; Lietzmann, *Korinther*, 88).

26. An example is Dunn's edited volume, *Paul*. There are four references to 1 Cor 15:56, yet the essayists do little more than cite the verse (similarly also Martin, *Christ*; Westerholm, *Perspectives*; Wright, *Climax*; van Dulmen, *Theologie*). Hay's edited *Pauline Theology*, dedicated solely to the Corinthian epistles, mentions the verse but once. Dunn's *Theology*, Ridderbos's *Paul*, and Bruce's *Apostle* give little attention to the verse. McRay's *Paul* makes no reference at all. Hubner refers to the verse in a brief footnote in his *Law* (165), and Gorman mentions it only in passing (*Apostle*, 281). Sanders's *Law* makes no reference at all, nor does Bayes (*Weakness*). Räisänen devotes only a brief paragraph to it (*Paul and the Law*, 143). Schreiner gives a half page (*Theology*, 83; see also his *Paul*, 133). Schnelle, who discusses the relationship of the law-critical statement to the development of Paul's doctrine, is somewhat of an exception (*Paul*, 231–32). Thurén is another exception. Though the space he devotes to the verse is relatively minimal in the context of his wider discussion, I Cor 15:56 plays a part in his argument concerning the identity of the individual depicted in Rom 7:14–25 (*Derhetorizing*, 115–17, 122–25).

27. Besides the present writer's "Law, Sin, and Death: An Edenic Triad?" a scan of the last hundred years has revealed only four articles devoted solely to 1 Cor 15:56: Horn, "Stachel"; Hollander and Holleman, "Relationship"; Söding, "Kraft"; García Pérez, "1 Co 15,56." All of these have appeared within the last twenty years. This recent attention coincides with the current interest in Paul and the law (see Söding, "Kraft," 74).

28. Wilckens, "Entwicklung," 154.

Consequently, 1 Cor 15:56 becomes largely overlooked by scholars in favor of Romans 5 and 7. Why labor over a "cryptic throwaway line,"[29] "ein kleiner Exkurs,"[30] or "a thunderbolt from a Romans sky,"[31] when all that it says and more is elaborated elsewhere?[32] Thus Héring introduces it only to bypass it, "What is the role of the law? The reader will understand that we cannot embark here on a discussion of the Pauline conception (or conceptions) of the law, for this question, merely touched on here, is to be treated in the commentaries on the Epistles to the Romans and to the Galatians."[33]

Nevertheless, 1 Cor 15:56 would seem to deserve better than to be relegated to a footnote. Indeed, there are good reasons to argue that Paul's understanding of the law-sin nexus would be better approached initially by way of 1 Cor 15:56 than through Romans 7.[34] To begin with,

---

29. Wright, *1 Corinthians*, 227. Elsewhere Wright pegs 1 Cor 15:56 as a "tendentious assertion" (*Climax*, 9). Byrne calls Rom 3:20b ("for through the law comes the knowledge of sin") "the first of a series of 'throw-away' lines Paul offers about the ill effects of the law" (*Romans*, 121; he includes in this series Rom 4:15b; 5:20a; 6:14; 7:5). If this comment is any indication, Byrne would most certainly label 1 Cor 15:56 in a similar manner. Donaldson regards 1 Cor 15:56 as "a Roman thunderbolt in a Corinthian sky" ("'The Gospel,'" 168).

30. Lietzmann, *Korinther*, 88. First Corinthians 15:56, according to Lietzmann, "ist eine exegetische Anmerkung, ein kleiner Exkurs, in welchem die Rm 7,7ff. behandelten Gedanken gestreift werden" (ibid.).

31. Westerholm, *Perspectives*, 363 n. 39.

32. Weima views 1 Cor 15:56 as a "cryptic claim of what Paul says elsewhere" ("Function," 234).

33. Héring, *First Corinthians*, 182. Luther's words to his congregation on 1 Cor 15:56 are similar: "Das ist S. Paulus' Theologie. Welche zu verstehen wir dazu nehmen müssen das 5., 6. und 7. Kapitel an die Römer. Da der Apostel solches weiter und reichlich auslegt" (quoted in Brecht, "Lied," 58; note also Olshausen, *First and Second Corinthians*, 264; Strobel, *Korinther*, 261–62; Thrall, *First and Second Corinthians*, 115).

34. The phrase "law-sin nexus" is used in this study to refer to a connection between law and sin in which the law functions in a non-salvific or less than positive way with regard to sin, i.e., it serves in a capacity other than to curtail it, Such a relationship is detected in Rom 3:20; 4:15; 5:14; 5:20; 7:5, 7–11; 1 Cor 15:56; Gal 3:19. In passages linking law and sin, the law is generally understood by Paul to be functioning in one of the following three ways: 1) a *defining* function; i.e., the law transforms sin into a more clearly defined act of transgression (Rom 4:15b; 5:14b; Gal 3:19); 2) a *cognitive* function; i.e., the law reveals either one's sinful condition or sin for what it is (Rom 3:20b?); 3) a *causative* function, i.e.; the law incites transgression (Rom 3:20b?; 5:20; 7:5, 7–11; 1 Cor 15:56) (see discussions in Räisänen, *Paul and the Law*, 141 and Weima, "Function," 222–23). A fourth function is often added—a *condemning* function; i.e., the law serves to indict sin. However, in light of Rom 4:15b, a verse often linked to this notion, it may

Romans 7 is a large theological parcel that has been well scoured. First Corinthians 15:56, to the contrary, provides fresh soil and a more narrow thematic field for the scholar to examine. Secondly, the very feature that causes the verse to go unheeded, viz., its diminutiveness, is its virtue.[35] Precisely because it is embryonic, the verse presents the opportunity to analyze the "molecular structure" of Paul's law-sin notion that appears full-blown elsewhere. Something salient may be noticed by retreating from the complexities and re-approaching the topic in its *essential* and *axiomatic* state.[36] Thirdly, the contextual setting of 1 Corinthians provides an opportunity unique to the epistle. As Thielman notes, the fact that the law does not appear to have been a problem in the Corinthian congregations makes the letter an ideal laboratory to investigate Paul's view of the law: "The relatively minor place of the law in the argument of this letter actually enhances its usefulness for understanding Paul's view of the law generally. The absence of an argument between Paul and the Corinthians over the significance of the law, and the subsequent scarcity of highly polemical language about the law in the letter, allow us to see what Paul's statements about the law look like when the law itself is not a topic of debate."[37] Finally, we have in 1 Cor 15:56 the first explicit instance

---

be better to consider this idea to he a corollary to the *defining* function; i.e., as a consequence of turning sin into transgression, the law serves to indict the transgressor (see Luz, *Geschichtsverstandnis*, 187–88). The present work will contend that the nexus in 1 Cor 15:56 is causative. It will, however, designate the function differently (see n. 15 above).

35. Kruse finds in I Cor 15:56 a potential importance for the study of Paul and the law "out of proportion to its brevity" (*Paul*, 143).

36. This is noted by Thurén: "Paul's letters often contain sentences, which are so condensed, that they are difficult to understand (e.g., Rom 1:3–4; 1 Cor 15:56). The original context is missing. It may well be that such 'kernel sentences' are summaries of Paul's (or somebody else's) teaching or tradition, of which we have too little knowledge. However, the doctrines or ideas mentioned were presumably so well known to the original addressees that a short reference sufficed. By studying these 'tips of the icebergs' one could approach even such teaching of Paul, as was not acute in any of the situations of his letters, but still important, even crucial, for him" (*Derhetorizing*, 16).

37. Thielman, "Coherence," 236. This has also been observed by Thurén: "While the law is not discussed as a theological topos, we may assume that occasional references at least to some extent reflect Paul's unbiased view thereof. They can also enable us to visualize his ordinary teaching concerning law, . . . 1 Cor and Paul's other letters are thus valuable, when their 'main stream' theology concerning the law is compared with the biased Galatians and Romans" (*Derhetorizing*, 105–6).

in Paul's writings of the relationship between law, sin, and death.³⁸ In fact, if 1 Corinthians predates Galatians, 1 Cor 15:56 would be the first hint in Paul's extant letters of a dark role for the law in salvation-history.³⁹ It would appear to be important, therefore, to analyze the topic in its primitive stage, seeking to answer the question of what contextual factors originated the negative reference to the law.⁴⁰ Indeed, in light of the significance that the question of origins raises for the study of Paul and the law,⁴¹ a solution to the riddle of 1 Cor 15:56 may well serve to answer the greater question of what contributed to Paul's particular understanding of the Torah and his polemic against it.

## 1 CORINTHIANS 15:56—AN EDENICALLY INFORMED AXIOM

Among the commentators and theologians who have ventured to unravel the exegetical knot, the perplexing nature of 1 Cor 15:56 has given rise to an assortment of explanations. Some suggest that the verse resonates with Hellenistic or Jewish ideas with which Paul presumed his readers would have been familiar.⁴² Some assume Paul's notion regarding law and sin, though unrelated to the argument of the chapter or epistle, was a well known dictum of his theology that he could hardly refrain from mentioning, especially in a thematic context of sin and death.⁴³ One study

---

38. Galatians 3:19 is no exception. There Paul discusses the connection between νόμος and παράβασις, which is a similar but different notion, as will later be discussed. Furthermore, θάνατος, the third entity of the 1 Cor 15:56

39. See Thielman, "Coherence," 250 n. 49; Stanley, *Corinthians,* 322. if indeed, it occupies a role in *salvation* history at all (see below, pp. 230–36).

40. Though, as we will see, García Pérez argues otherwise, most commentators would agree with Thielmann that "the verse is undeniably negative in its attitude toward the law" ("Coherence," 250; idem, *Paul and the Law,* 107; note, e.g., Söding's description of the verse: "die offenkundig massive Gesetzeskritik" ["Kraft," 76]). Indeed this negative attitude is what tangles the exegetical yarn. What accounts for such a dark statement in a letter where the law does not appear in a bad light?

41. See below, pp. 224–26.

42. Hollander and Holleman suggest a Hellenistic backdrop ("Relationship," 270–91). Grundmann argues for a rabbinic background (see Grundmann, "Gesetz," 52–65) as do Kummel and Lietzmann (*Korinther,* 196). Sandelin finds the verse understandable in light of Jewish wisdom traditions (*Auseinandersetzungl,* 72). Farina finds 1 Cor 15:56 understandable with the Targum Jonathan of Hos 13:14 as its backdrop (*Leihlichkeit,* 312).

43. See e.g., Thielman, *Paul and the Law,* 108; C. K. Barrett, *First Corinthians,* 383;

attempts to ease the passage into its setting by proposing an entirely new translation of the verse.[44] Still other exegetes claim to have located a direct link between the verse and the letter in general or the immediate context in particular.[45] And finally, many put a sword to the knot by asserting that the verse is an interpolation, either by Paul himself or by a later redactor.[46]

In the following chapters, we will weigh these attempts to explain the appearance of 1 Cor 15:56, but find them mostly wanting. The study will argue, as others do, that v. 56 bears a contextual and theological relationship to its immediate context. It will also agree with those who assume that Paul states a dogma with which the Corinthians would have likely been familiar. However, unlike previous investigations, the present study proposes that the "puzzling" epigram in 15:56b concerning the law being the power of sin is related to the preceding *Adamic* discussion in 1 Cor 15:21–22, 45–49 and is immediately stimulated by the *edenic* nexus of sin and death in 15:56a. Paul, we will argue, based on his reading of Genesis 3,[47] not only considered there to be a *sin-death* nexus in the garden but a *law-sin* nexus as well. For Paul, rather than being a barrier to keep sin out of the system, the law was the means by which sin gained entry,[48] and far from keeping the first couple from disobedience, the commandment provided the serpent with the platform from which to provoke it. Indeed, it was law, in the form of the garden prohibition, that drew the snake out of the bush. Thus, though 1 Cor 15:56 might appear to be an intrusion, an axiom regarding the catalytic operation of the law in a setting endued with edenic scenery may not be as unwelcome as would initially seem.

Our contention that Paul molded his law-sin axiom in 1 Cor 15:56 from the theological soil of Eden will find support from an overview of vv. 54–57, a careful scan of v. 56 itself, and an analysis of the paragraphs

---

Räisänen, *Paul and the Law*, 143; Hays, *First Corinthians*, 277.

44. García Pérez, "1 Co 15,56," 405–14.

45. See Söding, "Kraft," 74–84; Gertner, "Midrashim," 282–83; Morissette, "Midrash," 176–84; Matand Bulembat, *Noyau et enjeux*, 124–25; Collins, *First Corinthians*, 578.

46. See Straatman, *Kritische Studiën*, 284; Heinrici, *Korinther*, 509; Moffatt, *First Corinthians*, 265, 268; Gaston, *Paul and the Torah*, 195 n. 24; 231 n. 9; Schmithals, *Bride*, 32; idem, *Theology*, 47; Carter, *Power*, 75; Horn, "Stachel," 88–105; Horsley, *I Corinthians*, 215; Weiß, *Korintherbrief*, 380.

47. It will later be argued that Paul was primarily, if not solely, dependent on the Genesis account itself rather than intertestamental literature for his theology of the Fall.

48. See Carter, *Power*, 187.

preceding the verse. Additional support will be drawn from passages outside the epistle where law, sin, and death similarly appear in relationship. Thus in Rom 5:12–21, where these entities are in view, edenic events are similarly present.[49] Likewise, in Rom 7:7–11, a passage that we will argue portrays in *dramatic* form the catalytic operation of law that 1 Cor 15:56 expresses in *axiomatic* form,[50] edenic imagery permeates the landscape.[51] The thesis will find its ultimate confirmation, however, in the Genesis account itself. It will not only be maintained that Genesis 3 is present in 1 Cor 15:56 but that the law-sin nexus of 1 Cor 15:56 is present in Genesis 3. Indeed, it will become evident that in the Fall narrative sin had no opportunity of seducing the woman until the command "you shall not eat of it" was issued. The prohibition itself became the means by which the snake incited in Eve the desire to transgress it. As we will argue, this primal relationship between law and sin depicted in Genesis 3 provided the theological substructure to Paul's catalytic notion of law.[52]

## THE SIGNIFICANCE OF 1 CORINTHIANS 15:56

Although 1 Cor 15:56 presents the interpreter with an exegetical riddle, discovering the solution has the potential to provide more than the satisfaction of solving a puzzle; the theological implications for Paul's understanding of the law could be significant. First, if Genesis 3 is the source from which the Apostle's catalytic notion of the law is ultimately

---

49. On the validity of using one Pauline epistle to help interpret another, see below, p. 111 n. 113.

50. This last point has been long recognized. 1 Corinthians 15:56, notes Findlay, "throws into an epigram the doctrine of Rom iv-viii and Gal iii respecting the interrelations of Sin, Law, and Death" ("First Corinthians," 942). The present study will argue this as well, but will differ by linking 1 Cor 15:56 to Romans 7 rather than to Galatians 3 or Romans 4–6, 8 and, more importantly, by arguing that the epigram in 1 Cor 15:56 respecting law, sin, and death finds its source in Old Testament history (Genesis 3).

51. If the verb γινώσκω in Rom 7:7 carries an experiential sense, such a sense should, perhaps, be read back into Rom 3:20b (see Schlier, *Römerbrief*, 101; Sloan, "Paul and the Law," 47–48). If so, and if (as we will argue) the phrase ἐπίγνωσις ἁμαρτίας in Rom 3:20b alludes to the paradisiacal knowledge of good and evil, an edenic allusion would again be found in the vicinity of a reference to the catalytic operation of the law. See below, pp. 108–13.

52. Explanations of particular methods and assumptions will be discussed as they arise in the course of our study (e.g., authorship, interpretation theory, relevance of Second Temple sources, and the definition of and criteria for discerning an "allusion").

derived, not only would the referent of 1 Cor 15:56 be identified, but a *primordial* source of his law problematic would be located. By locating a law problematic as far back as Eden, Paul would be reaching the historical high water mark of his polemic against the saving efficacy of the law. Furthermore, a law-sin nexus in Eden would suggest that Paul deemed the law-problematic to be *archetypical*. It would be in the very nature of the case that divinely sanctioned law exacerbates sin. This in turn would not only account for the *old realm* relationship between law and sin in Romans 6–7 but would explain the role that freedom from the law plays in the chapters' logic regarding freedom from sin. For if it was the prohibition that drew the serpent out of the bush, than deliverance from the jurisdiction of the law would necessarily and inevitably defang sin of its power.

Even though reading the Genesis narrative from over Paul's shoulder could open up fresh theological applications, theological examinations of the law, batting from both Old and New Testament sides of the plate, have tended to bypass Eden. Concerning Old Testament studies, Bruckner notes: "Clearly missing from most OT scholarship on law is specific reference to law in Genesis 1 through Exodus 18. The primary reason for this neglect is methodological; i.e., the predominant interest has been in the history of composition. This means that any reference to law in these texts is treated in its literary-historical context (e.g., as the addition of a late redactor) rather than in its literary narrative context."[53] New Testament scholarship, as we will later note, fares little better. While many recognize the influence of the Genesis Fall account on Rom 7:7–11, few Pauline scholars have attempted a careful re-reading of the narrative itself—a narrative, we believe, that profoundly shaped the Apostle's understanding of law and sin.[54]

---

53. Bruckner, "Creational Context," 93. As an example, the treatments of Old Testament law by Levenson, Daube, and Clark make no references to Gen 2:16–17 ("Theologies of Commandment," *Studies in Biblical Law*, "Law") nor do the more recent treatments by Patrick, Brin, and Jackson *(Old Testament Law, Studies in Biblical Law, Studies in the Semiotics of Biblical Law)*. Recent exceptions to this pattern are Bruckner himself and Pedersen's "Biblical Law," although the latter goes too far in his reading of Paul by often misreading as allusions to the garden commandment what are certainly references to the Mosaic law (e.g., in Rom 5:12, 20 [see Bruckner, "Creational Context," 19, 21]), and the former does not go far enough; he inexplicably neglects Gen 2:16, 17 in his survey of law in Genesis 1 through Exodus 19!

54. Peter Stuhlmacher, in his discussion of the biblical theology of the law, notes that,

In spite of this neglect, it is the contention of the present study that a biblical theology of law must take Eden into account and even begin there. For if Paul considered the law to be present in the Eden account (as will be argued), and if he understood the catalytic operation of the law to have been active there (the major premise of this study), and, indeed, if the catalytic notion of the law is discovered in the story line of Genesis itself (as an examination of Fall narrative will suggest), then a biblical theology of law will be missing its foundation if this seminal interaction between law and sin is overlooked or ignored.

---

for Paul, law existed in paradise and "with the Fall came under the power of sin" ("Topic," 127). He goes on to assert how the law through Christ has now been freed for the first time "to fulfill the 'life-sustaining' function accorded it in paradise" (ibid.). Setting aside his notion that sin's co-opting of the law was the *result* of the Fall rather than the *cause* of it, and apart from the life-sustaining role that he contends that the Mosaic law plays in the life of the believer, it is significant that Stuhlmacher not only links Paul's law-sin nexus to Eden but also ponders the importance that such a link might have to the biblical theology of law as a whole. Yet, he pursues the topic no further. A more recent study that does attempt a pursuit, however, is "The Figure of Eve in Romans 7:5–25," by Austin Busch. Busch not only explores the manner in which Paul employs the role of Eve in the Fall account but, taking his cue from Paul, re-reads the Genesis narrative and seeks to explore the relation of law aid sin there. Indeed, he argues that interpreting Romans 7 with reference to Eve's experience "opens up new hermeneutical possibilities for comprehending sin, the (split) self, and the law" ("Eve," 24). Busch concludes that a "careful exegesis of the Genesis passage that has so influenced Paul's argument shows how law is complicit with sin in alienating persons from God" (ibid., 24). While the term "complicit" here is offensive to Paul's vindication of the law in Rom 7:12–13, Busch is correct, we believe, that "competent interpretation [of Romans 7] must comprehend the coming of the commandment or law in the context of Eve's temptation" (ibid., 19–20), and although Busch, as we will contend below, distorts Paul's catalytic notion of the law by his peculiar interpretation of the Fall account, he is one of a few who have laid spade to the ground in a biblical-theological attempt to analyze Genesis 3 from over the shoulder of Paul's catalytic operation of the law. Inherent in our thesis that the law-critical axiom of 1 Cor 15:56 is drawn from edenic soil is the intent to steer the conversation of Paul and the law Edenward, to the primeval event that, we believe, provided the backdrop to the Apostle's perception of the law. For if, as we will argue, Paul discerned a catalytic operation of the law in the Garden, then his understanding of law and sin can not be fully understood and applied unless we take a closer look with him at the prototypical event that transpired in Eden—where the prohibition against partaking of the knowledge of good and evil led to the knowledge of sin.

# 2

# Interpretations of 1 Corinthians 15:56

## A GLOSS

IN LIGHT OF THE apparent dissonance of 1 Cor 15:56 within its context, it is not surprising that some scholars would consider the verse to be an interpolation.[1] The critical apparatus of the NA[27] at v. 56 refers to the nineteenth-century Dutch proponent of *Konjekturalkritik*, J. W. Straatman, who was likely the first to suggest such a theory.[2] Since then many others have rallied around the notion.[3] Among these, Moffatt contends that 1 Cor 15:56 "is a prose comment which could not have occurred to him [Paul] in the passionate rush of triumphal conviction."[4] Likewise, Kuss argues that "der v. 56 paßt mit seiner doktrinären Pedanterie schlecht in den beinahe hymnischen Zusammenhang."[5] Weiß argues similarly. Verse 56, he maintains, is "ein völlig aus dem begeisterten Ton fallende theologische

---

1. This chapter will treat interpretations of 1 Cor 15:56 that are notable and/or most often cited. Additional writers and commentators, both ancient and modern, who have given attention to v. 56 will be considered in the exegetical portion of our study. Unless otherwise noted, New Testament Greek references and textual abbreviations used in the present study are taken from the NA[27]. LXX references come from LXXR.

2. Depending on his conclusions (which are unstated), Ewald may have preempted Straatman by eight years: "Liest man hier die kurzen Worte v. 22, 56, so könnte man meinen, der B. an die Römer müsse früher geschrieben seyn und unsre Worte seien nur wie ein wiederhall daraus" (*Sendschreiben*, 219 n. 1).

3. See above, p. 9 n. 46. Clemen, von Soden, Schmiedel, Bousset, and Völter can be added to the names noted above (see citations in Horn, "Stachel," 89).

4. Moffatt, *First Corinthians*, 268. Hence the verse does not appear in his New Testament translation.

5. Kuss, *Paulus*, 378 n. 1.

Glosse, die eine genaue Kenntnis der paulin. Theologie voraussetzt."[6] Paul could have written it, he concedes, "aber dann erst nachträglich. Besser fasst man die Worte als eine fremde Exegese auf."[7] Carter finds the marked change in style to be "intrusive" and thus evidence of "an insertion made by a follower of Paul on the basis of the apostle's letter to Rome."[8] Horsley likewise contends that the verse, which contains "topics of importance in the later letter to the Romans," is utterly out of place "in a letter otherwise completely and closely devoted to burning issues in the Corinthian assembly."[9] Indeed, Horn, the most prolific exponent of a gloss,[10] puts the burden of proof on those who would defend its authenticity. The verse, he contends, is not only contextually intrusive, but the genuiness of such a "prägnante Formel" in 1 Corinthians would necessitate what he considers to be the unlikely scenario that a law-sin nexus was at this early date a fixed notion for Paul.[11]

The main reasons that Horn and others suspect a gloss are thus twofold: the verse does not seem to suit the literary and thematic context of

---

6. Weiß, *Korintherbrief*, 380.

7. Ibid. Heinrici postulates here "eine nachträgliche Beischrift" (*Korinther*, 509). Similarly, Schmithals argues that "mit v. 56 erläutert eine sekundäre Hand v. 55" (*Briefe*, 32). In a later work, he considers there to be "no doubt" that we have in v. 56 a secondary marginal gloss (*Theology*, 47).

8. Carter, *Power*, 75.

9. Horsley, *1 Corinthians*, 215. Horsley bases his thesis that the verse is a gloss on the lone fact that there is no indication that there was a law problematic in Corinth (ibid.).

10. Horn considers the verse to be out of sync with the surrounding argument: "Will also hinsichtlich der formalen Rhetorik v. 55 das 'Nicht-mehr-Bestehen' des Todes ansagen, welches bereits jetzt proklamiert, zukünftig (τότε v. 54) aber erwartet wird, so verweist der prädikatlose, aber wohl auf die Gegenwart zu beziehende v. 56 in völligem Widerspruch zu dieser rhetorischen Absicht auf die Präsenz des Todes kraft der Sünde und des Gesetzes. Spricht v. 55 von einem Ende des Stachels, so benennt v. 56, worin er besteht. Erst v. 57 schließt sich nahtlos an die rhetorische Absicht des v. 55 an, insofern ausgeführt wird, daß der proklamierte Sieg und das Ende des Todes mit der Person Jesu Christi bereits gegenwärtig den Glaubenden verbürgt ist" ("Stachel," 98).

11. Ibid., 101–3. Horn writes, "Eine gesetzeskritische Einstellung und ein Verständnis der ἁμαρτία als einer feindlichen Macht findet sich erst im Kontext der Ausbildung der Rechtfertigungslehre. Daß aber die Sünde sich zur Tötung des Gesetzes bedient, diese über die Anfänge der paulinischen Gesetzeskritik noch hinausführende rein negative Folie der Rechtfertigungsaussage steht innerhalb der gesamten paulinschen Theologie mit Ausnahme des Röm isoliert" (ibid., 101). Early A.D. 54 is widely accepted as the most likely date for 1 Corinthians (see, e.g., Wolff, *Erste Brief*, 12–13; Witherington, *Conflict*, 73).

the chapter or epistle,[12] and, more importantly,[13] it reflects Pauline notions regarding law and sin that are too negative for that time period.[14] Though many writers, almost by default, argue for these reasons against the authenticity of 1 Cor 15:56, the conjecture is highly unlikely.[15] The theory must overcome the virtually insurmountable fact that there is no textual evidence to support it.[16] In Horn's own words, the thesis "bleibt freilich eine subjecktive Überlegung des Exegeten *ohne jeglichen textgeschichtlichen Anhalt*."[17] To maintain his premise, Horn is forced to suppose that the gloss was placed in the original letter by Paul or by one of his students in "all!" of the early copies.[18] The latter scenario must in

12. "It interrupts the train of thought," writes Conzelmann. "It looks like a gloss" (*1 Corinthians*, 293; see also Lang, *Korinther*, 241). At least it initially appears as such to Conzelmann and Lang. Upon closer examination both conclude otherwise.

13. The latter concern carries more weight with theorists of a gloss than the former. Schrage notes: "In neuerer Zeit ist mehrfach versucht worden, v. 56 als eine sekundäre Glosse zu erweisen: Das Hauptargument dabei ist nicht ein unpaulinscher Charakter des sentenzhaften Verses, sondern die fehlende Einbettung in den Kontext und die Rekonstruktion einer Entwicklung der paulinschen Theologie, die z.Zt. des 1 Korintherbriefes noch keine Rechtfertigungslehre mit ihren Koorodnaten von Sünde und vor allem Gesetz ausgebildet habe" (*Korinther*, 4:365–66). Verburg similarly detects this, "Das Problem hier ist nicht, daß Paulus seinen eigenen Gedankengang unterbricht, sondern das in diesem Kontext unerwartete, erstmalige Auftauchen des paulinschen Gedankens, daß νόμος negativ zu bewerten sei" (*Endzeit*, 89).

14. Söding frames the arguments in favor of a gloss in this two-fold manner, "Die Interpolations-These hängt an zwei Argumenten. Das erste: Für Paulus sei das Gesetz zur Zeit des 1 Kor noch kein brennendes Problem gewesen; zumindest die Vorstellung, es diene der Sünde als Werkzeug, sei noch nicht ausgebildet. Das zweite: Sowohl die Vorstellung der ἁμαρτία (im Singular) als Todesmacht wie *a fortiori* die Deklaration des Nomos als Unheilsgröße, die mit dem Tod und der Sünde im Bunde ist, habe weder im Duktus von 1 Kor noch im Corpus des gesamten Briefes einen Anknüpfungspunkt, geschweige daß sie im 1 Thess vorbereitet wäre" ("Kraft," 76).

15. Söding assures us that "zu dieser *ultima ratio* braucht man nicht Zuflucht zu nehmen" (ibid.).

16. $\mathfrak{P}^{46}$, the oldest extant manuscript containing 1 Cor 15:56, exhibits at v. 56 no variations from the NA$^{27}$ (see Kenyon, *Chester Beatty Papyri*, 91). Orr and Walther assert that "the sequence would be simpler if vs. 56 were omitted as a theological gloss of later editors, but there is no evidence for such an emendation" (*1 Corinthians*, 352). Though our later examination will reveal the verse to be less difficult than Orr and Walther would make it appear, the authors are correct that the theory of a gloss is out of favor with the evidence.

17. Horn, "Stachel," 104, italics mine.

18. Ibid., 90, exclamation mark his. Since Romans appears at the head of early collections of the Pauline epistles (e.g., $\mathfrak{P}^{46}$), Horn assumes that portions of the later letters

fairness be deemed improbable. It is nearly unthinkable that one could have retrieved and emended *all* the early copies once they had been scattered to the wind. Similarly, Horn's assumption that the original text was emended by Paul is unlikely and, moreover, immaterial. Not only does 1 Cor 1:16 show that Paul "was not concerned to check and revise what he had dictated,"[19] but even if the statement were later inserted by Paul, it should not be treated as a gloss any more than Lincoln's spoken words "under God" in the Gettysburg Address are, even though the phrase is missing from Lincoln's earliest drafts and perhaps even from his delivery text.[20] Authors who modify their own work would more appropriately be described as making edits rather than interpolating glosses. This would be especially so in the case of an autograph prior to distribution.[21]

In addition, the verse contains implicit evidence of authenticity rather than the telltale signs of inauthencity. An analysis of the text below will reveal the passage to be intricately woven into the syntactical fabric of the verses that immediately precede it,[22] and rather than being out of keeping with its rhetorical surroundings, it will be discovered that the verse contains two rhythmic epigrams that fit precisely within the lyrical strain of the context.[23] Furthermore, an analysis of the wider context will

---

would have been adapted to conform to the lead epistle (ibid., 91).

19. Räisänen, *Paul and the Law*, 143 n. 78.

20. See Wills, *Lincoln*, 192.

21. Reicke argues that "the very practice of dictation implies that disconnections, interpolations, and fluctuations may, for psychological reasons, have emerged in the original composition and are not necessarily the result of scribal errors or deliberate changes of a later hand" (*Re-examining*, 31).

22. Horn concedes this: "Literarkritisch beurteilt ist v. 56 also in den umgreifenden Kontext eingebunden, nicht spannungsfrei, aber doch mit syntaktischer und sprachlicher Verzahnung" ("Stachel," 93) and goes further: "Ein vollständig vorliegender Kettenschluß in v. 56f., in dem die Einzelglieder untereinander fest verzahnt sind, wäre freilich ein starkes Argument für die ursprüngliche Integrität des Abschnitts" (ibid., 97). Since, in contrast to v. 57, the key words θάνατος and νῖκος in vv. 54–55 *both* occur in v. 56, Schneider notes "daß rein auf der Ebene der Stichwortverbindungen *V. 56 enger mit der Zitatkombination verbunden ist als V 57!*" (Schneider, *Vollendung*, 45 italics his; see also Furnish, *Theology of First Corinthians*, 119; Morissette, "Midrash," 176).

23. Bachmann notes that the verse is "in Wirklichkeit keine trockene dogmatische Glosse" (*Korinther*, 472); see also Barrett, *First Corinthians*, 384. Regarding Moffatt's comment that a prosaic comment could not have occurred in such an emotionally charged context (see p.13, above), Fee responds that "such a comment says far more about the commentator than about Paul: Paul could not be imagined to write differently from our better selves!" (*First Corinthians*, 805).

find the verse to be organic to the thematic flow of the chapter.[24] In the end, an axiom regarding law and sin, which seems to have no relationship to its context, will be found to be in tune with the themes that precede it.[25]

Finally, concerning Horn's ultimate and, perhaps, driving concern,[26] we agree that an axiom in 1 Corinthians regarding a catalytic function of the law would necessitate the conclusion that the notion was already fixed in Paul's mind and preaching, perhaps well before the law controversy erupted in Galatia.[27] Truisms, such as we have in 1 Cor 15:56, are indeed

---

24. Even if the verse appears to be introduced abruptly, this would not be the only place in the chapter where Paul made such an excursion (see vv. 9-11; 23-28; 32-34). Nor is the way in which the verse is left unexplained without precedent. In Romans Paul inserts comments about the law that he does not explain until later (Rom 4:15; 7:5), and in Galatians phrases regarding the law occur that are never explained (διὰ νόμου, 2:19; τῶν παραβάσεων χάριν προσετέθη, 3:19). Horn himself allows for such spontaneity in Paul: "Unsere Kenntnis der paulinischen Gedankenführung weiß um abrupt eingefügte Zwischenaussagen oder um Anakoluthe" ("Stachel," 101). It is revealing that Horsley, who himself considers the verse to be a "probable" gloss, allows that v. 56 can be harmonized with its surroundings. He postulates that, if original, the verse could be viewed as an aside reflecting on the cause of human death: "Over against the view that the body is *naturally* mortal and perishable he would be saying that death is brought about by the historical powers of sin and the law" (*1 Corinthians*, 215). This interpretation is reasonable and will appear more so when the verse is later examined. Assuming the *possibility* of Horsley's harmonization, there would seem to be no pressing reason to suspect a gloss, especially with no textual evidence in its support. Verburg correctly notes that the theory of a gloss is only justified "wenn es keine andere Erklärung gibt, weshalb der negative bewertete νόμος-Begriff hier auftaucht" (*Endzeit*, 90). Since Horsley concedes that the verse can be reasonably harmonized with its context, it is puzzling that he deems it "probable" that the verse is a gloss. Under the circumstances it appears that an interpolation would at best be considered "possible," if not "improbable."

25. See Allo, *Corinthiens*, 436; Wolff, *Erste Brief*, 209; Collins, *First Corinthians*, 582.

26. This is Horn's stumbling stone: "Unsere Kenntnis der paulinschen Gedankenführung weiß um abrupt eingefügte Zwischenaussagen oder um Anakoluthe. Vielmehr ist letztlich zu fragen, ob die Voraussetzungen innerhalb der paulinschen Theologie z.Zt. des 1 Kor eine solche Aussage möglich erscheinen lassen" ("Stachel," 101).

27. Klein notes that this would be especially so if (as it indeed appears) the statement emerged during a nomistic lull (see "Gesetz," 65; see also Fee, *First Corinthians*, 806; Söding, "Kraft," 74-76). On the dating of 1 Corinthians in relation to Galatians, see Lüdemann, *Paul*, 108-9; Suhl, *Paulus*, 343; Kümmel, *Introduction*, 252-55; 278-79, 304; Lührmann, *Galatians*, 3; Price, *New Testament*, 335, and the survey in Fiensy, "Roman Empire," 48-50. While we offer no opinion regarding the comparative dating of 1 Corinthians and Galatians, we note that 1 Corinthians is among the earlier letters of Paul and, as is almost unanimously argued, predates Romans.

the products of time, experience, and reflection.[28] However, the fact that the strong textual witness for the verse requires that a gloss would need to have been made while Paul's ink was virtually still wet would necessitate the same conclusion.[29]

## A HELLENISTIC BACKGROUND

Assuming the integrity of 1 Cor 15:56, but being unable to discern a direct connection to the chapter, others argue that the verse can be best understood against the backdrop of Hellenistic thought. This is the approach taken by Hollander and Holleman. For them, 1 Cor 15:56 should not be understood as a brief compendium of Paul's theology of law and sin that he elsewhere works out in detail in Galatians and Romans.[30] Nor should the term νόμος be taken as a direct reference to the Torah or the Jewish Law. Instead, they argue that both the connection in v. 56 between death and sin and the relation between sin and law in v. 56 are to be understood "in the context of Paul's communication with the Christians in the community of Corinth,"[31] i.e., against the background of Hellenistic popular philosophy regarding *law in general*.

Specifically, for Hollander and Holleman, Paul subscribed not only to the Jewish-Hellenistic notion that mortality and decay came through one man (i.e., Adam),[32] but he embraced the negative attitude toward the law that was part and parcel of the Cynic concept of *Ursprung und*

---

28. See below, pp. 64–65 n. 87.

29. Wolff finds the verse to be "durchaus paulinisch formuliert" (*Erste Brief*, 209; note again Weiß's statement [quoted above, p. 13–14] that the verse assumes an exact knowledge of Pauline theology). Even Horn concludes that the verse could only have been written by one who knew the theology that underlies Romans ("Stachel," 95). Surely Wilckens's wry conclusion is appropriate: "Ja, da der Glossator ein exzellent paulinisch denkender und formulierender Theologe gewesen sein müßte, ist es immer noch wahrscheinlicher, in ihm Paulus selbst zu sehen" ("Entwicklung," 161). Indeed, if one detects the fingerprints of Paul on the text, and since there is no textual evidence of a gloss, and if there are valid explanations of how the verse fits into its context, would it not be reasonable to assume the presence of Paul himself in the autograph? For further critique of the gloss theory, see Schneider, *Vollendung*, 44–54.

30. Hollander and Holleman, "Relationship," 272–73.

31. Ibid., italics mine.

32. Hollander and Holleman cite *4 Ezra*, *2 Baruch*, and especially Philo (ibid., 275–79).

*Entartung* and its antithetical notions of φύσις and νόμος.³³ According to the authors' assessment of Cynic thought, though there was a god-given order with which humanity was originally in harmony,³⁴ society degenerated over time,³⁵ and laws were enacted to stem the degeneration.³⁶ However, since these νόμοι were human products, they were deemed to be in conflict with the primitive order of nature (φύσις), and, as such, were regarded as ineffective means to regulate society.³⁷ They were thus considered to have little value beyond that of providing evidence of humanity's inborn wickedness.³⁸ Indeed, since laws were the result of human degeneration, they were associated with this depravity and were themselves deemed to be depraved.³⁹ For Hollander and Holleman,

33. See ibid., 280. The phrase *Ursprung und Entartung* is taken by Hollander and Hollemann from Reinhardt's *Poseidonios über Ursprung und Entartung*.

34. The authors appeal to writers such as Strabo, Seneca, Posidonius (as quoted by Strabo, Diodorus Siculus, and Athenaeus), and Philo to document the widespread Greek belief of a past golden age ("Relationship," ibid., 284–86).

35. Ibid., 284–86.

36. Though there were some philosophers (e.g., Posidonius) who believed that god-given laws existed during the golden era, Hollander and Holleman note the classic Cynic view that the process of degeneration began *before* any laws were in existence ("Relationship," 286). They cite Seneca, who, they contend, "regarded the laws as a reaction to the degeneration of mankind" (ibid.). The authors likely have in mind Seneca's assertion, "When once vice stole in and kingdoms were transformed into tyrannies, a need arose for laws" (*Lucil.* 90. 6 [Gummere, LCL]).

37. See Hollander, "'Law,'" 132. Among other primary sources, Hollander and Holleman cite in this regard Plutarch (*Sol.* 5.2), who considered the laws of Lycurgus, for example, to be "efficacious in producing valor, but defective in producing righteousness" ("Relationship," 287).

38. See ibid., 289. Strabo, indeed, cites Plato to this effect: "Where there are very many laws, there are also very many lawsuits and corrupt practices, just as where there are many physicians, there are also likely to be many diseases" (*Geogr.* 6.1.8 [Jones, LCL]). See also Hollander and Holleman's quotation of (pseudo) Diogenes of Sinope (*Ep.* 28): "You admit them [laws] as witnesses to your ingrained evil" and the line attributed to Heraclitus (*Ep.* 7): "The things which seem to be preeminently the symbols of justice among you, the laws, are evidence of vice" ("Relationship," 288) . Hollander and Holleman do, however, recognize that the Cynics conceded at least some value to laws. Though they do not teach righteousness, laws at least repel *some* wickedness (ibid.).

39. Hollander and Holleman quote Epictetus (*Diatr.*1.13.5) and his assessment of human law as "wretched" (ταλαίπωρος) and "laws of the dead" (ibid., 284). See also their quote from Xenophon (*Mem.* 4.iv.13–14) in which Hippias objects to Socrates that, "laws can hardly be thought of much account, Socrates, or observance of them, seeing that the very men who passed them often reject and amend them" (ibid., 281). The authors similarly cite Plato (*Prot.* 337 D) where Hippias depicts the law as the "despot [τύραννος] of

the upshot of such a philosophy that combined the concept of *Ursprung und Entartung* with the antithesis of φύσις versus νόμος was a longing among the philosophers to return to the primeval bliss of life κατὰ φύσιν, i.e., free from law.[40]

Believing that these negative notions regarding the law were shared by Paul and were well-known to the Corinthians, Hollander and Holleman propose that 1 Cor 15:56 is to be understood from a Cynic perspective:[41] "Paul rejects any law, subscribing to the negative view of law that was current among the Cynics who regarded laws as part of the degeneration of humanity. In Paul's opinion, death operates in the present age, and its 'sting,' through which it brings mortality to all men, is sin. Law is the stimulus, the catalyst of men's wickedness. Paul sympathized with this negative attitude towards the law because it fitted quite well in his apocalyptic world-view."[42] According to Hollander and Holleman, then, the Jewish law was not at issue in 1 Corinthians 15. Rather, the term "law" in v. 56, placed, as it is, alongside the universal powers of "death" and "sin," is best understood as a reference to "law in general, or to the (written) laws that are found in all sorts of cultures and among all kinds of nations."[43] For Paul, all laws, Torah included, were part of human culture and convention and "are characteristic of the old order and will pass away together with death and sin at Christ's return."[44]

---

mankind" (ibid.)

40. See Hollander and Holleman, "Relationship," 286. In his *Lives* (2.20), observe Hollander and Holleman, Diogenes Laertius notes Aristotle's response when asked what advantage he had gained from his pursuit of philosophy: "This, that I do without being ordered what some are constrained to do by their fear of the law" (ibid., 289 n. 74). Cicero, we can add, ascribes a similar reply to Xenocrates when asked what his disciples learned: "To do of their own accord what they are compelled to do by law" (*Rep.*1.3 [Keyes, LCL]). Note also here Hollander and Holleman's quote of Democritus in Epiphanius (*Pan.* 3.2. 9): "Laws are a bad invention, and it befits the wise not to obey the laws but to live freely" ("Relationship," 282 n. 41). Indeed, we can also add that to the Cynics, the wise had no need of laws, because they would do good anyway, as Demonax argues: "In all likelihood the laws were of no use, whether framed for the bad or the good; for the latter had no need of laws, and the former were not improved by them" (Lucian, *Demon.* 59 [Harmon, LCL]).

41. See ibid., 290–91.
42. Ibid., 290.
43. Hollander, "'Law,'" 132.
44. Hollander and Holleman, "Relationship," 290.

Though the article of Hollander and Holleman is one of the most frequently cited examinations of 1 Cor 15:56, its argument finds few supporters.⁴⁵ This is not surprising. The Cynic notion to which Hollander and Holleman allude is almost certainly not Paul's referent. Even if it were likely that the Corinthians were acquainted with a Hellenistic philosophy that denigrated human laws as "unrighteous" and "insufficient" means to curb wickedness, this notion goes further then 1 Corinthians 15:56, and yet not far enough. It goes beyond Paul's statement by disparaging the law. Paul does not do so in 1 Cor 15:56 (nor elsewhere). As we will later argue, the law, for Paul, is not itself evil but becomes an instrument in the hands of an evil entity, viz., sin. And yet the Hellenistic philosophies depicted by Hollander and Holleman fall short of Paul's thought. It is not that the law for Paul is an *ineffective* means of *inhibiting* human wickedness; rather, the law is an *effective* means of *empowering* human wickedness.⁴⁶ However much Hollander and Holleman try to turn the Cynics into Paulinists, the philosophy they sketch went no further than to assert that laws were the result and evidence of humanity's wickedness. This comes nowhere near to what Hollander and Holleman (rightly) consider to be Paul's notion in 1 Cor 15:56, that the law serves as "the *catalyst* of men's wickedness."⁴⁷

But more importantly, ὁ νόμος in 1 Cor 15:56 almost certainly refers to something other than mere human laws and institutions en-

---

45. Among major commentators, only Collins appears tempted to second their motion (*First Corinthians*, 582–83).

46. See Carter, *Power*, 75 n. 86. Thus Kleinknecht notes: "No Gk. could speak of the νόμος τῆς ἁμαρτίας as Pl. does in R. 7:23 (cf. 1 Cor 15:56)" ("νόμος, ἀνομία, κτλ.," in *TDNT* 4:1035 n. 36).

47. Hollander and Holleman, "Relationship," 290, italics mine. In his later essay, Hollander admits that this sin-engendering function of the law was underestimated in his collaboration with Holleman ("Law," 133 n. 67). A Hellenistic notion that may seem to go as far as 1 Cor 15:56 does in linking law to a *catalytic* outworking of wrong-doing is the concept of counter-suggestibility, a notion that is well attested in Greco-Roman antiquity (see, e.g., Plutarch, *Mor.* 71A, *Am.* 2.19.3; 3.4.17.18; *Metam.* 3.566; Livy, *Livy*, 34.4.20 and other citations in von Gemünden, "Affekt," 70 n. 88). Nevertheless, though Greek readers may well have identified Paul's statement regarding law and sin with a forbidden desire scenario, greater powers are at work for Paul, and matters of far greater consequence are at issue in 1 Cor 15:56. As will become evident, the concern of the verse is not the mundane struggle between pleasures and prohibitions, but the role divine law plays in the outworking of *sin*. And the relationship between law and sin to which the verse alludes is not analyzed psychologically, but eschatologically. The law-sin connection for Paul is a nexus that inevitably leads to *death*.

acted after humanity's golden age had become tarnished. Hollander and Holleman may be correct that the appearance in v. 56 of ὁ θάνατος and ἡ ἁμαρτία as abstract entities cautions us against restricting ὁ νόμος there to the Mosaic law. Indeed, we will later argue similarly. Nevertheless, it is problematic to assume without further ado that Paul had *human* laws in mind. Not only does such an interpretation correspond poorly to the theological use of νόμος in 1 Corinthians (cf. 9:8–9, 20; 14:21, 34),[48] but it would seem to bode ill with Paul's earlier depiction of the Gentiles as being ἄνομος (1 Cor 9:20).[49] Furthermore, if, as we will suggest, ἡ ἁμαρτία and ὁ θάνατος appear in 15:56 as primeval entities, what would likely be in view is a notion of law that is *primordial* rather than merely ancient or cultural.

## A JEWISH BACKGROUND

### Grundmann

While Hollander and Holleman look to Hellenistic thought, others, who similarly contend that Paul's notion in 1 Cor 15:56 did not originate from and cannot be explained by its immediate context, argue that the verse reflects Jewish ideas with which Paul assumed his readers would have been familiar.[50] The most cited of such theories is that proposed by

48. See Wolff, *Erste Brief*, 418 n. 3.

49. See Verburg, *Endzeit*, 91; van Bruggen, *Paul*, 358 n. 10.

50. Though the thesis has not been applied directly to 1 Cor 15:56, one might suppose that the rabbinic notion of counter-suggestability provided the source to Paul's law-sin nexus in 1 Cor 15:56. Carter, for example, argues (regarding the law-sin nexus of Rom 7:7–11) that Paul's Jewish readers in Rome would have identified with a struggle between sin and the commandment. As evidence he cites the story recorded in the Jerusalem Talmud of R. Mena's visit to R. Haggai, who was ill. R. Haggai said, "I am thirsty." R. Mena responded, "Drink," and then left him. Upon returning, R. Mena asked R. Haggai about his thirst, to which R. Haggai replied: "No sooner had you permitted me to drink than the thirst left me" (*Power*, 186–87; see the discussion of this passage in Montefiore and Loewe, *Rabbinic Anthology*, 302). The Talmud relates the incident to the axiom, "The evil impulse craves only what is forbidden" (*y. Yoma 6:4* [Neusner]). The alleged exchange would have occurred, however, in the fourth century (see "Haggai," *Encyclopaedia Judaica*, 7:1114) and would thus be an uncertain indication of what Jews believed three centuries prior. Yet, even if it be assumed that Paul's Jewish readers were familiar with a notion regarding the evil inclination being stimulated by forbidden fruit, this would indicate how 1 Cor 15:56 could have been understood by some in Corinth but would not

Grundmann, who contends that Paul was acquainted with the rabbinic axiom: "The power of Yahweh is the Torah" and in 1 Cor 15:56 turns it on its head: "the power of *sin* is the law."[51] By this move, Paul shifts the center of divine power from the *law* to the *gospel*.[52] The evidence that Grundmann cites to support this scenario, however, is unconvincing. His primary source is *Mek. Shirata* 9:43–48: "'Thou hast guided them in thy strength.' For the sake of the Torah which they were destined to receive, for *'Thy strength'* here is but a designation for the Torah, as in the passage, 'The Lord will give strength unto His people.'"[53] Not only is it difficult to assume that the Corinthians would have been familiar with this late Jewish midrash,[54] but even if they were, Grundmann turns a mere expression, "thy strength," into a fixed Rabbinic axiom, "The power of Yahweh is the Torah."[55] It is hardly imaginable that Paul would have done the same and then expected his readers to understand his axiom with the original Jewish midrash in mind.[56]

---

tell us why Paul included the verse here (see Garland, *1 Corinthians*, 749). An additional Jewish reference to counter-suggestability will be discussed below though the reference is likely post-Pauline (see pp. 198–99).

51. See Grundmann, "Gesetz," 54–55; see also Watson, *First Corinthians*, 180; Barrett, *First Corinthians*, 384; Wilckens, "Entwicklung," 161. Kümmel and Lietzmann contend that Grundmann's scenario argues for the authenticity of the verse (see *Korinther*, 196).

52. Grundmann asserts "daß er die Aussage des Midraschs 'Kraft Jahwes ist die Torah' . . . kennt . . . und sie antitoralogisch-negativ verwendet 1 Cor 15:56: ἡ δὲ δύναμις τῆς ἁμαρτίας ὁ νόμος· sowie antitoralogisch-positiv Rom 1:16: . . . τὸ εὐαγγέλιον, δύναμις γὰρ θεοῦ ἐστιν εἰς σωτηρίαν (vgl. auch 1 Cor 1:18)" (ibid., 54–55; see also Grundmann, *Kraft*, 89). Díaz Rodelas also adopts Grundmann's argument: "Judaism sees in the law the ultimate expression of the divine power for salvation; evoking implicitly or explicitly Ps 28,8, the law is considered as a power that God gives his people. The unity between the nouns עוז or תורה to express the vision makes one think that Paul is directly opposing it when he asserts that it is the law that sets the δύναμις of sin into action" (*Pablo*, 29–30, translation mine).

53. Lauterbach, trans., *de-Rabbi Ishmael*, 2:70, italics mine.

54. Although Grundmann presents the *Mekilta* as the earliest of the Midrashim, it can only with difficulty be dated in the second century (see Söding, "Kraft," 82 n. 29), and, as Wacholder argues, the final redaction can be dated as late as the early ninth century (Wacholder, "Date," 117–44). A late third century date appears to be the most likely (see Stemberger, *Introduction*, 253–55).

55. Conzelmann calls Grundmann on this leap as well (*First Corinthians*, 293 n. 42).

56. In a later article, Grundmann appears to be more cautious. He cites the expression rather than an axiom: "Paulus . . . nimmt den jüdischen Ausdruck für die Tora עוז יהוה auf" ("δύναμαι, δυνατός, κτλ.," in *TWNT* 2:309). Yet even here, can he be so sure that Paul was tapping into this tradition*

## Sandelin

Another theorist arguing for a Jewish backdrop to 1 Cor 15:56 is Sandelin, who finds v. 56 to be intelligible when viewed against the background of Philo and the Wisdom of Solomon. According to his reading of these sources, the Torah, by way of its identification with Wisdom, is a power that leads to life and salvation.[57] Paul, Sandelin argues, was contending against this legalistic notion in his statement, "the power of sin is the law":[58] "Von einer paulinschen Sicht aus führt aber eine solche weisheitliche νόμος-Lehre nicht zum Heil, sondern Unheil. Für Paul führt das Gesetz zum Tode wegen der Sünde. . . . Eine Macht wie die in Sap. und bei Philo gezeichnete Sophia wäre in der Tat eine Todesmacht. Die Gerechtigkeit, die durch die Befolgung ihrer Gebote zustandekommt, könnte vom paulinischen Standpunkt aus nicht zum leben führen."[59]

Although the background sources differ, Sandelin's nomistic reconstruction runs similar to Grundmann's and, in the end, fares the same. First of all, it faces the difficulty of conceiving that Paul would have presumed that the Corinthians would make the subtle Wisdom associations that Sandelin assumes they did.[60] Furthermore, Sandelin's interpretation suffers from the fact that a Torah-Wisdom notion, which he argues v. 56 contains in embryo, does not appear full-blown, as we would expect, in Romans where Paul elaborates on the law-sin nexus. Finally, as Räisänen quips, if Paul in v. 56 were indeed engaged in a polemic against a nomistic front in Corinth such as Sandelin suggests, "so indirect a comment would be an unintelligibly mild reply."[61] Sandelin, to be sure, opens himself to

---

57. See Sandelin, *Auseinandersetzung*, 72, 84–85. For references to the Torah as both a barrier against sin and a source of life, see Morissette, "Midrash," 181–82.

58. For Sandelin, this scenario fits well into the Christological context: "Der Satz: 'die Kraft der Sünde ist aber das Gesetz,' zeigt eine der Grenzen der Sophia-Christologie, denn er taucht gerade in einem Zusammenhang auf, wo Christus als Herrscher nach dem Bilde der Sophia der jüdischen Weisheitstradition gezeichnet ist" (*Auseinderandersetzung*, 72).

59. Ibid., 85.

60. A concern raised against Sandelin by Schrage (*Korinther*, 4:382 n. 1914).

61. Räisänen, *Paul and the Law*, 143 n. 77. This is also noted by Wolff: "Ein Nomismus der Korinther ist im Brief sonst nicht nachzuweisen; Paulus würde dagegen auch viel energischer polemisieren, wie der Galaterbrief zeigt" (*Erste Brief*, 418). This concern, of course, has damaging relevance to Gründmann's scenario as well (see Horn, "Stachel," 103).

Räisänen's counter-punch when he himself observes "wie energisch Paulus . . . Versuche bekämpft, die der Gesetzesgehorsam als Heilsweg aufstellen wollen, zeigt der Galaterbrief."[62]

## Farina

Finally, Farina argues that a reference to "law" following a quotation of Hos 13:14 in 1 Cor 15:55 should come as no surprise since, he claims, a logical connection between νόμος and Hos 13:14 is "well attested" in the literary traditions of Judaism.[63] As evidence, Farina cites the "Targum Jonathan" of Hosea 13:14:[64] "I have delivered the house of Israel from the power of death and rescued them from the destroyer. But now my Memra shall be against them to kill, and my decree will be to destroy. *Because they have transgressed my law*, I shall remove my Shekinah from them."[65] Farina is confident that this interpretative tradition provides the backdrop to 1 Cor 15:56 and, in fact, is puzzled that this explanation has not received the consideration of commentators that he thinks it deserves.[66] Farina's thesis, however, is difficult to accept. As was the case with the rabbinic source appealed to by Grundmann, Farina's source post-dates Paul.[67] We cannot in fairness assume that Paul or the Corinthians had access to this tradition, written or oral.[68] Furthermore, though there may be points of contact between 1 Cor 15:56 and the Targum, they do not appear precise enough to support Farina's conclusions, as Horn aptly notes:

---

62. Sandelin, *Auseinderandersetzung*, 63.
63. Farina, *Leiblichkeit*, 312.
64. The origin of the *Targum of the Prophets* remains shrouded (see *ArBib* 14:1).
65. *Tg. Neb.* 13:14 (*ArBib* 14:59–60). I have italicized the phrase highlighted by Farina.
66. The theory, he notes, has until now either been "unknown" or "disrespected" by commentators (*Leiblichkeit*, 312).
67. The preponderance of evidence appears to favor an AD second century date (see *ArBib* 14:13–18).
68. This is especially so since it does not appear that Hos 13:14 was considered very often in the intertestamental and rabbinical literature (see Str-B 3:483). Schade, who ponders Farina's theory, can certainly not be faulted for being unable to decide its merits: "Ich sehe mich außerstande, zu beurteilen, ob v 56 aus einer Auslegungstradition von Hos 13, 24 [sic] wirklich erklärt werden kann" (*Apokalyptische Christologie*, 210).

> Jedoch ist die exegetische Bemerkung des v. 56 zu v. 55 kaum von der rabbinischen Auslegung zu Hos 13,14 abhängig. Zwar begegnen in dieser Auslegung die Faktoren Tod-Tora-Übertretung, jedoch wird die Sonderstellung der ἁμαρτία als personifizierter aktiver Größe allein in 1 Kor 15,56 in Entsprechung zu Aussagen des Röm angezeigt, nicht aber in der rabbinischen Auslegung.... Eine auslegungsgeschichtliche Vorgabe von v. 55–56 über Hos 13:14 und die rabbinische Auslegung ist eine vage Vermutung, die als solche keinesfalls die Annahme, die exegetische Bemerkung v. 56 zu v. 55 sei in der Tradition vorgegeben, unterstützen kann.[69]

Finally, and most importantly, to embrace Farina's theory would be to assume that Paul's axiom, "The power of sin is the law" was based on a rabbinical interpretation that may or may not have been familiar to the Corinthian churches. It is hardly imaginable that Paul would mint a *truism* from material so remote.[70]

## A DIGRESSION IRRELEVANT TO THE CONTEXT

### Räisänen, Thielman, and Barrett

While the previous interpretations sought connections with 1 Cor 15:56 outside of the letter, some exegetes assume that the referent is Paul himself, or more precisely, his inner theological framework.[71] Thus, rather

---

69. Horn, "Stachel," 98–99 (see also Verburg, *Endzeit*, 90).

70. See pp. 64–65 n. 87, below. Klauck observes that even if one were to assume a relation to the Targum, one must still account for the pithy nature of the verse and its relation to Romans: "Aber auch dann müßte sagen, daß Paulus in änigmatischer Kürze, als Chiffre nur, einen Gedankengang hinwirft, mit dem er sich schon länger beschäftigt hat und den er im Römerbrief erst entfalten wird" (*Korintherbrief*, 122).

71. The theory of Chester regarding 1 Cor 15:56 is worth noting briefly even if it is not representative (see *Conversion*, 169–70). He detects in the verse a settled "theological opinion" of the Apostle concerning the law and sin (ibid. 169). While most, he notes, connect Paul's notion to Rom 5:13 and 7:7 and to the law-sin nexus that appears there, Chester argues that Paul's *conversion experience* is the source of his notion in 15:56: "Given that this opinion is that the law is the power of sin, and given that in Gal 1:11–17 and Phil 3:4–12 we have seen Paul connect his persecution of the church to his zeal for the law, then it is difficult to see a valid case against there also being a connection between Paul's theological opinion and his conversion experience" (ibid.). Chester's thesis, however, appears unlikely. Whatever parallels there may be between 1 Cor 15:56 and Galatians 3 and Philippians 3 they are not explicit enough to override the seemingly obvious echoes of v. 56 in Romans 5 and 7. Thus, the catalytic notion of the law that Paul would later expand

than the notion of law and sin having an immediate relationship to the context or to a Hellenistic or Jewish literary tradition, Paul, as Räisänen asserts, "just could not help spelling out this connection, although it was of no relevance for his present purpose."[72] In other words, the mention of sin and death in vv. 55–56a prompted Paul to recall the relationship between law and sin in v. 56b, which, it is assumed, was irrelevant to the discussion at hand. As Thielman describes it: "like a runner unable to stop at the finish line, Paul goes beyond the fitting climax to his argument to reveal an important conviction about the law which has not emerged in the rest of the letter."[73] Likewise, Barrett contends that "once embarked upon the theme, Paul though he does not develop it, cannot refrain from mentioning the third factor in the complex in which sin and death are two members."[74]

The manner in which v. 56b appears, however, argues against the contention that Paul's reference to the law there was an irrelevant digression appearing *ex nihilo*. The clause is first of all anything but rhetorically out of place. Rather than detecting evidence of a rhetorical blip at v. 56b, a scan of vv. 54–57 will reveal a clause that emerges smoothly from within its context. The statement, as will be shown, stands in a rhetorically balanced relation to v. 56a and fits comfortably within the rhetorical flow of the context as a whole. Its conformity to the rhetorical style of its context, in fact, is so exact that were 56b to be extrapolated, a rhetorical pattern begun in v. 51 and running through v. 56 would be

---

on in Romans 5 and 7, *not* his former zeal for the law and consequent persecution of the church, would be the theme lying closest at hand to 1 Cor 15:56. Furthermore, and more importantly, while it ought not be denied that "the fact that an issue is discussed in a theoretical manner does not of itself exclude the influence of experience upon one's conclusions" (ibid.), the settled nature of the axioms in 1 Cor 15:56 regarding sin and death and law and sin suggests that the truisms depicted there are informed by a reality that transcends Paul's personal experience.

72. Räisänen, *Paul and the Law*, 143.

73. Thielman, *Paul and the Law*, 108; see also Stanley, *Corinthians*, 323; Schnelle, *Paul*, 231. Though unexpected, Thielman finds Paul's statement regarding law in v. 56b understandable: "It is easy to see how, having introduced the subject of sin, he could deviate even further from his argument to say something more specific about where it gets its effectiveness" (ibid., 108). Nevertheless, though he appreciates the relation between v. 56b and Paul's inner logic, Thielman considers the clause to be "anti-climactic," "excursive," and "beyond the fitting climax to his argument" (*Paul and the Law*, 107–8).

74. Barrett, *First Corinthians*, 383.

broken.⁷⁵ Indeed, v. 56b bears no likeness to the typical Pauline "digression."⁷⁶ Rather, in contrast, the reference to the law in v. 56b "appears as a natural, undisputed element in the train of thought."⁷⁷ Nor is the topic of law in v. 56b thematically irrelevant to the discussion at hand. As will be shown, the notion of the catalytic operation of the law is not only relevant to 1 Corinthians 15 but is a perfectly fitting climax to Paul's argument there. In fact, Romans 5:20a, which "abruptly" introduces the catalytic function of the law,⁷⁸ concludes a discussion of Adam's sin and universal death, precisely as does 1 Cor 15:56. The latter verse should no more be considered an irrelevant afterthought than the former.⁷⁹

Nevertheless, while we will argue that 1 Cor 15:56 was prepared for by its preceding context, the perception among these exegetes that Paul in v. 56b could not help but recount the story of Christ's victory over "sin" and "death" without also mentioning "law" is quite telling. It suggests how closely Paul at this time had come to associate law with the entities of sin and death; the triad had already become for him "a systematically

---

75. See below, p. 62. García Pérez believes that nothing would be lost were v. 56 to be eliminated from the chapter (see "1 Co 15,56," 405). This, in our opinion, would only appear to be so. It fails to appreciate how the verse fits squarely into the rhetorical style and structure of the chapter.

76. Note, e.g., that the digression that begins in Eph 3:2 and runs through 3:21 is clearly parenthetical in nature: in Eph 4:1, Paul returns to where he left off in 3:1. In contrast, our next chapter will reveal intricate rhetorical and syntactical traits that strap 1 Cor 15:56 tightly into its immediate context.

77. Thurén, *Derhetorizing*, 116.

78. Some commentators understand Rom 5:20 to mean that the law serves in a *cognitive* capacity to identify sin as a violation (e.g., Morris, Black, Barth). Others argue that the verse depicts the law *intensifying* the seriousness of sin (e.g., Cranfield, Moo, Byrne). It appears more likely, however, that in Rom 5:20 the *quantitative* multiplication of sin is in view since Paul compares the increase of "sin" with the superabundant increase of "grace." Weima, in our view, correctly notes that "since the latter refers to an increase in quantity (not an increase in knowledge or intensity), the same is likely to be true of the former" ("Function," 232). Furthermore, a reference in Rom 5:20 to a *quantitative* increase of sin is a notion that most likely leads to the misunderstanding regarding licensciousness addressed in Rom 6:1-2 (see further, Brandenburger, *Adam und Christus*, 252–53; Bandstra, *Elements*, 127–28; Hofius, "Antithese," 203–4). Nevertheless, whatever be the relation of law to sin in Rom 5:20 (even if, though unlikely, v. 20 is speaking of the *result* rather than the *purpose* of the law's coming [see BDR §391.11; Esler, *Galatians*, 240–43]), the verse serves notice that the reference in 1 Cor 15:56 to *law and sin* following after a discussion of *sin and death* is not without precedent.

79. See p. 53, below.

established relationship."[80] And that this perception is correct is likely in view of the absence of outer conflict in Corinth over the role of the law. Here is a statement, unlike much of 1 Corinthians,[81] that transcends the immediate circumstances. It is therefore reasonable to assume that the reference to law in 1 Cor 15:56 was theologically motivated rather than circumstantially driven.[82] Even during this season of nomistic cease-fire, Paul, notes Hays, "cannot recount the story of Christ's victory over one of these powers without also mentioning the others, for the full story includes the good news that all three have been subdued by Jesus Christ."[83]

## A POLEMICAL STATEMENT RELEVANT TO THE CONTEXT

### Gertner, Matand Bulembat, and Morissette

Finally, other exegetes seek to bring the context of 1 Corinthians explicitly into the discussion of 15:56. One such attempt is that which considers v. 56 as part of a Pauline midrash on Hos 13:14, which is quoted (or alluded to) in 15:55. Collins heralds this approach with his statement that "there can be little doubt . . . that 15:54b–57 has the characteristics of a midrash.

---

80. Conzelmann, *First Corinthians*, 293; see also Stanley, *Corinthians*, 323.

81. Dunn notes that more than any of Paul's letters: "1 Corinthians indicates how much of Paul's theology as we have it was contextually conditioned" (*1 Corinthians*, 21).

82. While it does not appear that Paul was faced with a Judaizing opposition in Corinth, it is probable that opposition came from the other side of the fence, viz., from a libertine element (1 Cor 6:12ff.; 8:1ff; 10:23ff.). Drane postulates that the group, having a "Gnostic" bent, "maintained that by virtue of the pneumatic character of its members it was released from the normal rules of society and ethics" (*Libertine*, 105; see also Fee, *First Corinthians*, 11; Bruce, *1 and 2 Corinthians*, 90; Käsemann, *Essays*, 116–17)]. Thurén, on the other hand proposes that Paul himself was at least partially responsible for the libertinism (*Derhetorizing*, 102–3); i.e., the Apostle's rhetoric led to misunderstanding (cf. 1 Cor 5:9–13; 1 Cor 7:1). Whether the source of the libertinism in Corinth was a proto-Gnostic influence or a misunderstanding of Paul himself or something else (e.g., Christian Sophists? See Hall, *Unity*, 3–29 ), passages such as 3:1ff.; 5:1ff.; 6:5ff.; 11:17ff.; make it clear that there were serious ethical problems in the Corinthian camp (Wenham, "Whatever Went Wrong?" 137–41; contra Hurd, *Origin*, 277). Thus, not only is it likely that 1 Cor 15:56 appears in a setting where *legalism* was not a threat, but it emerges in a context where *licentiousness* was a threat. In such a setting one would expect Paul to be more "positive" toward the law, yet in 1 Cor 15:56 we encounter an extremely negative reference, where law is depicted alongside of sin. This suggests that 1 Cor 15:56 hovers above and beyond the external circumstances in Corinth.

83. Hays, *First Corinthians*, 277.

It is an applied commentary on a specific passage of Scripture."[84] There are three notable representations of this midrashic approach—those of Gertner,[85] Matand Bulembat,[86] and Morissette.[87] Gertner's study, the shortest of these, presents 1 Cor 15:55–56 as a prime example in the New Testament of a "covert" midrash,[88] i.e., one that "has been divested . . . of all midrashic appearance."[89] Indeed, he contends that it is only by recognizing the midrashic nature of the text that a coherent connection between 15:56 and the preceding verses can be discerned. In short, according to Gertner, Paul plays on the variegated interpretations of אֱהִי and דְּבָרֶיךָ in Hosea 13:14 by utilizing the midrashic techniques of *double reading* (*ʾal tiqrey*) and *double meaning* (*tartey mashmaʿ*). Thus, in his "first" interpretation of Hos 13:14, Paul emends the verb to אַיֵּה,[90] i.e., "where is" (as in the LXX) and interprets דְּבָרֶיךָ as "your plague or penalty."[91] This yields: "Where is thy sting, O death?" From there Paul moves to a second interpretation in which he this time reads the verb יְהִי, i.e., "it shall be" or

---

84. Collins, *First Corinthians*, 578. Collins cites 1 Cor 1:18—2:16; 10:1–13; and 15:20–28, which "clearly contain elements that show the midrashic technique at work" (ibid.). He thus concludes that "the remark [v. 56] is not incidental to his argument" (ibid., 582).

85. Gertner, "Midrashim," 267–92.

86. Maand Bulembat, *Noyau et enjeux*, 124–25.

87. Morissette, "Midrash," 161–88. Though Vicuña also argues in favor of a midrashic interpretation of 1 Cor 15:54–57 ("1 Corintios 15:54b-57," 4–19), he will not receive consideration here since his article is, to put it kindly, a mirror image of Morissette. Perhaps this is why his study is all but ignored in the literature.

88. Gertner, "Midrashim," 271; see also 282–83. Along with 1 Cor 15:56, Gertner examines Mark 4:1–22, Luke 1:67–75, and the letter of James as a whole (ibid., 271–201). Gertner argues that all these examples have three essential points in common: 1) In all of them the there is an apparent incoherence; 2) there has been no satisfactory explanation for this incoherence; 3) a solution is sought and found by uncovering their "veiled midrashic nature" (ibid., 271).

89. Ibid., 291. Gertner surmises that in his doctrinal discourses Paul would have presented this midrash in its entirety. In 1 Cor 15:55–56, however, "the literary form of the Epistle required the omission of the detailed midrashic apparatus" (ibid. 283). This begs the question, however, why such midrashic details do not appear in Romans 5–7.

90. The meaning of the form אֱהִי in Hos 13:14 is notoriously difficult. Most consider it a dialectical variant of אַיֵּה (see discussions in Stuart, *Hosea-Jonah*, 200 n. 10.a; Andersen and Freedman, *Hosea*, 639–40).

91. Cf. LXX: ἡ δίκη (i.e., "judgment/penalty/punishment"). Wolff following *KB* reads דֶּבֶר as "thorns" (*Hosea*, 221 n. gg). Since the word occurs in tandem with קֶטֶב in Ps 91:6, the traditional translations "plague" or "destruction" would seem preferable.

"it is" (as in the Targum) and interprets דְּבָרֶיךָ as "thy word, the Torah." He then affixes to this *covert* reading a doctrinal explanation in v. 56. This leads Gertner to the following paraphrase: "'Thy word, the Torah, will be, or is, death' *because* (he adds his doctrinal explanation) 'the sting of death is sin, and the strength of sin is the law.'"[92] According to Gertner, by means of this interpretative technique, Paul reads (and re-reads) the words of Hosea in a manner that serves both his doctrine concerning immortality and his negative evaluation of the law's role. Although this yields no "logical coherence" of thought between v. 56 and the preceding, there is, for Gertner, a "midrashic" coherence:[93] "In reading the first word of his quotation in two different versions (*'ayyeh-yehiy*) and in interpreting the second word of it (*debharekha*) in two different senses (Torah and penalty) Paul could thread on this Hosea verse two doctrines both important in their own right, but both belonging to different spheres of religious teaching, linked only by the biblical reference."[94]

In response to Gertner, though it is certainly possible that his scenario is correct, it is difficult not to be skeptical. First, there is no discernible evidence that Paul is doing a double reading of Hos 13:14 in the way in which Gertner argues. Indeed, the modifications that Paul *does* make of Hos 13:14 in v. 55 are *overt*, not covert.[95] Secondly, it need be fairly asked whether Gertner's theory provides the most probable solution to the riddle of 1 Cor 15:56. Is it reasonable to entertain covert testimony when, as we will see, there are overt parallels to consider from other Pauline texts, i.e., Romans 5 and 7? Thirdly, in light of the tight rhetorical stitching together of the clauses and the step parallelism in vv. 55–56, where Paul moves from *death* to *sting*, from *sting* to *sin*, and from *sin* to *law*,[96] there appears to be more "logical coherence" than Gertner detects.[97] Fourthly, though an analysis of the particle must await the exegesis of 1 Cor 15:56 below, it can at least be stated here that Gertner has no basis to translate δέ "because." Finally, what is perhaps most problematic

---

92. Gertner, "Midrashim," 283, italics mine.

93. Ibid.

94. Ibid., 283.

95. See below, pp. 59–60 n. 71.

96. Schrage also notes this "kettenartiger Form" (*Korinther*, 4:381). Cf. similar chain linking in Rom 5:3–5; 8:29–30; 10:13–15.

97. It is in light of this coherent movement in the text that Fee chooses to decline Gertner's proposal (*First Corinthians*, 805 n. 42).

about Gertner's proposal is that the theory has the inherent quality of being virtually unverifiable;[98] *hidden* midrashim are no easier to see than ghosts. Thus, in trying to assess what Gertner calls a "covert" midrash, it becomes almost impossible to move beyond possibilities to probabilities, which is the goal of the present study.

Matand Bulembat, who, like Gertner, recognizes the apparent dissonance that 1 Cor 15:56 brings to its context, also argues for a midrashic solution.[99] Unlike Gertner, however, who relies on lexical subtleties, Matand Bulembat builds on what he perceives to be thematic links between v. 56 and the context surrounding Hosea as a whole. Thus, citing Hos 12:15; 13:1–2, 12; 14:2, he notes that God threatens to deliver Israel over to the power of death because of her sin against the first commandment. Indeed, as long as she remained in an idolatrous state, the commandment to remain loyal to God would only aggravate the rebellion and thus bury Israel deeper under the threat of destruction.[100] It is this perceived story line regarding sin, death, and the first commandment in Hosea 12–14 that provides, for Matand Bulembat, the seguey into 1 Cor 15:56.[101] Following upon his declaration of victory in v. 55, Paul, remembering the context surrounding Hos 13:14, concedes (δέ = "certes") in v. 56 that in spite of this future victory, sin continues to exist in the believer, and the law continues to aggravate the situation.[102] Realizing, however, that this fact could douse the assurance of the victory announced in v. 55, Paul immediately follows in v. 57 with a response to the *concession* of v.

---

98. As Horn notes: "Unüberprüfbar ist natürlich die Vermutung von M. Gertner" ("Stachel," 98 n. 26).

99. "Ce verset constitue . . . une affirmation qui semble sortir de son contexte. Mais le modèle midrashique peut . . . expliquer comment le v. 56 n'est pas une interpolation. Il nous semble qu'il s'agit d'un commentaire paulinien basé sur le contexte d'Os 13,14" (*Noyau et enjeux*, 124).

100. "Tant qu' Ephraïm ne se convertissait pas," Matand Bulembat notes, "cela ne pouvait qu'aggraver son péché et—selon la logique prophétique—entraîner inéluctablement la mort" (ibid., 125).

101. Matand Bulembat also appears to suggest a link between Hosea and 1 Cor 15:56 via the notion of *power*: "La force (la gravité: δύναμις) de ce péché, consiste dans la non observation de la Loi" (ibid.). The term δύναμις, however, does not appear in LXX Hosea nor is the notion of power explicitly or implicitly associated with sin in the book.

102. See ibid. 1 Cor 15:56 thus "fonctionne comme une sorte d'objection au chant de victoire exprimé dans les versets précédents où le regard est posé sur le futur, sur le pas encore" (ibid.). Matand Bulembat does not specify the manner in which the law serves to aggravate sin in the believer.

56.¹⁰³ Matand Bulembat paraphrases the verses thus: "Certes, l'aiguillon de la mort, c'est le péché; et la puissance du péché, c'est la loi. Mais, grâce soit à Dieu qui nous donne la victoire par l'intermédiaire de notre Seigneur Jésus Christ."¹⁰⁴ Though 1 Cor 15:56, for Matand Bulembat, primarily comprises a reaction to the context surrounding Hos 13:14, it is nevertheless indisputable for him that the verse fits quite well within the thematic, i.e., *edenic*, context of 1 Corinthians 15 itself: "Qui douterait du fait que l'allusion à l'origine du péché et l'affirmation de la victoire sur la mort renvoient à la typologie Adam-Christ déjà exprimée dans les unités littéraires centrales des deux macro-unités précédentes (vv. 20–28 et vv. 44–49)?"¹⁰⁵ It should be noted, however, that, for Matand Bulembat, the themes that 15:56 has in common with its edenic context are *sin* and *death*. He considers Hosea, not Eden, to be the thematic antecedent of *law* in v. 56.

Some of the specifics of Matand Bulembat's interpretation will be assessed later in the exegesis of 1 Cor 15:55–57, including the (unsubstantiated) proposal that the δέ in v. 56 introduces a concession and should be translated "admittedly." For now, however, we can say that the epigram in 1 Cor 15:56 appears to define the *inherent* relationship between law and sin, not necessarily of law to the believer and, more importantly, that the links that Matand Bulembat proposes between 1 Cor 15:56 and Hosea appear to be tenuous. While arguing on the basis of audience competence can itself be tenuous, it is, nevertheless difficult to assume that Paul would have expected the Corinthians to make the associations from Hos 13:14 to the wider context of Hosea that Matand Bulembat suggests or that he would have assumed they would readily recognize Hosea as the source for the precise categories in 1 Cor 15:56 of law, sin, and death. Thurén correctly notes, for example, that the reference to "law" in v. 56 "appears as a natural, undisputed element in the train of thought; its role is implied to be easily accepted, maybe even self-evident for the addressees."¹⁰⁶ It is difficult to imagine that the link between law and Hosea that Matand

---

103. Matand Bulembat contends that v. 57 "est posé comme une antithèse (cf. δέ) à l'objection sournoise contenue dans le v. 56. Il est une réponse au doute qui est exprimé dans ce constat-ci: le péché est encore à l'oeuvre, rendu puissant par l'existence même de la Loi" (ibid., 126).

104. Ibid., 125.

105. Ibid., 126.

106. Thurén, *Derhetorizing*, 116.

Bulembat suggests would have been self-evident to the Corinthians. Nor is it plausible that the story line itself in Hosea served as the derivative of Paul's seemingly universal axioms concerning sin and death and law and sin. A source with more global relevance would seem to be expected to sustain such truisms.

Yet, in contrast to the improbability that the notions of law, sin, and death in v. 56 were quarried from Hosea, Matand Bulembat's passing observation that v. 56 "returns" to the edenic themes of vv. 20–28 and 44–49 inadvertently points to a more likely source. Would not Paul's Adam typology be a more obvious source of an *axiom* regarding sin and death than the prophets? And, rather than assuming that the law in v. 56 has Hosea, not Eden as its antecedent, should not Paul's theology of the Fall also be considered as a source of his axiom regarding law? This would seem all the more reasonable in light of the fact, to be later noted, that edenic, not Hosaic, shadows are observed elsewhere in Paul where the law-sin nexus appears.

Perhaps the most extensive case for a Pauline midrash, however, is Morissette's study.[107] Though his primary focus is vv. 54–55, Morissette devotes considerable attention to v. 56 and proposes that the verse is a Pauline commentary on Hosea 13:14. Crucial to this assessment are certain "faits littéraires relatifs à la structure du morceau" that suggest to Morissette that v. 56 is intimately linked to Hosea 13:14.[108] Specifically, the key terms in v. 56 (δύναμις and κέντρον) are stitched to Hos 13:14, and thus to v. 55, by means of the Hebrew terms יָד and קֶטֶב in Hos 13:14a:

> "Du fragment *Os.*, xiii, 14*a* et *b*, l'ApHtre reprend, en un *climax* à deux membres axé sur le terme ἁμαρτία, les deux expressions déterminées par le *nomen rectum SheEl* et dont l'une ouvre et l'autre referme le double parallélisme qui s'y trouve: la יָד du *SheEl* (cf. v. 56*b*: δύναμις) et sa קֶטֶב (voir v. 56*a*: κέντρον). Marqué ainsi par deux nouvelles métaphores, le commentaire paulinien consiste à appliquer celle de la "puissance" à Loi et celle de l' 'aiguillon' au Péché."[109]

---

107. Paul's argument in these verses, according to Morissette, offers "un exemple assez typique des habitudes littéraires et théologiques de l'ApHtre. Il illustre en particulier sa façon d'exploiter l'Écriture sous la forme midrashique" ("Midrash," 161).

108. Ibid., 176.

109. Ibid. (see also, 174 n. 51). In addition to the link he perceives between יָד and δύναμις, Morissette argues: "Quelle que soit sa signification, propre ou métaphorique, le mot κέντρον contient toujours l'idée d'une δύναμις, d'une certaine souveraineté même,

After proposing this link, Morissette proceeds to examine v. 56 and Paul's doctrine of law there. Though, for Morissette, the verse is *rhetorically* linked to Hos 13:14, it is *theologically* connected to and aimed at Jewish theology of sin, death, and law in general; i.e., v. 56a parallels rabbinic notions of sin and *death*,[110] and v. 56b counters rabbinic notions of sin and *law*.[111] Regarding these latter notions, though Paul is possibly using the term "law" to refer to "any law,"[112] *as he does, according to Morissette, in his "midrash" in Rom 7:9, 11 of Adam's experience with the Garden commandment*,[113] his law-sin axiom in v. 56 is polemically directed, he believes, at the traditional manner of speaking of the *Mosaic* law among the rabbis, viz., as a protective barrier against sin and death.[114] The Apostle in v. 56b, according to Morissette, bluntly denies this notion with a counter thought: rather than deterring sin and fostering life, the law, in fact, is the *power* of sin. Drawing from passages in Galatians, 2

---

dont est dotée une personne, un animal ou une situation" (ibid., 174).

110. Morissette asserts that "le contenu idéel de la métaphore du 'Péché, aiguillon de la Mort' est tout aussi rabbinique d'origine que l'image qui l'exprime" (ibid., 179). In regard to *sin*, Morissette argues that v. 56a draws from popular ideas regarding the evil inclination and the personification of sin (ibid., 177–79). Similarly, the notion of death's venomous *sting* finds parallels in the variegated rabbinic references to the angel of death and "the prick of his lance," the "spike" in his hand, or the "drops of poison" he causes the sick to swallow and die (ibid., 179). The link between *sin and death* reflects the well-known Jewish supposition that death is the consequence of sin (Morissette cites Sir 25:24; *Apoc. Mos.* 14:2; 4 *Ezra* 3: 7; 7:116–119; 2 *Bar.* 23[sic, 33?]:4; 48:42–43; *Sifr. Deut* 323 [138b]; *Sifr. Lev* 5:17; *Gen. Rab.* 16.6; 21.1, 5; *Deut. Rab.* 9.8 [ibid.]).

111. "Au verset 56a," writes Morissette, "Paul trahit ses dépendances juives concernant les rapports du péché et de la mort; en 56b, au contraire, il oppose en quelques mots le fait chrétien à la face du Judaïsme tout entier en stigmatisant la Loi comme 'la puissance du Péché'" (ibid., 176). See also Díaz Rodelas, *Pablo*, 29.

112. Morissette, "Midrash," 180. In light of similar contexts within Romans 5–7 where the law appears at times to assume cosmic dimensions (e.g., in Rom 7:9b), Morissette argues that law is likely being depicted by Paul in 1 Cor 15:56 as a "Puissance cosmique" in the service of sin and death (ibid.).

113. Ibid., 180–81. Italics here to stress a key point that will be revisited.

114. For rabbinic citations regarding the law as a prophylactic against sin, see ibid., 181 nn. 95–98. For references to the law as life preserving, see ibid., 181–82 nn. 99–105. Regarding the latter, Morissette quotes a statement attributed to R. Jose: "The Israelites accepted the Torah only so that the Angel of Death should have no dominion over them" (b. 'Abod. Zar. 5a [BTal. 29:21]) and a verse from Qumran: "And on the day on which one has imposed upon himself to return to the law of Moses, the angel Mastema [of hostility] will turn aside from following him, should he keep his words" (4QDa 15 XVI, 4–5 [*DSSSE* 1:565]; for Qumran text abbreviations, see *SBL Handbook*, 183–218).

Corinthians, and Romans,[115] Morissette argues that this *power* refers not to a catalytic function, but to the law's death-inflicting capacity of turning sins into identifiable and condemnable transgressions.[116] Thus, contrary to the rabbinic view that law leads to life, for Paul, "le Péché puise sa vigueur mortifère dans la loi."[117]

While some of Morissette's exegetical and hermeneutical insights will enjoy favor later during the exegesis of the text itself, especially his perception that νόμος in 1 Cor 15:56 is perhaps not a direct reference to the Torah,[118] the scenario that he proposes for 1 Cor 15:56 is implausible. First of all, again, while an audience competence argument has its limits, one can at least ask whether Paul would have expected the Corinthians to have drawn a syntactical line from δύναμις in 1 Cor 15:56 back to יָד in Hos 13:14. While Paul could assume that they were familiar with the Old Testament, would he have presumed that they would make the subtle connections that Morissette makes? Secondly, though the notion of *power* can be, and likely is, inherent in the expression *hand* in Hos 13:14a,[119] Paul does not, in fact, quote Hos 13:14a in 1 Cor 15:55. The antecedent יָד or χείρ (LXX) would thus have to be *assumed*. This would be out of step with the explicit rhetorical pattern that is exhibited in 1 Cor 15:55–57:

---

115. Unlike Gertner, who avoids bringing into the discussion Pauline passages parallel to 1 Cor 15:56, Morissette has no qualms with interpreting Paul with Paul. Thus, in regard to parallels in Galatians, Morissette argues: "Par conséquent, nous ne craignons pas, pour rendre compte du sens de la clause *1 Cor.*, xv, 56b, de recourir à l'*Épître aux Galates* qui, du reste, appartient à la même époque que *1 Cor.*, xv. Paul y fournit le motif pour lequel le Péché tire de la Loi sa puissance mortelle" (ibid., 182). Morissette cites Gal 3:10, 18, 22; 5:3; 2 Cor 3:6, 9; Rom 4:15; 7:7–11.

116. Morissette argues that the law "par l'information qu'elle fournit, fait des moindres désordres des 'transgressions,' multiplie ainsi les fautes formelles et conduit, par conséquent, à la 'mort' ou à la condamnation" (ibid., 183). Morissette likely draws this notion of "information" and "condemnation" from Benoit, to whom he earlier acknowledged his indebtedness (ibid., 181 n. 94). Regarding the manner in which sin utilizes the law to inflict its sting, Benoit argues: "If man dies, it is because the 'sting' of death has regained its deadly venom thanks to the Law and the moral information it brings" ("Law," 20).

117. Morissette, "Midrash," 182.

118. Also his methodology of considering parallel passages in the interpretation of 1 Cor 15:56 (on the latter, see above, n. 115). On the other hand, Morissette's notion that law in v. 56b is functioning in a condemning capacity rather than catalytically will not find a favorable reception.

119. See, e.g., AV, NASB, ESV, NRSV, NIV.

θάνατος (v. 55) → θάνατος (v. 56)

κέντρον (v. 55) → κέντρον (v. 56)

νῖκος (v. 55) → νῖκος (v. 57)

[יָד/χείρ (Hos 13:14)] → δύναμις (v. 56)

Finally, rather than being prompted by Hos 13:14, it is more likely that v. 56b receives its *entrée* from v. 56a. As will be noted, the two clauses are virtually antiphonal.

Yet, even if Morissette were correct that the axiom "the power of sin is the law" was consciously or unconsciously triggered by the term יָד in Hos 13:14a,[120] he misses the ultimate background to the phrase itself. And he does so in the face of a significant observation that he himself makes in passing, viz., Rom 7:7–11, a passage regarding law, sin, and death that he deems parallel to 1 Cor 15:56,[121] "se développe en effet sous la forme d'un *midrash* dont l'expérience adamique du 'précepte' et de la 'mort' constitue la base."[122] Indeed, based on the link between the passages, Morissette suggests that νόμος in 1 Cor 15:56, like the edenically nuanced ἐντολή in Rom 7:7–11, may apply to law *in general*, rather than only to Jewish law.[123] With these insights in mind, Morissette might have looked past Hos 13:14 and rabbinics and searched the Genesis account itself for a notion or episode more likely to have informed Paul's axiom that the power of sin is the law. However, Morissette fails to follow the sign posts he himself erects and pursues particulars to the exclusion of the universal. By interpreting the law-sin epigram in 15:56 from the perspective of rabbinics, he would have us believe that a particular misunderstanding of the Torah by certain Jews underlies what Paul presents as a universal truth regarding divine law and sin.[124]

---

120. Or by a notion of power implicit in the term קֶמַב. See n. 101, above.

121. See Morissette, "Midrash," 176–77.

122. Ibid., 180–81.

123. Ibid., 180.

124. It is not difficult to pinpoint the high water mark where Morissette recognizes that v. 56 appears to have universal application and yet recedes to become engrossed in legalistic *anti*-parallels to v. 56b: "S'il n'est pas impossible que l'énoncé *1 Cor., xv, 56b* se réfère à toute loi, il reste que son expression même vise, et non sans polémique, la manière traditionnelle de parler de la Loi mosaïque parmi les rabbins" (ibid., 181).

## García Pérez

A more recent attempt to bring the context of 1 Corinthians into the discussion of 15:56, and, next to Horn's interpolation theory, the most radical, is that of García Pérez. Arguing that 1 Corinthians is devoid of any polemic whatsoever against the Mosaic law,[125] García Pérez concludes that v. 56 cannot contain a reference to the law of the old covenant and proceeds to give the verse a novel makeover. To begin with, he contends that τῆς ἁμαρτίας refers in v. 56 not to *sin* but to an "error," or "lapse in knowledge."[126] Moreover, the definite article is best understood as a possessive. In the second clause, the genitive τῆς ἁμαρτίας is best rendered as the object of δύναμις, i.e., "the power *against* the error."[127] Regarding νόμος, he argues that the term in v. 56b is alluding to the "Written Law," i.e., "those writings that testify to the resurrection of Jesus,"[128] and since, for García Pérez, the article that accompanies νόμος can be translated as a possessive pronoun, he argues that Paul is referring in v. 56b to "our law," i.e., "the holy Christian writings."[129] The entire verse should thus be

---

125. After noting that νόμος, besides 15:56, occurs eight times in 1 Corinthians, García Pérez dismisses the four occasions where the term introduces an Old Testament quotation or allusion (1 Cor 9:8, 9; 14:21, 34) and argues that the other occurrences in 1 Cor 9:19–23 are unconcerned with the Torah (see "1 Co 15,56," 410–11). Regarding these latter verses, citing 1 Macc 7:5; 9:23, 58, 69; 11:25; 14:14; and Luke 22:37, García Pérez contends that ἄνομος in v. 21 refers not to Gentiles but to unbelieving (i.e., apostate) Jews (see ibid., 410). Conversely, citing LSJ 570 (though the lexicon deems the term in 1 Cor 9:21 to mean *subject to law*) and *TDNT* 4:1087 (though the volume states that in Judaism the term "mostly refers to the OT law" and that in 1 Cor 9:21 the notion of νόμος is implicit in ἔννομος), he argues that the adjective ἔννομος is descriptive of one who is "justo" (ibid., 411 n. 12). He thus suggests the following paraphrase of the heretofore obscure words in 1 Cor 9:21: "'not being godless (i.e., accursed) of God, but instead, righteous of Christ [justo de Cristo], i.e., made righteous by Christ'" (ibid. 411, translation here and following mine). Having this perspective of 1 Cor 9:19–23, García Pérez concludes that "neither is the Mosaic law in question nor the Paul's attitude towards it" (ibid.). He likewise finds no reference to the Torah in 1 Cor 7:19. Rather than denoting the Mosaic Law, the phrase ἐντολῶν θεοῦ is "a plural of excellency," i.e., "the definitive precept that God has revealed, and that is nothing else but to believe in Christ Jesus" (ibid., 408). He cites 1 John 3:22–24 and Gal 5:6 as parallels.

126. Ibid., 412. García Pérez appeals to LSJ 77; *TDNT* 1:267–316; and the classical scholar Kendall, "Oedipus," 195–97.

127. He finds in Matt 12:31 (ἡ δὲ τοῦ πνεύματος βλασφημία) and Mark 6:7 (ἐξουσίαν τῶν πνευμάτων τῶν ἀκαθάρτων) precedents for doing so ("1 Co 15,56," 413).

128. Ibid. 414.

129. I.e., a written gospel that circulated among the churches of Paul (see ibid., 414

translated: "The sting of death is our error, and the strength against our error is our Law."[130] Understood thus as an encouragement against the fear of death, 1 Cor 15:56 is reconciled to the discussion of death within the context.

Though García Pérez is confident that his translation reflects Paul's thought, the probability that he is correct is less than slim. Since he proposes so many improbable renderings, it would necessitate a virtually impossible lexical and syntactical alignment for his translation to fall on all fours.[131] And with regard to his assertion that ὁ νόμος in v. 56 is a

---

n. 20).

130. "El aguijón de la muerte es nuestro error y la fuerza contra el error es nuestra Ley" (ibid. 144).

131. To begin with, it is highly unlikely that the articles with ἁμαρτία and νόμος should be translated as possessive pronouns. Though instances of this usage are numerous in the New Testament (see, e.g., Matt 4:20, 21; 8:3; 13:36; 27:24; Mark 1:41; 7:32; Luke 13:13; 18:15; John 1:41; 3:17; 7:30; Acts 5:19; 21:40; Rom 4:4; 7:25; 16:23; 1 Cor 5:1; 2 Cor 8:18; 12:18; Eph 5:25; Phil 1:7), the notion of possession is almost always obvious (see Wallace, *Grammar*, 215–63; Nunn, *Syntax*, 58; Brooks and Winbery, *Syntax*, 72). There is no such implication in v. 56. Furthermore, there is little, if any, precedent for the article functioning as a possessive pronoun with abstract entities such as ἁμαρτία and νόμος (Wallace notes that the idiom is especially used when human anatomy is involved [*Grammar*, 215]). To the contrary, as will be later noted, the article in v. 56 with θάνατος, ἁμαρτία, and νόμος likely serves a generic function (see Verburg, *Endzeit*, 234). Moreover, with regard to the genitive τῆς ἁμαρτίας, it is unlikely that the words should be rendered as the object of ἡ δύναμις, i.e., "the power *against* sin." Though Mark 6:7 (ἐξουσίαν τῶν πνευμάτων τῶν ἀκαθάρτων), which García Pérez cites, might appear to contain a precedent (see also Matt 10:1; John 17:2), such a precedent is unlikely since the noun ἐξουσία here is probably following in the steps of the verb ἐξουσιάζω, which takes the genitive. It is also far from certain that δύναμις is a suitable lead noun in an objective genitive construction. Neither the noun δύναμις nor the verb δύναμαι follow this pattern. For a genitive noun to be categorized as an objective genitive (in the sense that García Pérez intends), most grammars require a verbal notion implicit in the head noun (see, e.g., Moule, *Idiom Book*, 39–41). More precisely, as Wallace notes, "*an objective genitive can only occur with verbal nouns which imply a transitive verb*" (*Grammar*, 117, italics his). Neither the New Testament nor Paul's usage elsewhere of δύναμις with the genitive provide precedent for García Pérez's translation (see Rom 1:16; 1 Cor 1:18, 2 Cor 12:9). Apart from rare exceptions where the verb takes the accusative (though in these cases the verb ποιεῖν is probably to be supplied [see BDAG 262. c.]) the verb δύναμαι is intransitive. It would appear that the noun δύναμις is likewise inherently intransitive. Furthermore, to render τῆς ἁμαρτίας as an objective genitive and not also τοῦ θανάτου in the previous clause may disrupt the evident parallelism within the verse (see further below, p. 67 n. 99). What is even less likely is García Pérez's contention that ἁμαρτία in v. 56 refers not to sin, but to an "error." Though LSJ does indeed pose the translations *failure, fault,* or *error*, it assumes for ἁμαρτία the definitions *guilt*

reference to Christian Scriptures—if, with García Pérez, we assume that Paul here is referring to writings, it is almost unthinkable that the Apostle would apply without qualification to Christian writings a term he uses elsewhere in the letter to designate the Hebrew scriptures.[132] And, in any case, to what *Christian* writing does García Pérez assume Paul is alluding to at this early date? If Paul, as García Pérez contends, did have in mind a written gospel that testified to Christ's resurrection, would he not have employed γραφαί,[133] a term that he uses in 1 Cor 15:3 when he argues for Christ's resurrection?[134] As with his thesis as a whole, García Pérez here is asking too much. Though the law, to be sure, seems not to have been an issue in Corinth and though this fact may provide a reason to assume that νόμος in v. 56 does not refer explicitly to the Mosaic law, this does not necessitate that the Torah cannot lie implicit.[135] And it certainly does not justify the inconceivable translation that García Pérez proposes.

## Söding

The most notable and sustained attempt to bring the context of 1 Corinthians explicitly into the discussion of 15:56 is that of Söding.[136]

---

and *sin* for contexts "in Philos. and Religion" (LSJ 77). Likewise, while *TDNT* indeed affirms that in secular Greek ἁμαρτία was the "least sharp" word for wrongdoing, it notes that the term in the LXX becomes a moral and religious concept of guilt, i.e., "there is seen in it an evil will and intention, . . . a conscious apostasy from and opposition to God" (Stählin, "ἁμαρτάνω, ἁμάρτημα, κτλ.," in *TDNT* 1:294). The same meaning is noted by *TDNT* in the New Testament (ibid., 1:295–96). And with regard to García Pérez's appeal to classical Greek, he offers no explanation why Paul in v. 56 would use ἁμαρτία in an Aristotelian sense and expect his readers to recognize the nuance. Since García Pérez admits that Paul in the Adam-Christ typology of Rom 5:12:21 employs the term ἁμαρτία to reflect upon the universal dimension of *sin* (see "1 Co 15,56," 405–6), it would seem reasonable to assume that this notion of sin is implicit in 1 Cor 15:21–22 and 45–49, verses parallel to Rom 5:12–21, and that these passages provide the antecedent to ἁμαρτία in v. 56. And finally, as will be argued, what is likely at issue in 1 Cor 15:56 are entities, not particulars and thus not individual errors or even sins, but *sin* (see Gaventa, "Cosmic Power," 229–40).

132. See 1 Cor 9:8, 9; 14:21, 34.

133. As he apparently does of Luke's gospel in 1 Tim 5:18.

134. See also 2 Peter 3:16.

135. See Morissette, "Midrash," 181.

136. Although Söding is often mentioned, his arguments are rarely engaged. García Pérez's article, one of the more recent treatments of 1 Cor 15:56, typifies the norm; he merely cites Söding in a footnote ("1 Co 15,56," 406 n. 2).

Though he recognizes the abruptness of the verse, he sees no need to presume it to be a gloss or to seek outside contexts to explain its meaning. For Söding, "die offenkundig massive Gesetzeskritik" is written against the background of Paul's implicit antinomism that can be detected within the context and in the letter as a whole.[137] Before turning to this wider context, Söding examines the place 1 Cor 15:56 occupies in its immediate setting and what may have triggered the reference to the law there. Specifically, he argues that in 1 Cor 15:20-28 and 41-49 Paul's Adam-Christ typology and consequent argument for the resurrection is a *polemical reinterpretation* of early Jewish Adam-traditions that 1) differentiated (with reference to Gen 1:27 and 2:7) two classes of humans: heavenly/immortal and earthly/transitory (Philo, *Creation* 134; *QG* 1.8; *Alleg. Interp.* 1.31),[138] 2) regarded Adam's sin as a transgression of the law (*4 Ezra* 3:6-7; 7:11; 8:52; Philo, *QG* 1.10; *Leg.* 1.59; *Tg. Neof.* Gen 3:23), and 3) identified Adam as the source of universal death (*4 Ezra* 3:26; 7:116-126; *2 Bar.* 23:4; 54:15).[139] Since Paul, he believes, is evidently tapping into these Jewish Adam-speculations, Söding assumes that he had to have also been aware of their tendency to consider strict law obedience to be a necessary prerequisite for salvation since Adam's transgression of it led to ruination:[140]

> "Wenn Paulus zur Begründung seiner Auferweckungstheologie auf die apokalyptisch geprägte Adam-Tradition von Gen 3 und unter ihrem Vorzeichen dann auf die mythologische Adam-Spekulation über Gen 1,27 und 2,7 rekurriert, begibt er sich auf ein theologisches Themenfeld, das im Frühjudentum von einer durch und durch positiven Wertung der Tora wie des Gesetzesgehorsams als der einzigen Möglichkeit eschatologischer Rettung besetz ist."[141]

---

137. See Söding, "Kraft," 76.

138. Söding argues that Paul turns the tradition on its head: "Paulus hingegen stellt den Mythos vom Kopf auf die Füße: Als den ersten Menschen weist er den sterblichen Adam aus, zu dem jeder Mensch seiner physischen Abstammung nach gehört, als den 'letzten Adam' aber Jesus Christus, der in dynamischer Wirk-Einheit mit dem Pneuma den Glaubenden das eschatologische Leben vermittelt" ("Kraft," 78-79).

139. See ibid., 78. Citations are Södings.

140. See ibid., 79. Söding cites *4 Ezra* 3:11; 7:17, 20-21, 24-25; 9:31.

141. Ibid.

For Söding, the upshot of the presence of Jewish Adam-traditions in 1 Corinthians 15 and Paul's critique and reworking of them is the lead-in this provides for the negative reference to the law in v. 56. Not only does v. 56a make explicit what was implicit in vv. 20-28 and 41-49,[142] viz., the mortality and transitoriness of all humans is the result of sin, but v. 56b climaxes, according to Söding, with a broadside against the legalistic notions that were present in these Jewish traditions.[143] With this reading of the text, Söding thus finds 1 Cor 15:56 to be a "genuiner Bestandteil" of Paul's train of thought.[144]

Though Söding contends that Jewish Adam-speculations within the immediate context triggered the negative reference to the law in v. 56, he argues that an antinomistic rhythm had, in fact, been pulsating from the letter's beginning. Paul, according to Söding, portrays the γραμματεύς in 1:20 as a legalistic prototype,[145] implies in 1 Cor 1:17-18, 24 and 2:5 that legalism stands in implicit contrast to ὁ λόγος τοῦ σταυροῦ,[146] and implicitly asserts in 1 Cor 7:18f. and 1 Cor 9:20ff. the abrogation of the law.[147] When Paul finally comes to his resurrection chapter and

142. Specifically, according to Söding, by way of vv. 3 and 17 (ibid., 80).

143. "Da Paulus," writes Söding, "durch einschlägige frühjüdische Positionen, möglicherweise auch durch problematische korinthische Rezeptionen veranlaßt, seine Argumentation auf eine Adam-Christus-Typologie abstellt und (bezeichnender Weise) zuerst die apokalyptische Auslegungstradition von Gen 3, danach dann die hellenistisch-spiritualische Exegese von Gen 1,26f.; 2,7 im christlichen Sinn umdeutet, liegt es aber auch nahe, daß er auf das Gesetz zu sprechen und den gut alttestamentlichen und jüdischen Gedanken, daß Toraobservanz zum ewigen Leben führt, von Christus her als irrig zu erweisen trachtet" (ibid).

144. Ibid.

145. I.e., since the scribes interpret the law as the epitome of the God's wisdom, they are blind to the eschatological and salvific event of Christ (see ibid., 83).

146. The term "law" does not occur in these verses, yet, for Söding the notion is implicit: "Das Stichwort Gesetz fällt zwar in 1 Kor 1-4 nicht. Dazu bestand auch kein Anlaß. Wohl aber ist davon die Rede, daß die Kreuzespredigt nicht nur den Griechen, die Weisheit suchen, als Torheit erscheint, sondern auch den Juden, die Zeichen fordern, als Skandal gilt (1, 22ff.). Dafür ist der Nomos zumindest mitverantwortlich" (ibid.).

147. With regard to the former verse, Söding asserts that "1 Kor 7,18f. bestreitet ausdrücklich jede soteriologische Relevanz der Beschneidung ... und explizit damit, was in Tauftraditionen wie Gal 3,26ff. und 1 Kor 12,13 angelegt ist. Wenn der Apostel im Gegenzug auf das Halten der Gebote Gottes abhebt, verpflichtet er die Korinther nicht auf Tora-Obervanz, sondern auf die Erfüllung des Willens Gottes, wie er in der Verkündigung des Evangeliums zur Sprache kommt" (ibid., 81) and regarding the latter, "Auch 1 Kor 9:20ff. stellt die Freiheit des Apostels vom Gesetz ausdrücklich fest; sie wird dadurch, daß er in seinem apostolischen Verkündigungsdienst den Juden wie ein Jude

is prompted by his recollection of the legalistic Jewish Adam-traditions, the antinomism that had been gaining steam boils over in vv. 56–57 with the declaration that victory over sin and death does not come by obedience to the law but by the death of Christ.[148] However, unlike Rom 7:7ff., which, according to Söding, describes the havoc the law works when it *provokes* one to do things that are forbidden,[149] the law in 1 Cor 15:56 is depicted as empowering sin by disrupting the relationship between God and humanity; i.e., when approached legalistically, the law contributes to sin's schemes by eclipsing God's design to save humanity through Christ alone. This, for Söding, is the very essence of sin:

> Auf der Seite der Sünde und des Todes kommt es [Das Gesetz] zu stehen, insofern (und soweit) es auf eine Vorstellung vom Willen Gottes festlegt, die ihn nicht mehr als den *Deus semper maior* wahrnehmen läßt und deshalb am auferweckten Gekreuzigten scheitert, in dem Gott seine ganze δύναμις und σοGα in einer Weise offenbart, die jeglicher Weltweisheit, auch einer am Gesetz orientierten, zuwiderläuft. Das tiefe Wesen der Sünde ist nach Paulus die Störung der Beziehung zu Gott (wie dann zum Nächsten). Zu dieser Störung trägt das Gesetz bei, *wenn* die Orientierung an ihm den Blick däfur versperrt, daß Gott sich entschlossen hat, die Menschen durch den auferweckten Gekreuzigten zu retten.[150]

Whether or not he is correct to discern allusions to legalism in the earlier chapters of Corinthians and in 1 Cor 15:20–8, 40–9, Söding, in

---

wird, nicht im mindesten aufgehoben—so wie auch seine Praxis im Umgang mit den Heiden nicht das geringste mit Libertinismus zu tun hat" (ibid.). In both verses it is clear to Söding that Paul implicitly deduces the abrogation of the law on Christological grounds; i.e., since Christ, through his death, has "qualified" and "quickened" those who believe, the requirements of the law have *de facto* been abrogated (ibid.).

148. Söding argues that the law-negative statement is Christologically situated: "Der adversative Anschluß von v. 57 macht klar, daß die Gesetzeskritik von 15,56 christological begründet ist: Während das Gesetz der Sünde dient und deshalb zum Tod führt, ist es der auferweckte Kyrios als πνεῦμα ζῳοποιοῦν (1 Kor 15,45), durch den Gott den Sieg schenkt, der in der Überwindung der Sünden (15,3.17) und schließlich auch des Todes in der endzeitlichen Auferstehung der Toten besteht (vgl. 15:20–28)" (ibid., 82). Goulder alights on a similar interpretation. He argues that the "driving power" of the law had dominated the discussion as far back as chapter 1, when Paul contrasted the word of the cross with the interpretations of the Jerusalem sages and scribes (*Competing Mission*, 196).

149. Söding cites the counter-suggestibility statement in Ovid, *Am.* 3.4.17, as an illustration. See above, n. 47.

150. Söding, "Kraft," 84.

our opinion, correctly identifies the *edenic* background of 1 Cor 15:56a-b.[151] He is one of the few to argue for this,[152] and in doing so he has discovered a key, heretofore neglected, that we believe helps unlock the verse's significance. Yet, for all this, Söding, we believe, makes a serious methodological error and drops the key by focusing on *Jewish* Adam-traditions rather than paying more careful attention to 1 Cor 15:56 and to the *Genesis* account itself. By transposing assumed Jewish legalistic notions onto 1 Cor 15:56, Söding precludes the possibility that Paul is, in fact, depicting a scenario there where the law is functioning *catalytically,* rather than being approached nomistically. Since Söding perceived a catalytic operation of the law in Rom 7:7ff.,[153] a passage that most every exegete associates with 1 Cor 15:56,[154] a better course, it seems, would have been to entertain a catalytic notion in 15:56 and follow the trail to see if a catalytic scent could be detected in the Genesis Fall narrative itself, especially since he detects edenic themes in the context. As it is, however, Söding makes the mistake of focusing on secondary sources to the exclusion of the primary sources. As a result, as close as he gets to unraveling the exegetical mystery of 1 Cor 15:56, he is thrown off track by incidental, if not irrelevant, themes.

---

151. Söding, we believe, is correct to affirm that there is "für Paulus durchaus einen plausiblen Grund, sie [die gesetzes-kritische Sentenz] in 1 Korinther 15 zu zitieren" (ibid., 76).

152. See also Schade, *Christologie*, 210.

153. See Söding, "Kraft," 80.

154. See, e.g., Wolff, *Erste Brief,* 209; Conzelmann, *First Corinthians,* 293; Fee, *First Corinthians,* 806; Garland, *1 Corinthians,* 746; Héring, *First Corinthians,* 182; Stanley, *Corinthians,* 322–33. Ortkemper finds that the Corinthian statement anticipates the entire theology of Rom 5:12f.; 7:7–13 (*Korintherbrief,* 166).

# 3

# 1 Corinthians 15:56 and Its Context

## CHAPTER OVERVIEW

ALTHOUGH IT SEEMS TO many that 1 Cor 15:56 appears out of thin air, this is not the case; the verse, as we will now see, appears within the context of a climactic unit of thought and fits precisely into its rhetorical structure.[1] The unifying theme of the fifteenth chapter is, of course, the resurrection of the dead,[2] and with this topic Paul comes to the last major subject of

---

1. Conzelmann notes, "Chap. 15 is a self-contained treatise" (*1 Corinthians*, 249). Mitchell asserts that "the integrity of 15:1-58 itself remains unchallenged" by partition theorists (Mitchell, *Rhetoric*, 284; see also Barth, *Resurrection*, 11). On the unity of the chapter, see Saw, *Rhetoric*, 181; Watson, "Strategy," 231-49; Bünker, *Briefformular*, 60; Eriksson, *Traditions*, 233. Sandelin identifies an overarching chiasm that begins at v. 12: A (vv. 12-21), B (vv. 22-28), C (vv. 29-34), C' (vv. 35-44a), B' (vv. 44b-49), A' (vv. 50-58) (*Auseinandersetzung*, 13). Whether or not Sandelin's blueprint is correct, there are some relatively clear indicators of the chapter's unity: the theme of *futility* likely functions as an inclusio marking the unit's beginning (v. 2) and end (v. 58) as do the phrases ἐν ᾧ καὶ ἑστήκατε (v. 1) and ἑδραῖοι γίνεσθε (v. 58) and the designations ἀδελφοί (v. 1) and ἀδελφοί μου ἀγαπητοί (v. 58). In addition, the terms ἐγείρω (vv. 4, 12, 13, 14, 15, 15, 15, 16, 16, 17, 20, 29, 32, 35, 42, 43, 43, 44, 52), νεκρός (vv. 12, 12, 13, 15, 16, 20, 21, 29, 29, 32, 35, 42, 52), and ἀνάστασις (vv. 12, 13, 21, 42) serve as connecting threads. For stylistic features that also serve to connect the chapter, see Saw, *Rhetoric*, 239-43. Among the devices Saw notes are Paul's use of the recurrence of the same letter (*alliteration*), the repetition of the same word (*transplacement*), and the continuous series of words with similar endings (*homoeoptoton*) (ibid., 242-43). Other characteristic rhetorical features in the chapter, particularly those that relate to v. 56, will be discussed below.

2. The four occurrences in 1 Corinthians of ἀνάστασις, all but one of the twenty occurrences of ἐγείρω, and all thirteen occurrences of νεκρός appear in this chapter. Though the matter has been hotly debated (see Fee, *First Corinthians*, 715 n. 6), the dualistic terminology in vv. 44-54 would make it appear that some in Corinth were express-

the letter.³ While Paul in the previous chapters addressed moral, cultural, and ecclesiastical concerns, he treats here a theological issue.⁴ The law-sin axiom of v. 56 thus appears in a chapter in which Paul's attention turns to doctrine. This is not to say that doctrine was absent prior to chapter 15. The repeated phrase, "Do you not *know*?" indicates the extent to which doctrine underlay Paul's earlier paraenesis,⁵ and the discussions regarding men and women in 11:3–12 and spiritual gifts in 12:4–31 are certainly doctrinal.⁶ Nor is it to imply that axioms are unwelcome in non-doctrinal contexts. Far from it. The axiom "a little yeast leavens the whole batch of dough" in 1 Cor 5:6 is both natural and obviously appropriate in its context.⁷ Yet, unlike elsewhere in the epistle, in 1 Corinthians 15 the discussion turns almost exclusively to doctrine, indeed deep doctrine. In

---

ing doubts about the *corporeal* reality of the resurrection (See Wright, *Resurrection*, 316; for a listing of proponents of this theory, see Thiselton, *First Corinthians*, 1174). Another possible scenario is that there were those (like Hymenaeus and Philetus in 2 Tim 2:17–18) who considered the resurrection already to have taken place (see von Soden, "Sakrament," 1–40; Schniewind, "Leugnung," 110–39; Käsemann, *Questions*, 108–37 and Bünker's argument in n. 26 below). Thiselton concludes that there were likely those in Corinth who were offended by *both* the bodily and future features of the traditional view (*First Corinthians*, 1176) as does Gillespie (*Theologians*, 205–18). Vos argues for a third scenario in which some at Corinth denied the possibility that there even is life after death ("Argumentation," 313–33; see also Schmithals, *Gnosticism*, 156; Moiser, "1 Corinthians 15," 12–14; Barrett (who sees two errors in Corinth: a denial of a resurrection *and* a denial of a bodily resurrection), "Significance," 121–22). The fact, however, that there were those being baptized for the dead (1 Cor 15:29) would seem to imply a belief in the afterlife. For a history of interpretation and analysis of the precise nature of the Corinthian heresy, see Spörlein, *Leugnung*, 1–19; Johnson, "Resurrection Rhetoric, 37–38 n 119; de Boer, *Defeat*, 96–104; Wilson, "Corinthians," 90–107; Plank, "Resurrection Theology," 41–54; Wedderburn, "Problem," 229–41. For a discussion of why a belief in the bodily resurrection held such importance to Paul, see Setzer, *Resurrection*, 66–70.

3. Fee finds an immediate repetition of two themes from the previous chapter (14:33–38): 1) what Paul is expounding is the common ground of *all* who believe and preach Christ, and 2) his apostolic ministry is the source of their life in Christ (*First Corinthians*, 713; see also Schrage, *Korinther*, 4:7–8; Barth, *Resurrection*, 11–13). For examples of other thematic threads to earlier chapters, see Saw, *Rhetoric*, 183 n. 17.

4. See Kistemaker, *First Corinthians*, 524. Hays observes that Paul is not concerned here to correct *behavior* but *beliefs* (*First Corinthians*, 252; see also Garland, *1 Corinthians*, 678). This is correct, yet note the paraenesis at the end of vv. 1–34 and vv. 35–58.

5. See 3:16; 5:6; 6:2, 3, 9, 15, 16, 19; 9:13, 24.

6. See further, Furnish, "Theology in 1 Corinthians," 59–89.

7. See also 6:12, 13; 10:26.

such a setting one should not be surprised, therefore, to meet in v. 56 "ein sentenzhafter Lehrsatz."[8]

The following formulae introduce various transitions of thought in 1 Corinthians 15:

Γνωρίζω δὲ ὑμῖν, ἀδελφοί (v. 1)

Εἰ δέ (v. 12)

Νυνὶ δέ (v. 20)

Ἀλλὰ ἐρεῖ τις (v. 35)

Τοῦτο δέ φημι, ἀδελφοί (v. 50)

Ὥστε, ἀδελφοί (v. 58)

Based on these grammatical markers, the chapter might be schematized as follows:[9]

1. "The good news that I proclaimed to you" (vv. 1-11)

2. "There is no resurrection of the dead" (vv. 12-19)

3. "Christ, . . . the first fruits of those who have died" (vv. 20-34)

4. "How are the dead raised?" (vv. 35-49)

5. "Listen, I will tell you a mystery!" (vv. 50-57)

6. "Therefore, my beloved, be steadfast" (v. 58)

Most scholars recognize the textual markers,[10] and most note these divisions, though they may choose to section the chapter into larger or smaller portions.[11] Most commentators also note the major shift that

8. Schrage, *Korinther*, 4:361.

9. See Gillespie, *Theologians*, 218-19.

10. Sandelin, however, is more impressed with various repeated words or thoughts that demarcate an end of one section and the beginning of another (*Auseinandersetzung*, 13). Note, for example, κηρύσσομεν/κηρύσσεται (vv. 11, 12); ἀπαρχή (vv. 20-23); θάνατος/ἀποθνῄσκουσιν (vv. 21, 22); νεκροί, ἐγείρονται (vv. 32, 35); σῶμα ψυχικόν and σῶμα πνευματικόν (vv. 44a, 44b).

11. E.g., Mack: vv. 1-2, 3-11, 12-19, 20, 21-28, 29-34, 35-44, 45-50, 51-58; Sandelin: 1-11, 12-21, 22-28, 29-34, 35-44a, 44b-49, 50-58; Bünker: vv. 1-2, 3a, 3b-11, 12-28, 28-34, 35-49, 50-58; Eriksson: vv. 1-2, 3-9, 12-19, 20-34, 35-49, 50-57, 58; Wegener: vv. 1-2, 3-11, 12, 13-34, 35-49, 50-57, 58; Lindemann: vv. 1-11, 12-19, 20-28, 29-34, 35-49, 50-57, 58; Schrage, Garland, and Johnson: vv. 1-11, 12-19, 20-28, 29-34, 35-49, 50-58; Vos: vv. 1-11, 12-21, 22-28, 29-34, 35-58; Watson: vv. 1-2, 3-11, 12-34, 35-57,

takes place between v. 34 and v. 35.[12] It demarcates the two main sections of the chapter—vv. 1–34 and vv. 35–58.[13] In the first section Paul is concerned with the resurrection on a general level, "specifying the relationship between the resurrection of Christ and the Christian."[14] Thus, in vv. 1–11 Paul appeals to the traditional belief in the resurrection of Christ,[15] and in vv. 12–34 he relates Christ's resurrection to the believer's.[16] In the second section he "takes up the specific problem caused by the second finite question, the resurrection of the body,"[17] i.e., how is the resurrected body to be defined?[18] At v. 35 the question is indirectly addressed by way of analogies concerning seeds and types of bodies (vv. 35–44) and in turn

---

58; Furnish, Stenger, and Saw: vv. 1–11, 12–34, 35–49, 50–57, 58; Wright: vv. 1–11, 12–28, 29–34, 35–49, 50–58; Aletti: vv. 1–2, 3–11, 12–34, 35–58; Allo, Witherington, and Fee: vv. 1–11, 12–34, 35–58; Mitchell: vv. 1–34, 35–49, 50–58; Verburg and Hays: vv. 1–34, 35–58.

12. Thiselton regards v. 34 as the logical "linchpin" of the chapter (*First Corinthians*, 1178). Bultmann finds the phrase ἀλλ' ἐρεῖ τις in v. 35 to be a characteristic turning point signal of the stoic-cynic diatribe (*Stil*, 66–67; see also Verburg, *Endzeit*, 58–59). Note Jas 2:18. Barrett contends that vv. 29–34 are a digression in that they begin with *ad hominem* arguments in support of Paul's doctrine of the resurrection and then move to moral exhortation in light of the disorder that might follow if the doctrine is denied. The doctrine itself has yet to be fully developed. In vv. 35–49, Barrett argues, Paul begins to do so (*First Corinthians*, 369).

13. See Hays, *First Corinthians*, 254.

14. Eriksson, *Traditions*, 267. The section as a whole turns on the logical absurdity of believing in Christ's resurrection while denying one's own. Note the recurring εἰ in vv. 12, 13, 14, 16, 17, 19, 29, 32, 32.

15. Paul appears to be establishing common ground here. Note the reiteration in vv. 1–2 and in v. 11 that the tradition cited is something that *they too* have believed. It is relatively certain that Paul is repeating here an early creedal formulation. Fee notes: 1) the terms παραλαμβάνω (vv. 1, 3) and παραδίδωμι (v. 3); 2) the stylized form of four statements in two balanced sets; 3) the repeated ὅτι before each clause, which implies a quotation; 4) the appearance of several non-Pauline words in such a short span (*First Corinthians*, 717 n. 21; see also Conzelmann, "Analysis," 15–25; Jeremias, *Eucharistic Words*, 101–5; Kloppenborg, "Analysis," 351–67; Webber, "Note," 265–69). Sibinga theorizes that Paul in vv. 1–11 consciously used a composition technique on the basis of the number 160 ("Divisions," 54–59). Sibinga's theory, at best, seems impossible to verify.

16. Collins notes a chiastic pattern in vv. 12–34: A (vv. 12–19), B (vv. 20–28), A' (vv. 29–34). Elements A and A' presume that the resurrection of Christ is related to that of the believer. Element B seeks to explain this link (*First Corinthians*, 527).

17. Eriksson, *Traditions*, 267.

18. The section treats both the logical possibility and the conceivability of the resurrection of the dead (see Thiselton, *First Corinthians*, 1178).

by the *Adam-Christ* analogy (vv. 45-49), which picks up from vv. 21-22.[19] Indeed, as Wright observes, the entire second half of 1 Corinthians 15 is built on the foundation of Genesis 1-2.[20]

Most writers identify vv. 50-58 as the climax of the chapter.[21] How (or if) the phrase τοῦτο δέ φημι, ἀδελφοί in v. 50 relates to the previous section is unclear. For Jeremias, whereas vv. 35-49 addressed the question *how* (πῶς) in relation to the body, vv. 50ff. address the question *how* in relation to the beatific vision, i.e., how could they see God at all?[22] This may be correct since it seems that Paul introduces the "metaphysical road-block" in v. 50 to set up the dramatic proclamation that follows.[23] In any case, in light of the use of τοῦτο δέ φημι in 1 Cor 7:29 and 10:19, the phrase is likely introducing a new phase in the argument,[24] yet in doing so it signals a summary and conclusion of the argument.[25]

Scholars, viewing the chapter from different vantage points, have, of course, observed and emphasized various features in the logical flow.[26] Of direct relevance to the present study, however, is an insight of

19. It appears that the pivot point of vv. 35-49 is v. 42, "So it is with the resurrection of the dead," while the summary and punch-line is v. 49, "Just as we have borne the image of the man of dust, we will also bear the image of the man of heaven."

20. Wright, *Resurrection*, 340.

21. Fee, e.g., finds the passage to be a "magnificent crescendo" (ibid., 797). Wright notes that the paragraph has "the sustained excitement of a celebration" (*Resurrection*, 356; see also Schrage, *Korinther*, 4:361; John Gillman, "Comparison," 443).

22. Jeremias, "'Flesh and Blood,'" 151-59. Jeremias detects a chiastic structure signaled by the questions in v. 35: "How are the dead raised? With what kind of body do they come?" Paul, argues Jeremias, takes up the second question in vv. 35-49 and the first in vv. 50-57. It is difficult, however, to assess whether the two questions are distinct or whether the second amplifies the first; the latter appears to be more likely from the context (see Schrage, *Korinther*, 4:279 n. 1363). More importantly, Jeremias's interpretation misses the climactic nature of vv. 50-57(8).

23. Garland, *1 Corinthians*, 742; see also Lang, *Korinther*, 238-39.

24. See Eriksson, *Traditions*, 273.

25. See Wright, "Adam," 367; BDAG 1053.2.

26. Gillespie, for instance, has noted the way in which the argument contained in vv. 12-49 is bracketed by an appeal to apostolic tradition in vv. 1-11 and by prophetic revelation in vv. 50-57. He concludes that since the *kerygma* is interpreted by *revelation*, chapter 15 may be identified as an instance of "prophetic discourse" (*Theologians*, 219). Many others in recent years, to greater or lesser degrees, have sought to identify and organize the argument of chapter 15 in terms of classical Greek rhetoric (see, e.g., Wegener, "Rhetorical Strategy," 438-55; Aletti, "Rhetorique," 396; Mack, *Rhetoric*, 56-59; Verburg, *Endzeit*, 255-69; Schrage, *Korinther*, 4:3-421; Saw, *Rhetoric*, 176-289; Watson, "Strategy,"

Conzelmann that is taken up by Chester and applied to the structure of chapter 15 as it relates to v. 56.[27] Chester writes:

> The sequence of Paul's references to sin in 1 Cor 15 . . . repays observation. Conzelmann . . . says of 15:56 that "in content it is prepared for by vv. 3–5; the hearer, when it is read out, hears the creed in the background; then v. 17." Thus there is first a statement that Christ died for concrete sins (15:3), and finally a statement concerning the power of sin (15:56), with an intervening statement which seems to bridge the two by stating that if Christ has not been raised then the Corinthians are still in their sins (15:17). This corresponds to the sequence of the argument of Romans 1–8, which first deals primarily with sin as transgression (chapters 1–4), and finally with sin as power (6–8), but has chapter 5 as a bridge between the two. Note also the similarity

---

231–49; Eriksson, *Traditions*, 232–78, 310–13; Mitchell, *Rhetoric*, 175–7; Collins, *1 Corinthians*, 525–84; Witherington, *Conflict*, 291–312; Thiselton, *First Corinthians*, 1169–1306; Bünker, *Briefformular*, 59–72; Matand-Bulembat, *Noyau et enjeux*, 33–129). Along this vein, for instance, Collins sees vv. 1–11 as an introduction of Paul's argument regarding the resurrection with vv. 1–2 serving as the *exordium* and vv. 3b-5 functioning as a kind of *narratio*. The next two sections, vv. 12–34 and 35–57, function as proofs (*pisteis*) of the argument in vv. 1–11. The former is set forth in a chiastic pattern: A (vv. 12–19), B (vv. 20–28), A' (vv. 29–34) the latter joins a "midrashic" exposition of Genesis 1–2 (vv. 35–49) to an apocalyptic scenario that provides Paul with the language to answer his imaginary interlocutor (vv. 50–57). The argument is then brought to a close with the *peroratio* of v. 58 (see *First Corinthians*, 526–27). With eyes also tuned to rhetorical style, Bünker detects a parallel between the style of 1 Corinthians 15 and 1 Corinthians 1–4 (*Briefformular*, 72):

| 1:10–17 | = | 15:1–3a | exordium |
| 1:18–2:16 | = | 15:3b-11 | narratio |
| 3:1–17 | = | 15:12–28 | argumentatio I |
| 3:18–23 | = | 15:29–34 | peroratio I |
| 4:1–15 | = | 15:35–49 | argumentatio II |
| 4:16–21 | = | 15:50–58 | peroratio II |

From this, he deduces that those that Paul opposed in 1 Corinthians 15 were sacramentalists who assumed that eschatological existence (including resurrection) could be experienced in the present (ibid.; see also Sandelin, *Auseinandersetzung*, 147–49). Aside from the interpretative conclusions of Collins, Bünker and others, it is highly questionable whether they are justified in taking classical rhetorical categories that were applied to oral discourses and ascribing them wholesale to Paul's *writings* (see Weima, "Aristotle," 458–68; Stamps, "Rhetorical Criticism," 129–69; Porter, "Rhetorical Categories," 100–122).

27. Conzelmann's reference is found in *1 Corinthians*, 293 n. 43. Eriksson makes the same observation as Conzelmann (*Traditions*, 274).

between Paul's exclamation of thanksgiving at 1 Cor 15:57, and that at Rom. 7:25.[28]

Chester's observation is insightful, and with the following fine-tuning it becomes, in our view, even more so. First, if, as Chester contends, the sequence of 1 Corinthians 15, *sins — resurrection — power of sin*, is reflected in the first half of Romans, the culmination point would be Romans 7 rather than Romans 8. Since, as Chester notes, 1 Cor 15:57 marks the conclusion to the argument preceding it, and it parallels Rom 7:25,[29] which, in turn, concludes the argument of Romans 7, the logical end point of the parallel would be Romans 7:25.[30] Secondly, rather than identifying the theme of 1 Cor 15:56 and Romans 6–7 as *the power of sin*, it would seem more precise to view *law and sin* as the theme. 1 Corinthians 15:56 concerns more than the power of sin; there is a predicate: the power of sin *is the law*. Similarly, on the Romans end, it is not the power of sin, but law and sin that occupies center stage in Romans 7.[31] In addition, a statement concerning law and sin (Rom 5:20) indirectly precipitates the discussion in Romans 6, and another (Rom 6:14) recharges it. Indeed, the question contained in Rom 7:1,[32] the hinge verse between chapters 6 and 7,[33] indicates that the law had been a part of the discussion in chapter 6 and would continue to be in chapter 7.[34] Thirdly, both in 1 Corinthians 15 and Romans 1–8, in between the notions of *sins* and *the power of sin*, Chester sees a linking theme or "bridge," viz., *the resurrection of Christ*. It would seem better to adjust the focus of the parallel by recognizing the bridge in each composition to be the *Adam-Christ analogy*. While eter-

---

28. Chester, *Conversion*, 170 n. 70.

29. Banks argues that the thanksgiving in Rom 7:25 bears the "closest formal, verbal and conceptual resemblance" to 1 Cor 15:57 than to any of Paul's other *Charisspruchen*, ("Romans 7.25a," 38).

30. Rather than being a continuation of the argument of Romans 7, Romans 8 appears to return to the themes Paul took leave of at the end of Romans 5 (see Moo, *Romans*, 469–70; and below, pp. 238–39 n. 6).

31. See Stendahl, "Introspective Conscience," 92–93.

32. "Do you not know, brothers and sisters—for I am speaking to those who know the law—that the law is binding on a person only during that person's lifetime?"

33. Romans 7:1–6 appears to be an elucidation of Rom 6:14 with 7:7–25 serving as a clarification (see Kuss, *Römerbrief*, 2:432).

34. See below, pp. 237–53.

nal life may be a discernible theme in Rom 5:12-21,[35] the Adam-Christ motif is pervasive there. Both Romans 5 and 1 Corinthians 15 (and in the New Testament, only these chapters) share this cosmic plot line,[36] even though, like Paul's statement in v. 56 regarding law and sin, the Adam-Christ analogy appears only in axiomatic form in 1 Corinthians 15.[37] Finally, Chester observes that the keynote in 1 Cor 15:3 that *Christ died for our sins* is reflected in Romans 1-4. Thematically this appears to be the case,[38] and lexical matches between 1 Cor 15:1-3 and Romans 1-4 are, in fact, present.[39] Yet, if the scope of the analysis is allowed to extend into the first half of Romans 5, as it should,[40] Chester would find that his case is strengthened by further parallels that emerge. Though the precise string Χριστὸς ἀπέθανεν ὑπὲρ τῶν ἁμαρτιῶν ἡμῶν does not occur in Romans 1-4 (nor elsewhere in the New Testament),[41] similar phrasing occurs in 5:6 (Χριστὸς ... ὑπὲρ ἀσεβῶν ἀπέθανεν) and in 5:8 (Χριστὸς ὑπὲρ ἡμῶν ἀπέθανεν). In addition, a key word in 15:2,

---

35. De Boer, *Defeat*, 141-80.

36. Fee sees the Adam-Christ analogy in 1 Corinthians 15 as "the key to everything" (*First Corinthians*, 777).

37. See Scroggs, *Last Adam*, 82-84.

38. Indeed, based on the introductory premise in Rom 1:2 that the gospel was "promised beforehand through his prophets in the holy scriptures," what follows in Romans 1-4 could be viewed as an argument leading to the conclusion that *Christ died for our sins according to the Scriptures*.

39. E.g., εὐαγγέλιον: 15:1/Rom 1:1, 9, 16, 2:16; εὐαγγελίζομαι: 15:1/Rom 1:15; σῴζω: 15:2/Rom 1:16 (σωτηρία); πιστεύω: 15:2/Rom 1:16, 3:2, 22; 4:3, 5, 11, 17, 18, 24; γραφή: 15:2/Rom 1:2; 4:3.

40. There is no valid reason why it should not. Although the οὖν of 5:1 is transitional (see Fitzmyer, *Romans*, 394), the central theme of Romans 1-4 (justification through faith in the redemptive work of Christ) is *revisited* even as the implications are applied. Dunn notes this. In Rom 5:1-11 he identifies deliberate "backward links" to Romans 1-4 (*Romans*, 1:242). E.g., δικαιοσύνη/δικαιόω ἐκ πίστεως announced in 1:17 and developed in 3:21-4:25 is summed up in Rom 5:1 and 9; the "salvation" language in 5:9-10 recalls 1:16; echoes of the central argument of 3:21-26 are present in 5:2 (χάρις), 5:9 (ἐν τῷ αἵματι αὐτοῦ), and 5:9, 11 (νῦν); central themes contained in the: indictment of 1:18-2:29 appear in reverse: ὀργή (1:18/5:9), ἀσέβεια/ἀσεβής (1:18/5:6), δόξα (1:21, 23/5:2), ἀδόκιμος/δοκιμή (1:28/5:4), καυχᾶσθαι ἐν θεῷ (2:17/5:11), ἀσθενής, ἀσεβής, ἁμαρτωλοί, ἐχθροί (1:19-32/5:6-10).

41. If, as suggested above (see n. 15), 1 Cor 15:3-5 is a pre-Pauline creed, we would not necessarily expect Paul to quote it to his (Jewish?) interlocutor in Romans 1-4.

σῴζω, appears in 5:9, 10, and a reference in 15:1 to the posture of the saved (ἵστημι) is found in Rom 5:2.

When 1 Corinthians 15 is, therefore, placed alongside of Romans 1–7 (with the nuances that we have suggested), a parallel thematic progression emerges, especially between the second and third stages:[42]

| 1 Cor 15:3 | 1 Cor 15:21–22 (45–49) | 1 Cor 15:56 |
|---|---|---|
| *Christ died for our sins* | *As in Adam all die* | *The power of sin is the law* |
| Romans 1–5:1–11 | Romans 5:12–21 | Romans 6–7 |

There are three inferences to post here before proceeding. First, though the embryonic statement in 1 Cor 15:56 regarding law and sin might initially appear to be out of context, it appears at the same point in its setting that Paul's law-sin discussion appears in the thematic sequence mirrored in Romans. This, as Thielman contends, should "serve as a warning that Paul can make compressed statements about the law which have underneath them a coherent—albeit unexpressed—foundation."[43] Secondly, though some look elsewhere for parallels,[44] it would seem that any analysis of 15:56 must consider both the thematic flow of Romans 1–7 and, especially, the argument contained in Romans 6–7,[45] with which 15:56 shares a lexical, thematic, *and* sequential affinity.[46] Kruse's quip is appropriate: "It is very debatable whether recourse to Hellenistic popular philosophy to interpret this text is better than recourse to Paul's letters to the Galatians and the Romans."[47] Finally, the fact that the law-sin nexus of 15:56 reappears in Romans within a similar sequential movement provides us with a recurrence of the phenomenon. This gives us the op-

---

42. By itself, the fact that Christ's death is expounded in both Romans 1–4 and 1 Cor 15:3 might hold little significance. After all, it would be expected that the heart of Paul's gospel would appear in a letter such as Romans, whose theme is the gospel and in 1 Cor 15:3, where the gospel is being elucidated. Yet, when 1 Corinthians 15 is placed against the backdrop of Romans 1–7, Chester appears to be correct that a corresponding sequence emerges.

43. Thielman, "Coherence," 249.

44. E.g., Hollander and Holleman, Gertner, Matand-Bulembat, García Pérez.

45. Even as a study of the embryonic axiom "In Adam all die" in v. 21 must consider Rom 5:12–21.

46. Lexemes shared between 15:56 and Romans 6–7 include νόμος, ἁμαρτία, and θάνατος. The relationship between δύναμις and the verbs ἐνεργέω (Rom 7:5) and κατεργάζομαι (Rom 7:8) will be discussed below.

47. Kruse, *Paul*, 143.

portunity to examine both settings to determine what common themes surround and may have prompted Paul's mention of the law-sin nexus. Before we do this, however, we now zoom in on the closing unit in 1 Corinthians 15 and then more closely still on 15:56 itself.

## 1 CORINTHIANS 15:54-58—A CLIMACTIC UNIT

Having argued in vv. 35-44 for the reasonableness of a bodily resurrection and in vv. 45-49 for its certainty based on Christ's heavenly body, Paul in vv. 50-58 emphasizes the necessity of change and the inevitability of victory over law, sin, and death.[48] Most scholars, as noted earlier, recognize that these verses contain the climactic conclusion to the chapter.[49] The passage consists of two sub-sections (vv. 50-53 and 54-57) and a closing admonition (v. 58), whose reference to futility may hearken back to v. 2 and serve as the end marker of an inclusio.[50] In the first sub-unit we encounter a recurring contrast between mortality and immortality that serves as a linking motif.[51] In order to be suitable for the celestial

---

48. See Fee, *First Corinthians*, 797.

49. Saw identifies the passage as a *peroratio*, which amplifies, recapitulates, and excites the emotions of his audience (*Rhetoric*, 238; see also Bünker, *Briefformular*, 71). Whether or not the designation is appropriate (see n. 26, above), almost every commentator senses the climactic nature of these words (see n. 76, below).

50. See Morissette, "Midrash," 163. Although vv. 50-58 are generally recognized as the final unit, most observe the shift indicated in v. 58 by ὥστε and thus note the verse's independence from the preceding. Thus, Bünker finds v. 58 to be functioning as the resolution to the argument of the chapter in its entirety: "Die Abschlußmahnung v. 58 nimmt . . . exordiale Gedanken und Wendungen wieder auf, womit sich 1 Kor 15 als in sich geschlossener Argumentations-prozeß, als wohldurchdachte und durchaus kunstvoll disponierte Rede erweist" (*Briefformular*, 72). Grosheide suggests that the verse marks the conclusion of the epistle (*First Corinthians*, 395). Mitchell argues similarly, since, in her view, it recapitulates the central argument of the letter itself (*Rhetoric*, 290; see also Collins, *First Corinthians*, 578-79). In light of the inclusionary themes noted above (see n. 1), however, it is more likely that the verse serves as the conclusion to chapter 15 (see Watson, "Strategy," 248). The conclusion to the letter likely appears in 16:13-24.

51. I.e., σὰρξ καὶ αἷμα . . . οὐδὲ ἡ φθορά/ἡ ἀφθαρσία (v. 50); τὸ φθαρτὸν τοῦτο/ἀφθαρσία . . . τὸ θνητὸν τοῦτο/ἀθανασία (v. 53). Note: σὰρξ καὶ αἷμα not σάρξ. At issue is the mortal nature, not the evil nature. Jeremias argues (famously) for a contrast between σὰρξ καὶ αἷμα, i.e., (in his view) the living and ἡ φθορά, i.e., the dead ("'Flesh and Blood,'" 151-59). Thus, the thought of v. 50 would be that "neither the living nor the dead can inherit the kingdom of heaven as they are" (ibid., 154). "Suggestion intéressante," quips Senft (*Corinthiens*, 211). Barrett embraces it (*First Corinthians*, 379) as does Eriksson (*Traditions*, 273). Yet, while a contrast between the living and deceased

environment, it is imperative that all, living or dead, undergo a radical transformation;[52] the perishable *must* (δεῖ, v. 35) assume imperishability and the mortal, immortality.[53] The presence of this unifying theme in v. 50 and vv. 52b-53 encloses the sub-section:[54]

---

is certainly apparent in vv. 51-52, the parallelism in v. 50 is more likely to be synonymous rather than synthetic; i.e., rather than σὰρξ καὶ αἷμα being a reference to those alive at the parousia, the phrase is essentially synonymous with ἡ φθορά (see Gillman, "Transformation," 316; Asher, *Polarity*, 152-53; Perriman, "Parousia," 513-14; Usami, "1 Cor 15:35-58," 489-90). To argue with Jeremias ("1 Cor. 15.50," 152) that the abstract noun ἡ φθορά refers to "corpses in decomposition" forces Paul's language "into such a narrow sense that it simply cannot be sustained" (Fee, *First Corinthians*, 798 n. 11). Note, e.g., how φθορά in v. 42 applies to *the living* not the dead (contra Eriksson, *Traditions*, 273 n. 158). The prior string of *contrasting* pairs (44, 45, 47, 48) and the entire train of thought of vv. 50-53 is also against Jeremias's thesis (see Conzelmann, *1 Corinthians*, 290; Verburg, *Endzeit*, 57-61) as are numerous commentators (see listing in Garland, *1 Corinthians*, 741 n. 1).

52. The verb ἀλλάσσω in vv. 51, 52 serves as a *stichwort* (Sellin, *Streit*, 223).

53. Conzelmann sees here an "apocalyptic" order rather than a necessity of nature (*1 Corinthians*, 291; see also Senft, *Corinthiens*, 212). That is, "Δεῖ bezeichnet auch hier keine Naturnotwendigkeit, sondern umschreibt apokalyptisch die eschatologische Notwendigkeit bzw. den göttlichen Heilsplan" (Schrage, *Korinther*, 4:376 n. 1876; note v. 25; see also Gillman, "Comparison," 444).

54. See W. Stenger, "Beobachtungen zur Argumentationsstruktur von 1 Kor 15," *LB* 45 (1979): 122-23; Verburg, *Endzeit*, 84. Collins notes this pattern as well (*First Corinthians*, 573). Gillman also observes a chiastic structure but lays it out according to whole verses, i.e., A (v. 50), B (vv. 51-52), A′ (v. 53) ("Transformation," 321). Stenger proposes an $A^{xy}$ B C B′ $A'^{yx}$ structure (vv. 50/51/52ab/52cd/53) in which vv. 51-52 focus on the future whereas vv. 50 and 53 are timeless presents ("Beobachtungen," 121). Matand Bulembat detects a more complex structure:

| | | |
|---|---|---|
| A (*propositio*) negatively | v. 50b: | σὰρξ καὶ αἷμα βασιλείαν θεοῦ κληρονομῆσαι οὐ δύναται |
| | v. 50c: | οὐδὲ ἡ φθορὰ τὴν ἀφθαρσίαν κληρονομεῖ |
| B (*ratio*) | a: v. 51b: | πάντες οὐ κοιμηθησόμεθα |
| | v. 51c: | πάντες δὲ ἀλλαγησόμεθα |
| | b: v. 52aα: | ἐν ἀτόμῳ, ἐν ῥιπῇ ὀφθαλμοῦ, |
| | c: v. 52aβ: | ἐν τῇ ἐσχάτῃ σάλπιγγι |
| B′ (*conformatio*) | c′: v. 52bα: | σαλπίσει γὰρ |
| | b′: --------- | ---------------- |
| | a′: v. 52bβ: | καὶ οἱ νεκροὶ ἐγερθήσονται ἄφθαρτοι |
| | v. 52bγ: | καὶ ἡμεῖς ἀλλαγησόμεθα |
| A′ (*propositio*) positively | v. 53a: | δεῖ γὰρ |
| | v. 53bα: | τὸ φθαρτὸν τοῦτο ἐνδύσασθαι ἀφθαρσίαν |
| | v. 53bβ: | καὶ τὸ θνητὸν τοῦτο ἐνδύσασθαι ἀθανασίαν |

A  ⁵⁰Τοῦτο δέ φημι, ἀδελφοί, ὅτι σὰρξ καὶ αἷμα βασιλείαν θεοῦ κληρονομῆσαι οὐ δύναται οὐδὲ **ἡ φθορὰ τὴν ἀφθαρσίαν** κληρονομεῖ.

B  ⁵¹ἰδοὺ μυστήριον ὑμῖν λέγω· πάντες οὐ κοιμηθησόμεθα, πάντες δὲ ἀλλαγησόμεθα, ⁵²ἐν ἀτόμῳ, ἐν ῥιπῇ ὀφθαλμοῦ, ἐν τῇ ἐσχάτῃ σάλπιγγι·

A′  σαλπίσει γὰρ καὶ οἱ νεκροὶ ἐγερθήσονται **ἄφθαρτοι** καὶ ἡμεῖς ἀλλαγησόμεθα. ⁵³ Δεῖ γὰρ **τὸ φθαρτὸν τοῦτο** ἐνδύσασθαι **ἀφθαρσίαν** καὶ **τὸ θνητὸν τοῦτο** ἐνδύσασθαι **ἀθανασίαν**.

The next section (vv. 54–57), "the climactic conclusion of the chapter,"[55] is linked to vv. 50–53 by the virtually exact,[56] and likely emphatic,[57] recurrence of v. 53 in v. 54:

⁵³δεῖ γὰρ τὸ φθαρτὸν τοῦτο ἐνδύσασθαι ἀφθαρσίαν καὶ τὸ θνητὸν τοῦτο ἐνδύσασθαι ἀθανασίαν.

⁵⁴ὅταν δὲ τὸ φθαρτὸν τοῦτο ἐνδύσηται ἀφθαρσίαν καὶ τὸ θνητὸν τοῦτο ἐνδύσηται ἀθανασίαν

Besides the change from the infinitive to the subjunctive, the only noticeable difference between the verses are the lead words δεῖ γάρ (v. 53) and

---

Verburg, for his part, observes a chiastic correspondence between v. 50b and v. 50c on the one hand and v. 53a and v. 53b on the other (*Endzeit*, 85). He tabulates it thus:

| | | |
|---|---|---|
| ⁵⁰ᵇ σάρξ καὶ αἷμα | → | βασιλεία θεοῦ |
| ⁵³ᵇ τὸ θνητόν | → | ἀθανασία |
| ⁵⁰ᶜ ἡ φθορά | → | ἀφθαρσία |
| ⁵³ᵃ τὸ φθαρτόν | → | ἀφθαρσία |

55. De Boer, *Defeat*, 129.

56. Wright notes that repetition such as of v. 53 in v. 54 is rare in Paul: "Clearly this is a point he wants to underline, to rub in as hard as he can" (*Resurrection*, 357).

57. Regarding v. 54, Eriksson quotes Cicero on the use of repetition (*epanaphora*) and reduplication (*Rhet. Her.* 4.28.38): "The reiteration of the same word makes a deep impression upon the hearer and inflicts a major wound upon the opposition—as if a weapon should repeatedly pierce the same part of the body" (*Traditions*, 274 n. 162). Schrage suggests that "die Wiederholung von v. 53 in der Protasis des Konditionalsatzes in v. 54a unterstreicht die Gewichtigkeit der Aussage von v. 53" (*Korinther*, 4:378; see also Weiß, *Korintherbrief*, 379). Calvin asserts that we have in v. 54 not a mere "amplification" but a "confirmation" of the previous sentence; "what the prophets have been told is bound to be fulfilled" (*First Corinthians*, 344).

ὅταν δέ (v. 54).⁵⁸ Yet by embedding the statement into a temporal clause the temporal aspect becomes dominant.⁵⁹ Having spoken in v. 53 of the inevitability of the transformation, Paul turns in vv. 54ff. to its eschatological realization.⁶⁰ The syllable-by-syllable match between the colae of v. 54 parallels that of v. 53 and from here on will be a distinctive stylistic feature throughout vv. 54–57. The chapter culminates with a flourish of rhetorical passion and eloquence.⁶¹

Yet, while stitched to the previous verses, vv. 54–57 comprise a distinct, climactic, and, as just noted, stylistic unit. By way of "step parallelism,"⁶² the sequence moves from a quotation of Isa 25:8 in v. 54

---

58. There are variants in the textual tradition of v. 54. The reading adopted above is supported by ℵ² B C²ᵛⁱᵈ D Ψ 075 1739ᶜ·⁽ᵐᵍ⁾ 1881 𝔐 vgᵐˢˢ *al*. Some manuscripts (with slight variations) support a shorter reading: ὅταν δὲ τὸ θνητὸν τοῦτο ἐνδύσηται ἀθανασίαν (𝔓⁴⁶ ℵ* C* 088 0121a 0234 1739* itᵃʳ vg copˢᵃᵐˢ, bo goth eth Marcion Irenaeusᵍʳ,ˡᵃᵗ *al*). This was probably the result of homoeoarcton or homoeoteleuton. Metzger suggests that the readings of A 326 copˢᵃᵐˢ (cf. also F G 365 614* 629*) arose after this oversight was noticed, but the omitted clause was restored in the wrong sequence (*Textual Commentary*, 502-3). The omission of the entire verse (F G 614* 1877* itᵍ copᵇᵒᵐˢ) is almost certainly explained from homoeoteleuton with v. 53 (ibid., 503). If the longer reading is accepted, this would be an occasion where the suspicion of homoeoteleuton would outweigh the canon that the shorter reading is to be preferred (see Aland and Aland, *Text of the New Testament*, 281).

59. See Verburg, *Endzeit*, 86; Watson, "Strategy," 247. The use of ὅταν with the aorist subjunctive in v. 54 strengthens the notion of future eventuality (BDF §382.3). For other instances of ὅταν (with an aorist subjunctive) followed by τότε, see 15:28; Col 3:4.

60. Gillman notes: "The repetition of the mortal/immortal, corruptible/incorruptible and clothing terminology in v. 54ab does not merely connect ideas; it signals a subtle, though significant, advance in thought" ("Comparison," 444; see also Collins, *First Corinthians*, 582; Ortkemper, *Korintherbrief*, 166). Conzelmann sees v. 54 moving beyond the "formal statement (the mortal puts on immortality) to the apocalyptic conception" (*1 Corinthians*, 292). Allo contends that the repetition of τοῦτο in vv. 53–54 underlines the continuity of the present body: "L'adjectif démonstratif τοῦτο est répété *quatre fois*, pour inculquer fortement l'identité du corps ressuscité avec celui qui est maintenant, ou qui a été, corruptible et mortel; ainsi l'image intiale du grain (voir vv. 35–38) est toujours applicable pour l'essential" (*Corinthiens*, 434; see also Sider, "Resurrection Body," 437; Dahl, *Resurrection*, 10, 94–95; Héring, *First Corinthians*, 181). That vv. 53–54 denote an eschatological experience is evident from the subordinate clauses there that describe the cause of death's defeat and from the trumpet imagery (v. 52; cf. v. 23), which, like 1 Thess 4:16, marks death as an event occurring on the *last* day (see Wright, *Resurrection*, 359; Asher, *Polarity*, 173 n. 51; Gillman, "Comparison," 443; Schrage, *Korinther*, 4:378-79).

61. Meyer notes its "elevated and emotional tone" (*Corinthians*, 107; see also Schrage, *Korinther*, 4:361 n. 1796).

62. Fee's designation (*First Corinthians*, 805).

to a quotation in v. 55 of Hos 13:14. Both quotations are connected by a key word association;[63] all three colae contain the term θάνατος.[64] The focal issue of the passage, as in the chapter as a whole, remains death.[65] Paul's line of thought, linked by an explanatory δέ,[66] then proceeds to two "concise and powerful statements" in v. 56 regarding death, sin, and law.[67] The final term in each line becomes the key word that leads to the phrase found on the next rung.[68] The pattern is Pauline.[69] Though the step parallelism could have continued with the term νόμος leading to a further clause, the passage climaxes on the reverberating note of "law."[70] After reaching the furthest step with νό-

63. See Ellis, *Paul's Use*, 50.

64. The reading in v. 55 of ᾅδη for θάνατε in ℵ[c] A[c] K P Ψ 88 104 614 𝔐 syr[p, h] goth arm *al* is likely a scribal attempt to conform the text to LXX Hos 13:14; Paul never uses ᾳ ῞δης. For an earlier example in 1 Corinthians of multiple Old Testament quotations connected by a *stichwort*, note: σόφοι: 1 Cor 3:19 (Job 5:13; Ps 93:11). Compare also: λίθος: Rom 9:33 (Isa 8:14; 28:16); λαός: Rom 9:25–26 (Hos 2:23; 1:10); ὀφθαλμούς: Rom 11:8, 19 (Isa 29:10; Deut 29:4; Ps 68:23–24); ἔθνη: Rom 15:9–12 (Ps 17:40; Deut 32:43; Ps 116:1). See Vollmer, *Alttestamentlichen Citate*, 36; Ellis, *Paul's Use*, 50 n. 2.

65. See de Boer, *Defeat*, 132.

66. Morissette asserts that the particle "signale la distance . . . entre la situation présente du chrétien (v. 56) et l'achèvement définitif du dessein divin (vv. 54 s.)" ("Midrash," 176). This may be reading too much into the conjunction (and context). Since the thoughts of v. 56 are conveyed in axiomatic form it would be difficult to limit the application to Christians (contra also Thurén, *Derhetorizing*, 122–25). Rather, it would appear that Paul is expressing universally applicable truisms: *it is in the very nature of things* that sin is the cause of death, and law empowers sin. Rather than functioning adversatively, the conjunction is functioning continuatively ("als bloß Übergangspartikel ohne irgendwie bemerkbaren Ggs." [Bauer, *Wörterbuch*, 342.2]) or more specifically, as in 1 Cor 10:4, 11a, in an explanatory manner (see BDAG 213.2). It is left untranslated by major English versions.

67. Godet, *First Corinthians*, 444. Fee comments: "Not only has *death* been overcome by resurrection; but *mutatis mutandis* so have the enemies that have brought death to all — sin and the law" (*First Corinthians*, 805).

68. The sequence νῖκος . . . κέντρον, supported by 𝔓[46] ℵ* B C 1739*[vid] vg cop[sa, bo] *al*, is to be preferred to the reverse sequence found in D* Ψ K P 88 *al*. The latter most likely arose as a correction intended to conform Paul's wording to LXX Hos 13:14.

69. See, e.g., Rom 5:3–5; 8:16–17, 29–30; 10:8–9; 10:13–15; 2 Cor 3:16–17; Eph 4:8–11. Koch finds the pattern to be common in Greek literature (see *Schrift*, 230). In 2 Cor 3:16–17; Rom 10:8–9; Eph 4:8–11, and as in 1 Cor 15:54c-56, Paul takes up in his interpretation/application a term from an Old Testament citation.

70. In Rom 2:14, where Paul links together four clauses by means of the catch word νόμος, he similarly ends the final clause with the term νόμος:

ὅταν γὰρ ἔθνη τὰ μὴ νόμον ἔχοντα
φύσει τὰ τοῦ νόμου ποιῶσιν,

μος, v. 57 returns to the theme of *victory* that was sounded in v. 54b.⁷¹

οὗτοι νόμον μὴ ἔχοντες
ἑαυτοῖς εἰσιν νόμος·

Though the syntactical pattern is dissimilar to that of 1 Cor 15:56b, the rhetorical effect served by placing νόμος in the final position is not.

71. The reading νεῖκος in 𝔓⁴⁶ B D* 088 is most likely the result of *itacism*. The term occurs nowhere else in the New Testament (see Aland and Aland, *Text*, 286). How to relate Paul's "quotations" of Isa 25:8 and Hos 13:14 to the Old Testament texts is notoriously difficult (see discussions in Stanley, *Language*, 209–15; Matand-Bulembat, *Noyau et enjeux*, 117–21; Morissette, "Midrash," 168–76; de Boer, *Defeat*, 127). As his preface suggests (τότε γενήσεται ὁ λόγος ὁ γεγραμμένος), Paul is citing these passages rather than "writing freely, in scriptural language, of the ultimate victory over death" (Thus Barrett, *First Corinthians*, 383; see also Morris, *First Corinthians*, 229). Yet, this is where the difficulty begins. The versions, including Theodotion (θ′) and Aquila (α′), read as follows:

| | |
|---|---|
| 1 Cor 15:54c: | κατεπόθη ὁ θάνατος εἰς νῖκος |
| LXX Isa 25:8: | κατέπιεν ὁ θάνατος ἰσχύσας |
| MT Isa 25:8: | בִּלַּע הַמָּוֶת לָנֶצַח |
| θ′ Isa 25:8: | κατεπόθη ὁ θάνατος εἰς νῖκος |
| α′ Isa 25:8: | καταποντίσει τὸν θάνατον εἰς νῖκος |
| 1 Cor 15:55: | ποῦ σου, θάνατε, τὸ νῖκος; |
| | ποῦ σου, θάνατε, τὸ κέντρον; |
| LXX Hos 13:14: | ποῦ ἡ δίκη σου θάνατε; |
| | ποῦ τὸ κέντρον σου ᾅδη; |
| MT Hos 13:14: | אֱהִי דְבָרֶיךָ מָוֶת אֱהִי קָטָבְךָ שְׁאוֹל |

With regard to Isa 25:8, Paul appears to be influenced by the sense of the Hebrew reading rather than the LXX. His quotation of Isa 25:8 may be a free rendering of the Hebrew comparable to the Greek versions of Theodotion or Aquila, a direct quote of a Ur-Theodotion textual tradition (see Stanley, *Language*, 211; Gillman, "Comparison," 445; for recent theories identifying Ur-Theodotion with the first century *Kaige*, see Jobes and Silva, *Septuagint*, 284–87), or it may reflect the occasional LXX idiom of substituting the phrase εἰς νῖκον for לָנֶצַח (2 Sam 2:26) and νίκος for נֶצַח (Job 36:7; Amos 1:11; 8:7; see Caird, "Septuagint, 24; Harrelson, "Death," 1990], 155; Morissette, "Midrash," 168–70). In any case, the Apostle appears to be in step with an interpretive tradition and found it applicable to the *victory* procured by Christ (15:25–26, 57). Thus Ellis argues that "the idea of death 'being swallowed up in victory' is so intimately connected with the 'victory' of Christ's resurrection that, if a conjecture must be made, the probability is that this interpretation of the Hebrew is one created (or recovered) in the early church" (Ellis, "Hermeneutics," 131). With regard to v. 55, if Paul changed the LXX δίκη (דְּבָר) in the MT) to νῖκος it would have been to link Hos 13:14 to the notion of victory found in Isa 25:8 (Hollander and Holleman, "Relationship," 274). Yet, Paul may not have enacted a *change*. The possibility "cannot be lightly dismissed" that "Paul found τὸ νῖκος already in his Greek *Vorlage*" (Stanley, *Language*, 212–13). The advancement of σου is almost certainly done for emphasis (see BDF §473). Koch aptly remarks that "die außergewöhnlich weite Voranstellung des Possessivpronomens, das jeweils durch den Vokativ θάνατε vom Bezugswort getrennt ist, verleiht dem Zitat eine stark rhetorische Wirkung, was

As in every case in which it occurs in Paul's *charisspruchen*,[72] the δέ that introduces the thanksgiving in v. 57 stands in contrast to what precedes.[73] The law-sin-death triumvirate is doomed. The particle also serves to connect the exclamation back to proclamation of victory in vv. 54c-55.[74] The thought progression in 1 Cor 15:54–57 is observed in the following layout:

```
┌─ ⁵⁴ᶜ Κατεπόθη ὁ θάνατος εἰς νῖκος.
│                    │
│    ⁵⁵ ποῦ σου, θάνατε, τὸ νῖκος; ποῦ σου, θάνατε, τὸ κέντρον;
│                                                   /
│            ⁵⁶ᵃ τὸ δὲ κέντρον τοῦ θανάτου ἡ ἁμαρτία,
│                                              /
│                  ⁵⁶ᵇ ἡ δὲ δύναμις τῆς ἁμαρτίας ὁ νόμος
│
└─ ⁵⁷ τῷ δὲ θεῷ χάρις τῷ διδόντι ἡμῖν τὸ νῖκος διὰ τοῦ κυρίου
   ἡμῶν Ἰησοῦ Χριστοῦ.
```

Evident at the first reading and especially upon closer examination is the rhetorical passion that surges in vv. 54–57. The unit, "débordant

---

seiner Funktion als Schlußaussage von 1 Kor 15 insgesamt voll entspricht" (*Schrift*, 107). Though θάνατος and ᾅδη are rhetorically synonymous, by replacing θάνατε ... ᾅδη (מָ֫וֶת ... שְׁאוֹל) with the double vocative θάνατε, Paul heightens the object of his taunt and achieves a rhetorical emphasis. A common view argues that Paul made the substitution to avoid any association with the Greek deity ᾅδης (Pluto), the god of the inferno (see e.g., Kistemaker, *Corinthians*, 585; Morissette, "Midrash," 172–73). This theory, however, is unfounded. The term ᾅδης was widely used in both Jewish and early Christian religious writings (see *TDNT* 1:146–49). In light of the rhetorically charged nature of 15:54–57, Stanley is likely correct that the reason behind the change was *rhetorical* rather than *religious* (*Language*, 215). The resulting parallelism, as noted, heightens the rhetorical pitch and (linked with the occurrence of the term in vv. 54, 56 and united to the key word νῖκος) achieves a rhetorical flourish that signals not just the end of the *discussion* (contra Koch, *Schrift*, 115; Stanley, *Language*, 215), but the end of *death* itself.

72. See Rom 6:17; 7:25; 2 Cor 2:14; 8:16.

73. It is difficult to explain away the awkwardness of the adversative δέ in v. 57 were v. 56 an interpolation.

74. Schneider observes this: "Von dieser Aussage hebt sich, wiederum mit einem δέ, noch einmal V 57 ab, um im Blick auf die Glaubenden den so entstandenen Gegensatz zwischen den VV 54c-55 einerseits und V 56 anderseits zu überbrücken, indem er betont, daß der erst am Ende völlig überwundene Tod gleichwohl grundsätzlich niedergeworfen ist" (*Vollendung*, 48).

d'enthousiasme à la fin d'un exposé théologique de grande envergure,"[75] erupts in a burst of poetical fervour.[76] Along with the overall rhythm noted in the above layout, the following rhetorically-charged features are evident in vv. 54-57: 1) the attributive σου in v. 55 is twice advanced to the head of it clause and separated from its noun for emphasis;[77] 2) rhyme occurs at the end (v. 54a and v. 54b) and/or in the middle of the members (v. 54a and v. 54b, v. 55a and 55b);[78] 3) a double chiasm can be detected within the fabric of vv. 55-57, i.e., A: **τὸ νῖκος** ποῦ σου, B: **θάνατε**, τὸ κέντρον; τὸ δὲ κέντρον τοῦ **θανάτου** κτλ., A':... **τὸ νῖκος**;[79] 4) the parallel members in vv. 55, 56, carry the same number of syllables.[80]

## 1 CORINTHIANS 15:56—TWO AXIOMS

Looking more closely now at v. 56, the syntactical structure of each of its clauses is mirrored in the other. Each contains the pattern, art.-conj.-nom.-art.-gen.-art. nom:

```
56a  τὸ  δὲ  κέντρον  τοῦ  θανάτου  ἡ  ἁμαρτία,
56b  ἡ   δὲ  δύναμις  τῆς  ἁμαρτίας  ὁ  νόμος.
```

Though prosaic, there is a distinct rhythm. As we noted above, each cola contains the same number of syllables (as is the case in the parallel members in vv. 53, 54, 55). This rhetorical feature, known as *isocolon*,[81] though

---

75. Morissette, "Midrash," 165; Saw, *Rhetoric*, 257.

76. See Stanley, *Corinthians*, 321. Not a few commentators have noted the rhetorical surge that takes place here. De Wette deems the passage "ein lyrischer Schluss" (*Erklärung*, 143). Morissette observes that the passage "présage ceux, hymnniques, de l'Épître aux Romains (cf. viii, 31-39; xi, 33-36)" ("Midrash," 165). Robertson notes: "There is the perfection of poetic form in the noble prose in... 1 Cor 15:54-57" (*Grammar*, 1200). Horsley deems the strophe an "ecstatic exultation" (*1 Corinthians*, 214). Hays marks the "resonant climax" (*First Corinthians*, 275). Bünker asserts that the passage is expressed "mit stark affektischer Sprache, ja mit großer Emphase" (*Briefformular*, 71). Díaz Rodelas refers to its "vigor axiomático" (*Pablo*, 28). See also above, n. 23.

77. See n. 71, above.

78. I.e., at the end: ἀφθαρσίαν (v. 54a) and ἀθανασίαν (v. 54b); in the middle: τὸ φθαρτόν (v. 54a) and τὸ θνητόν (v. 54b). See Morissette, "Midrash," 165.

79. I have placed the inner chiasm in italics. See Verburg, *Endzeit*, 89. Stenger recognizes only the overarching chiasm ("Transformation," 321).

80. See Saw, *Rhetoric*, 257; Morissette, "Midrash," 165.

81. Though *isocolon* and *parisosis* are often viewed as synonymous (e.g., Lausberg treats both devices under the heading of *isocolon* [*Handbook*, §§719-54]), *isocolon*

present elsewhere in 1 Corinthians,[82] is primarily discovered, along with *parisosis*,[83] in chapter 15, clustering at vv. 39–56:[84]

| | |
|---|---|
| 11b | οὕτως κηρύσσομεν |
| 11c | καὶ οὕτως ἐπιστεύσατε. |
| | |
| 14b | κενὸν ἄρα τὸ κήρυγμα ἡμῶν, |
| 14c | κενὴ καὶ ἡ πίστις ὑμῶν· |
| | |
| 21a | ἐπειδὴ γὰρ δι' ἀνθρώπου θάνατος, |
| 21b | καὶ δι' ἀνθρώπου ἀνάστασις νεκρῶν. |
| | |
| 22a | ὥσπερ γὰρ ἐν τῷ Ἀδὰμ πάντες ἀποθνήσκουσιν, |
| 22b | οὕτως καὶ ἐν τῷ Χριστῷ πάντες ζῳοποιηθήσονται. |
| | |
| 39b | ἄλλη μὲν ἀνθρώπων, |
| 39c | ἄλλη δὲ σὰρξ κτηνῶν, |
| | |
| 39d | ἄλλη δὲ σὰρξ πτηνῶν, |
| 39e | ἄλλη δὲ ἰχθύων. |
| | |
| 40a | καὶ σώματα ἐπουράνια, |
| 40b | καὶ σώματα ἐπίγεια· |
| | |
| 40c | ἀλλὰ ἑτέρα μὲν ἡ τῶν ἐπουρανίων δόξα, |
| 40d | ἑτέρα δὲ ἡ τῶν ἐπιγείων. |

---

(ἰσόκωλον, *having equal members*) is more precisely defined as a "figure comprised of cola ... which consist of a virtually equal number of syllables" (Cicero, *Rhet. Her.* 4.20.7 [Caplan, LCL]; see also Smyth, *Grammar*, §3031; Spencer, *Literary Style*, 297–98).

82. See, e.g., 1 Cor 1:22, 23, 24. None of these examples, however, is as precise as those that appear in 1 Corinthians 15.

83. Smyth defines *Parisosis* (παρίσωσις, *almost equal*) as "the approximate equality of clauses as measured by syllables" (*Grammar*, §3038; see also Lanham, *Handlist*, 93, 109). Besides 1 Corinthians 15, see 1:18, 19, 25; 7:17, 38; 8:1; 9:26; 10:21; 14:15.

84. There may be other examples of this pattern in the chapter. Saw, e.g., also cites vv. 12–13, 16–17. But in vv. 12–13 a chiastic structure seems to dominate: ἐγήγερται ... ἀνάστασις νεκρῶν ... ἀνάστασις νεκρῶν ... ἐγήγερται, and v. 16b breaks up the pattern in vv. 16–17. The instances of *parisosis/isocolon* cited here are, we believe, self-evident.

| | |
|---|---|
| 41a | ἄλλη δόξα ἡλίου, |
| 41b | καὶ ἄλλη δόξα σελήνης |
| 42b | σπείρεται ἐν φθορᾷ, |
| 42c | ἐγείρεται ἐν ἀφθαρσίᾳ· |
| | |
| 43a | σπείρεται ἐν ἀτιμίᾳ, |
| 43b | ἐγείρεται ἐν δόξῃ· |
| | |
| 43c | σπείρεται ἐν ἀσθενείᾳ, |
| 43d | ἐγείρεται ἐν δυνάμει· |
| | |
| 44a | σπείρεται σῶμα ψυχικόν, |
| 44b | ἐγείρεται σῶμα πνευματικόν. |
| | |
| 47a | ὁ πρῶτος ἄνθρωπος ἐκ γῆς χοϊκός, |
| 47b | ὁ δεύτερος ἄνθρωπος ἐξ οὐρανοῦ. |
| | |
| 48a-b | οἷος ὁ χοϊκός, τοιοῦτοι καὶ οἱ χοϊκοί, |
| 48c-d | καὶ οἷος ὁ ἐπουράνιος, τοιοῦτοι καὶ οἱ ἐπουράνιοι· |
| | |
| 49a | καὶ καθὼς ἐφορέσαμεν τὴν εἰκόνα τοῦ χοϊκοῦ, |
| 49b | φορέσομεν καὶ τὴν εἰκόνα τοῦ ἐπουρανίου. |
| | |
| 51b | πάντες οὐ κοιμηθησόμεθα, |
| 51c | πάντες δὲ ἀλλαγησόμεθα, |
| | |
| 53a | Δεῖ γὰρ τὸ φθαρτὸν τοῦτο ἐνδύσασθαι ἀφθαρσίαν |
| 53b | καὶ τὸ θνητὸν τοῦτο ἐνδύσασθαι ἀθανασίαν. |
| | |
| 54a | ὅταν δὲ τὸ φθαρτὸν τοῦτο ἐνδύσηται ἀφθαρσίαν |
| 54b | καὶ τὸ θνητὸν τοῦτο ἐνδύσηται ἀθανασίαν, |
| | |
| 55a | ποῦ σου, θάνατε, τὸ νῖκος; |
| 55b | ποῦ σου, θάνατε, τὸ κέντρον; |
| | |
| 56a | τὸ δὲ κέντρον τοῦ θανάτου ἡ ἁμαρτία, |
| 56b | ἡ δὲ δύναμις τῆς ἁμαρτίας ὁ νόμος· |

Findlay well states the case when he notes that 15:56 delivers its ideas "in a rhythmical, imaginative turn of expression harmonizing with the context."[85] The verse, we can see, is part and parcel of the rhetorical flavor of the chapter and of the immediately preceding verses: the syllabic pattern of v. 56 perfectly echoes v. 55, which in turn echoes v. 54, which echoes v. 53. Indeed, without v. 56b, v. 56a would be left void of a rhetorical echo. Hence, while Findlay correctly states the case, others, who argue for a gloss, misstate the case. A rhetorical work-up of v. 56 provides no reason to suspect an interpolation. On rhetorical grounds alone, the verse appears genuine.[86]

In addition to the stylistic rhythm, it is noteworthy that the impact of the thought in v. 56 is delivered by the nouns; there are no linking verbs. Like Rom 6:23a (τὰ γὰρ ὀψώνια τῆς ἁμαρτίας θάνατος); Rom 3:20b (διὰ γὰρ νόμου ἐπίγνωσις ἁμαρτίας); and Rom 7:8b (χωρὶς γὰρ νόμου ἁμαρτία νεκρά), which contain similar thoughts and syntax, the omission of the verb in both clauses of 15:56 accents the *axiomatic* nature of each statement.[87] The relationship of sin to death *and*

---

85. "First Corinthians," 943, italics mine. Allo finds the verse to be "tout à fait organique" (*Corinthiens*, 436).

86. Stenger argues that the presence of v. 56 produces an effective chiastic pattern within vv. 55-57: "'Sieg'—'Stachel'—'Stachel'—'Sieg.'" This, in his view, argues against the thesis that the verse is an interpolation ("Beobachtung," 126; see also Schneider, *Vollendung*, 47; Lindemann, *Korintherbrief*, 371). Verburg ends his examination of the text with the conclusion, "Aus syntaktisch-sigmatischen Gründen muß Vers 56 keineswegs unbedingt als Glosse angesehen werden, sondern aufgrund inhaltlicher Erwägungen kann der Vers als paulinischen angesehen werden" (*Endzeit*, 91; see also 235). A semantic and pragmatic analysis will lead Verburg to the same conclusion (ibid., 232-36; 268-69).

87. "The total absence of a temporal reference" notes Díaz Rodelas, "gives the phrase a general sense" (*Pablo*, 29, translation mine). The addition of ἔστιν after θάνατος by A Ψ and Eusebius or of *est* after *peccatum* by the old Latin versions (except It [d e g]) and all the vg. mss. (except c) misses what virtually every commentator recognizes, viz., the axiomatic nature of the verse (see comments, e.g., in Findlay, "Corinthians," 942; Klein, "Gesetz," 65; Horn, "Stachel," 101; Wilckens, "Entwicklung," 161; Schrage *Korinther*, 4:361; Lang *Korinther*, 241; Räisänen, *Paul and the Law*, 149; Watson, "Strategy," 247). Aune defines axioms as "concise, autonomous sayings that give pithy expression to an insight about life, the validity of which is generally recognized or approved" (Aune, "Aphorism," 40). Gross defines an aphorism as a "comment on some *recurrent* aspect of life, couched in terms which are meant to be permanently and universally applicable" (*Aphorisms*, vii-viii, italics mine; see also Saw, *Rhetoric*, 263). Notable, according to Gross, is its "highly idiosyncratic or self-conscious form" (ibid., viii). That Paul regularly drops the verb when expressing truisms suggests such idiosyncrasy and self-conscious-

law to sin, in other words, are expressed in v. 56 in terms of universally applicable truisms.

## The Sting of Death Is Sin (v. 56a)

With the defiant questions of v. 55 it might appear that Paul has reached the climax to his argument. But he has not. As at the end of the first major section (vv. 33-34), a word of exhortation is due, and in v. 58 Paul will give one. In the meantime "the final words of the taunt in v. 55 apparently touch off a theological chord that must be given a moment's hearing."[88] Paul has taunted death, asking what had become of its sting. In v. 56a he now appends to his taunt an explanatory epigram that identifies the source of death's capacity to mortally wound.[89]

---

ness. Turner notes that the absence of the verb can appear "when there is a striving after rhetoric in epigrammatic phrases and those which express general or abstract truths" (*Syntax*, 297). For examples of truisms in 1 Corinthian 15 being expressed without the verb, see vv. 21, 39, 40, 41, 47, 48 (see also Rom 2:13, 29; 3:20, 4:8; 6:23; 7:8, 12; 8:6, 10; 9:6; 10:4, 15; 11:6, 16, 29, 33; 13:10; 14:14, 21, 22; 1 Cor 3:19; 6:13; 10:26; 11:6, 11; 2 Cor 3:17; 1 Tim 1:8; 4:4; 5:18; Titus 1:12, 15). For discussion of the omission of the verb in proverbial statements see also BDF §127 (1); Winer, *Grammar*, 584-88. For a helpful study of the use of aphorisms in ancient Greek, see Barnes, "Aphorism," 91-109. Hippocrates's *Aphorisms*, which presents more than 400 medical maxims, provides a virtual syntax of this rhetorical device. The opening line exhibits the non-copulative style that pervades the book: ὁ βίος βραχύς, ἡ δὲ τέχνη μακρή, ὁ δὲ καιρὸς ὀξύς, ἡ δὲ πεῖρα σφαλερή, ἡ δὲ κρίσις χαλεπή ("Life is short, the Art is long, opportunity fleeting, experiment treacherous, judgment difficult" [*Aph.* 1.1 (Jones, LCL)]).

88. Fee, *Corinthians*, 805. Edwards observes that "the two questions in v. 55 give the Apostle an opportunity to introduce the only element that seems wanting hitherto to the completeness of his doctrine of resurrection, the characteristic Pauline notion of the moral relation in which believers stand to Christ" (*First Corinthians*, 459). This thought brings us full circle to Chester's observation cited earlier (see above, pp. 50-51) that the sequence in the argument of 1 Corinthians 15 ends by focusing on deliverance from the *power* of sin.

89. The δέ in v. 56a likely functions in an explanatory manner. See above, n. 66. Wolff notes: "Man wird v. 56 am ehesten als paulinische Interpretation des voranstehenden Zitats zu fassen haben, mit der Paul den Ursprung der Macht des Todes und zugleich damit den Sieg über den Tod als umfassenden Sieg über Gesetz und Sünde darlegen will" (*Erste Brief*, 418). Conzelmann considers v. 56 to be "an exegetical remark; hence the compressed style" (*1 Corinthians*, 293) as does Lietzmann (*Korinther*, 88).

τὸ δὲ κέντρον τοῦ θανάτου

Though the tone of v. 56a is clear,[90] the details are not. The term κέντρον can refer to a *goad* (Acts 26:14; Prov 26:3; Sir 38:25; *Pss. Sol.* 16:4),[91] to the *sting* of insects or scorpions (4 Macc 14:19; Rev 9:10), or, perhaps, metaphorically to the *power to rule*.[92] In light of the depiction in v. 26 of death as a combatant and the position that τὸ κέντρον occupies parallel to τὸ νῖκος in v. 55, it would seem that the word is being used in v. 56 in the second sense.[93] Though the term κέντρον may assume within itself the idea of a certain sovereignty,[94] and while one can say that mortality prods one along throughout life,[95] what appears to be at issue in vv. 54-56 is not death's rule or prodding, but its ultimate "victory," i.e., its fatal capacity to bring an end to life, physically and spiritually.[96] The sense of the metaphor is that death's wound is severe—indeed, gravely so.[97]

90. See Conzelmann, *1 Corinthians*, 293; Senft, *Corinthiens*, 214.

91. Note the Greek proverbial phrase πρὸς κέντρα λακτίζειν (see LSJ 939). Etymologically, the term refers to "any sharp point" (ibid.). The verb κεντέω means *to prick, spur on* (BDAG 539).

92. By its association with νῖκος in the previous clause and δύναμις in the following, Wolff and others argue that κέντρον metaphorically denotes here the power to rule (*erste Brief*, 209-10; see also Müller, "Leiblichkeit," 241; Schrage, *Korinther*, 4:381; *TDNT* 3:664-65, 668). Yet, while the notion of death's dominion is certainly be assumed (see Rom 5:14, 17, 21), de Wette is likely correct that v. 56b does not repeat, but advances the thought of v. 56a: "Nicht ist es parallel mit δύναμις . . . denn κέντρ. τ. θάν. ist der Stachel, mit welchem der Tod tödet, nicht, mit welchem seine Kraft geweckt wird" (*Corinther*, 143; see also Kling, *First Corinthians*, 348).

93. See De Moor, "'O Death,'" 105-6. All major English versions translate the term "sting." The notion of death possessing a sting is present in later rabbinic depictions of the angel of death "pricking" the soon to be deceased as with a lance (see *b. Moʿ ed Qat.* 28a) or approaching with a sword or spike in hand (*b. Ber.* 51a; *Deut. Rab.* 11). However, the imagery is a "transcultural metaphor" (BDAG 539.1). *NewDocs* cites a second century Greek epitaph in which an individual describes the "unceasing sting" (κέντρον ἄπαυστον) he bears over the loss of his deceased friend (4:157 no. 64).

94. See, e.g. the linking of κέντρον and ἐξουσία in Rev 9:10.

95. "La Mort," writes Matand-Bulembat, "exerce une telle menace sur les vivants par la peur qu'elle inspire de la fin de la vie et de la corruption qui s'en suit" (*Noyau et enjeux*, 123).

96. See Laato, *Paul*, 102-3.

97. See Ellicott, *First Corinthians*, 327. De Wette deems the κέντρον "eine verderbliche Waffe" (*Corinther*, 143). See also Morissette, "Midrash," 175; Calvin, *First Corinthians*, 346; Hodge, *First Corinthians*, 358. The Hebrew term in Hos 13:14b, קֶטֶב (*sting, HALOT* 3:1092), is used in both Deut 32:24 (parallel with רֶשֶׁף) and Ps 91:6 (parallel with דֶּבֶר) to

The terms κέντρον and θάνατος from v. 55 are combined in v. 56a to form the phrase τὸ κέντρον τοῦ θανάτου. The genitive τοῦ θανάτου might be subjective since θάνατος in v. 55 appears as a subject of address.[98] However, like the genitive τῆς ἁμαρτίας in v. 56b, it is more likely a possessive genitive.[99] Indeed, in light of the emphatic and repeated possessive pronouns in v. 55, a possessive understanding of θάνατος in v. 56a should be the default interpretation.[100] Thus, though it might initially appear from the syntax of v. 56a that Paul's meaning is: *it is death that brings about sin*,[101] the clause may be better paraphrased: *what gives death its sting is sin*.[102] The causal relation between sin and death depicted here assumes a staple of Jewish theology (based on Gen 2:17; 3:19) that is "such a commonplace as to be formulaic in Paul's letters,"[103]

denote an *epidemic* and in Isa 28:2 to denote *destruction* (see *HALOT* 3:1091–92). In each case, whatever the precise translation the versions employ, annihilation is at the door.

98. See Schrage, *Korinther*, 4:382.

99. So Hollander and Holleman, "Relationship," 277 n. 22. As is the case with an objective genitive (see above, n. 131), for a genitive noun to be categorized as a subjective genitive, most grammars require a verbal notion implicit in the head noun. Wallace, e.g., argues that "a *subjective* gen. takes precedent over possession *when* a verbal noun is involved" (*Grammar*, 82). It is not clear that κέντρον is a verbal noun, and as noted above (see n. 131), δύναμις, which stands in parallel to κέντρον, is almost certainly not a verbal noun. Similarly, Dana and Mantey assert that a subjective genitive *produces* the action implicit in the noun (*Grammar*, 78). While Paul's syntax in v. 56 can comfortably convey the notion of "death's sting," the reading "death *produces* a sting" appears awkward in light of the reading it would seem to necessitate for the parallel clause: "sin *produces* a power"). This, coupled with the possessive pronoun modifying κέντρον in the immediately preceding clause, makes it difficult to identify the genitive in v. 56a as anything but a possessive.

100. See Verburg, *Endzeit*, 235 n. 578.

101. This would be the sense if the genitive were taken as a subjective. Hence Schrage, who does so, writes: "Bei der Aussage von v. 56a, daß "der Stachel des Todes" die Sünde ist, könnte man zunächst vermuten, daß es die Sünde ist, die den Tod bewirkt und ihm seine qualvolle und das Leben vergiftende Macht verleiht. . . . Hier aber scheint es eher so zu stehen, daß der Genitive τοῦ θανάτου wie in v. 55 ein *gen. subj.* ist, der Tod unabhängig als eine selbstmächtige Größe agiert, der seinerseits die Sünde als Herrschaftsinstrument benutzt und zur Sünde antreibt" (*Korinther*, 4:381–82). Olshausen takes a similar route in stating that "the slumbering power of death awakens sin" (Olshausen, *Corinthians*, 264; see also Grosheide, *First Corinthians*, 394).

102. Wendland notes: "Das, was dem Tode seine tödlich wirkende Angriffskraft verleiht, ist die Sünde" (*Korinther*, 158). A similar thought is expressed by Pop: "It is sin, by which death has power over humans. It is the weapon, with which death harms its victims" (*Corinthiërs*, 403, translation mine; see also Beker, *Paul*, 190).

103. Sampley, "First Corinthians," 989.

viz., that death is the consequence of sin.[104] Yet if, as seems likely, the imagery in v. 56 is of death's poisonous sting, Paul may be more precisely reflecting here on the fatal capacity that sin imparts to death;[105] i.e., without sin, death loses its terror.[106]

In 1 Cor 15:26 death is depicted as a "cosmological power":[107] ἔσχατος ἐχθρὸς καταργεῖται ὁ θάνατος. Paul similarly views it as such in Romans 5.[108] There it is pictured as a reigning tyrant (5:14, 17, 21). This same notion is found in 1 Cor 15:55, where death is addressed in the vocative as an entity in its own right.[109] One need not assume from this that Paul is describing salvation in terms of a "mythological conflict between the savior-god and the voracious death-god."[110] Yet, one should neither merely conclude that "we are . . . not in the realm of supernatural

---

104. E.g., Rom 5:12–21; 6:16, 21, 23; 7:7–20. Thus, Bultmann argues that for Paul "it is axiomatic that sin draws death after it" (*Theology*], 1:246). Note also Strobel, who sees here a "unauflöslich" relationship between sin and death (*Korintherbrief*, 262) and Martin who tags death as "the Sacrament of sin" (*Spirit*, 141). See below, pp. 88 n. 5.

105. So Kling: "Death, like a scorpion, has a sting, a fatal power imparted to it by means of sin" (*First Corinthians*, 348). Speaking more theologically, *TDNT* notes: "Death rules over the human race. The reality of its awful rule rests on the reality of sin. What gives death its power . . . is sin. When sin is overcome, death is robbed of its power. Like an insect which has lost its sting, it is helpless" (Lothar Schmid, "κέντρον," in *TDNT* 3:668). In simpler terms, Theodoret writes: "Αὕτη γὰρ τῷ θανάτῳ τὴν φύσιν παραδέδωκεν" (*epistolae ad Cor.* [PG 82: col. 368]; see also Trail, *Summary*, 366–67).

106. Thus Moffatt asserts: "Were it not for sin, death could not reach us" (*First Corinthians*, 265; see also Chrysostom, *NPNF*1 12:257; Benoit, "The Law," 19–20; Ellicott, *First Corinthians*, 328; Lang, *Korinther*, 241). Similarly, and typically laconic is Bengelii's dictum: "*Si peccatum non esset, mors nil posset*" (*Gnomon* , 673). More recently, but no less rhetorically, Heim states: "Der Tod kann nur solange herrschen, wie die Sünde herrscht" (*Gemeinde*, 239). The imperical reality for Paul is that when sin is conquered (15:3–5, 57), death loses its terror and authority to condemn (see Bruce, *Corinthians*, 156; Robertson and Plummer, *First Corinthians*, 378). Indeed, for Paul (Phil 1:21–23), death becomes a *gain* not a loss; being redeemed, it is "a mere transition from a lower to a higher state" (Hodge, *First Corinthians*, 358; see also Beet, *Corinthians*, 302; Morris, *First Corinthians*, 229). The interpretation proposed above appears more suitable to the context (of death gaining entrance into the world by way of sin) than the psychological interpretation suggested by Godet, who understands the sting of vv. 55–56 as "the *consciousness* of sins committed" (*First Corinthians*, 444–45; see also Clark, *1 Corinthians*, 315; Barclay, *Corinthians*, 160).

107. De Boer, *Defeat*, 132.

108. See Brandenburger, *Adam und Christus*, 158–68.

109. See Gillman, "Comparison," 444–45; Schrage, *Korinther*, 4:382; Verburg, *Endzeit*, 235.

110. Healey, "Canaanite," 211.

powers, but within the realm of history."[111] It will become increasingly clear as the study proceeds that, for Paul, behind the reality of death and dying there is an inimical, cosmological power at work.[112]

In Romans 5:15-18 death and judgment coincide. This can be deduced from the manner in which θάνατος and κατάκριμα oscillate in an A B A′ B′ pattern:

[15c] εἰ γὰρ τῷ τοῦ ἑνὸς παραπτώματι οἱ πολλοὶ **ἀπέθανον** ...

[16b] τὸ μὲν γὰρ κρίμα ἐξ ἑνὸς εἰς **κατάκριμα** ...

[17a] εἰ γὰρ τῷ τοῦ ἑνὸς παραπτώματι ὁ **θάνατος** ἐβασίλευσεν διὰ τοῦ ἑνός ...

[18a] Ἄρα οὖν ὡς δι᾽ ἑνὸς παραπτώματος εἰς πάντας ἀνθρώπους εἰς **κατάκριμα**.[113]

In view of the Adam-Christ axioms of 1 Cor 15:21-22 that are developed in Rom 5:12-21, it can be assumed that the notion of death occupies the same corridor of meaning in 1 Corinthians 15 as it does in Romans 5.[114] And since Paul in 15:56a explicitly introduces ἡ ἁμαρτία into the equation, a key term that envelops the exposition of Rom 5:12-21,[115] it becomes almost certain that Paul, as in Romans 5,[116] understands ὁ θάνατος in 1 Corinthians 15 not merely in terms of corruption and mortality,[117] but of sin and judgment.[118]

---

111. Carr, *Angels*, 91. Carr bases this conclusion on his observation that in the taunts of v. 55, death "is connected not with any power of evil or of the Devil, but with sin" (ibid.). It will become evident, however, that where sin is present, something fiendish is also at hand.

112. See de Boer, *Defeat*, 138.

113. The contrast in Rom 5:21 between ὁ θάνατος with ζωὴ αἰώνιος suggests that Paul is referring to "spiritual" death, i.e., eternal estrangement from God.

114. Observed by Sellin: "Implizit [in v. 56] ist . . . der Sündengedanke im Adam-Christus-Schema (vv. 44b-50) enthalten" (*Streit*, 227).

115. The noun ἡ ἁμαρτία launches the discussion (vv. 5:12-13) and brings it to a close (vv. 5:20-21), though, of course, it is in the end trumped by χάρις.

116. Note how ὁ θάνατος is linked with ἡ ἁμαρτία in the inclusio: [12]Διὰ τοῦτο ὥσπερ δι᾽ ἑνὸς ἀνθρώπου **ἡ ἁμαρτία** εἰς τὸν κόσμον εἰσῆλθεν καὶ διὰ **τῆς ἁμαρτίας ὁ θάνατος** .... [21b]ἵνα ὥσπερ ἐβασίλευσεν **ἡ ἁμαρτία** ἐν τῷ θανάτῳ.

117. For Paul, mortality is bound up with sin: "Mit 1 Kor 15,56 expliziert Paul, was er in 15,20-28 und 15,41-49 (zumal 5:3, 17) voraussetzen konnte: daß die Sterblichkeit und Vergänglichkeit aller Menschen in ihrer Sündenhaftigkeit begründet ist" (Söding, "Kraft," 80).

118. Barrosse's logic is apt: "The idea of total death [i.e., both physical and spiritual]

## ἡ ἁμαρτία

In v. 56a Paul proceeds to identify what it is that gives death its capacity to inject mortality into the human race: ἡ ἁμαρτία. The term ἁμαρτία occurs earlier in 1 Cor 15:3, 17, but in the plural and with a possessive pronoun. The singular occurs in the epistle only here, and the articular singular form occurs elsewhere in Paul only in Romans 5–8.[119] The definite article serves to generalize the notion.[120] In many of these verses in Romans,[121] Paul depicts sin as a personified power,[122] reminiscent of חַטָּאת in Gen 4:7 and the *yēṣer hâraʿ* of Jewish thought.[123] This is espe-

---

seems ... to fit more satisfactorily the Apostle's long passage on the resurrection to the Corinthians. Death through and in Adam, life through and in Christ (1 Cor 15:22f.). This life is certainly not merely the body's at the resurrection. And therefore the death which is its contrary is hardly merely physical death. Especially since the glorious resurrection sets the just not only beyond the reach of sickness and infirmities but beyond that of *sin*, the sting death uses to kill" ("Death and Sin," 455; see also Beker, who argues that Paul in 1 Corinthians 15 is referring to death as a "physico-spiritual" reality [*Paul*, 224]).

119. Rom 5:12, 12, 20, 21; 6:1, 2, 6, 6, 7, 10, 11, 12, 13, 17, 18, 20, 22, 23; 7:7, 8, 9, 11, 13, 13, 14, 23, 8:2, 3. Of the 64 occurrences of the term ἁμαρτία in Paul, 42 occur in Romans 5–8, and all are singular.

120. See BDF §252.

121. See, e.g., Rom 5:12, 21; 6:6, 12, 13, 14, 16, 17, 18, 20, 21, 22; 7:8, 9, 11, 13, 14, 17, 20, 23; 8:2, 3, 10.

122. See Hofius, "Antithese," 172 n. 23; Morissette, "Midrash," 177. The manner in which Paul depicts sin in these chapters as an entity acting in the world makes it difficult for some to reduce Paul's depictions to mere literary expressions (see, e.g., Morissette, "Midrash," 178): sin came into the world (5:12); it was in the world" (5:13); it reigns (5:21); it exercises dominion (6:13–14); it enslaves (6:6, 17, 20; 7:14); it can be rendered service (6:13, 16–17); it pays wages (6:23); it resides (7:17, 20); it comes to life (7:9); it seizes the occasion (7:8, 11); it deceives (7:11); it kills (7:13). Yet, even if Paul's manner of depiction is merely a rhetorical device alluding to a *propensity* to sin, the manner in which Paul personifies it is reminiscent of sin in Gen 4:7 and the *yēṣer hâraʿ*, which are likewise personified (see ibid., 176–78). We will build on this below (see pp. 190–91).

123. On the former, see below, pp. 151–53, 190. For the latter, see Marcus, "Evil Inclination," 13–17); Morissette, "Midrash," 177–78. Morissette notes that the *evil inclination* was generally personified in the literature (see ibid., 178 n. 64). Thus, it exercises a reign (see *Midr. Eccl.* 4:13–16; *b. Ber.* 61b; *b. Sanh.* 91b; *b. Sukkah* 52a; *b. Qidd.* 30b, 80b); it seduces humans (*Gen. Rab.* 22; *Midr. Pss.* 32:4; *Sifr. Deut.* 11:16; *ʾAbot. R. Nat.* 25a); it craves (*y. Yom.* 6:5); it is depicted as a king (see *b. Ned.* 32b; *Num. Rab.* 15; *Midr. Eccl.* 4:13; 9:15; *Midr Ps.* 41:1; *ʾAbot R. Nat.* 25a), a thief (*Gen. Rab.* 22; *Midr. Ps.* 34:2; *Pesiq. Rab.* 9), a strange god (*b. Šabb.*105b), or an enemy (*m. Pirqe ʾAbot* 4:1). Morissette notes that the rabbis looked forward to a future point, as does Paul in 15:55 regarding death, when the evil impulse would come to an end (*Gen. Rab.* 48:11; *Exod. Rab.* 41:7; *Num.*

cially the case in Rom 7:9, 11, where sin, analogous to the edenic serpent, is the entity in the drama that exists prior to,[124] and independently of the individual's act of transgression and that rises from the shadows to beguile its victim into breaking the freshly given commandment: ἡ γὰρ ἁμαρτία ἀφορμὴν λαβοῦσα διὰ τῆς ἐντολῆς ἐξηπάτησέν με καὶ δι' αὐτῆς ἀπέκτεινεν. In light of the affinity between 1 Corinthians 15 and Romans 5 and 7,[125] and in view of the explicit shift from *lower case* transgressions (vv. 3, 17) to an *upper case* entity,[126] it appears clear that in 1 Cor 15:56 ἡ ἁμαρτία is being depicted alongside of its cosmic ally, θάνατος, as "one of the anti-God powers whose final defeat the resurrection of Jesus Christ inaugurates and guarantees."[127] While it may not be entirely certain whether Paul is personalizing sin here rather than merely personifying it, further comparison with Rom 7:7-11 will suggest that he is all but doing so here as there.[128]

---

*Rab.* 15:16; 17:6; *Midr. Deut.* 2:30; *Midr. Song.* 1:2; 7:8), and sometimes the rabbis cited Isa 25:8 as a proof text (*Deut. Rab.* 2:30). Though it is uncertain to what extent Paul was influenced by such thought, it is likely that he was aware of the *evil inclination* notion (see, e.g., Sir 15:11-14; *T. Ash.* 1:3-9; cf. *4 Ezra* 3:21; 4:30). For the *evil inclination* as a fixed notion by the first century A.D., see Porter, "Sin," 109.

124. Contra Moo, *Romans*, 319 n. 25. See n. 128, below.

125. "La présentation du Péché dans *Rom.*, v à viii," notes Morissette, "et celle que contient notre énoncé doivent être rapprochées: l'une et l'autre ont le même objet et trahissent le même milieu littéraire d'origine" (Morissette, "Midrash," 176-77).

126. See Gaventa, "Cosmic Power," 231. Scott argues that while ἁμαρτία in the plural carries for Paul the meaning of individual and personal acts of sin: "'Sin' is not for him a synonym for a sinful status; it is a power invading, attacking, subjugating men from without" (*Christianity*, 47). In light of Rom 7:17, Scott ought to have added that sin also subjugates from *within*.

127. Gaventa, "Cosmic Power," 231. Beker recognizes 15:56 to be an exception to the overall absence in 1 Corinthians of allusions to sin as an apocalyptic power ("Relationship," 59). Drawing from Romans, Gaventa highlights Paul's personification of sin by assembling a veritable résumé of sin's achievements: 1) *Sin entered the world* (5:12-21), 2) *Sin became an enslaving power* (Romans 6); 3) *Sin unleashed its cosmic partner, Death* (Rom 5:12-21; 6:23; 1 Cor 15:56); 4) *Sin exerts its power over* [better: *through*] *the law* (Rom 7:7-8, 13) (see "Cosmic Power," 232-36). She concludes that failure to take seriously Paul's notion of *Sin* as an anti-God power trivializes Paul's understanding of the dynamics of sin (see ibid., 238-40). Sin is not strictly a human activity or experience; a force of cosmic proportion is at work.

128. Moo doubts that Paul ever views sin "as a 'demon' that exists prior to, and independent of, personal acts of rebellion against God" (*Romans*, 319 n. 25). The "demon" issue aside, it appears clear that Rom 7:8-11, at least, contains an example of "sin" existing *prior to*, and *independent of*, the personal and initiatory act of transgression depicted

### The Power of Sin is the Law (v. 56b)

In her essay on the cosmic power of sin, Beverly Gaventa more than once calls attention to the ability of sin to use the law as an occasion to provoke disobedience to it.[129] Her cases in point are Rom 7:8, 11, and 13:

> [8] But sin, seizing an opportunity in the commandment, produced in me all kinds of covetousness . . .

> [11] For sin, seizing an opportunity in the commandment, deceived me and through it killed me.

> [13] It was sin, working death in me through what is good . . .

Yet Gaventa might have also considered 1 Cor 15:56 in her résumé of sin. While Romans 7 depicts this diabolically perverse process *in action*, 1 Cor 15:56 presents it as a *dictum*. So typical is the pattern in Paul's mind that even as early as the first Corinthian correspondence, the Apostle encapsulates it in epigrammatic form.

ἡ δὲ δύναμις τῆς ἁμαρτίας

The second clause in 1 Cor 15:56, ἡ δὲ δύναμις τῆς ἁμαρτίας ὁ νόμος, receiving a boost from the first clause, τὸ δὲ κέντρον τοῦ θανάτου ἡ ἁμαρτία, repeats the word ἁμαρτία and introduces two terms that occurred previously in the epistle, δύναμις and νόμος.[130] In general, δύναμις refers in the letter to the ability to function in a particular way; i.e., *power, might, strength, force,* or *capability*.[131] We meet its antonym, ἀσθένεια,[132] in 2:3 and 15:43. Having this understanding of δύναμις there.

---

129. See Gaventa, "Cosmic Power," 234–35, 239.

130. The term δύναμις occurs elsewhere in the letter in 1:18, 24; 2:4, 5; 4:19, 20; 5:4; 6:14; 12:10, 28, 29; 14:11; 15:24, 43, while νόμος appears in 9:8, 9, 20, 20, 20, 20, 14:21, 34.

131. See BDAG 262.1; *TDNT* 2:284–85; *NIDNTT* 2:601. The term δύναμις in the singular occurs in 1:18, 24 of Christ and the gospel being the power of God, in 2:4 of demonstrations of power in Paul's preaching, in 2:5; 5:4; 6:14 of the power of God or Jesus, in 4:19 of the alleged power of Paul's opponents, in 4:20 of the power in which the kingdom of God exists, in 15:24 of the worldly power that will be abolished in the eschaton, and in 15:43 of the power by which the body will be resurrected.

132. I.e., *incapacity, ineffectualness* (BDAG 142.2).

and taking τῆς ἁμαρτίας as a possessive genitive,[133] the phrase, ἡ δύναμις τῆς ἁμαρτίας, should probably be understood as *the inherent strength possessed by sin*.[134] Yet a nuance is in order. Typical of its usage in Paul, the term δύναμις assumes *activity* will follow.[135] In other words, unlike ἀσθένεια, which is inert, δύναμις, for Paul, is a power that *works*.[136] This is evident in all of its occurrences in 1 Corinthians.[137] Thus, while the rendering *the inherent strength possessed by sin* conveys the gist of the phrase, it is significant, and will become more so as the

133. As we most likely should, contra Schrage, *Korinther*, 4:382. The term δύναμις itself is intransitive and thus is unlikely to be subjective. See above, pp. 39-40 n. 131.

134. Verburg attempts to link δυνάμις here to δύναμαι in v. 50: "Entspricht diese Aussage, daß die Tora Kraft der Sünde sei, der bisherigen Argumentation? Wichtig ist in diesem Zusammenhang Vers 50b. Nicht zufällig ist hier wie dort von δύνασθαι beziehungsweise δύναμις die Rede. Das Lexem δύναμις ist schon bekannt aus Vers 43, dort antonym zu ἀσθένεια. Hintergrund der Aussage von Vers 50b ist, daß alle Menschen vor dem Gesetzt schuldig geworden sind, also gesündigt haben. Grund dafür ist ihre Schwachheit" (*Endzeit*, 235). This appears too subtle. If *human* weakness were the concern we would expect a phrase such as appears in Rom 8:3: τὸ γὰρ ἀδύνατον τοῦ νόμου ἐν ᾧ ἠσθένει διὰ τῆς σαρκός. Also, at issue in v. 56 is not ἡ ἀσθένεια τοῦ ἀνθρώπου but ἡ δύναμις τῆς ἁμαρτίας.

135. In defining δύναμις BDAG is careful to mark that along with the notion of capability there is an "emphasis on function" that is assumed in the term (601). This need not conflict with our earlier conclusion that δύναμις is intransitive (see above, pp. 39-40 n. 131). Power is the source into which transitive action taps.

136. On the linking of δύναμις with ἐνέργεια/ἐνεργέω/κατεργάζομαι, see below, n. 193. *NIDNTT* notes that δύναμις not only suggests the *capacity* to carry something out but also denotes "the largely spontaneous *expression* of such *dynamis*" (Betz, "δύναμις," 2:601, italics used in first two words mine). Thielman understands the term in this manner: "The word . . . refers to that which enables something to accomplish a particular feat—that which makes something else effective" (*Paul and the Law*, 107).

137. In 1 Corinthians δύναμις issues in action that *saves* (1:18), *calls* (1:24), *manifests the workings of Spirit* (2:4-5), *issues in deeds* (4:19-20), *judges* (5:4), *raises the dead* (6:14; 15:24), and *works miracles* (12:10, 28; 14:11).

study proceeds, that the strength that sin possesses emanates in action.[138] Once energized, sin does not lie dormant.[139]

## ὁ νόμος

That which "gives sin its power to function,"[140] according to v. 56b, is *the law*.[141] As noted earlier,[142] v. 56b contains the last link in the thematic chain that spans vv. 54-56. The idea of *victory* over death (v. 54) leads to the thought of death deprived of its *sting* (v. 55), which in turn draws attention to *sin* (v. 56a), which in turn elicits the notion of *law* (v. 56b).[143] In the culminating movement from *sin to law* Paul makes what for him is a ready linkage.[144] As death acquires its sting through sin, sin is provided leverage through the law.[145] The natural overflow of the latter clause not

---

138. Morissette's paraphrase of ἡ δύναμις τῆς ἁμαρτίας captures this nuance: "la puissance dont dispose et qu'exerce le Péché" ("Midrash," 180). Similarly, though even more nuanced, Hollander and Holleman understand δύναμις here as the "'power' through which sin is brought about" ("Relationship," 279). They cross reference to the term's use in *Test. Dan* 4:1: σύνετε τὴν δύναμιν τοῦ θυμοῦ, i.e., "understand how anger works" (ibid., 279 n. 30). Another example in this regard is the phrase "the power of sin" (כח עבירה), words which are attributed in *Sifr. Num.* (see *Sifr. d'be Rab* 4.14) to Rabbi Jose the Galilean (first-second century?). Levertoff translates the Hebrew here "the *effect* of sin" (*Numbers*, 2).

139. Ellingworth and Hatton suggest that the term here implies "power to hurt" or better, "power to kill" (*Corinthians*, 324).

140. BDAG 262.1.

141. Paraphrased by Hofius: "Das, was die Sünde so stark und mächtig werden läßt, weil es sie zwingt, sich in ihrer ganzen Gewalt und Schrecklichkeit kundzutun,—das ist das Gesetz" ("Antithese," 202 n. 233). Thurén conveys the sense yet more expressively: "In the verse sin is the sting of a scorpion, and the power of this sting, viz. the poison injected thereby, is the *law*" (*Derhetorizing*, 116).

142. See above, pp. 58.

143. When v. 56b is then clipped to v. 57, and to its theme of *victory* over death, the thematic chain comes full circle:

144. Thurén rightly observes that "the law appears as a natural, undisputed element in the train of thought" (*Derhetorizing*, 116).

145. "Sans la loi," observes Lagrange, "le péché perdrait une bonne arme" (*Romains*, 169). Similarly Wolff: "Wie der Tod durch die Sünde seine Herrschaft ausübt (vgl. v. 17), so die Sünde durch das Gesetz, das Gesetz verhilft der Sünde zur Macht" (*Erste Brief*,

only suggests Paul's familiarity with the notion,¹⁴⁶ but reveals how fluently he can move from the idea of sin to that of law.¹⁴⁷

*Divine Law in a General Sense*

By way of the precedents set in the epistle, ὁ νόμος in v. 56 could refer to the Mosaic legislation, the Pentateuch, or the Old Testament Scriptures.¹⁴⁸ The manner in which the term νόμος is used in Romans in like settings might tip the interpretative scales of an interpreter toward the first of these options. In Rom 5:20, for example, after a discussion of Adam and Christ similar to that in 1 Corinthians 15, Paul clearly has the law of Moses in mind when he expresses the relationship of the law to the trespass: "Now the law came in to increase the trespass."¹⁴⁹ In the similar context of Rom

---

418).

146. Thus, Beet observes "that the mention of *death* recalls *sin* and *the Law*, shows how deeply inwoven in the mind of Paul was the teaching of Rom vii.7ff." (*Corinthians*, 302).

147. See Stanley, *Corinthians*, 323. Later in our study we will observe how Paul moves between these notions in Romans 6–7.

148. In 9:8b-9 the term is used of the Mosaic legislation: ὁ νόμος ταῦτα οὐ λέγει; ἐν γὰρ τῷ Μωϋσέως νόμῳ γέγραπται, Οὐ κημώσεις βοῦν ἀλοῶντα. In 9:20 Paul argues that when among Jews, he adopts their customs, although in Christ he has the freedom not to do so: καὶ ἐγενόμην τοῖς Ἰουδαίοις ὡς Ἰουδαῖος, ἵνα Ἰουδαίους κερδήσω· τοῖς ὑπὸ νόμον ὡς ὑπὸ νόμον, μὴ ὢν αὐτὸς ὑπὸ νόμον, ἵνα τοὺς ὑπὸ νόμον κερδήσω. Since τοῖς ὑπὸ νόμον refers here to Jews, the references in this verse to "the law" are likely to the Jewish law, i.e., the law of Moses. In 14:21, on the other hand, Paul introduces a quotation from Isa 28:11-12 by the phrase ἐν τῷ νόμῳ γέγραπται ὅτι. The term "law" in this case is almost certainly a reference to the Old Testament Scriptures even though, as Fee notes, Paul rarely appeals to the Old Testament by this designation (*First Corinthians*, 406; Fee points to 9:8; 14:21; 14:34 as the only possible exceptions in the extant letters, though he might have added Rom 3:19 and Gal 4:21). Finally, Paul's appeal in 14:34 to the law (καθὼς καὶ ὁ νόμος λέγει) in support of his admonition that the women should maintain silence in the churches is also a likely allusion to the Old Testament Scriptures, or more precisely to the Pentateuch (see Thiselton, *First Corinthians*, 1153-54). Although no specific text is cited, Paul is probably appealing to the order of creation in Genesis 2:20-22 as the basis for his admonition that the women are to submit in the church to the male leadership. This can be compared to 1 Tim 2:13, where the sequence of creation in Genesis 2 is cited in response to a similar situation regarding the women's silence and submission in the church. 1 Tim 2:13 appears to make explicit what is implicit in 14:34.

149. Contra Pedersen, who reads the garden commandment into Rom 5:12, 20 ("Biblical Law," 19-21). That the Mosaic law is in view in 5:20 is evident from the fact

## 76  THE LAW AND THE KNOWLEDGE OF GOOD AND EVIL

7:7-11, where the law-sin nexus is again the focus, ὁ νόμος is likewise used of the Mosaic law, or at least predominantly so.[150] That this is the case is evident since a specific commandment of the Mosaic code is cited in v. 7, viz., the tenth commandment: "I would not have known what it is to covet if the law had not said, you shall not covet."[151]

In keeping with Paul's normal usage of the term in 1 Corinthians and in similar contexts, then, an argument can be made that ὁ νόμος in 15:56 is none other than the Mosaic Law.[152] However, in spite of Paul's typical use of the term, there are indications that ὁ νόμος in v. 56 refers, in fact, to *divine law in general*,[153] i.e., of divine demands made known,

---

that the arrival of the law depicted in 5:20 signals the end of the period from Adam until Moses mentioned by Paul in 5:13-14.

150. See below, pp. 77-79 for a possible exception in v. 7:8b.

151. That this is a citation from the decalogue is argued below, pp. 100-102 n. 68.

152. Winger concludes that "the other uses of νόμος in this letter imply strongly that this ordinary, unspecified reference is to Jewish νόμος" (*Νόμος*, 72). See our response below, n. 165.

153. So, Schneider, *Vollendung*, 53; Hollander, "'Law,'" 132; Hollander and Holleman, "Relationship," 279; Collins, *First Corinthians*, 582-3; Hodge, *First Corinthians*, 358. Morissette seriously entertains the possibility that 15:56 concerns law in general ("Midrash," 180-81). Thiselton appears to draw away from applying the reference in v. 56 to the Torah. He assigns three "distinct conceptual grammars of ὁ νόμος determined contextually": 1) the law as "Torah," 2) the law as "a moral indicator, making it possible to realize the gravity of sin," 3) the law as "a broader principle or rule of cause and effect" (*First Corinthians*, 1303). He observes that the first of the three categories has been receiving the most attention since Sanders's "new look" (ibid.). A careful reading of his application appears to indicate that Thistleton applies only the second and third category to v. 56b. He writes: "The major problem about a judicial or *de facto* law of cause and effect [i.e. the third category] is that it *ties* a human being to the effects of his or her *past actions*. Consequences of destruction, self-contradiction, guilt, and ultimately death are set in train. Both for this reason and on the ground of the second conceptual grammar of 'moral indicator' ἡ δὲ δύναμις τῆς ἁμαρτίας ὁ νόμος in this way arms death with its deadly κέντρον" (ibid.). While there are exceptions (e.g., Garland [*1 Corinthians*, 749] and Fee [*First Corinthians*, 806] *appear* to identify ὁ νόμος in a Mosaic sense by way of cross referencing 1 Cor 15:56 to 2 Cor 3:6 [see also Bachmann, *Korinther*, 472; de Boor, *Korinther*, 291]; Grundmann, as noted above, sees an inverted reference to the power of the Torah ["Gesetz," 54-55; see also Kümmel and Lietzmann, *Korinther*, 196; Watson, *First Corinthians*, 180]; and Witherington assumes a Mosaic reference [*Conflict*, 311 n. 73]), most commentators do not specify the sense in which they understand ὁ νόμος in 1 Cor 15:56. Thus Lindemann dismisses a secular connotation to νόμος in v. 56 (*a la* Hollander and Holleman) yet fails to specify beyond that (*Korintherbrief*, 371). Robertson and Plummer merely discuss the verse in the context of there being sin where "there is a law to be transgressed" and no rebellion "where there is no law" (*First Corinthians*, 378; so also Godet, Orr and Walther, Lias). Thrall cross references Rom 7:7-11 and speaks

but without reference to any specific manner of expression.[154] This possibility is not only suggested by the fact that the Jewish law had not been a front burner issue in 1 Corinthians,[155] but it finds support when this axiomatic statement regarding law and sin is compared to the law-sin axioms of Rom 3:20b; 4:15b; 5:13b; and 7:8b:

3:20 διότι ἐξ ἔργων νόμου οὐ δικαιωθήσεται πᾶσα σὰρξ ἐνώπιον αὐτοῦ,
**διὰ γὰρ νόμου ἐπίγνωσις ἁμαρτίας.**

4:15 ὁ γὰρ νόμος ὀργὴν κατεργάζεται·
**οὗ δὲ οὐκ ἔστιν νόμος οὐδὲ παράβασις.**

5:13 ἄχρι γὰρ νόμου ἁμαρτία ἦν ἐν κόσμῳ,
**ἁμαρτία δὲ οὐκ ἐλλογεῖται μὴ ὄντος νόμου.**

7:8 ἀφορμὴν δὲ λαβοῦσα ἡ ἁμαρτία διὰ τῆς ἐντολῆς κατειργάσατο ἐν ἐμοὶ πᾶσαν ἐπιθυμίαν·

---

of "moral laws which ought to govern human behavior" (*First and Second Corinthians*, 115). Commenting on v. 56, Schlatter asserts that "Gesetz, Sünde, Tod sind die Mächte, die wider uns sind und gegen die wir ringen müssen" (*Paulus*, 446; see also Schrage, Hays). Kling applies the verse to "the revelation of the divine will in the form of a command or prohibition" (*First Corinthians*, 348). Barrett speaks merely of anarthrous "law" (*First Corinthians*, 383; see also Conzelmann). Kay applies the verse to "the law" in the garden prohibiting the eating of the fruit (*Corinthians*, 83). Luther is non-specific ("1 Corinthians," 28:208–10) as is Chrysostom (*NPNF1* 12:257) and Calvin. Each merely alludes to "the law." Similar in their commentaries are Wolff, Senft, Stanley, Kistemaker, Ellicott, de Wette, Edwards, Strobel, Grosheide, Pop, Beet, Olshausen, Héring, Heinrici, Goudge, Sampley, Allo, Morris, Bruce, Wendland, and Lang. While some of these writers possibly consider νόμος in v. 56 to be Mosaic (does the capital letter L in "Law," for example, imply such for Beet or Héring?), most seem to assume a theologically general sense.

154. For such an understanding of *law qua law*, see Démann, Burton, *Galatians*, 456, "Moïse," 218; Burton, *Rhetoric*, 51–58.

155. See Hollander and Holleman, "Relationship," 279; García Pérez, "1 Co 15,56," 411–12. The possibility that νόμος in 1 Cor 15:56 does not refer to Jewish law provides the climax to Schneider's critique of Horn's thesis that, for theological reasons, a reference to the Torah in v. 56 can only be an interpolation. Schneider argues: "Außerdem ist zu bedenken, daß die von Horn selbstverständlich vorausgesetzte Annahme, Paulus meine in V 56 mit νόμος das jüdische Gesetz, keineswegs so sicher ist, wie es den Anschein hat. Im Gegenteil! Da der Apostel es in Korinth hauptsächlich mit Heidenchristen zu tun hat und im ganzen Kapitel nichts erwähnt, das deutlich in die Richtung des Judentums weist, ist es viel wahrscheinlicher, daß er, wie etwa auch in Röm 7,1a.b, hier von dem Prinzip Gesetz schlechthin spricht, zu dem die Tora ebenfalls gehört, ohne diese jedoch besonders im Blick zu haben" (*Vollendung*, 53).

χωρὶς γὰρ νόμου ἁμαρτία νεκρά.

When these four verses are examined, two inferences emerge. First, Paul consistently conveys his law-sin (or law-transgression) notion by way of axioms. The absence of the copulative verb in the second clause or the present tense there accents the epigrammatic nature of the expressions.[156] Secondly, while the first clause in each verse makes an explicit reference to the Mosaic law,[157] the second clause presents a general proposition, or truism, in light of its implication for the particular case in view.[158] In view of this, it is appears as though the term νόμος in the truism bears the sense of divine *law qua law*.[159] This is almost certainly the case in 4:15b and 5:13b.[160] By way of analogy, 3:20b and 7:8b likely follow suit.[161]

---

156. See n. 87, above. On the aphoristic use of the present tense with νόμος, see Winger, *Νόμος*, 83-84. Burton notes that the present tense may be used to express "general truths" (*Syntax*, 8; see also Fanning, *Verbal Aspect*, 208-18; Schwyzer, *Grammatik*, 270). Additional examples of the aphoristic use of the present tense in regard to *law* are found in Rom 7:1 (ὁ νόμος κυριεύει τοῦ ἀνθρώπου ἐφ' ὅσον χρόνον ζῇ), Gal 5:23 (κατὰ τῶν τοιούτων οὐκ ἔστιν νόμος) and Tim 1:9 (δικαίῳ νόμος οὐ κεῖται). The exact nature of the term νόμος in each of these verses is debatable, but the fact that the statements are axiomatic in nature would be consistent with a generic meaning of the term.

157. Burton is overly specific in identifying the referent of νόμος in Romans with the Decalogue (*Rhetoric*, 60-67). Though he correctly notes that several passages cite the Decalogue (e.g., Rom 2:21-22; 7:7-12; 9:31-32), these could just as well be considered as references to the *Torah* since the Decalogue, in fact, is contained in the Torah. In addition, it is clear from Gal 2:16 (cf. Rom 3:28) that the works of the "law" that do not justify include circumcision and other ritual observances. Suffice it to say that the usual referent of νόμος in Romans is sinaitic.

158. See Winger, *Νόμος*, 83-84. An additional example of this is likely found in Gal 3:21b, though the proposition is stated hypothetically: ὄντως ἐκ νόμου ἂν ἦν ἡ δικαιοσύνη (see Hong, *Law*, 122-23). In Burton's appendix listing the anarthrous occurrences of νόμος in Romans he designates all to be references to the Decalogue but those in 7:23, 25 (*Rhetoric*, 106). Although he distinguishes between the *meaning* of νόμος and the *referent* of νόμος (see ibid., 49-67), he fails to consider the axiomatic structure of Rom 3:20b; 4:15b; 5:14b; 7:8b and the possibility that these verses contain examples of νόμος used in both senses.

159. See Winger, *Νόμος*, 83-84; Poirier, "Universality," 352-53; Hollander, "'Law,'" 133 n. 68; Käsemann, *Romans*, 121; Zahn, *Römer*, 228; Aletti, *Israël*, 110; Turner, *Syntax*, 177.

160. Contra Hofius on 4:15b and 5:13b ("Antithese," 193, 195). Most every English version renders νόμος in 4:15b and 5:13b in a general sense.

161. The word in 7:8b is rendered in a generic manner in NEB, NIV, NJB, REB, TEV, Barclay, Goodspeed, Moffatt. A generic sense for 3:20b is found in JB, NEB, REB, Barclay.

When 1 Cor 15:56b, itself an axiom, is thus viewed alongside of these four axioms, it seems reasonable to conclude that "law" possesses a general sense in the clause as it likely does in these others.[162] And this possibility is strengthened by the fact that the terms ὁ θάνατος and ἡ ἁμαρτία, to which ὁ νόμος is intimately linked in 15:56, depict abstract entities. Morissette catches this:

> "'La Loi' représente-t-elle la Loi mosaïque ou toute loi? ... Notons d'abord qu'il nous semble devoir maintenir le fait de la personnification de la Loi, Puissance cosmique au service du Péché et de la Mort. Dans le contexte, similaire, de la réflexion contenue dans l'*Épître aux Romains* sur les rapports entre le Péché, la Mort et la Loi (cf. v ss), cette dernière accuse en effet *une dimension cosmique*."[163]

In tune with the use of the article with these entities of θάνατος and ἁμαρτία, the article with νόμος would serve a generic function to deemphasize specific identity.[164] The axiom in v. 56b, then, would not be confined to Jewish law but would concern law as such.[165]

---

Jewett likewise understands νόμος in 3:20b and 7:8b in a broad sense (see *Romans*, 266; 450). While Winger is open to the possibility of a generic reference in these two verses, he hesitates because "these phrases lack the present tense that was decisive for 4:15b and 5:13b" (*Νόμος*, 84). But do they? In point of fact, 7:8b and 3:20b are verbless. Though the tense in Rom 7:8b could be deemed an imperfect (TNIV), the precedent set in 4:15b; 5:13b makes an axiomatic *present* sense more likely. Indeed, this is the way most versions translate 4:15b. The same applies to 3:20b. Virtually all versions render the clause in the present tense, which is appropriate of an axiom. Jewett understands νόμος in 3:20b and 7:8b as a reference to and beyond Jewish law (see *Romans*, 266; 450)

162. Commenting on ὁ νόμος in 15:56, Hodge argues, "This must be the law of God in its widest sense; not the Mosaic law, which would make the declaration amount to nothing" (*First Corinthians*, 358). See references to other commentators above, n. 153.

163. "Midrash," 180, italics in last phrase mine. See also Schneider, *Vollendung*, 50; Hollander and Holleman, "Relationship," 279; Hollander, "'Law,'" 131.

164. See Abel, *Grammaire*, 120-21; Porter, *Idioms*, 104-5; Robertson, *Grammar*, 757-58.

165. See further discussion, below, pp. 114-16. Winger considers νόμος to be generic in Paul's writings when, in context, a verse contains "a statement about νόμος *as such*" (*Νόμος*, 68 n. 16, italics mine). While Winger sees a reference to "Jewish law" in 1 Cor 15:56 (ibid., 72), it would appear that the verse fits his generic definition precisely. Though he asserts that the unspecified reference there assumes a specific understanding of Jewish νόμος on the part of the readers (ibid.), he fails to take into consideration both the association in v. 56 of ὁ νόμος with the global entities of ἡ ἁμαρτία and ὁ θάνατος and the *axiomatic* nature of v. 56. Also, unlike the other references in 1 Corinthians to

If 15:56 is indeed utilizing ὁ νόμος generally, this would not assume a reference to "law as a part of human culture and convention";[166] the thoroughly theological use of νόμος in 1 Corinthians would suggest rather a *divine* notion.[167] Nor would a general notion in 15:56 exclude the Mosaic law from being encompassed within the axiom; the Mosaic law would be a specific, indeed, for Paul's contemporaries, the most relevant, application of divine law. Hong is surely correct to note that Paul "cannot think of it [divine law] without an awareness of the Mosaic law as its supreme example."[168] Yet this being so, Paul does not appear to be pondering Mosaic law in his Corinthian epigram, but divine law in general and its relation to sin. As we will later suggest, this linking of law and sin in 15:56 has *universal* relevance, rather than merely *sociological* pertinence.[169] For Paul, we argue, it is in the very nature of reality that the divine imperative empowers sin. In what setting and why it does so will be explored below.

*Law in a Catalytic Sense*

Taking v. 56b now in its entirety, with regard to the law being ἡ δύναμις τῆς ἁμαρτίας, some exegetes interpret this energizing capacity of the

---

νόμος, v. 56 does, in fact, appear to be making a statement about νόμος *as such*. As we have seen, the statement resembles the axiomatic statements in Rom 3:20b, 4:15b, 5:13b, and 7:8b, verses in which Winger himself either perceives a generic meaning of νόμος (4:15b, 5:13b) or remains open to the possibility (3:20b, 7:8b). The evidence, therefore, should have given Winger pause. He should not have so quickly assumed that Paul in 15:56 was speaking in Jewish categories. Paul's embryonic and axiomatic statement (as well as the primordial scenery that we will see) suggests that he may have had something inclusive of, but beyond Sinai in mind. Likewise, while Jewett correctly, we believe, argues for a generic sense of the anarthrous νόμος in Rom 7:8b, he assumes Jewish categories in 1 Cor 15:56 by missing what is likely a generalizing function of the article there (see *Romans*, 450).

166. Hollander and Holleman, "Relationship," 290.

167. Note 9:8–9, 20; 14:21, 34, especially 9:8. See Verburg, *Endzeit*, 91; Wolff, *Erste Brief*, 418 n. 3.

168. Hong, *Law*, 123; see also Morissette, "Midrash," 181.

169. Thus Winger, who argues that 15:56 concerns Jewish law (see *Nόμος*, 36 n. 87), contends that *Jewish law* describes what *Jews* do as a way of life. Therefore, since it is not the *command* of God as such but rather a sociological or ethnic norm, it would be irrelevant, and indeed, inappropriate for Gentiles to be placed under its jurisdiction; hence Paul's critique of the law in his Gentile context (see ibid., 109–113; 157–58, 196–201).

law in a cognitive sense, i.e., the law *reveals* sin for what it is. Orr and Walther, for instance, contend that sin would have no power were it not for the "awareness of God's purpose revealed by *the law*."[170] The law is thus "the agent that fills with guilt."[171] Witherington similarly understands Paul to be speaking here of the (Mosaic) law's function "to reveal and warn against sin,"[172] as does Thiselton, who views the *law* in v. 56 primarily as a "moral indicator."[173] Fee, on the other hand, while perceiving in v. 56 this cognitive function of the law to reveal "the depth of one's depravity and rebellion against God" suggests that it also functions conversely as a *nomistic* agent of sin since "it leads to pride of achievement."[174] Likewise, Ortkemper asserts that "der Tod begegnet uns auf tausenderlei Art, in den vielen Formen schuldhafter Zerstörung menschlichen Lebens, wie in dem zerstörerischen Wahn, den Sinn des eigenen Lebens ganz aus eigener Kraft 'leisten' zu müssen (das meint im Kern die Chiffre 'Gesetz'),"[175] and Schrage, arguing along similar lines, states that the law in v. 56, among other things, empowers sin "denn das Gesetz stachelt zum sich rühmenden Gesetzeseifer an."[176]

A more common understanding regarding the law's power in relationship to sin in v. 56 is that which considers its capacity to bring condemnation upon those who transgress it. The thought follows the line set out by Rom 4:15 and 5:13.[177] Without law to *define* sin there would be no

---

170. Orr and Walther, *1 Corinthians*, 353.

171. Ibid. The authors quote here from Hamlet's soliloquy (*Hamlet* III. i. 83): "Conscience does make cowards of us all."

172. Witherington, *Conflict*, 311 n. 73.

173. Thiselton, *First Corinthians*, 1302–3; see also Trail, *Summary*, 367. Bengelii, succinctly as usual, writes concerning v. 56: "sine lege peccatum non sentitur" (*Gnomon*, 673). It appears that Luther understands 15:56 along cognitive lines. Commenting on the verse, he writes: "Sin is not properly recognized and felt unless this light is kindled in the heart; nor can sin attain its power unless it is awakened by the Law. But when the Law appears, it shows us that we are completely steeped in sin and lying in God's wrath" ("1 Corinthians," 28:210). See also Ellicott, *First Corinthians*, 328; Barclay, *Corinthians*, 160.

174. Fee, *First Corinthians*, 806.

175. Ortkemper, *Korintherbrief*, 166.

176. Schrage, *Korinther*, 382. See also Senft, *Corinthiens*, 214, and recall Söding's nomistic theory concerning 1 Cor 15:56.

177. Morissette thinks the notion is better traced to Gal 3:10–13: "Nous ne craignons pas, pour rendre compte du sens de la clause *1 Cor.*, xv,56b, de recourir à l'*Épître aux Galates* qui, du reste, appartient à la même époque que *1 Cor.*, xv. Paul y fournit le motif pour lequel le Péché tire de la Loi sa puissance mortelle" ("Midrash," 182). In light of the

accountable trespass. In the presence of law, however, non-imputed sin is transformed into prosecutable violation. Thus, Ambrosiaster comments on v. 56: "ideo virtus peccati lex [est], quia peccatum non imputaretur, si lex non esset,"[178] Schlatter's comments regarding 15:56 are similar: "Weil die Sünde Übertretung ist, ist sie Schuld, und weil das Gesetz als Gottes Gebot heilig ist, fällt auf den, der es übertritt, das Urteil des Tods,"[179] as are Lang's: "Die Gesetz macht die Sünde anrechenbar (Röm 5,13) und klagt den Sünder an im eschatologischen Gericht."[180]

When Paul's theology of law as a whole is taken into consideration, one could easily read into 1 Cor 15:56 any of these functions that Paul attributes to the law.[181] To be sure, Paul elsewhere argues that violating the law will lead to condemnation,[182] recognizes the possibility that it may lead to pride,[183] and may ascribe a cognitive function to it.[184] Nevertheless, it is unlikely that any of these notions convey the meaning of 1 Cor 15:56.[185] That a cognitive sense is in view is improbable in light

---

stronger affinity that 1 Cor 15:56 has with Romans 5–7, Romans, not Galatians, should receive the first glance.

178. Ambrosiaster, *Epist. ad Cor.* Similarly, in his homily on 15:56 Chrysostom states: "Without the law sin was weak, being practiced indeed, but not able so entirely to condemn: since although the evil took place, it was not so clearly pointed out. So that it was no small change which the law brought in, first causing us to know sin better, and then enhancing the punishment" (*Hom. 1 Cor.* 42.4 [*NPNF*1 12:257]; see also Theodoret, *epistolae ad Corinthios* [PG 82: col. 309]). Benoit emphasizes this last point regarding *knowing* and *enhancing* sin. There are for him two essential roles of the law attributable to 15:56, viz., "information and condemnation" ("The Law," 15).

179. Schlatter, *Paulus*, 446.

180. Lang, *Korinther*, 241. See also, e.g., Blocher, *Péché*, 50, 141, 306; Somerville, *Corinthiens*, 214; Moule, "'Justification'," 183; Whitely, *Theology*, 81.

181. See above, p. 6 n. 34. Although he need not assume self-contradiction, Räisänen is correct that Paul "seems to understand the relation between the law and sin in different ways in different passages" (*Paul*, 148). Perhaps this is why Díaz Rodelas in his study of 15:56 hesitates to say exactly how the power of sin is actuated by the law (*Pablo*, 30). He is wrong to assume, however, that the context is ambiguous. As will become evident, the term δύναμις in itself points to the meaning of the phrase in v. 56b.

182. Rom 4:15a; 5:14a; 2 Cor 3:7, 9; Gal 3:10.

183. See Rom 3:27.

184. Most understand Rom 3:20b in this manner, though the *knowledge of sin* there, we will argue, probably has an experiential connotation, as in Rom 7:7-8 (see Klein, "Sündenverständnis," 261; Kuss, *Römerbrief*, 2:109; Schlier, *Römerbrief*, 101; Käsemann, *Romans*, 89). See below, 108–13.

185. Rather than committing themselves to assigning one sense to the law in its relation

of the term δύναμις, which, we noted above, connotes activity, not cognition.[186] Nor is condemnation likely in view in v. 56b since that appears to have been the focus of 56a: "The sting of death is sin." The step parallelism would be expected to progress, not repeat the thought. And more importantly, if Paul were addressing the condemning function of the law we would expect Paul to say that "the power of the law is sin" or to employ a παράβασις-ἁμαρτία nexus as he does in Rom 4:15b and Gal 3:19:[187]

4:15b οὗ δὲ οὐκ ἔστιν **νόμος** οὐδὲ **παράβασις**.

3:19 Τί οὖν ὁ **νόμος**; τῶν **παραβάσεων** χάριν προσετέθη.

Nor is the nomistic pride of keeping the law the likely theme of 15:56. If so, one might expect to find the term ἔργα here, which in Paul comports more with the notion of boastful activity.[188]

It is improbable, then, that the focus of v. 56b is cognition, condemnation, or nomism. Rather, Paul is almost certainly alluding to the most startling of the capacities that he ascribes to the law. In 15:56, we believe, Paul is portraying ὁ νόμος in a *catalytic* sense. As Martin maintains: "Texts like Rom 7:7–11, 4:15, 5:20, 1 Cor 15:56 indicate more than man realizing his sinfulness by means of the law, or that the law makes sin a conscious and willful activity and thereby makes man guilty, *the law is the catalyst that helps to bring about sinning*."[189] Indeed, notes Wendland

---

to sin, some exegetes suggest that multiple functions are present in 15:56. Thus, Schrage in his interpretation of v. 56b encapsulates three capacities of the law in one sentence: "Was aber der Sünde zur Macht verhilft, ist nach anderen paulinischen Grundaussagen das Gesetz, denn das Gesetz stachelt zum sich rühmenden Gesetzeseifer an, dient aber auch der Vermehrung und Offenbarung der Gesetzesübertretungen" (*Korinther*, 4:382; for similar approaches [indecision?], see Garland, Barrett, Fee, Senft, and Lang).

186. See also n. 193, below.

187. Rom 2:23 also employs παράβασις with its lexical partner ἁμαρτία: ἐν νόμῳ καυχᾶσαι, διὰ τῆς παραβάσεως τοῦ νόμου τὸν θεὸν ἀτιμάζεις. The two other occurrences of παράβασις (Rom 5:14; 1 Tim 2:14) will be discussed below.

188. See, e.g., Rom 3:27 (Ποῦ οὖν ἡ καύχησις; ἐξεκλείσθη. διὰ ποίου νόμου; τῶν ἔργων;); 4:2 (εἰ γὰρ Ἀβραὰμ ἐξ ἔργων ἐδικαιώθη, ἔχει καύχημα, ἀλλ' οὐ πρὸς θεόν); and Eph 2:9 (οὐκ ἐξ ἔργων, ἵνα μή τις καυχήσηται). In Rom 2:17, 23 νόμος and καυχάομαι occur together, but the boasting there appears to be in regard to possession rather than activity. The assumption in Rom 2:23 is that Paul's Jewish debating partners, in fact, were *not* keeping the law.

189. Martin, *Christ and the Law*, 97, italics mine. Since παράβασις occurs in Rom 4:15b the verse should probably not be assigned by Martin to the catalytic category. It more likely is expressing the defining (i.e., condemning) function of the law. On the cata-

of 1 Cor 15:56, with the law as its power source, "die Sünde kommt zum Leben;"[190] or in Cranfield's words, it "springs into activity."[191] And in doing so, argues Bandstra, sin through the law "becomes *actualized* and *realized* in the concrete transgression."[192]

That 15:56b indeed depicts a catalytic notion is evident from the semantic domain that δύναμις shares with the ἐργ- verbs ἐνεργέω and κατεργάζομαι that are found in Rom 7:5, 8, 13,[193] verses which, like 15:56, expound on the *law-sin-death* triad and, as most exegetes agree, depict the sin-stimulating operation of the law:

7:5 ὅτε γὰρ ἦμεν ἐν τῇ σαρκί, τὰ παθήματα τῶν ἁμαρτιῶν τὰ διὰ τοῦ νόμου **ἐνηργεῖτο** ἐν τοῖς μέλεσιν ἡμῶν, εἰς τὸ καρποφορῆσαι τῷ θανάτῳ·

7:8 ἀφορμὴν δὲ λαβοῦσα ἡ ἁμαρτία διὰ τῆς ἐντολῆς **κατειργάσατο** ἐν ἐμοὶ πᾶσαν ἐπιθυμίαν· χωρὶς γὰρ νόμου ἁμαρτία νεκρά.

---

lytic function of the law in 15:56, see also Bruce, *Apostle*, 194; idem, "St. Paul," 47; Heim, *Gemeinde*, 239; Räisänen, *Paul and the Law*, 143; Luz, *Geschichtsverständnis*, 188; Napier, "Analysis," 23; Hollander and Holleman, "Relationship," 279; Schreiner, *Paul*, 133, idem, *Law*, 83; Deluz, *Companion*, 249; Bandstra, *Elements*, 126-27; Weima, "Function," 234; see also the following commentators: Sampley, Pop, Thrall, Kling, Héring, Grosheide, Goudge, Moffatt (though he assumes the notion was interpolated by Paul or another); Wendland, Barrett, Johnson. Mention here should, of course, also be made of Augustine, who practically owns this topic. Though Romans 7 was his primary scriptural source on the subject of counter-suggestibility and the law (see, e.g., *Exp. quaest. Rom.* 37, 39, 40; *Div. quaest. Simpl.* 1:4; *Div. quaest. LXXXIII* 66:4), he more than once comments on 15:56. Thus in *The City of God*, after quoting the verse, Augustine states that the strength of sin is the very thing that prohibits sin, i.e., the law: "Most certainly true; for prohibition increases the desire of illicit action, if righteousness is not so loved that the desire of sin is conquered by that love" (*Civ.* 13.5 [*NPNF*1 2:248]). Likewise, after a reference to 1 Cor 15:56 in *On Grace and Free Will*, Augustine notes that "concupiscence is increased and receives greater energies from the prohibition of the law, unless the spirit of grace helps" (*Grat.* 8 [*NPNF*1 5:447]; see also *Contin.* 7; *Mor. eccl.* 30.64; *Spir. et Litt.* 56; *C. du. ep. Pelag.* 3.2.

190. Wendland, *Korinther*, 158.

191. Cranfield, "St. Paul," *SJT* 17 (1964): 47. Cranfield's words here are directed at 1 Cor 15:56 and Rom 7:8.

192. Bandstra on 15:56, *Elements*, 127, italics mine. See also Hollander and Holleman, "Relationship," 279.

193. Note also the linking of δύναμις with ἐνέργεια/ἐνεργέω/κατεργάζομαι in Rom 15:18-19; 2 Cor 12:12; Eph 1:19-20; 3:7, 20; Col 1:29; 2 Thess 2:9). See above, pp. 73-74.

7:13 Τὸ οὖν ἀγαθὸν ἐμοὶ ἐγένετο θάνατος; μὴ γένοιτο· ἀλλὰ ἡ ἁμαρτία, ἵνα φανῇ ἁμαρτία, διὰ τοῦ ἀγαθοῦ μοι **κατεργαζομένη** θάνατον, ἵνα γένηται καθ' ὑπερβολὴν ἁμαρτωλὸς ἡ ἁμαρτία διὰ τῆς ἐντολῆς.[194]

The relationship between the notion of *power* and these *energy* verbs suggests that 1 Cor 15:56 is alluding to the same sin-empowering capacity of the law that is depicted in Rom 7:5, 7–11.[195] This thesis is all the more strengthened by the close affinity that 1 Cor 15:56 has with Romans 7.[196]

The thought in 15:56 thus does not appear to be that the law makes people realize they behave badly or condemns those who behave badly but rather becomes part of the reason that they behave badly.[197] Rather than defusing sin, the law, in the manner described in Rom 7:7–11, provides sin with "powerful leverage by which it may bring people under its sway."[198] The dynamic at work here between law and sin will be explored later, though understanding the dynamic may not be as simple as identifying the dynamic itself. Yet for now we will announce our course by proposing that Paul's understanding of the law-sin nexus may be best

---

194. The use of the verb κατεργάζομαι, in fact, continues into the depiction in 7:15–20 of the struggle with sin (7:15, 17, 18, 20).

195. See Wilckens, *Römer*, 2:69; Weima, "Function," 233–34.

196. Dodd remarks that "by content, 1 Cor 15:56–57 is the closest Pauline parallel to Romans 7" (*Paradigmatic*, 233). Indeed, he concludes: "1 Cor 15.56 could function as a partial summary of Romans 7" (ibid., see also Lietzmann, *Korinther*, 88; Räisänen, *Paul and the Law*, 143; Weima, "Function," 233–34). In light of this affinity between 1 Cor 15:56 and Romans 7, δύναμις in 1 Cor 15:56 is more likely to be linked to the ἐργ- verbs of Romans 7:5, 8, 13 and the *catalytic* setting there than to κατεργάζομαι in Rom 4:15a and its *defining/condemnatory* context.

197. Benoit argues that one can only introduce a catalytic notion into 1 Cor 15:56 with violence ("The Law," 15). In light of the evidence we have gathered, we consider this an ill-informed statement.

198. Sampley, "1 Corinthians," 989. "Gesetz," writes Jülicher, "ist für die Sünde Zufuhr von Lebenskraft (Rom 5:20!) für den Menschen Hinführung in den Tod" ("Römer," 2:41; see also Anders Nygren's reference to 1 Cor 15:56 in his exposition of Rom 7:7–13 [*Romans*, 280]). "The norms and models contained in the law," writes Theissen, "themselves evoke behavior contrary to the norm, even though their authentic purpose is to promote behavior corresponding to the norm" (*Aspects*, 223).

explicated for scholars of Paul and the law by reference to the Fall account itself, which, it would appear, contains the *story* behind the *moral* of 1 Cor 15:56.

# 4

# The Power of Sin Is the Law: An Edenic Axiom

HAVING EXAMINED 1 COR 15:56, its context, and various approaches to understand it, we will now suggest what may have been the thematic precursor to Paul's axiomatic statements, "the sting of death is sin, and the power of sin is the law." Since, as we have discovered, v. 56 appears to be an undisputed element in the train of thought,[1] it would not be unreasonable to expect to find such a thematic link.

## EDENIC LINKS IN 1 CORINTHIANS 15 TO THE SIN-DEATH NEXUS OF 1 CORINTHIANS 15:56A

Looking again at the step parallelism that led up to v. 56, it is clear that ὁ θάνατος in v. 56a is linked to the occurrences of the term in v. 55, which are linked back to the statement κατεπόθη ὁ θάνατος εἰς νῖκος in v. 54,[2] which in turn picks up the thought in v. 26 of death (as in v. 56, personified) as the last enemy to be defeated.[3] The mention of ὁ θάνατος in v. 56, then, comes as no surprise; the reference there is an overflow of the statements regarding its defeat that culminate in vv. 54–55.[4]

---

1. Thus Thurén, *Derhetorizing*, 116.

2. Schrage likens the sequence of thought in vv. 54–56 to "chain links" (*Korinther*, 4:381). Using a similar metaphor, Díaz Rodelas notes that the phrase τὸ κέντρον τοῦ θανάτου serves to link v. 56 to 55 as "un lazo estrechísimo" (*Pablo*, 27).

3. Fee asserts that the decisive pronouncement in v. 26 is precisely the point that is made again in vv. 53–57 (*First Corinthians*, 757). Sandelin's insights are similar: "Dieser Kontext von v. 56 steht . . . inhaltlich zu den Gedanken in vv. 26–28 parallel" (*Auseinandersetzung*, 71–72).

4. See Thielmann, *Paul and the Law*, 107–8; Barrett, *First Corinthians*, 383; Sellin, *Streit*, 227.

## 1 Corinthians 15:21-22

> ²¹ For since death came through a human being, the resurrection of the dead has also come through a human being; ²² for as all die in Adam, so all will be made alive in Christ.

Though launched by vv. 54-56, the antecedent of "death" in v. 56a, however, may likely be traced back ultimately to vv. 21-22, where Paul epigrammatically identifies Adam as the origin of ὁ θάνατος in the world: δι' ἀνθρώπου θάνατος . . . ἐν τῷ 'Ἀδὰμ πάντες ἀποθνῄσκουσιν. As noted earlier, Paul's viewpoint here is in step with a common Jewish understanding of Genesis 2-3 in which Adam was rergarded as the source of universal death.[5] It is likely that the notion of death in v. 56 reaches back past the prophetic oracles quoted in vv. 54-55 to the *primordial* reference in vv. 20-21.[6] Indeed, since, as Wright observes, the entire section comprising vv. 20-28 (and 35-49) "is built upon the foundation of Genesis 1-2," and vv. 50-57 primarily "sum up" what he writes there,[7] and seeing that Paul's teaching in vv. 20-28 concerning Adam is recognized by commentators to be the preparation for all that follows,[8] it

---

5. *4 Ezra*, for instance, attributes physical death to Adam's transgression of the divine command (Gen 2:17): "And you laid upon him one commandment of yours; but he transgressed it, and immediately you appointed death for him and for his descendants" (*4 Ezra* 3:7 [*OTP* 1:528]; see also 3:10, 21; 7:116-26). The identical thought is found in *2 Baruch*: "For what did it profit Adam that he lived nine hundred and thirty years and transgressed that which he was commanded? Therefore, the multitude of time that he lived did not profit him, but brought death and cut off the years of those who were born of him" (*2 Bar.* 17:2-3 [*OTP* 1:627]; see also 19:8; 23:4; 48:42; 54:15; 59:5-6). Note also *2 En.* 30:16-17; *Syb. Or.* 1:50-53; 8:259-62; *Apoc. Adam* 1:10; *T. Ab.* 8:9; *T. Adam* 3:2-3; *Jub.* 3:17-32; 4:29-30; *L.A.E.* 26:2; 34:1-3; 44:2-4; *Apoc. Mos.* 7:1; 17:5; *L.A.B.* 13:8; 37:3; *Hel. Syn. Pr.* 3:24-27; *Sir* 15:14-17; 17:11; 25:24; *Wis* 2:23-24; Philo (*Creation* 152, 156; *Alleg. Interp.* 1:33.105-108; *QG*. 1.16, 51); *Pirqe R. El.* 13; *Midr. Pss.* 25:8; 92:3, 14; *Tanh. Lev* 13:1; *Sifr. Deut.* 32:50, 339; *Pesiq. Rab.* 46:1; *y. Qidd.* 4:1 IV. See further Str-B 3:227-30; Morissette, "Midrash," 180 n. 90; Brandenburger, *Adam und Christus*, 15-64; Scroggs, *Last Adam*, 17; Tobin, "Context," 159-75; Wedderburn, "Structure," 344-46; Levison, *Portraits*, 116-17; 122-23; 133-40; 142-43; 156-59; 188-89, etc; Aletti, *Israël*, 122-33.

6. The term θάνατος skips along from v. 21, to v. 26, to v. 54, to v. 55 (2x), and then to v. 56. There are no occurrences of the term after chapter 15. The nearest reference prior to 1 Cor 15:21 is the reference to Christ's death in 11:26.

7. Wright, "Adam," 367; see also idem, *Resurrection*, 340; Asher, *Polarity*, 151. Note the phrase τοῦτο δέ φημι in v. 50, which likely introduces a fuller explanation of what precedes (see BDAG 1053.2).

8. See e.g., Wolff, *Erste Brief*, 382. Sellin suggests that vv. 20ff. "handelt sich hier um

would appear that the climactic expression concerning death in v. 56a has these earlier edenic expressions as its basis. Indeed, the fact that the principles concerning mortality in both v. 56a *and* vv. 21-22 are expressed in axiomatic form may indicate that each truism is reflecting the other.[9]

The notion of ἡ ἁμαρτία in v. 56a likely also alludes back to vv. 21-22. Though it may initially appear that the occurrence of the term in the plural in vv. 3 and 17 prepared for its appearance in v. 56,[10] this is unlikely since v. 56 is addressing *sin* as an entity rather than *sins* as transgressions.[11] And though the term ἁμαρτία does not appear in vv. 21-22, the notion of sin can nevertheless be assumed there if what Paul makes explicit in Rom 5:12-17 is implicit in his Corinthian reference to Adam being the origin of death.[12] And that Adam's sin does, in fact, lie implicit in vv. 21-22 is virtually certain.[13] Seeing that the Adamic sin-death nexus in Romans 5 "is surely to be taken as determinative of Paul's meaning" in vv. 21-22,[14] the emphatic and repeated linking in Romans 5:12-21 of Adam's transgression with death makes it hard to deny that the notion is embedded in vv. 21-22:[15]

Romans 5

[12] as sin came into the world through one man and death through sin . . .

[15] many died through the one man's trespass . . .

---

den zentralen Teil der paulinischen Argumentation" (*Streit*, 261). Indeed, G. Barth argues that vv. 20-28 must be seen as the "Höhepunkt der Argumentation des ganzen Kapitels" ("Erwägungen," 516), and Aletti contends that "les v. 20-28 ne sont pas seulement le centre *matériel* de la composition, mais aussile centre *sémantique*" ("L'argumentation," 66). The term θάνατος is certainly among the semantically significant terms introduced there (v. 21).

9. Note the elliptical language in v. 21 and the use of the present tense in v. 22. Both, as shown above, are characteristic features of axioms (see pp. 64-65 n. 87). The introductory ἐπειδή (see 1:22) indicates that the principle is generally recognized (see BDAG 360.2; BDF §455.1; also Wilckens, *Weisheit*, 29).

10. See Conzelmann, *1 Corinthians*, 293.

11. See Schade, *Christologie*, 210 and above, pp. 39-40 n. 131.

12. Quotations here are taken from the RSV since the NRSV breaks the uniformity by using the phrase "human being" in 1 Cor 15:21 while using "man" in Rom 5:12, 15, 17.

13. See Blocher, *Original Sin*, 47-48.

14. Scroggs, *Last Adam*, 84. Barth argues that 1 Cor 15:21-22 provides the reader with a clarification of Rom 5:18-19 (see *Christ and Adam*, 43).

15. See Jervell's discussion (*Imago Dei*, 265). He concludes that "die Aussage hier [1 Cor 15:20-22] ist in einer Linie mit Röm 5, 12-20 zu sehen" (ibid.).

[17] by the trespass of the one man, death reigned through that one man . . .

1 Corinthians 15

[21] as by a man came death . . .

[22] as in Adam all die . . .

The difference between the Romans 5 context and that of 1 Corinthians 15 is that in the latter Paul is not making the point that Adam's *sin* brought death, but that Adam's sin brought *death*.[16] That is, in 1 Corinthians 15 the effect of the fall is at issue, not its cause.[17] Thielman, also noting the different contexts, observes a movement from plight to solution that is vigorous in Romans 5–8, yet tacit in 1 Corinthians 15: "In First Corinthians 15 the Corinthian objection to the resurrection is Paul's primary concern, and so his argument centers upon the resurrection itself, only mentioning the plight from which the resurrection rescues believers in vv. 17 and 56. In Romans 5–8, however, Paul has the leisure to discuss fully the role of sin, death, and the law in the plight as well as the role of the resurrection in the solution."[18]

Hence, while in the salvation-historical setting of Romans 5 Paul identifies Adam's *sin* as the source of mortality in the world,[19] in 1 Cor 15:21-22 he makes this same identification, though in an abbreviated, axiomatic manner that focuses on *death*. In v. 56a, we argue, Paul proceeds to make explicit the primal relation between sin and death that is assumed in vv. 21–22.[20] This is all more suggested by the aphoristic

---

16. See Garland, *1 Corinthians*, 706.

17. See Holleman, *Resurrection*, 56; Goossens, "Immortalité," 332; Sellin, *Streit*, 227; Scroggs, *Last Adam*, 84.

18. Thielman, "Coherence," 249. Beker argues that, unlike Romans where death, as in Jewish thought, is seen as the consequence of sin: "there is no speculation [in 1 Corinthians 15] about the relation of sin to death" ("Relationship," 59). Rather, he asserts, "in 1 Corinthians Paul's argument stresses the contrast between the finite-transient character of the created world and the coming apocalyptic glory" (ibid.). One might as well say that Paul, unlike in Romans 7, nowhere in 1 Corinthians 15 mentions a causal relation between law and sin. Evidently, Beker misses a causal relation between sin and death in 1 Corinthians 15 because he elsewhere misreads ὁ θάνατος in v. 56a as a subjective genitive, i.e., sin issues from death rather than death from sin (see *Paul*, 190).

19. That physical death is at least partially in mind in Romans 5 is evident from 5:14 where the term likely bears this meaning. Nevertheless, in view of the contrast between death and eternal life in 5:21, spiritual death is probably in focus as well.

20. Schlatter comments, "Nun aber fügt Paulus einen Satz ein, der die Botschaft vom Leben mit der von der Gerechtigkeit vereint" (*Paulus*, 446).

manner in which Paul expresses himself in 56a. Apart from the universal reign of death initiated by Adam's sin, no other reality would seem to support the truism *the sting of death is sin*.[21] And it is within ear-shot of v. 56a that we find this Adamic reality expressed in vv. 21–22.

## 1 Corinthians 15:45–49

> [45] Thus it is written, "The first man, Adam, became a living being," the last Adam became a life-giving spirit. [46] But it is not the spiritual that is first, but the physical, and then the spiritual. [47] The first man was from the earth, a man of dust; the second man is from heaven. [48] As was the man of dust, so are those who are of the dust; and as is the man of heaven, so are those who are of heaven. [49] Just as we have borne the image of the man of dust, we will also bear the image of the man of heaven.

First Corinthians 15:21–22 contains the first occurrence of the Adam-Christ typology in Paul's extant letters. In vv. 45–49 the Apostle returns to the theme, though with a different emphasis or, perhaps, *refinement* of his Adam-Christ contrast.[22] The fact that he varies his use of the theme in vv. 45–49, and later still in Rom 5:12–21, suggests that the Adam-Christ typology is a "commonplace" with Paul.[23] This is made all the more evident by the poetic manner in which the formulations appear.[24] Paul's use of isocolon and parisosis is in full bloom at this point in the chapter. The notions thus appear to have had some time to incubate, if not dance, in his mind.[25]

The likelihood that vv. 21–22 and its Adamic theme underlies the axiom of 15:56a would suggest that vv. 45–49 and its similar Adamic setting is a prime area to investigate for antecedents to v. 56a. Yet, to turn aside here to a full discussion of the verses and the issues they raise would be impossible. The section is "one of the most controversial passages in the New Testament,"[26] and a "jungle of misinterpretations" has grown up

21. See further below, pp. 95–96.
22. See Sampley, "1 Corinthians," 988.
23. Fee, *First Corinthians*, 750. See below, pp. 229 n. 41.
24. See above, pp. 62–63.
25. It is unlikely, however, that the statements are pre-Pauline. The language is *too* Pauline to be so (see Barrett, "Significance," 107).
26. Asher, *Polarity*, 110.

around it.²⁷ A basic overview, however, reveals that the situation depicted in vv. 45–49 appears to provide a point of reference for v. 56a and its statement regarding sin and death.

The section opens in v. 45 with a slightly adapted quotation of LXX Gen 2:7b: ἐγένετο ὁ πρῶτος Ἀδὰμ εἰς ψυχὴν ζῶσαν.²⁸ What follows, perhaps a midrash of some sort,²⁹ supports the contention in v. 44 that believers will be raised with a *spiritual* body.³⁰ The two kinds of bodies described in v. 44 are represented in vv. 45–49 in terms of two archetypical "Adams."³¹ They are respectively described in vv. 45–46 by the words

---

27. Wright, *Resurrection*, 352.

28. The LXX reads, καὶ ἐγένετο ὁ ἄνθρωπος εἰς ψυχὴν ζῶσαν. The addition of the adjective πρῶτος and the noun Ἀδάμ serves to balance the references to Christ, whom Paul describes as the *last Adam* (see Stanley, *Language*, 208; Barrett, *First Corinthians*, 373).

29. Similar, perhaps, to 1 Cor 14:21 (see Ellis, *Paul's Use*, 141–43. Scroggs presumes Paul is playing off a rabbinic midrash found in *Gen. Rab.* 14.5, which postulated that the two *yods* of וַיִּיצֶר in Gen 2:7a denoted the two natures of a person: the one in this world and the other in the world to come (*Last Adam*, 86). Though the tradition may be early since the schools of Hillel and Shammai are associated with the context, the theory seems to wobble on a point that is raised by Scroggs himself, viz., Paul does not quote from Gen 2:7a but from Gen 2:7b (see ibid., 87). Paul could hardly have expected his readers to follow such logic when the key part of the equation was missing. For other Jewish traditions concerning Gen 2:7, including those regarding Adam and the *primal man*, see Conzelmann, *1 Corinthians*, 284–86. It may be possible, though, that Paul's use of Gen 2:7b in v. 45 is limited to the nature of Adam. The verse would thus be paraphrased: "The Scripture says that the first Adam 'was made a living soul;' the last Adam (*as we know*) was made a life-giving spirit" (see Hodge, *1 Corinthians*, 350). The reference to the *first* Adam would imply a *last*, just as the principle enunciated in 1 Cor 15:44b that the the natural body requires an opposite counterpart, the natural body (see Garland, *1 Corinthians*, 735; Barrett, *First Corinthians*, 374). This would allow for an extension of the Genesis quotation to Christ in v. 45b.

30. I.e., raised on account of Christ's resurrection. Note in v. 45 the repetition of the verb ζωοποιέω, which was used of Christ in v. 22. The linking would appear to imply that Christ assumed his "life-giving" capacity after the resurrection (see Dunn, "1 Corinthians 15:45, 140; Fee, *First Corinthians*, 789; Conzelmann, *1 Corinthians*, 287), though *when* Christ became so seems not to be as important to Paul as that he *was* so. The context, in any case, places the emphasis on *resurrection* life, not the "believers' experience of new life" (Dunn, "Last Adam," 132).

31. In vv. 45 and 47 Paul, reverting back to v. 22, uses the term "Adam" of both Adam and Christ and adds the adjectives πρῶτος and δεύτερος. Paul is clearly connecting what he says here with what he had said in vv. 20–21 (see Wright, *Resurrection*, 354).

ψυχή/ψυχικός and πνεῦμα/πνευματικός,[32] drawn from Gen 2:7,[33] and in vv. 47-48, alluding again to Genesis,[34] with the phrases ἐκ γῆς χοϊκός and ἐξ οὐρανοῦ. The midrash then concludes in v. 49 with an analogy contrasting, as it would seem,[35] tense (ἐφορέσαμεν/φορέσομεν) and, once more with Genesis in mind,[36] image (ἡ εἰκὼν τοῦ χοϊκοῦ/ἡ εἰκὼν τοῦ ἐπουρανίου).[37] The verse serves as both a summary of vv. 45-48 and a threshold into the final section of the chapter, vv. 50-58, which takes up the preceding argument and carries it to its climactic conclusion.[38]

---

32. Though v. 46 is difficult (a contrast between two bodies, or between Christ and Adam, or both?), the idea, at least as it relates to believers, appears to be that the *spiritual* follows the *natural/human* mode of existence in terms of "the two forms of somatic existence people will bear" (Fee, *First Corinthians*, 790). BDAG defines ψυχικός as that which "pertains to the life of the natural world and whatever belongs to it, in contrast to the realm of experience whose central characteristic is πνεῦμα, *natural, unspiritual, worldly* (1100)." It is not at all certain that Paul's statement here was aimed at individuals who were claiming to be already πνευματικοί (Watson, "Rhetoric," 246; Fee, *First Corinthians*, 790). It is likewise uncertain if Paul was consciously contradicting Philo's notions of a heavenly man of Gen 1:27 and an earthly man of Gen 2:7 (see *Creation* 134; *Alleg. Interp.* 1.31-32). In favor of this scenario, see Allo, *Corinthiens*, 427-81; Barrett, *First Corinthians*, 374-75. Against it, see Wedderburn, "'Heavenly Man,'" 301-26; Scroggs, *Last Adam*, 791.

33. While Paul quotes Gen 2:7b in v. 45, there may be a faint allusion to Gen 2:7a in v. 46: ἐνεφύσησεν εἰς τὸ πρόσωπον αὐτοῦ πνοὴν ζωῆς. There would thus be a parallel between the Lord, who gave life to Adam, and Christ, who gives resurrection life to the believer. The allusion, however, appears dim at best.

34. Gen 2:7a: καὶ ἔπλασεν ὁ θεὸς τὸν ἄνθρωπον χοῦν ἀπὸ τῆς γῆς. By using the noun χοϊκός rather than the adjective χοῦς, Paul emphasizes the *earthiness* and, perhaps, the susceptibility towards decay of Adam's body (see Collins, *First Corinthians*, 571). Garland (probably following *TDNT* 9:472) suggests that Paul may have coined the adjective as a contrast to ἐπουράνιος. This may be so since the term seems not to predate Paul (*1 Corinthians*, 736 n. 13).

35. Although the aorist subjunctive φορέσωμεν has better textual support than the future indicative φορέσομεν, exegetical factors have convinced many that the latter is the original reading (see Thiselton for discussion [*First Corinthians*, 1289]).

36. Though the reference almost certainly draws from the language of Gen 1:27 (καὶ ἐποίησεν ὁ θεὸς τὸν ἄνθρωπον κατ' εἰκόνα θεοῦ ἐποίησεν αὐτόν), an allusion to Gen 5:3 (καὶ ἐγέννησεν κατὰ τὴν ἰδέαν αὐτοῦ καὶ κατὰ τὴν εἰκόνα αὐτοῦ) should not be missed, since the likeness of which Paul speaks is that of Adam (see Schrage, *Korinther*, 4:311).

37. In light of the saturation of vv. 45ff. with Genesis imagery, Fee's "may perhaps" in regard to a reference here to Gen 1:27 seems overly cautious (*First Corinthians*, 794 n. 34).

38. See above, p. 54 n. 50.

How might vv. 45-49 prepare for the epigram concerning sin and death in v. 56a? Although there is no mention of sin or death in the passage, the depiction of the first Adam there is of one who seems, at least, to be *susceptible to mortality*. That is, in contrast to the last Adam, who is *life-giving*, the first Adam in v. 45 is deemed to be merely *living*,[39] and unlike the second man, who is from the heavenly sphere, the first man is considered as *dust*.[40] While there is nothing inherently evil here,[41] there is a possibility that this life can be readily lost.[42] The distance, thus, between ψυχικός and θνητός is little, as is the distance between v. 49, with its emphasis on dust and what is merely human, and v. 50, with its focus on mortality and decay. Being taken out of the earth presents the possibility of returning to it.[43] This *all but mortal* constitution depicted in vv. 45-49 naturally, it seems, leads to v. 56a and its statement regarding sin and death. Though the terms sin and death do not appear in vv. 45-49, the notions of sin and death are virtually assumed in the depictions that Paul uses there of Adam. "The *psyche* is linked with Adam," writes Hays, "the initiator of death and decay."[44] We tread carefully here. It would seem incorrect to assert with Meyer that Adam was "*created mortal*,"[45]

39. Thiselton understands the term ψυχή here (as he does the Hebrew נֶפֶשׁ) as denoting "earthly life that can be lost in death" (*First Corinthians*, 1283).

40. See Beker, "Relationship," 59.

41. Nor, to the contrary, is there anything inherently inclining towards the good, as *TDNT* asserts: "The psychical is neither sinful as such nor does it incline to the πνεῦμα. . . . But it is corruptible and finds no access into God's kingdom" (Schweizer, "ψυχικός," in *TDNT* 9:662). Contra Schrage, it does not appear from the context that Adam is being characterized in vv. 45-49 in a "fast positiv" manner (*Korinther*, 4:345).

42. Blocher comments: "Originally death was a possibility arising from his [Adam's] constitution, but he was not subject to it, not destined to it by nature" (*In the Beginning*, 186-87). Regarding the fallen couple, Erickson suggests that before the Fall "they *could* die; now they *would* die" (*Theology*, 630).

43. Thiselton catches the subtle nuance in the allusion to *dust*, which "describes the σῶμα which is laid in the grave in weakness and sorrow, to disintegrate into bones and powder" (*First Corinthians*, 1287; see Jones, "Paganism," 726 and also n. 34, above).

44. Hays, *First Corinthians*, 272.

45. Meyer, *Corinthians*, 2:96, italics his; see also Heinrici, *Korinther*, 488, criticized by Schrage (*Korinther*, 4:308). Bray, who assumes that animal death is not the result of sin, asks why the "animal" part of humans could not also have been mortal by nature ("Significance," 216). Hence he deduces that Adam was "a mortal being who was protected from death as long as he was obedient to the commands of God: disobedience removed the protection, and Adam was allowed to complete the life cycle which was normal to his physical being" (ibid.). Note also Goossens, who is representative of the common Roman

and it is certainly theologically risky for Sellin brazenly to conclude from vv. 45–49 that "Adam ist schlecht von Natur."[46] In light of Rom 5:12–21 (and Rom 8:18–22), mortality and decay appear to be a result of the Fall. Earthiness and soulishness, on the other hand, are part and parcel of creation. Indeed, in v. 45, when Paul refers to Adam's *psychical* nature, he quotes a verse from Genesis 2, not Genesis 3,[47] and all the allusions in vv. 45–49 are to the creation portions of Genesis rather than the Fall narratives. Yet all this being said, and being careful in how we say it, a reading of 1 Corinthians 15 as a whole reveals how closely intertwined in Paul's mind are the notions of ψυχικός, ἀτιμία, ἀσθένεια, γῆ, χοϊκός, σὰρξ καὶ αἷμα, φθορά, *and* ἁμαρτία and θάνατος. The span between between corruptibility and mortality is short. The distance is as close as sin.[48]

## Sin and Death—An Edenic Nexus

Therefore, while in Rom 5:12–21 the nexus of *sin and death* is presented at the commencement of Paul's Adamic exposition (i.e., in v. 12), it appears at its climax in 1 Corinthians 15 (v. 56a). In both cases, however, the nexus appears within an edenic milieu. The Adamic milieu in vv. 21–22 and 45–49 serve the present study by highlighting the *primordial* context from which Paul's statement regarding sin and death in v.

---

Catholic position that unfallen humans were mortal by nature but a gift of grace enabled them to ascend above their transient constitution (see "Immortalité," 298–313, 328–32). See below, p. 136 n. 32.

46. Sellin, *Streit*, 227. Jervell rightly chastises such speculation: "Es liegt Paulus gar nicht daran, das Psychische genetisch zu erklären" (*Imago Dei*, 265).

47. See Jones, "Paganism," 720–23. Contrast this with Rom 8:20–21 and the reference there to the ματαιότης and φθορά to which the creation is subject. Paul is almost certainly alluding in this case to Gen 3:17–19 (see Wilckens, *Römer*, 2:154).

48. Similarly observed by Söding: "Mit 1 Kor 15,56 expliziert Paulus, was er in 15,20–28 und 15,41–49 (zumal nach 15,3.7) voraussetzen konnte: daß die Sterblichkeit und Vergänglichkeit aller Menschen in ihrer Sündhaftigkeit begründet ist" ("Kraft," 80; see also Robertson and Plummer, *First Corinthians*, 379). Söding's statement, however, needs two minor tweaks. Though he correctly identifies the role that v. 56a plays in bringing to the surface the notion that was close at hand in the previous verses, in point of fact, Paul uses the term *Sünde* in v. 56a rather than *Sündhaftigkeit*, and, though the word "their" might be assumed, he, in fact, affixes no pronoun to the noun. The Apostle seems to be speaking in broad terms, i.e., he is identifying what it is that lies behind the reality of death in the world and what gives mortality its sting, viz., *sin*.

56a arises. "Perhaps with Adam again in mind," notes Furnish of v. 56a, "[Paul] takes the opportunity to identify sin as the means through which humanity is infected with mortality."[49] In a context in which Adam and things Adamic loom large, it is, therefore, not unnatural or surprising for a statement regarding sin and death to appear.[50] For Paul, "the nexus between sin and death goes all the way back to the story of Adam's fall."[51] And it is also not surprising that the statement appears in epigrammatic form. Such a mode of expression is appropriate, and, indeed, significant. It is appropriate since a truism is a suitable mode for expressing a bedrock reality that has universal relevance.[52] It is in turn significant since, as Fee notes, "its appearance here in this fashion is the sure indication that this essential dictum of Pauline theology had long been in place."[53] It can be reasonably assumed that the Corinthians would have been familiar with the notion through prior contact with Paul.

## EDEN AND THE LAW-SIN NEXUS IN ROMANS

Although the nexus of sin and death in 1 Cor 15:56 was likely prepared for by 15:21–22 and 45–49, the appearance of a *law-sin* nexus in such a setting may seem inexplicable, especially since the law does not appear to have been a serious issue in the Corinthian church and was certainly not an issue in the chapter.[54] However, the catalytic function of the law

---

49. Furnish, *Theology of First Corinthians*, 119 (similarly noted by Díaz Rodelas: see *Pablo*, 29).

50. The nexus would seem to apply both corporately (cf. Rom 5:12, 14, 17) and individually (cf. Rom 6:23; 8:13).

51. Hays, *First Corinthians*, 277. For commentators who conclude that the sin-death nexus in v. 56a is informed by the Genesis Fall account, whether directly or by way of rabbinic thought, see, e.g., Barrett, Collins, Trail, N. Watson, Garland, Kay; for other scholars, see Barrett, *First Adam*, 20; Pate, *Reverse*, 426; Hollander and Holleman, "Relationship," 277–78; Deluz, *Companion*, 249; Schlatter, *Paulus*, 445; Díaz Rodelas, *Pablo*, 29; Schick, *Allen*, 307; Söding, "Kraft," 77–81; Morissette, "Midrash," 177–80; Heim, *Gemeinde*, 239.

52. It is also an effective mode. Regarding aphorisms, Barnes notes, "They catch the attention and capture the mind" ("Aphorism," 91; see also Aune, "Aphorism," 37 and above, p. 64 n. 87).

53. Fee, *Corinthians*, 806; see also Furnish, *Theology of First Corinthians*, 119.

54. Wilckens sees nothing in the chapter that prepares for 1 Cor 15:56b: "Zwar ist der Zusammenhang von Sünde und Tod vorbereitet (1 Cor 15:21f.) keineswegs jedoch der von Sünde und Gesetz" ("Entwicklung," 161).

and the Fall may not have been concepts unassociated in Paul's mind. Indeed, if Hays rightly concludes from his study of v. 56a and its context that "the nexus between sin and death goes all the way back to the story of Adam's fall" and if Furnish is correct to suggest that Paul in v. 56a had "Adam again in mind," it is possible that the edenic allusion carries over into v. 56b, and a nexus between law and sin *also* goes all the way back to the story of Adam's fall.[55] An examination of the contexts within Romans where the catalytic operation of the law is explicated will suggest the likelihood of this possibility.[56]

## Romans 5:20

> But law came in, with the result that the trespass multiplied; but where sin increased, grace abounded all the more.

As noted earlier, Rom 5:20, which introduces the catalytic function of the law,[57] follows closely after a discussion of Adam and the realities of sin and death, as does 1 Cor 15:56b.[58] That Adam is half the focus of Rom 5:12-21 is famous. He is mentioned twice by name in v. 14,[59] al-

---

55. Furnish can do no more than to assume that Paul, after identifying Adam's sin in v. 56a as the means by which death infected humanity, added, "*as if to round off the thought*, that sin is empowered by the law" (*Theology of First Corinthians*, 119, italics mine). It does not appear to Furnish that *law* may have also played a part in the edenic story. He assumes that any edenic imagery ceases half way through v. 56.

56. Thurén's words serve as an appropriate introduction to our jaunt into Romans: "We know very little about the probably oral teaching about the law, on which Paul counts in 1 Cor 15:56. But it is reasonable to infer that since the law is so frequently discussed in the Corpus Paulinum, corresponding ideas could be found elsewhere.... Romans in particular may be expected to provide us with good material" (*Derhetorizing*, 116-17).

57. That v. 20 is catalytic is argued above (p. 28 n. 78). The singular παράπτωμα is likely meant to convey a reminiscence of Adam's sin's (cf. vv. 15, 17, 18) but is considered here corporately (see Martin, *Christ and the Law*, 75; Luz, *Geschichtsverständnis*, 202-3; Moo, *Romans*, 348) or, perhaps, typically, i.e., "no longer, of course, the one transgression of Adam, but the act characteristic of the whole epoch which his transgression began and typifies" (Dunn, *Romans*, 1:286; Wright, *Climax*, 39).

58. Though anarthrous, it is misleading for the NRSV to render νόμος in Rom 5:20 "law," as though Paul were speaking of *law* in a generic sense. The reference is surely to the Mosaic law given at Sinai as specified in vv. 13-14 (see Winger, *Νόμος*, 79). In addition, the verb παρεισέρχομαι is reminiscent of προστίθημι in Gal 3:19.

59. Besides 1 Cor 15:22 and 45, Paul designates Adam by name only in 1 Tim 2:13, 14 (assuming, as we do, the Pauline authorship of the pastorals, for which, see Carson and Moo, *Introduction*, 555-68).

luded to indirectly as the "one man" in vv. 12, 15, 16, 17, 18, 19, and his deed (whether it be deemed *sin, transgression,* or *disobedience*) is mentioned in vv. 12, 14, 15, 16, 17, 18, and 19. The relation between sin and death in Rom 5:12–21, as we have seen, mirrors a similar discussion in 1 Corinthians 15. The term ἁμαρτία occurs in vv. 12, 13, 20, 21 while θάνατος appears in vv. 12, 14, 17, 21.[60] Both terms, it can be observed, are found together in 5:12 and 5:21, thus providing a thematic inclusio for the passage.

It is within this context that the catalytic notion of the law appears in 5:20. And true to its 1 Cor 15:56 counterpart, the notion occurs abruptly at the conclusion of the argument and is presented without any explanation. Together with these similarities, however, lies a significant difference. While the catalytic notion of the law appears in 1 Cor 15:56 as a verbless and timeless expression (ἡ δὲ δύναμις τῆς ἁμαρτίας ὁ νόμος), in Rom 5:20 it is expressed in the past tense (νόμος δὲ παρεισῆλθεν, ἵνα πλεονάσῃ τὸ παράπτωμα). Hence while 1 Cor 15:56 is *axiomatic*, Rom 5:20 is *historic*, i.e. *Mosaic*. It will be argued that the latter may be best considered as an historical expression of the former—a case history, as it were, reflecting the thesis. We will return to Romans 5, particularly vv. 13–14, below. Sufficient here is to note the Adamic context in which the catalytic reference in Rom 5:20 appears.

### Romans 7:7–11

> 7 What then should we say? That the law is sin? By no means! Yet, if it had not been for the law, I would not have known sin. I would not have known what it is to covet if the law had not said, "You shall not covet." 8 But sin, seizing an opportunity in the commandment, produced in me all kinds of covetousness. Apart from the law sin lies dead. 9 I was once alive apart from the law, but when the commandment came, sin revived 10 and I died, and the very commandment that promised life proved to be death to me. 11 For sin, seizing an opportunity in the commandment, deceived me and through it killed me.

More significant to the present study, Eden appears to be close at hand in Rom 7:7–11, the passage that bears the closest resemblance to 1 Cor 15:56 and contains the most sustained exposition of the catalytic func-

---

60. The verb ἁμαρτάνω occurs in vv. 12, 14, 16, while ἁμαρτωλός appears in v. 19.

tion of the law. Ernest Käsemann may be justly accused of overstating the case when he asserted with regard to Rom 7:7–11 and its depiction of the relationship between the law and sin that "there is nothing in the passage that does not fit Adam, and everything fits Adam alone."[61] A more recent student of the passage, however, may not have been exaggerating in his assertion that edenic references there are "omnipresent."[62] It is, indeed, difficult not to discern at least some shadows of Eden in Paul's first person account of the Mosaic law's role in the outworking of sin. Allusions to the Garden narrative appear to be dispersed throughout each and every layer of the Apostle's account.[63] Not only do specifics of the Genesis story appear in the Apostle's terminology,[64] but overarching

61. Käsemann, *Romans*, 196.

62. Grappe, "Qui me délivrera," 488. Cranfield states: "Paul no doubt has the narrative of Genesis 3 in mind" (*Romans*, 1:350; see also idem, "St. Paul," 46–47). Byrne detects "unmistakable allusions" to the Genesis 2–3 narrative that lend the "I" an "Adamic aura" (*Romans*, 218) and Busch more recently finds allusions in Romans 7 to Genesis 3 to be "indisputable, especially since Paul has recently established a connection between the two texts by discussing the entry of sin into the world through Adam in Rom 5:12–21" ("Eve," 13; see also 12–36). Lichtenberger correctly observes that the view which (even if only to some extent) sees Adam's shadow in Rom 7:7–11 "hat heute weitgehende Zustimmung gefunden" (*Das Ich*, 266; Kümmel, an opponent of an edenic interpretation, acknowledges it to be the majority view among interpreters [*Römer 7*, 54]).

63. The term "allusion" in this context is used here and throughout of a conscious reference to an Old Testament passage that the New Testament author assumes the reader will recognize and that consists of words, themes, or plot lines distinctive enough to be traced to an Old Testament passage and yet not verbatim reproductions of the text in part or whole (see Morner and Rausch, *Dictionary*, 5; Paulien, *Decoding*, 165–73; Hollander, *Figure*, 64–66). By nature an allusion is *allusive* rather than *explicit* (see Dunn, "Christ," 75). Though he makes no claim to be exhaustive, it is surprising that Hays does not treat Rom 7:7–11 in his examination of Old Testament echoes in the New Testament. It would have provided an instructive case study since the passage meets most, if not all, of the seven tests that he proposes as indicators of an intertextual allusion: 1) *availability* of the source to the author and readers; 2) *volume* or degree of explicit repetition of words or syntax patterns; 3) *recurrence* of the passage allegedly alluded to elsewhere in the same author; 4) *thematic coherence*, i.e., how well the proposed allusion fits into the line of argument; 5) *historical plausibility*, i.e., the likelihood that Paul's readers could have discerned the echo; 6) *history of interpretation*, i.e., whether others have discerned an allusion; 7) *satisfaction*, i.e., whether the alleged allusion make sense (*Echoes*, 29–32).

64. The following are notable: 1) ἐντολή (vv. 8, 9, 10, 11) recalls ἐντέλλομαι in LXX Gen 2:16; 3:11, 17; 2) the durative ἔζων (v. 9) is reminiscent of ζῶσαν in LXX Gen 2:7; 3) the commandment οὐκ ἐπιθυμήσεις in v. 7 recollects Eve's desiring after the forbidden fruit (at Gen 3:6 the verb חָמַד occurs, which is the verb used in Exod 20:17: לֹא תַחְמֹד; although not the case in Gen 3:6, in the LXX the verb is usually translated by ἐπιθυμέω) ; 4) ἡ ἁμαρτία ... ἐξηπάτησέν με (v. 11) echoes LXX Gen 3:14, ὁ ὄφις ἠπάτησέν

*motifs* are observed in the very fabric of the story itself: 1) life, 2) death, 3) prohibition, 4) desire, 5) deceit, and 6) knowledge. In addition, the Fall *sequence* of life-commandment-sin-death reemerges in the narrative's course of events,[65] and edenic *images* seem to appear behind the subjects of the drama and behind its story line: i.e., behind the *I*,[66] Adam (and Eve);[67] behind *the Mosaic commandment* against coveting,[68]the

---

με; 5) εἰς θάνατον (v. 10) recalls LXX Gen 2:17, θανάτῳ ἀποθανεῖσθε; 6) sin "seizing" (λαβοῦσα) the opportunity in vv. 8 and 11 recalls the woman "seizing" (λαβοῦσα) the fruit in LXX Gen 3:6; 7) Paul's combined use of γινώσκω and οἶδα in v.7 is reminiscint of τὸ ξύλον τοῦ εἰδέναι γνωστὸν καλοῦ καὶ πονηροῦ in LXX Gen 2:9.

65. Stott lists six parallel stages in the story of Eden and the "I" in Rom 7:7-11: 1) an age of innocence, 2) prohibition, 3) the arousal of sin, 4) deceit, 5) the awakening of lust, 6) disobedience and death (*Romans*, 200) see also Bussini, *L'homme*, 125-31 and below, pp. 186-90. Strictly speaking, the sequence of *life → law* would apply to Adam, not Eve. On whether the allusion in vv. 7-11 is to Adam or Eve, see below, n. 67.

66. For a discussion of the identity of the "I" in Rom 7:7-11, see below, pp. 203-6.

67. Barrett argues that "it is impossible to mistake the figure of Adam" (*Romans*, 135). As will be later argued (see below, pp. 207-10), Paul appears to speak on two levels, referring both to Adam (and Eve) and to the "I." Thus Theissen asserts that "Adam is not the *subject* of the conflict in Rom 7:7ff. but rather its *model*" (*Aspects*, 203; see also Espy, "Robust Conscience," 169; Ziesler, *Romans*, 184; Haacker, *Römer*, 143-44; Brandenburger, *Adam und Christus*, 216; Kuss, *Römerbrief*, 2:444, 448-49; Laato, *Paul*, 138; Lichtenberger, *Das Ich*, 127). For a discussion of the precise referent of the allusion, i.e., Adam or Eve, see Busch, "Eve," 12-36; Garlington, *Faith*, 118-19; Laato, *Paul*, 137-39. In 7:7-11 Paul appears to be identifying himself with the circumstances leading up to the Fall without distinguishing formally between Adam and Eve. To maintain this inclusiveness, we will speak of Rom 7:7-11 in terms of "edenic," rather than "Adamic" imagery.

68. An encounter with the *Mosaic law* is most certainly the immediate plot line of Rom 7:7-11 (contra, e.g., Oltramare, *Romains*, 54-80; see Romanello, "Rom 7:7-25," 514 n. 10; Kümmel, *Römer 7*, 86). The abbreviated form of the prohibition cited by Paul (οὐκ ἐπιθυμήσεις) has led some, however, to see in Rom 7:7 a *direct* reference to the garden prohibition rather than the Decalogue (see, e.g., Causse, "Le renversement," 368; Kühl, *Römer*, 230; S. Lyonnet, "'Tu ne convoiteras pas,'" 157-65). The manner in which Paul cites the prohibition in Rom 7:7, however, is reproduced exactly in Rom 13:9 with unquestionable reference to the Decalogue (see Lichtenberger, *Das Ich*, 130 n. 47; Esler, *Conflict*, 230; Stendahl, "Introspective Conscience," 92-94). In addition, the way in which Paul depicts the law as "speaking" is reminiscent of his references to the Jewish law in Rom 3:19; 1 Cor 9:8; 14:34. Furthermore, Paul's statement in 7:10 that the commandment "promised life" recalls Lev 18:5. Thus, though there are almost certainly edenic shadows behind the drama depicted in Rom 7:7-11 and a possible "fusion" there of the garden story with that of Sinai (see Wright, "Romans," 10:563; Hofius, "Mensch," 115-16; Grappe, "Qui me délivrera," 487), it is almost unquestionable that the commandment cited by Paul in Rom 7:7 is none other than the tenth commandment of the Decalogue (see Moo, "Israel and Paul," 123; Napier, "Analysis," 19). Jervis, however, argues that

though ἐντολή in Rom 7:7 refers to the Torah command, the term from 7:9 onwards is "transmuted" and refers from then on to the obedience required in the Christian life ("'Commandment,'" 193-216). Her rationale for doing so is her assumption that Paul's attribution of *life* to the commandment in 7:10 suggests that ἐντολή here is a Christian commandment, not a sinaitic decree. After all, she contends, Gal 3:21 argues that the Mosaic Law is incapable of producing life (ibid. 205). Yet, while the Mosaic law, to be sure, was never intended to bestow life, verses such as Lev 18:5; Deut 6:24; 30:15-20; Neh 9:29; Ps 19:7-10; Ezek 20:11; Rom 10:5; Gal 3:12 suggest that the Mosaic law did indeed hold out a promise of life to those who obeyed it, though, as Westerholm notes: "only the threat [of the law] can be operative among those in the flesh" (*Perspectives*, 419; see below, p. 186 n. 62, p. 233 n. 56). The seemingly contradictory statements ("the law cannot give life" and "the law can give life"), in other words, are based on the same syllogism, by adding a premise: "the law can give life, but since nobody keeps the law, the ability is never realized" (thus Thurén, *Derhetorizing*, 114). It would not be inconsistent, therefore, for Paul in Rom 7:10 to ascribe a life promise to a Sinai commandment that, in fact, can only bring death (see Spanje, *Inconsistency*, 226-27). Furthermore, if Jervis allows that contexts elsewhere require that Paul uses the term "commandment" there of requirements intrinsic to the Christian life (see, e.g., 1 Cor 7:19; 14:37), she ought similarly to respect the context surrounding Rom 7:7, where Paul specifies the commandment that he has in mind there, viz., the tenth commandment of the Decalogue. Stated differently, while Jervis is critical of those who search in the "shadows" for "a phantom appearance of the Genesis Fall" in Romans 7 (ibid., 214), she fails to note both a *direct* quotation from the Old Testament that determines the meaning of ἐντολή within the context and 7:1, 4, which, she admits, directs the readers attention "to issues specific to *Jewish* believers in Christ" (ibid., 196-97, italics mine; see also Napier, "Analysis," 19). Gundry, for his part, argues famously that Rom 7:7-11 is not only strictly biographical, but the reference to coveting in 7:8-9 is to *sexual* lust, the one vice against which he was powerless as he was coming of age ("Moral Frustration," 228-45). Gundry's thesis, however, has little support and, it seems, for good reasons. First, there is no doubt that Paul is citing the Decalogue here, yet neither Exod 20:17 nor Deut 5:21 confine "desire" to sexual lust. Secondly, in the LXX and New Testament, neither ἐπιθυμία nor ἐπιθυμέω carry sexual connotation in themselves. Indeed the verb in Paul is never used in such a sense (see Rom 13:9; 1 Cor 10:6; Gal 5:17; 1 Tim 3:1) and the noun as such in only three of its seventeen occurrences in his letters (Rom 1:24; 2 Tim 2:22; 3:6). Thirdly, and most fatal to Gundry's thesis, is v. 8b itself: ἡ ἁμαρτία διὰ τῆς ἐντολῆς κατειργάσατο ἐν ἐμοὶ πᾶσαν ἐπιθυμίαν. The phrase πᾶσαν ἐπιθυμίαν, which Gundry fails to mention, makes it clear that Paul is contemplating coveting *in general* rather than limiting ἐπιθυμία to sexual desire (see Ziesler, "Role," 45-46; Schreiner, *Romans*, 369-70). More recently Nanos has argued that the "coveting" in Rom 7:8-9 refers to a "*covetous* insistence on Jewish priority among Jews in Christ . . . the one human sin that the Law cannot help one overcome" (*Mystery*, 358; see also Segal, *Convert*, 243-44). Nanos's interpretation is a little puzzling within the context of his monograph since it appears to contradict his earlier conclusion that Paul is addressing a Gentile church (see *Mystery*, 10). His interpretation of Rom 7:8 would appear to be more applicable if it were addressed to Jews who were not accepting Gentiles (see Burnett, "Individual," 179). Furthermore, Nanos understands ἐπιθυμέω not as "wanting what is not one's own, and especially wanting it at the expense of one's neighbor" (Nanos quoting Ziesler's "Role," 47) but "wanting what *is* one's own *but ought*

garden prohibition against partaking of the forbidden fruit;[69] behind *sin coming to life* after the arrival of the law, the appearance of the serpent subsequent to the giving of the commandment;[70] and behind Paul's expe-

---

*to be no longer regarded as only* one's own so as to *be denied* to the neighbor *also*," viz., "the privilege of sonship for gentile neighbors" (*Mystery*, 359 n. 48, italics his). Though his argument is well-nuanced, Nanos offers no lexical evidence to support his definition of ἐπιθυμέω nor does he account for the use of the term in Exod 20:17 (Deut 5:21?), the very passage that Paul is citing. In the tenth commandment, the prohibition is clearly against desiring after what one does *not* have. We likewise find it difficult to embrace Jewett's theory that the ἐπιθυμία in Rom 7:7-11 denotes Paul's pre-conversion zeal for the law (*à la* Gal 1:14) as well as distinctively Gentile forms of competition for honor (see *Romans*, 443-53, etc.). Romans 7:7-8 must certainly be linked to Rom 5:20. The latter verse, which speaks of the multiplying of "transgression" and "sin" rather than "a zeal for honor," would seem to undercut Jewett's sociological reading of Romans 7. What appear to be universal truisms in Rom 3:20b and 1 Cor 15:56 regarding law and *sin* offer Jewett no support as well. Furthermore, Jewett faces the same difficulty that beleaguers Gundry and Nanos. The phrase πᾶσαν ἐπιθυμίαν in Rom 7:8b delimits any theory that would limit ἐπιθυμία to any single vice, be it sexual desire, ethnic pride, or a competitive zeal for honor. See further discussions, below, p. 217 n. 91, pp. 220-21 n. 105.

69. The noun ἐντολή in 7:8-11 is either synonymous with νόμος (see van Dülmen, *Theologie*, 108 n. 118) or, more likely, the latter refers to the Mosaic code in general and the former to the specific command cited in v. 7 (see Moo, *Romans*, 436), which may also serve as a paradigm of the whole (see Ziesler, "Role," 49-50). Nevertheless, Theissen appropriately ponders whether it is coincidental that Paul "in a place where one thinks most readily of Adam's fall, uses the term *entole*" (*Aspects*, 204; see also Pedersen, "Biblical Law," 16-19; Lagrange, *Romains*, 170-71; Weber, "Geschichte," 156-59). Although the Mosaic Law is the primary subject of 7:7-11, the garden commandment can well be regarded as anticipatory of the tenth commandment. Bruce writes: "It could be argued that covetousness (ἐπιθυμία) is the quintessential sin" ("Law of Moses," 269). This may be why Paul chose the tenth commandment; no other command can be so naturally fused to the Paradise command: "L'interdiction de convoiter et celle de manger de l'arbre du bien et du mal ne sont pas étrangères l'une à l'autre" (Bussini, *L'homme*, 127; see also Lichtenberger, *Das Ich*, 242-51). Lyonnet contends that Paul quotes only the verb because he meant to speak of the essence of covetousness, i.e., the exaltation and substitution of self over God, which was the sin of Adam ("'Tu ne convoiteras pas,'" 159; see also Barrett, *Romans*, 132). See further below, p. 194 n. 110.

70. Dunn perceives an unmistakable allusion in 7:9 to the sequence in Genesis 2-3, where following the command, the serpent comes on the scene "with the commandment on its tongue" (*Romans*, 1:383). "The contrast here," writes Cranfield, "between νεκρά and ἀνέζησεν in the next verse well suits the serpent lying motionless and hidden, and then stirring itself to take advantage of its opportunity" (*Romans*, 1:351). Leenhardt's often quoted words are worth repeating: "Nothing resembles a dead serpent more than a living serpent so long as it doesn't move!" (*Romans*, 186). For νεκρά in the sense of "inactive, powerless" see Jas 2:17, 26 (see Kuss, *Römerbrief*, 2:444, Dunn, *Romans*, 1:381). Although the verb ἀναζάω means "to rise again" in its only other occurrence in the New Testament (Luke 15:24; see similar examples in MM 32), there is nothing in the context

riential *knowledge of sin*,[71] the first couple's acquisition of the knowledge of good and evil.[72] Furthermore, in both accounts the subjects fall prey to

---

of Paul's tale that assumes a "prior life" of ἡ ἁμαρτία (see Romanello, "Rom 7:7-25," 516). In light of the thought pattern in vv. 8-9 where ἁμαρτία νεκρά stands opposite of ἁμαρτία ἀνέζησεν, it is more likely (contra Moo [*Romans*, 438 n. 53]) that the verb does not stand in contrast to a *prior life* but to a *prior inactivity* (so BDAG 62.2). The preposition ἀνά would thus either lose its temporal force and be simply translated "come to life" (see Cranfield, *Romans*, 1:352; note the use of the term by Nilus: οἱ γὰρ κόκκοι μετὰ τήν ἐκ σήψεως νέκρωσιν καὶ φθορὰν ἀναζῶσι, "for the seeds *come to life* after death and destruction by decay" [quoted in Deissmann, *Light*, 98]; note also ἀναβλέπω in John 9:11; 15:18), or the preposition would seem to strengthen the simple form (see Lohse, *Römer*, 216 n. 19) and be translated "*sprang* to life" (see BDAG 62.2) or "awoke" (see Käsemann, *Romans*, 197).

71. On Rom 3:20b and the phrase "the knowledge of sin," see below, pp. 108-11. That the two verbs γινώσκω and οἶδα in Rom 7:7 point to *an acquaintance with sin learned by experience* is evident from v. 8, which fleshes out what the knowledge of sin included, viz., lust (see Lambrecht, "Man," 23; Caird, *Principalities*, 42 n. 5; Barth, *Romans*, 242; Bornkamm, "Sin", 90; *Römer*, 172; von Gemünden, "Affekt," 70; Gaugler, *Römerbrief*, 1:199; Dunn, *Romans*, 1:379; Klein, "Gesetz," 701; Haacker, *Römer*, 142; van Dülmen, *Theologie*, 107; Romanello, "Rom 7:7-25," 514-18; contra van Spanje, *Inconsistency*, 225). Brunner is correct, we believe, to note that there is more here than mere intellectual comprehension: "The intertwining of law and sin is much closer and more of a unity. The law *enters into the process of the formulation of sin, it is itself a factor in becoming sinful*" (*Romans*, 59, italics mine; contra Weima, "Function," 224-25) and Wright's perception that the term here denotes knowing "from the inside, what sin meant in practice" appears sound ("Romans," 562). The phrase used by Paul thus encompasses both cognitive and experiential elements; i.e., the "I" knows "what it is to covet" (Rom 7:7 NRSV; contrast the merely cognitive "known what sin was" [NIV, TNIV]) because it, in fact, *experienced* coveting (see Espy, "Robust Conscience," 169). This is all the more confirmed since Rom 7:7-11 appears to be an elaboration (see Bandstra, *Elements*, 127) or "drastic working out" of Rom 7:5 (Lambrecht, "Man," 21), which, as virtually all commentators agree, depicts the *provocation* of sinful deeds (see, e.g., Käsemann, *Romans*, 189; Romanello, "Impotence," 512-13; Elliott, *Rhetoric*, 247). For other occurrences in Paul of γινώσκω being used in an experiential sense, see Rom 1:21; 1 Cor 8:3; 2 Cor 5:21; Gal 4:9; Phil 3:10; for οἶδα see 1 Cor 2:2; Gal 4:8; 1 Thess 4:4, 5; 5:12; 2 Thess 1:8; Titus 1:16. That Paul is depicting here the knowledge of *sin* derails Theissen's argument that "Romans 7 depicts how the once-unconscious conflict with *the law* became conscience" (*Aspects*, 229, italics mine; see further below, p. 215).

72. Theissen ponders, "That Rom 7:7-13 contains so many reminiscences of the story of the Fall leads one to ask if... the motif of knowledge does not also become intelligible on the basis of Genesis 2-3" (ibid., 207). Kuhl is more blunt, "Das theoretische Erkennen von Gut und Böse liegt natürlich im Hintergrunde" (*Römer*, 230. An allusion in Rom 7:7-8 to the Garden motif of knowledge is also perceived, e.g., by Pesch, *Römerbrief*, 63; Espy, "Robust Conscience," 169, Haacker, *Römer*, 144; Dodd, *Paradigmatic*, 225; Lichtenberger, *Das Ich*, 163; Ziesler, *Romans*, 182). See further discussion below, pp. 111-13; 179-82.

deceit,[73] and in each narrative a prohibition, which was intended to foster life,[74] becomes the means of provoking of forbidden desires.[75] De Boer well captures the analogies in 7:7-11 to the Eden story: "Paul suggests . . . that the situation of Adam's descendants to whom the universally applicable Law came is analogous to the situation of Adam to whom the commandment came. Paul evidently thinks that 'the commandment' of the Mosaic Law functioned or functions in a way similar to the commandment given to Adam (cf. 7.11), i.e., the commandment caused sin to come to life and thus paradoxically to bring about the fatal result it sought to prevent, death."[76] It would seem "all but inescapable,"[77] then, that the story of Adam is incorporated into the drama depicted in Rom 7:7-11. Edenic terminology, motifs, shadows, and sequencing appear too

---

73. See Zeller, *Römer*, 1985), 140-41. The term ἐξαπατάω in 7:11 occurs in 2 Cor 11:3 and 1 Tim 2:24, which describe the serpent's role in the Fall. Regarding 7:11 ("For sin . . . deceived me"), Wright argues that "it is at this point that the disguise of the personified 'sin' is close to disappearing: we are clearly talking about the serpent in the garden, though Paul has told the story in such a way as to allow other levels to be heard as well, which, had he been more explicit, might have been drowned out" ("Romans," 563-64).

74. Though the phrase εἰς ζωήν in Rom 7:10 is likely alluding on the surface to Lev 18:5, it is reminiscent of the motive clause in Gen 2:17: "for in the day that you eat of it you shall die." This phrase provides a clear example of a direct reference in 7:7-11 to the Torah under which lies "hidden" an allusion to Eden (Wright, "Romans," 563). Yet Ziesler, who argues strongly for an edenic backdrop in Rom 7:7-11, finds it hard to detect a promise of life in Gen 2:16-17 since, explicitly, there is only the threat of death if the command is disobeyed. He thus concludes that in Rom 7:10 the emphasis is more on Sinai than Eden. There is no need, however, to thus eclipse Eden from v. 10. The Garden prohibition was indeed life-preserving (see Thurén, *Derhetorizing*, 113). "If Adam," notes Dunn, "had lived according to the commandment . . . he would have enjoyed free access to the tree of life" (*Romans*, 1:384). The phrase εἰς ζωήν can thus aptly apply to the Garden prohibition when viewed as a life-preserving/sustaining prohibition. See below, p. 186 n. 62 and pp. 134-35.

75. The phrase πᾶσαν ἐπιθυμίαν recalls the threefold repetition of Gen 3:6: לְמַאֲכָל . . . לָעֵינַיִם . . . לְהַשְׂכִּיל (see Lyonnet, *Les étapes*, 125).

76. De Boer, *Defeat*, 241 n. 66. Commenting on the inevitable operation of both the Adamic commandment and Mosaic law to serve as an occasion for sin, Weber writes: "Wesen und faktische Funktion des adamitischen Paradiesgebotes und der Mosethora sind ja auch im Zentrum völlig parallel: Begierdeverbot und eben dadurch Provokation derselben" ("Geschichte," 158; see also Lichtenberger, *Das Ich*, 131; Lyonnet, *Les étapes*, 125; Lagrange, *Romains*, 171).

77. Dunn on the edenic backdrop of Rom 7:7-11, *Romans*, 1:200.

suggestive to be unintentional and too pervasive for the Fall not to be in the background of the conflict described there.[78]

To be sure, there are those who either fully deny or radically downplay any edenic allusions in Rom 7:7-11.[79] Esler, for example, presents a sustained critiques of an edenic interpretation of Rom 7:7-11. Beginning by quoting Moo,[80] he asks "how could Paul feature Adam's experience in a discussion about a law which he presents as entering the historical arena only with *Moses*?"[81] This concern, however, appears irrelevant. As we will later argue, Adam is not the *subject* but appears to be the *model* of 7:7-11.[82] As Espy contends, Paul seems to be speaking "on two levels, referring both to Adam and to a more contemporary party."[83] Thus contrary to Esler's assumption, an edenic interpretation of Romans 7 does not necessarily argue for direct references *to* Adam, but reminiscences *of* Adam.[84]

Esler further argues that when Paul does speak explicitly of Adam in Romans 5 "he does not even mention the commandment of Gen 2:16-17"

---

78. See Milne, "Genesis 3," 15. Some see Sinai as the *primary* backdrop in Rom 7:7-11 rather than Eden (see, e.g., Watson, *Hermeneutics*, 356-80; Moo, "Israel and Paul," 122-35; Strelan, "Note," 23-25; Esler, *Conflict*, 237-38; Karlberg, "History," 65-74). The reference to the tenth commandment certainly is a bolt from Sinai (see Lichtenberger, *Das Ich*, 133; Wright, *Climax*, 227). Nevertheless, in light of the thick edenic imagery, Paul's account has more affinity, we believe, with the Eden temptation narrative than with the account of the law's arrival at Sinai. See discussion below, pp. 195-97.

79. See, e.g., Bläser, *Gesetz*, 114-15; Middendorf, *Storm*, 21, 140-43; Das, *Solving*, 216-18; Gundry, "Frustration," 229-32; Légasse, *Romains*, 446-51; Maillot, *Romains*, 183-91; Osborne, *Romans*, 173; Finsterbusch, *Thora*, 51; Schreiner, *Romans*, 361); Burnett, "Individual," 196; Jervis, "'Commandment,'" 193-216; Esler, *Conflict*, 236; Gottlob Schrenk, "ἐντέλλομαι, ἐντολή," in *TDNT* 2:550-51; Benoit, "The Law," 13; Blocher, *Original Sin*, 47-48; Kümmel, *Römer 7*, 86-87; Moo, "Israel and Paul," 124-25; idem, *Romans*, 425, 428-30 (though he allows that there may be allusion to Adam "in that the situation depicted parallels Adam's" [ibid., 429]; similarly Watson, *Hermeneutics*, pp. 354-411, note p. 360).

80. "Israel and Paul," 124; see also Kümmel, *Römer 7*, 55-56, 87.

81. Esler, *Conflict*, 234. See also Middendorf, *Storm*, 21, 140-41.

82. See Theissen, *Aspects*, 203.

83. Espy, "Robust Conscience," 169. See further discussion below, pp. 203-10.

84. Esler's assumption is typical. Objections raised against an edenic understanding of Rom 7:7-11 are often aimed at the belief that the verses are describing the *actual* garden of Eden story (see e.g., Moo, *Romans*, 429; Das, *Solving*, 216-18). Our contention (see below, 207-10) that the "I" of Rom 7:7-11 is *not* Adam, but speaks *as* Adam would be exempt from such objections.

but is "content merely to refer to Adam's 'transgression' (Rom 5:15, 17, 18)."[85] Hence, for Esler, what took place in Eden was of no concern to Paul in Romans 5 or 7 and, in any case, Esler insists that Paul unambiguously places the arrival of the law at Sinai rather than Eden.[86] Esler's contention that the Eden commandment is not present in Rom 5:12–21 appears incorrect, however. While in the verses he cites, Paul contrasts Christ's righteous deed with Adam's "transgression" (παράπτωμα), in Rom 5:14, where Paul explains the relationship of sin to the law, he indeed alludes to law in the garden by way of the carefully chosen term παράβασις, which, as will later be discussed,[87] assumes the presence of *law* in Eden, though *Jewish* law, of course, first made its appearance at Sinai.[88]

With regard to terminology parallels between Genesis 3 and Rom 7:7–11, Esler dismisses two of the verbal similarities (ἐντολή and ἐξαπατάω) as mere coincidence.[89] This response seems to lose its force, however, when it is observed, as above, that there are more than just *two* verbal parallels and when these parallels are viewed against the totality of the analogies. Not only are there similarities in the details, but parallel motifs, themes, and sequencing are present as well.

85. Esler, *Conflict*, 235.
86. Ibid.
87. See below, pp. 114–16.
88. See Laato, *Paul*, 135; Byrne, *Romans*, 218. Schreiner, like Esler, is anxious that an edenic interpretation of Rom 7:7–11 would grant that Adam himself possessed the Torah, which in turn would cause Paul's argument in Galatians 3–4 to be "shipwrecked, since he there designates the arrival of the Torah to have occurred some 430 years *after* Abraham" (*Romans*, 361; see also Moo, *Romans*, 428–29). There need be no such anxiety on Schreiner's part. In Rom 5:12–21 Paul appears to perceive the following scenario [NL 1-3]: 1) a commandment in Eden (vv. 13–14); 2) no law between Adam and Moses (vv. 13–14); and 3) Torah at Sinai (v. 20). The presence of law in Eden would not contradict Paul's argument in Galatians regarding the coming of Jewish law at Sinai. The point for Paul in Galatians 3 is that Moses followed Abraham in Jewish-salvation chronology, not vice versa. Eden is not an issue.
89. Esler rightly notes that although ἐξαπατάω is used in 2 Cor 11:3 [and 1 Tim 2:24] of the Fall, the term also occurs in Rom 16:18 and 1 Cor 3:18 in senses unrelated to Eden (*Conflict*, 235; see also Moo, *Romans*, 440). This is not surprising. It is rare that a single word or phrase is used in only one sense. Thus, though the phrase "dearly beloved" is used elsewhere than in weddings, it would likely convey a nuptial nuance if it occurred within a context containing wedding motifs. In Rom 7:7–11, therefore, a passage in which edenic motifs appear to flourish, it is difficult for the verb "beguile" not to evoke edenic associations in the reader. See above, n. 73.

All that Esler can say about the relationship between Genesis 3 and Romans 7 is that there are resemblances. Paul, however, "did not intend *any* allusion to, or echo of, the fall, *nor was his audience likely to hear one.*"⁹⁰ These assertions, however, are surely too strong. Can we really conclude that Paul did not intend *any* allusions to Eden? Even Moo, who argues against edenic *descriptions*, concedes that "there may be allusion to Adam's situation in vv. 7–11,"⁹¹ and Watson, who interprets the verses against "the event at Sinai and its aftermath, as reenacted in individual experience," nevertheless acknowledges that Paul uses "motifs drawn from Genesis" to describe this experience.⁹² And does Esler's assertion regarding Paul's audience beg the question of why it would have been unlikely for his readers to perceive *any* edenic allusions or echoes in Rom 7:7–11 when a multitude of scholars have discerned *many*?⁹³ Though Esler claims that the Fall was "simply irrelevant" to Paul's account in Romans 7 of the "increased ferocity that sin gained through its manipulation of the law of Moses,"⁹⁴ Paul, we noted, indeed draws conclusions about the Mosaic law from *truisms* concerning law.⁹⁵ In light of the edenic imagery that scholars perceive in 7:7–11, Esler and others who deny or downplay any edenic allusions may want to reconsider whether Paul's narrative discloses in dramatic form a *primeval* reality by which these truisms are informed.⁹⁶ We will return to Rom 7:7–11 below and throughout the following chapters.

90. Esler, *Conflict*, 236, italics mine.
91. Moo, *Romans*, 429.
92. *Hermeneutics*, 360; see also idem, *Paul*, 151–53.
93. See n. 62, above and excursus below pp. 123–30.
94. Esler, *Conflict*, 235.
95. See above, pp. 77–78.

96. Along with posing concerns similar to Esler's, Middendorf objects to the view that Rom 7:7–11 paradigmatically alludes to Adam's fall, since Adam's sin, in his view, is depicted in Rom 5:14 "in a way unlike the sin of others" (*Storm*, 143). Contrary to Middendorf, to be precise, Adam's sin was unlike the sin of those who lived *from Adam to Moses* (Rom 5:14). Paul does, however, draw an analogy between Adam's sin and sins committed under the jurisdiction of the sinaitic law (see Moo, "Israel and Paul," 132 n. 21). Finsterbusch, for her part, lodges a syntactical objection against an edenic interpretation of Rom 7:7–11, which is unique to her: "Es [das 'Ich'] kann sich kaum auf Adam beziehen, denn Adam hat nach Gen nicht dauerhaft ohne Gebot außerhalb des Paradieses gelebt (duratives Impf ἔζων)" (*Thora*, 51). Apart from the fact that no exegete (to my knowledge) contends that Adam spent time *outside* of Paradise prior to receiving the paradisiacal command, Finsterbusch reads too much into the meaning of the im-

## Romans 3:20b

An *edenic* referent might also be present in Rom 3:20b, a verse that appears to be expressing a *catalytic* notion of the law in an axiomatic manner similar to 1 Cor 15:56: διὰ νόμου ἐπίγνωσις ἁμαρτία. That a catalytic idea is present in the statement is first of all suggested by the verse's connection to Rom 7:7 and the experiential use there of γινώσκειν τὴν ἁμαρτίαν.[97] The terms (νόμος, ἐπίγνωσις/γινώσκω, ἁμαρτία), prepositional phrase (διὰ νόμου), and theme (ἐπίγνωσις ἁμαρτίας/τὴν ἁμαρτίαν οὐκ ἔγνων) that are shared between Rom 3:20b and Rom 7:7 could hardly be more suggestive of a kinship between the verses, as is the manner in which the motif of *knowledge* occupies the rhetorical center position between law and sin in each statement:

διὰ γὰρ νόμου **ἐπίγνωσις** ἁμαρτίας (3:20b)

τὴν ἁμαρτίαν οὐκ **ἔγνων** εἰ μὴ διὰ νόμου (7:7b)

Secondly, support for a practical meaning of knowledge in Rom 3:20b is found in 2 Cor 5:21, the only other occurrence in Paul of the phrase γινώσκειν ἁμαρτίαν: "For our sake he made him to be sin who knew no sin, so that in him we might become the righteousness of God."[98] The experiential sense in 2 Cor 5:21, notes Klein, is unmistakable: "Wenn der Apostel Jesus hier den μὴ γνόντα ἁμαρτίαν nennt, so will er ja nicht sagen, daß Jesus nicht wußte, was Sünde sei, sondern: daß er keine Sünde *getan* hat."[99] In light of the affinity between 2 Cor 5:21 and Rom 3:20-26,[100]

---

perfect. The imperfect is functioning here to emphasize the duration of time apart from law, i.e., while the "I" was *living* (Goodwin notes that in narration the imperfect "dwells on the course of the event instead of merely stating its occurrence" [*Syntax*, 12]). Within such a setting the durative sense of the imperfect likely stands in contrast to the aorist ἀνέζησεν in v. 9 and, perhaps most importantly, serves to evoke the ψυχὴν ζῶσαν of Gen 2:7 (see Dunn, *Romans*, 1:381).

97. See above, n. 71.

98. See also Rev 2:24: οἵτινες οὐκ ἔγνωσαν τὰ βαθέα τοῦ σατανᾶ; Herm. *Sim.* 9.29.1: ὡς νήπια βρέφη εἰσίν, οἷς οὐδεμία κακία ἀναβαίνει ἐπὶ τὴν καρδίαν οὐδὲ ἔγνωσαν, τί ἐστι πονηρία, ἀλλὰ πάντοτε ἐν νηπιότητι διέμειναν (LCL 25: 456).

99. Klein, "Sündenverständnis," 261. See also Harris, *Second Corinthians*, 450; Windisch, *Zweite Korintherbrief*, 197-98; Carrez, *Corinthiens*, 155; Thrall, *Second Corinthians*, 1:439; Wolff, *Zweite Brief*, 132; Héring, *Deuxièmes Corinthiens*, 54; Furnish, *2 Corinthians*, 339; Str-B 3:520.

100. Note the following parallels:

such a notion should probably be read back into ἐπίγνωσις ἁμαρτίας in Rom 3:20b.[101] The idea would, therefore, not be that one merely gains the knowledge of what sin *is* through the law (though the cognitive, perceptual meaning inherent in the term would assume at least as much),[102] but that through the law one also becomes, in an Old Testament sense of יָדַע,[103] experientially acquainted with sin.[104] "Certainly," comments Käsemann on Rom 3:20b, "ἐπίγνωσις is the knowledge of experience which leads to acknowledgement of a situation."[105] We will have more to say about 2 Cor 5:21 below.

Finally, if, as we will ponder, Paul's knowledge of sin motif in Rom 3:20b is linked to the knowledge of good and evil notion in Genesis 2–3 and if, as we will propose, the latter notion depicts an experiential knowl-

| 2 Cor 5:21 | | Rom 3:20-26 |
|---|---|---|
| γνόντα ἁμαρτίαν | → | ἐπίγνωσις ἁμαρτίας (v. 20) |
| τὸν ... ἁμαρτίαν ἐποίησεν | → | ὃν προέθετο ὁ θεὸς ἱλαστήριον (v. 25) |
| δικαιοσύνη θεοῦ | → | δικαιοσύνη θεοῦ (vv. 21, 22, 25, 26) |
| γενώμεθα δικαιοσύνη θεοῦ | → | δικαιούμενοι (v. 24) |
| ἐν αὐτῷ | → | ἐν Χριστῷ Ἰησοῦ (v. 24) |

101. See Grundmann, "Gesetz," 57; Hofius, "Gesetz," 269; Althaus, *Römer*, 32; van Dülmen, *Theologie*, 84; Bläser, *Gesetz*, 138-39; Schlier, *Römerbrief*, 101; Schmithals, *Römerbrief*, 114; Jülicher, "Römer," 40; Sloan, "Paul and the Law," 47-48; Kuss, *Römerbrief*, 1:109; Käsemann, *Romans*, 89-90. Though Hodge considers ἐπίγνωσις to be the stronger term (*Romans*, 86), it is difficult to discover a difference between ἐπίγνωσις and γνῶσις in the NT or LXX (see *TDNT* 1:707). A case in point in Paul is the obvious parallel between the phrase οἵτινες τὸ δικαίωμα τοῦ θεοῦ ἐπιγνόντες (Rom 1:32) and καὶ γινώσκεις τὸ θέλημα (Rom 2:17).

102. See Kümmel, *Römer 7*, 44-46; Bandstra, *Elements*, 126 n. 40; Espy, "Robust Conscience," 169.

103. See von Rad, *Genesis*, 89; Stern, "Knowledge," 409; Vogels, "'Like one of us,'" 147; Speiser, *Genesis*, 26. See below, pp. 139-40 n. 49.

104. As Klein observes of 3:20b: "Paul also das Gesetz nicht als Spiegel, sondern als Auslöser konkreter Sünde verstanden wissen will" ("Sündenverständnis," 261). Similarly, Bultmann writes: "This sentence does not, of course, mean that *through the law* man is led to knowledge of what sin is, but does mean that by it he is *led into sinning*" (*Theology*, 1:264; see also Schlier, *Römerbrief*, 101). We quote Bultmann without embracing the hubristic notion he attaches to the verse. The "sinning" that one is led into through the law is not the attempt to observe it, but the failure to keep it. Stated differently, sin does not employ the law to fuel *pride* but *passions*. See below, pp. 216-17.

105. Käsemann, *Romans*, 89. Stower's rereading of Rom 3:20 to mean that "the law only informs [Gentiles] of their captivity to sin" is inadequate (*Rereading*, 193). If we link the verse to Rom 7:7-11, it would appear that the unhappy role of the law according to 3:20b is not to *inform*, but to *acquaint* the individual experientially with sin, both Jew and Gentile.

edge of evil, the Genesis Fall narrative might bring light to the interpretation of 3:20b. An experiential notion behind *the knowledge of good and evil* in Genesis 3 in other words would suggest an experiential sense of *the knowledge of sin* in 3:20b.

In spite of what appears to be a link to Rom 7:7 and thus to the catalytic notion depicted there, Weima argues against a catalytic understanding of the law in 3:20b (though he accepts it in 7:7).[106] Since the verse serves as the conclusion to the *preceding* argument of 1:18–3:20, the cognitive recognition of sin and guilt, in his view, would be more appropriate to Paul's forensic argument than the law's role in the outworking of sin. Cranfield also argues that "it is a mistake to read into ἐπίγνωσις here a special meaning which is often thought to attach—but more probably does not—to the use of γινώσκειν and εἰδέναι in 7:7."[107] He concludes that "there is no suggestion at all in this context of the thought of the law as ἀφορμή, which Paul introduces in 7:5, 7–11."[108] Dunn concurs that an experiential sense in 3:20b is unlikely since he assumes that such a notion would be "a huge leap in his [Paul's] argument (not otherwise properly reached till chap. 7), which would be likely to confuse the listener and detract from the point being made."[109]

Concerning Weima's argument, while 3:20 does in fact serve as a conclusion to 1:18–3:20, the phrasing διὰ νόμου ἐπίγνωσις ἁμαρτίας, as we have seen, has more of an affinity with τὴν ἁμαρτίαν οὐκ ἔγνων εἰ μὴ διὰ νόμου in Rom 7:7 then with anything that precedes.[110] Indeed, though, as with 1 Cor 15:56, few words are given to 3:20b in the commentaries,[111] commentators usually make a b-line from 3:20b to 7:7–8 where, they say, v. 3:20b is unpacked.[112] With regard to Cranfield,

---

106. See "Function," 223–24; see also Zeller, "Zusammenhang," 198; Räisänen, *Paul and the Law*, 145.

107. Cranfield, *Romans*, 1:199 n. 1.

108. Ibid.

109. Dunn, *Romans*, 1:155; similar concerns are raised by Zeller, *Römer*, 81; Moo, *Romans*, 210.

110. See p. 108, above.

111. Especially in comparison to 3:20a: "For no human being will be justified in his sight by deeds prescribed by the law."

112. See, e.g., Black, who briefly notes in passing that the idea expressed in 3:20b "seems to be a characteristically Pauline one: it is worked out more fully by St. Paul at 7:7ff." (Black, *Romans*, 56–57; see also Bruce, *Romans*, 94; Stuhlmacher, *Romans*, 56; Theobald, *Römerbrief*, 1:94; Fitzmyer, *Romans*, 339; Michel, *Römer*, 145; Byrne, *Romans*,

while it is true that the idea of the law as ἀφορμή is not explicitly present in 3:20b, in light of the verbal and thematic kinship between 3:20b and 7:7-11, this notion, we believe, should be read back into 3:20b,[113] in the same manner in which one reads 1 Cor 15:56 in light of Rom 7:7-8.[114] And in reference to Dunn's argument about "huge leaps," 1 Cor 15:56 is itself such a leap.[115] Yet we have learned from the verse that Paul can make embryonic statements about the law that will later come to full term.[116]

Moving now from an *experiential* sense in Rom 3:20b to an *edenic* sense, though some scholars perceive Paul's "knowledge of sin" in 3:20b to be an allusion to "the knowledge of good and evil" in Genesis 2-3,[117]

---

121).

113. Schreiner is methodologically correct, we believe, to seek light from another passage when interpreting a passage containing the same subject. Regarding interpreting Galatians in light of Romans he writes: "It would be methodologically suspect to impose Romans upon Galatians. But New Testament scholars have exercised too much care to hermetically seal off each Pauline letter from one another. Such an approach is artificial. When Paul speaks on the same subject (for example, the law) in a similar context, one letter can shed light on another. . . . Some scholars think that to interpret each letter without any consideration of the others will yield more objective results, but it is more probable that it will simply yield more interpretive hypotheses, with little agreement on the meaning of each text" (*Law*, 76-77).

114. Caird comments that 1 Cor 15:56 "would hardly be intelligible if we did not have Romans to provide a commentary on it" (Caird, "Everything," 389). Yet we *do* have Romans to comment on it, and we likewise have Rom 7:7-11 to provide commentary on Rom 3:20b.

115. Not to mention Rom 5:20b, a verse designated by Wright as a "throwaway" line ("Romans," 460).

116. Recall Thielman's observation quoted above (see p. 53). Snodgrass also observes this tendency in Paul's methodology: "Frequently he introduces a point briefly only to return to it later for detailed treatment" (Snodgrass, "Spheres," 104; see also Conzelmann, *1 Corinthians*, 293). Byrne calls Rom 3:20b "the first of a series of 'throw-away' lines Paul offers about the ill effects of the law (see also 4:15b; 5:20a; 6:14; 7:5) before formally sorting out the connection between law and sin in 7:7-25" (*Romans*, 121).

117. See, e.g., Theissen, *Aspects*, 207; Lichtenberger, *Das Ich*, 241; Byrne, *Romans*, 220). Lichtenberger identifies a link between the law and the tree of knowledge in *3 Gospel Philip* (*Das Ich*, 240-41). Since the Nag Hammadi codex II, *3 Gospel of Philip* is badly mutilated at 73, it is difficult to be certain of the original reading as it pertains to the tree of the knowledge of good and evil and the law (see Ménard, "Philippe" 211-12). It appears clear, however, at *Gos. Phil.* 74 that the law is depicted negatively by way of its association with the tree of the knowledge of good and evil, which was the source of death for Adam: "The law was the tree. It has power to give the knowledge of good and evil. It neither removed him from evil, nor did it set him in the good, but it created death for those who ate of it. For when he said, 'Eat this, do not eat that,' it became the

it is curious that such a link is not considered more often by those who with reason, we believe,[118] perceive such an allusion in 7:7-11.[119] That edenic interpreters of 7:7-11 do not entertain an edenic allusion in 3:20b is especially surprising since the phrase ἐπίγνωσις ἁμαρτίας clearly stitches the verse to the latter passage (via τὴν ἁμαρτίαν οὐκ ἔγνων in 7:7) and in turn to the edenic setting landscaped there.[120] In addition, since edenic allusions are also in the vicinity of 5:20, another instance in Romans where the catalytic operation appears, it is worth considering whether 3:20b and its motif of *knowledge* may be informed to some extent by Eden as well. Furthermore, it is possible that Adamic undertones are present in 2 Cor 5:21, a passage, as we observed, that runs parallel to 3:20b. Not only is it conceivable that the phrase τὸν μὴ γνόντα ἁμαρτίαν is inclusive of Christ's preexistence,[121] but an allusion there to a heavenly man becomes suggestive when 2 Cor 5:21 is compared to 2 Cor 8:9 and to the adamically nuanced Phil 2:6-11.[122] Such an Adam-

---

beginning of death" (*NHL* 53). The most that can be said, however, is that this is strongly reminiscent of Rom 3:20b; 7:7-11 (see Lichtenberger, *Das Ich*, 241; Ménard, "Philippe," 212). It really sheds no light on whether there are allusions to Gen 2:15 in Rom 3:20b; 7:7-11.

118. See discussion below, pp. 179-82.

119. For references to those who see such an allusion in 7:7-11, see above, n. 72.

120. An edenic allusion is likely present in Rom 3:23: πάντες γὰρ ἥμαρτον καὶ ὑστεροῦνται τῆς δόξης τοῦ θεοῦ. Though its date is uncertain (see below, p. 198), it is possible that *Apoc. Mos.* 20:2; 21:6 (or similar traditions and speculations current with Paul) provides the conceptual substructure linking Paul's statement to Genesis 3 (see Hafemann, *Letter/Spirit*, 434-45; Adams, "Paul's Story," 26; Scroggs, *Adam*, 26; 48-49; Jervell, *Imago Dei*, 180-83; Grappe, "Qui me délivrera," 480-81; Dunn, *Theology*, 93-94).

121. The aorist participle is timeless. For the view that the phrase is descriptive of Christ's preexistence, see Windisch, *Zweite Korintherbrief*, 197-98.

122. Branick lays the verses out in the following manner (see "Sinful Flesh," 255).

2 Cor 5:21:   τὸν μὴ γνόντα ἁμαρτίαν
              ὑπὲρ ἡμῶν ἁμαρτίαν ἐποίησεν,
              ἵνα ἡμεῖς γενώμεθα δικαιοσύνη θεοῦ ἐν αὐτῷ.
2 Cor 8:9:    πλούσιος ὤν,
              ἵνα ὑμεῖς τῇ ἐκείνου πτωχείᾳ πλουτήσητε.
Phil 2:6-11:  ὃς ἐν μορφῇ θεοῦ ὑπάρχων
              οὐχ ἁρπαγμὸν ἡγήσατο τὸ εἶναι ἴσα θεῷ, . . .
              ἑαυτὸν ἐκένωσεν . . .
              ἐταπείνωσεν ἑαυτὸν . . .
              ὁ θεὸς αὐτὸν ὑπερύψωσεν . . .
              καὶ ἐχαρίσατο αὐτῷ . . .
              ἵνα ἐν τῷ ὀνόματι Ἰησοῦ πᾶν γόνυ κάμψῃ . . .

Regarding a possible Adam-Christology in 2 Cor 5:21 (especially as it relates to mo-

Christology in 2 Cor 5:21 may explain Paul's use there of the consciously nuanced phrase "who *knew* no sin"; i.e., "He made him sin, who, *unlike the first man*, never experienced an acquaintance with sin."[123]

If the phrase ἐπίγνωσις ἁμαρτίας in Rom 3:20b indeed contains an allusion to the knowledge of good and evil, not only would this suggest a relationship between the law-sin nexus and the primordial sin, but Paul's adage διὰ γὰρ νόμου ἐπίγνωσις ἁμαρτίας would deem this primordial operation of the law axiomatic; i.e., as through the Garden commandment came *the knowledge of good and evil*, so by the Mosaic law comes *the knowledge of sin*.[124] Romans 3:20b and 7:7-11 would thus cross-pollinate one another: 7:7-11 would "edenize" the statement in 3:20b, while 3:20b would "axiomatize" the drama regarding the Mosaic law depicted in 7:7-11. We will revist Rom 3:20b and 7:7-11 and the edenic motif of knowledge later in our study.

## A CATALYTIC OPERATION OF THE LAW IN EDEN: A PAULINE REREADING OF THE GENESIS FALL NARRATIVE

From this brief excursion into Romans, it has become apparent that in each location where Paul discusses the catalytic operation of the law,[125]

---

tifs in Rom 5:12-21), see, e.g., Pate, *Adam*, 142-44; Dunn, *Christology*, 112-13; idem, *Theology*, 221-23; Hooker, "Interchange," 349-61; Schnackenburg, *Baptism*, 115-21; Kim, *Origin*, 306; Scroggs, *Last Adam*, 791; Branick, "Sinful Flesh," 252-56.

123. 2 Corinthians 5:21 may also contain the notion of an exchange of the earthly image for the heavenly as in 2 Cor 3:18 (see Hooker, "Interchange," 355) as well as an exchange of the curse as in Gal 3:13 (see Dunn, "Understanding," 136-37).

124. Laato writes: "Consequently, Gen. 3 suffices at least for the apostle to the Gentiles to prove that sin—just as it once took advantage of the 'law' in Paradise—now makes use of the Mosaic law in provocation of evil works in man" (*Paul*, 135).

125. Though some contend that the statement τῶν παραβάσεων χάριν προσετέθη in Gal 3:19 expresses a catalytic notion (see, for example, Betz, *Galatians*, 165; Kuula, *Law*, 151-54; Hübner, *Law*, 26; Räisänen, *Paul, and the Law*, 144), the presence of the term παράβασις indicates that Paul is more likely depicting a *defining* or *condemning* operation of the law there (concerning these designations, see above, p. 6-7 n. 34; on the term παράβασις in Gal 3:19, see Longenecker, *Galatians*, 138-39; Drane, *Libertine*, 34; Burton, *Galatians*, 188).

Adam appears near. The fact that edenic themes are also present in 1 Corinthians 15, the first setting in which Paul's law-sin nexus appears, quietly suggests that the catalytic function of the law and the Fall may have long been associated in Paul's mind. That Paul appears to have indeed assumed a primeval, catalytic operation of the law is inferred by two additional factors that can be deduced from his representation of law in Romans 5–8: 1) The logic of Paul's argument in Rom 5:12-14 assumes that *law* was present in the garden, and 2) Paul choreographs with *edenic* motifs the law-sin nexus to which the "I" in Roman 7:7-11 falls victim.

## Law in Eden

With regard to law in Eden, the fact that Paul in Rom 5:14b designates the edenic sin as παράβασις assumes for him that ὁ νόμος, i.e., explicit legislation sanctioned with consequences,[126] was present in the garden: τοὺς μὴ ἁμαρτήσαντας ἐπὶ τῷ ὁμοιώματι τῆς παραβάσεως Ἀδὰμ ὅς ἐστιν τύπος τοῦ μέλλοντος.[127] Though the term νόμος does not appear in the verse, the notion of divine legislation is presupposed by the fact that Paul considered Adam to have committed παράβασις, which by definition requires a law to be transgressed (4:15).[128] "Παράβασις," correctly notes Wright, "is what happens when miscellaneous sin (ἁμαρτία) is confronted by a specific command."[129] Furthermore, the logic of Rom

---

126. The verb ἐλλογέω would suggest by definition that there were santions to be reckoned. See n. 131, below.

127. Note also 1 Tim 2:14: ἡ δὲ γυνὴ ἐξαπατηθεῖσα ἐν παραβάσει γέγονεν.

128. Paul is consistent in his use of the noun to connote the transgression of a divinely revealed "requirement or obligation which is legally valid or has legal force" (J. Schneider, "παραβαίνω, παράβασις, κτλ.," in *TDNT* 5:739; see Rom 2:23; 4:15; 5:14; Gal 3:19; 1 Tim 2:14).

129. Wright, *Climax*, 172 n. 58; see also Hultgren, *Paul's Gospel*, 87–89; Wedderburn, "Adam," 421; Kuula, *Law*, 140–43; Grundmann, "'Gesetz,'" 57–58; Winger, *Νόμος*, 149 n. 105; Poirier, "Universality," 354; Martin, *Christ and the Law*, 73–74. Brandenburger describes the distinction between Adamic and post-Mosaic sin and that of humanity between Eden and Sinai: "Die Situation der Menschen zwischen Adam und Mose war eine andere und besondere. Auch in dieser Menschheit im ganzen gab es Sünde—als Macht und persönliche Tat in eins—, aber eben nicht παράβασις. Denn es fehlte das spezifische Gegebensein des Gotteswillens im νόμος qua Mosetora oder Paradiesesgebot, angesichts dessen das Sündetun auch den objektiven Tatbestand der παράβασις (τοῦ νόμου) erfüllen konnte" (*Adam und Christus*, 192).

5:13-14 argues that Adam transgressed *law*. In Rom 5:14 Paul writes, ἀλλὰ ἐβασίλευσεν ὁ θάνατος ἀπὸ Ἀδὰμ μέχρι Μωϋσέως καὶ ἐπὶ τοὺς μὴ ἁμαρτήσαντας ἐπὶ τῷ ὁμοιώματι τῆς παραβάσεως Ἀδὰμ ὅς ἐστιν τύπος τοῦ μέλλοντος. The phrase here, μέχρι Μωϋσέως, parallels ἄχρι γὰρ νόμου in v. 13.[130] Since the period between Adam and Moses was *law-less*,[131] it follows that Adam's sin, in contrast to the sins committed during this interim, was related to law.[132]

Paul seems to acknowledge, then, two law traditions linked to Adam and Moses respectively.[133] In light of the implicit reference in Rom 5:12-14 to law in Eden, it may not be surprising, therefore, if in 1 Corinthians 15, a chapter in which thoughts of Eden likely evoked the reference in v. 56a to the entities of sin and death, the edenic context would have also prompted in v. 56b a reference to divine law, *of which Edenic law was paradigmatic*. Understanding ὁ νόμος in 1 Cor 15:56 in this manner is probably more accurate than seeing a direct reference there to the garden commandment.[134] As we have argued,[135] the generic manner in which Paul appears to use νόμος in the axioms of Rom 3:20b; 4:15b; 5:13b; and 7:8b coupled with the axiomatic nature of 1 Cor 15:56 itself, suggest that Paul is likely using the term in v. 56 in a theological rather than salvation-historical sense, i.e., as a *divine demand*.[136] The Edenic commandment

---

130. Aletti is correct to note that Paul is evidently referring here to *divine* law rather than *human* law (*Israël*, 112 n. 4). Otherwise he would not be speaking in terms of *sin* and *transgression* (ibid., 110).

131. According to Rom 5:13, sin was "not reckoned" (οὐκ ἐλλογεῖται) during this *law-less* era. Individual sins (the Flood and Sodom and Gomorrah notwithstanding) thus could not account for the sway of death, to which all eventually succumbed. Weima is likely correct that the coming of the law did not bring about a change from innocence to guilt but rather "a change from sin to transgression" ("Function," 229; see also Bergmeier, "Gesetz," 64). After Sinai, God judged scrupulously "according to the book" (see, e.g., Amos 3:1-2).

132. Theissen argues, "If, first, people in the interim period between Adam and Moses did not sin like Adam and if, second, they sinned without law, then the sin of Adam and the sin under the law must be comparable" (*Aspects*, 203; see also Poirier, "Universality," 354; Winger, *Νόμος*, 149 n. 105; Martin, *Christ and the Law*, 73-75).

133. See Pedersen, "Biblical Law," 17.

134. As we earlier proposed in "Law, Sin, and Death," 294. See also Kay, *Corinthians*, 83.

135. See above, pp. 77-78.

136. For a definition of terms regarding "law," see Moo, "'Works of the Law,'" 88-90. We adopt for 1 Cor 15:56 what Moo deems the "theological sense"; see also Schneider,

and the Mosaic code would each be regarded in their respective revelatory periods as historical embodiments or particularizations of divine law.[137]

## A Catalytic Operation of the Law in Eden

That Paul not only viewed *law* to be present in Eden but saw it serving also in a *catalytic* role seems implicit in what appears to be a rereading of the Genesis account in the drama of Rom 7:7-11.[138] There, as in Rom 5:12-14, Paul seems to present the Fall as a prototype for sins under the Mosaic law.[139] In this "once upon a time" depiction,[140] Paul casts a story of an individual abiding in a law-free and life-filled setting.[141] The individual, however, encounters a command, which if kept, promises life.[142]

---

*Vollendung*, 53.

137. Thus, Longenecker suggests that, for Paul, "God's Torah in a pre-Mosaic prototype was from the beginning: a prototype of basic instruction minus the particular national and ceremonial features" (*Paul*, 95; see also Pedersen, "Biblical Law," 17. Similarly, Kay, commenting on 1 Corinthians 15, places the edenic command in the mouth of *the law* in v. 56: "The law said, 'In the day thou eatest, thou shalt die'" (*Corinthians*, 83 n. 4), as does Brown: "What the apostle here refers to is the influence which the law of God, broken by Adam, has, in giving power to his sin as the dart of death" (*Resurrection*, 270; see also Lockwood, who takes v. 56 as a departure to discuss the law-sin scenario in Eden (*1 Corinthians*, 604).

138. For Bussini, "Nous pouvons considérer notre passage comme une relecture du récit yahwiste" (*L'homme*, 119). Although there may be one exception (see below, pp. 197-99), there appears to be no clear evidence of a Jewish belief in a catalytic function of the law in Eden. As will be argued, the Genesis account itself was most certainly Paul's referent.

139. Käsemann contends that Paul "made Adam the prototypical recipient of the law" (*Romans*, 196; see also Espy, "Robust Conscience," 169; Lyonnet, *Les étapes*, 128; Jülicher, "Römer," 40).

140. The adverb ποτέ in Rom 7:9 may have been used by Paul to set a *story telling* ambience (see LSJ, III. I; Dunn, *Romans*, 1:382). Brandenburger views Paul's narrative as "Urgeschichte" and the statement in v. 9a to be "freilich mythologisch geprägt" (*Adam und Christus*, 206, 211). For Lietzmann, the time of "paradiesischen Unschuld" comes to mind (*Römer*, 74).

141. In view of the contrast with ἀπέθανον in v. 10, it is almost certain that ζάω in v. 9 is used in the theological sense of "being alive" rather than in the prosaic sense of "passing one's life" (see discussions in Cranfield, *Romans*, 1:351; Byrne, *Romans*, 222). Yet, the life depicted here likely stops short of life in a *fully* eschatological sense (see discussion below, pp. 186-87 n. 65, p. 136 n. 31).

142. On the phrase εἰς ζωήν in Rom 7:10 see below, p. 186 n. 62. The phrase appears

Yet, upon hearing the commandment's "thou shalt not covet," sin was aroused, and once awakened, seduced its victim into transgressing the commandment by deceptively using the commandment as a means to provoke the very desires it prohibited.¹⁴³ As a result, the individual violates the prohibition and suffers the loss of life in the process. Ultimately, the law, which was intended to foster life, became the means by which sin wrought death.¹⁴⁴

Looking behind the scenes of the narrative in Rom 7:7-11, it appears that Paul considered this nexus of law and sin to have been present in Eden.¹⁴⁵ It is improbable that he would have sounded so many edenic notes otherwise.¹⁴⁶ Paul, apparently reading his experience in light of the Genesis story,¹⁴⁷ "where the tempter plied his seductions vis à vis God's commandment ('Has God said?'),"¹⁴⁸ likely wanted his readers to read between the lines that in the beginning, the garden commandment (and hence "law") paradoxically was the catalyst that set the first sin in motion and the means by which sin and death gained its entrance into humanity. Thus Carter asserts: "Paul casts the ἐγώ in the role of Adam here in order to make the point that, far from effectively serving as a boundary keeping sin at bay, the law in fact proved to be the loophole through which sin entered the system."¹⁴⁹ Witherington depicts the scene even more strongly: "We have here . . . a vivid retelling of the Fall that shows that there was a problem with the commandments and the Law from the very beginning

---

to have salvific overtones (see van Spanje, *Inconsistency*, 227 n. 45).

143. Napier refers to this perverted strategy as "sin's sneak attack" ("Analysis," 23).

144. See similar paraphrases by Laato (*Paul*, 137) and Neyrey (Neyrey, *Paul*, 173-74).

145. See Jülicher's exposition of Paul's narrative in Rom 7:7-11 ("Römer," 40-41).

146. Watson argues that "the correspondences are so close that there can be little doubt that Paul has the Genesis story in mind throughout" (*Paul*, 152-53; see also Dodd, *Paradigmatic*, 225; Laato, *Paul*, 135-37). Sloan draws the same conclusion: "The biblical history of the temptation, sin, and death of Adam and Eve . . . provides a plausible narrative substructure to Paul's theological construct regarding sin and law" ("Paul and the Law," 51).

147. Laato is careful to note that, contrary to Theissen (*Aspects*, 251-60; contra also an interpretation that assumes Paul is utilizing *speech in character* rhetoric [see, e.g., Talbert, *Romans*, 186-87]), the "I" does not *play the role* of Adam and Eve, but *identifies* with them (see *Paul*, 139 n. 347). See discussion below, pp. 203-10.

148. Sloan, "Paul and the Law," 51.

149. Carter, *Power*, 187; see also Aletti, *Israël*, 141-42.

of the human story."¹⁵⁰ This scenario will be later developed, though nuanced. While we believe there was a law problematic, there was, in fact, no "problem" with the law.¹⁵¹ What produced the problematic was *sin/serpent*.

It might be objected that a rereading of the Genesis account in which the commandment provided *latent sin* with an opportunity to entrap humanity would assume that Adam and Eve resided in an environment where sin had already found entrance.¹⁵² This would seemingly depict as polluted an environment deemed "good" by God (Gen 1:4, 10, 12, 18, 25, 31) and would appear to contradict the Apostle's statement in Rom 5:12 that "sin came into the world through one man."¹⁵³ As will be later noted, however, while there is no suggestion in the Genesis narrative of anything inherently evil *within* Adam or Eve,¹⁵⁴ and while it remains true that sin entered into the human race through Adam,¹⁵⁵ in the Genesis Fall sequence, as in the sequence of events in Rom 7:7–11, sin/serpent makes its entrance onto the stage *in between* the giving and transgression of the commandment.¹⁵⁶ In other words, the Genesis drama, we will suggest, portrays sin slithering through the garden *before* its poison penetrated the human race.¹⁵⁷ As to the origin of this evil, like the Genesis writer,¹⁵⁸ "Paul,"

---

150. Witherington, *Romans*, 186. This is a conclusion towards which Lichtenberger also argues (*Das Ich*, 265–69; see also Lyonnet, *Les étapes*, 135).

151. As Paul in Rom 7:7, 12–13 can hardly emphasize more strongly.

152. See, e.g., Althaus, *Römer*, 75; Feuillet, "Loi," 33.

153. Blocher is concerned about those who argue for a connection between Rom 7:7–11 and Genesis 2–3. "Nowhere else," he argues, "does Paul suggest the presence of dormant sin *before* the moment when sin entered into the world" (*Original Sin*, 48). This may be true, though Rom 5:12 appears to suggest the existence of sin prior to its entrance into the human realm. Nevertheless, whether or not Paul elsewhere alludes to dormant sin prior to the Fall, the writer of the Fall narrative, as we will see, appears to do so.

154. Contrast this to the life of the "I" of Romans 7 in whom "sin dwells" (7:17, 20b). See below, p. 212 n. 61.

155. That "world" in 5:12 = "humanity" is implied by the repeated references to the "all" and the "many" in vv. 12c, 15–19.

156. Brandscheidt argues that the abrupt and sudden appearance of the serpent in Gen 3:1 signals "daß . . . die von der Schlange vertretene Macht des Bösen eine der menschlichen Entscheidung vorausliegende Größe ist" (Brandscheidt, "Mensch," 4).

157. Longenecker aptly notes that "the Devil was not invented to test the commandment, but the commandment was given in the presence of lurking evil" (*Paul*, 95; see also Hübner's discussion, *Law*, 73).

158. As will be noted, though Genesis describes the manner in which sin invaded hu-

observes Lichtenberger, "rührt hier ohne in protologische Spekulationen zu verfallen, an die Frage, die auch von der Paradiesgeschichte her offen bleibt: Woher kam die Sünde?"[159] Likewise while the presence of a prohibition need not in itself be problematic,[160] the Apostle provides no explanation of why the Lord would provide a commandment that latent sin would use as a beachhead from which to invade humanity.[161] Perhaps he had no answer,[162] or he considered it inappropriate to speculate.[163] It was sufficient for Paul's purpose to note that sleeping evil was not left to slumber; it was aroused at the sight of the law as part of a deeper design,[164]

---

manity, the account contains no etiology of the origin of evil itself. The narrator's object, like Paul's, is not the fall of Satan but that of man (see below, p. 154 n. 131).

159. Lichtenberger, *Das Ich*, 131-32; see also Hofius, "Gesetz," 270.

160. The prohibition, writes Blocher, is "the reminder to the man of his limits and of his creaturely dependence" (*In the Beginning*, 126; see also Bonhoeffer, *Creation*, 52-53; and below, p. 213 n. 66).

161. If we place a catalytic operation of the law in Eden, unavoidable questions arise. Žižek, indeed, raises one for us: "If it is prohibited to eat of the Tree of Knowledge in Paradise, why did God put it there in the first place? Is it not that this was a part of His perverse strategy first to seduce Adam and Eve into the Fall, in order then to save them? That is to say: should one not apply Paul's insight into how the prohibitive law creates sin to this very first prohibition also?" (Žižek, *Puppet*, 15) It is difficult to brush Žižek's remarks aside as just those of an atheistic postmodernist, especially since we would give a "yes" (albeit qualified) to his final question.

162. See Rom 11:33?

163. Blocher writes: "We would argue that the mystery of evil is the one unique inscrutable mystery, as unique as evil itself, *sui generis*. Far from being absurd, it corresponds precisely with the experience of evil, with its two facets: unjustifiable-reality . . . . We do not understand the why of evil. But we can understand that we cannot understand. Human reason is made to trace the connections in God's created order, and to weave harmonious patterns from them; to understand means to integrate. A rational solution to the problem of evil would necessarily imply that evil was an integral part of the harmony that came forth from God! . . . But evil is disruption, discontinuity, disorder, alienness, that which defies description in creational terms (except negatively!). Seeking its causal explanation, its ontological reason, its why, is tantamount to seeking, by the very nature of that seeking, to reconcile it with the rest, in other words to justify it (The 'rest' is in fact what is 'just.'). To understand evil would be to understand that evil is not ultimately evil. The French have a saying, that to understand all is to forgive all; here, understanding all would mean to *excuse* everything. Evil is not there to be understood, but to be fought" (*Evil*, 102-3).

164. The ἵνα clauses in Rom 7:13 are final (see Kümmel, *Römer 7*, 57; Käsemann, *Romans*, 198) and express divine intention (see Cranfield, *Romans*, 1:354-55). Note also Rom 11:32: συνέκλεισεν γὰρ ὁ θεὸς τοὺς πάντας εἰς ἀπείθειαν, ἵνα τοὺς πάντας ἐλεήσῃ.

viz., that sin's evil character might be unmasked by the manner in which it works death through that which is good.[165]

## 1 Corinthians 15:56—an Edenic Axiom

Taking into consideration, then, both the edenic imagery with which Paul choreographs his depiction of the catalytic operation of the law in Romans and the edenic themes present within 1 Corinthians 15 itself,[166] it appears that the statement "the power of sin is the law" in 1 Cor 15:56b expresses an axiom rooted in edenic experience:[167] *Ever since the beginning it has been in the very nature of things that divine law energizes sin.*[168] This is all the more suggested by the manner in which Paul links ὁ νόμος in 1 Cor 15:56 to the generic and ancient entities of ὁ θάνατος and ἡ ἁμαρτία, which in turn, as noted, almost certainly hearken back to the Adamic references in 1 Cor 15:21-22, 45-49. In addition, ὁ νόμος is

---

165. See Rom 7:13: ἀλλὰ ἡ ἁμαρτία, ἵνα φανῇ ἁμαρτία, διὰ τοῦ ἀγαθοῦ μοι κατεργαζομένη θάνατον, ἵνα γένηται καθ' ὑπερβολὴν ἁμαρτωλὸς ἡ ἁμαρτία διὰ τῆς ἐντολῆς. Lichtenberger brings in Rom 5:20a as well: "Offen bleibt die Frage, warum das Gebot überhaupt gegeben wurde; auch darauf antwortet Paulus nicht, er geht vom Faktischen aus: eben daß es kam. In 5,20 gibt er einen Grund an: νόμος δὲ παρεισῆλθεν, ἵνα πλεονάσῃ τὸ παράπτωμα" (*Das Ich*, 132). Lichtenberger might have also included 5:20b: οὗ δὲ ἐπλεόνασεν ἡ ἁμαρτία, ὑπερεπερίσσευσεν ἡ χάρις (see Hofius, "Antithese," 203-5). Romans 5:20a and Rom 7:13 are not the final expressions on the subject (see Pate, *Curse*, 427; Martin, *Christ and the Law*, 97; Bandstra, *Elements*, 128-29; Beker, *Paul*, 244-45).

166. Indeed, Wright considers the entire chapter to be "an appeal to Genesis 1-3 in light of the events concerning Christ" (*Fresh Perspective*, 28).

167. Even as 1 Cor 15:56a expresses an edenic truism concerning sin and death (see above, pp. 95-96). Regarding v. 56a, Schlatter asserts: "Er stellte mit dieser Formel die Korinther zum Schluß noch vor die Frage, woher der Tod seine Macht über den Menschen habe. *Seine Antwort ist die, die Genes. 3 gegeben hat; der Mensch steht unter dem Gericht Gottes, das ihm den Tod zuteilt, weil er sündigt* (*Paulus*, 445, italics mine; see also Hays, *First Corinthians*, 277).

168. While Schade considers Hos 13:14 as the immediate fuse that launched v. 56, he finds the law-critical statement in v. 56 to be a natural outgrowth of the edenic setting of chapter 15: "ja durch die Adam-Gestalt auch die Gesetzesproblematik in dem Blick kommen kann (Adam übertritt das Gebot Gottes)" (*Christologie*, 210). Jervell arrives at a similar conclusion: "Die Aussagen in vv. 54c-58 zeigen, daß der Tod hier nicht einfach als Naturvorgang, sondern als von Sünde und Gesetz bestimmt dargestellt ist. Endlich haben wir hier die Adam-Christus-Parallele in v. 20-22, wo der Tod mit dem Gesetzesübertreten des ersten Menschen zusammenhängt" (*Imago Dei*, 265; see also Grelot, *Péché*, 124-25).

woven together with ἡ ἁμαρτία in v. 56b into a timeless adage: ἡ δὲ δύναμις τῆς ἁμαρτίας ὁ νόμος. The epigrammatic form of expression linked with the edenic allusions in the chapter would accord well with an experience rooted in primal history. It would appear, then, that 1 Cor 15:56 expresses in *axiomatic* form what Rom 7:7-11 discloses in *dramatic* form because the Fall, for Paul, was the ultimate reality upon which his law-sin axiom was drawn.¹⁶⁹ Being *primordial* the catalytic operation of law becomes *prototypical*:¹⁷⁰ "[Adam's] Begegnung mit dem Gesetz zeigt auf, was die Funktion des Gesetzes immer ist, wenn es zum Menschen spricht."¹⁷¹ Thus, rather than being a polemical construct, i.e., a response to a problematic issue in the Corinthian church, or a "violent" attempt to attribute to the law a negative function,¹⁷² or even an interpretation of the citations in vv. 54-55,¹⁷³ *Paul's law-critical statement in 1 Cor 15:56b is linked to v. 56a and to the preceding edenic context as a theological construct.*¹⁷⁴ Such a conceptual link to the foregoing would suggest that Paul not only recognized *sin* as the ultimate origin of death but that he envisioned *law* to be a fundamental factor in the outworking of sin.¹⁷⁵ Indeed, the curt manner in which he presents the dogma implies

---

169. Lyonnet, we believe, hits the peg squarely. Regarding the catalytic function of the law in Eden he argues: "Tel est le rôle qu'en fait, selon l'Ecriture, joue le premier précepte, la première 'loi,' prototype de toutes les autres, comme le péché d'Adam et d'Eve,—tout en ayant bien d'autres effets—, est visiblement aussi, dans la pensée de l'hagiographe, le protoype de tous les péchés" (*Les étapes*, 128; see also Thurén, *Derhetorizing*, 128-29).

170. For Paul, Eden occupied a seminal position within his theological universe. See below, pp. 201 n. 2, pp. 201-2 n. 6.

171. Lichtenberger, *Das Ich*, 267. More specifically: "wo immer *die adamitische Existenz* dem Gebot Gottes begegnet" (ibid., 134, italics mine). Jülicher similarly catches from Rom 7:7-11 the axiomatic relevance of the law-sin nexus: "Und wiederum ist das kein zufälliger Zusammenhang; *sondern ein ewiger*: Gebot (Gesetz) ist für die Sünde Zufuhr von Lebenskraft (5:20!), für den Menschen Hinführung in den Tod" ("Römer," 41, italics mine).

172. Räisänen, *Paul and the Law*, 150.

173. Contra the conclusion of Schneider (*Vollendung*, 54), and, of course, the midrashic interpretation examined above.

174. See Fee, *1 Corinthians*, 806. Stanley notes that "the natural overflow of the sentence into this thought shows its familiarity to his mind. It is as if he could not mention Sin, without adding that 'the strength of sin is the law'" (*Corinthians*, 323; see also Hays, *First Corinthians*, 277). The δέ in v. 56b functions to connect the clauses. Moiser inexplicably excludes the conjunction in his translation (see "1 Corinthians 15," 14).

175. See Laato, *Paul*, 135-36.

his readers' prior education on the matter,[176] and it virtually assumes that the doctrine was part and parcel of Paul's theological understanding.[177] Thus, regarding the "theological aside" in v. 56b, Fee observes: "This . . . means that the essential matters that surface in a thoroughgoing way in Galatians and are spelled out at length in Romans had been essential to Paul's theology long before the Judaizing controversy erupted—at least in the tangible form in which we know it from Galatians."[178] In 1 Cor 15:56, therefore, we do not seem to be confronted with a statement about the law that was merely part of the arsenal Paul employed against Jewish objectors to his gospel, and therefore something that could be jettisoned once there was a nomistic lull.[179] Instead, as Kruse notes: "These statements were integral to Paul's whole understanding of salvation, in particular his understanding of what it was from which people needed to be saved."[180]

It would seem, then, that an excursus regarding law and sin that follows a reference to the Fall earlier in the chapter and comes after an epigram concerning sin and death in the preceding clause may not be as puzzling as it first appeared. When the puzzle piece is inserted into an edenic scenario, the exegete discovers a fit. Nevertheless, though the

---

176. Thurén argues that "it is feasible, that short references to the law tell us something about the addressees' prior Christian education. When the issue is not clarified, Paul must count on what he has previously taught. He would hardly introduce new theology without a reason and a proper explanation" (*Derhetorizing*, 106; see also Lindemann, *Korintherbrief*, 371; Wolff, *Erste Brief*, 418; Schreiner, *Paul*, 133). Johnson suggests that Paul's audience already had attributed a negative status to the law. The implication of Paul's use of σῴζω in 9:22b, he argues, is that those in the categories mentioned in vv. 19–22a are in need of salvation, including those ὑπὸ νόμον. This would seem to imply that Paul's readers would be open to entertaining the notion that ὁ νόμος had an alliance of some sort with death in hindering salvation ("Resurrection Rhetoric," 292).

177. Conzelmann observes that "the connection between sin and law is for Paul a systematically established relationship" (*1 Corinthians*, 293; see also Furnish, *Theology of First Corinthians*, 119; see also Hengel and Schwemer, *Paul*, 13).

178. Fee, *First Corinthians*, 806 (see also Lindemann, "Toragebote," 94; Klein, "Gesetz," 13:65; Söding, "Kraft," 74–76). Though this assumes a later dating of Galatians (see above, p. 17 n. 27), the gist of Fee's conclusion remains valid nevertheless. The axiom does not appear to have been polemically spawned. Schnelle downplays a connection between 1 Cor 15:56 and Romans since "the thematic combination of law-Torah/sin/death is dealt with in a unique form in 1 Corinthians" (Schnelle, *Apostle*, 231). To the contrary, we find find the themes of law, sin, and death in 1 Cor 15:56 to be mirrored, albeit amplified, in Rom 5:12–21; 7:7–11.

179. See Garland, *1 Corinthians*, 749.

180. Kruse, *Paul*, 143.

Fall narrative may be discerned in Paul's catalytic notion of the law, it remains to be found if Paul's catalytic notion of the law is discernible in the Fall narrative, or, to reverse Grappe's statement quoted above,[181] if a law-sin nexus is *omnipresent* in Gen 3:1-7. Are there indications in the Fall account itself of a catalytic operation of the law? Was it the garden commandment, in fact, that provided the occasion by which the serpent seduced Eve? While scholars until now have asked these questions of Paul and Rom 7:7-11, it is pertinent to a biblical-theological study of law also to ask them of Moses and Genesis 2-3.[182] The next chapter will undertake an exegetical expedition into the Genesis text itself to determine whether a match of Paul's catalytic notion of the law can be discovered there.

## EXCURSUS: INTERPRETERS OF EDENIC ALLUSIONS IN ROMANS 7:7-11

The following is a comprehensive, yet inexhaustive, bibliography of modern scholars who to greater or lesser degrees discern edenic allusions in Rom 7:7-11. For citations in the Fathers, see Karl Hermann Schelkle, *Paul, Lehrer der Väter: Die altkirchlich Auslegung von Röm 1–11* (Düsseldorf: Patmos, 1956), 232-41; Karl Staab, *Pauluskommentare aus der Griechischen Kirche: aus Katenenhandschriften gesammelt und herausgegeben*, NTAbh (Münster: Aschendorff, 1933), 3, 219, 370.

**Paul J. Achtemeier**, *Romans*, Interpretation (Atlanta: John Knox, 1985), 122; **Edward Adams**, "Paul's Story of God and Creation: The Story of How God Fulfills His Purposes in Creation," in *Narrative Dynamics in Paul: A Critical Assessment*, edited by Bruce W. Longenecker (Louisville: Westminster John Knox, 2002), 27-28; **Jean-Noël Aletti**, *Israël et la loi dans la lettre aux Romains*, LD 173 (Paris: Cerf, 1998), 141-42; **P. Althaus**, *Der Brief an die Römer*, 11th ed., NTD 6 (Göttingen: Vandenhoeck & Ruprecht, 1970), 75; **C. K. Barrett**, *The Epistle to the Romans*, BNTC (London: A. & C. Black, 1991; reprint, Peabody, MA.: Hendrickson, 1991), 133-36; **David Lyon Bartlett**, *Romans*, WBComp (Louisville: Westminster John Knox, 1995), 69-71; Paul Beauchamp, *La loi de Dieu: d'une montagne à l'autre* (Paris: Seuil, 1999), 212-17; **Jürgen Becker**,

---

181. See above, p. 99.
182. See above, pp. 10-12.

*Paul: Apostle to the Gentiles*, translated by O. C. Dean (Louisville: Westminster John Knox, 1993), 397; **Samuel Bénétreau**, *L'Épître de Paul aux Romains*, 2 vols., CEB (Vaux-sur-Seine, Fr.: Edifac, 1996–1997), 1:198–99; **Roland Bergmeier** "Röm 7,7–25a (8,2): Der Mensch-das Gesetz-Gott-Paulus--die Exegesis im Widerspruch?" *KD* 31 (1985), 162; idem, "Das Gesetz im Römerbrief," in *Das Gesetz im Römerbrief und andere Studien zum Neuen Testament*, WUNT 121 (Tübingen: Mohr/Siebeck, 2000), 69–70. **Ernest Best**, *The Letter of Paul to the Romans*, CBC (Cambridge: Cambridge University Press, 1967), 81–82; **C. Clifton Black**, "Pauline Perspectives on Death in Romans 5–8," *JBL* 103 (1984): 424; **Matthew Black**, *Romans*, 2d ed., NCB (Grand Rapids: Eerdmans, 1989), 97–98; **Günther Bornkamm**, "Sin, Law and Death: An Exegetical Study of Romans 7," in *Early Christian Experience*, translated by Paul L. Hammer, NTL (London: SCM, 1969), 93–94, 87–104; **Egon Brandenburger**, *Adam und Christus: Exegetisch-religionsgeschictliche Untersuchung zu Röm. 5,12–21 (1 Kor 15)*, WMANT 7 (Neukirchen-Vluyn: Neukirchener, 1962), 205–17; **F. F. Bruce**, *The Letter of Paul to the Romans: An Introduction and Commentary*, 2d ed., TNTC 6 (Grand Rapids: Eerdmans, 1985), 141–42; idem, "Paul and the Law of Moses," *BJRL* 57 (1974–1975): 268–69; **Rudolph Bultmann**, *Theology of the New Testament*, translated by K. Grobel (New York: Scribner, 1951), 1:250–51; **Austin Busch**, "The Figure of Eve in Romans 7:5–25," *BibInt* 12 (2004): 12–36; **François Bussini**, *L'homme pécheur devant Dieu: Théologie et anthropologie* (Paris: Cerf, 1978), 115–31; **Brendan Byrne**, *Romans*, SP 6 (Collegeville, MN: Liturgical, 1996), 218; **D. H. Campbell**, "The Identity of ἐγώ in Romans 7:7–25," in *Studia Biblica 1978: Sixth International Congress on Biblical Studies, Oxford 3–7 April 1978: Papers on Paul and Other New Testament Authors*, edited by E. A. Livingstone, JSNTSup 3 (Sheffield: JSOT Press, 1979–80), 61; **J. D. Causse**, "Le renversement diabolique du symbolique: Réflexions à partir de Romains 7," *ETR* 75 (March 2000): 366–69; **Hans Conzelmann**, *An Outline of the Theology of the New Testament*, NTL (London: SCM, 1969), 170, 233; **C. E. B. Cranfield**, *A Critical and Exegetical Commentary on the Epistle to the Romans*, 2 vols. ICC (Edinburgh: T. & T. Clark, 1973, 1975), 1:350; idem, "St. Paul and the Law," *SJT* 17 (1964): 46–47; **W. D. Davies**, *Paul and Rabbinic Judaism: Some Rabbinic Elements in Pauline Theology*, rev. ed. (London: SPCK, 1955, reprint, New York: Harper, 1967), 32; **Martinus C. de Boer**, *The Defeat of Death: Apocalyptic Eschatology in 1 Corinthians*

15 *and Romans 5*, JSNTSup (Sheffield: Sheffield Academic, 1988), 241 n. 66; **Paul Démann**, "Moïse et la loi dans la pensée de saint Paul," in *Moïse, l'homme de l'alliance*, edited by H. Cazelles (Paris: Desclée, 1955), 204–6; **T. J. Deidun**, *New Covenant Morality in Paul*, AnBib 89 (Rome: Biblical Institute, 1981), 196–98; **W. M. L. de Wette**, *Kurze Erklärung des Briefes an die Römer*, KEHNT 2/1 (Leipzig: Weidmannsche, 1847), 94–95; **Brian Dodd**, *Paul's Paradigmatic "I": Personal Example as Literary Strategy*, JSNTSup 177 (Sheffield: Sheffield Academic, 1999), 224–26; **C. H. Dodd**, *The Epistle of Paul to the Romans*, MNTC (London: Fontana, 1959), 124; **James D. G. Dunn**, *Christology in the Making: A New Testament Inquiry into the Origins of the Doctrine of the Incarnation* (Grand Rapids: Eerdmans, 1989), 103–4; idem, *Romans*, WBC 38a,b, 2 vols. (Waco, Tex.: Word, 1988), 1:376–85; idem, *The Theology of Paul the Apostle* (Grand Rapids: Eerdmans, 1998), 98–100; **James R. Edwards**, *Romans*, NIBCNT 6 (Peabody, MA: Hendrickson, 1992), 188–89; **John Espy**, "Paul's Robust Conscience Re-Examined," *NTS* 31 (1985): 169–72; **André Feuillet**, "Loi de Dieu, loi du Christ et loi de l'Esprit d'après les épîtres pauliniennes: Les rapports de ces trois lois avec la loi Mosaique," *NovT* 22 (1980): 32–33; idem, "Le plan salvifique de Dieu d'après l'Épître aux Romains: essai sur la structure littéraire de l'épître," *RB* 57 (1950): 369; **Joseph A. Fitzmyer**, *Romans*, AB 33 (Garden City, N.Y.: Doubleday, 1993), 468; **Martin H. Franzmann**, *Romans*, ConC (St. Louis: Concordia, 1968), 125; **Donald B. Garlington**, *Faith, Obedience, and Perseverance*, WUNT 79 (Tübingen: Mohr/Siebeck, 1994), 116–18; idem, "Romans 7:14–25 and the Creation Theology of Paul," *TJ* 11 (1990): 207–10; **Alfred E. Garvie**, *Romans: Introduction, Authorized Revised Version with Notes, Index, and Map*, CB (Edinburgh: Jack, n.d.), 177; **E. Gaugler**, *Der Römerbrief*, 2 vols. Prophezei (Zurich: Zwingli-Verlag, 1958), 1:204–5; **F. Godet**, *Commentary on St. Paul's Epistle to the Romans*, translated by A. Cusin and Talbot W. Chambers, (New York: Funk & Wagnalls, 1883), 277; **Michael J. Gorman**, *Apostle of the Crucified Lord: A Theological Introduction to Paul and His Letters* (Grand Rapids: Eerdmans, 2004), 372; **Christian Grappe**, "Qui me délivrera de ce corps de mort? L'Esprit de vie! *Romains* 7,24 et 8,2 comme éléments de typologie adamique," *Bib* 83 (2002): 488; **Pierre Grelot**, *Péché originel et rédemption examinés à partir de l'épître aux Romains: Essai théologique* (Paris: Desclée, 1973), 122–27; **Klaus Haacker**, *Der Brief des Paulus an die Römer*, THKNT 6 (Leipzig: Evangelische Verlagsanstalt, 1999), 143–44; idem, *The Theology of Paul's Letter to the*

*Romans*, NTTh (Cambridge: Cambridge University Press, 2003), 126; **Th. Haering**, *Der Römerbrief des Apostels Paulus* (Stuttgart: Calwer, 1926), 70–71; 127; **Robert Hamerton-Kelly**, "Sacred Violence and Sinful Desire: Paul's Interpretation of Adam's Sin in the Letter to the Romans," in *The Conversation Continues: Studies in Paul and John*, edited by Robert T. Fortna and Beverly R. Gaventa (Nashville: Abingdon, 1990), 47–50; **Everett F. Harrison**, "Romans," in *EBC*, edited by Frank Gaebelein (Grand Rapids: Zondervan, 1976), 10:80–81; **Roy A. Harrisville**, *Romans*, ACNT (Minneapolis: Augsburg, 1980), 111; **John Paul Heil**, *Romans: Paul's Letter of Hope*, AnBib 112 (Rome: Biblical Institute, 1987), 47 n. 30; **Otfried Hofius**, "Das Gesetz des Mose und das Gesetz Christi," *ZTK* 80 (1983): 262–83, 269–71; idem, "Der Mensch im Schatten Adams," in *Paulusstudien II*, WUNT 143 (Tübingen: Mohr/Siebeck, 2002), 114–21; **Glenn S. Holland**, "The Self Against the Self in Romans 7.7–25," in *The Rhetorical Interpretation of Scripture: Essays from the 1966 Malibu Conference*, edited by Stanley E. Porter and Dennis L. Stamps, JSNTSup 180 (Sheffield: Sheffield Academic, 1999), 265; **Hans Hübner**, *Law in Paul's Thought*, translated by James C. G. Greig, SNTW (Edinburgh: T. & T. Clark, 1984), 70–76; **A. M. Hunter**, *The Epistle to the Romans: Introduction and Commentary*, TBC (London: SCM, 1961), 70–72; **Walter Jens**, *Der Römerbrief* (Stuttgart: Radius, 2000), 36; **Adolf Jülicher**, "Der Brief an die Römer," in *Die Schriften des Neuen Testaments*, edited by Johannes Weiß, 2 vols. (Göttingen: Vandenhoeck & Ruprecht, 1907–1908), 40–41; **Leander E. Keck**, *Romans*, ANTC ) Nashville: Abingdon, 2005), 183–84; **Seyoon Kim**, *The Origin of Paul's Gospel*, 2d ed., WUNT 4 (Tübingen: Mohr/Siebeck, 1984), 52–54; **Günter Klein**, "Gesetz III. Neues Testament," in *TRE*, edited by Gerhard Krause and Gerhard Müller, 36 vols. (Berlin: de Gruyter, 1976–2004), 13:70; **Heiko Krimmer**, *Römerbrief*, BKNT 10 (Neuhausen-Stuttgart: Hänssler, 1983), 181–84; **Ernst Kühl**, *Der Brief des Paulus an die Römer* (Liepzig: Quelle & Meyer, 1913), 229–32; **Timo Laato**, *Paul and Judaism: An Anthropological Approach*, translated by T. McElwain (Atlanta: Scholars, 1995), 102–6; **Paul Lamarche and Charles Le Dû**, *Épître aux Romains V–VIII: structure littéraire et sens* (Paris: Centre National de la Recherche Scientifique, 1980), 49–51; **M.-J. Lagrange**, *Saint Paul épître aux Romains* (Paris: Gabalda, 1950), 168–71; **Jan Lambrecht**, *The Wretched 'I' and Its Liberation: Paul in Romans 7 and 8*, LTPM 14 (Grand Rapids: Eerdmans, 1992), 47; **F. J. Leenhardt**, *The Epistle to the Romans* (Cleveland: World,

1961), 184-88; **Hermann Lichtenberger**, *Das Ich Adams und das Ich der Menscheit: Studien zum Menschenbild in Römer 7*, WUNT 164 (Tübingen: Mohr/Siebeck, 2004), 125-35; **Hans Lietzmann**, *Die Briefe des Apostels Paulus. I. An die Römer*, HNT (Tübingen: Mohr-Siebeck, 1906), 73; **Barnabas Lindars**, "Paul and the Law in Romans 5-8: An Actantial Analysis," in *Law and Religion: Essays on the Place of the Law in Israel and Early Christianity by Members of the Ehrhardt Seminar of Manchester University* (Cambridge: Cambridge University Press, 1988), 134; **Richard N. Longenecker**, *Paul, Apostle of Liberty: The Origin and Nature of Paul's Christianity* (Grand Rapids: Baker, 1976), 92-95; **Ulrich Luck**, "Das Gute und das Böse in Römer 7," in *Neues Testament und Ethik: für Rudolph Schnackenburg*, edited by Helmut Merklein (Freiburg: Herder, 1989), 220-37; **Ulrich Luz**, *Das Geschichtsverständnis des Paulus*, BeVT 49 (Münich: Kaiser, 1968), 166-67; **Stanislas Lyonnet**, *Les étapes de l'histoire du salut selon l'épître aux Romains*, Bibliothèque œcuménique 8 (Paris: Cerf, 1969), 121-37; idem, "L'histoire de salut selon le chapitre VII de l' épître aux Romains," *Bib* 43 (1962): 117-51; idem, "'Tu ne convoiteras pas' (Rom vii, 7)," in *Neotestamentica et Patristica: Eine Freundesgabe, Herrn Professor Dr. Oscar Cullmann zu seinem 60. Geburtstag überreicht*, edited by W. C. van Unnik, NovTSup 6 (Leiden: Brill, 1962), 157-65; **Bruce J. Malina**, "Some Observations on the Origin of Sin in Judaism and St. Paul," *CBQ* 31 (1969): 30-33; **Brice L. Martin**, "Some Reflections on the Identity of ἐγώ in Rom. 7:14-25," *SJT* 34 (1981): 43; **Heinrich August Wilhelm Meyer**, *Critical and Exegetical Handbook to the Epistle to the Romans*, 2 vols, edited by William Dickson, translated by John C. Moore and Edwin Johnson (Edinburgh: T. & T. Clark, 1879), 2:12; **Paul W. Meyer**, "The Worm at the Core of the Apple," in *The Conversation Continues*, edited by Robert T. Fortna and Beverly R. Gaventa (Nashville: Abingdon, 1990), 73; **Otto Michel**, *Der Brief an die Römer*, KEK 4 (Göttingen: Vandenhoeck & Ruprecht, 1955), 226-28; **D. J. W. Milne**, "Genesis 3 in the Letter to the Romans," *RTR* 39 (1980): 15-17; **O. Modalsli**, "Gal 2, 19-21; 5, 16-18 und Röm 7, 7-25," *TZ* 21 (1965): 32; **Robert Morgan**, *Romans*, NTG (Sheffield: Sheffield Academic, 1997), 35, 45; **Rodolphe Morissette**, "Un Midrash sur La Mort: (1 Cor. 15, xv, 54c à 57)," *RB* 79 (1972): 180-81; **D. Napier**, "Paul's Analysis of Sin and Torah in Romans 7:7-25," *ResQ* 44 (2002): 17-23; **Jerome H. Neyrey**, *Paul in Other Words: A Cultural Reading of His Letters* (Louisville: Westminster John Knox, 1990), 172-74; **Barclay M. Newman, and Eugene A. Nida**, *A*

*Handbook on Paul's Letter to the Romans.* UBSHS (New York: United Bible Societies, 1973), 134–35; **C. Marvin Pate**, *The Reverse of the Curse: Paul, Wisdom, and the Law*, WUNT 111 (Tübingen: Mohr/Siebeck, 2000), 310–11; **Sigfred Pedersen**, "Paul's Understanding of the Biblical Law," *NovT* 44 (January 2002): 16–19; **Pheme Perkins**, "Pauline Anthropology in Light of Nag Hammadi," *CBQ* 48 (1986): 517–18; **Rudolph Pesch**, *Römerbrief*, NEchtB 6 (Würzburg: Echter, 1983), 63–64; **Erik Peterson**, *Der Brief an die Römer*, AusSch (Würzburg: Echter, 1997) 218–19; **Heikki Räisänen**, *Paul and the Law* (Philadelphia: Fortress, 1983), 230 (though note the qualification in n. 9); **Marius Reiser**, "Sünde und Sündenbewusstsein in der Antike, bei Paulus und bei uns," *Erbe und Auftrag* 77 (2001): 464; **Herman Ridderbos**, *Paul: An Outline of His Theology* (Grand Rapids: Eerdmans, 1975), 144; **William Sanday and Arthur Headlam**, *A Critical and Exegetical Commentary on the Epistle to the Romans*, ICC (Edinburgh: T. & T. Clark, 1902), 180; **Heinrich Schlier**, *Der Römerbrief*, HTKNT 6 (Freiburg: Herder, 1977), 223–26; **Hans Wilhelm Schmidt**, *Der Brief des Paulus an die Römer*, THKNT 6 (Berlin: Evangelische Verlagsanstalt, 1966), 123–25; **Walter Schmithals**, *Der Römerbrief: Ein Kommentar* (Gütersloh: Mohn, 1988), 213–15; **Rudolph Schnackenburg**, "Römer 7 im Zusammenhang des Römerbriefes," in *Jesus und Paulus: Festschrift für Werner Georg Kümmel zum 70. Geburtstag*, eds. E. Earle Ellis and Erich Gräßer (Göttingen: Vanenhoeck & Ruprecht, 1978), 293–95; **Udo Schnelle**, *Apostle Paul: His Life and Theology*, translated by M. Eugene Boring (Grand Rapids: Baker, 2003), 334–36; **Christophe Senft**, "Paul et Jésus," *ETR* 84 (1985): 52 n. 7; **Robert B. Sloan**, "Paul and the Law: Why the Law Cannot Save," *NovT* 33 (1991): 51; **D. M. Stanley**, "Paul's Interest in the Early Chapters of Genesis," in *SPCIC 1961*, AnBib 17–18, 2 vols. (Chicago: Loyola University Press, 1963): 1:248–49; **Krister Stendahl**, *Final Account: Paul's Letter to the Romans* (Minneapolis: Fortress, 1995), 28; **John R. W. Stott**, *Romans: God's Good News for the World* (Downers Grove, IL: InterVarsity, 1994), 200–201; **G. Strelan**, "A Note on the Old Testament Background of Romans 7:7," *Lutheran Theological Journal* 15 (1981): 23–25; **Peter Stuhlmacher**, "The Law as a Topic of Biblical Theology," in *Reconciliation, Law, and Righteousness* (Philadelphia: Fortress, 1986), 127; idem, *Paul's Epistle to the Romans: A Commentary*, translated by Scott J. Hafemann (Louisville: Westminster John Knox, 1994), 106–7; **Charles H. Talbert**, *Romans*, SHBC (Macon, GA: Smyth & Helwys, 2002), 187–88; idem, "Tracing

Paul's Train of Thought in Romans 6-8," *RevExp* 100 (2003): 5; **Gerd Theissen**, *Psychological Aspects of Pauline Theology*, translated by John P. Galvin (Philadelphia: Fortress, 1987), 202–11; **Michael Theobald**, *Studien zum Römerbrief*, WUNT 136 (Tübingen: Mohr/Siebeck, 2001), 426–27; idem, *Römerbrief*, 2 vols., SKKNT 6 (Stuttgart: Verlag Katholisches Bibelwerk, 1992), 1:203–10; **Frank Thielman**, *Paul and the Law: A Contextual Approach* (Downers Grove, IL: InterVarsity, 1994), 295 n. 15; *Theology of the New Testament: A Canonical and Synthetic Approach* (Grand Rapids: Zondervan, 2005), 363–64; **Lauri Thurén**, *Derhetorizing Paul: A Dynamic Perspective on Pauline Theology and Law*, WUNT 124 (Tübingen: Mohr/Siebeck, 2000), 121, 127–29; **Chris Alex Vlachos**, "Law, Sin, and Death: An Edenic Triad? An Examination with Reference to 1 Corinthians 15:56," *JETS* 48 (2004):291–92; **Andrea van Dülmen**, *Die Theologie des Gesetzes bei Paulus*, SBM (Stuttgart: Katholisches Bibelwerk, 1968), 110; **Samuel Vollenweider**, *Freiheit als neue Schöpfung: Eine Untersuchung zur Eleutheria bei Paulus und in seiner Umwelt*, FRLANT (Göttingen: Vandenhoeck & Ruprecht, 1989), 349–52; **P. von der Osten-Sacken**, *Römer 8 als ein Beispiel paulinischer Soteriologie*, FRLANT 112 (Göttingen: Mohr/Siebeck, 1975), 198; **Petra von Gemünden**, "Der Affekt der ἐπιθυμία und der νόμος: Affektkontrolle und soziale Identitätsbildung im 4. Makkabäerbuch mit einem Ausblick auf den Römerbrief," in *Das Gesetz im frühen Judentum und im Neuen Testament: Festschrift für Christoph Burchard zum 75 Geburtstag*, edited by Dieter Sänger and Matthias Konradt, SUNT (Göttingen: Vandenhoeck & Ruprecht, 2006), 69. **Francis Watson**, *Paul, Judaism and the Gentiles*, SNTSMS 56 (Cambridge: Cambridge University Press, 1986), 151–53; idem, *Paul and the Hermeneutics of Faith* (London: T. & T. Clark, 2005), 360; **N. M. Watson**, "The Interpretation of Romans VII," *ABR* 21 (1973): 28; **Reinhard Weber**, "Die Geschichte des Gesetzes und des Ich in Römer 7,7—8,4: Einige Überlegungen zum Zusammenhang von Heilsgeschichte und Anthropologie im Blick auf die theologische Grundstellung des paulinischen Denkens," *NZSTR* 29 (1987):155–59; **A. J. M. Wedderburn**, "Adam in Paul's Letter to the Romans," in *Studia Biblica 1978: Papers on Paul and Other New Testament Authors*, edited by Elizabeth A. Livingstone, JSNTSup 3 (Sheffield: JSOT Press, 1980), 419–22; **Hans Weder**, "Gesetz und Sünde: Gedanken zu einem qualitative Sprung im Denken des Paulus," *NTS* 31 (1985): 374 n. 23; **Ulrich Wilckens**, "Zur Entwicklung des paulinischen Gesetzesverständnisses,"

*NTS* 28 (1982): 183; idem, *Der Brief an die Römer: Röm 6–11*, EKKNT (Neukirchen-Vluyn: Neukirchener, 1980), 2:78–83; **Ben Witherington III**, *Paul's Letter to the Romans: A Socio-Rhetorical Commentary* (Grand Rapids: Eerdmans, 2004), 185–92; idem, *Paul's Narrative Thought World* (Louisville: Westminster John Knox, 1994), 24–28; **N. T. Wright**, *Climax of the Covenant: Christ and the Law in Pauline Theology* (Minneapolis: Fortress, 1992), 196–98; idem, "The Letter to the Romans: Introduction, Commentary, and Reflections," in *NIB*, edited by Leander E. Keck (Nashville: Abingdon, 2002), 10:562–64; **Theodor Zahn**, *Der Brief des Paulus an die Römer*, KNT (Leipzig: Deichert, 1910), 340–44; **Dieter Zeller**, *Der Brief an die Römer* (Regensburg: Pustet, 1985), 138–41; **John Ziesler**, *Paul's Letter to the Romans*, TPINTC (London: SCM, 1989), 180–84; idem, "The Role of the Tenth Commandment in Romans 7," *JSNT* 33 (1988): 44–49.

# 5

## The Genesis Fall Narrative Revisited

### GENESIS 2

THOUGH THE STORY OF the Fall begins in Gen 3:1, Genesis 2 marks the starting point for an investigation of law and sin in Eden.[1] It is in Gen 2:17 that a *commandment* is introduced for the first time into the primeval narrative.[2] It is also in Gen 2:17 that the motif of *knowledge* appears

---

1. While not denying the possibility that various sources were woven together in the construction of the Genesis narrative, this study will examine the finished form of the text in its own right, i.e., as a coherent literary unity (similar, e.g., to the approaches of Gordis, "Knowledge," 129-30 n. 27; Moberly, "Serpent," 2-3; Frye, *Code*, xvii; Childs, *Crisis*, 99).

2. Although the sentences pulsate with "poetic rhythm" (Blocher, *In the Beginning*, 32), Genesis 2-3 is presented as a *narrative*, i.e., as a description of an event portrayed within defined limits that "moves up to a climax and tapers down to a conclusion" (Westermann, *Genesis*, 1:190; see also Gunkel, *Genesis*, xl; Beauchamp, *Création*, 384), or more specifically, as a "primeval tale," i.e., a short, prose narrative within a larger saga intended to preserve and convey "real world" traditions that present models for the believing community's behavior (see Coats, *Genesis*, 5-8, see also 58-59). Yet, approaching Genesis 2-3 as a narrative tale need not assume the absence of figurative language nor does assuming the historicity of the primordial events depicted there, as we do with Paul (see below, p. 201 n. 2) and his tradition (see, e.g., Matt 19:4-8; Mark 10:6; John 8:44; Heb 11:2, 4-7; 1 John 3:12), presume that the language used to picture these events is to be taken only literally (see, e.g., below, p. 154 n. 130). The present study will find reason to approach the narrative as somewhat of a *mixed-genre*, i.e., a saga containing some typology where unspecified realities stand behind certain depictions (see Blocher, *In the Beginning*, 36-37, who, with reference to examples of mixed genres in Scripture, cites the works of Thompson, ["Genesis 1," 17] and Dubarle, *Le péché originel*, 51 n. 2]). Although the genres are unlike (an apocalypse looks ahead whereas a saga look back), Revelation can at least be cited as an example of an account that, according to Rev 1:1, records "events which must take place" (ἃ δεῖ γενέσθαι) yet conveys these literal events in

in Scripture—a motif, as we have seen, that emerges in Paul's edenically-colored discussion of the law-sin nexus in Romans 7. Moreover, Gen 2:18–25 contains the account of the creation of Eve. Rather than impeding or slowing the movement of the narrative, this event, as we will argue, serves as a curt and necessary transition in the story between the giving of the law and its violation.[3] Since, therefore, Genesis 2 sets the stage for the drama depicted in Genesis 3, an analysis of the Fall account must begin with an examination of the related scenes contained there.[4]

## The Garden Commandment

In Gen 2:9 we read that the primeval paradise contained trees that were pleasant to the eyes and produced fruit that was good to eat. In vv. 16–17 the Lord God now permits the consumption of fruit from every tree,[5] except for one:[6]

---

symbolic terms (note καὶ ἐσήμανεν in Rev 1:1).

3. Westermann identifies 2:18–24 as an "intermediary passage" (*Genesis*, 1:191).

4. The term "scene" is used here and throughout to designate "those smaller portions of an account distinguishable from one another through the change of persons, of place, or of action" (Gunkel, *Genesis*, xxx). Brueggemann demarcates four scenes: 1) 2:4b-17; 2) 2:18–25; 3) 3:1–7; 4) 3:8–24 (*Genesis*, 44–45) as does Coats: 1) 2:4b-7; 2) 2:8–17; 3) 2:18–25; 4) 3:1–24 (*Genesis*, 49–50) and van Wolde: 1) 2:4b-6; 2) 2:7–25; 3) 3:1–7; 4) 3:8–24 (*Analysis*, 132–34). Hinschberger stretches this to five: 1) 2:5–17; 2:18–25; 3:1–7; 3:8–21; 3:22–24 ("Synchronique," 1); Walsh identifies seven scenes in the garden of Eden narrative: 1) 2:5–17; 2) 2:18–25; 3) 3:1–5; 4) 3:6–8; 5) 3:9–13; 6) 3:14–21; 7) 3:22–24 ("Synchronic," 161–62); Stordalen recognizes seven scenes but considers 2:4 as a *superscript* and 3:20–21 as an *interplay*: [2:4]; 1) 2:5–7; 2) 2:8–17; 3) 2:18–24; 4) 2:25–3:7; 5) 3:8–13; 6) 3:14–19; [3:20–21]; 7) 3:22–24 (Stordalen, *Echoes*, 219–20); Gunkel discerns nine scenes: 1) 2:4b-7; 2) 2:8–15; 3) 2:16–17; 4) 2:18–24; 5) 2:25; 6) 3:1–7; 7) 3:8–13; 8) 3:14–21; 9) 3:22–24 (*Genesis*, 4–25). While an eye will remain upon 2:4b-15 and 3:8–24, the present chapter will primarily examine three connected scenes: 1) the giving of the commandment (2:16–17); 2) the creation of Eve (2:18–25); 3) the transgression of the commandment (3:1–7).

5. There is no indication in the text itself that the permission did not include partaking of the tree of life (contra Barth, 3:256). Being later prohibited from going near the tree (Gen 3:22) need not imply that the couple had never eaten from it (see Lauer, "Tree," 42–50; contra Zimmerli, *1. Mose*, 1:132; Starke, "Tree," 23–24).

6. If one reads 2:16–17 in its canonical position and considers 1:28–30 to be a general blessing, the prohibition is the first direct, personal address by God to his human creatures (see Moberly, "Serpent," 4 n. 8). The latter verse, however, appears to contain more than a blessing. The man and woman receive a commission and mandate.

¹⁶ And the LORD God commanded the man, "You may freely eat of every tree of the garden; ¹⁷ but of the tree of the knowledge of good and evil you shall not eat, for in the day that you eat of it you shall die."

This is the first time that צָוָה occurs in the Scriptures. The verb occurs twenty-seven times in Genesis,⁷ but its occurrence here is the only time where a divine commandment is introduced with the formula וַיְצַו יְהוָה אֱלֹהִים.⁸ We also find here one of the few places in the Scriptures where the verb occurs with the preposition עַל and the object.⁹ This construction may emphasize the gravity of the commandment and the authority of the one who issues it.¹⁰ The verb is commonly found in the pentateuchal laws, especially in Deuteronomy where God, through Moses, "commanded" Israel and issued commandments (מִצְוָה).¹¹ This key term in the Garden narrative (recurring again in 3:11, 17) should probably not be applied to both the permission (אָכֹל תֹּאכֵל) and prohibition (לֹא תֹאכַל) but only to the prohibition, as in 3:11, 17.¹² The infinitive absolute can be used in legislative contexts,¹³ but it is used there independently rather than joined with a finite verb as in v. 16,¹⁴ and although it is possible that the phrase implies that Adam *must* eat of the trees, it is unlikely since the disjunctive ו, which begins v. 17, establishes a contrast.¹⁵ Rather than

---

7. The subject of the verb is divine in 2:16, 3:11, 17; 6:22; 7:5, 9, 16; 18:19; 21:4, while the subject is human in 12:20; 26:11; 27:8; 28:1, 6; 32:5, 18, 20; 42:25; 44:1; 45:19; 47:11; 49:21, 33; 50:2, 12; 50:16, 16.

8. Old Testament Hebrew references are taken from *BHS*.

9. וַיְצַו יְהוָה אֱלֹהִים עַל־הָאָדָם.

10. See Budde, *Paradiesesgeschichte*, 21. Note, e.g., the use of צָוָה and עַל in Gen 28:6; 1 Kgs 2:42; 11:11; Jer 35:6; Amos 2:12.

11. With minor variations, the expression "[all] which the Lord commanded" is particularly frequent in the account of the tabernacle's construction in Exodus 39–40 (see Exod 39:1, 5, 7, 21, 26, 29, 31–31, 42–43; 40:16, 19, 21, 23, 25, 27, 29, 32; note also 29:35; 31:6, 11; 34:4, 18; 35:1, 4, 10, 29; 36:1, 5; 38:22).

12. Westermann comments that v. 16 "is a not a restriction, but a release" (*Genesis*, 1:222; see also von Rad, *Genesis*, 80; Zlotowitz and Scherman, *Bereishis*, 100). Craig, to the contrary, unites both permission and prohibition in a double command ("Misspeaking," 238) as does Trible (*Sexuality*, 87) and Blocher (*In the Beginning*, 121).

13. See, e.g., Exod 20:8; Lev 2:6; Num 4:2; Deut 1:16, 5:12.

14. See GKC §113.*bb*. Deut 6:17 and 7:18 seem to be exceptions, but they likely fall into the category of exhortation rather than legislation.

15. See *IBHS* §392.3.b n. 12. The RL captures this: "Du *darfst* essen von allen Bäumen im Garten, aber von dem Baum der Erkenntnis des Guten und Bösen *sollst* du nicht

there being two commandments in tandem, therefore, there appears to be one, a single prohibition that is set against the background of a bounteous provision.[16] Besides the fact of the prohibition, the authority of the one who speaks, and the expectation of obedience,[17] nothing is here said or implied concerning the purpose of the divine command.[18] "The snake," notes von Rad, "was the first to open discussion about the prohibition."[19]

The Hebrew לֹא תֹאכַל in v. 17 matches precisely the form of the negative commandments in the Decalogue, i.e., לֹא coupled with the imperfect.[20] Attached to the prohibition is a motive clause,[21] which stipulates here a negative consequence, "for in the day that you eat of it you shall die."[22] Though the exact formulation מוֹת תָּמוּת is not found in legal texts,[23]

---

essen."

16. The infinitive absolute contained in the phrase אָכֹל תֹּאכֵל may signify Adam's freedom to eat from all the trees without restraint, i.e., "entirely at will" (Gunkel, *Genesis*, 10). This is reflected in the translation "you are free to eat" (NIV, NJB) or "you may eat freely" (NASB). See Joüon and Muraoka, *Grammar*, § 123 h., *IBHS* §35.3.1g n. 31. Ruppert ruefully observes that "die Eingrenzung ist minimal. . . . Nur ein einziger Baum unter so vielen" (*Genesis*, 1:135; see also von Rad, *Genesis*, 80; Westermann, *Genesis*, 1:222; Fretheim, "Genesis," 1:351). Note the similar contrast between provision and prohibition in Gen 10:3-4: "Every moving thing that lives shall be food for you; and just as I gave you the green plants, I give you everything. Only, you shall not eat flesh with its life, that is, its blood."

17. See Brueggemann, *Genesis*, 46.

18. Yet the inference is that God knows what is good (טוֹב) for the man (see Sailhamer, "Genesis," 2:45; von Rad, *Genesis*, 81; Moberly, "Serpent," 4).

19. Von Rad, *Genesis*, 81.

20. Note, for example, לֹא תַחְמֹד in Exod 20:17. For a discussion of the use of this form in Old Testament law, see Gerstenberger, *Wesen*, 73-74; Liedke, *Gestalt*, 101-3. In the LXX a similar pattern occurs; the commandment in 2:17 (οὐ φάγεσθε) resembles the Decalogue pattern of οὐ followed by the future (note οὐκ ἐπιθυμήσεις in Exod 20:17). The second person form of address in 2:17 perhaps underscores its authoritative nature and may stress the immediate and personal relationship between the Lord and Adam (See Westermann, *Genesis*, 1:187; Mathews, 210; see below, p. 179 n. 19).

21. I.e., a grammatically subordinate sentence in which the motivation for the commandment is given (see Gemser, "Motive," 50).

22. The conjunction כִּי is used here for the first time in Genesis to introduce a consequence.

23. Legal texts characteristically employ the infinitive plus the Hophal form of a third person verb (see Exod 19:12; 21:12, 15, 16, 17; 22:18; 31:14, 15; Lev 20:2, 9, 10, 11, 12, 13, 15, 16, 27; 24:16, 17; 27:29; Num 15:35, 35:16, 17, 18, 21, 31; the non-legal occurrences of the Hophal are found in Gen 26:11; Judg 21:5; Ezek 18:13). The phrase מוֹת תָּמוּת in Gen 2:17 is used elsewhere of divine or royal threats contained in narrative and prophetic

the pattern of appending a threat to a sanction likewise finds parallels in the Decalogue (Exod 20:5, 7, 11) and is a characteristic feature in Old Testament law in general.[24] Gerstenberger, nevertheless, denies any legal inferences in the threat of Gen 2:17b (nor in any Old Testament divine death threats) and deems the clause to be a *death stipulation* conveyed within the context of a *life setting*, i.e., "a wonderful example of how divine threats are to function. They protect a given order and thus promote life."[25] While Gerstenberger misses the fact that the Garden prohibition is, in fact, formulated in legal terms and, as such, serves as a judicial sanction,[26] his take is, nevertheless, noteworthy. Though a death threat,[27] it is undoubtedly correct that the motive clause in 2:17b is meant to function in a *preservative* capacity.[28] To be sure, the presence of the tree of life in the middle of the Garden attests to the divine concern to foster life.

---

texts (see Gen 20:7; 1 Sam 14:44; 22:16; 1 Kgs 2:37, 42; 2 Kgs 1:4, 6, 16; Jer 26:8; Ezek 3:18; 33:8, 14). The more rare third person singular (מוֹת יָמוּת) occurs in similar contexts (see 1 Sam 14:39; 2 Sam 12:14; 2 Kgs 8:10) as does the third person plural (מוֹת יָמֻתוּ) in Num 26:65 and the first person plural (מוֹת נָמוּת) in Judg 13:22; 2 Sam 14:14. The second person plural paragogic nun (לֹא־מוֹת תְּמֻתוּן) appears in Gen 3:4 on the lips of the serpent. In the Pentateuch, the infinitive with the Qal form of the finite verb (תָּמוּת) may emphasize the *divine* infliction of the penalty, whereas the infinitive and the Hophal form (always occurring in the third person) appears to be used of the *human* implementation of capital punishment, i.e., in contexts where situations are cited in which a transgressor is to be "put to death" (see Delitzsch, *Genesis*, 1:139). Hamilton points to the use of the infinitive absolute coupled with the Qal form of the verb in Gen 20:7 (מוֹת תָּמוּת) in contrast to the infinitive absolute with the Hophal verb form in Gen 26:11 (מוֹת יוּמָת). The latter ("he shall be put to death") implies that Abimilech himself will mete out the punishment, whereas the former ("you shall surely die") denotes death at God's hands (*Genesis*, 1:173). Milgrom, citing more thorough evidence (noting particularly how the Qal stem is used in reference to crimes committed against the sanctuary), concludes that "P is most scrupulous in the use of the *qal* and *hofʿal* of מות to distinguish between death by God or man" (*Studies*, 5–7). This distinction appears to carry throughout the Pentateuch and Ezekiel, but not in other narrative/prophetic texts. While the usage of the Hophal comports to this pattern in its appearances outside the Pentateuch (Judg 21:5; Ezek 18:13), the Qal is used there of both divine and human implementation of the sanctions.

24. See Milgrom, *Studies*, 50–66; Liedke, *Gestalt*, 103–5, 107–14; 127–30 and especially Zimmerli, *Law and Prophets*, 51–65.

25. Gerstenberger, "Threats," 47.

26. I.e., where crime is served with punishment. See, e.g., Exod 31:14; Lev 24:16. See verses cited in n. 23, above.

27. See the discussion of this verse in reference to retribution in Gathercole, "Justified," 173–74.

28. See also Zlotowitz and Scherman, *Bereishis*, 100.

Genesis 2:17 contains the first mention of death in Genesis.[29] Like the verb "command," it is a key term in the story, reappearing in 3:3 and twice in 3:4, and since the narrative opens in 2:7 with a description of the newly created man as a "living being,"[30] the reference to death in 2:17 signals a potential turn in the story. In light of the use of מוּת in the immediate context,[31] the term, it would seem, refers primarily to physical death.[32] This conclusion receives additional support from the way the infinitive absolute is used in the Pentateuch. The phrase "he shall surely die" occurs repeatedly there, for instance, where criminals are sentenced to death.[33] The expression בְּיוֹם, however, does not necessarily mean that the divine decree would be carried out on Adam immediately. The phrase here can convey a temporally indefinite, rather than specific sense.[34] What seems

29. It appears unduly speculative for Sarna to presume that the threat of death would have been unintelligible to the man if he had not already witnessed the demise of animals (*Genesis*, 21). Certainly Adam understood *life* and, it can be safely assumed, he would thus comprehend that disobedience to the commandment would bring its cessation. Death, as Hinschberger notes, is "la valeur contraire à la vie" ("Synchronique," 3).

30. לְנֶפֶשׁ חַיָּה (LXX 2:7: ψυχὴν ζῶσαν).

31. See especially the refrain וַיָּמֹת in Gen 5:5–31. Note also the similar phrasing in Pharaoh's threatening words to Moses in Exod 10:28: כִּי בְּיוֹם רְאֹתְךָ פָנַי תָּמוּת. It is thus difficult to argue, as does Moberly, that the reference to death in 2:17 is metaphorical ("Serpent," 16–18; similarly Gowan, *Genesis 1–11*, 44). While the Hebrew notion of death may entail more than the termination of physical life (see, e.g., Deut 30:15, 19), there is no justification from the context to understand the concept in Genesis 2–3 to mean anything less.

32. Jobling, to the contrary, argues that upon eating the forbidden fruit Adam would not die but become *mortal*, i.e., forfeit his immortality ("Myth," 31). Aside from the question of whether or not Adam was created immortal, there does not appear to be anywhere in the Scriptures where the phrase מוֹת תָּמוּת unambiguously means "to become mortal" (see the discussion in Moberly, "Serpent," 14–16; see also n. 39, below).

33. See, e.g., Gen 20:7; Exod 31:14; Lev 24:16. See also the citations in n. 23, above.

34. Note the NIV rendering "when." It appears to bear this meaning, e.g., in Gen 2:4; 5:1; Exod 6:28; 10:28; 32:34; Num 3:1; 2 Sam 22:1; Isa 11:6. Wenham denies that the phrase bears an indefinite sense in Gen 2:17 and argues from its use in 1 Kgs 2:37, 42 (a passage, he notes, that bears close similarity to 2:17) that בְּיוֹם tends to emphasize *promptness* of action (*Genesis*, 1:68). There it is stated that Shimei would be put to death "on the day" he crossed the Wadi Kidron, and he indeed suffered this fate when he returned on donkey from Gath where he traveled in pursuit of his runaways slaves. But surely 1 Kgs 2:37–42 does not support Wenham's contention. Although the precise location of Gath is difficult to determine, there is a present consensus that it lay near Tel Miqne (Ekron), i.e., twenty five miles more or less south-west of Jerusalem (see Seger, "Gath," 2:909; Aharoni and Avi-Jonah, *Atlas*, 113). If this location is correct, Shimei, in Wenham's scenario, would had to have journeyed over 50 miles round trip in one day

to be at issue is the *certainty* of death, not its chronology.[35] This is the notion likely conveyed here by the infinitive absolute coupled with the finite verb.[36]

Unlike the mandate in 1:28 to procreate and subjugate, Adam is now faced with a commandment to which is appended a death threat;[37] he would inevitably suffer the cessation of life if he were to partake of the forbidden tree. In the present narrative this divine sentence will be carried out against the first couple when they are ejected from the garden and denied access to the rejuvenating benefits of the tree of life (3:22-24).[38] Without such access to life's fruit they are doomed to die.[39]

---

on his donkey, a feat that could not have been possible. The phrase בַּיּוֹם thus appears to carry an indefinite sense in 1 Kgs 2:37, 42. What is underscored in the scene is the *certainty* of judgment were Shimei to violate the terms of his probation (see Ramban, *Commentary*, 74).

35. See, e.g., Exod 10:28; Num 30:6, 8, 9. Cassuto, *Genesis*, 125; see also Budde, *Paradiesesgeschichte*, 22-23; Hamilton, *Genesis*, 1:172.

36. See Keil and Delitzsch, *Pentateuch*, 85. Although in 1 Sam 14:44 and Jer 26:8 the threatened execution is not carried out, in each instance the announcement of a death sentence is conveyed. The sense in Gen 2:17, would appear to be, then, that Adam's fate would be sealed; i.e., he would be "doomed to die" (NJB) if he partook of the forbidden fruit. This is how most major English versions render the phrase in 2:17 (note "surely die," AV, ESV, NASB, NIV and "certainly die," NEB). The general use of the phrase in the Old Testament does not appear to support Soggin's translation "des Todes würdig" (*Genesis*, 70).

37. Steck assumes that 2:16-17 does not mark the first time where the man faced an ethical crossroads between obedience and disobedience (*Paradieserzählung*, 87-88). The narrative itself, however, does not support such a presumption. There are no red lights posted prior to 2:16-17.

38. Sarna argues that since the couple did not immediately die, and there is no indication that God rescinded the penalty, it is best to see the denial of access to the tree of life as the infliction of the penalty (*Genesis*, 18-19). This appears to be the case. In light of 3:19, which foretells Adam's fate of returning to the dust; 3:22-24, where the couple's access to the tree of life is cut off; and 5:5, which publishes Adam's obituary, there is no reason to assert with Westermann that the disobedient couple experienced an "inconsequence" of their transgression (*Genesis*, 1:225) or to conclude with Gunkel that the death penalty was never exacted (see *Genesis*, 10) or to agree with Skinner that God changed his purpose and modified the penalty (see *Genesis*, 67; see also Clines, "Themes," 490) or to contend with Beattie that God is depicted as having lied (see "*Peshat*," 73).

39. Narrowe comments that "Adam and Eve could no longer continually lengthen their days. Their nature had not been altered but their source of rejuvenation was no longer available" ("Tree," 187; see also Blenkinsopp, *Pentateuch*, 64). The Genesis story appears to assign to Adam a *derivative* rather than an *ontological* immortality; i.e., Adam received life by the divine inbreathing (2:7), and the perpetuation of that life was

However, at this point in the story Adam is alive, and the implication is that his life would be perpetuated as long as he does not trespass this one command.[40]

## The Knowledge of Good and Evil

Just as the terms "command" and "die" occur here for the first time in the Scriptures, the mention of the "tree of the knowledge of good and evil" in 2:9, 17 marks the first references in Scripture to *knowledge*.[41] Outside Genesis 2–3 there is no reference to this tree in biblical literature,[42] and the precise phrase טוֹב וָרָע appears elsewhere in the Old Testament only in Deut 1:39.[43] There is also no exact analogue to the tree among Israel's neighboring peoples. The exact significance of the second tree, therefore, has proven to be difficult to discern,[44] although numerous theories have

---

made possible by appropriating the "tree of life" (3:22) (see Wallace, *Eden*, 103; Fretheim, "Genesis," 1:350). Kidner notes: "the presence of the tree of life in the garden indicates that if man is to share the boon it must be an added gift" (*Genesis*, 1:65; see also Vriezen, *Outline*, 1970], 410; Sailhamer, "Genesis," 2:48). See above, pp. 94-95.

40. This notion is assumed in *Tg. Neof.* Gen 3:23: "If he had observed the precept of the Law and fulfilled its commandment he would live and endure forever like the tree of Life" (*ArBib* 1A:63).

41. The phrase occurs again in 3:5 and 22. The manner in which the phrase וְעֵא הַדַּעַת טוֹב וָרָע is attached to the end of the verse should not be considered as evidence of a later edition to a story that contained only one tree (so, e.g., Budde, "Baum," 46-88). Similar syntax is found in 1:16; 12:17; 34:29; Num 13:23, 26, etc. (see Dillmann, *Genesis*, 1:122-23).

42. In contrast, the "tree of life," which is introduced in Gen 2:9; 3:22, 24, resurfaces subsequently in the Old Testament (Prov 3:18; 11:30; 13:12; 15:4) and in the New Testament (Rev 2:7; 22:2, 14, 19).

43. I.e., without a preposition and collocated with the verb "to know." Note, however, the parallel phrases: רַע אוֹ־טוֹב (Gen 24:50); מִטּוֹב עַד־רָע (Gen 31:24, 29); בֵּי/ טוֹב וּבֵי/ רָע (Lev 27:12, 14); טוֹבָה אוֹ רָעָה (Num 24:13); הַטּוֹב וְהָרָע (2 Sam 14:17); בֵּי/־טוֹב לְרָע (Lev 27:33; 2 Sam 19:36; 1 Kgs 3:9); לְמֵרָע וְעַד־טוֹב (2 Sam 13:22); and בָּרַע וּבָחוֹר בַּטּוֹב (Isa 7:15).

44. Not only is the meaning of the tree elusive, but the name of the tree itself presents syntactical difficulties. At issue is whether הַדַּעַת is a substantive or infinitive and how it relates to the phrase טוֹב וָרָע. If it is a noun it could either be in the absolute state governed by עֵא or in the construct state affixed to טוֹב וָרָע. The latter option has the difficulty of explaining the article being attached to a noun in the construct state. The former option faces the problem of how טוֹב וָרָע relates to it. On the other hand, הַדַּעַת could be taken as an infinitive construct of יָדַע preceded by the article and followed by a direct object. This construction is paralleled in Jer 22:16 and appears to have been understood as such by

been proposed.[45] Nevertheless, it appears to us that the phrase "the knowledge of good and evil" in Genesis 2–3 can be understood in ethical or moral terms and may merely be a description of *what would experientially ensue* upon obedience or disobedience to the commandment; i.e., Adam would either gain the experiential knowledge of good through obedience or receive a first hand knowledge of evil through disobedience.[46] Thus Delitzsch argues that "the emphasis is more on the knowledge than on the objects. Good: obedience with its happy consequences; evil: disobedience with its evil consequences."[47] Similarly, Kidner suggests that "the tree plays its part in the opportunity it offers, rather than the qualities it possesses; like a door whose name announces only what lies beyond it."[48]

Along with being somewhat of a straight forward understanding of the text, this view has in its favor what commentators have noted about יָדַע, that it is often used to express experiential knowledge, as, e.g., in Ps 101:4: "A perverse heart shall depart from me; I will know no evil."[49]

---

the LXX translators, who translated the term with the articular infinitive τοῦ εἰδέναι in Gen 2:9 and τοῦ γινώσκειν in Gen 2:17. Because Speiser considers the phrase to be "extremely awkward syntactically, especially in a writer who is otherwise a matchless stylist" he assumes the phrase in 2:9, 17 is secondary (*Genesis*, 20, 26). This seems extreme. The term is likely an infinitive construct (see *IBHS*, 36.2.1.e).

45. See Excursus pp. 167–74. Indeed, Westermann devotes over a half page to a bibliography of interpretations of the phrase "good and evil" (*Genesis*, 1:240–41), and Coppens wearily comments on the subject that "il a été traité tant de fois et, si vous me permettez l'expression, il a été mis à tant de sauces, qu'il ne peut plus guère provoquer de l'appétit" (*La Connaissance*, 13).

46. See, e.g., Kidner, *Genesis*, 63; Heinisch, *Genesis*, 114; Jacob, *Genesis*, 19; Ross, *Genesis*, 123; Coppens, *La Connaissance*, 13–46, 73–86; Heppe, *Dogmatics*, 292–93; Hodge, *Theology*, 2:125–26; Young, *Genesis* 3, 40–41; Lagrange, "L'innocence," 344; Köhler, *Theology*, 168–69; Schaeffer, *Genesis*, 71–73.

47. Quoted in Westermann, *Genesis*, 1:242; see also Heinisch, *Genesis*, 114.

48. *Genesis*, 63. Note also Trible, who maintains that the tree's meaning resides "not in its content but in its function. It symbolizes obedience and disobedience" (*Sexuality*, 87; a view similar to Augustine's [see *Civ.* 14.12]) and Vogels, who theorizes that the tree "may be the symbol of experiencing or tasting what is good and what is bad" (Vogels, "'Like one of us,'" 150).

49. NASB. The Hebrew reads: לֵבָב עִקֵּשׁ יָסוּר מִמֶּנִּי רָע לֹא אֵדָע. Von Rad observes: "So far as knowledge of good and evil is concerned, one must remember that the Hebrew *yd'* never signifies purely intellectual knowing, but in a much wider sense an 'experiencing,' and 'becoming acquainted with'" (*Genesis*, 89; see also Stern, "Knowledge," 409; Vogels, "'Like one of us,'" 147; Speiser, *Genesis*, 26). For "knowing" in the sense of *becoming acquainted with* (excluding *sexually* [for which, see n. 216, below]), see, e.g., Gen 18:19; 41:31; Exod 23:9; 33:13; Num 14:31, 34; 24:16 Deut 7:15; 8:3, 16; 33:9; Josh 24:31;

Furthermore, the depiction in Gen 3:7 of what immediately ensued upon the transgression, viz., the consciousness of guilt, would appear to coincide with an experiential notion.[50] Additionally, this interpretation coincides with Deut 1:39, the only passage outside Genesis 2–3 where the exact phrase טוֹב וָרָע occurs: "And as for your little ones, who you said would become a prey, and your children, who today have no knowledge of good or evil, they shall go in there. And to them I will give it, and they shall possess it."[51] Here, the phrase "knowledge of good and evil" appears to connote a loss of innocence, as Coppens notes: "La locution 'ne connaître ni le bien ni le mal' y signifie 'être entièrement innocent,' 'n'avoir commis aucun crime, aucune faute.' Le correspondant positif sera donc: 'avoir transgressé,' 'avoir eu la connaissance du péché.'"[52] More importantly, there may also be an affinity between the phrase in Genesis 2–3 and the scene depicted in Deut 30:15–19,[53] a passage that appears to contain numerous verbal and thematic parallels to Eden.[54] The Israelites

---

Judg 2:10; 3:1, 2, 2; 1 Sam 3:13; 2 Sam 19:35; 1 Kgs 9:27; 2 Chr 8:18; 12:8; Job 20:20; 21:19; 28:7; 34:4; Ps 101:4; 138:6; Ecc 8:5; Isa 47:8; 51:7; 59:8, 8; Ezek 25:14; Hos 9:7; Mic 3:1; 6:5; Zeph 3:5. In the broadest sense, the verb can be defined as the taking of "various aspects of the world of one's experience into the self, including the resultant relationship with that which is known. The fundamentally relational character of knowing (over against a narrow intellectual sense) can be discerned, not least in that both God and human beings can be subject and object of the vb." (Fretheim, "ידע" 2:410; see also *TLOT* 2:514).

50. See discussion on Gen 3:7, below.

51. ESV.

52. Coppens, *La Connaissance*, 17. This appears to be a less strained interpretation than understanding the phrase in Deut 1:39 of those "not yet twenty years old" (Buchanan, "Good and Evil," 116) or of "*the total dependence* which makes children unsuitable to answer for their actions or to control their own conduct" (Blocher, *In the Beginning*, 132, italics mine).

53. See Jacob, *Genesis*, 19; Emmrich, "Temptation Narrative, 8–9; Henry, "'Tod' und 'Leben,'" 9; Orbe, "El dilema," 512–13.

54. Note, e.g., יוֹם (Gen 2:17; 3:5/Deut 30:15, 16, 18), צָוָה (Gen 2:16; 3:11, 17/Deut 30:16), טוֹב (Gen 2:9, 17; 3:5, 22/Deut 30:15), רָע (Gen 2:9, 17; 3:5, 22/Deut 30:15), הַחַיִּים (Gen 2:17; 3:5/Deut 30:15, 19), מוּת (Gen 2:17; 3:3, 4/Deut 30:15, 19). In addition to these verbal matches, compare the references in Deut 30:16 to "multiplying" (רבה) and being "blessed" (בר) to Gen 1:22, 28 and the mention of possessing the "land" (אֶרֶץ) to Gen 2:5, 6, etc. Thematically, the reference to being "lead astray" (Deut 30:17) is reminiscent of Eve being deceived by the serpent, the threat of being cursed and banished from Canaan (Deut 30:18) is similar to the curses and banishment from the Garden, and the statement in Deut 30:18 "you shall not live long" (לֹא־תַאֲרִיכֻן / יָמִים) evokes the phrase "you shall surely die" in Gen 2:17. Furthermore, in both accounts God issues a command to which is appended a warning meant to preserve life. Canonically, the Deut

in the desert, like Adam and Eve before the tree, stood at a crossroads. Their obedience or disobedience, like the first couple's, would determine what they would experience—good or evil, life or death:[55]

> [15] See, I have set before you today life and good, death and evil. [16] If you obey the commandments of the LORD your God that I command you today, by loving the LORD your God, by walking in his ways, and by keeping his commandments and his statutes and his rules, then you shall live and multiply, and the LORD your God will bless you in the land that you are entering to take possession of it. [17] But if your heart turns away, and you will not hear, but are drawn away to worship other gods and serve them, [18] I declare to you today, that you shall surely perish. You shall not live long in the land that you are going over the Jordan to enter and possess. [19] I call heaven and earth to witness against you today, that I set before you life and death, blessing and curse. Therefore choose life, that you and your offspring may live.

Finally, this interpretation comports with what appears to be a key feature of the two trees themselves, viz. they get their names from their *effects*;[56] i.e., just as partaking of the first tree would result in life, so eating from the second tree would emanate in knowledge.[57] It would seem that a correct interpretation of the phrase "the knowledge of good and evil" must coincide with this pattern.

Nevertheless, though interpreting the phrase in an experiential sense appears reasonable, it, of course, raises the question of how a God

---

30:15ff. passage may combine with the drama in Genesis 2–3 to create an inclusio. If one assumes Mosaic authorship of both Genesis and Deuteronomy, an inclusio may become even more likely.

55. ESV.

56. As argued at length by Hodge (*Theology*, 2:125–26) and noted by Heinisch: "Wenn der eine imstande war, dem Menschen das Leben zu vermitteln, so muß der andere imstande gewesen sein, ihm ebenfalls etwas zu geben: die Erkenntnis des Guten und Bösen" (*Genesis*, 114). Rather than the genitive carrying an attributive meaning (i.e., "the living tree," "the good and evil tree"), it would seem that the grammatical constructions (עֵץ הַחַיִּים . . . וְעֵץ הַדַּעַת טוֹב וָרָע) indicate what the trees *produced*, viz., life and knowledge (see Ross, *Creation and Blessing*, 123). The use of the articular infinitive in the LXX, which mirrors the Hebrew infinitive construct (see above, n. 44), coincides with a notion of result: τὸ ξύλον **τοῦ εἰδέναι γνωστὸν** καλοῦ καὶ πονηροῦ (Gen 2:9), τὸ ξύλον **τοῦ γινώσκειν** καλὸν καὶ πονηρόν (Gen 2:17).

57. Note Gen 3:6: "When the woman saw that the tree was . . . to be desired *to make one wise*."

who is depicted in the canonical Scriptures as being experientially unacquainted with sin could be deemed conversant with both good *and* evil (Gen 3:22).[58] Yet, need the likeness in Gen 3:22 be exact?[59] Might the first couple have gained by an act of disobedience what God had known in his omniscience?[60] Coppens argues for this: "Dieu la [la science du péché], doit la posséder puisque rien ne lui échappe selon les écrivains bibliques, mais seulement d'une science spéculative, incluse dans l'omniscience; l'homme, par contre, ne pouvait arriver à la posséder que par un acte de péché."[61] Similarly, Kidner describes the fallen humans' consciousness of good and evil as both like and unlike the divine knowledge, "differing from it . . . as a sick man's aching awareness of his body differs . . . from the insight of the physician."[62]

Whatever the exact significance of the tree of the knowledge of good and evil (and the existence of so many interpretations reveals its elusiveness),[63] the tree of knowledge looms large in the narrative. References to it occur twice in the introductory scene (2:9, 17), once during the seduction of Eve (3:5), and finally in the closing scene (3:22). Indeed, it over-

58. See, e.g., Exod 3:1-6; 1 Sam 2:2; Job 36:23b; Ps 99:9; Isa 6:3; 57:15; Heb 1:13; 1 Pet 1:15; Rev 4:1-11; etc.

59. Hamilton writes: "One suspects that these words ["knowing good and evil"] in the serpent's mouth convey one thing and the same words in God's mouth say another" (*Genesis*, 1:208).

60. Hodge argues: "Adam had, by eating the forbidden fruit, attained a knowledge in some respects analogous to the knowledge of God, however different in its nature and effects. . . . God knew the nature and effects of evil from his omniscience. Adam could know them only from experience, and that knowledge he gained when he sinned" (*Theology*, 2:127).

61. Coppens, *La Connaissance*, 15-16.

62. Kidner, *Genesis*, 69. It may be appropriate to add here that although interpreting the phrase in an experiential manner raises difficulties, if, as we think, Rom 7:7-11 is "best understood as exposition of the Genesis narrative" (Cranfield, *Romans* 1:350; see also the similar assessments of Kühl [*Römer*, 230] and Haacker [*Römer*, 143]) and if, as we believe, Paul's exposition is itself canonical, it would appear to be more warranted to read the Genesis account from over the Apostle's shoulder and confront any theological tensions that might ensue, than to leave Romans 7 out of consideration altogether. Indeed, from a biblical-theological perspective (i.e., from a perspective that assumes an underlying coherence and theological unity of the two Testaments) Romans 7 and its notion of the experiential knowledge of sin may provide interpretative insight without which the meaning of "the knowledge of good and evil" in Eden cannot be fully grasped (see below, pp. 179-83).

63. Mayes ponders whether the wide variety of interpretations suggests that the narrator intended to be vague at this point ("Nature," 257).

shadows the tree of life, becoming the touchstone on which the narrative turns.[64] The attention that the narrator fixes on it, to be sure, indicates that knowledge is among the primary motifs in the Fall story line.[65] We will revisit the phrase below and consider what relevance it may have to Paul's notion of the law leading to *the knowledge of sin*.

## The Creation of Eve

The next scene in Genesis 2 comprises the creation of the animals (vv. 18–20) and the creation of the woman (vv. 21–25). Though these may appear to be two unrelated events, they are presented as a unified episode.[66] The creation of the animals, which provided no suitable counterpart for the man, serves as a soft foil leading up to the central theme of the passage, the creation of Eve.[67] The phrase עֵזֶר כְּנֶגְדּוֹ, which opens the section, strikes this note. It recurs in v. 20 after it is apparent that the animals brought to Adam fail to provide him with a mirror of himself. The tension which began in v. 18a is thereby intensified and is only alleviated in vv. 21–25 with the creation of the woman for the man.[68]

In addition to being a unit, 2:18–25 is *transitional*.[69] It serves as an interlude between "the two main pillars of the narration," 2:8–17 (paradise

---

64. For Speiser, the tree is the narrative's "focal point" (*Genesis*, 26).

65. Vawter views it similarly; the tree "bears the burden of the narrative" (*Genesis*, 68). Westermann notes that the expression "the knowledge of good and evil" is a *leitmotif* that "must color the whole narrative" (*Genesis*, 1:242).

66. Most view vv. 18–25 as a unit (see, e.g., Calvin, Cassuto, Brueggemann, Kidner, Skinner, Walsh, Culley), though v. 25 is sometimes placed alone (Westermann, Sailhamer; Sarna) or with 3:1ff. (Trible, Speiser).

67. Kidner, in his commentary, entitles the section comprising vv. 18–25, "The Making of the Woman" (*Genesis*, 65). Sarna, Cassuto, and Fretheim similarly designate it, "The Creation of Woman." Gunkel utilizes the subtitle, "The Man's Helper" (*Genesis*, 11), and Mathews dubs vv. 18–25 "The Man's Companion, the First Woman" (*Genesis*, 212). Clearly, the creation of the animals is recognized by many to be a sub-plot. Curiously, there is no other account in ancient Near East literature of the creation of the woman. Genesis 2 is not only unique in this regard, but it devotes more space to the creation of the woman than of the man. Sarna observes that this detail "is extraordinary in light of the generally nondescriptive character of the biblical narrative and as such is indicative of the importance accorded this event" (*Genesis*, 21).

68. See Westermann, *Genesis*, 1:229; Sailhamer, "Genesis," 2:47.

69. Westermann identifies 2:18–24 as an "intermediary passage" (*Genesis*, 1:191).

gained) and 3:1–24 (paradise lost).[70] The transitional nature of the passage is observed in the manner in which it is linked to both the preceding and following scenes. Thus, divine speech in 2:18 connects the beginning of this scene to the end of the previous one—both scenes contain the only direct discourses of God in 2:4–25.[71] The two scenes are also chiastically related: 2:4–17 begins with third person narration and ends with direct discourse; 2:18–25 begins with direct discourse and ends in narration.[72] Furthermore, most commentators recognize that 2:25 is a pivot that joins the forgoing to what follows by means of a word play between "naked" (עֲרוֹם) and "shrewd" (עָרוּם) and by an anticipatory hint at the couple's later recognition of their nakedness.[73] The author, notes Westermann, "with great ingenuity and simplicity, constructed a bridge passage, 2:25, which joined the narratives [i.e., 2:16–17 and 3:1–7] firmly together."[74]

Furthermore, the transitional nature of 2:18–25 is perceived in what appears to be the fact that 2:16–17 and 3:1–7 are cut from the same cloth and comprise the story line of Genesis 2–3, crime and punishment.[75] Indeed, observes Coats: "the two elements stand together as one unit, the one a reflex to the other."[76] This is suggested not only by the presence of recurring motifs, such as the tree of life and the tree of the knowledge of good and evil but also by Culley's observation that both scenes together comprise an *action sequence* that moves from *wrong* to *wrong punished*.[77]

---

70. Coats, *Genesis*, 53. Ruppert finds that Gen 2:18–24 "supplements" ("hat ergänzt") the account of Adam's fall (*Genesis*, 138). Westermann deems vv. 18–24 "an inset" (*Genesis*, 1:194).

71. See Trible, *Sexuality*, 89.

72. Ibid.

73. See van Wolde, *Analysis*, 165; Brueggemann, *Genesis*, 47. Moberly observes that "before we come to the *main narrative* there is the *intervening paragraph* concerning the creation of animals and of woman. Without preempting what follows, we simply note that the paragraph is integrated into the story as a whole; one of the animals created together with the woman takes centre stage as the story continues, and the concluding note about the nakedness of the man and the woman sets the stage for what follows" ("Serpent," 5, italics mine; see also Walsh, "Synchronic," 164; Ruppert, *Genesis*, 1:144; Westermann, *Genesis*, 1:234; Sailhamer, "Genesis," 2:49; Mathews, *Genesis*, 224–25).

74. Westerholm, *Genesis*, 1:194.

75. See ibid., 1:236. Recall also Coats's designation quoted above of Gen 2:8–17 and 3:1–24 being the main "two pillars" that recount the story of "paradise gained" and "paradise lost."

76. Coats, *Genesis*, 51.

77. Culley, "Action Sequences," 32.

In contrast, 2:18–25, an action sequence whose plot proceeds from *difficulty* to *difficulty removed*, is a distinct account that "functions as background information setting the stage for the main sequence."[78] What appears then, is a chiastic pattern in which the creation and deception of Eve forms the center piece between the two key scenes of the drama:

    **A** Adam receives the commandment

        **B** Eve is created

   **A'** Eve is deceived by the Serpent

       **B'** Adam violates the commandment

Thus, both the transitional character of vv. 18–25 and the thematic relation between 2:16–17 and 3:1–7 would seem to indicate that, far from being unrelated to what precedes and follows, 2:18–25 serves as a bridge between the giving of the commandment and its transgression. In the flow of the narrative, therefore, what intervenes between 2:16–17 and 3:1–7, viz., the creation of Eve, does not disconnect these scenes, but links them.[79] Indeed, the plot line could not proceed without her.[80]

Finally, not only is the movement between commandment and transgression not diverted by the account of Eve's creation,[81] it is neither unduly *lengthened*.[82] In the flow of the narrative, little time elapses

---

78. Ibid.; see also Wenham, *Genesis*, 1:71.

79. Von Rad identifies 2:18–25 as part of the milieu in which the commandment is set: "In the narrative as a whole, the prohibition (v. 17) is completely embedded in the description of God's fatherly care for man" (*Genesis*, 82). He had previously noted that the "great release" in 2:16 established this fatherly care prior to the prohibition (ibid., 80). Thus the prohibition is padded on both sides with God's provision.

80. Westermann argues that 2:18–24 provides key background information for the Fall account of 3:1ff.; i.e., since it is only the man who heard the command in 2:16–17, while in 3:3 the woman knows of it, the author, by means of 2:18–24, "enables the action of Gen 3 to presuppose the community of man and woman as partners before God" (*Genesis*, 1:194). Similarly, Heinisch argues that "Gn 1 will die Schöpfung darstellen, Gn 2 will auf den Sündenfall vorbereiten und ihn verständlich machen, indem der weitgehende Einfluß des Weibes auf den Mann begründet wird" (*Genesis*, 120; see also Coats, *Genesis*, 53; Ruppert, *Genesis*, 1:138). Along the same vein, but somewhat further out on the limb, *2 En.* 30:17 states: "And I assigned a shade for him, and I imposed sleep upon him, and he fell asleep. And while he was sleeping, I took from him a rib. And I created for him a wife, so that death might come [to him] by his wife" (*OTP* 1:152; see also *Gk. Apoc. Ezra* 2:10).

81. The conjunctive ו in 2:18 splices and moves the action from scene to scene.

82. Though, in a sense, Coats is correct to consider the passage to be a "delay in the plot" (*Genesis*, 53).

from the time that Adam receives the commandment until the serpent appears.[83] After the giving of the commandment,[84] the narrator quickly introduces Eve and places her next to the man in a state together of childlike innocence.[85] This "when there was not yet" prepares for the drama of Genesis 3 and introduces the element of suspense that reaches it ominous climax there.[86] "Bref," observes Hinschberger, "tout s'est mis progressivement en place pour l'actualisation d'un méfait."[87]

---

83. The Genesis text is silent concerning how long the state of innocence in the Garden lasted; indeed "no hour strikes in Paradise" (Herder, quoted in Gunkel, *Genesis*, 15). Yet, in terms of "scene-editing," the narrator portrays the action moving rather quickly from the before to the after. This no doubt led to the later rabbinic tradition that the giving of the commandment, the creation of Eve, and the sin and expulsion from Eden took place on the same day (an exception to this common notion is found in *Jub.* 3:15 and *2 En.* 71:28, where the state of innocence is depicted as lasting seven years). Indeed, notes one rabbi, Adam "did not remain obedient to the commandment for a single hour" (*Tanh. Lev.* 11:1 [Townsend]; see also *Tanh. Gen.* 3:22; *Pirqe R. El.* 11; *b. Sanh.* 38b; *Pesiq. Rab.* 46.2; *Exod. Rab.* 32.1; *Lev. Rab.* 29.1; *Midr. Pss.* 92:3; *ʾAbot R. Nat.* 17b.8; see also Scroggs, *Last Adam*, 33 n. 2 and especially the discussion in Lichtenberger, *Das Ich*, 232–34). Early church literature contains similar speculation. Irenaeus, for example, believed that Adam sinned on the sixth day of creation (*Haer.* 5.23; for other references in the Fathers, see Ginzberg, *Haggada*, 48–50).

84. As noted, the commandment makes its appearance with the prohibition at Gen 2:16–17 rather than with the mandate to be fruitful and multiply at 1:28 (contra Heppe, *Dogmatics*, 281–300).

85. The ו establishes a disjunctive relation between being naked and *yet* not being ashamed (see Sasson, "Gen 2:25," 418). Gunkel suggests that the force of the Hithpael form (יִתְבֹּשָׁשׁוּ) expresses reciprocity, i.e., "they were not ashamed in each other's presence" (*Genesis*, 14; see also Sasson, "Gen 2:25," 420; GKC §72.*m*; *IBHS* §26.2g). Skinner considers the imperfect to be frequentative (*Genesis*, 70), i.e., the couple was not at any time ashamed before each other. There is no good reason to assume with Gunkel that this lack of shame signified that the couple, like children, had not yet recognized their sexual differences nor had engaged in sexual relations (*Genesis*, 14; see also Procksch, *Theologie*, 633–64). Rather, there appears here a connotation of childlike *innocence* in contrast to their coming recognition of guilt (Gen 3:7). Cassuto notes: "Since they did not yet know good or evil, nor had they yet learned that sexual desire could also be directed towards *evil ends*, they had no cause to feel ashamed at the fact that they were naked; the feeling of shame in regard to anything is born only of consciousness of the evil that may exist in that thing" (*Genesis*, 137).

86. Westermann, *Genesis*, 1:235.

87. Hinschberger, "Synchronique," 5.

## GENESIS 3

Although the story line of crime and punishment continues into chapter 3,[88] at this point in the narrative a new actor *suddenly* rises onto the scene, the serpent.[89] Yet while the plot progresses, a line from the previous chapter appears again in the script; the snake emerges on the stage with *the commandment* of 2:17 on its tongue.[90] Westermann notes, most likely correctly, that one could excise the temptation episode contained in vv. 1–5 and read vv. 6–7 immediately after 2:17, since temptation does not necessarily belong to the course of events of crime and punishment.[91] Nevertheless, the temptation account has its purpose in the Genesis story. It is an elaboration of the narrative; "the narrator wanted to use it to explain *how* the transgression came about."[92]

---

88. Westermann notes that Genesis 3, together with 2:9, 15–17, is a narrative of crime and punishment (*Genesis*, 1:236; see also Culley, "Action Sequences," 28). He thus divides chapter 3 into two parts, the transgression (3:1–7) and its penalty (3:8–24). Fretheim separates the chapter into four parts: 1) transgression (3:1–7); 2); inquest (3:8–13); 3) sentence (3:14–19); 4) expulsion (20–24) ("Genesis," 1:359, 364). Coats's outline is similar, though he follows Westermann by isolating vv. 1–5: 1) temptation (3:1–5); 2) the fall (3:6–7); 3) accusation (3:8–13); 4) judgment (3:14–24) (*Genesis*, 1:50).

89. Numerous commentators have observed the manner in which the serpent suddenly appears in the narration. Thus, Hinschberger exclaims: "Voilà qu'un nouvel acteur entre en scène" ("Synchronique," 5). Note also Fretheim: "the author introduces the serpent abruptly" ("Genesis," 1:360); Brueggemann: the scene "moves quickly into a new agenda" (*Genesis*, 47); Ruppert: the appearance of the snake occurs "plötzlich" (*Genesis*, 145); Brandscheidt: "das unvermittelte und plötzliche Auftreten der Schlange" ("Mensch," 4); and Skinner: attention is "at once" diverted to the serpent" (*Genesis*, 71; see also Zimmerli, *1 Mose*, 1:163; Mathews, *Genesis*, 232).

90. See Dunn, *Romans*, 1:383.

91. Westermann, *Genesis*, 1:236.

92. Ibid., italics mine. Drewermann draws an application from Westermann's observation: "Wenn es wahr ist, daß Gn 3,1–5, die Versuchungsgeschichte, 'eine Erweiterung der Erzählung' darstellt und anzunehmen ist, 'daß der Erzähler durch sie besonders hervorheben wollte, wie es zu der Verfehlung kam,' dann muß es von besonderer Bedeutung sein, *den Ablauf des Prozesses zu erfassen*, durch den die Menschen schuldig wurden" (*Strukturen*, 54, italics mine; see also van Wolde, *Analysis*, 111).

## THE SERPENT

As the narrator introduces the new character into the primordial drama a circumstantial clause is deployed that describes its character and origin:[93]

> 1a Now the **serpent** was more crafty than any other wild animal that the LORD God had made.

The term עָרוּם, which bears an acoustical likeness to עָרוֹם in 2:25 and thus links the two scenes,[94] is not necessarily a negative term in the Scriptures; shrewdness can, in fact, be a virtue worthy of pursuit.[95] The term, however, carries a negative connotation in contexts where shrewdness is misused,[96] and from the ominous manner in which the garden drama unfolds,[97] the author is likely using the slippery term pejoratively.[98] Indeed, the phonetic and stylistic parallels between 3:1 (מִכֹּל חַיַּת הַשָּׂדֶה עָרוּם) and 3:14 (אָרוּר אַתָּה מִכָּל־הַבְּהֵמָה) appear to link the craftiness of the snake to its curse.[99]

---

93. In spite of von Rad's contention that "we are not to be concerned with what the snake is but with what it says" (*Genesis*, 88), the fact that the narrator was concerned enough to describe it is sufficient reason to note its hiss as well as its words. This may be especially so since, according to Wenham, explicit characterization of actors is rare in Hebrew narrative (*Genesis*, 1:72).

94. The "craftiness" of the serpent contrasts with the couple's *naive* innocence. Wenham describes the impending irony: "They will seek to be shrewd (cf. 3:6) but will discover themselves 'nude'" (3:7, 10) (*Genesis*, 1:72).

95. See, e.g., Prov 1:4; 8:5; 12:16; 13:16; 14:8; 15:5. The ability of the snake to be *aware* of the tree and to *speak* suggests that the connotations of עָרוּם when describing the snake are not *solely* negative; it clearly possesses intelligence (see Niehr, "עָרְמָה, עֵירוֹם, עָרוֹם" in *TDOT* 11:363).

96. See Exod 21:14; Josh 9:4; Job 5:12; 15:5.

97. The story line certainly elicits no sympathy from the reader towards the serpent. The snake is villainous. However the term עָרוּם is understood upon first reading, it is difficult not to read it in a negative light in view of the evil that transpires.

98. Emmrich observes: "No matter whether we are here dealing with a neutral term or not, a contextual analysis will lead us to the conclusion that the serpent is depicted not only as being rebellious against God, but also as displaying an evil kind of cleverness in engaging the woman" ("Temptation Narrative," 12).

99. Rashi observes that the serpent's cunning was his ultimate downfall: "more cunning than all . . . cursed more than all" (*Genesis*, 69).

Though the serpent itself may not have aroused the woman's suspicions,[100] and while some ancients viewed snakes positively,[101] the Jewish reader, at least, probably would have been suspicious that a villain was now on stage. That this would have been the case is likely for the following reasons: First, an evil connotation may be latent in the term itself; the Hebrew נָחָשׁ is reminiscent of both the verb נָחַשׁ, "to divine" and the noun נַחַשׁ, "divination."[102] And even if there be no actual etymological connection between the two words, a "'popular' etymology would undoubtedly have been felt."[103] Second, in the classification of animals in Leviticus 11:41–45 the snake is among the unclean animals. Wenham notes that the snake in the human food chain "must count as an archetypal unclean animal. Its swarming, writhing locomotion puts it at the farthest point from those pure animals that can be offered in sacrifice."[104] Third, the snake was associated with the judgment of God against Israel for her complaints against him in the wilderness.[105] Fourth, an association of serpents with God's enemies may be evident in the references to the antagonist Leviathan.[106] Fifth, elsewhere in the Old Testament, with the exception of the bronze serpent made by Moses,[107] snakes consistently represent hostility to humans.[108] Sixth, as noted, the term by which the

---

100. The term נָחָשׁ is the general term for "snake" in the Scriptures (see Num 21:7–9; Deut 8:15; Prov 23:32; etc.). It would have been (at least originally) among the "good" animals God had created in Genesis 1.

101. In the ancient world the snake was often venerated and worshipped as an emblem of health, fertility, and immortality (see Joines, *Symbolism*, 19–29). On the other hand, the Babylonian *Epic of Gilgamesh* indicates that the snake could be perceived in ancient times as an antagonist to humans. In the account, Gilgamesh is told by the immortal Utnapishtim, the survivor of the flood, that there is a sea plant that can rejuvenate his life. Gilgamesh finds the plant, but, unfortunately, while swimming in a pond a snake appears and devours it, thereby depriving him of his chance at immortality (see *ANET*, 96).

102. For נָחַשׁ, see Gen 30:27; 44:5, 15; Lev 19:26; Deut 18:10; 1 Kgs 17:17; 20:3; 21:6; 2 Chr 33:6; for נַחַשׁ, see Num 23:23; 24:1. Interestingly, Ancient Near Eastern divination formulae often employed incantations involving serpents (see Joines, *Symbolism*, 22).

103. Hartman, "Sin," 39–40.

104. Westermann, *Genesis*, 1:73.

105. See Num 21:6.

106. See Job 26:12–14; Isa 27:1.

107. See Num 21:4–9.

108. See, e.g., Gen 49:17; Exod 4:3; Num 21:6; Isa 14:29; 27:1; Jer 8:17; Amos 9:3. Moberly points out that one of the notable marks of a transformed world according to

snake is designated, i.e., "crafty," most certainly turns a dark shade in the light of the nefarious context. Emmrich appropriately asks: "How would the Israelite audience react to the tempter's questioning of God's command, which gives expression to the snake's craftiness?"[109] For these reasons, then, the Jew would likely have been leery of this new character in the story. For a Hebrew, an animal more likely than a snake to seduce and lead the first couple away from their creator could hardly be imagined.

The snake is further described as a "wild animal that the LORD God had made." The fact that it owes its existence to God removes any notion in the primordial saga of a competing dualism.[110] Furthermore, being a beast of the field, "it is not outside the circle of those already mentioned in the narrative; it is one among the animals created by God."[111] This latter fact has led some to disassociate any supernatural or demonic elements from the snake.[112] Yet the preposition /מ in some sense marks the serpent out from the group. Although it can be rendered as a comparative,[113] or as a superlative,[114] the preposition might be best understood as a partitive: "subtle as none other of the beasts."[115] In favor of this rendering is the use of /מ in 3:14: אָרוּר אַתָּה מִכָּל־הַבְּהֵמָה וּמִכֹּל חַיַּת הַשָּׂדֶה. Since it is the snake that is cursed in v. 14 rather than the other animals, the comparative and superlative notions would seem to be inappropriate here. Reading /מ as a partitive in v. 1, then, would suggest that the serpent was not totally within the circle of those already mentioned in the narrative. Distinguished by a certain craftiness, this particular creature is, it would seem, in a class by itself.[116]

---

Isa 8:11 is the absence of such enmity ("Serpent," 13).

109. Emmrich, "Temptation Narrative," 12.

110. Hamilton notes that "Genesis 1–3 makes no room for the idea that in the beginning there were two" (*Genesis*, 1:188; see also Gruenthaner, "Demonology," 8–9).

111. Westermann, *Genesis*, 1:239; see also Zimmerli, *1. Mose*, 1:163. This depiction is maintained throughout the account (see v. 14).

112. Brueggemann writes: "It is not a phallic symbol or satan or a principle of evil or death" (*Genesis*, 47). Sarna similarly argues that "the serpent is here reduced to an insignificant, demythologized stature. It possesses no occult powers. It is not demonic, only extraordinarily shrewd" (*Genesis*, 24).

113. As in the ESV, NIV, NRSV.

114. *IBHS* §14.5d.

115. GKC §119w; see also BDB 582.

116. See Sailhamer, "Genesis," 2:50.

It is hard from the narrative alone, however, to arrive at any specificity beyond this.[117] Late Jewish and early Christian interpretation, of course, associated the snake with the devil.[118] While this view is a legitimate extension of the relationship between the serpent and temptation,[119] the narrative itself does not make such an association.[120] Nevertheless, it is hard to see nothing more than an animal, albeit a shrewd one.[121] There is something nefarious here. The serpent not only speaks and is cognitive (and perhaps privy to hidden knowledge) but is adversarial towards God and humans alike.[122] A possible clue, we believe, to the serpent's identification is found in Gen 4:7: "If you do well, will you not be accepted? And if you do not do well, sin is lurking at the door; its desire is for you, but you must master it."[123] In the passage, *sin* (הַטָּאת) is personified, if not

117. A common view, repackaged by Ruppert (*Genesis*, 146), that the snake was included into the narrative in Solomonic times as a polemic against Egyptian or Canaanite snake cults is purely speculative. There appears to be no indication in the text, nor between the lines, that the narrator is taking such a shot. To the contrary, in this *primeval* saga, whose perspective is more worldwide (see Westermann, *Genesis*, 1:5), a more rudimentary evil appears to be in view, whose function in the account is to progress the plot of the story (see Brueggemann, *Genesis*, 47).

118. Wis 2:24 is usually cited as the first extant identification of the devil and the garden snake. An earlier identification may be detected in *1 En*. 69:6, where the seduction of Eve is ascribed to a fallen angel called Gader'el (see also *2 En*. 31:3-6; *3 Bar*. 4:8; *Apoc. Mos*. 16:1-5; 17:4; *Pss. Sol*. 4:9). An identification of the serpent with the devil is found at the outset in Christianity (see John 8:44; Rom 16:20; 2 Cor 11:3; 1 John 3:12; Rev 12:9; 20:2).

119. See Skinner, *Genesis*, 73; Fretheim, "Genesis," 1:360.

120. Westermann lays out four main interpretative options: 1) The serpent is Satan in disguise; 2) the serpent is purely symbolical; 3) the serpent is a mythological form; 4) the serpent is merely a clever animal (*Genesis*, 1:237). Cassuto proposes the theory that "the duologue between the serpent and the woman is actually, in a manner of speaking, a duologue that took place in the woman's mind, between her wiliness and her innocence" (*Genesis*, 1:142). Fretheim argues that the serpent *represents* "anything in God's good creation that could present options to human beings, the choice of which can seduce them away from God" ("Genesis," 1:360; see also Cassuto, *Genesis*, 142). More traditionally, Luther sees a literal snake possessed by Satan (see "Genesis," 1:151; see also Calvin, *Genesis*, 139-42).

121. Skinner sees no more than this. The snake, he argues, "is simply a creature of Yahwe distinguished from the rest by his superior subtlety" (*Genesis*, 73; see also Ruppert, *Genesis*, 146).

122. See Gunkel, *Genesis*, 15.

123. The syntax of the verse is notoriously difficult to unravel (for discussions, see Ramaroson, "Gn 4,7," 233-37; van Wolde, "Story," 29-32; Janowski, "Gen 4:1-16," 143-48; Deurloo, "Gen 4,7," 405-6; Wöller, "Gen 4,7," 436; idem, "Gen 4,7," 271-72; Yasher,

personalized,[124] and the depiction of it as an animal lurking and ready to strike is reminiscent of the serpent in 3:1.[125] What makes it likely that the "serpent" of Genesis 3 and "sin" of Genesis 4 are to be linked are the parallels that link the two chapters themselves.[126] Note, for example: 1) Like Adam before the tree of good and evil (Gen 2:17), Cain stands at a moral intersection in 4:7 between the doing or not doing of *good* (טוב). 2) The closing words of 4:7 (וְאֵלֶיךָ תְּשׁוּקָתוֹ וְאַתָּה תִּמְשָׁל־בּוֹ) bear an unmistakable resemblance to God's words to Eve in 3:16 (וְאֶל־אִישֵׁךְ תְּשׁוּקָתֵךְ וְהוּא יִמְשָׁל־בָּךְ). 3) God's question "*Where* is your brother Abel?" (4:9) recalls his earlier question "*Where* are you?" (3:9). 4) The question "*What* have you done?" (4:10) recalls "*What* is this that you have done?" (3:13). 5) Both Adam and Cain provoke God's *curse* (3:17; 4:11). 6) Both Adam and Cain are *driven* from God's presence (3:24; 4:14). 7) Both Adam and Cain settle to the *east of Eden* (3:24; 4:16). Other parallels abound.[127] Hauser concludes

---

"Gen 4,7," 635–37). Nevertheless, in the end, the major English versions render the clause in question similarly: "sin lieth at the door" (AV); "sin is lurking at the door" (NRSV); "sin is crouching at the door" (ESV, NET, NASB, NJB, NIV). The RL likewise translates, "so lauert die Sünde vor der Tür."

124. While הַטָּאת is feminine, רֹבֵץ and אַתָּה are masculine.

125. The verb רָבַץ is used in Ezek 29:3 of a sea serpent (/תַּנִּי, δράκων LXX) lying in the river. Some commentators see an allusion in Gen 4:7 to the Mesopotamian demon *rābiṣu* that was thought to lie in wait near the threshold to ambush its victim (see van der Toorn, Becking, and van der Horst, *Dictionary*, 682–83).

126. See Hauser, "Links," 297–305.

127. Hauser, who has done a careful analysis of Genesis 2–3 and Gen 4:1–16, argues that the story of Cain and Abel is *structurally, linguistically,* and *thematically* interwoven with the Fall narrative. He suggests the following parallels: 1) *Structural*: a) a description of the functions performed by the principal characters [e.g., tilling the ground, keeping of sheep, etc.]; b) an interplay between the two human figures whose originally harmonious relations are disrupted; c) a warning from God before the transgression and offense is committed; d) an exchange in which God confronts the guilty parties with their deed; e) a pronouncement of a sentence; f) the removal of the guilty parties from God's presence; g) the subsequent dwelling of the offenders east of Eden. 2) *Linguistic*: a) the use of "know" in 4:1 and 3:5-6, 7; b) the use in 4:1 of "conceive" and "bear," which echo the sentence pronounced in Gen 3:16; c) the name "Abel," i.e., "fleeting breath, in 4:2 in contrast to "breath of life" in 2:7; d) the use of "fruit" in 4:3, which evokes 3:2-6; e) the use of "his brother" in 4:2, 8-11 and "his wife"/"the woman" in Genesis 2-3, which express both intimacy and subsequent alienation; f) the use of "driven" in 4:14 as a parallel to its use in 3:24; g) the use of "face" in 4:14 as a parallel to 3:8; 3) *Thematic*: the motif of initial intimacy and subsequent alienation—from God, man, and ground (ibid. 304–5). For other examinations of the links between the two accounts, see Cassuto, *Genesis*, 212, 218, 225, 228; Ruppert, *Genesis*, 1:184–86; van Wolde, "Cain," 25–26; Fishbane, *Texture*, 26–27; Wenin, "Adam," 3–16. Significantly, the Cain story is closely linked in the Targumim with

his detailed analysis of Genesis 2–3 and 4:1–16 by arguing that "the two narratives have been written by one highly-skilled writer who has interwoven all major aspects of the two stories so that structurally, linguistically and thematically they form one unit. Any attempt to interpret the accounts without reference to their unity is likely to obscure and distort what the writer intended to say."[128] Such associations, then, between the Fall narrative and the Cain and Abel account strongly suggest that the tempter of Gen 3:1 is none other than the tempter of Gen 4:7.[129] If so,

---

Adam's fall. This is so much the case that in the Neofiti Targum, the Targum Yerushalmi (Geniza fragment), and the Fragmentary Targum (Second Jerusalem Targum) Cain's murder of Abel is virtually seen as a *fall* or, perhaps, *the* Fall, in and of itself (see Vermes, *Studies*, 104–5). Note, e.g., *Tg. Neof.* Gen 4:16; *Tg. Onq.* 4:16; *Tg. Ps.-J* 4:16). Some modern Jewish theology continues to identify Genesis 4 as the point at which the Fall occurred (see, e.g., Novak, *Natural Law*, 31–36).

128. Hauser, "Linguistic and Thematic Links," 305.

129. Wénin argues that the animal that tempts Cain with envy in Gen 4:7 "n'est autre que 'la semence ou l'engeance du serpent'" ("Genèse 1–4," 12). Regarding 4:7, Fishbane writes: "This image of sin recalls Genesis 3; coiled now at the root of Cain's will, the serpent is in external enmity with man, as was foretold (3:15)" (*Texture*, 26). Mangan, noting in 4:7 the use of masculine pronouns though "sin" is feminine, also perceives a reference here to the serpent of Genesis 3 ("Genesis 4:7," 92; for similar linkings of the "serpent" in Gen 3 with "sin" in Gen 4, see Ramaroson, "Gn 4,7," 236 n. 4; Zimmerli, *1. Mose*, 1:214; Ruppert, *Genesis*, 1:199). Duhm, perceiving an association between the "moralisch böses Wesen" in 4:7 and the serpent of 3:1, even postulates that in earlier versions, רב occupied the place of the serpent in 3:1 (*Geister*, 10 n. 1). A possible early identification of the serpent of 3:1 with the tempter of 4:7 is found in *Apoc. Ab.* 24:5: "And I saw, as it were, Adam, and Eve who was with him, and with them the crafty adversary and Cain, who had been led by the adversary to break the law" (*OTP* 1:701). Note also 1 John 3:12, which places the devil on the scene in Genesis 4.

the narrator associates the snake with *sin*,[130] and, without any etiological explanation,[131] he places *sin* in the primeval garden prior to the Fall.[132]

## The Serpent's Seduction of Eve

What now follows is the first dialogue recorded in Scripture,[133] and the topic is God's *commandment*:

> ¹ᵇ He said to the woman, "Did God say, 'You shall not eat from any tree in the garden'?"

The serpent leads by making an insinuation regarding God's words to Adam. The appellation אֱלֹהִים rather than יְהוָה אֱלֹהִים, which is characteristic of Genesis 2–3, appears to distance the creator from Eve,[134] and the

---

130. It is likely, then, that we see here in the Garden narrative an instance where the author may be alluding to a reality behind the symbol. Yet, the allusion to *sin* in Gen 3:1 is as misty as the garden itself and as elusive as the serpent (Wenin concedes that the nature of the parallel between the serpent in Genesis 3 and sin in Genesis 4 "ne saute pas aux yeux" ["Genèse 1–4," 5]). It appears that the first couple, as we learn from Gen 4:7, is in reality being tempted by *sin*, but the story teller pictures this in terms of being beguiled by a *snake*. This opens the possibility, though not the necessity, that other elements in the narrative are likewise figurative, e.g., the two trees, the partaking of their fruit, the fig leaves, etc.

131. The presence of sin at 3:1 apparently assumes that something bad had penetrated God's "good" creation. The account, nonetheless, contains no etiology of the origin of evil itself. Zimmerli notes: "Die Verführung . . . steht als etwas absolut Unerklärtes unversehens da inmitten der guten Schöpfung Gottes. Sie wird als Rätsel stehen gelassen" (*1. Mose*, 163; see also Westermann, *Genesis*, 1:239; von Rad, *Genesis*, 87–88; Moberly, "Serpent," 24–25). Calvin argues that the narrator's object is not Satan's fall but that of man (see Calvin, *Genesis*, 142).

132. See above, pp. 118–20.

133. Bonhoeffer calls this "the first conversation about God" (*Creation*, 70). Brueggemann adds that theological talk "which seeks to analyze and objectify matters of faithfulness is dangerous enterprise. . . . This is not speech *to* God or *with* God, but *about* God. God has been objectified. The serpent is the first in the Bible to seem knowing and critical about God and to practice *theology* in the place of *obedience*" (*Genesis*, 47–48).

134. Ibn Ezra claims that the serpent did not utter God's personal name because the Tetragrammaton was unknown to him (*Genesis*, 67). This conjecture, however, is doubtful. The account reveals that the serpent was anything but ill-informed. Wenham suggests that the absence of the appellation reveals the distance that exists between God and the serpent: "God is just the remote creator, not Yahweh, Israel's covenant partner" (*Genesis*, 1:73). Westermann similarly perceives that יְהוָה "belongs only to the context of the relation of humans to God" (*Genesis*, 1:239). Skinner, to the contrary, doubts that any such significance can be discerned since he detects no uniform patterns of usage in

terms אַף כִּי and מִכֹּל עֵץ הַגָּן/ seem to convey a sympathetic sense of shock and surprise at such restrictiveness on God's part.[135] Yet the statement is a distortion of God's original generous permission (2:16) and illustrates the serpent's craftiness. Whether or not it is significant that the snake uses אָמַר rather than צִוָּה in reference to the prohibition,[136] it appears clear

---

Genesis (*Genesis*, 74, see e.g., Gen 4:25). Yet, the full designation is a hallmark of Genesis 2–3, and it appears as recently as 3:1a. Its absence, therefore, appears to be significant. If the snake is insinuating that God is uncaring, the omission of his personal name would be a natural corollary (see Moberly, "Serpent," 6).

135. The words אַף כִּי are the first words spoken by the serpent. Immediately the reader is confronted by ambiguity, which will be a typical ploy of the snake (Drewermann, indeed, suggests the notion of "Doppeldeutigkeit" is inherent in the term עָרוּם itself, which is applied to the serpent [*Strukturen*, 54]). The phrase, which occurs 19 times in the Old Testament, is difficult since there exists no exact parallel for its use here. The words are exclusively used to introduce the second half of an argument (see 1 Sam 14:30; 2 Sam 4:11; 1 Kgs 8:27; 2 Chr 6:18; 32:15; Neh 9:18; Job 9:14; 15:16; 25:6; 35:14; Prov 11:31;15:11; 17:7; 19:7, 10; 21:27; Ezek 14:21; 15:5). Only in Gen 3:1 does the phrase introduce a new thought. The compound generally means "how much more/less," "not to mention," etc. (see, e.g., 1 Sam 14:30; 1 Kgs 8:27; Prov 11:31). This could be the sense here if it is assumed that some previous conversation took place (see Ibn Ezra, *Genesis*, 66–67; Dillmann, *Genesis*, 1:150). This conjecture, though, appears unwarranted. The opening words וְהַנָּחָשׁ הָיָה indicate that a new section of the narrative has begun, not that a previous section has resumed (see Cassuto, *Genesis*, 143; Skinner, *Genesis*, 73 n. 1). Luther detects bitter sarcasm: "I cannot translate the Hebrew either in German or in Latin; the serpent uses the word *aph-ki* as though to turn up its nose and jeer and scoff at one" (quoted by von Rad, *Genesis*, 86). This is a possible translation, yet it seems too brazen for the subtleties otherwise employed by the reptile. If, as understood by the LXX (τί ὅτι), numerous scholars (e.g., Savran, *Telling*, 63; Moberly, "Serpent," 5–6; Westermann, *Genesis*, 1:239), and all major English versions, the phrase functions to introduce a question, this would be the only time in Scripture that the words carry an interrogative force (on אַף כִּי as an interrogative, see BDB 65a; Joüon, 157aN). *BHS* proposes the addition of the interrogative ה, thus הַאַף, and Cassuto retains the question by regarding כִּי as the interrogative after the analogy of Isa 54:6 with אַף employed for emphasis in accord with Gen 18:13 (*Genesis*, 1:144). Mathews responds, however, that there is no need for such emendations and conjectures. Intonation alone, he argues, is a sufficient explanation since for yes/no questions there is no need for the interrogative (*Genesis*, 235; see *IBHS* § 40.3.b). This may be true, but the clever manner in which the statement is phrased leaves no room for a simple yes or no response. Speiser, thus, suggests that "the serpent is not asking a question; he is deliberately distorting a fact" (*Genesis*, 23). With such an interpretive log jam, perhaps it is best to consider the statement to be "a half-interrogative, half-reflective exclamation" (Skinner, *Genesis*, 73; see also Delitzsch, *Genesis*, 1:147). What is clear is that the serpent leads with a deceptive innuendo. The first words out of serpent's mouth are meant to cast a web of doubt around God's intentions in issuing the prohibition (see Emmrich, "Temptation Narrative," 13).

136. Though אָמַר can connote a command (see, e.g., Exod 8:27; 2 Chr 14:4; 31:4;

that he purposefully inverts the permission and prohibition and shifts the negative injunction. Thus, God's words "you may freely eat of every tree of the garden" are now in the mouth of the serpent: "you shall not eat from any tree in the garden"[137] By this crafty recontextualization, the snake "ingratiates itself through pretended sympathy and sows mistrust and suspicion toward God in the heart of the unsuspecting wife."[138] In addition, and more importantly, the misrepresentation, cleverly dangled before Eve, lures her into a discussion about the prohibition.[139] The innuendo cannot be replied to with a simple yes or no.[140] Indeed, the woman's attention now cannot help but be drawn to the forbidden tree.[141] Thus, "naïvement," observes Hinschberger, "la femme mord à l'hameçon."[142]

The next two verses, which contain Eve's response to the snake, are linked to each other in the same manner as 2:16 is to 2:17, i.e., a prohibition follows upon a permission:

> ² The woman said to the serpent, "We may eat of the fruit of the trees in the garden; ³ but God said, 'You shall not eat of the fruit of the tree that is in the middle of the garden, nor shall you touch it, or you shall die.'"

In her response Eve, attempts to correct the snake. Many commentators, however, argue that in doing so she makes misrepresentations and exaggerations as the snake had done, though not with the same mali-

---

Job 9:7; 36:10; ), it may be telling that the snake changes the original verb "command" to "say." What was first *commanded* is now merely *spoken* (see Craig, "Misspeaking," 240; Jacob, *Genesis*, 103–4). God will return to the verb "command" in 3:11, 17.

137. See Craig, "Misspeaking," 240. The negative at the beginning of the serpent's citation along with the "any" at the end expresses an *absolute* prohibition (GKC §152b). Noticeably absent is the emphatic "freely" conveyed by the infinitive absolute in Gen 2:16, and the clause /מִכֹּל עֵץ הַגָּן which appears at the end of the sentence rather than at the head as in 2:16, appears to be another deceptive ploy on the serpent's part to obscure God's liberality (see Emmrich, "Temptation Narrative," 13; Matthews, *Genesis*, 235).

138. Gunkel, *Genesis*, 16; see also Moberly, "Serpent," 6.

139. Zimmerli comments: "Das ist die Raffiniertheit des Versuchers, daß er der Frau zunächst einmal Gelegenheit gibt, recht zu haben und sich für Gott zu wehren. Wer möchte night gerne recht haben!" (1. Mose, 1:153; see also Westermann, *Genesis*, 1:239; Hamilton, *Genesis*, 1:189; von Rad, *Genesis*, 88; Kidner, *Genesis*, 67; Skinner, *Genesis*).

140. See Trible, *Sexuality*, 109.

141. See Zimmerli, *1. Mose*, 1:154; Emmrich, "Temptation Narrative," 14.

142. Hinschberger, "Synchronique," 6.

ciousness.¹⁴³ Indeed, her phrasing may even imply that she has begun to drift from God. A number of features contained in Eve's reply might appear to support these conclusions. First, by omitting "any" and "freely," elements are missing that placed the prohibition in a context of liberality. Wenham remarks that "the creator's generosity is not being given its full due, and he is being painted as a little harsh and repressive."¹⁴⁴ Second, the woman refers to the deity merely as "God," as the serpent had done. This may suggest that she is already edging away from the Lord.¹⁴⁵ Third, she identifies the tree according to its location rather than by its name or significance. Cassuto surmises that Eve is particularly grieved that such a "special tree in a special location" is off limits.¹⁴⁶ Fourth, the woman adds the phrase "nor shall you touch it."¹⁴⁷ This might suggest that she was consciously or unconsciously exaggerating the strictness of God.¹⁴⁸ Fifth, like

143. "While the command of God is being discussed," notes Westermann, "it is altered in the very act of defending it" (*Genesis*, 1:239; see also Waltke, *Genesis*, 91; Wenham, *Genesis*, 1:73; Hamilton, *Genesis*, 1:189; von Rad, *Genesis*, 88; Kidner, *Genesis*, 67–8).

144. Wenham, *Genesis*, 73.

145. Trible suggests that using the general appellation establishes "that distance which characterizes objectivity and invites disobedience" (*Sexuality*, 109; see also Brandscheidt, "Mensch," 6–7).

146. Cassuto, *Genesis*, 144. Cassuto notes that though there was in the center of the garden also the tree of life, "her interest is focused at the moment on the *forbidden tree*, and for her it is *the tree*—with the definite article—in the center of the garden" (ibid., 145).

147. Sarna suggests that the woman may be merely repeating what Adam had told her (*Genesis*, 24). Townsend perceives nothing inappropriate in Eve's words. After suggesting that the verse be read within the context of the Levitical uncleanness codes, he argues that Eve considered the fruit of the tree to be unclean and therefore unlawful to be touched (see Townsend, "Eve's Answer," 399–420). Cassuto argues (based on Gen 20:6 and 26:11) that the verb נגע often has a graver connotation than mere touching. The clause "neither shall you touch it" would merely be synonymous with "you shall not eat the fruit" (*Genesis*, 145). Hinschberger associates Eve's concern about touching the tree with her concern not to die; she would naturally avoid any contact that would place her life in jeopardy ("Synchronique," 6). Trible and others see the embellishment as an indication of Eve's faithfulness: "The woman 'builds a fence around the Torah,' a procedure that her rabbinical successors developed fully to protect the law of God and to insure obedience to it" (*Sexuality*, 110; see also Moberly, "Serpent," 7). This is possible, though the Talmud and most rabbis, in point of fact, explicitly denied Eve's was a valid "preventative fence" around the commandment since she attributed the prohibition against touching the tree *to God*. It would thus not be *her* fence, but *God's* commandment. Rabbinical commentators, therefore, generally perceived Eve to have inappropriately added to the word of God (see Zlotowitz and Scherman, *Bereishis*, 116).

148. There is no suggestion in the text that would warrant Lapide's attraction to the

the serpent, Eve's uses אָמַר rather than צִוָּה in reference to the prohibition. It might appear that the serpent had successfully moved the woman's understanding of the prohibition away from the idea of a commandment.[149] Finally, the way in which she expresses the warning, "or you shall die" (פֶּן־תְּמֻתוּן/), seems to fall short of the urgency and certainty of the original phrase, "you will *surely* die" (מוֹת תָּמוּת). The Hebrew phrasing here implies for Calvin that Eve is beginning to waver; "her perception of the true danger of death was distant and cold."[150]

These variations may or may not suggest that the woman has at this point moved towards the serpent's attitude. Interpreters, in fact, may be reading too much into her words.[151] Her expressions, rather, may be sincere and reflect God's intention concerning the forbidden tree.[152] Indeed, with the exception of the phrase פֶּן־תְּמֻתוּן/, which provides the snake with the keynote for his second speech,[153] none of her statements or embellishments appears to play a part in the subsequent narrative, and the fact that some of the ancient versions tended to assimilate the woman's wording in 3:2 to the wording of 2:16 would suggest that the early translators, at least, were unaware of any particular significance in her words.[154]

What *is* significant, however, is the way in which the serpent has succeeded in drawing Eve into a discussion about the prohibition and especially the consequence of disobeying it.[155] This makes her vulnerable

---

theory that the serpent successfully induced Eve into *touching* the tree to prove to her that there was no immediate danger (see "Touching," 43). Sarna concludes that however her words are explained, Eve "introduces into her own mind the suggestion of an unreasonably strict God" (*Genesis*, 24). Kidner ruefully adds that "she was to have many successors" (*Genesis*, 68). For even graver assessments of Eve's frame of mind at this stage in the account, see Knight, *Genesis*, 36; Stigers, *Genesis*, 74; Steck, *Paradieserzählung*, 103; Vawter, *Genesis*, 78.

149. See Savran, *Telling*, 133 n. 65.

150. Calvin, *Genesis*, 149.

151. Stigers, Vawter, Steck, and Knight even impute "resentment" or "exasperation" at this point to Eve (for references, see n. 148, above). This, as Townshend notes, may be going too far ("Eve's Answer," 401).

152. Blocher sees Eve taking liberties in her paraphrase but sees no definite misrepresentation of the commandment on her part (*In the Beginning*, 144–45). To greater or lesser degrees Eve's initial response is also viewed positively by Calvin, Cassuto, Trible, Fretheim, Walsh, Townshend, Bonhoeffer, and Gunkel. See n. 147, above.

153. See Walsh, "Synchronic," 165.

154. See Moberly, "Serpent," 6 n. 13. For variants in the versions at 2:16, see *BHS*.

155. See Savran, *Telling*, 64.

to his surrejoinder.¹⁵⁶ Rather than refusing to engage in dialogue with the serpent, she presents it with a "point of attack,"¹⁵⁷ and he strikes:

> ⁴ But the serpent said to the woman, "You will not die; ⁵ for God knows that when you eat of it your eyes will be opened, and you will be like God, knowing good and evil."

While the serpent began the dialogue with an insinuation that feigned curiosity and surprise, he here makes bold assertions that reveal that he is more dogmatic than Eve was originally led to believe. The snake's statements, though, are laden with ambiguities. Is he negating the commandment of 2:17 or Eve's rendition of it?¹⁵⁸ Is he telling the truth or uttering blatant lies?¹⁵⁹ Should אֱלֹהִים in 3:5b be interpreted as a singular

---

156. "Satan now springs more boldly forward," writes Calvin, "and because he sees a breach open before him, he breaks through in a direct assault" (*Genesis*, 149). Luther comments that the serpent observes that Eve has begun to totter, and "he now exerts himself with his utmost power, as though against a leaning wall, in order to overwhelm her altogether" ("Genesis," 1:155). Brueggemann similarly perceives a downward slide: "By then the misquotation [by the serpent] has opened up to consciousness the possibility of an alternative to the way of God. From that point on, things become distorted" (*Genesis*, 48). "One who defends a command," observes Westermann, "can already be on the way to breaking it" (*Genesis*, 1:239-40).

157. *Angriffsfläche*, Zimmerli, *1. Mose*, 1:154.

158. The serpent's words are: /לֹא מוֹת תְּמֻתוּן. According to GKC §113v, the normal order is for the negative לֹא to appear between the infinitive absolute and the finite verb, not before both verbs as here (see also Joüon, §123.0). The exception to this norm occurs only in Gen 3:4; Ps 49:8; Amos 9:8. The significance, according to GKC, is that the clause here is negating the threat pronounced in Gen 2:17 since it contains the same words as there (מוֹת תָּמוּת). Cassuto notes, however, that the words are in fact not the same; the verb in 2:17 is singular, while in 3:4 it is plural (*Genesis*, 145; see also Skinner, *Genesis*, 74 n. 4). Cassuto takes the phrase as a denial of Eve's statement (/פֶּן־תְּמֻתוּן), which does contain the plural form and is only a verse away. Perhaps it is best to see 3:4 as the immediate antithesis to 3:3, though 2:17 is, of course, at issue. The question remains, however, exactly how the phrase is to be understood; does it mean "You certainly will not die!" or "It is not certain that you will die"? Vawter argues for the former (*Genesis*, 78). Roth argues for the latter ("Double-Meaning," 245–54). Eve perhaps could have understood it either way. In any case, the divine threat was being minimized.

159. The snake appears to be launching a bald challenge, i.e., "a direct frontal attack on God's earlier threat" (Hamilton, *Genesis*, 1:189), "an open challenge of the divine veracity" (Skinner, *Genesis*, 74), "a flat contradiction" (Kidner, *Genesis*, 68). But it may be more subtle than this. In keeping with his craftiness, the snake was likely uttering half truths, i.e., speaking only of gains and not losses (see Fretheim, "Genesis," 1:361). The couple did not suffer immediate death, but they were denied access to life; and their eyes were indeed opened, but they saw only their nakedness; and they did become like God in that they had a heightened sense of moral awareness, but it came at the expense of

or plural?¹⁶⁰ And, a question previously encountered, what exactly does it mean in the account to *know* good and evil? Though answers to these questions do not come easily, if at all, there may be an inherent significance to the ambiguities. Since the whole tenor of the serpent's speech is marked by cleverness,¹⁶¹ it might be expected that he would now speak in double-entendres rather than launch direct challenges to God's veracity.¹⁶² Such ambiguity could prove deadly, as Steck notes: "With tiny shifts of accent, with half-truth and double meaning, it can bring the unsuspecting partner to the point when she joins in and acts of her own volition, which is precisely what is intended."¹⁶³

In spite of the mist of ambiguities, the reader can clearly see the snake's strategy—to lure the woman into partaking of the fruit by inciting within her a *desire* for what is forbidden. He attempts this by impugning the motivation behind the prohibition; God issued the command with his own interests in mind, not theirs.¹⁶⁴ To be precise, God was keeping back from them and had not told them the whole truth. Indeed, he was jealous of them becoming his equals.¹⁶⁵ The serpent's shrewdness reaches

---

separation from him. Wenham catches the irony: "The snake's promises have come true but in a very different way from the way one might have expected, had they come from God" (*Genesis*, 1:74).

160. The plural may be used not only for "God," but also for "gods," as the LXX renders the term here: καὶ ἔσεσθε ὡς θεοὶ γινώσκοντες καλὸν καὶ πονηρόν. Verse 22 supports the plural, if it is taken of the angelic host. Yet, the speaker there is God. While the plural יֹדְעֵי would seem to be decisive (see Sarna, *Genesis*, 25), the singular can be retained if the participle is predicative: "You will be as God, *that is*, you shall know good and evil" (Hamilton, *Genesis*, 1:189; *IBHS* §37.6a indicates, however, that the subject is usually explicitly expressed in such constructions). In favor of taking the term as a singular is the implausibility that the term *God* would be used differently in the same verse (see Cassuto, *Genesis*, 146–47). However, this too is inconclusive. As noted, the serpent's words are elusive.

161. Recall the misrepresentation and exaggeration met in 3:1.

162. See Vawter, *Genesis*, 78; Mathews, *Genesis*, 236 n. 183; Gowan, *Genesis 1–11*, 54.

163. Quoted in von Rad, *Genesis*, 90.

164. Gunkel contends that φθονερὸν τὸ θεῖον was a wide-spread idea in Greek thought (*Genesis*, 17; see also von Rad, *Genesis*, 88). Perhaps so, but it would have no bearing on the Hebrew Genesis account. More relevant to the narrative is the irony that the snake implies that God was holding back good from the couple when it had been a central theme of chapters 1 and 2 that God will provide good if they would only trust him (see Sailhamer, "Genesis," 2:51).

165. Von Rad correctly asserts: "What the serpent's insinuation means is the possibil-

the high water mark here. He appears not as a deceiver, but as a *truth-teller*.¹⁶⁶ And there is no coercion. Indeed, the serpent never explicitly invites the woman to eat of the tree. By merely broaching the issue, he seduces her into focusing on what is forbidden and why it is forbidden in order to lead her to partake of what is forbidden.¹⁶⁷ That this indeed was his strategy and that he accomplished his aims is evident in what follows.¹⁶⁸

## The Transgression of the Commandment

The narrative now reaches its climax. There are no words spoken, only the woman standing before the tree in contemplation. The serpent, now silent, leaves "the fascination of sense to do the rest."¹⁶⁹

> ⁶ So when the woman saw that the tree was good for food, and that it was a delight to the eyes, and that the tree was to be desired to make one wise, she took of its fruit and ate; and she also gave some to her husband, who was with her, and he ate.

That the woman observed the tree to be "good for food" and "a delight to the eyes" indicates that the forbidden tree had become like the other trees to her.¹⁷⁰ That the tree was a source of wisdom, however, marks

---

ity of an extension of human existence beyond the limits set for it by God at creation, an increase of life not only in the sense of pure intellectual enrichment but also of familiarity with, and power over, mysteries that lie beyond man" (*Genesis*, 89). To "have their eyes opened" is a metaphor suggesting a newfound acquisition of awareness not previously possessed, i.e., "to see what was up to then not there" (Westermann, *Genesis*, 1:240; see, e.g., Gen 21:19; Num 22:31; 2 Kgs 6:17, 20). Sarna adds that this would entail the capacity for reflection that allows one to make decisions independently of God (*Genesis*, 25).

166. See Fretheim, "Genesis," 1:361; Zimmerli, *1. Mose*, 1:156.

167. See Gunkel, *Genesis*, 17. "Dabei," writes Ruppert, "stiert sie, *durch die Schlange erst aufmerksam gemacht*, auf Gottes Verbot von 2,17" (*Genesis*, 147, italics mine; see also Savran, *Telling*, 64).

168. Craig mourns the downward spiral: "the serpent's interrogative begins a process of moving the woman from answering the elusive question, to doubting God's truthfulness, to desiring the forbidden fruit, to ultimately desiring to be God-like, knowing good and evil" ("Misspeaking," 241).

169. Skinner, *Genesis*, 75. The serpent no longer speaks. Zimmerli soberly notes that there is no need for it to say anything more: "Die Schlange kann jetzt ruhig verstummen. Das Giftkorn keimt" (*1. Mose*, 1:157; see also von Rad, *Genesis*, 90; Steck, *Paradieserzählung*, 104).

170. See Wenham, *Genesis*, 1:75; Fretheim, "Genesis," 1:361.

it out as special.¹⁷¹ The threefold repetition of the particle preposition (לְמַאֲכָל ... לָעֵינַיִם ... לְהַשְׂכִּיל) intensifies and "disperses" the multiple desires welling up within Eve;¹⁷² she is enticed physically, aesthetically, and sapientially.¹⁷³ Furthermore, her desire for the tree is described in language that foreshadows the tenth commandment.¹⁷⁴ She begins to *covet* after what she assumes is being held back from her—divine enlightenment. This becomes the "highest and decisive enticement."¹⁷⁵ That Eve stood before the forbidden tree reflecting on its capacity to impart wisdom indicates that the serpent's words were resonating in her ears. Such a desire for enlightenment was not, apparently, stimulated by sight alone.¹⁷⁶ It is during the discussion about *the commandment* that she develops an appetite for the forbidden fruit.

The account now moves rapidly,¹⁷⁷ and almost anticlimactically: "the woman *saw* ... *took* ... *ate* ... *gave* ... and he *ate*."¹⁷⁸ The sin of the

---

171. The NRSV "desired to make one wise" is preferable to Skinner and Gunkel, who after the analogy of Gen 2:9, translate the Hebrew "desirable to look at." This would assign an unparalleled meaning to שָׂכַל (see Wenham, *Genesis*, 1:75).

172. Beauchamp, *La loi*, 218. Blocher notes that "the temptation played upon the whole range of human desire" (*In the Beginning*, 140).

173. See Trible, "Sexuality," 112.

174. The verb חָמַד in 3:6 occurs in Exod 20:17 and Deut 5:21 (לֹא תַחְמֹד). It is usually translated in the LXX by the term ἐπιθυμέω. LXX 3:6 reads ὡραῖόν ἐστιν τοῦ κατανοῆσαι.

175. Citing 1 John 2:16, "the lust of the flesh and the lust of the eyes and the pride of life," von Rad traces the scale of emotions through which the woman passed, "'Good for food,' that is the coarsely sensual aspect; 'a delight to the eyes,' that is the finer, more aesthetic stimulus; and 'desired to make one wise,' that is the highest and decisive enticement" (*Genesis*, 90).

176. See Zimmerli *1. Mose*, 1:158; Delitzsch, *Genesis*, 1:155; Heinisch, *Genesis*, 121; Skinner, *Genesis*, 75; Jacob, *Genesis*, 25. Whether or not Gen 3:1–5 played an independent literary role prior to the final formation of the text (see Westermann, *Genesis*, 1:195; Drewermann, *Strukturen*, 70), the serpent's dangling of the prohibition before Eve is crucial to the Genesis story line. Without the snake's insinuations regarding the prohibition, the woman would not even be standing before the forbidden tree. "Das Versprechen der Schlange," observes Albertz, "löst v. 6 in der Frau einen übermächtigen Drang aus" ("'Ihr werdet sein wie Gott,'" 20).

177. "Quickly to its sorry resolution" (Brueggemann, *Genesis*, 48).

178. Narratively little, if any, time transpires between Eve's pondering the fruit and her partaking of it. "Perception and flight of imagination," notes Cassuto, "were followed immediately by decision and action" (*Genesis*, 147). It is probably best to conclude with Blocher that Eve's doubt and desiring are not antecedent acts but form part of the first sin (See *Genesis*, 141).

couple is described here with eight Hebrew words that release the tension "in a rush."¹⁷⁹ The first four (three of which are reversing *vav* imperfects) contain six doubled consonants, all of them being voiceless plosives: וַתִּקַּח מִפִּרְיוֹ וַתֹּאכַל וַתִּתֵּן/ גַּם־לְאִישָׁהּ עִמָּהּ וַיֹּאכַל. Walsh notes that the "extremely difficult pronunciation . . . forces a merciless concentration on each word."¹⁸⁰ The fact that the man is depicted as having been with the woman (עִמָּהּ) seems to assume his presence throughout the dialogue.¹⁸¹ This assumption is strengthened throughout by the serpent's use of the plural "you" (vv. 1, 4, 5) and the woman's use of "we" (v. 2). It also accords with the author's depiction in 2:24 of the man cleaving to his wife.¹⁸² In any case, Adam's eating is the determinative act of disobedience; immediately after *he* eats,¹⁸³ the initial consequences of their transgression are described.

## The Aftermath of the Transgression

The immediate results of the Fall are as swift as the transgression itself:¹⁸⁴

> ⁷ Then the eyes of both were opened, and they knew that they were naked; and they sewed fig leaves together and made loincloths for themselves.

The first consequence was the literal fulfillment of the serpent's prediction. The phrase וַתִּפָּקַחְנָה עֵינֵי in 3:7 mirrors וְנִפְקְחוּ עֵינֵיכֶם in 3:5, though,

179. Walsh, "Synchronic," 166.

180. Ibid.

181. Cassuto argues that עִמָּהּ or אֵת occur "as a rule" when a person is said to associate themself in a given action with someone who leads them (*Genesis*, 148). He cites Gen 6:18; 7:7; 13:1. In the case of 3:6, the particle preposition and the flow of the narrative suggests that Adam was present throughout the dialogue. Gunkel, citing the common motif of a woman *seducing* a man (the harlot seducing Eabani, Isis Ra, Delilah Samson) goes too far in assuming that such was the case here (*Genesis*, 17). Though she was, needless to say, of no help to her husband at this point (cf. 2:18, 20), there is no indication that Eve seduced Adam (as von Rad also assumes, *Genesis*, 90). It may be better to conclude with Hamilton (and Paul [1 Tim 2:14]) that Eve's was a sin of initiative, whereas Adam's was a sin of "acquiescence" (*Genesis*, 1:191).

182. See Ruppert, *Genesis*, 152.

183. The LXX reads here ἔφαγεν καὶ ἔδωκεν καὶ τῷ ἀνδρὶ αὐτῆς μετ' αὐτῆς καὶ ἔφαγον. The plural would appear to imply that Eve ate a second time.

184. The connection between action and result appears to be evident in the interplay between תַאֲוָה in v. 6 and תְאֵנָה in v. 7.

notes Soggin, "in einer fast karikaturhaften Weise."[185] The irony would be comical, if it were not so tragic. Instead of becoming wise, the couple merely becomes aware that they are naked. Here is a "grotesque anticlimax to the dream of enlightenment."[186]

The couple's sudden awareness of their nakedness assumes that they have now attained to the knowledge of good and evil.[187] This is suggested by the use of the verb יֵדַע as well as by the reference to the opening of their eyes, which would imply illumination (see 3:5).[188] Since this enlightenment pertains to the couple's sudden awkwardness over being naked, a sense of shame seems to be the result,[189] if not the essence, of their new found knowledge.[190] That this embarrassment implies a consciousness of guilt and a loss of innocence appears evident from the fear of God that Adam expresses in 3:10, "I heard the sound of you in the garden, and I was afraid, because I was naked; and I hid myself."[191] There is no

---

185. *Genesis*, 84.

186. Kidner, *Genesis*, 69 (see also Williams, "Genesis 3," 277). For Hamilton, "This is hardly the knowledge for which they bargained" (*Genesis*, 1:191).

187. See Steck, *Paradieserzählung*, 104.

188. See Niehr, *TDOT* 11:352–53; Callender, *Adam*, 73 n. 143.

189. Blocher muses: "The narrative does not take up the word 'shame,' but the deliberate contrast between 3:7 and 2:25 suggests it immediately, and it is confirmed by the couple's behavior. For what is shame, other than a feeling of embarrassment which makes us hide?" (*In the Beginning*, 173).

190. The slight move from עָרוֹם in 2:25 to עֵירֹם in 3:7 may be significant in this regard. The latter term, rare in the Old Testament, is distinguished by its use with reference to the exiles who have been punished for their sin (Deut 28:48; Ezek 16:39; 23:29). The word appears to convey the notion of total (and usually shameful) exposure (see BDB 735–36). The effect of the Fall, Sailhamer notes, "was not simply that the man and the woman come to know they were naked (ʿārûm). The effect is rather that they come to know they were naked (ʿărûmmîm) in the sense of being under God's judgment" ("Genesis," 2:49). Niehr notes that the choice of עֵירֹם in 3:7, 10–11 "makes clear the negative connotation of the motif of nakedness" (*TDOT* 11:352). Though nakedness can denote poverty (Job 24:7, 10; 31:19; Ezek 18:16 ) it likely carries here a connotation of guilt. This is evident from the common relation that nakedness bears to guilt in the Old Testament (Hamilton suggests that a connotation of guilt was perhaps suggested by the stripping of slaves and prisoners of war [*Genesis*, 1:181; see 2 Sam 10:4; Jer 13:36; see also Ezek 16:22, 37, 39; 23:29; Hos 2:3; Amos 2:16; Mic 1:8a and from the coupling in Gen 3:7 of nakedness and shame [see Isa 20:4; 47:3; Mic 1:11; Nah 3:5] and in Gen 3:10 of nakedness and fear). Davidson concludes that "the human pair find themselves 'utterly naked,' bereft of the garments of light and glory" ("Theology," 123).

191. See Delitzsch, *Genesis*, 156; Drewermann, *Strukturen*, 79; Calvin, *Genesis*, 158–9. Westermann denies this. He argues that the fear in v. 10 encompasses something

inference here of the male's modesty before the female;[192] there is only fear and dread before God.[193] The response of the couple to their nakedness is a self-protective and, perhaps, self-atoning, attempt to cover their shame.[194] Why they choose fig leaves to cover themselves is unclear.[195]

---

much broader and more basic than the consciousness of sin or guilt. Rather, it is the couple's fear, i.e., "shame," of having their nakedness unmasked before God (*Genesis*, 1:253–54; see also idem, *Creation*, 94–95). The weakness of this interpretation is the lack of lexical support for "fear" being a synonym of "shame." It is more natural to interpret the couple's fear as the anxiety that resulted from their guilt, i.e., "just as the child who has transgressed his father's commandment" (Gunkel, *Genesis*, 19; see a similar scene in Gen 18:15). Nevertheless, Westermann is certainly correct to stress that the situation becomes *different* at 3:7; a dramatic change has clearly taken place (*Genesis*, 1:251; see also Culley, "Action Sequences," 31).

192. Contra Moberly, who deems their making of loincloths in a positive light, i.e., as a result of the couple's new found vision they now possess a pious modesty in the presence of each other and appropriately clothe themselves ("Serpent," 8–9; see also Westermann, *Genesis*, 1:251).

193. This is the first reference to *fear* in the canon. Albertz claims that in the Old Testament *shamelessness*, not *shame*, is equated with sin (see "Ihr werdet sein wie Gott," 20). This may be true (see Lev 18:17; 20:14; Ezek 16:27; etc.). Yet, though the man seems to be experiencing shame (see above, n. 189), he is described here not as being *ashamed*, but as being *afraid*. The latter condition can certainly be indicative in the Old Testament of a bad conscience (see, e.g., Gen 18:15; 43:18, 23; Exod 2:14; Deut 13:11; 17:13; cf. 1 John 4:18; see *NIDOTT* 2:528).

194. The verbs יַעֲשׂוּ and חֲגֹרֹת anticipate 3:21 where God "made" (יַּעַשׂ) "garments" (כָּתְנוֹת) for the couple. The verb עשׂה has been been used up until now of the creative acts of God (occurring eleven times in 1:1–2:4 and again of the creation of Eve [2:18]) and the animals [3:1]). While it is possible that God's clothing of the couple with animal skins is solely meant to meet their immediate need of clothing "in a more permanent way" (Culley, "Action Sequences," 33; see also Walton, *Genesis*, 230; Hamilton, *Genesis*, 1:207; Kidner, *Genesis*, 72), the act may represent something more *salvific* than a concern for physical covering and modesty. Since a connection between animal skins and animal sacrifice can well operate within the ancient pattern that underlies 3:21 (so, Westermann, *Genesis*, 1:270), and noting that the language of the verse is reminiscent of the tabernacle setting (for כָּתֹנֶת, see Exod 28:4, 39–40; 29:5, 8; 39:27; 40:14; Lev 8:7, 13; 10:5; for לבשׁ, see Exod 28:41; 29:5, 8, 30; 40:13–14; Lev 6:3, 3, 4; 8:7, 13; 16:4, 4, 23, 24, 32; 21:10; Num 20:26, 28, note also how Lev 7:8 stipulates that the skin of a sacrificed animal was reserved for the officiating priest), and having concluded that more than mere modesty lies behind the couple's shame, the divine act may also intimate the covering of *guilt* and anticipate the *sacrificial* system itself (see Davidson, "Theology," 123; Keil and Delitzsch, *Pentateuch*, 106; Mathews, *Genesis*, 254–55). In any case, the gesture of personally making garments and clothing for the errant couple would at least seem to demonstrate that God "wishes to remain the God of sinners, for their good and not for their ill" (Blocher, *In the Beginning*, 191).

195. Some rabbinic traditions considered the tree of knowledge to be a fig tree (see Evans, *Paradise Lost*, 45–46).

Since the fig tree produces large leaves, the couple may have chosen them to gain maximum coverage.[196] In any case, the scene concludes with a reversal of the condition depicted in 2:25.[197] Guilt has replaced innocence. Although, in fact, now clothed, the man and woman consider themselves to be utterly naked in the presence of the Lord God, and they flee.[198]

And yet the story does not end here. While the particular scene concludes with the first couple reacting to their newly found vision by hiding, they are sought out, found, and finally expulsed from the garden and from all access to the tree of life (3:22–24). And this brings us full circle back to 2:16–17 and to where our excursion into Eden began. For prior to 2:16–17 and the issuing of the prohibition that threatened death, life language is pervasive. Up until then there are no references to death, whereas allusions to life occur nine times.[199] Indeed, the Fall narrative itself opens in 2:7 with a description of the newly created man as a *living* being. From 2:16–17 on, however, though references to life (through chapter 11) occur eight times,[200] allusions to death occur nineteen times.[201] Clearly 2:16–17 marks a critical and transitional point in the story.

Having now briefly examined the Genesis Fall narrative, it remains to analyze the data. While all the diverse issues encountered in a reading of Genesis 2–3 cannot be discussed in one chapter, the exegetical and theological soundings taken here should be sufficient enough to determine whether or not a match of Paul's catalytic notion of the law can be detected in Eden. The next chapter will dust for prints.

---

196. See Sarna, *Genesis*, 26; Hamilton, *Genesis*, 191. Wenham wonders, however, whether the use of חֲגוֹרָה, which is used elsewhere of a belt (see 1 Kgs 2:5; 2 Kgs 3:21; Isa 3:24), rather than אֵזוֹר, the usual term for a loin cloth, emphasizes the skimpiness of their clothing (*Genesis*, 1:76).

197. The mention of nakedness in 3:7 links the scene to the end of chapter 2, the beginning of chapter 3 (the play between עֲרוּמִּים and עֲרוֹם), and to the end of chapter 3 (3:21). But 3:7 primarily serves to reverse the condition of 2:25 (see Sasson, "Gen 2:25," 420; see also Brueggemann, *Genesis*, 47).

198. See Davidson, "Theology," 123.

199. 1:20, 21, 24, 28, 30, 30; 2:7, 7, 9.

200. 3:20; 6:19; 8:21; 9:3; 10, 12, 15, 16.

201. 2:17; 3:3, 4, 4; 4:8, 14, 23, 25; 5:5, 8, 11, 14, 17, 20, 27, 31; 7:22; 9:29; 11:28, 32.

## EXCURSUS: THE TREE OF THE KNOWLEDGE OF GOOD AND EVIL

While we presented our understanding of the phrase above, we list and briefly evaluate here other common interpretations of "the knowledge of good and evil" in Genesis 2–3:

1. The knowledge of good and evil in the Fall narrative is a *magical* knowledge, i.e., an occultic or mantic knowledge communicated by the tree.[202] Such a dabbling would have been repulsive to God and would explain the expulsion from the garden. God alone is to be the channel of knowledge. Among the arguments in favor of this view, Stordalen offers the following:[203] a) The phrase טוֹבָה אוֹ רָעָה occurs in Num 24:13, a chapter that not only contains the account of Balaam's manticism but contains (in 24:5‑7) a blessing that, some argue, portrays Eden imagery.[204] b) There are, according to Stordalen, numerous references in the Old Testament to cultic trees that communicated insight and knowledge.[205] c) The "cultic trees" in Isa 1:29 (like the tree in Gen 3:6) are characterized as desirable (חמד), and, more importantly, according to Isa 8:19–22,[206] extraordinary knowledge would be conferred by them in times of distress.[207] d) The typical verb

---

202. In a note not appearing in the English editions, Wellhausen remarks, "Es ist freilich möglich, daß Gen. 4 und 11 über den Sinn von Gen. 2.3 nicht entscheidet und daß das den Menschen versagte Wissen dort wenigstens ursprünglich Zauber und Zaubermacht war" (*Prolegomena*, 302). See also Stordalen, *Echoes*, 462–65; Müller, "Erkenntnis," 68–87; Vriezen, *Onderzoek*, 147; Baudissin, *Studien*, 2:227; Lenormant, *Beginnings*, 93–96.

203. See Stordalen, *Echoes*, 462–65.

204. I.e., Num 24:5–7, "How fair are your tents, O Jacob, your encampments, O Israel! 6 Like palm groves that stretch far away, like gardens beside a river, like aloes that the LORD has planted, like cedar trees beside the waters. 7 Water shall flow from his buckets, and his seed shall have abundant water, his king shall be higher than Agag, and his kingdom shall be exalted" (see ibid., 442–43; Eichrodt, *Hoffnung*, 104–5; Zobel, "Bileam," 147; Emmrich, "Temptation Narrative," 5).

205. Stordalen offers the following: Gen 12:6–7; 18:1–16; Judg 6:11–24; Hos 4:11–15a; Isa 57:5 (see *Echoes*, 463, 122–36).

206. Or, rather, according to Stordalen's understanding of Isa 8:19–22 (see ibid. 463).

207. Presumably in the form of necromancy argues Stordalen, if אֱלֹהִים, as in 1 Sam 28:13) denotes ghosts (ibid., 463).

for practicing magic or divination is נַחַשׁ.²⁰⁸ The term נָחָשׁ (serpent) may thus suggest in Gen 3:1 a verbal association to a magical tree.²⁰⁹ e) The mediums are called הַיִּדְּעֹנִים in Lev 19:31. The Eden story, with its motif of "knowledge," could be "punning upon the magic category ידענים."²¹⁰

Though an impressive argument can seemingly be made on behalf of this interpretation, much of the scriptural evidence that Stordalen cites is, upon closer examination, unimpressive. It is far from certain, for example, that the trees to which he alludes (Gen 12:6; 18:1; Hos 6:11; Isa 1:29) are cultic, let alone communicative, nor does burning with lust "under the oaks " (Isa 57:5) or looking "to the earth" (Isa 8:22) imply magical activity.²¹¹ Yet even if these trees were cultic oracles, there is no necessary correlation to Eden here. Furthermore, echoes of Eden in Num 24:5–7 are faint, if audible at all,²¹² and while the mediums in Lev 19:31 are deemed הַיִּדְּעֹנִים, and the tree of Isa 1:29 is considered to be desirable (חמד), these facts need not imply magical qualities in the Paradise tree. The same applies to a possible etymological relation between נַחַשׁ and נָחָשׁ.²¹³ To read magical qualities in the Garden tree may be to read back into the Genesis story a polemic against a tree cult that did not exist in the narrative's world.²¹⁴ It also misses the point that the couple was expelled

---

208. See, e.g., Lev 9:26.

209. Stordalen also points to a possible connection between נָגַד (reveal, report), which is used in connection with tree cult in Hos 4:12, and God asking the couple who told (נָגַד) them they were naked (Gen 3:11). Stordalen suggests that the tree had been rather "revealing" (ibid., 463).

210. Ibid., 464.

211. Hamilton argues that Genesis nowhere says that the Patriarchs engaged in cultic practices among the trees (*Genesis* 1:377).

212. A scan of the comments on Num 24:5–7 by Ashley, Budd, Cole, Milgrom, and Levine turned up only two brief asides in reference to Eden. Levine observes regarding Num 24:6, "In several biblical sources, we read that YHWH or ʾ*Elohim* 'God' plants trees or gardens, like the garden of Eden, for example" (*Numbers*, 2:197). Milgrom, regarding the same verse, comments that the phrase *gardens beside a river* is "a reminder of the Garden of Eden" (*Numbers*, 204). Such insights are hardly significant enough to support an argument that the reference in Num 24:13 to Balaam not being able "to do either good or evil of my own will" is an echo of the Eden narrative that in turn implies magical qualities in the edenic tree.

213. See p. 149, above.

214. Thus Westermann responds, "Such a polemic has its place after the human race has divided itself into peoples and religions; this makes opposition possible. But the uniqueness of the primeval narratives consists in this, they are concerned with the world

from Eden not to prohibit further dabbling with the tree of knowledge but to seal off access to the tree of life.

2. The knowledge associated with the tree is *carnal knowledge*, i.e., the experience of sexual relations.[215] Several arguments are offered in support of this view: a) In Gen 3:7, after the couple partook of the tree, they *knew* (יֵּדְעוּ) they were naked; i.e., they, perhaps, for the first time became *sexually* aware. b) In Gen 4:1, the first reference in the Scriptures to sexual intercourse, the verb יָדַע is used.[216] c) The fertile garden is considered to be suggestive of sexual fertility.[217] d) A corroborating account is said to exist in the Epic of Gilgamesh, where Enkidu acquired wisdom and became like a god after a week of cohabitation with a harlot.[218]

Without responding to each point,[219] there are two inherent difficulties that would seem to make this theory "quite untenable."[220] First, since Gen 3:22 states that the man has become like God, knowing good and evil, this interpretation would seemingly imply that God is a sexual being. Yet, this concept is entirely foreign to the Old Testament delineation of God. Gordis attempts to avoid this problem by asserting that the implied counterpart to human procreation is divine creation and, secondly, by noting that "in primitive thought the gods are always pictured as possessing . . . the sexual appetites and capacities of men."[221] Though the former

---

and its inhabitants before and beyond such divisions" (*Genesis*, 1:244).

215. See Gordis, "Knowledge," 123–38; Coppens, *La Connaissance*, 118–22; Reicke, "Knowledge," 193–201; Bailey, "Initiation," 144–47; Engnell, "'Knowledge,'" 116; Michel, "Ihr werdet sein wie Gott," 63–87.

216. "Now the man knew his wife Eve, and she conceived." See also Gen 4:1; 17, 25; 19:5, 8, 33, 35; 24:16; 38:26; Num 31:17, 18, 35; Judg 11:39; 19:22, 25; 21:11, 12; 1 Sam 1:19; 1 Kgs 1:4.

217. Reicke's contentions are typical on this point, "The scenery is a fertile garden and the forbidden power is deposited in a tree. Comparative anthropology suggests that in such cases one has to do with the idea of vegetation and agricultural fertility which, in ancient civilizations, was associated with human procreation" ("Knowledge," 197).

218. See Gordis, "Knowledge," 134–35. The account can be found in *ANET*, 75.

219. For detailed responses, see Westermann, *Genesis*, 1:242–45; Emmrich, "Temptation Narrative," 7; Mathews, *Genesis*, 204; Kidner, *Genesis*, 63; Stern, "Knowledge," 407–8; Sarna, *Genesis*, 19; Hamilton, *Genesis*, 1:164; Cassuto, *Genesis*, 111; Wenham, *Genesis*, 1:63–64.

220. Westermann, *Genesis*, 1:243.

221. Gordis, "Knowledge," 134.

assertion may be a valid counter-argument, it, as Hamilton notes, seems strained.[222] The latter notion, however, by appealing to a primitive and pagan notion behind the text, would, contrary to a principle that Gordis himself espouses, both "fail to recognize the unity of the biblical text as it has reached us" and "avoid the duty of comprehending its meaning *in its present form*."[223] In other words, while seeking to understand the text as a unity, Gordis's interpretation would amount to pitting contradictory source traditions against each other.[224] A more serious problem with a sexual interpretation, however, appears to be the insurmountable difficulty it has explaining why God would prohibit sexual awareness when the institution of marriage was a part of the divinely ordained order (Gen 1:27–28; 2:25).[225] As Kidner notes, this would imply that "God instituted marriage after forbidding the use of the tree that is said to symbolize it."[226]

3. The knowledge of good and evil in Eden refers to moral or ethical *discernment*, i.e., knowing the difference between right and wrong.[227] This has in its favor 1 Kgs 3:9 and Isa 7:16, where the references to knowing good and evil are likely to be understood in this way. A fundamental problem with this interpretation, however, is that it would imply that Adam lacked a moral capacity to begin with, which would presumably make him unaccountable for violating the divine will.[228] Furthermore, as Gordis notes, it is inconceivable that biblical thought, "with its over-

---

222. See Hamilton, *Genesis*, 164.

223. See Gordis, "Knowledge," 130 n. 27, italics his.

224. See Gispen, *Schepping*, 132–33.

225. This is a point raised by Sapp, "Such a position assumes that sexuality itself occasions shame by its very nature (once one is aware of it). But this suggests that sexuality was *not* part of God's intention for humans in creation," whereas the creation narratives "consider sexuality to be a purposeful part of God's good creation, with no indication whatsoever that sexual experience was jealously withheld from Adam and Eve" (*Sexuality*, 18).

226. Kidner, *Genesis*, 63.

227. See Driver, *Genesis*, 41; Goldingay, *Theology*, 2003), 132–33; Walton, *Genesis*, 170–72; Buchanan, "Good and Evil," 114–20. This sense if attested to in *Tg. Neof.* Gen 2:9, 17; *Tg. Onq.* 2:9; *Tg. Ps-J.* 2:9; 3:5.

228. Hodge ruefully observes, it is unlikely that the knowledge attained consisted of the ability to determine between right and wrong since it would appear that "he had less of that knowledge after than before the fall" (*Theology*, 2:127).

powering moral consciousness," could conceive of God creating humans without a moral sense, "which is the essence of humanity."[229] This view also snags on the quandary that there is no adequate explanation as to why the Lord would have forbidden humans from the acquisition of ethical discernment or exile them from the garden as a result of it.[230]

4. The "knowledge of good and evil" in Genesis 2–3 refers to the knowledge of everything, i.e., *omniscience*. This interpretation understands good and evil as a merism, i.e., a figure of speech where the totality of something is expressed by two constituent parts.[231] Good and evil would thus denote knowledge "in the widest sense."[232] The strength of this view is that it accords with at least some biblical usage,[233] and it explains the prohibition; omniscience is an attribute enjoyed by God alone. Nevertheless, this interpretation also faces difficulties. Not all the occurrences of "good and bad" in the Old Testament are conjunctive (Deut 1:39; Isa 7:15–16; 2 Sam 19:35).[234] It need not be assumed, then, that such is the case in Genesis 2–3. Moreover, the man and woman did not, in fact, acquire unlimited or even "immeasurably expanded" knowledge as a result of eating the fruit.[235] Rather, the narrative presents them as acquiring no more than shame and a recognition of their nakedness (Gen 3:7–8).[236]

---

229. Gordis, "Knowledge," 125; Mathews quips that the man and woman "are in a state of moral innocence, not moral ignorance" (*Genesis*, 204; see also Wenham, *Genesis*, 1:63; Ruppert, *Genesis*, 148).

230. See Michel, "Ihr werdet sein wie Gott," 67; Cassuto, *Genesis I-VI*, 111; Sarna, *Genesis*, 19. Walton, who understands the phrase to denote *mature* discernment, i.e., of one who has passed through adolescence, argues that the couple is not yet *ready* for it; "Autonomy and sexuality should come only at the end of an appropriate process" (*Genesis*, 216). Buchanan, based on 1Q 1.10–11, in which the age when one knows good and evil is said to be twenty years, argues similarly ("Good and Evil," 114–20). This, however, may be going against the sense of the text. The narrative gives no indication to assume that the prohibition against seizing the fruit of the tree was temporary or conditional.

231. See Honeyman, "*Merismus*," 11–18; Krašovec, *Merismus*.

232. Von Rad, *Genesis*, 81; see also Soggin, *Genesis*, 65; Wallace, *Eden*, 128; Callender, *Adam*, 69–70; Harrison, *Introduction*, 556.

233. See, e.g., Gen 24:50; 31:24; 2 Sam 14:17, 20; Jer 42:6; Lam 3:38; Eccl 12:14.

234. See Albertz, "'Ihr werdet sein wie Gott,'" 14–15.

235. Sarna, *Genesis*, 19.

236. See Wenham, *Genesis* 1:63.

5. The knowledge of good and evil in the Fall narrative symbolizes *autonomous wisdom*, i.e., the privilege or power to decide for oneself what is right and wrong.[237] Though Wisdom literature sees the acquisition of knowledge as one of the highest goals of the godly (Prov 3:13; 8:10–11), it is not to be sought independently from the Lord (Prov 2:1–6; 3:3–6; 9:10), and, indeed, there is a wisdom beyond the realm of human comprehension that one should never covet (Job 15:7–9, 40; 28:12–28; 40:1–5; Prov 30:4). For Adam, therefore, the independent pursuit of wisdom or the snatching after divine wisdom would be a bald assertion of human autonomy. Thus Calvin observes, "We now understand what is meant by abstaining from the tree of the knowledge of good and evil; namely, that Adam might not, in attempting one thing or another, rely upon his own prudence; but that cleaving to God alone, he might become wise only by his obedience."[238] More recently Vawter writes, "For the Yahwist the only proper posture of man if he would be truly wise and lead a full life is faith in God and not a professed self-sufficiency of knowledge. It is in this latter acceptation, then, that man is forbidden 'the tree of the knowledge of good and evil.'"[239] Clark arrives at a similar interpretation, though he understands the phrase to have an adjudicatory nuance based on 1 Kgs 3:9 and 2 Sam 14:17. The emphasis in the Genesis narrative, he writes, "is not on the content of knowledge but on man's moral autonomy. Man takes upon himself the responsibility of trying apart from God to determine whether something is good for himself or not."[240] Finally, Blocher concludes that the tree represents "ingratitude and rebellion against God's provision, the absurd pretension to abolish dependence; and the disastrous misuse of the privilege of being freely accountable to God."[241]

---

237. See, e.g., Barth, *Dogmatics* 3.1:284–88; Steck, *Paradieserzählung*, 34–36 n. 43; Wenham, *Genesis*, 1:63; Blocher, *In the Beginning*, 130–34; Westermann, *Genesis*, 1:244–48; Fretheim, "Genesis," 349–50; Moberly, "Serpent," 25; Vawter, *Genesis*, 72–73; Procksch, *Theologie*, 634–65; Hamilton, *Genesis*, 1:165–66; Mathews, *Genesis*, 205–6; Emmrich, "Temptation Narrative," 8; Clines, "Tree," 8–14; Renckens, *Beginning*, 273–77; Buber, *Good and Evil*, 67–80.

238. Calvin, *Genesis*, 118; see also idem., *Institutes*, 2.1.2.

239. Vawter, *Genesis*, 73; see also Cassuto, *Genesis I–VI*, 113.

240. Clark, "Legal Background," 277.

241. Blocher, *In the Beginning*, 133; see also Hamilton, *Genesis*, 1:165–66.

There are strong arguments in favor of this final interpretation: a) There is a growing recognition that features of the garden story bear a resemblance to Wisdom literature and themes.[242] b) This interpretation fits well with the depiction in Gen 3:6 of Eve being lured by the desire to become wise (וְנֶחְמָד הָעֵץ לְהַשְׂכִּיל) and perhaps with the statement in Gen 3:6, "when the woman saw that the tree was good," since up until then such language had only been used of God.[243] Thus now, instead of God, it is the woman who determines what is good.[244] c) It is favored by the analogy of Ezekiel 28, where the king of Tyre is expelled from Eden for aspiring after the wisdom of God.[245] d) This view may find a parallel in the refrain of Ecclesiastes that an autonomous pursuit of wisdom leads only to vanity and toil.[246] e) It is difficult to deny that there was a coveting after wisdom in Eden and that a quest for autonomy was implicit in that pursuit.[247]

In spite of the strength of these arguments the interpretation appears to be vulnerable, and in our view, fatally so, at a significant point. Although the quest for autonomy may be present in Eve's pursuit of the fruit, the notion of autonomy or *hubris* does not appear to be a notion implicit in the tree itself. As we noted above, the trees appear to get their names from their *effects*; i.e., just as partaking of the first tree would result in life, so eating from the second tree would emanate in knowledge. Thus, although a desire for autonomy may have been a root *cause* of what led

---

242. See Mendenhall, "Wisdom," 319–34; Schökel, "Themes," 468–80; Carmichael, "Myth," 50–54; Dubarle, *Les sages*, 7–24; Perdue, *Wisdom*.

243. See Gen 1:10, 12, 18, etc.

244. See Sailhamer, "Genesis," 51; Emmrich adds that she does so in blunt contradiction to God's command; i.e., in reality, "the tree was *not* 'good for food' in that God had prohibited the eating of its fruit" ("Temptation Narrative," 8 n. 23).

245. See Ezek 28:2, 6, 15–17 (see Albertz, "'Ihr werdet sein wie Gott,'" 24).

246. See Clemens, "Law," 5–8.

247. Coppens notes the serpent's role in provoking this, "il est clair qu'elle fut commise sous l'angle précis de la tentation. Or, celle-ci fut provoquée . . . par les propos d'orgueil tenus par le serpent à Eve, la pécheresse" (*La Connaissance*, 19).

the couple to disobey God and take a bite of the forbidden fruit, it was not its *effect*. The fallen couple seems to be anything but autonomous as a result of partaking of the forbidden tree.[248]

---

248. Mayes counter is similar: "If we define it as knowledge which leads to moral autonomy, then there is the difficulty that it was precisely this ability to decide for himself which led man to eat of the tree; such ability did not derive from eating of the tree" ("Nature," 257; see also Hartman, "Sin," 33). Blocher himself observes that in point of fact it is impossible for the couple "not to discover at once the gulf between their intent and their resources. How vulnerable are they in their finitude, how tender and defenseless is their flesh" (*In the Beginning*, 173).

# 6

# A Catalytic Operation of the Law in Eden

HAVING CANVASSED THE GENESIS Fall narrative, it remains now to draw some general conclusions concerning Eden and Paul's notion of the catalytic operation of the law. If, as was earlier proposed, Paul considered the grim events that transpired in the Garden to be prototypical of sin under the law, whether recapitulated at Sinai or in the life of an individual, this would suggest that he envisioned law to have been a fundamental factor in the outworking of the first sin. The question at hand is whether the Genesis account itself would concur. Is Paul's catalytic operation of the law present in Eden? Did the Garden commandment awaken dormant sin, and did sin in turn seize the commandment as an opportunity to produce all manner of covetousness? To seek an answer we will now look more broadly at the Fall narrative and to its key motifs and sequencing and more especially to the relation between the commandment and sin depicted there.

## THE MOTIF OF LAW IN THE FALL NARRATIVE

Our examination of Rom 5:13–14 above concluded that Paul took for granted the existence of two law traditions linked to Adam and Moses respectively.[1] For Paul, the presence of law in the Garden is presupposed by the fact that Adam committed a παράβασις there, which by his own definition requires a law to be breached.[2] In addition, we noted that the logic of 5:13–14 argues that Adam transgressed law, i.e., explicit divine

---

1. See above, pp. 115–16.
2. See Rom 4:15.

legislation.³ For since the period between Adam and Moses was without law,⁴ it follows that Adam's sin, unlike the sins committed during this period and like those committed after Sinai, was related to law. Now it could be that Paul's theology of law in Romans 5 was influenced by Jewish traditions that regarded law, particularly, *the* Law (i.e., the Torah), to have been present in Eden.⁵ One need not presume this, however.⁶ Indeed, one should not assume this. A pivotal point of Paul's argument in 5:12-14 regarding the reality of death in the world is driven by his understanding that the Jewish Torah did not appear on the world stage until Sinai.⁷

3. To which is affixed sanctions. It would appear that the logic of Paul's argument and his use of ἐλλογέω in 5:13 presumes that those who commit sin in the presence of law are liable since law is comprised of *specific* legislation sanctioned with stated *consequences*. Such was the case in both Eden and Sinai. See also above, p. 115 n.131.

4. Though Bruckner points out that natural law existed between Eden and Sinai in such forms as judicial, commercial, and contractual procedures, he notes that the post-Eden and pre-Sinai narratives are not ostensibly "about" law, and they do not contain law codes "nor are specific statutes and ordinances presented as such" ("Creational Context," 97).

5. See, e.g., *Tg. Neof.* Gen 2:15: "And the Lord God took Adam and had him dwell in the garden of Eden to toil in the Law and to observe its commandments" (*ArBib* 1A:58). For other references to Adam and Eve being given either the Torah or other divine commandments and prohibitions, see *Tg. Neof.* Gen 3:9, 22-24; *2 En.* 30:15; 31; *Syb. Or.* 1:38-39; 1:42-45, 50-53; *4 Ezra* 3:7; 7:11; *2 Bar.* 4:32; 7:2; *L.A.E.* 18:1; 26:2; 34:1-3; 37:2; 38:2; 49:1-3; *L.A.B.* 13:8; *Apoc. Mos.* 7:1; 8:2; 10:2; 11:1-3; 21:2; 23:3; 24:1, 4; 25:1; 39:1; *Apoc. Sedr.* 4:4; *Hist. Rech.* 6:8; *Hel. Syn. Pr.* 12:44-46; *Tg. Ps.-J.* 2:15; 3:9, 10, 22, 24; Sir 17:11-12, 14; Josephus (*Ant.* 1:40-47); Philo (*Creation* 1.3; *Alleg. Interp.* 1.30. 90-31.97; *QG* 1.15); 4QpHosb 7-8, 1-2; 4QpapPrQuot 8 *recto* I, 4-8. Rabbinic thought is also replete with references to Adam and law (see e.g., *Gen. Rab.* 8:2; 16:5-6; 24:5; *Deut. Rab.* 2:25; *b. Sanh.* 56b; *Pirqe R. El.* 13; *Midr. Pss.* 1:10; 6:2; *Midr. Prov.* 8:4; *Pesiq. Rab Kah.* 12.1). Maimonides's ascription to Adam six of the seven *Noahide* laws typifies rabbinic thought: "Six precepts were given to Adam: prohibition of idolatry, of blasphemy, of murder, of adultery, of robbery, and the command to establish courts of justice. . . . An additional commandment was given to Noah: prohibition of (eating) a limb from a living animal" (*Mish. Tor.* 14.5.9.1); see also *Gen. Rab.* 16:6; 24:5; 34:13; *Deut. Rab.* 2:25; *b. Sanh.* 59a,b; and citations in Ginzberg, *Legends*, 5:92-93). Other traditions depict God considering giving Adam the complete Torah (613 commandments) but then hesitating after reflecting on Adam's inability to keep the six commandments that were given to him (*Gen. Rab.* 24:5). See Moore, *Judaism*, 1:274. For more recent discussions of Jewish notions regarding law in Eden as they relate to Rom 7:7-11, see Lichtenberger, *Das Ich*, 205-41; Grappe, "Qui me délivrera," 480-87; Hofius, "Mensch," 115-18.

6. As does Tobin, "Context," 159-75.

7. Note also Rom 5:20: "The law was added so that the trespass might increase" (NIV). Moo correctly, we believe, argues: "That Paul viewed Adam as, in some sense, a 'prototype' of man under the law is suggested by Rom 5:14, but the similarity consists in

Moreover, Paul's contention that the Torah appeared *after* rather than *before* the promise given to Abraham serves elsewhere as a salvation-historical linchpin to his argument that salvation comes through faith, not works of the Torah.[8]

A Jewish tradition that placed the Torah in the Garden, then, ought not to be assumed behind 5:13–14 and, in any case, Jewish traditions need not be assumed. The Genesis account alone would have been a sufficient enough guide to mentor Paul on the subject of law in the Garden. This is evident in Gen 2:16, for example, in the statement that God "commanded" Adam. Though the term "law" does not appear here, it may be logically implied in the thought conveyed.[9] The verb צָוָה assumes the existence of מִצְוָה which in turn suggests the notion of תּוֹרָה, i.e, תּוֹרָה either as a synonym of מִצְוָה or in the sense of *legislation* of which the particular מִצְוָה would be a specific expression.[10] Such a linkage is suggested by the semantic field that the terms share in the Old Testament.[11] Furthermore, as noted in the previous chapter (and by most commentators), both the

---

the situation of confrontation with the divine demand; nothing indicates that the analogy must be extended to include possession of the same *body* of demands" ("Israel and Paul," 124; see also Esler, *Conflict*, 234; Schreiner, *Romans*, 361).

8. See Gal 3:17.

9. *Law* is not the only motif that lay implicit in the Genesis narrative but becomes explicit later in Scripture. Although the term itself is absent from the account, *marriage*, e.g., is implied in the notion of the first couple becoming "one flesh" and in their role as the prototype of those who would "leave and cleave" (Gen 2:24). In addition, although the term *sin* does not appear until Gen 4:8, few, if any, would suggest that *sin* did not occur in Eden. Indeed, Paul argues in Rom 5:12 that it was through Adam that sin gained access into the world.

10. As the examples in the following note indicate, the notion of *torah* can be understood in either sense. Greidanus defines *torah* as "that which demands a prescribed response" ("Dimension," 39).

11. For passages in which צָוָה is used together with מִצְוָה and תּוֹרָה, see Lev 6:2; Num 19:3; 31:21; Josh 22:5, Deut 32:46; 33:4; 2 Kgs 14:6;17:13, 34; 21:8; 1 Chr 16:40; 22:12; 2 Chr 25:4; 33:8; Neh 8:1; 8:14; 9:14; Jer 23:23. Passages where תּוֹרָה serves as the object of צָוָה include Deut 32:46; Num 19:2; 31:21; Josh 1:7; 8:31; 22:5; 2 Kgs 14:6; 17:13, 34; 2 Kgs 21:8, 8; 1 Chr 16:40; 2 Chr 25:4; 33:8; Neh 8:14; Ps 78:5; Jer 32:23; Mal 4:4. For verses in which מִצְוָה and תּוֹרָה are juxtaposed, if not used interchangeably, see, e.g., Gen 26:5; Exod 16:28; 24:12; Lev 27:34; Num 36:13; Deut 30:10; Josh 22:5; 2 Kgs 17:37; 2 Chr 14:4; 19:10; 31:21; Ezra 10:3; Prov 6:23; 13:13; 19:16; Ecc 8:5 (See *NIDOTT* 2:1070; 3:77; *TDOT* 8:506; 11:281). Note also here the interchange of the terms νόμος and ἐντολή by Paul in Rom 7:8–11 (see above, p. 102 n. 69). That תּוֹרָה can denote *law qua law* rather than the Sinai code itself is evident from Exod 12:49; Lev 7:7; Num 15:16, 29; Prov 3:1; 4:2; 6:23; 7:2; etc.

form of the commandment in Gen 2:17 and the motive clause appended to it are mirror images of the legal formulae found in the Decalogue and in Old Testament law language in general.[12] Indeed, Cassuto argues that the commandment in Eden serves "as a symbol of, and introduction to, similar injunctions that were to be given to Israel in the future."[13] Moreover, the punishment inflicted on the couple in Gen 3:16-19 assumes disobedience to a divine demand. While the common scriptural terms for *sin* are absent from the narrative,[14] this does not suggest that God was presenting the couple with "a conditional offer rather than a categorical imperative."[15] Not only does the narrative frame the prohibition in *legal* language and define it as a "command," but Adam explicitly suffers consequences: "because you have . . . eaten of the tree about which I commanded you" (3:17). Disobedience and punishment assumes an imperative.

It would thus seem apparent from the language and story line of Genesis that *law*, whether defined loosely as an authoritative standard of instruction or more precisely as a divine demand with an affixed sanction,[16] was as present in Eden as it was at Sinai,[17] though the former lacked

---

12. Westermann observes that the two sentences in 2:17 conform to the two basic forms of command and law: "The prohibition (= command) has the form of the commandments of the Decalogue . . . , and the second sentence that of apodictic law consisting of condition (case) and consequence (punishment)" (*Genesis* 1:223). House regards the verse as a "law code" (*Theology*, 62).

13. Casutto, *Genesis*, 124. Greidanus argues similarly but widens the analogy of the law in Eden to *natural law* applicable to all people (see "Dimension," 43-44). Whether or not this is the case, Greidanus is correct, in our view, to observe the presence of *law* in Eden.

14. Though not absent from Paul's reading of it (see the terms "sin," "transgression," "trespass," and "disobedience" in Rom 5:12-19).

15. Novak, *Natural Law*, 32. I.e., before the couple can face specific moral choices they must first become moral beings knowing good and evil. At Gen 2:16-17 God presents Adam with this possibility: "If you eat of this tree you will know good and evil."

16. See the range of meanings of *torah* discussed in *NIDOTTE*, 4:893; *HALOT* 4:1710-12; *TLOT* 3:1415-22. See also above, n. 3, p. 79 n. 165.

17. A further link between Eden and Sinai may be discerned when the garden setting is read against the sinaitic tradition. We observed the parallels between Deut 30:15-19 and the temptation narrative (see above, pp. 140-41). Additionally, as the tabernacle represented the place of fellowship with God, Eden was where God and the first couple enjoyed communion (see Clines, "Tree," Wenham, "Sanctuary," Beale, "Eden," 7-12, 15-19). Emmrich, indeed, suggests that the two trees in Genesis function like the Mosaic blessing and curse respectively (see "Temptation Narrative," 6-9). See also below, nn.

the national, civil, and cultic features of the latter,[18] and the latter was expressed through a mediator unlike the former.[19] Consequently, it is quite possible that Genesis 2–3 and its references to the divine command,[20] not intertestamental literature, served as the primary, and perhaps sole, source behind Paul's assumption in Rom 5:13–14 of the presence of *law* in the Garden.[21] And this possibility becomes all the more probable—not only in view of the nature of Romans itself, an epistle saturated with Old Testament quotations and allusions,[22] but because the *other* law notion in Rom 5:12–20, the catalytic operation of divine law, as we will see,[23] finds no parallel in extant intertestamental Jewish literature.

## THE MOTIF OF THE KNOWLEDGE OF SIN IN THE FALL NARRATIVE

A further point of contact between Paul and Eden likely evident from the above examination of Genesis 2–3 is the motif of *knowledge*. As we argued,[24] it is difficult in light of the edenic reminiscences in Rom 7:7–11 not to see "the knowledge of good and evil" in the background of Paul's experiential "knowledge of sin" in Rom 3:20b and 7:7. Grappe writes, "On peut dès lors considérer à bon droit que l'histoire du paradis est ici,

---

126, 127.

18. Longenecker contends that, for Paul, "God's Torah in a pre-Mosaic prototype was from the beginning: a prototype of basic instruction minus the particular national and ceremonial features" (*Paul*, 95; see also Pedersen, "Biblical Law," 17).

19. Westermann observes that the authoritative form of the direct address in the second person "presumes a situation which is unique to Gen 2:17, namely that God is within call, and so the address 'Thou shalt not eat' is without mediator, spoken and direct. For that very reason the command of Gen 2:17 belongs to primeval time; there can be no such directness in historical times" (*Genesis*, 1:223).

20. The verb צָוָה in 2:16 is repeated in 3:11, 17. Clearly there is an emphasis on the term that would have been difficult for Paul to miss.

21. Prior to citing Jewish apocryphal works, Stuhlmacher cites Genesis 2–3 at the head of his list of traditions guiding Paul's edenic notions in Romans 5 and 7 ("Topic," 133 n. 38; so also Dunn, *Theology*, 82–84).

22. The note that Paul strikes in Rom 1:2 (ὃ προεπηγγείλατο διὰ τῶν προφητῶν αὐτοῦ ἐν γραφαῖς ἁγίαις) indicates that much of what follows is drawn from the Old Testament Scriptures. Waters doubts that Second Temple notions informed Paul's world view (see *Justification*, 157).

23. See below, pp. 197–99.

24. See above, pp. 103 n. 72, 112–13.

conjointement avec les récits relatifs au don de la Loi au Sinaï, en vue, Paul amalgamant, d'une part, le commandement du Décalogue et l'interdit de Gn 2,16–17 et, d'autre part, *l'histoire de la connaissance du péché* avec l'histoire de la chute en Gn 3."[25] Paul's references to the knowledge of sin are reminiscent not only of the tree itself but are descriptive of the first couple's experience after they had eaten the forbidden fruit and perceived the shame of their nakedness:[26]

ἐπίγνωσις ἁμαρτίας (Rom 3:20b)
ἀλλὰ τὴν ἁμαρτίαν οὐκ ἔγνων (Rom 7:7a)
ἐπιθυμίαν οὐκ ᾔδειν (Rom 7:7b)

τὸ ξύλον τοῦ εἰδέναι γνωστὸν καλοῦ καὶ πονηροῦ (LXX Gen 2:9)
τὸ ξύλον τοῦ γινώσκειν καλὸν καὶ πονηρόν (LXX Gen 2:17)
καὶ διηνοίχθησαν οἱ ὀφθαλμοὶ τῶν δύο καὶ ἔγνωσαν ὅτι γυμνοὶ ἦσαν (LXX Gen 3:7)

Since the terms καλός and πονηρός are absent from Paul's statements, however, an allusion in Romans to the primeval tree of good and evil might appear uncertain.[27] Yet, even though the tandem of καλός and πονηρός does not appear in Romans 7, the presence of the verbs γινώσκω and οἶδα amidst the *edenic* scenery of 7:7–11 along with Paul's employment there of the rare phrase *to know sin*,[28] may be more significant than the absence of the pair of ethical opposites.[29] As to why the tandem

25. Grappe, "Que me délivera?" 487, italics mine. For the experiential nature of the verbs γινώσκω and οἶδα in Rom 3:20b; 7:7, see above, p. 103 n. 71, 108–11.

26. See Espy, "Robust Conscious," 169.

27. A concern that causes Theissen some hesitation in embracing an allusion he otherwise fancies (*Aspects*, 208; see above, p. 103 n. 72).

28. The phrase occurs in the New Testament only in Rom 3:20; 7:7; and 2 Cor 5:21. The closest parallel in the Old Testament appears to be the Genesis Eden narrative itself (see below, n. 124). In Second Temple Judaism the phrase appears to be used only with reference to the Eden account (see, e.g., *1 En.* 32:3–6; *Syb. Or.* 1.39–41; 8.259–262; *Jub.* 3:19–22; 4:30; *Tg. Neof.* Gen 2:9, 17; 3:5; *Tg. Onq.* 2:9; *Tg. Ps.-J.* 2:9; 3:5; Sir 17:7; Josephus [*Ant.* 1:40–47]; Philo [*QG* 1:36]; 1QS IV, 26; 1 Qsa I, 10; 4Q303, 8–9; 4Q305, 2–3. Though Str-B cites several rabbinic parallels to the phrase "to know sin" in 2 Cor 5:21, the references cited speak of "tasting" rather than "knowing" sin (see Str-B 3:520).

29. It is worth considering Paul's use of *both* γινώσκω and οἶδα in Rom 7:7. Though he uses the verbs interchangeably and in near proximity elsewhere (see Rom 7:14–15; 1 Cor 2:11; Gal 4:8–9), he nowhere else employs the pair in quite as close a proximity as he does in Rom 7:7. While the interchange of terms there may be merely stylistic, in

does not appear if Paul did, in fact, intend an allusion to the knowledge of good and evil, Theissen is likely correct that the "knowledge of good and evil" motif in the story of the Fall may have been modified by Paul into "knowledge of sin" in 7:7 to adapt to his mode of thought in 3:20.[30] This may be correct. At issue for Paul is the nexus of law and *sin*. Nevertheless, though the exact LXX tandem καλός and πονηρός are absent, the edenic notion of *good and evil* may, in fact, be echoed in the contrasts of ἀγαθός and κακός in 7:17, 18 and καλός and κακός in 7:19, 21.[31] While containing by themselves at best only a glimmer of the Fall motif of good and evil, the references to *good and bad* in 7:17-19, 21 take on an edenic hue in the shade of the Garden imagery of 7:7-11. This may be all the more suggested, as Lichtenburger argues, by the *knowledge* motif that recurs in v. 14, 15, 18:[32] "Gleichwohl finden sich Hinweise, die auch 14-25 mit Gen 2f. verbinden. Aus dem Motiv des γινώσκειν καλὸν καὶ πονηρόν von Gen 2,17 (vgl. 3,5) wird in 7,15 οὐ γινώσκω und in 7,19 der Gegensatz 'Gutes-Bösen' aufgenommen. Daß die Gebotsübertretung nach Gen 2,17 den Tod zur Folge hat (vgl. Gen 3,3f.19), ist Zielpunkt in Röm 7,24. Es handelt sich dabei nicht um bloße stichwortartige Anspielungen, sondern um Leitwörter, die die beiden Texte strukturieren."[33]

Looking back again to the Eden account, in the previous chapter we suggested that the Genesis phrase "the knowledge of good and evil," signified an acquaintance with good and evil learned by experience. A number of considerations were presented that supported this understanding, including the observation that the depiction in Gen 3:7 of what immediately ensued upon the transgression, viz., a consciousness of wrongdoing,

---

light of his edenic landscaping in Rom 7:7-11, Paul may have chosen to use both terms in v. 7 to echo LXX Gen 2:9, where both stems appear: τὸ ξύλον τοῦ εἰδέναι γνωστὸν καλοῦ καὶ πονηροῦ.

30. See Theissen, *Aspects*, 207.

31. The former tandem is found outside of Genesis 2–3 more frequently in the Old Testament than καλός and κακός (see Gen 24:50; 1 Kgs 22:8, 18; Prov 15:2, 23) or καλός and πονηρός (see Gen 44:4; Lev 27:10, 12, 14, 33; Num 13:19; 24:13; Josh 23:15; Ps 34:12; Amos 5:14, 15; Mic 3:2; Mal 2:17; cf. Sir 42:6). This is especially so in the poetic sections. See Num 14:23; 32:11; Deut 1:39; Deut 30:15; 1 Sam 24:18; 2 Sam 17:14; 19:36; 1 Kgs 3:9; 2 Chr 18:7, 17; Ps 33:15; Ps 36:27; 37:21; 108:5; Prov 6:11; 11:27; 13:21; 14:19, 22; 15:3, 15; 17:13, 20; 28:10; Ecc 9:2; Job 2:10; 30:26; cf. Tob 12:7; 1 Macc 16:17; Sir 11:14, 25, 31; 12:3; 13:25; 17:7; 18:8; 33:14; 39:4.

32. I.e., οἴδαμεν γὰρ ὅτι ὁ νόμος πνευματικός ἐστιν (7:14a); ὃ γὰρ κατεργάζομαι οὐ γινώσκω (7:15a); οἶδα γὰρ ὅτι οὐκ οἰκεῖ ἐν ἐμοί (7:18a).

33. Lichtenberger, *Das Ich*, 163; see also Luck, "Gute," 220-37.

coincides with this interpretation.³⁴ Now if Paul indeed alluded in Rom 3:20b and 7:7–8 to the Eden motif of knowledge, the experiential notion found in his re-reading of the Fall story would suggest that he interpreted the phrase in an experiential manner. In other words, whatever else the "knowledge of good and evil" might convey in the Garden narrative, *the experiential knowledge of sin* may have comprised for Paul the essence of where the theft of the fruit led Adam and Eve.³⁵ It is on such an experiential note that Paul's knowledge of sin motif seems to intersect with the Eden account. Alluding to this, Byrne writes: "Sin played the role of the serpent, exploiting the onset of the commandment as a chance to portray the prohibition, not as a life-preserving measure of a benevolent Creator, but as a restriction keeping the creature from discovering and usurping divine 'knowledge.' What followed, in fact, was not knowledge of divinity but 'knowledge of sin.'"³⁶ Haacker argues similarly: "Wenn in Röm. 7,7 das "Kennen" der Sünde als Folge der Konfrontation mit dem Gesetz bezeichnet wird, so erinnert das daran, daß nach Gen 3,5.22 das Wissen um Gut und Böse als Wirkung des Sündenfalls erscheint."³⁷ In any event, whatever the tree of the knowledge of good and evil signifies in the Temptation narrative, what is important for this study is the possibility of an allusion to it in Rom 3:20b and 7:7. A reverberation of Eden in Paul's axiomatic assertions that the law leads to the knowledge of sin would suggest that this law-sin nexus for him is *primeval* and thus *archetypal*.³⁸ We will pursue this point in our later reflections.

---

34. The use of יָדְעוּ in v. 7 to denote the couple's sudden awareness of their nakedness assumes that they have now attained the knowledge of good and evil (see Hodge, *Theology*, 2:126; Niehr, "עָרוֹם, עֵירוֹם, עֲרֻמָּה" 11:3523; Callender, *Adam*, 73 n. 143).

35. Notice how in both accounts *knowledge* of sin appears at the end of the process.

36. Byrne, *Romans*, 220.

37. Haacker, *Römer*, 144.

38. Feuillet notes: "Ce qui s'est passé aux origines de l'humanité . . . se répète d'une certaine façon dans l'existence de chaque homme mis en présence d'une loi divine positive" ("Loi," 33–34). Thus also Aquinas: "A prototype should serve as the model for all the subsequent members of the class. In every sort of sin the same order of temptation is found as in the first" (*SumT*, 2a2æ.165.2.4).

## THE MOTIFS OF DECEIT AND DEATH IN THE FALL NARRATIVE

Concerning the motifs of *deceit* and *death*,[39] Genesis 3 and Rom 7:7-11 echo each other.[40] Though ἐξαπατάω in 7:11 is not an exact match of ἀπατάω in LXX Gen 3:13,[41] the verb appears in Theodotion,[42] and it is used in reference to the serpent's seduction of the woman by Josephus,[43] Philo,[44] and elsewhere in his epistles by Paul himself.[45] Indeed, while Paul can use the verb on occasion without any allusion to the Eden narrative,[46] he uses no term for the beguiling of Eve by the serpent but ἐξαπατάω.[47] Considered along with the edenic reminiscences in 7:7-11, the appearance of the verb in v. 11 makes an allusion there to Eden virtually certain.[48] That Paul has an eye on the Fall motif of deception becomes even more apparent, however, when the respective clauses in Rom 7:11 and Gen 3:13 are juxtaposed. Paul only adds an editorial comment regarding the role that the commandment played in the process of deception:[49]

39. The motif of *desire* will be discussed below (see p. 194).

40. See Milne, "Genesis 3," 16.

41. ὁ ὄφις ἠπάτησέν με. There does not appear to be a great difference in meaning between the two verbs (see *TDNT* 1:384-85), though ἐξαπατάω is likely intensive. They occur side by side in 1 Tim 2:14: καὶ 'Αδὰμ οὐκ ἠπατήθη, ἡ δὲ γυνὴ ἐξαπατηθεῖσα ἐν παραβάσει γέγονεν. Although Paul employs ἐξαπατάω there for stylistic reasons, a slightly emphatic sense fits the context well (see Marshall, *Pastoral Epistles*, 464).

42. See Wevers, *Text*, 92. Paul's acquaintance with a Ur-Theodotion text tradition may be evident from the affinity of his quotation of Isa 28:5 in 1 Cor 15:54 with θ' Isa 28:5 (see above, pp. 59-60 n. 71 and the discussion in Marcos, *Septuagint*, 142-53).

43. Josephus, *Ant.* 1:48, 49.

44. Philo, *Alleg. Interp.* 3:109; *QG* 1:31.

45. See 2 Cor 11:3 (ὡς ὁ ὄφις ἐξηπάτησεν Εὔαν) and 1 Tim 2:14 (see n. 41, above).

46. The verb is rare in biblical Greek. It is applied elsewhere by Paul to deceptive doctrines (Rom 16:18; 2 Thess 2:3) and self-deception (1 Cor 3:18). The term occurs in LXX Exod 8:25 of Pharoah's deception of the Jews and in Θ Sus 1:56 of the seduction of beauty (τὸ κάλλος).

47. The term as defined by BDAG means "to cause someone to accept false ideas about someth." (345). As will be noted, the term can be applied to *enticement*. See p. 220 n. 104.

48. Nevertheless, Moo considers an allusion to Eden in v. 11 to be "not at all clear" (*Romans*, 440), and Esler finds a suggested reminiscence there to be "interesting" but "unpersuasive" (*Conflict*, 235).

49. Viewed in this manner, it would appear that the phrase διὰ τῆς ἐντολῆς in v. 11 belongs with ἀφορμὴν λαβοῦσα (Lietzmann, *Römer*, 74; Schreiner, *Romans*, 367

ἡ γὰρ ἁμαρτία *ἀφορμὴν λαβοῦσα διὰ τῆς ἐντολῆς* ἐξηπάτησέν με
(Rom 7:11)

ὁ   ὄGς                                      ἠπάτησέν  με
(LXX Gen 3:13)

In both accounts, then, the motif of *deception* is a notable plot line.[50] Qualitatively speaking, both Eve and the "I" of Rom 7:7-11 were *deceived*. How so and in what way does deceit relate to the law-sin nexus will be considered below. At this point we merely note that in the motif of *deceit* we have what appears to be a precise match between Rom 7:7-11 and Genesis 3.

In addition, the motif of *death* is common to both narratives.[51] Death terminology occurs in Rom 7:8, 10-11,[52] and, of course, it is a recurring theme that spans the opening chapters of Genesis.[53] In the Fall narrative, while spiritual death and separation may be indirectly in view,[54] the notion of physical death is prominent.[55] As a result of violating the prohibition, Adam and Eve are doomed to die. In Rom 7:10-11,

---

n. 14; Theissen, *Aspects*, 225) rather than with ἐξηπάτησεν (Tobin, *Rhetoric*, 239 n. 56; Cranfield, *Romans*, 1:350; Dunn, *Romans*, 1:380; Lambrecht, *Wretched*, 45-46). By analogy, the phrase διὰ τῆς ἐντολῆς in v. 7 likely belongs with with ἀφορμή (Moo, *Romans*, 435 n. 40; Kümmel, *Römer 7*, 44; Wilckens, *Römer*, 2:81 n. 319) rather than with κατειργάσατο (Cranfield, *Romans*, 1:350; Dunn, *Romans*, 1:380). In either case, however, the law plays a factor in the process of sin. Even though the latter notion may not be inherent in 7:7, 11, it is explicit in Rom 7:5 (τὰ παθήματα τῶν ἁμαρτιῶν τὰ διὰ τοῦ νόμου ἐνηργεῖτο ἐν τοῖς μέλεσιν ἡμῶν) and 7:13 (ἡ ἁμαρτία, ἵνα φανῇ ἁμαρτία, διὰ τοῦ ἀγαθοῦ μοι κατεργαζομένη θάνατον). The coming of the commandment in Romans 7, then, as in Genesis 3, presented sin with an opportunity *and* a means to beguile its victim (see Dunn, *Romans*, 1:380). With regard to the noun ἀφορμή in vv. 8, 11, the term suggests "a base or circumstance from which other action becomes possible" (BDAG 158; see also 2 Cor 5:12; 11:12, 12; Gal 5:13; 1 Tim 5:14). Barrett notes that the law is depicted by Paul as "the jumping-off ground from which sin operates" (*Romans*, 383). While it is unclear to what, if any, extent a military motif is present, Dunn notes that the use of this term with sin is "one of the most vigorous of the personifications of sin as a power" (see *Romans*, 1:382).

50. See Bussini, *L'homme*, 128-30.

51. See Theissen, *Aspects*, 206-7, 209-10.

52. Note ἀποθνήσκω and θάνατος in v.10 and ἀποκτείνω in v.11. The term νεκρός, which is applied to dormant sin in v. 8, carries a different nuance (see above, p. 102 n. 70) as do the references to death in 6:2, 7, 8; 7:4 (see Cranfield, *Romans*, 1:352).

53. Note: "You shall die . . . you will not die . . . and he died" (Gen 2:17, 3:4; 5:5).

54. See Moberly, "Serpent," 16-27; Gowan, *Genesis 1-11*, 44; Milne, "Genesis 3," 16.

55. See above, p. 136.

eschatological death (i.e., *condemnation*) is the primary focus since the verses are enveloped by vv. 5 and 13 where such a state is in view.⁵⁶ Yet, like the Genesis account, the notion of physical death as an impending reality is present, for as Cranfield notes, physical death "is but the fulfillment of the sentence already passed."⁵⁷ Indeed, the reference in 7:24 to τὸ σῶμα τοῦ θανάτου τούτου, while perhaps expressing the *spiritual* condition of condemnation from which Paul cries for deliverance,⁵⁸ is suggestive of the state of dissolution to which the body is doomed: "It is the final outworking and end of death's rule over this age, and so defeat of the last enemy (1 Cor 15:56), for which Paul longs here."⁵⁹

In each narrative, then, not only is *death* a dominant feature in the story line,⁶⁰ but in both accounts the chicanery of the serpent/sin leads to death, and this is in spite of the fact that in each case a prohibition had been issued to serve de facto as *a life-bestowing or -sustaining measure*. If Adam and Eve had lived according to the commandment and heeded its warning they would have enjoyed (continued) access to the tree of life. Similarly, obedience to the commandment held out to Paul the promise of life.⁶¹ Unfortunately, however, for both Paul and the first parents such would not be the outcome. Whatever the divine intention

---

56. See Moo, "Israel and Paul," 125; Kuss, *Römerbrief*, 448–49; Wilckens, *Römer*, 2:82. Assuming as we do, that the "ἐγώ" of Rom 7:7-11 is *not* Adam (see above, p. 100 n. 67, and below, pp. 207-10) but an individual under law *like* Adam, the death here describes "that situation according to which the law, by turning 'sin' into 'transgression', confirms, personalizes, and radicalizes the spiritual death in which all find themselves *since* Adam" (Moo, *Romans*, 438, italics mine; contra Milne, who understands the notion in "subjectivist and attitudinal terms" ["Genesis 3," 16] as does Calvin, *Romans*, 265; Murray, *Romans*, 1:251; Bandstra, *Elements*, 137; Schreiner, *Romans*, 364; Hodge, *Romans*, 224).

57. *Romans*, 1:352; Dunn, *Romans*, 1:383. Byrne likewise notes that the allusion in v. 11 "is not to immediate physical death but to coming under the liability to physical death (mortality) and to the prospect of this becoming eternal death" (see *Romans*, 222).

58. So Moo, *Romans*, 466; Gundry, "Moral Frustration," 239.

59. Dunn, *Romans*, 1:397; see also Cranfield, *Romans*, 1:367; Banks, "Rom 7.25a," 34-42. In this view, the phrase τὸ σῶμα τοῦ θανάτου τούτου in 7:24 would hearken back to τὸ σῶμα τῆς ἁμαρτίας (6:6) and ἐν τῷ θνητῷ ὑμῶν σώματι (6:12).

60. See Milne, "Genesis 3," 16.

61. I.e., the phrase εἰς ζωήν of Rom 7:10 parallels the expression מוֹת תָּמוּת in Gen 3:17. Though Paul's depiction in Rom 7:10 of the *life-promising* commandment may be drawn from Lev 18:5, both verses are themselves reminiscent of the motive clause in Gen 2:17 (see above, p. 104 n. 74). Wright finds an allusion to the Genesis tree of life to be "hidden" in 7:10 under the more direct reference to Lev 18:5 ("Romans," 563).

behind the command, [62] "the serpent/sin in using the commandment to provoke disobedience to that command . . . used it to bring the warning into operation and effect."[63]

## THE SEQUENCE OF EVENTS IN THE FALL NARRATIVE

With regard to the overall *sequence* of events, the Fall narrative in Genesis 2–3 is a virtual image of Rom 7:7-11.[64] Each narrative begins on the note of *life*,[65] and both accounts pass through the phases of *life-commandment-*

---

62. Although εἰς ζωήν in Rom 7:10 has a telic force ("intending to bring life"), Paul's intention in using the phrase here is difficult to determine (see *TDNT* 2:429). It could be that the phrase signifies a regulating of a life already possessed — like Adam's prior to the Fall and in some sense (see n. 65, below) like that of the ἐγώ before its encounter with the commandment (see Hofius, "Mensch," 132; Dunn, *Romans*, 1:384). Moo, on the other hand, argues that the law, if kept perfectly, held out the promise of a life not yet attained (see *Romans*, 439; see also Westerholm, *Perspectives*, 419-20). In light of the parallel phrase εἰς θάνατον, it would appear that the phrase conveys the idea that the commandment was intended to bring about a spirtual quality of life not yet possessed, viz., *eternal life* (the antonyms death and life in 7:10, as in Gal 2:19, would thus denote *eschatological* life and death). This may be the thought conveyed by Paul in Rom 10:5 and Gal 3:12, 21b (see also Lev 18:5; Deut 30:15ff.; Ps 19:7-10; Ezek 20:11; *4 Ezra* 7:21; 14:29-30; *2 Bar.* 38:2; *Tg. Neof.* Gen 3:23; Sir 17:11; 45:5; Wisd 6:18; Bar 3:9; 4QDa 15 XVI, 4-5; *m. ʾAbot* 2:7-8; *b. Yoma* 72b; *b. Šabb.* 88b; *Sifr. Deut* 11:18; *Midr. Pss.* 119:64; *Midr. Song* 6:11; see further StrB 1:129-32; 917; 2: 482-83; 3:118-237, 277, 498, 502). In principle, the law could be a path to life (as in Lev 18:5; Ps 19:7-10; Ezek 20:11; etc.), but it is incapable of achieving this end because of the inability, indeed, the hostility, of the flesh (Rom 8:3, 7, see above, p. 100 n. 68). In any case, whatever the divine intention behind the law, it is clear for Paul (in light of the Eden account?) that the law neither leads to life nor maintains it; rather, it is the means by which sin brings about death (see Morissette, "Midrash," 181-84).

63. Dunn, *Romans*, 1:385; see also Zeller, *Römer*, 140; Hofius, "Mensch," 132; Haacker, *Römer*, 144.

64. See Bussini, *L'homme*, 125-31; Laato, *Paul*, 136; Dunn, *Romans*, 1:383; Lyonnet, *Les étapes*, 126; idem, "Tu ne convoiteras pas," 161-62; Stott, *Romans*, 200; Dodd, *Paradigmatic*, 225.

65. Like the ἐγώ in Rom 7:9 (ἐγὼ δὲ ἔζων), Adam is described in LXX Gen 2:7 as ζῶσαν. Given the use in Genesis of the phrase "living being" in regard to the animals (see, e.g., 1:20; 2:19; 9:9), it may be that the designation by itself in 2:7 means no more than that "the man began to live" (TEV). Yet, since only the man in the story (cf. 2:9 and 2:19) was animated directly by God with the breath of life (נִשְׁמַת חַיִּים), it would seem that he enjoyed more than mere existence. "The correspondence between man and his maker," observes Mathews, "is expressed both by the language of 'image' (1:26-27) and by the metaphor of a shared 'breath'" (*Genesis*, 1:197; see also Gunkel, *Genesis*, 6; Blocher, *In the Beginning*, 77; Hofius, "Mensch," 131; Espy, "Robust Conscience," 169). This is all the

*sin-death.*⁶⁶ Indeed, one could even sharpen the focus and detect eight parallel stages in the story of Adam/Eve and the "I" in Rom 7:7-11: 1) a period of life without the law; 2) prohibition; 3) the emergence of the serpent/sin; 4) deceit; 5) the arousal of lust; 6) disobedience; 7) the knowledge of sin; 8) death. Not only do the two accounts share virtually every major motif, but these motifs are recounted in precisely the same order.⁶⁷ This resemblance between the accounts remains evident even though the creation of Eve intervenes between the arrival of the commandment and

more suggested by the fact that נִשְׁמַת is applied in the Old Testament only to God and humans. The verb ἔζων in Rom 7:9 should probably likewise be understood in a theological manner in view of the position it occupies in contrast to ἀπέθανον (7:10), which almost certainly bears a theological sense (see above, n. 62). Yet, unlike ζωή in 7:10, ἔζων may not be used here by Paul in a *fully* theological sense (i.e., "wahren Lebens," Kümmel, *Römer 7*, 52). While the verb stands opposite to ἀπέθανον, in the structure of vv. 9-10 its chiastic counterpart is ἀνέζησεν, which is prosaic. The connection between the terms ἔζων and ἀνέζησεν may thus relativize the theological connection that exists between ἔζων and ἀπέθανον. Accordingly, ἔζων in 7:9 may be best viewed in a *relative* theological sense; i.e., of life in relationship with God that stops short of full eschatological life (see Kuss, *Römerbrief*, 448; Benoit, "The Law," 17). This is all the more probable since 1) the verb ζάω is rarely used by Paul of theological life in its fullest sense (of the 59 occurrences, perhaps only in Rom 1:17; 6:13; 8:13; 10:5; Gal 2:19; 3:11, 12; 5:25); 2) the phrase ἔζων ποτέ in itself lacks specificity (see Wilckens, *Römer*, 2:81; Schlier, *Römerbrief*, 224); 3) the notion of *life* plays no significant role in Romans 7 (unlike *death* [compare the sparse occurrences of ζάω (v. 9), ἀναζάω (v. 9) and ζωή (v. 10) with θάνατος (vv. 5, 10, 13, 13, 24), ἀποθνῄσκω (vv. 6, 9), νεκρός (vv. 4, 8), and θανατόω (v. 4)]); and 4) as the above layout suggests, the role of ἔζων is rather unremarkable; it primarily serves to set up the deadly situation that ensues with the giving of the law. Notes Kuss: "Es wird sich bei dem 'ich lebte' also doch wohl um ein 'leben' handeln, welches lediglich dem 'ich starb' v. 10 eine Folie schaffen soll, ohne daß damit—von Paulus wenigstens—weitergehende Überlegungen verknüpft worden wären. Es ist einfach der Zustand gemeint, welcher der tödlichen Begegnung des Menschen mit dem Gesetz vorausgeht, aber eben auf dem 'ich starb' liegt der Ton und das, was vorher war, beschäftigt die Aufmerksamkeit des Apostels offenbar nicht im geringsten" (*Römerbrief*, 448; see also Légasse, *Romains*, 450; Wilckens, *Römer*, 2:82). Thus, while some argue that a *full* theological meaning can be assigned to ἔζων in Rom 7:9 if there is a *direct* reference there to Adam (see discussions in Wilckens, *Römer*, 2:81; Moo, *Romans*, 437), a *relative* theological sense, in fact, better suits the depiction in Gen 2:7 of Adam, as a "living being" who was animated by God with the breath of life. Although there may be anthropological differences between humans before and after the Fall, each narrative likely depicts no more, though no less, than an individual at a point during which existence in relation to God was enjoyed. See further below, pp. 200-221).

66. See above, p. 99-100.

67. "Schrift für Schrift," notes Kühl of Paul, "folgt er der Sündensfallsgeschichte" (*Römer*, 230). Kühl could say the same about the Fall story line in relation to Paul's account.

the appearance of the serpent. As was noted above,[68] rather than being unrelated to what precedes and follows, Gen 2:18–25 serves as a transitional bridge between the giving of the commandment and its transgression. Thus, Paul's sequence of *life-commandment-sin-death* is not incompatible with the Genesis sequence of *life-commandment-(creation of Eve)-sin-death*. Though explanatory, 2:18–24, we observed, appears unessential to the narrative structure of the Fall account.[69] Paul (if we assume an allusion) would be appropriately subsuming a subsidiary motif and highlighting the key components of the drama. In addition, the distance from commandment to sin is not unduly lengthened by the account of Eve's creation.[70] In the flow of the narrative, little time elapses from the time that Adam receives the commandment until the serpent appears. Indeed, commentators have noted the quickness with which the snake emerges onto the stage.[71] Paul's depiction, then, of sin springing to life at the arrival of the commandment (Rom 7:9) would not (if it were an allusion) ignore the Genesis choreography but, in fact, would appreciate the pace at which it changes scenes.[72]

68. See above, pp. 143–45.
69. See Westermann, *Genesis*, 1:191–92.
70. See discussion above, pp. 145–46.
71. See, e.g., Brandscheidt, "Mensch," 4; Ruppert, *Genesis*, 145; Westermann, *Genesis*, 1:239; Zimmerli, *1. Mose*, 163 (see above, p. 147 n. 89).

72. This is not to deny that intervals exist in the Genesis narrative, as Gundry does in the argument he lodges against those who discern an allusion to Eden in Paul's statement ἐγὼ δὲ ἔζων χωρὶς νόμου ποτέ. He contends that there can bo *no* allusion in 7:9 to the Eden story since there is *no* hint in Genesis 2–3 of an interval between the creation of man and the giving of the commandment, and if such an interval were supposed, "its extreme brevity militates against Paul's making it a discreet period of salvation-history and describing life during it with an imperfect tense" ("Moral Frustration," 231). In response to Gundry, in point of fact, there *is* in the story an implicit temporal interval between man's creation and the appearance of the prohibition. In Gen 2:7 man is created a ψυχὴν ζῶσαν (LXX), and in v. 8 God plants a garden and places the man in it. In v. 9 the author proceeds to describe how God caused trees to grow in the garden, including the tree of life and the tree of the knowledge of good and evil. Unless we presume that the trees sprouted over night, we may reasonably assume that there was a natural season of time during which the plants grew. Verses 10–14 go on to describe the rivers that flowed through Eden, and in v. 15 we read that God placed Adam there to cultivate and keep it. It is not until vv. 16–17 that the prohibition is given. Thus, between the creation of man and the giving of the commandment an interval exists, although the narrative evidently (and, perhaps, typically [as in 2:18ff.]) has telescoped the length. Consequently, there appears a law-less interval in the Eden story after which Paul's depiction in Rom 7:9 may have be modeled. Paul use of the imperfect ἔζων is, indeed, a suitable counterpart of the

A further parallel in regard to the succession of events is the focal point that the *law* occupies in each sequence. Such a case is certainly apparent in Rom 7:7-11.[73] Not only do the terms νόμος and ἐντολή appear nine times in these five verses, but the law's arrival marks the center point of the drama chiastically depicted in 7:9-10a:[74]

    ἁμαρτία νεκρά                               ἁμαρτία ἀνέζησεν
                  ἐλθόντες τοῦ νομοῦ
    ἐγὼ ἔζων                                      ἐγὼ ἀπέθανον

The giving of the commandment in Gen 2:16-17 is likewise a pivotal and transitional element in the Fall narrative. It is, indeed, the linchpin that links chapters 2 and 3.[75] The prohibition, notes Coats, "foreshadows the development of the plot and thus *represents the principle point of tension which moves the story.*"[76] It reappears in 3:1 on the tongue of the serpent, in 3:3 when the woman responds, and in 3:17 when God speaks, and, observes Craig, it evokes the series of questions that appear in 3:1, 9, 11, 11, 13.[77] Genesis 2:16-17, as seen above,[78] is also the divide or point at which the narrative begins to darken. An account that earlier glistened with *life* becomes overshadowed with *death*, and this turn in the narrative begins at 2:16-17, the point at which God issues the commandment to Adam. Regarding the issuing of the prohibition, Bruckner notes: "It is a link, but not *simply* a link; it is the hyphen between creation (in chapter 1) and the fall (in chapter 3).... It is the pivot point of the text. Before it

---

durative ζῶσαν in Gen 2:7.

73. See Romanello, "Rom 7,7-25," 512-13. The numerous references in vv. 14-22 to the law (or to τὸ ἀγαθόν and τὸ καλόν) would indicate that the law continues to be in discussion in 14-25 despite its more anthropological character.

74. See Légasse, *Romains*, 450; Kümmel, *Römer* 7, 51; Wilckens, *Römer*, 2:82.

75. Westermann, *Practical Commentary*, 17, 20.

76. Coats, *Genesis*, 53, italics mine. Similarly, "Die Funktion dieses Gebotes," notes Steck, "ist deutlich: mit ihm ist das dramatische Element für den weiteren Handlungsverlauf exponiert" (*Paradieserzählung*, 87, see also 32–33).

77. See Craig, "Misspeaking," 238. Westermann also observes the manner in which the drama depicted in chapter 3 "is prepared" by 2:16-17 (*Genesis*, 1:194) as does Culley, who identifies the central sequence in Gen 2:4b-3:24 to be the "wrong/wrong punished" action sequence that centers around the commandment issued in 2:16-17 (see "Action Sequences," 28).

78. See pp. 144–45, 166.

(1–2:15) the positive dynamic between boundary and freedom is sung. After it (2:25–3:24), the dynamic becomes dissonant."[79]

## THE RELATION BETWEEN LAW AND SIN IN THE FALL NARRATIVE

Most peculiar to Paul's account in Rom 7:7–11, however, is the relationship that exists between the *law and sin*. In the experience of the "I", sin found occasion *through the commandment* to produce the very desires that the prohibition was meant to deter.[80] Does a *law-sin* nexus of a similar sort appear in the Fall story? Based on our examination of Genesis 2–3, and the observations of others, it would appear so. First, in the Genesis account, as in Rom 7:7–11, a personalized entity emerges, and it does so on the heels of the commandment. In Genesis 3 what appears in the tale is a crafty serpent, but, as in Paul's account, what is present (either *in* the serpent or represented *by* the serpent) is *sin*.[81] This is, of course, hinted at by the serpent's virtually supernatural craftiness and "bitterly evil" opposition to God.[82] Something crooked is present here, even diabolical, as later Jewish and Christian tradition recognized.[83] Yet, it can also be deduced from the noticeable links between Gen 3:1ff. and Gen 4:7.[84] The parallelism between the Eve and Cain accounts suggests that the entity that lay in wait for Cain, i.e., "sin" (חַטָּאת), is considered by the Genesis author to be the tempter that beguiled Eve.[85] While, therefore, a snake

---

79. Bruckner, "Boundary," 30. It is not surprising that Bruckner regards 2:16–17 as the *interpretive fulcrum* for chapters 1 and 2 (ibid., 21).

80. "Sin, seizing an opportunity in the commandment, produced in me all kinds of covetousness" (Rom 7:8).

81. See above, pp. 148–54 and the discussion by Westermann (*Genesis*, 1:237–39).

82. Gunkel, *Genesis*, 16. That the serpent appears as a dialogue partner with the woman may suggest a deviation from the order assigned by God to the animals, and its seduction of the woman can hardly suggest anything but hostility toward God. Brandscheidt observes that the crafty snake is depicted by the author "als Inbegriff einer satanischen Alternative zu den Schöpfungsbestimmungen Jahwes" ("Mensch," 5).

83. See above, p. 151 n. 118.

84. See above, pp. 151–54.

85. It is perhaps noteworthy that Wright identifies allusions in Romans 7 to both the first parents (7:7–12) and Cain (7:13–20). He too sees a connection between Genesis 3 and 4 and of both to Romans 7 (*Climax*, 226–30; see also Mathews, who is reminded by the Cain story of Rom 7:15–25 and 1 Cor 15:56 [*Genesis*, 271]).

appears in the foreground and a fiend perhaps lies in the background (the devil?),[86] the writer of Genesis 3 seems to present a picture of *sin* at work. It may be noteworthy, therefore, that Paul designates the deceiver in Rom 7:7-11 as "sin" rather than the "serpent." By doing so, the Apostle would seem to be linking his account to Gen 3:1ff. (and 4:7) in such a way that indicates he recognizes the subtle nuances and yet not so closely that it would detract from the present application he intends to make.[87] And it may be further significant that Paul does not designate the villain in Rom 7:7-11 as "Satan," as much Jewish thought had identified the serpent.[88] That Paul labels the foe simply as "sin" suggests *edenic* rather than intertestamental nuancing of his allusions and thus may indicate his dependence on the primeval account rather than on later Jewish writings.

Secondly, the serpent, like awakened sin in Rom 7:7-11, is *set in motion* by the commandment and in turn finds in the commandment a means *to set covetousness in motion*.[89] Indeed, though the narrative does not explicitly say why the snake springs into action at this point in the story,[90] the depiction of the tempter arriving on the scene "with the commandment on its tongue" would imply that it was the commandment and the opportunity that it afforded that drew the serpent out of the bush.[91] This has not gone unnoticed by commentators. After describing how the serpent made use of the prohibition to incite rebellion,[92] Bussini observes that "le surgissement du précepte donne l'occasion au serpent ou au pé-

---

86. The devil may, in fact, also lie behind Paul's personalization of sin in Rom 7:7-11. That the devil remains covert in both accounts may be due to the fact that each drama concerns the *process* of sin, rather than the ultimate origin of evil.

87. As we suggested earlier and will argue later, Paul is not *directly* describing the garden experience, but his own (and that of others faced with divine law) in edenic terms: "The I assumes the role of Adam and structures it in light of personal experience of conflict" (Theissen, "Aspects," 203). If Paul used the appellation "serpent," his readers could, perhaps, be more apt to detach the account from present experience. The designation "sin," however is relevant to both Eden and present experience.

88. Nor does Paul explicitly identify the villain in 7:7-11 as the *evil inclination* (*yēṣer hâraʿ*), though such a notion may lie in the background here and in vv. 7:18, 25 (see Davies, *Paul*, 19-27 and above, pp. 70-72).

89. See above, n. 49.

90. A fact noted by Steck, *Paradieserzählung*, 99.

91. See Dunn, *Romans*, 1:383.

92. "Gen 3,1-3 décrit avec beaucoup de finesse comment un précepte, auquel on obéissait sans contrainte, peut soudain être ressenti comme un interdit discutable qui pèse de l'extérieur" (Bussini, *L'homme*, 126).

ché de séduire l'homme."[93] Zimmerli refers to this opportunity afforded by the Garden commandment as an *Angriffsfläche* or "point of attack."[94] Unconsciously, perhaps, he echoes Paul's reference in Rom 7:8, 11 of sin finding in the commandment "a base of operations" (ἀφορμὴν).[95] Once on the scene, it appears that the serpent uses the prohibition in a twofold manner to provoke the first transgression. First, its deceitful misrepresentation of the commandment is what initially lures the woman into conversation. Secondly, by fixing her attention on the prohibition, the serpent incites her into disobeying the prohibition. Regarding the former ploy, as was noted above,[96] the serpent crafts its question in such a way that it would have been virtually impossible for the woman to answer with a simple yes or no.[97] The serpent, thus, dangles the bait, and she seizes it.[98] With regard to the latter scheme, the prohibition, otherwise out of the picture, now becomes the focus of Eve's attention.[99] If it be assumed that this was not the first time the woman saw the tree of the knowledge of good and evil, it would not be the mere sight of the tree that now entices her. The narrative portrays the snake's innuendoes regarding the commandment to be the stimulus of Eve's appetite and actions.[100] "Das Weib," notes Heinisch, "nähert sich dem Baume und sieht ihn jetzt mit andern Augen an."[101] Albertz speaks of the "übermächtigen Drang" that the serpent's spin on the commandment brings about in Eve.[102] Or,

93. Ibid., 128.

94. Zimmerli, *1. Mose*, 154.

95. Also reminiscent of ἀφορμήν in Rom 7:8, 11 is the statement attributed to Eliezer: "when the serpent heard the words of Eve, he found a way [lit. "opening"] through which he could enter" (*Pirqe R. El.* 13 [Friedlander]).

96. See pp. 154–56.

97. See Zimmerli, *1. Mose*, 1:153; see also Westermann, *Genesis*, 1:239; Hamilton, *Genesis*, 1:189; von Rad, *Genesis*, 88; Kidner, *Genesis*, 67; Skinner, *Genesis*, 73.

98. "Klug hat die Schlange es zu vermeiden gewußt," writes Zimmerli, "selber das erste Wort vom verbotenen Baum zu sagen, sie hat die Frau verlockt, in ihrer Verteidigung Gottes das erste Wort von diesem Baum zu sagen. Sie hat es erreicht, daß die Frau in ihrer arglosen Verteidigung sich an die Stelle lokken ließ, wo die Schlange sie haben möchte" (*1. Mose*, 1:154); see also Sarna, *Genesis*, 24; Emmrich, "Temptation Narrative," 14. See above, pp. 154–56, 160–61.

99. "Dabei stiert sie, durch die Schlange erst aufmerksam gemacht, auf Gottes Verbot von 2:17" (Ruppert, *Genesis*, 147; see also Budde, *Paradiesesgeschichte*, 46).

100. See Zimmerli *1. Mose*, 1:158; Delitzsch, *Genesis*, 1:155.

101. Heinisch, *Genesis*, 121; see also Skinner, *Genesis*, 75; Jacob, *Genesis*, 25.

102. Albertz, "Ihr werdet sein wie Gott," 20.

again to quote Ruppert: "Die Frau macht die urmenschliche Erfahrung: 'Nitimur in vetitum, semper cupimusque negata.'"[103] Brueggemann, indeed, sees the serpent engaging here "in a bit of sociology of *law*."[104] Judging, then, from the narrative itself, far from keeping the couple from disobedience, Genesis commentators observe that the prohibition provided the occasion through which the serpent provoked it:[105] "Durch die 'Frage' der Schlange," writes Drewermann, "ist das Verbot Gottes in den Mittelpunkt des Interesses gerückt; zum ersten Mal ist die Möglichkeit, die bisher schlummerte, geweckt worden, gegen das Verbot Gottes zu handeln."[106] Though Westermann does not mention the similarity of the Genesis narrative to Rom 7:7–11 in this regard, his words would well serve as a commentary on either passage: "The narrator, with economy of detail, manages to describe the woman as she allows herself to be led astray by simply gazing at the fruit side-by-side with the temptation by the serpent. It is a case of the general human phenomenon of the attraction of what is forbidden. The prohibition itself fixes attention on what

---

103. Ruppert, *Genesis* 151, quoting here Ovid, *Am.* 3.4.17: "We ever strive for what is forbid, and ever covet what is denied" (Showerman, LCL).

104. Brueggemann, *Genesis*, 47, italics mine.

105. Numerous New Testament scholars reading the Genesis narrative over Paul's shoulder are particularly perceptive of this as well. Stuhlmacher comments: "Only when the commandment from God came on the scene did sin spring to life, since like a parasite, it could make use of the commandment for its own purposes" (*Romans*, 107–8). "It was precisely by means of this command, the prototype of all law and religion," notes Barrett, "that the serpent tempted man" (*Romans*, 143). Bruce, similarly observes that "Adam and his wife lived a carefree life *until* they were tested by the commandment banning the fruit of the tree of knowledge: *that very commandment*, brought to their remembrance by the tempter, directed their attention to the forbidden fruit and made it so irresistibly attractive that they ate it" ("Paul," 268–69, italics mine). Commenting on the allusion to Genesis 3 in Rom 7:7–8, Zahn similarly remarks that "Schon hier, wie noch deutlicher v. 11, schreibt Paulus in Erinnerung daran, daß die Schlange im Paradies mit ihrer Versuchung des Weibes an das Verbot Gottes, von dem Baum der Erkenntnis des Guten und Bösen zu essen, anknüpfte und dadurch das erste gottwidrige Begehren in eines Menschen Brust erregte" (*Römer*, 340) as does Cranfield, who observes that "the serpent found in God's explicit prohibition (Gen 2:17) the very opportunity he wanted and was able to use the commandment as a means of deceiving and ruining Adam" ("St. Paul," 46; see also Hofius, "Mensch," 128; Bussini, *L'homme*, 123; Lyonnet, "Tu ne Convoiteras pas," 163; idem, *Les étapes*, 128).

106. Drewermann, *Strukturen*, 59.

is forbidden, making it in a mysterious way seductively and irresistibly attractive."[107]

Finally, Paul's statement that "sin seizing an opportunity in the commandment produced in me *all kinds of coveting*" (7:8) could easily have been Eve's own description of the situation that unfolded in Gen 3:4–5. As sin used the commandment as an occasion to stimulate coveting within Paul, the serpent used the prohibition to conjure up desire within Eve.[108] In Paul's case, the "thou shalt not covet" hearkens back to Sinai, in Eve's case the "thou shalt not eat of it" foreshadows Sinai.[109] In each case covetousness was at issue,[110] and in both cases the result was the generation of *multiple desires*; with Paul, coveting of every kind; with Eve, sensual, aesthetic, and sapiential desires.[111]

---

107. Westermann, *Genesis*, 1:249.

108. In *Apoc. Mos.* 19:3 the devil in the form of the serpent spits out "desire" (τὸν ἰὸν τῆς κακίας αὐτοῦ, τοῦτ' ἐστι τὴν ἐπιθυμίαν) on the forbidden fruit before Eve partakes of it. Neither Paul nor the Genesis author postulate exactly how a sinless being can be successfully tempted into sinning. Nor do the accounts specify the exact point at which the line of disobedience was crossed. Sufficient for each author is the fact that sin by means of the commandment successfully lured its victim into crossing that line.

109. Note again the grammatical link between the Garden prohibition and the Sinai prohibitions and the lexical link between Gen 3:6 and Exod 20:17 (Deut 5:21) via the verb חָמַד (see above, pp. 100–102 n. 68, p. 162 n. 174).

110. Lyonnet points out that the word used by the narrator (חמד) is the only term in 3:6 that is cataloged among the biblical vocabulary of sin (see *Les étapes*, 132; "Tu ne convoiteras pas," 161). Although the term ἐπιθυμία does not occur in LXX Gen 3:6, it is apparent that the idea of desire is "powerfully present" there (Hamerton-Kelly, "Sacred Violence, 53 n. 26; see also Lyonnet and Sabourin, *Sin*, 53). The belief that covetousness was the root of all sin was well established among Paul's contemporaries, even to the point where in *Apoc. Mos.* 19:3 lust is directly related to Eve's disobedience: ἐπιθυμία γάρ ἐστι κεφαλὴ πάσης ἁμαρτίας (see also 3 *Bar.* 4:8–17; *Apoc. Ab.* 24:9, 10; 4 Macc 2:6; *Tg. Neof.* Exod 20:17; Philo [*Decal.* 142, 149–150, 173; *Creation* 152; *Spec.* 4.79–94, 130–131; *QG* 1.47]; *b. Šabb.* 145d–146a and the discussions in Ziesler, "Role," 41–56; Grappe, "Qui me délivrera," 487; Hofius, *Paulusstudien II*, 115–18; Lyonnet, *Les étapes*, 129–33; idem, "Tu ne convoiteras pas," 157–65). Paul's use of the term "covet" thus does double duty: it stitches Rom 7:7–11 to both Sinai and Eden. See above, pp. 100–102 n. 68, p. 102 n. 69.

111. Recall the threefold repetition in Gen 3:6: לְמַאֲכָל ... לָעֵינַיִם ... לְהַשְׂכִּיל (see Beauchamp, *La loi*, 218).

## A LAW-SIN NEXUS IN THE FALL NARRATIVE

That there is a law-sin nexus of some sort in the Genesis temptation narrative would thus seem clear from an examination of the account.[112] The serpent used the commandment "intended as a check on man's inquisitiveness actually to stimulate that inquisitiveness, to transform inquisitiveness into acquisitiveness."[113] Scholars reading the text on its own terms have noted this plot twist. Westermann, indeed, after analyzing the Fall narrative, distills the entire temptation scene down to the axiom: "What is prohibited is especially enticing."[114] Since Paul seems to follow the Fall account almost line by line in Rom 7:7-11,[115] and the idea of "sin seizing opportunity through the commandment" appears to be present in Eden, it is almost certain, we argue, that the Apostle recognized a catalytic notion of the law in the Genesis story itself.[116] While the analogy between Rom 7:7-11 and Gen 3:1-7 may not stand on all fours (e.g., the first couple is tempted by sin without while the "I" is tempted by sin within),[117] "the Biblical history of the temptation, sin, and death of Adam and Eve, wherein the tempter plied his seductions vis-à-vis God's commandment ('has God said?'), provides a plausible narrative substructure to Paul's theological construct regarding sin and the law."[118]

An edenic substructure to Paul's depiction of his experience in Rom 7:7-11 would seem to hold even though Rom 5:20 explicitly describes a catalytic operation of the law at Sinai and sinaitic themes appear to be

---

112. Busch's conclusion is strong: "Careful exegesis of the Genesis passage that has so influenced Paul's argument shows how law is complicit with sin in alienating persons from God" ("Eve," 24).

113. Dunn, *Romans*, 1:400.

114. Westermann, *Practical Commentary*, 22; see also idem, *Genesis*, 2:249; Ruppert, *Genesis*, 151.

115. Haacker views Rom 7:7-11 as "eine stillschweigende Auslegung von Genesis 2-3" (*Römer*, 143). Recall Kühl's observation quoted earlier (above, n. 67).

116. Thurén reaches this conclusion as well: "The law can, however, provoke sin, *as it did with Adam*" (*Derhetorizing*, 129, italics mine). See also the comments cited in n. 105, above.

117. See p. 212 n. 61.

118. Sloan, "Paul and the Law," 51. Elliott correctly, we believe, argues that the rhetorical function of Rom 7:7-11 does not depend on "exact salvation-historical analogue" (*Rhetoric*, 249). Sufficient for Paul's purposes are the analogies that *are* present.

present in 7:7-11.¹¹⁹ In a setting such as 7:7-11, where Paul, it seems, casts the "I" in tones evocative of both Sinai *and* Eden,¹²⁰ Eden would naturally provide the determinative backdrop to the notions there because of the paradigmatic nature of the Fall.¹²¹ The prototypical character of the primeval account is evident, for example, in 5:12ff., where Paul presents Adam as a paradigm of those under the law.¹²² Indeed, in the historical sweep of 5:12-21, Eden and Calvary are *epochal*, whereas Sinai is *parenthetical*.¹²³ Furthermore, while Paul's motif of *knowledge* finds a match in Eden, such a theme, if not missing altogether from the Sinai and wilderness accounts,¹²⁴ is certainly not as notable there as it is in the Eden narrative. The knowledge motif thus would appear to be a distinct *edenic* thread that strings the allusions in Romans 7 past Sinai and ultimately to the Fall narrative and to its conspicuous motif of the knowledge of good and evil. The allusions in 7:7-11, therefore, may be reminiscent of the

---

119. Most clear is the quotation in 7:7 of Exod 20:17 (Deut 5:21) in the phrase in "You shall not covet." In addition, the sequence of *life-law-sin-death* may reflect the course of events leading up to and after the giving of the law at Sinai. Similarly, the motif of *coveting* appears in the wilderness accounts (see, e.g., LXX Num 11:4, 34; Ps 105:13-14) and in Paul's midrash (1 Cor 10:6-13), and the notion of *deceit* is present in the golden calf episode (see Watson, *Hermeneutics*, 354-80).

120. While some writers, based on the sinaitic motifs, see Sinai rather than Eden as the backdrop in Rom 7:7-11 (see above, p. 105 n. 78) or deny allusions to Eden altogether there (see above, pp. 105-7), we agree with Wright that this is a false either-or (*Climax*, 227). If, as we will contend (see below, pp. 200-221), the temptation and sin of Adam and Eve is prototypical (i.e., it "transcends" history [Feuillet, "Loi," 34]) and Paul is describing the experience of a Jew faced with the Torah, we can expect to discover the Apostle deliberately "meshing in the story of Israel" (Dunn, *Theology*, 99).

121. See below, p. 227 n. 30. It appears from the manner in which Paul elsewhere cites Genesis 2-3 (see, e.g., Eph 5:22-33; 2 Cor 9:13; 1 Tim 2:14) that he deemed the events there to be both historical and archetypical. See below, p. 201 n. 2, pp. 201-2 n. 6.

122. As Moo acknowledges, "Israel and Paul," 124; see also Espy, "Robust Conscience," 169.

123. Romans 5:20a: νόμος δὲ παρεισῆλθεν. In the New Testament period the verb παρεισέρχομαι most often assumed negative overtones (see BDAG 774). Note also its (only other NT) use in Gal 2:4 of the Judaiziers. It almost certainly has a negative tinge in 5:20 (see Wilckens, *Römer*, 1:328-29; Dunn, *Romans*, 1:286). Moo suggests that Paul chose the term to "relativize" the role of the law in salvation history (*Romans*, 347).

124. The only major *knowledge* motif in the wilderness accounts appears to be the refrain "that you may *know* that I am the LORD" (NET, italics mine) or similar phrases (see, e.g., Exod 8:10, 22; 9:14, 29; 10:2; 11:7; 16:12, 29:46; 31:13; etc.). There does not appear to be a *knowledge of sin* motif, however, as there is in Genesis 2-3 and Rom 3:20b; 7:7-8. See above, n. 28.

coming of the law at Sinai, but they do not seem to be drawn from there. Paul seems to view the catalytic operation of the law at Sinai (Rom 5:20) as a recapitulation of the primal story,[125] i.e., almost as a repeat of the Fall itself.[126] "Instead of recapitulating Adam's creation as distinct from the beasts," observes Napier, "the arrival of the Torah [at Sinai] effected the recapitulation of Adam's fall."[127] And as for the possible punch-line behind Paul's reflections on a catalytic scenario at Sinai, "Israel, Paul is saying, is in Adam too—and the Torah proves it."[128]

If the ultimate source of Paul's catalytic notion of the law and his allusions in Rom 7:7-11 is unlikely to be sinaitic, it is even less likely to be *Judaic*. While a counter-suggestability notion may be present in post-biblical Jewish writings,[129] the references, with one possible exception, post-date Paul. There is thus little, if any, support for a Pauline dependency on such sources for his law-sin notion.[130] Yet the one possible exception is intriguing. It is found in the *Apoc. Mos.* 19:1 and interestingly, it occurs in the account of the serpent's temptation of Eve. There Eve recalls the snake's seduction of her by way of a counter-suggestive ploy of holding back the promised fruit:

> "After we had walked a little, he turned and said to me 'I have changed my mind and will not allow you to eat.' He said these things, wishing in the end to entice and ruin me."[131]

---

125. Moo concedes this, although he downplays edenic allusions in Rom 7:7-11 (*Romans*, 438-39; see also Modalsli, "Gal 2 und Röm 7," 32).

126. Strelan finds both Eden and Sinai to be "places of creation, of the giving of the law, and of the Fall" ("Note," 23; see also Urbach, *Sages*, 1:425-26 and above, n. 17 and next note).

127. Napier, "Analysis," 21. One need but think of how quickly the golden calf incident followed upon the arrival of the Torah (Deut 4:13; 9:10; see Watson, *Hermeneutics*, 364; Wright, *Climax*, 227; Strelan, "Note," 23-25; Lyonnet, *Les étapes*, 118; Toews, *Romans*, 195-99). According to *Exod. Rab.* 32.1, these idolatrous Israelites were like Adam, who could not even withstand three hours of temptation.

128. Wright, *Climax*, 227; similarly Dunn, *Theology*, 100.

129. Note, e.g., the statement, "The evil impulse craves only what is forbidden" (*y. Yoma* 6:4 [*JTal.* 14:179]). See also above, pp. 22-23 n. 50.

130. Besides *Apoc. Mos.* 19:1, which we will presently discuss, a search of Jewish sources uncovered nothing even remotely related to a catalytic notion of the law in Eden.

131. *Apoc. Mos.* 19:1 (*OTP* 2:279). A Greek text appears in *Concordance Grecque de Pseudépigraphes*, 815-18.

What makes this edenic reference especially attractive as a possible influence on Paul is the near reference in 19:3 to "covetousness" as "the origin of every sin."[132] This is reminiscent of Rom 7:7. Nevertheless, the uncertainties surrounding the text render its relevance to our subject questionable. First, the source may be post-Pauline. While some consider the *Apocalypse of Moses* to be a pre-Christian document,[133] parallels to early rabbinic traditions, 2 Enoch, Josephus, and even to Paul himself,[134] may imply a date towards the end of the first Christian century.[135] It is possible, therefore, that the *Apocalypse* was influenced by Paul rather than vice versa. Secondly, the relevant phrase "He said these things, wishing in the end to entice and ruin me" is absent from several of the oldest manuscripts.[136] Thus, *APOT* reads: "I have changed my mind and I will not give thee to eat until thou swear to me to give also to thy husband."[137] If we apply the dictum *lectio brevior lectio potior*, as we probably should since the longer reading appears to be an explanatory reading,[138] this would

---

132. *OTP* 2:279.

133. See Sharpe, "Second Adam," 35.

134. Note, e.g. 17:1 and 2 Cor 11:14; 19:3 and Rom 7:7; 37:5 and 2 Cor 12:2. See discussions in *OTP* 2:255; *APOT* 2:130; Sharpe, "Second Adam," 35–46.

135. See, e.g. *OTP* 2:252 and the sources cited in Stone, *Jewish Writings*, 116.

136. See Sharpe, "Prolegomena," 125.

137. *APOT* 2:146. This shorter reading is recently followed by both Tromp, *Life*, 142 and Dochhorn, *Apokalypse*, 106; Knittel, *Leben*, 156–57.

138. So Knittel, *Leben*, 157 n. 113. Following mss. A1, 2 and B (Sharpe's designations), Sharpe's full text here reads: και περιπατησας ολιγον εστραφη και λεγει μοι· μεταμεληθεις ου δωσω σοι φαγειν. ταυτα δε ειπεν θελων εις τελος δελεασαι και απολεσαι με. και λεγει μοι· ομοσον μοι οτι διδεις και τω ανδρι σου (with the exception of the initial letter here, Sharpe's text has no accents). Manuscripts E1 E2 omit μεταμεληθεις ... και λεγει μοι. This could be the result of homeoteleuton due to the repeated phrase και λεγει μοι. Manuscripts C D2 D4 M1 M2 omit only the explanatory phrase ταυτα ... και λεγει μοι (Levison lays out a synopsis of textual tradition [see Levison, *Texts*, 72]). While there appears to be a good reason why E1 and E2 could have mistakenly omitted the words in their entirety, it is difficult to explain why C D2 D4 M1 M2 would have deleted an explanatory phrase. It would thus appear that μεταμεληθεις ... και λεγει μοι is original and ταυτα ... και λεγει μοι is an interpolation. A possible scenario then is that the C family is primary, the A and B traditions added the explanation and inserted the phrase και λεγει μοι as an introduction to the serpent's words regarding the husband, and the E tradition, while copying a manuscript from the B tradition, dropped μεταμεληθεις ... και λεγει μοι due to homeoteleuton. Taking into consideration its textual history, the most recently published edition of the Greek text of *L.A.E.* (Tromp, *Life*) omits ταυτα ... και λεγει μοι.

gut the reference of a counter-suggestive sense.[139] Finally, although the longer reading of *Apoc. Mos.* 19:1 places a counter-suggestability idea in Eden, it is unlikely that the reference, even if known to him, provided Paul with his law-sin notion. It is not the *divine* commandment that is the catalyst in the apocalyptic tale but the *serpent's* permission or lack thereof. Yet, despite these uncertainties, the cryptic and lone reference is nevertheless curious. If the counter-suggestive phrase was present in a manuscript available to Paul, the verse would provide one early Jewish source, at least, that pictures counter-suggestability as the dynamic that led to the Fall. It would not have been impossible in this case that the verse stimulated Paul to revisit and interpret the Genesis story in a similar, albeit disparate, manner. If on the other hand the counter-suggestive phrase was influenced by Paul, it could be a once-removed and slightly degenerated clone that provides an early witness to the Apostle's law-catalytic understanding of the Fall.

Having, then, discerned what appears to be a law-sin nexus in the Garden narrative and having suggested that the Genesis account itself was the soil from which Paul's law-sin truism sprouted, the final chapters will consider the significance that a catalytic operation of the law in the Eden account might have held for Paul and will weigh the potential importance that it could have for the discussion of Paul and the law today. Or to state it more succinctly, having examined Paul's law-sin axiom and identified its likely *source*, we conclude our study by considering what may be its theological *relevance*.

---

139. The textual uncertainty of the verse seems to have escaped the notice of scholars who have appealed to it as an example of a countersuggestability notion in Judaism and thus a possible influence on Paul catalytic notion (e.g., Theissen, *Aspects*, 224).

# 7

# Reflections: The Axiomatic Nature of the Catalytic Operation of the Law

WE HAVE ARGUED THAT the statement "the power of sin is the law" in 1 Cor 15:56b presents in epigrammatic form Paul's catalytic notion of the law. We proposed that the theological soil from which Paul molded this epigram was the Genesis Eden narrative. This conclusion was suggested by the relation that v. 56 appears to share with the edenic references in 1 Corinthians 15, a comparison with the law-sin nexus present in the edenic contexts of Romans (3) 5 and 7, and an examination of the Genesis narrative itself, where we found the serpent expropriating the prohibition to incite the first transgression. Our final three chapters will attempt to draw out some implications that a law-sin nexus rooted in edenic experience might have for Paul's theology of law. We will consider there three issues: 1) the axiomatic nature of the nexus; 2) the relation of the nexus to Paul's assessment of the law's role in relation to salvation history; and 3) the relation of the nexus to Paul's understanding of the individual's freedom from sin. Although the theological applications to be drawn are tentative, they are pursued with the conviction that our findings to this point suggest that there is theological pay dirt relevant to Paul's theology of law to be found in Eden.

## THE CATALYTIC EXPERIENCE IN EDEN AS A PROTOTYPE

We begin with the axiomatic character of Paul's statement regarding the power of sin and the law. If, as appears to be the case, Paul discerned a catalytic operation of divine law in Eden, this would seem to imply for him the prototypical nature of the law-sin relationship that existed there.

Paul, in other words, would almost inevitably have considered the edenic commandment-transgression scenario to be archetypal, i.e., indicative of "a general human phenomenon."[1]

That Paul considered the catalytic activity in Eden to be prototypical follows first of all from the seminal position that Eden occupied within his biblical-theological universe.[2] That the Fall was, for Paul, paradigmatic, and not merely illustrative is suggested by the arguments in such passages as Rom 5:12, 18–19, where humanity, in some manner, participates in Adam's sin and its consequences;[3] Rom 5:12–14, where Israel's transgression at Sinai is a recapitulation of the primal transgression in Eden;[4] and 1 Tim 2:14,[5] where Paul depicts the beguiling of Eve to be, in some sense, typical.[6] For Paul, it appears, the sin of Adam and Eve set

---

1. Westermann, *Genesis*, 1:349.

2. The seminal position that Eden occupied within Paul's thinking has been appropriately noted (see, e.g., Pedersen, "Biblical Law," 17; Milne, "Genesis 3," 12–16; Hooker, "Adam," 297–306; idem, "Further Note," 181–3; Stanley, "Paul's Interest," 1:242–52; and references cited below in this note). For Adam as a prototype in Judaism, see *4 Ezra* 3:21–22; *4 Ezra* 3:25–26; *4 Ezra* 7:118; *Gk. Apoc. Ezra* 2:10; *2 Bar.* 7:2–3; *2 Bar.* 18:2; *2 Bar.* 48:42; *2 Bar.* 54:15; *2 Bar.* 54:19; *3 Bar.* 5:16 (Greek); *Pesiq. Rab Kah.* 15.1. Stanley observes that Paul's abundant references and allusions in his letters to Genesis 1–3 is a feature that distinguishes him from other New Testament writers (see ibid., 241). Similarly, Milne argues that "the Fall narrative excercises an influence with Paul out of proportion to its length in the Old Testament" (see "Genesis 3," 10). There can be little doubt that Paul considered Adam to be historical and that he took for granted the determinative events of the Genesis Fall account (see Hofius, "Mensch," 112–13). Not only does the phrase "from Adam to Moses" in Rom 5:14 fix Adam within history, but Paul's Adam-Christ analogies follow only if Paul deemed Adam to be historical (see Moo, *Romans*, 325; Versteeg, *Adam*; Carson, "Adam," 28–43; Wedderburn, "Adam," 413–3; Milne, "Genesis 3," 10–18; Wright, "Climax," 18–40).

3. See Hofius, "Mensch," 113.

4. See Thielman, "Story," 180.

5. ἡ δὲ γυνὴ ἐξαπατηθεῖσα ἐν παραβάσει γέγονεν (cf. 2 Cor 11:3.). See Bénétreau, *Romains*, 1:199.

6. Paul's use of Genesis 3 in 1 Tim 2:14 appears to assume for him the paradigmatic nature of Eve's experience. If they were not careful to heed the role assigned to them in creation and respect their male counterparts, certain women in Ephesus could find themselves replaying the role of Eve. His use of γυνή instead of Εὔα likely serves to make a transition from Eve to women *in general* (see Marshall, *Pastoral Epistles*, 464; Knight, *Pastoral Epistles*, 144). The perfect γέγονεν appears to stress the abiding effects of the deception. The verse may be implying that women are ontologically vulnerable to deception (so interpreted by Johnson, *Timothy*, 208). Such an interpretation, however, is contested (see, e.g., Moo, "Authority," 190). In any case, Paul appears to depict the Fall as a paradigm. Kelly notes: "Like other exegetes, Jewish and Christian, he regards

the pattern for all subsequent transgressions and provides a template of the way in which temptation and sin operate in human life.⁷ Käsemann's words in this regard are virtually legend: "Every person after Adam is entangled in the fate of the protoplast. . . . Before Christ Adam is continually repeated."⁸ Barrett's remarks are hardly less quotable: "It is clear that Paul believed that everything that could be said about Adam as a (supposed) historical figure could also be said about mankind as a whole; he took his Hebrew (*ādām*-man[note accents, etc.]) seriously."⁹

Beyond this, the prototypical character of the *catalytic* experience can be deduced from the part that the prohibition played in the first sin. If Paul considered the primal sin to be archetypal, it would seem to follow for him that the divine command would repeat its primeval role in subsequent temptation scenarios, i.e., it would continue to provide the occasion through which sin is stimulated. This has been duly noted among commentators. According to Lichtenberger, "Adams Geschichte der Begegnung mit dem Gebot zeigt auf, was *immer* gültig ist, wenn der Mensch dem Gesetz begegnet."¹⁰ Westermann, indeed, reads back into the Fall account the common phenomenon of being attracted to what is divinely forbidden. In the author's mind, what took place in Eden was "not the extraordinary, the shocking, the 'unthinkable and terrible'

---

Adam and Eve as historical persons, but also as archetypes of the human race" (*Pastoral Epistles*, 68). For a historical sketch of the interpretation of 1 Timothy 2:14, see Doriani, "1 Timothy 2," 215-69.

7. See Milne, "Genesis 3," 17-18. Scholars have also discerned allusions to Genesis 3 in Rom 1:18-32 (see, e.g., Garlington, "Creation Theology," 202; Dunn, *Christology*, 101-2; idem, *Theology*, 91-93; Grappe, "Qui me délivrera," 480; Hooker, "Adam," 297-306; idem, "Further Note," 181-83; Stanley, "Paul's Interest," 247-48; Milne, "Genesis 3," 10-18). Nevertheless, while faint echoes of Genesis 3 may be discerned in Rom 1:18ff., it is improbable that the passage can be pinned down to any one point in history (see Wedderburn, "Adam," 413-19).

8. Käsemann, *Romans*, 197.

9. Barrett, *First Adam*, 19. According to Barrett, "Paul sees history gathering at nodal points, and crystallizing upon outstanding figures — men who are notable in themselves as individual persons, but even more notable as representative figures" (ibid., 5).

10. Gerstenberger, *Das Ich*, 134. This echoes Lyonnet's words: "Tel est le rôle qu'en fait, selon l'Écriture, joue le premier précepte, la première 'loi,' prototype de toutes les autres, comme le péché d'Adam et d'Ève, — tout en ayant bien d'autres effets —, est visiblement aussi, dans la pensée de l'hagiographe, le prototype de tous les péchés" (*Les étapes*, 128; see also Kühl, *Römer*, 231).

[quoting von Rad], but the completely natural and perfectly human."[11] Bornkamm also perceives Paul's description of the catalytic operation of the law to be a throw-back to a *primal* scenario: "Only under law, sin and death does man really become an 'I,' and in such a way that he is forced back to the basic nature of human existence in general."[12] The "I" here is the ἐγώ of Rom 7:7–11, a passage to which we now turn, since it is there that the prototypical nature of the edenic and catalytic scenario appears most evident.

## ROMANS 7:7–11—AN AXIOMATIC NARRATIVE

Though von der Osten-Sacken may be exaggerating to assert that "die Frage nach dem Subjekt der Aussagen [in Rom 7:7–11] nach der umfassenden Untersuchung von Kümmel als grundsätzlich gelöst gelten kann,"[13] Lichtenberger is probably safe to say that since Kümmel there has been "einen weitgehenden Konsens."[14] In particular, the consensus lies in the denial that the "I" in Rom 7:7–11 is *strictly* autobiographical of Paul either before or after his conversion.[15] To hurdle, if possible, all the obstacles facing such an interpretation would leave the interpreter virtually breathless.[16] Kümmel, of course, went further. He argued that there is no personal reference to Paul whatsoever in the "I" of 7:7–11.[17]

11. Westermann, *Genesis*, 1:349.
12. Bornkamm, "Sin," 94.
13. Osten-Sacken, *Römer 8*, 195.
14. Gerstenberger, *Das Ich*, 125.
15. Most commentators argue for the former. The latter view is argued by Segal (*Convert*, 241–45), Campbell ("Identity," 61–62), and more recently by Jervis ("'Commandment,'" 193–216).
16. Kümmel lays out these obstacles (*Römer 7*, 1–60). Among them, he argues that 1) the statement of 7:9 regarding the "I" being once alive "apart from the law" cannot be reconciled with Paul's pre-Christian life (ibid., 78–84); 2) since Phil 3:4–6 is autobiographical and Romans 7 depicts a seemingly contrary pre-conversion scenario, the latter cannot be autobiographical (ibid., 111–17); 3) examples of a *fictive* "I" are present elsewhere in Paul (and outside the New Testament) (ibid., 67–90; 118–32). While the second point may be overstated (the contrast between the passages is likely located in the difference in Paul's perspectives, i.e., before and after conversion [see Espy, "Robust Conscience," 161–88; Causse, "Le renversement," 364; Thielman, *Plight*, 110]; etc.), and the third point is inconclusive (see below, n. 23), Rom 7:9 appears to be a formidable barricade against a strictly autobiographical interpretation (see below, n. 31).
17. "Ob Paulus von sich allein oder von sich als Typus redet, jedenfalls redet er von

Paul did not experience the situation depicted there; "er benütze die erste Person zur Schilderung allgemein menschlicher Erlebnisse."[18] Paul's use of ἐγώ in a general or typological sense elsewhere might, initially at least, seem to lend support to such an interpretation.[19] The change of voice at 7:7 following a rhetorical question also appears to signal a rhetorical change.[20] Nevertheless, while it seems improbable that 7:7-11 is *strictly* autobiographical,[21] it is difficult to remove *all* autobiographical elements from the narrative.[22] Typical traits may at times be present, but it is *Paul's* voice that we hear elsewhere in his uses of ἐγώ in positive (i.e., indicative) statements in the past tense.[23] In fact, whenever Paul uses ἐγώ typically, it virtually necessitates the inclusion of his experience precisely because

---

sich, und das scheint mir der Text nicht zuzulassen" (*Römer 7*, 84).

18. Ibid., 89.

19. See, e.g., 1 Cor 6:12, 15; 9:26; 10:29-30; 11:31-32; 13:1-3, 11-12; 14:11; Gal 2:19-20; 4:12.

20. Witherington notes the change of voice at v. 7 and appeals to the rhetorical device known as *enallagē* or *metabolē*. Readers, he suggests, would expect a difference in characterization (*diaphonia*) to follow (*Romans*, 186).

21. See Dodd, *Paradigmatic*, 224.

22. See Campbell, "Identity," 59-60; Lambrecht, *Wretched*, 73-91; Segal, "Romans 7," 362.

23. See Theissen, *Aspects*, 199, for an analysis of occurrences that meet the criteria of Rom 7:7-11, i.e., declarative statements in the past tense using ἐγώ. In the end, what may appear to be *fictive* first persons in Paul (see Kümmel's list [*Römer 7*, 121]) may not be true parallels of 7:7-11 since they appear in present, hypothetical, deliberative, or interrogative constructions or include Paul (see, e.g., Rom 3:5, 7, 8 and vv. cited in n. 19, above). Likewise, most of the references to a *fictive* "I" outside the New Testament cited by Kümmel (see ibid., 126-31) or more recently by Stowers, *Diatribe*, 136, 232) occur in questions or statements in the present tense and are connected with dialogical signals or include the author (see Theissen, *Aspects*, 200). However, in what is likely the closest parallel to Paul's use of ἐγώ in 7:7-11, viz., Gal 2:19-21, the "I" undoubtedly includes Paul despite typical features. The structural similarity between the Galatians 2 passage and 7:7-11 is highlighted by Theissen (ibid., 197; see also Wilckens, *Römer*, 2:77; Kertelge, "Überlegungen," 107). It is noteworthy that [NL 1-4] 1) each passage is introduced by a thesis statement in the first person plural (7:4-6, Gal 2:15-16); 2) a question is then raised regarding an absurd consequence (7:7a, Gal 2:17); 3) a rebuttal using μὴ γένοιτο follows (7:7b, Gal 2:17); 4) a basis for the rebuttal is given that begins with a contrary-to-fact first person singular (7:7; Gal 2:18) that is followed by a past tense with ἐγώ (7:9; Gal 2:19) and closes with a present tense with ἐγώ (7:14ff., Gal 2:20-21). Since the passages share such similarities, Gal 2:15-20 must certainly be given weighty consideration by those endeavoring to identify the ἐγώ in Romans 7.

it is typical.²⁴ Furthermore, the existential character that permeates 7:7ff., i.e., its "liveliness and intensity,"²⁵ appears to be more than bare rhetoric,²⁶ and since Paul picks up in 7:7 with the first person singular what he had summarized in 7:5 using the first person plural,²⁷ it can hardly be assumed that he is excluded from the former when he is included in the latter.²⁸

It would seem best, then, to think in Rom 7:7–11 of an "I" that "combines personal *and* typical traits."²⁹ While Paul writes "I," in other words, he implies "we."³⁰ The narrative would thus contain an account of Paul's general situation,³¹ and yet what Paul experienced as a devout

---

24. Dunn quips: "It seems to me a rather convoluted process of reasoning which argues both that the 'I' does not denote Paul's personal experience but that it does denote the experience of everyman—everyman, except Paul!" ("Rom. 7:14–25," 260). Theissen distinguishes three possibilities of understanding the ἐγώ (*Aspects*, 191): *a personal "I"* by which Paul means himself as an individual in opposition to others (see 1 Cor 15:8); *a typical "I"* by which Paul means himself though as a representative of others (see Gal 2:20); *a fictive "I"* by the use of which Paul presents a general idea without including himself (see 1 Cor 10:29b). While Kümmel argues for the third use in Rom 7:7ff., the affinity of Gal 2:20 to the passage would seem to suggest the second (see preceding note).

25. Theissen, *Aspects*, 178.

26. Contra Sanders, *Law*, 71–81. Dodd aptly notes that "a man is not moved like that by an ideal construction" (*Romans*, 1959], 125); see also Watson, "Romans VII," 29; Kertelge, "Überlegungen," 106–7).

27. Lambrecht notes that 7:7–25 is "a drastic working out of 7:5" ("Man," 21; see also Hofius, "Mensch," 112).

28. See Longenecker, *Paul*, 91–92; Lichtenberger, *Das Ich*, 128–29.

29. Theissen, *Aspects*, 201, italics mine; see also Dunn, *Christology*, 104; Espy, "Robust Conscience," 170. While the nearest analogy, in our view, is Gal 2:15–20, some find analogies in the "I" of the Old Testament Psalms (see Wilckens, *Römer*, 2:77–78; Dunn, *Romans*, 1:382; Michel, *Römer*, 225) or of the Qumran psalms (see Kuhn, "New Light," 102; Theissen, *Aspects*, 201 n. 37). Others, of course, point to ancient rhetorical technique (see e.g., Stowers, *Rereading*, 16–22, 264–84; Johnson, *Reading Romans*, 107–8).

30. And "you" (see Rom 8:2). Thus Ambrosiaster: "Sub sua quasi persona generalem agit causam," i.e., "Within himself, as it were, he carries on a general process" (*epist. ad Rom.* 7,7). Despite attempts to identify and emphasize a salvation-historical model in 7:7–11 (see, e.g., Moo, "Israel and Paul," 122–35; Wright, *Climax*, 196–98; Napier, "Analysis," 17–22) or socio-historical concerns there (see, e.g. Stendahl, *Romans*, 28–20; Nanos, *Mystery*, 358–71; Wright, "Theology," 42–43, 50; Elliot, *Liberating Paul*, 131–39; Stowers, *Rereading*, 258–84), the use of ἐγώ and the overtly personal nature of 7:7f. suggests an application to *individuals*. "The experience is directly his own," argues Burnett, "but it can also be said to represent the experience of his readers as well" (Burnett, "Individual," 198, 212–13; see also Thielman, *Theology*, 364).

31. As opposed to a point by point account of his specific experiences (see Dunn,

Jew,[32] viz., the arousal of sin by means of the Mosaic law, is typical of all people in the situation depicted.[33] The *axiomatic* nature of 7:7-11 (and 1 Cor 15:56), in other words, suggests that the experience of Paul and Jews with the Mosaic law is "symptomatic of that of all people who, in various ways, are confronted with God's 'law.'"[34]

---

"Rom 7:14-25," 201). To be sure, there are details that are hard to pinpoint or to ascribe without qualification to Paul; e.g., the "I" in v. 9 being "once without the law." As Origen pointed out (see *Comm. Rom.* 6.8.7), it is hard to believe that Paul, who was circumcised on the eighth day, would refer to himself in this way (see also BDF §281; Kümmel, *Römer 7*, 78-84; Ziesler, "Role," 43-45; and the survey by Lichtenberger of Jewish sources regarding children and the Torah [*Das Ich*, 257-63]; see further discussion on v. 9 above, p. 116 n. 141, pp. 186-87 n. 65 and below, n. 35). On the phrase "I died" as applied to Paul in v. 10, see above, p. 185 n. 56. Perhaps at vv. 9-10, Paul's personal account is virtually overshadowed by the allusion there to Adam (as "sin" in 7:11 is almost eclipsed by the allusion there to the serpent? [see Wright, *Romans*, 563-64]). Dodd suggests that it is because of the various layers, i.e., the "creative combination of elements" that Paul weaved, that the precise circumstances involving the "I" are not easily discerned (*Paradigmatic*, 234).

32. Thus Milne: "While respecting the unique and unrepeatable position of Adam in Genesis 3 Paul also allows the passage there [Rom 7:7-11] to address everyman on an individual basis. In particular, it speaks to the man who is under the Law" ("Genesis 3," 17). Unlike the "I" of 7:7-11, not all people have been confronted by the Decalogue, nor are Gentiles ("god-fearers" to boot) bound in a do-or-die relationship with the Torah as is the "I" of 7:7-11 (see Lambrecht, "Man," 29; Moo, *Romans*, 428). As Toews notes: "The text unit . . . introduces Jewish agenda. Here the specific issue is the status of the covenant law, hardly a universal concern of men and women outside Judaism" (*Romans*, 195; see also Käsemann, *Romans*, 195; Lambrecht, "Man," 32; Rudolph Bultmann, "Romans 7," 199; contra Stowers, *Rereading*, 273-84; Gaston, *Paul and the Torah*, 62-64; Tobin, *Rhetoric*, 237-38; Gager, *Origins*, 220-23; Das, *Solving*, 223-35). See further below, n. 34.

33. See Byrne, *Romans*, 217; Cambier, "Le 'moi,'" 24.

34. Moo, *Romans*, 441. Since Paul appears to have the Jewish situation in mind in Rom 7:7-11, his usage of the phrase "under the law" to include Gentiles (e.g., Rom 6:14-15; 7:4-6) may have been an unconscious generalization to picture Gentiles as sharing in the Jewish dilemma (see Westerholm, *Perspectives*, 417; Sanders, *Law*, 82). Yet, it is probable that Rom 2:14-15 suggests that his generalization was conscious. While Paul is not explicit, if asked how his encounter with the law depicted in 7:7-11 relates to Gentiles, the Apostle would perhaps respond that while the Gentiles do not have the Mosaic law, "what the law requires is written on their hearts" (see Moo, *Romans*, 417; Donaldson, "'Curse,'" 95-96; Ebeling, *Word*, 275-80; Michel, *Römer*, 227).

## ROMANS 7:7-11—AN EDENICALLY NUANCED NARRATIVE

However, along with being *typical*, the ἐγώ of 7:7-11 (however we identify it) is *edenic*, i.e., it "bears the traits of Adam."[35] This is evident, as we argued above,[36] by the manner in which Paul "uses motifs drawn from Genesis" to describe the experience depicted there.[37] Thus, though the ἐγώ, we believe, is Paul,[38] the Apostle seems to present himself under the guise of Adam,[39] or perhaps in a manner that suggests solidarity with

---

35. Wilckens, *Römer*, 2:79. Along the same vein, Theissen remarks: "Even if Paul does not speak directly of Adam in Rom 7:7ff., the figure of Adam stands clearly in the background" (*Aspects*, 206). A case in point is 7:9 ("when the commandment came"), which Theissen dubs as "nonbiographical" (ibid., 201). It is hard to attach the verse to a specific point in Paul's life, though it may recall his first truly mature encounter with the Torah (see Burnett, *Individual*, 192-95 and above, n. 31) or a moment of crisis, such as he had on the way to Damascus (see Espy, "Robust Conscience," 175). In any case, Paul's utilization of the *life-law-sin-death* sequence suggests that he views his personal experience with the law as a recapitulation of the edenic story.

36. See pp. 98-107.

37. Watson, *Hermeneutics*, 360. Though Watson argues that 7:7-11 speaks "of the event at Sinai and its aftermath, as reenacted in individual experience" (ibid.), recall that he nevertheless acknowledges that Paul uses *edenic* motifs to describe this experience (see above, p. 107).

38. Dodd writes: "While motifs from the Genesis story about Adam have been employed here, he is not the subject. Rather, Adam is a model that Paul has woven into the fabric of his argument" (*Paradigmatic*, 225-2) and Espy: "The first point to be noted here is that Paul speaks on two levels, referring to Adam and Eve and to a more contemporary party" ("'Robust Conscience,'" 169; see also Senft, "Paul et Jésus," 52 n. 7; Lambrecht, *Wretched*, 83-84). Lichtenberger is similar, though he sees Adam and *humanity* occupying the two levels (*Das Ich*, 267; see also 127-29). We, like Dodd (see also Theissen, *Aspects*, 203, 206; Ziesler, *Romans*, 184), identity the subjects as Adam (and Eve) and Paul, though because of his solidarity with Adam's race, Paul does not stand alone; his experience with the law typifies that of others. Perceiving two character levels in 7:7-11 provides an answer to the question of why Paul did not specify Adam by name there if, in fact, he was the direct referent (a question raised by Middendorf, *Storm*, 140). Indeed, Adam is almost certainly *not* the direct referent, Paul is. As we argued above (see pp. 100-101 n. 68), the Mosaic law, and thus Paul's experience with it as a Jew, seems to be the primary topic of 7:7-11. It would, therefore, likely have obscured both the immediate and wider applications of the depiction if Paul were merely to retell the story of Adam's fall (see Lichtenberger, *Das Ich*, 129). On whether the allusion in 7-11 is to Adam or Eve, see above, p. 100 n. 67.

39. Indeed, the guise is such that scholars have had difficulty identifying the subject of the narrative.

Adam.⁴⁰ Indeed, by way of the "we" in 7:5,⁴¹ and in light of the edenic themes in 7:7-11, we likely have here a resumption of the themes of law, sin, death, and solidarity with Adam that were present in Rom 5:12-18.⁴² And though the account may not be *describing* the Fall,⁴³ Paul weaves into his past tense narrative *reminiscences* of the Fall.⁴⁴ By doing so, it would appear, he consciously describes his past experience with the

---

40. Thurén observes that the *Ego* is an appropriate literary device that both identifies Paul and addressees all humanity" (see *Derhetorizing*, 121 n. 132; see also Bussini, *L'homme*, 123). We use the phrase "solidarity with Adam" to highlight a contrast with Moo's salvation-historical view of the "I": "*Ego* is not Israel, but *ego* is Paul in solidarity with Israel" (*Romans*, 431). While the *immediate* situation is indeed Jewish, for reasons argued above (see pp. 98-107), we find that the "fall" of the ἐγώ is choreographed in terms more reminiscent of Eden than Sinai. Eden, in other words, appears to be the ultimate *Sitz-im-Leben* of the experience depicted in 7:7-11. Thus in Moo's terms, we would summarize it: "*Ego* is not Adam, but *ego* is Paul in solidarity with Adam."

41. Grelet considers Romans 7 to be a "knot" which binds together 5:12ff. and other earlier passages (*Péché*, 17; see also Hofius, "Mensch" 112-13, 121; Schnackenburg, "Römer 7," 294; Campbell, "Identity," 61).

42. See Schnackenburg, "Römer 7," 294; Witherington, *Romans*, 186, 191; Bornkamm's quip in this regard is legendary though not necessarily precise: "In dem *egō* von Röm 7:7ff. bekommt Adam von Röm 5:12ff. seinen Mund" (*Das Ende*, 59). Though we see 7:7-11 to be a resumption of the themes of *law, sin, and death* in 5:12ff., strictly speaking, *Paul*, not Adam, appears to be speaking in 7:7-11, albeit the Apostle's words could virtually be placed in Adam's (and Eve's) mouth.

43. See Brandenburger, *Adam und Christus*, 216; Lambrecht, "Man," 28, 32; contra Lyonnet, "'Tu ne convoiteras pas,'" 157-65; Witherington, *Thought World*, 24; et al.

44. See Kertelge, "Überlegungen," 108. In contrast to the *past* tense narrative of vv. 7-11 that is *retrospective* of primal history, the *present* tense statements of vv. 14-25, if still edenic (thus Lichtenberger, *Das Ich*, 136; Grappe, "Qui me délivrera," 472-92), appear much less so. They seem to be describing present *experience* under the law rather than identifying with a past *event* (see Witherington, *Thought World*, 24-28; Burnett, *Individual*, 201; Wright, "Romans," 565). In other words, vv. 14-25 narrate the situation of those under the law, who, like Paul, are identified with the primeval events alluded to in vv. 7-11. Along this line Hofius remarks: "Sie sprechen von dem durch Adams Fall für ihn selbst und eben damit für alle konstituierten ὑφ' ἁμαρτίαν εἶναι—also von der Konsequenz des Sündenfalls für Adam *und* seine Nachkommen" ("Mensch," 120). This would seem to suggest that a pre-conversion experience is depicted in vv. 14-25 as in vv. 7-11 (see next note and Lichtenberger, *Das Ich*, 136-50; Käsemann, *Romans*, 200; Esler, *Conflict*, 239; Moo, *Romans*, 442-51; et al.; contra Laato, *Paul*, 109-46; Dunn, *Romans*, 1:387-89; Cranfield, *Romans*, 1:344-47; et al.). Theissen is likely correct that the divide between vv. 7-13 and vv. 14-25 "is marked too weakly to be considered the transition between pre-Christian and Christian periods of life; above all, it lacks a reference to Christ, without whom this transition is inconceivable" (*Aspects*, 183).

Mosaic law,⁴⁵ and by analogy that of others, in terms of Adam and Eve's encounter with the edenic command.⁴⁶ What likely appears here, then, is not "the hidden Jew in all of us" nor "the hidden Adam in Israel,"⁴⁷ but *the hidden Adam in Paul and all*.⁴⁸ "Das Sein vorchristlichen Menschen," writes Vollenweider, "wird paradigmatisch in der *Gestalt Adams* zur Darstellung gebracht."⁴⁹

Thus, along with being typical, the narrative of Rom 7:7–11 is edenic. Yet, it is precisely because the account is edenic, we suggest, that it is typical. And this brings us back to the point being argued in this section: for Paul, it would appear, *primal* history becomes *human* history,⁵⁰ and Adam's story becomes *mine*.⁵¹ Therefore, the experience of Adam

---

45. That the "I" of 7:7–11 is stitched to the "we" of 7:5 indicates almost certainly (contra Campbell, "Identity," 59–60) that the narrative there describes the *past* experience of an unregenerate individual under the law, i.e., one who, according to v. 5, was "in the flesh" and whose "sinful passions" were "aroused by the law." This stands in contrast to v. 6: "But now we are discharged from the law, dead to that which held us captive, so that we are slaves not under the old written code but in the new life of the Spirit" (see Hofius, "Mensch," 110; Lichtenberger, *Das Ich*, 266; Elliott, *Rhetoric*, 247).

46. Or stated more succinctly by Theissen: "Paul reads his own nomist conflict with the law into Adam's conflict with the law" (*Aspects*, 209; see also Hofius, "Gesetz," 270).

47. The former, the words of Käsemann (*Questions*, 186), the latter the designation of Wright ("Messiah," 152).

48. We agree with Das, no friend of an edenic interpretation of Rom 7:7–11, and he with us, when he writes, "*If* Adamic motifs are present, as most commentators have thought . . . the Adam-like experience of the "I" would apply to *all* children of Adam as they encounter the command" (*Solving*, 218–19).

49. Vollenweider, *Freiheit*, 349.

50. As Hofius argues: "Adam ist, wie sowohl aus 1 Kor 15,21f.44b-49 wie auch aus Röm 5,12–21 ergibt, der *erste* Mensch und als solcher der am Anfang der Menschheitsgeschichte stehende Stammvater des ganzen Menschenge-schlechts. Die Geschichte dieses einen und erste Menschen ist für alle seine Nachkommen schlicksalbestimmend: Sie alle sind durch Adam als adamitsche" ("Mensch," 113; see also idem, "Gesetz," 270; Jülicher, "Römer," 40). Similar, though more laconic, is Michel: "Was sich einst geschichtlich und typisch abspielte, wird bestimmend für jeden Menschen" (*Römer*, 227).

51. Thus Wilckens: "Paulus [erzählt] hier Adams Geschichte als die 'meinige'; in der Geschichte des 'Ich' wird Adams Geschichte je existenziell konkret" (*Römer*, 2:79). Similar thoughts are expressed by Conzelmann: "The history of Adam is projected into the present as 'my' history" (*Theology*, 170; see also 233), Theissen: "The I assumes the role of Adam and structures it in the light of personal experience of conflict" (*Aspects*, 203), and Haacker: "Dieser Spur folgend, kann der ganze Abschnitt v. 7–11 als eine stillschweigende Auslegung von Gen. 2–3 verstanden werden, die 'Ur-geschichte' als allgemein-menschliche Grunderfahrung deutet" (*Römer*, 143; see also Dunn, *Romans*, 1:40; Käsemann, *Romans*, 197; Bornkamm, *Das Ende*, 59).

with the commandment becomes prototypical of every person's situation faced with divine law.[52] By his "autobiographical use of the Fall narrative" in 7:7–11,[53] Paul appears to craft his own story in such a way that it expresses this generality.[54] The abstract statement of 1 Cor 15:56 regarding the law being the power of sin thus finds a personal expression in the first person, past tense narrative of 7:7–11.[55] In Romans the Apostle portrays in *dramatic* form the catalytic operation of divine law that he had earlier expressed to the Corinthians in *axiomatic* form.[56] And he depicts the drama in *edenic* terms, we argue, because this law-sin scenario identifies with edenic experience.

## THE SETTING AND DYNAMIC OF THE CATALYTIC OPERATION OF THE LAW

Assuming that the Fall, for Paul, provides a prototype of the way in which "the norms and models contained in the law themselves evoke behavior

---

52. See Hübner, *Law*, 76; Sloan, "Paul and the Law," 51; Milne, "Genesis 3," 16–18; Wedderburn, "Adam," 421; Bornkamm, "Sin," 93; Nygren, *Romans*, 280; Dunn, *Romans*, 1:382; note also Lyonnet's response to Cambier in Cambier, "Le 'moi,'" 50.

53. Milne, "Genesis 3," 16.

54. As Theissen observes: "It [i.e., depicting his experience in Adamic terms] without doubt served him as a way of presenting his personal conflict with the law as a general human conflict" (*Aspects*, 255; see also Deidun, *Morality*, 198–99; Lamarche and Le Dû, *Structure*, 49; Grappe, "Qui me délivrera," 487). Bornkamm argues similarly. The "I" of Romans 7 "is *man under law and sin* . . . in whose history, of course, the story of Adam is repeated in a peculiar way" ("Sin," 93; see also Dodd, *Paradigmatic*, 226; Jülicher, "Römer," 40; Kühl, *Römer*, 231).

55. Leenhardt argues along a similar vein: "The function of the law has already been outlined in 3:20; 4:15; 5:20; quick indications which it was necessary to resume and amplify. They are now expressed in the form of a personal declaration" (*Romans*, 185; see also Elliott, *Rhetoric*, 247). Schlier's conclusion is similar, though, we believe, is in need of modification: "Die allgemeinen Formulierungen von 3,20; 4,15; 5,20 (7,5), die auf eine allgemeine Erfahrung der Menschen zielen, sprechen von vornehrein an unserer Stelle für ein generelles und nicht für ein individuelles oder gar autobiographisches 'Ich'" (*Römerbrief*, 221). While the general formulations suggest a common phenomenon, we disagree that this need negate all autobiographical elements in 7:7–11. What is common to all is experienced by each.

56. Indeed, the ἐγώ and the present tense combine to accentuate the universal and "timeless" condition depicted there (see Lambrecht, "Man," 32). Rather than labeling 7:7–11 a "hypothetical narrative" (see Elliott, *Rhetoric*, 247), we prefer the designation "axiomatic drama" since it better expresses the truistic nature of the narrative.

contrary to the norm,"⁵⁷ we are faced with the questions of *why* he assumes that such a scenario plays out in an individual and in *what setting* it does so. Since Paul does not elaborate,⁵⁸ we can do little more than speculate, and reservedly at that. Sufficient for him are pithy statements regarding the inevitability of the law-sin relationship and a narration of the nexus in motion. Nevertheless, though it is appropriate that our explanations here be similarly curt, there are implicit parameters and reasonable assumptions in which speculation can at least be framed.

In regard to the *setting* in which the catalytic operation of the law is operative, there appear to be four components that are on stage (or, in the case of the fourth, off stage) in the scenarios portrayed in both Genesis 3 and Romans 7.⁵⁹ Briefly stated, there is, first of all, the coterminous

---

57. Theissen (*Aspects*, 223). He continues: "even though their authentic purpose is to promote behavior corresponding to the norm."

58. A point noted by Romanello ("Rom 7:7–25," 515).

59. Attempting to comport with René Girard's theory of religion, Hamerton-Kelly identifies three ingredients that he considers to be central to Paul's catalytic notion: *desire*, *violence*, and *religion* ("Sacred Violence," 37). While the motif of *desire* is certainly present in Paul's account (and in Genesis 3), it does not comprise the *backdrop* to the law-sin scenario but is an *outworking* of it. In addition, though the notion of desire is present in Paul, few are convinced that the Pauline notion comports well with the Girardian notion (see discussion below, pp. 215–16 and Marrow, review of *Sacred Violence*, 137–38). A motif of *violence* in Romans 7 or Genesis 3, on the other hand, is not at all obvious, especially Girard's and Hamerton-Kelly's conception of it. Enmity, to be sure, is latent, as Rom 8:7 asserts. Yet the phrase τῷ γὰρ νόμῳ τοῦ θεοῦ οὐχ ὑποτάσσεται is explanatory of the statement τὸ φρόνημα τῆς σαρκὸς ἔχθρα εἰς θεόν. Enmity, in other words, manifests itself here primarily in disobedience to the law, not in violent and "mimetic rivalry." Even in Rom 5:12–21, where the sin of Adam is under discussion, the Fall is described in terms of *transgression* and *disobedience* rather than *violence*. With regard to *religion*, which Hamerton-Kelly associates with "the Mosaic Law" ("Sacred Violence," 38), there is nothing within the context of Romans 7 that warrants his assertion that the law is not the written record of God's revelation to man, but the religion of Judaism (ibid., 37). Not only does Hamerton-Kelly improperly apply to the sinaitic law what (he assumes) Paul says of the Old Testament in general (see the criticism of this common practice in Moo, "'Works of the Law,'" 88; Westerholm, *Perspectives*, 298–300), but he argues that the law code from which Paul quotes is a corruption and abuse of the primal command. It has been *sacralized* by religion, Paul has discovered, and *sanctioned* with vengeance (see "Sacred Violence," 38–39, 44). Suffice it to say in response that Paul insinuates no such thing. Indeed, Romans 7, may be viewed in part as a *defense* of the Mosaic law (see, e.g., Beker, *Paul*, 105; Bornkamm, "Sin," 88–89; Romanello, "Rom 7:7–25," 510–30). And certainly the Apostle's assertion in 7:12 that the "the law is holy, and the commandment is holy and just and good" allows no depreciation either in whole or in part.

*presence of sin.*⁶⁰ As we saw in the Genesis account, sin was externally present there in the form of the serpent; in Paul's depiction of himself, and by analogy of those in Adam, sin is not only present (7:8, 9, 11), but "evil is close at hand" (7:21b). Indeed, Paul exclaims: "sin dwells within me" (7:17, 20b).⁶¹ The context would seem to indicate that this indwelling sin is not so much associated with "a latent human readiness for anxiety,"⁶² but rather with an innate propensity to be hostile toward God and consequently disobedient to divine directives.⁶³ Second, there is law, i.e., a *divine demand*,⁶⁴ through which latent sin acquires stimulation and direction. In Eden the law appeared in the form of the command, "You shall not eat" (Gen 2:17); with Paul it was expressed through the Decalogue commandment, "You shall not covet" (Rom 7:8). There is no indication that either Genesis 3 or Romans 7 assumes a legalistic misuse of the law. Neither Eve nor the "I" were seduced into observing the law, but transgressing the law.⁶⁵ Next, with both Adam and Paul, there is a

---

60. See Pate, *Curse*, 427; Bandstra, *Elements*, 127; Theissen, *Aspects*, 225. Räisänen charges Paul with a "glaring contradiction" here: "On the one hand he states that the intervention of the law is necessary to induce man to sin [7:7-11]; on the other hand man is already 'sold under sin' [7:14] when he encounters the commandment of the law" (*Paul and the Law*, 142). Such a conclusion is ill-warranted. Romans 7:8-9 assumes the presence of latent sin *prior* to the commandment's arrival. A similar sequence occurs in Rom 5:13, 20. The law serves as the occasion that arouses existing sin (see Weima, "Function," 233). Van Spanje is incorrect, we believe, in his attempt to solve the alleged tension raised by Räisänen by altogether denying a catalytic function in 7:7-11 (see *Inconsistency*, 225). Besides the catalytic notion in 7:7-8, vv. 5 and 13, which envelop the narrative, make it clear that once aroused, existing sin uses the law to provoke actual transgression.

61. Lyonnet is careful to nuance the analogy between the "I" in Romans 7 and Adam/Eve: "Dans le récit de la Genèse, le diable-serpent demeure toujours extérieur à l'homme, tandis que pour saint Paul le péché, d'abord complètement étranger à Adam qui 'vivait' ... devient en lui un principe interne d'activité" (*Les étapes*, 125). Malina incorrectly assumes that Paul considered sin to have been dormant in Adam before the commandment arrived and sin sprang to life ("Observations," 30). Malina makes this mistake because he views Paul's narrative as "an account of the Genesis sin." It almost certainly is not. It is, we argue, an account of Paul's encounter with the law patterned after Adam's.

62. Theissen, *Aspects*, 229. Theissen argues that, for Paul, this propensity towards anxiety is elicited when sin dupes the recipient into unconsciously perceiving the moral demands to be life-threatening (ibid.). See below, p. 215.

63. See, e.g., Rom 5:10; 8:7.

64. The assumption of Hamerton-Kelly that the Mosaic law is a perversion of the primal command receives no encouragement from Paul (see above, n. 59).

65. Morris argues from Rom 7:7-8 that the knowledge of the law leads to the *desire* (ἐπιθυμία) for justification since this knowledge leads people to become aware of the

*sanction* attached to the law in which one's destiny hangs in the balance.[66] With Adam it was *do this and you will die* (Gen 2:17); with Paul it was *do not do this and you will live* (Rom 7:10).[67] There is nothing explicit, nor

---

possibility that they might be judged and found wanting (see "Law," 285-87). The difficulty with this is not only that knowledge stands at the *end* of the law-sin process in 7:7-8 rather than at its beginning, but that the "I" is being stimulated by sin to disobey the law not to establish its righteousness by observing the law. Paul's use of ἐπιθυμία here does not allow for the legalistic subtleties that Morris suggests. As Wilckens notes, the notion is certainly not *nomian*, but *a-nomian*: "Nicht weil ich das Gesetz erfüllen suche (was ich doch im Sinne des Gesetzes *soll*), bin Ich 'unter Sünde verkauft' (v. 14), sondern deswegen, weil ich tue, was das Gebot verbietet" (*Römer*, 2:80; see also Räisänen, *Paul and the Law*, 141; van Dülmen, *Theologie* 175-79). If Paul in 7:7-8 were pondering a catalogue of sins, he would have likely had in mind a list of behavior such as in Gal 5:19-21, where the ἐπιθυμίαν σαρκὸς (v. 16) is *concretized* in various forms of *misconduct*, not nomistic strivings (see Theissen, *Aspects*, 208). See further discussion below, pp. 216-17.

66. In contrast to "the righteousness that comes from faith" in Rom 10:6, Paul writes in 10:5: "Moses writes concerning the righteousness that comes from the law, that 'the person who does these things will live by them'" (ὁ ποιήσας αὐτὰ ἄνθρωπος ζήσεται ἐν αὐτοῖς). Likewise in Gal 3:12, the Apostle writes: "But the law does not rest on faith; on the contrary, 'Whoever does the works of the law will live by them' (ὁ ποιήσας αὐτὰ ζήσεται ἐν αὐτοῖς)." It would appear that a determinative feature of being *under* the law is being faced with the sanction attached to the commandment. It may be that Paul would not have considered the life described in Psalm 19 and 119 to be existence "under the law" in this sense. "Law" and "commandments" there may refer to divine directives and guidelines as opposed to stipulations in a do-or-die covenant issued in the presence of coterminous sin, and in any case, the psalmist is not, like Paul, speaking globally regarding the law in (un)salvation-history. What the psalmist sings, Paul likely states in Rom 7:13: "The law is holy, and the commandment is holy and just and good" and in 7:22: "I delight in the law of God." We might also mention here Calvin's view that the divine demand is an essential ingredient in life that has nothing to do with sin and disobedience (see *Genesis*, 125-26; see also the discussion in Hesselink, *Calvin's Concept*, 54-55; and above, p. 119 n. 160). Nevertheless, sparks fly, Paul seems to argue, when divine law is accompanied with death threats and is issued in the presence of sin.

67. See also Rom 10:5; Gal 3:10, 12. Such a "do-or-die" setting provides a partial answer to Räisänen's question of why it is only the Torah that incites sin. "Why," he asks "does not, say, the apostolic paraenesis—or paraclesis, if you like—lead to the same result?" (*Paul and the Law*, 148-49). In response, for Paul, the "death threat" has been overcome in the vicarious death of Christ (see Rom 8:1ff., Gal 3:13). Life and death, in other words, no longer hang in the balance. The relationship of the believer and unbeliever to the law are, thus, incomparable. With the latter the divine demand *threatens*; with the former it *regulates* (see below, p. 239 n. 9). The respective response to the divine imperative, therefore, would inevitably differ (see Theissen, *Aspects*, 228). In addition, it would seem that the law-sin syndrome has been disengaged in the lives of believers, who, according to Rom 7:6, are neither bound to the flesh (which is at enmity with God [Rom 8:7]) nor subject to the workings of the old age but are now aided by the Spirit (see Kertelge, "Überlegungen," 108; Wedderburn, "Adam," 421; Thurén, *Rhetorizing*, 135-37;

even implicit, in either narrative that would suggest that the sanction is anything but divinely prescribed.[68] Finally, in neither account does *the Spirit* appear as an aid against temptation. In the Genesis narrative we merely find a "living being";[69] in Paul, only an individual "alive" and "in the flesh."[70] These four features existing together, we suggest, comprise in general terms the scenario of life *under the law*,[71] i.e., subject to the rule of divine law and to its sanctions while being within the reach of sin and outside the realm of the Spirit. And, for Paul, it is within such a sphere of

---

Westerholm, *Israel's Law*, 215–16; and below, p. 246 n. 33).

68. Theissen argues that the death threat is not implicit in the divine demand but derives from sin itself, which overpowers the law and "conceals itself in the voice of the law." The recipient, in other words, is hood-winked into perceiving the law as a "hostile signal" that threatens one's life, or at least one's freedom (*Aspects*, 229). Hamerton-Kelly considers sanctioned prohibitions to have originated in the desire to imitate the violence committed and to enact revenge (see "Sacred Violence," 39). This, in his view, was a distortion of the primal sanction, which was minatory, rather than vengeful; i.e., transgressors were not threatened with the judgment of God (indeed, the notion of the "wrath of God" is "religion as violence in its aspect of vengeance" [ibid., 45]), rather they risked both the loss of limits that define creaturehood and the way being opened to rivalry with God and all other human beings (ibid., 44). Hamerton-Kelly appears to overlay an alien metanarrative over the Pauline narrative. Whatever may be the perception or response of the recipient to the divine demand, Paul depicts the death threat as a *divine* sanction rather than a *human* distortion, and in no sense is the motive depicted as a violent and vengeful reciprocity. In Paul's thought, and in accordance with Old Testament thought (see Zimmerli, *Law and Prophets*, 51–65), the divine curse is intrinsically related to divine law (see Gal 3:10, 13).

69. Gen 2:7 (נֶ֫פֶשׁ חַיָּ֫ה, LXX: ψυχὴν ζῶσαν). Noted by Paul in 1 Cor 15:44–45.

70. Rom 7:5. For the phrase "in the flesh," see below, n. 92.

71. The phrase "of the works of the law" (Gal 3:10) appears to be synonymous with "under the law" (Gal 4:5). Both cases imply being obligated to the Mosaic law's demands and liable to its sanctions (see below, p. 213 n. 45 and Westerholm, *Perspectives*, 300–21; idem, "'Letter' and 'Spirit,'" 242–43). While some understand Paul's phrase "under the law" (Rom 6:14) merely as a reference to being under the *condemnation* of the law (see, e.g., Calvin, *Romans*, 130; Wilckens, *Römer*, 2:23; Cranfield, *Romans*, 1:320; Hübner, *Law*, 134–35), the insinuation voiced in 6:15 that freedom from the law would inevitably lead to a licentious lifestyle suggests that being "no long under the law" entails freedom from the law's demands, not just its curses (see also 1 Cor 9:20; Räisänen, *Paul and the Law*, 47). An analogy may be found in Col 2:20–21, where Paul argues that an individual who "has died" to the world need no longer abide by its rules (see further discussion below, pp. n. 9). We are likewise to understand Paul's phrase "under the law" to include the ethical demands of the law, not merely its cultic or ethnic rites. Thus, Paul quotes the Decalogue in Rom 7:7, and, again, the reference to licence in 6:15 suggests that freedom from the moral demands of the Torah are included in Christian liberty.

influence,[72] prior to being "discharged from the law" (7:6), that the law-sin nexus thrived: "While we were living in the flesh, our sinful passions, aroused by the law, were at work in our members to bear fruit for death" (7:5).[73] This is the elixir of the catalytic operation of the law.

As to exactly *why* "the law produces the very attitudes and actions that it intends to proscribe,"[74] we can only postulate. Dodd appeals to modern psychology and the dynamic of repressed desires, which form a subconscious "complex" that eventually bursts into the conscious life.[75] Theissen likewise psychoanalyzes the "I" of Romans 7, though at greater length. He attributes a person's conflict with (the) law to the primitive fear of death. That is, we interpret the prohibition and threat of death as a "hostile signal." This life-threatening situation then elicits anxiety, which in turn leads to intolerance, distorted perception, and eventually to conflict with the law. Considering Paul's statements regarding law, self, and flesh to be in proximity to Freud's *superego*, *ego*, and *id*, Theissen theorizes that Rom 7:7–25 is an account of a once-unconscious conflict with the law becoming conscious.[76]

A more recent attempt to explain the dynamic that fuels the catalytic operation of the law is that of Hamerton-Kelly, who applies René Girard's theory of religion to Paul's theology of law.[77] According to Girard, human nature is imitative, and this propensity causes violence in the form of rivalry. Religion, with its prohibitions and doctrines of divine wrath, merely transformed this human violence into "sacred violence."[78] Hamerton-Kelly finds this scenario playing out in Judaism *par excellence* (and even in Paul whose references to eschatological wrath in Rom 2:5, 8; 3:5; 5:9; 12:19, he asserts, suggest that the Apostle was not entirely free from such sentiments).[79] The Mosaic law, he argues, originated in the ir-

---

72. A phrase used by Snodgrass (see "Spheres," 93–113; and below, p. 225). We will apply the phrase differently, however (see below, p. 228).

73. See Becker, *Paul*, 398.

74. Hamerton-Kelly, "Sacred Violence," 37.

75. Dodd, *Romans*, 110.

76. See Theissen, *Aspects*, 222–34. For other psychological exegeses of Romans 7, see, e.g., Crespy, "Psychanalyse," 169–79; Forsyth, "Freud," 476–87; Vergote, "Psychoanalyse, 73–116; Pfister, "Entwicklung," 243–90; Fischer, *Gespaltener*, 44–76.

77. Hamerton-Kelly treats the topic at length in *Sacred Violence*.

78. See ibid., 13–39.

79. See Hamerton-Kelly, "Sacred Violence," 45.

rational need to imitate the violence of the offender. Thus, Paul learned, its prohibitions stimulate rather than curb rivalry. The recipient sees a rival, not a benefactor behind the restriction and hence lashes out.[80]

Käsemann has strong words for psychologically-based exegeses of Romans 7 (like those of Dodd and Theissen), which he *in toto* labels "out of place."[81] His revulsion may itself be out of bounds, however. It is difficult not to ponder what psychological aspects are at work in the conflicted experience of the "I" in Romans 7. Nevertheless, at best, psychological phenomena have only a back burner interest for Paul.[82] Realistically, Paul says too little in our view to make a post-mortem psychological diagnosis such as Theissen's,[83] and his thesis regarding 7:7-25 does not seem to square with what little the Apostle does say.[84] Matters are even more precarious for Hamerton-Kelly's assessment. Many of his interpretative assumptions are anything but obvious,[85] and one gets the sense that the murkiness is due to his reading of Paul through the wrong lens.[86]

A more common attempt to explain the law-sin phenomenon appeals to nomistic strivings rather than psychological or primitive drives; i.e., Paul was deceived by sin into expecting life from something which could produce only death.[87] Playing on the contrast between εἰς ζωήν

---

80. See ibid., 37-39; idem, *Sacred Violence*, 140-60.

81. Käsemann, *Romans*, 193; see further, 193-211 and Barrett, *Romans*, 136.

82. See Dunn, *Romans*, 1:377. By "back burner" we mean that while Paul's reminiscence in 7:7-11 appears to be, so to speak, a "Pauline psychoanalysis" of the temptation and sin of Adam and Eve (Milne, "Genesis 3," the *subconscious* dynamics at play are left undeveloped.

83. See Ziesler, *Romans*, 183.

84. Theissen's understanding of vv. 7-25 as a psychological *coming out* is problematic. Not only does Paul's "knowledge of sin" in 7:7-8 suggest an *experiential acquaintance* with sin rather than mere *cognition* (see above, p. 103 n. 71), but the knowledge attained is, in fact, the knowledge of *sin*, not a conscious recognition of "the once-unconscious conflict with the law" (*Aspects*, 229).

85. See, e.g., nn. 59, 68, above.

86. Marrow's review of Hammerton-Kelly is merciless: "The Girardian theory, instead of being an obedient tool of elucidation, has become a tyrannous master of obfuscation" (review of Hamerton-Kelly, 138; see also Jewett, *Romans*, 448). We are similarly leery of Busch's use of Jacques Lacan's "mirror theory" to explicate Paul's law-sin notion (see "Eve," 30-35).

87. Of course, Bultmann virtually owns such an interpretation (see below, p. 225). See also, e.g., Garlington, "Creation Theology," 208; Middendorf, *Storm*, 83-84; Milne, "Genesis 3," 16, and the scenario of Morris noted above (see n. 65).

and εἰς θάνατον in 7:10, Moo, for example, suggests that Paul in a salvation-historical sense "thinks of the way that the 'promise of life' held out by the law 'deceived' Israel into thinking that it could attain life through it."[88] Bornkamm argues similarly, though from the perspective of an individual: "The deception of sin can only consist in the fact that it falsely promises life to me . . . which because of sin is never any longer truly an open possibility for me."[89] Barrett likewise argues that the law, used as a grounds of boasting, is deceptively shaped by sin into a false bridge across the gulf that separates humans from God.[90]

Such interpretations may find support from Rom 10:1-2, where Israel's zeal for the law is said to be "not enlightened" or from Gal 1:7, where Paul charges his opponents with seeking "to pervert the gospel of Christ." However, in contrast to Rom 7:11, the illusion in Rom 10:3 is a matter of *ignorance* (ἀγνοέω) not deception, and though Paul's opponents were misleading the Galatians, he describes them in Gal 1:7 in terms of *troubling* (ταράσσω) rather than deceiving the churches. Paul nowhere speaks of a *nomistic deception* with reference to the law. But more significant, as we noted above, the context of Romans 7 indicates that Paul was not misled into either keeping or trusting in the law but was tricked by sin into transgressing the law. What 7:7-11 addresses, in other words, is not *nomism* but *antinomism*.[91]

---

88. Moo, *Romans*, 440.

89. Bornkamm, "Sin," 91-92; see also Schlier, *Römerbrief*, 226; Cranfield, *Romans*, 1:353.

90. See Barrett, *Romans*, 135; Pate, *Curse*, 437. Pate suggests that the law provokes "a false confidence that one is obeying the law when, in fact, it is not" (ibid.). This we believe misunderstands the catalytic notion (see below, n. 104). Although Busch does not argue for this nomistic approach, he similarly proposes that Eve misconstrued the commandment. In her case, she made the error of *reflecting* upon it as *letter* instead of participating in it as *spirit* ("Eve," 25).

91. See Zeller, *Römer*, 140; Wilckens, *Römer*, 2:80-81; Theissen, *Aspects*, 208; and n. 65, above. Similar concerns can be expressed against Jewett's notion that sin misused the law by eliciting in the "I" of Rom 7:7-11a competitive zeal for the law (see *Romans*, 440-53). In light of the allusion to the serpent in Rom 7:11—an allusion that almost every commentator recognizes—and the fact that Paul nowhere spins his catalytic notion of the law in terms of "zeal for the law" (see above, p. 100 n. 68), we find it difficult to entertain Jewett's dogmatic assertion that "it is not the sin of disobedience, *as in the Genesis account*, but the sin of legalistic zealotism that leads to the death that Paul has in mind [in 7:11]" (ibid., 453, italics mine). See related discussion below, n. 105.

While the lack of elaboration on Paul's part may temper speculation on our part, some observations may at least point in the direction toward which guarded speculation about the dynamic of the catalytic experience should aim. Particularly significant, we believe, is Paul's assertion that it was while *in the flesh* that the sinful passions were aroused by the law (Rom 7:5).[92] Since Paul elsewhere identifies the flesh with *hostility towards God* (8:7), it may be fairly assumed that, for Paul, latent sin becomes actualized as a result of the divine restriction colliding with such enmity.[93] In other words, due to a profound and innate alienation from God, the divine command "calls out the opposition of man against God."[94] In addition, Paul, perhaps, considered that the mere forbidding of wrong-doing "so affects our perverse nature as to rouse in us a determination to indulge it."[95] The flesh responds perversely to the prohibition precisely because of its perversity.[96] Thus, innately, the divine prohibition likely functions counter-suggestively because of the propensity of the flesh to run counter to God.

Yet, in addition to this and in light of the edenic elements from which Paul appears to draw, Paul's understanding of the law-sin dynamic can perhaps be illuminated by the Fall scenario itself.[97] But how so? Qualitatively speaking, both Eve and Paul were deceived. She, it appears, was tricked into disobeying the commandment by being led to believe

---

92. The phrase "in the flesh" here likely denotes a "power-sphere" (Moo, *Romans*, 418 n. 51) that stands in contrast and opposition to the spiritual realm (see, e.g., 7:6; 8:5, 7, 12; 13:14; Gal 5:13–18; 6:8; Col 2:11, 13, 18, 23). The term σάρξ to greater or lesser degrees denotes a weakness and corruptibility that distances one from the Creator (see Dunn, *Romans*, 1:363). An ethically negative connotation is often apparent (see, e.g., Rom 7:5, 14; 8:6; Gal 5:19; 6:8; Eph 2:3), particularly when σάρξ is set in antithesis with πνεῦμα as here in Rom 7:6–7 (see, e.g., the verses cited immediately above and Rom 2:28; 8:9; Gal 3:19; 4:29; Phil 3:3, 4). Since the noun denotes what is corruptible and rebellious, the phrase "in the flesh" in 7:5 could simply be another way of saying "in Adam" and thus be the condition described in the various antitheses in Rom 5:12–21 (see Wright, "Romans," 560). For further discussions, see *TDNT* 7:98–151; Sand, 'Sarx'; Fee, *Presence*, 816–22; Brandenburger, *Fleisch und Geist*; Ridderbos, *Paul*, 93–95.

93. See Napier, "Analysis," 23.

94. So e.g., Kling, *First Corinthians*, 348; Goudge, *First Corinthians*, 160.

95. Simon, *First Corinthians*, 152.

96. Similar thoughts are expressed by Dodd (*Romans*, 109) and Bruce (*Romans*, 141).

97. See Dunn, *Christology*, 104. This is especially so if, as Cranfield argues, Rom 7:7–11 is best understood as "exposition of the Genesis narrative" (*Romans*, 1:350).

that she would not die but become enlightened with a divine knowledge that God had sought to withhold from her.⁹⁸ The Apostle, perhaps, felt himself the victim of a similar ruse; his covetousness, like Eve's, was aroused as a result of thinking of himself as the victim of God's jealousy and inhibitive restrictions.⁹⁹ Or more likely, perhaps like Eve, Paul found himself enticed by the lure of autonomy. While the motif of becoming like God plays no direct roll in Paul's narrative,¹⁰⁰ it is not impossible that the idea is latent. In light of the innate hostility toward God that resides in the flesh (Rom 8:7), divine law, which marks out the difference between creature and Creator, may have posed for Paul a limitation which led to resentment and a rebellious quest for autonomy and even divinity.¹⁰¹ Indeed, Moo, who is cool towards an edenic interpretation of Rom 7:7-11, nevertheless entertains the possibility that we should include in Paul's *every manner of coveting* (7:8) "the desire 'to be like God,' to usurp the place of the Creator."¹⁰²

While the topic beckons further study, it is perhaps best that the present study goes no further in an attempt to theo- or psychoanalyze the law-sin process, lest in our limited space we go too far.¹⁰³ While

---

98. "This precept," as Eliezer paraphrases the serpent, "is nought else except the evil eye" (*Pirqe R. El.* 13 [Friedlander]).

99. See Leenhardt, *Romans*, 189; Zeller, *Römer*, 138-40; Byrne, *Romans*, 220; Senft, "Paul et Jésus," 52. Finsterbusch likewise interprets v. 11 strictly in light of the serpent's seduction of Eve. For her, however, the subversion consists of sin dangling before the "I" the lie that transgression would not lead to death (*Thora*, 53; see also Zeller, *Römer*, 140-41). Dunn also applies the Eden narrative to the interpretation of v. 11, though he moves beyond Finsterbusch in the direction of Leenhardt, Byrne, and Senft: "The deception lay not merely in making God a liar ('You shall not die'), but also in misrepresenting God's motives in giving the commandment in the first place. It made the instruction 'intended to promote life' sound like the arbitrary command of a dictator fearful of losing his special status and prerogative" (*Romans*, 1:402; see also *Christology*, 104).

100. Rightly noted by Wilckens (*Römer*, 2:81).

101. See Cranfield, *Romans*, 1:350; Leenhardt, *Romans*, 189; Barrett, *Romans*, 134; Schmithals, *Römerbrief*, 214; Bussini, *L'homme*, 126; Zeller, *Römer*, 140; Senft, "Paul et Jésus," 52; et al.). Dunn traces the rebellious mind-set in 7:7-11 back to 1:18ff. and to the refusal to acknowledge human creatureliness and dependence on God (*Romans*, 1:427).

102. *Romans*, 436 n. 44; see also Lyonnet (*Les étapes*, 128). Dunn makes a similar application: "The serpent . . . twisted the instruction of the Creator given for man's good and made it sound like the legislation of a dictator fearful of losing his special status and prerogatives. Thus deceived, man clutched at a godlike life and grasped only death" (*Christology*, 104).

103. See our response to Hamerton-Kelly, above, p. 211 n. 59, pp. 215-16. We also

an innate enmity and a quest for autonomy may have driven the "I" to take the bait, Paul, in his brief account, does not *analyze* the process; he merely *describes* it: Like the serpent of old, sin used the commandment to entice him into transgressing the commandment.[104] In other words, while there is almost certainly a subplot between the lines, Paul does not unearth it. What strikes Paul, and for his purposes he highlights, is that the *law* led to *law-breaking*.[105] And rather than dissecting this scenario,

---

find that Busch goes too far by reading too much into Eve's re-wording of the prohibition ("Eve," 24-36). As we noted in our examination of the Fall narrative, one must be careful of reading too much into Eve's phrasing of the commandment. See further below, n. 105. Likewise, might Jewett's sociological reading of Rom 7:7-11 be drawing out of the text more than the text itself would justify? See above, n. 91.

104. See Zeller, "Zusammenhang," 200. We consider the notion of *enticement* to be implicit in Paul's use of ἐξαπατάω in v. 11. That it can convey such a sense is evident from θ ' Sus 1:56: τὸ κάλλος ἐξηπάτησέν σε καὶ ἡ ἐπιθυμία διέστρεψεν τὴν καρδίαν σου. Here Daniel says to the wicked judge who attempted to rape Susanna: "beauty has *beguiled* you and lust has perverted your heart." See also, e.g., Herodotus, *Hist.* 2.114 for this same meaning, LXX Judg 14:15; 16:15; Job 31:27; Jdt 13:16 for the notion of seduction in the verb ἀπατάω, and Strabo, *Geogr.* 11.2.10 for the connotation of "bait" in the noun ἀπάτη; see also the discussions in *TDNT* 1:384-85; *EDNT* 2:2; *TLNT* 1:153-55; *NIDNTT* 2:459.

105. Paul's didactic intentions appear to be simple; at issue is the *disobedience*, not the frame of mind—be it psychotic, legalistic, zealous, or autonomous—, that resulted from sin's deceptive use of the commandment. Such a direct line between *deceit* and *sin/transgression* is observed in 1 Tim 2:14 (ἡ δὲ γυνὴ ἐξαπατηθεῖσα ἐν παραβάσει γέγονεν) and in Rom 7:8a and 7:11a, where the phrases κατειργάσατο ἐν ἐμοὶ πᾶσαν ἐπιθυμίαν and ἐξηπάτησέν με run parallel:

ἀφορμὴν δὲ λαβοῦσα ἡ ἁμαρτία διὰ τῆς ἐντολῆς
**κατειργάσατο ἐν ἐμοὶ πᾶσαν ἐπιθυμίαν**
ἡ γὰρ ἁμαρτία ἀφορμὴν λαβοῦσα διὰ τῆς ἐντολῆς
**ἐξηπάτησέν με**

Note also Rom 5:12-21, where Adam's act is considered in terms of *disobedience* and *transgression*. In addition, as Räisänen correctly points out, the plural τὰ παθήματα in 7:5 suggests concrete *acts* (as does 5:20) rather than legalistic attitudes, and the parallel references in 6:21 to *fruitbearing* and in 6:19 to *members* suggest that Paul is referring in 7:5 to the slavery of *sin* described in chapter 6, as does the verb δουλεύω in 7:6 (see *Paul, and the Law*, 141). We should also note here that the theory of Busch, which argues that *the desire for knowledge* is the dynamic that drives Paul's catalytic operation of the law, also appears to break down on this point. In an attempt to understand Rom 7:7-11 from the perspective of the Fall narrative, Busch argues that the garden commandment drew Eve into *reflecting upon good and evil*, and yet *forbade* such reflection. It was in this way that Paul understood the catalytic operation of the law; the law forbids one to evaluate it and yet beckons such reflection (see "Eve," 30-33). Aside from a questionable interpretation of the Fall account (Eve was not guilty of *reflecting* on the commandment but *transgressing* the commandment, and knowing good and evil was not the *cause* of

Paul encapsulates it in epigrammatic form and immortalizes it in a first person narrative, and in so doing he generalizes the experience.[106] From the beginning, Paul reveals, rather than fostering a relationship with one's Maker, divinely sanctioned law, through no fault of its own, awakens latent sin to disobey the Creator.[107]

---

the Fall but the *result* of the Fall), it would seem that Busch misinterprets Paul's notion by taking the Fall narrative (or rather, his misinterpretation of it) into *too much* account. According to 5:20 and 7:4 the law prohibits and incites *numerous kinds of desires*, not just *cognitive desire*.

106. "The situation of the first man with the law," writes Malina, "is just like that of every man with the Law" ("Origin," 32).

107. "The law," writes Franzmann, "is the footstep of God upon the grass that rouses the serpent sleeping there to life" (*Romans*, 125).

# 8

# Reflections: The Catalytic Operation of the Law and Paul's Assessment of the Law

WE CONTINUE OUR REFLECTIONS. With regard to the relation of the law-sin nexus to Paul's assessment of the law's role in salvation history, if Paul assumed that the catalytic operation of the law dated to the childhood period of humanity, he would have likely considered both law and sin to be entities belonging to the era of the Fall. There would be, in other words, a primal, and hence seminal, law-problematic. Even in Paradise sin pressed the law into its service. In the following we will consider the role of the law in Eden and how it might relate to the *origin* of Paul's understanding of the law and to his *critical* assessment of it. We will begin by sketching some contemporary theories regarding Paul and the law and will then consider the place that the law/Torah occupies in salvation history, if it has a place there at all. Indeed, if the sting of death is sin and the power of sin is the law, it would appear that law, along with sin and death, would, strictly speaking, be an entity belonging to *Unheilsgeschichte* rather than *Heilsgeschichte*.[1]

---

1. We follow here Yarbrough's definition of *Heilsgeschichte*: "the personal redemptive activity of God within human history to effect his eternal saving intentions" ("Salvation History," 297). That Paul assumed a redemptive activity of God in history is evident from passages such as Galatians 3–4; 2 Cor 3:7–18; Rom 3:21–26; 9–11. See Bonneau, "Stages," 194; Goldsworthy, "Biblical Theology," 8; Schoeps, *Paul*, 219–58. For our definition of *Unheilsgeschichte*, see below, n. 63.

## PERSPECTIVES ON PAUL AND THE LAW

Scholars, too numerous to review in full here,[2] have proposed various scenarios regarding the origin and evolution of the Paul's critique of the law. Sanders, for example, proposes that Paul's reason for virtually equating the law with sin and death was his "black and white thinking." Since it was Christ, not the law that saves: "it becomes not just second best, but is ranged on the side of the forces of evil."[3] Wilckens, on the other hand, suggests that the pre-Christian Paul, while in the Hellenistic synagogue to which he belonged, encountered and persecuted Christians who claimed that the sacrifices prescribed by the Torah were made obsolete by the atoning death of Christ. After his conversion, his theological antagonism continued to exist but now in reverse: "Nun war es das Kreuz Christi, das die Geltung des Gesetzes ausschloß."[4] Others, like Drane and Hübner, likewise perceive a development in Paul's thinking. For Drane, Paul's concern for the Galatians resulted in a series of "devastating denunciations of the Old Testament Law and all that it stood for."[5] Being later faced with Corinthian libertinism, however, Paul modified his position, and finally, in Romans he attempts to give "a completely balanced exposition of his theological position, which would be susceptible of misunderstanding by neither Judaizers nor Gnosticizers."[6] Hübner assumes a similar mellowing, but postulates that it was due to criticism Paul received from the Jerusalem Apostles concerning his Galatian letter.[7] Räisänen, for his part, contends that Paul, at his conversion, adopted the Gentile's relaxed attitude toward Torah observance and over the years had fully identified himself with their point of view. When Jewish Christians later began to urge Gentile Christians to submit to the law, Paul was unable "to retrace his steps." He thus "came upon several *ad hoc* arguments for the termina-

---

2. For helpful summaries, see Moo, "Paul and the Law," 287–307; Westerholm, "'New Perspective,'" 1–38, idem, *Perspectives*, 101–258; Waters, *Justification*, 1–149.

3. Sanders, *Law*, 153.

4. Wilckens, "Entwicklung," 155.

5. Drane, *Libertine*, 5.

6. Ibid., 124; see also 65.

7. Hübner, *Law*, 60–65. Being "concerned to still the waves of indignation that had been whipped up in Jerusalem by his letter to the Galatians," Hübner postulates that Paul may have written Romans prior to his arrival in Jerusalem to make known his "new" theology (ibid., 64–65).

tion of the law . . . and its allegedly sin-engendering and sin-enhancing nature, etc."[8] Indeed, since, for Paul, Christ superseded the law, he "*had to show that the effects of the law are negative, and only negative, and he carried through his thesis with violence.*"[9] In attributing to the law a sin-provoking function "Paul," Räisänen argues, "*goes his own way, parting company with the prophets.*"[10]

In regard to how Paul would justify his critical attitude towards the law,[11] Sanders argues that Paul polemicized against the law for *dogmatic* reasons. For Paul, "doing the law, in short, is wrong only because it is not of faith. In itself obedience to the law is a good thing . . . and is faulted only when it seems to threaten the exclusiveness of salvation by faith in Christ."[12] Das, on the other hand, views Paul's polemic from a *salvation-historical* perspective; i.e., in Paul's understanding, the gracious framework of Judaism (election, covenant, sacrifice) has collapsed, without which non-Christian Jews are left to rely on the impossible task of keeping a law that demands perfect obedience.[13] For Moo, Paul's primary concern with the law is *anthropological*; i.e., humanity, by nature, is incapable of fulfilling the law. "'Works of the law,'" he writes, "cannot justify, not because they are inherently *wrong*, nor only because a decisive shift in salvation-history has occurred, but fundamentally because no man is able to *do* them in sufficient degree and number so as to gain merit before God."[14] Other scholars argue that Paul had a *qualitative* concern with the law.[15] Thus, for Bultmann, the doing of the law is wrong in and of itself, not "because, by reason of transgressions, it fails to reach its goal,

---

8. Räisänen, *Paul and the Law*, 261–62.

9. Ibid., 150.

10. Ibid., 161, italics mine.

11. See the survey in Snodgrass, "Spheres," 95–96.

12. Sanders, *Palestinian Judaism*, 550; see also 552. More specifically, Sanders argues that, for Paul, "what is wrong with the law, and thus with Judaism, is that it does not provide for God's ultimate purpose, that of saving the entire world through faith in Christ, and without the privilege accorded to Jews through the promises, the covenants, and the law" (*Law*, 47; see also 155).

13. See Das, *Covenant*, 69, 112, 214 n. 76, 273, etc.

14. Moo, "'Works of the Law,'" 98; see also Wilckens: "Was heißt bei Paulus," 81–104; Lambrecht, "Gesetzesverständnis," 112–27; van Dülmen, *Theologie*, 73–4; Das, *Covenant*, 226; idem, *Paul*, 151–55; Westerholm, *Perspectives*, 418–21; Schreiner, *Law*, 44–71.

15. On the distinction between Paul's *quantitative* (i.e., *anthropological*) and *qualitative* critiques of the law, see Moo, "Paul and the Law," 297–98.

... but rather that the *direction* of this way is perverse and, to be sure, because it intends to lead to 'one's own righteousness.'"[16] Somewhat similarly, Cranfield asserts that Paul was not negative toward the law itself but toward its "legalist misuse."[17] For Snodgrass, Paul's understanding of the law should be viewed from the "sphere of influence" it occupies. Paul's negative statements about the law describe "the usurped law in the sphere of sin, flesh, and death,"[18] whereas for the Christian, the law occupies the sphere of Christ, the Spirit, and faith, where it serves a positive role.[19] Lastly, Wright and Dunn argue famously that Paul objected to the law's abuse as a *nationalistic* barrier to exclude non-Jews. Thus for Wright, Paul's answer to the question of how Israel missed her vocation "is that she is guilty not of 'legalism' or 'works righteousness' but of ... 'national righteousness.'"[20] Similarly, Dunn speaks of the law's abuse as a Jewish "identity marker" or "badge of covenant membership."[21] In attacking the Judaism of his day, Dunn argues, "Paul was attacking neither the law, nor the covenant, ... but *a covenant nomism which insisted on treating the law as a boundary marker round Israel, marking off Jew from Gentile, with only those inside as heirs of God's promise to Abraham*. In short, it was the law abused to which Paul objected, not the law itself."[22] Even a later statement of Dunn's that Paul *also* critiques the law's "abuse by sin" becomes itself a

---

16. Bultmann, "Romans 7," 149. According to Bultmann, "*Man's effort to achieve his salvation by keeping the law* only leads him into sin, indeed this effort itself in the end *is already sin*" (*Theology*, 1:264, italics his; see more recently, Pate, *Curse*, 435-37).

17. Cranfield, "St. Paul," 56; see also idem, *Essays*, 203. Thurén labels such a view (and that of others who reject the law only with regard to certain functions) a *bifurcating* of the law (*Derhetorizing*, 54; see also Hong, *Law*, 12). Fuller takes a similar, though more radical approach. Paul's polemic against "works of the law" is directed against an attempt to do the law in the wrong spirit, i.e., in "all-out rebellion against God" (*Gospel and Law*, 96; see also Burton, *Galatians*, 120, 458; Moule, "Obligation," 393-95).

18. Snodgrass, "Spheres," 108-9; see also Tamez, "Justification," 187; Stuhlmacher, "Understandings," 99; idem, *Reconciliation*, 126.

19. See Snodgrass, "Spheres," 99.

20. Wright, "Paul of History," 65; see also Garlington, "Obedience" 265; Longenecker, *Eschatology*, 218-9.

21. For his use of the former designation, see Dunn's, *Jesus*, 192; for the latter, see his "New Perspective," 108-11.

22. Dunn, "'Covenantal Nomism,'" 138, italics his; see also idem, "Apostate," 26; *Theology*, 145-50, 354-71.

critique of boundary-marking: "Israel's clinging to its privileged position was itself a classic example of how sin abuses the law."[23]

## THE EDENIC LOCUS OF THE LAW PROBLEMATIC

It is difficult to assess reenactments of the historical circumstances surrounding the formation of Paul's theology of law. Pertinent information is limited.[24] We fare better when Paul's own writings comprise the scope of our study,[25] but even here there is no consensus, and there may not be one in sight.[26] With respect to the present study, however, whatever factors may have contributed in shaping Paul's theology of law, we find it significant among the theories outlined above that no researcher, it seems, has searched Eden for the Grail.[27] None, in other words, appear to have considered Genesis 3 as a seminal influence behind the Apostle's polemic against the law.[28] And this is not surprising. Most of the recent focus has been on Second Temple issues.[29] Yet, having detected what we believe to be traces of edenic soil in the axiom of 1 Cor 15:56 and significant amounts in the axiomatic narrative of Rom 7:7–11, we would propose that the source of the most notorious of the Apostle's law-critical notions

---

23. Dunn, *Theology*, 632, see also 155–60.

24. Though he ventures his own theory, Räisänen cannot help but be agnostic when it comes to identifying the origin of Paul's polemic against the law. Due to our lack of information, it is in the very nature of the case, he argues, that such theories will be merely conjectural (see *Paul and the Law*, 14, 229).

25. Moo argues that "the exegete has not done his job until he has searched *in the material* for clues to such larger, integrating models. It is when such a model is found that fairly handles the diverse material of the pauline letters that the 'problem' of Paul and the law will be solved" ("Paul and the Law," 306–7).

26. Snodgrass raises the concern that ecclesiastical and existential traditions have magnified presuppositional and methodological differences to the point that Paul's meaning has become difficult to discern (see "Spheres," 93).

27. Pate, however, comes close. He cites Eden as an example of law never being able to save, yet he does not develop the implications (see *Curse*, 427).

28. This is the case even among commentators who discern edenic allusions in Rom 7:7–11 (e.g., Cranfield and Dunn).

29. One need but scan the essays in the response to Sanders's covenantal nomism edited by Carson, O'Brien, and Seifrid (see *Variegated Nomism*) to appreciate the fact that even his critics recognize the importance that an understanding of the Second Temple milieu can have on Pauline interpretation.

at least, the catalytic operation of the law, [30] is the Genesis temptation narrative.

Now if the Eden account was indeed the source of the Apostle's catalytic notion of the law,[31] and he considered the law-problematic to be primeval, it would seem to follow that the fundamental problem which the law posed for Paul would not have been its "legalistic misuse";[32] Eve was enticed to *transgress* the law, not fulfill it. Nor would it have been its abuse as a Jewish "identity marker";[33] the law problematic *predated* the Patriarchs.[34] Neither would the problematic be attributed to the "compromise of Judaism's gracious framework";[35] a law problematic existed long before the collapse. Nor would Paul's polemic against the law have been solely due to "human inability";[36] the law's catalytic operation was set in

---

30. I.e., the very notion that, in Räisänen's opinion, has *no* Old Testament parallel. Weima responds to Räisänen by suggesting that parallels can be discovered in the wilderness accounts (see "Function," 234). Though Weima offers no examples, we can assume, on the basis of Rom 5:20 at least, that Paul assumed some such experiences (Wright suggests the golden calf incident [see *Climax*, 227]; see also Strelan, "Note," 23–25). Nevertheless, the *underlying* background to the phenomenon is more likely, we believe, to be Eden than Sinai since Paul's law-sin nexus in Rom 7:7–11 is garbed more in edenic than sinaitic attire and because a *primordial* event would be more apt to support the weight of Paul's law-sin generalization in 1 Cor 15:56 than would a merely *historical* event. This latter point is noted by Stanley, who argues that the universalism contained in the Garden story "would suggest itself to [Paul] as more apt than themes connected with Moses" ("Paul's Interest," 251; see above, pp. 195–97).

31. While the source of Paul's *personal acquaintance* with the catalytic workings of the law was evidently his own experience (as depicted in Rom 7:7–11), we are considering here the origin of his *universal truism* regarding the catalytic workings of the law (see above, p. 105 n. 78).

32. Cranfield, "Law," 56. Nor would the problem be its "zealous" misuse à la Jewett, *Romans*, 445–53.

33. Dunn, *Jesus*, 92. Dunn's position has been challenged from other angles as well (see, e.g., Kim, *New Perspective*, 1–84; Esler, *Galatians*, 87–88; Waters, *Justification*, 158–90; Westerholm, *Perspectives*, 380–84; Das, *Covenant*, 237–42).

34. Witherington writes: "One of the important corollaries of recognizing that Rom 7:7–13 is about Adam . . . is that it becomes clear that Paul is not specifically critiquing Judaism or Jews here" (*Romans*, 191). This may be an overstatement since the topic of the narrative is, in fact, Paul, himself a Jew, and the Mosaic law. Yet, we would agree to the point that an edenic backdrop to 7:7–11 would seem to push the law problematic *beyond* Judaism.

35. Das, *Covenant*, 45.

36. Moo, "Paul and the Law," 298. Note also Verburg's assessment of the law problematic in 1 Cor 15:56: "Insofern vor dem Hintergrund der ἀσθένεια der Menschen ist das Gesetz δύναμις der Sünde und damit des Todes" (*Endzeit*, 235).

motion prior to the Fall and before humanity's consequent plunge into depravity.³⁷ Neither would the basic problem with the law be related to what sphere the law occupies; the law problematic is rather determined by what sphere the individual occupies.³⁸ Nor is it necessary to assume that Paul's negative assessment of the law arose from the circumstances surrounding his apologetic or ecclesiastical ministries or was a "violent" attempt to attribute to the law a negative function. To the contrary, as our examination of 1 Cor 15:56 suggested,³⁹ Paul's notion of the catalytic operation of the law did not debut in his corpus on a polemical stage but quietly emerged as a theological construct amidst an edenic environment.⁴⁰

37. Thus, while Martin is correct that "since the fall, for the person outside of Christ, law (*nomos*) can only bring death" (*Christ and the Law*, 75), his conclusion needs to be re-tooled. The law has not only brought death *since* the Fall; it was what sin used *to bring about the Fall*. This is not to suggest that human inability plays no role in Paul's polemic against the law. Because of their slavery to sin and enmity towards God, none have the ability (Rom 8:3) nor inclination (Rom 3:10-12) to submit to God's law. Justification, therefore, must be received by grace through faith (see Laato, "Anthropological Considerations," 343-59). We only propose that the events in Eden provide Paul with a primordial and hence more rudimentary argument.

38. I.e., either like Adam, faced with a do-or-die commandment in the presence of a fiendish tempter, or, as the believer depicted by Paul in Romans 6-7, freed from obligation to the law and consequently from the homicidal schemes of sin (see below, pp. 237-53).

39. It is telling that Thompson fails to include 1 Cor 15:56 in his purview of the New Perspective (*New Perspective*). As a result, he makes the incorrect assertion that every time Paul speaks negatively about the law, it is in a context reflecting either the fundamental rejection of Jesus by Jews or the insistence by Jewish Christians that Gentile Christ believers had to adopt Jewish customs in order to join God's people (ibid., 15). Neither context is evident in 1 Corinthians.

40. Räisänen recognizes that the sudden appearance of Paul's law-critical statement in 1 Cor 15:56 "like a flash" shows how closely at this time Paul had come to associate the law with sin and death (*Paul and the Law*, 143; see also Kruse, *Paul*, 143). The notion, Klein argues, appears to have been well-established at the time of writing: "Nimmt man endlich hinzu, daß auch in der mit der Gesetzesfrage thematisch gar nicht befaßten korinthischen Korrespondenz der Zusammenhang von Gesetz, Sünde und Tod auf eine prägnante Formel gebracht ist . . . so spricht in der Tat 'alles dafür, daß die Gesetzesfrage von Anfang an in Brennpunkt des Denkens des Apostels gestanden hat'" (Klein, "Gesetz," 65 [quoting Wilckens, "Entwicklung," 154]; see alse Söding, "Kraft," 74-76). Although there may be echoes or allusions to Genesis 1-3 in Gal 3:28 (οὐκ ἔνι ἄρσεν καὶ θῆλυ), Gal 4:4 (γενόμενον ἐκ γυναικός), and Gal 6:15 (καινὴ κτίσις), there are no references to Adam or the Fall narrative in Galatians. As Hays notes: "Paul traces the story line backwards no farther than Abraham and forward no farther than the immediately controverted future of the Galatian churches" (Hays, *Faith*, 2002], 226). If Galatians pre-

Thus, rather than being merely polemically motivated, or being hatched in response to either legalistic or nationalistic tendencies or being due to anthropological inability or to a negative sphere of influence or salvation-historical shift, Paul's concern with the law, we suggest, was significantly driven by *primeval* considerations. At an early stage in his thinking,[41] Paul, perhaps while seeking an explication of his own innate

---

dates 1 Corinthians, it is not necessary to assume that Paul's Adam-Christ theology was as yet undeveloped. It is more likely that the short and fiery letter is preoccupied with Abraham and other figures of Jewish patriarchal history rather than with Adam and Eve because of the *Jewish* nature of the problem in Galatia (see ibid., 226; Stanley, "Paul's Interest," 247; Adams, "Paul's Story," 39–41).

41. That the subject of the law would come to occupy a place in the arguments of Rom 5:12–21 and 1 Corinthians 15 suggests that *the law* and his *Adam-christology* may not have been concepts unassociated in Paul's mind. Yet, approximately when Paul developed his Adam-Christ theology and his catalytic notion of the law is uncertain. The date of 1 Corinthians (c. AD 54) is, of course, the *terminus ad quem*. We argued above, however, that the axiomatic nature of Paul's expressions in 1 Cor 15:56 and the nonchalant manner in which he presents the axiom suggest his reader's prior knowledge of the dogma and that it had for some time been an essential dictum of Paul's theology (see above, pp. 91, 120–23). Kim, who argues from 2 Cor 4:4–6 and the alleged allusions there to Paul's Damascus road Christophany of Christ as the εἰκών of God, proposes that Paul, not long after his conversion, began to think of Christ as the Adam of the eschaton (ὁ ἔσχατος ʼΑδάμ) who restores what the first Adam all but lost through his transgression (see *Origin*, 260–68; idem, *New Perspective*, 165–74, 183). Wright proposes the alternate theory that "Paul's Adam-christology is basically an Israel-christology, and is predicated on the identification of Jesus as Messiah, in virtue of his resurrection" (*Climax*, 29). Yet, like Kim, Wright appears to suggest that Paul's Adam-Christ epiphany was related to his Damascus road Christophany. Regarding the Adam-Christ contrast of 1 Corinthians 15, Wright states: "Paul's belief in Jesus' resurrection . . . went back to his vision on the road to Damascus. . . . Paul believed Jesus to be alive as σῶμα πνευματικόν because he had seen him with his own eyes" (ibid. 26–27; see also Hultgren, "Two Adams," 366–70). If Paul's Adam-christology was incubating at such an early date, it is possible that it was at this stage that the Apostle was beginning to ponder the role of the garden commandment and its relation to Adam's sin. Rather than following the edenic lead he discovered at the Damascus road and searching the Genesis account itself for the origin of Paul's law-sin nexus, Kim, however, looks no further than Paul's conversion experience for the explanation. It was there, he argues, that Saul realized that his zeal for the law was, in fact, sin. Consequently, he was led to something that would have been unthinkable for him as a Pharisee, i.e., "associating the law with sin and the flesh" (*Paul*, 157). This scenario, though, does not seem to be descriptive of Paul's catalytic understanding of the law, i.e., where prohibitions stimulate the transgression of those very prohibitions. We believe that Kim would do better by following the Damascus road to Eden and then searching Genesis 3 itself for evidence of a catalytic relation between law and sin that may have stimulated Paul's thinking on the subject.

experience with the law,[42] was led to consider the Fall narrative, where he discovered that there was a law-problematic from the start.[43] It has always been in the very nature of the case—in Eden, when it was within earshot of the antagonistic serpent and now east of Eden, when it confronts Adamic flesh—that divinely sanctioned law becomes the instrument of sin rather than an antidote against it. And based on our study of the Genesis narrative, a reading of a catalytic operation of the law in Genesis 3 would not have been a reading *into* the story on his part but a deduction *from* the story. Indeed, as Paul scanned the Scriptures for its theology of law—and that Paul had conducted such a search is evident from his question concerning works of the law in Rom 4:3, "What does the scripture say?"—it would have been almost inevitable that *the first commandment* would appear on his screen. And as he pondered the role of the first commandment in the Genesis account, he could hardly have overlooked the manner in which the serpent commandeered the commandment to incite *the first sin*.

## Eden, the Law, and Unheilsgeschichte

What, then, would have been the contemporary significance for Paul if there was a law problematic in Eden, and why would he pattern his own experience with the Torah after the experience of Adam with the commandment? We argued in the previous chapter that the edenic axiom of 1 Cor 15:56 and the semi-autobiographical use of the Fall narrative in Rom 7:7-11 allows for a generalization of the Eden event and provides a paradigm of the manner in which the arrival of a divinely sanctioned demand sets in motion sin, temptation, and death. Taking this now a step further, it seems that the Apostle employs his epigrammatic and autobiographical applications of the Fall narrative as a means of denying the salvific role of the law in a manner more rudimentary than he has yet done.[44] The

---

42. See above, p. 26 n. 71.

43. Moo, like us, argues that Paul's critique of the law moves beyond its abuse as a social boundary marker to its inherent salvific inability: "The Apostle's criticism focuses on the law's failure to deliver sinful Jews (and all people, who find their best representation in the Jewish people) from the nexus of sin and death" ("Israel and the Law," 216). We would advance Moo by arguing that Paul finds that this inherent inability of the law in the presence of sin was evident even in Eden.

44. While the positive character of the law is, to be sure, defended by Paul in Rom

# Reflections: The Catalytic Operation of the Law and Paul's Assessment of the Law 231

edenic undertones, in other words, bring a *primordial* argument against works of the law to the fore.[45] *Even in Paradise* law did not promote life; "there was a problem with commandments and the Law from the very beginning of the human story."[46] While Paul, therefore, in Romans 5 cites the non-salvific outcome of the law's arrival at Sinai,[47] and in Romans 4 he evokes the experience of Abraham as evidence that works of the law do not justify,[48] in Rom 7:7-11 the Apostle, we argue, is establishing his argument by moving even further back in time, indeed, to the dawn of time.[49] With the exception of drawing back the curtain for a view of God's electing grace in eternity past,[50] *a law-problematic in Eden would be the high water mark of Paul's polemic against the saving efficacy of the law.*[51] If

---

7-7-11, it is nevertheless diminished. The main theme of the passage is the law's salvific *impotence* (see Romanello, "Rom 7:7-25," 510-30). Burnett likewise argues that Paul in 7:7-11 is seeking to complete his criticism of the law by focusing "specifically on the difficulty that any one individual person has, in seeking to live by it" ("Individual," 213). Yet by failing to sufficiently note the edenic nuances in the account, Burnett fails to appreciate the primordial basis for Paul's generalization. For Paul, as far as existence under the law goes, *as it was in the beginning it is and ever shall be.*

45. We use the phrase "works of the law" here as a synonym of "works," i.e., "commendable actions performed in obedience to the law" (Moo, "'Works of Law,'" 96; Gathercole, *Boasting?*, 216-51; Westerholm, *Perspectives*, 313-21). The former designation would be a particular subset of the latter (see Moo, "'Works of Law,'" 95). While Paul has in mind obedience to the Mosaic law in Romans 7, the edenic undertones and allusions to the garden commandment there would, we suggest, widen the *application* to "works of divine law in general" (see Schnackenburg, "Römer 7," 294).

46. Witherington, *Romans*, 186. Witherington argues that "the most satisfactory reading of these verses [7:7-11] is Paul the Christian rereading the story of Adam in the light of his Christian views about law and the Law" (ibid., 190).

47. Regarding Sinai law, Bornkamm states, "es hat also keine epochemachende Bedeutung, sondern nur die Funktion, die Krisis des adamitischen Menschseins zu aktualisieren und zu radikalisieren" (*Das Ende*, 88-89; see above, p. 196 n. 123).

48. Abraham, as "our forefather" is considered here as the paradigm *par excellence* for Israel (see Gathercole, *Boasting*, 233).

49. As Wedderburn remarks: "It is not surprising that Paul, seeking to show man confronted by a command of God, should go back to the story of man's beginning and his first encounter with God's command. Adam lies behind the first person singular of these verses, as the first to taste the bitter experience of an unaided confrontation with God's demand" ("Adam," 421; see also Käsemann, *Romans*, 197).

50. As he does in Rom 9:10-13; Gal 1:15-16; Eph 1:4.

51. Paul, it appears, depicts Adam not as *an* example but *the* example (for Adam as a prototype in Judaism, see Schäfer, "Adam," 71-72 and n. 2, above). Dunn finds this backward movement to Adam to be significant: "The further step back, already behind Moses (and the law) to Abraham (chap. 4), and now to Adam, is deliberate. . . . It highlights the

this indeed was the logic behind Paul's argument, it did not go unnoticed by Lyonnet, probably the most cited proponent of an edenic interpretation in Rom 7:7–11:[52]

> En Rm 4 Paul avait évoqué la figure d'Abraham en raison du rôle que les Juifs attribuaient à la loi dans la justification d' Abraham. . . . À propos d'Adam, la tradition juive attribuait à la loi un rôle analogue. . . . Si Paul fait allusion à Adam, ce serait pour réfuter une telle interprétation. . . . Voulant montrer la relation entre la loi et la péché, saint Paul s'inspire, me semble-t-il, de ce que l'Ecriture enseignait sur ce qui s'était passé aux origines de l'humanité lors du premier péché, qu' il avait évoqué deux chapitres auparavant, comme, au chapitre 4, voulant montrer la relation entre la justice et la foi, il avait invoqué ce que l'Ecriture enseignant sur la justification d'Abraham.[53]

We thus detect in 7:9 ("I was once alive apart from the law") what seems to be an *edenically nuanced* polemical point. Paul, it would appear, assumes here an interlocutor who considered adherence to the law to be a means of obtaining (or sustaining) life,[54] and he responds with edenic

---

universal sweep of God's saving purpose through Christ: God is Savior . . . as Creator . . . and not merely as the God of Israel" (*Romans*, 1:272). Yet we find the moral of Paul's story not to be that God, as Creator, is the Savior of all, but that *the law* was savior of neither Moses, Abraham, or Adam.

52. Although Lyonnet's edenic interpretation of 7:7–11 is often cited, his applications are not. While he wrote before the "paradigm shift" effected by Sanders and others (a phrase used by Robert Jewett to describe the current revision of the traditional anti-Judaic interpretation of Paul ["Coexistence," 341]), we believe that his conclusions, which are presented in part here and below, are relevant and bear (re)consideration.

53. Spoken in response to Cambier, "'Le moi,'" 49–50; see also Lyonnet, "L'histoire," 139–40.

54. That such notions were circulating within Judaism appears certain. Note, e.g., Sir 17:11: "He bestowed knowledge upon them, and allotted to them the law of life [νόμον ζωῆς]"; *t. Šabb.* 15:17 (*Tosef.* 2:63): "Lo, the religious requirements were given over to Israel only so that they may live by them . . . and not to die by them"; *4 Ezra* 7:21: "For the Lord strictly commanded those who came into the world, when they came, what they should do to live, and what they should observe to avoid punishment"; see also *4 Ezra* 14:29–30; *2 Bar.* 38:2; *Pss. Sol.* 14:2; *Tg. Neof.* Gen 3:23; Sir 15:11–20; 45:5; Wis 6:18; Bar 3:9; 4QD$^a$ 15 XVI, 4–5. For later testimony, see *m. Pirqe ʾAbot* 2:7–8; 6:7; *b. Taʿan.* 7a; *b. Yoma* 72b; *b. Šabb.* 88b; *b. ʿErub.* 52a; *Lev. Rab.* 16 (116b); *b. ʿAbod. Zar.* 5a; *Mek. Exod.* 20:19 (79a); *Exod. Rab.* 41 (97d); 51 (103d). See discussions in Schoeps, *Theology*, 175; Urbach, *Sages*, 1:424–26; Gathercole, *Boasting*, 37–111; Lichtenberger, *Das Ich*, 203–63; Hofius, "Gesetz," 270–71 n. 30; Morissette, "Midrash," 181–82; Str-B 1:129–32; 237; 917; 2: 482–83; 3:118–237, 277, 498, 502.

undertones that appear more than subliminally to accent the fact that Adam and Eve enjoyed life *prior* to the giving of the law.[55] Indeed, Paul seems to imply, it was only *after* the arrival of the commandment that the first couple experienced death.[56] To quote Lyonnet once more: "Aux Juifs, prétendant qu'Adam au paradis avait tiré sa justice de l'obervance de la loi, Paul fait donc remarquer que le précepte n'a pas été pour Adam la source d'une vie qu'il possédait déjà."[57] Indeed, "a en juger d'après le récit de la Genèse, la loi joua même un rôle fort différent: *loin de conférer à Adam la 'vie,' elle fut l'intrument dont se servit le serpent pour la lui ôter!*"[58] And while Paul recognizes the exclusive position of Adam,[59] the interplay of law and sin that he experienced was not unique, but typical of all who similarly fine themselves faced with do-or-die demands of divine

---

55. This is a point often overlooked by commentators, who understandably expend most of their energy in 7:9 attempting to chase down the subject and isolate the time referent (though see Jülicher, "Römer," 41).

56. See Pate, *Curse*, 427. "Paul clearly wishes to press the paradox," Dunn notes: "it was the command of God which sin has used to bring death into its dominant role on the stage of human life" (*Romans*, 1:385; see also Morissette, "Midrash," 181-84). Lichtenberger argues similarly: "Das Gesetz das zum Leben gegeben war, wurde also zum Tode. Ein breiter Traditionsstrom führt von Lev 18,5; Ez 20,11; Neh 9,29 durch die alttestamentlich-judische Überlieferung, wonach der Erfüller der Gebote in ihnen und durch sie Leben hat. Paulus greift darauf zürück, um gerade im Gegensatz dazu jenes unerhörte Geschehen zur Sprache zu bringen, daß das Kommen des Gebotes dem "Ich" nicht Leben, sondern den Tod bedeute" (*Das Ich*, 133). Lictenberger mentions here the influence of Lev 18:5 upon Jewish thought. By the manner in which Paul cites or alludes to the verse (Rom 7:10; 10:5, Gal 3:12), it appears clear that he was no less convinced than his contemporaries that the law promises life to those who observe its commands. It would appear, however, that his anthropology made him more pessimistic than others about the possibility of attaining life in this manner (see Becker, *Paul*, 396; Westerholm, *Perspectives*, 382-83; see above, pp. 101-2 n. 68).

57. *Les étapes*, 135.

58. "'Tu ne convoiteras pas,'" 163, italics mine. Commenting on 7:9, Dunn concludes: "Here in a nutshell is the sharpness of the human dilemma, and the depth of man's tragedy: *were it not for sin the law would promote life*" (*Romans*, 1:384, italics mine). True, but Paul's argument actually seems to be accented thus: *were it not for law Adam would not have died*. See the layout of 7:9-10a above, p. 189.

59. E.g., Rom 5:12-21; 1 Cor 15:21-22.

law.⁶⁰ None can gain life "by the strength of the 'thou shalt' of the law."⁶¹ Like Adam and Eve, they instead become victims of the irony that death comes by that which promises life.⁶²

Perhaps what is most significant about locating a law-sin nexus in Eden, however, and a point that leads into the final section of this chapter, is the implication that this would have had for Paul regarding the *unheilsgeschichtlich* nature of divinely sanctioned law,⁶³ whether it be the Garden commandment or the commandments given at Sinai.⁶⁴ If the Eden account was indeed the source of the Apostle's catalytic notion of the law, and he presented it as such, it would have been almost impossible for him more categorically to consign law/Torah to the present aeon and to the old creation purposes of God.⁶⁵ This would seem to be the case

---

60. See Aletti, "Romans 7,7-25," 81; Thurén, *Derhetorizing*, 128-29; Witherington, *Romans*, 186; "Hübner, *Law*, 76; Espy, "Robust Conscience," 170; Sloan, "Paul and the Law," 51; Milne, "Genesis 3," 16-18; Wedderburn, "Adam," 421; Bornkamm, "Sin," 93; Dunn, *Romans*, 1:382; note also Lyonnet's response to Cambier in Cambier, "Le 'moi,'" 50.

61. Ridderbos, *Paul*, 145.

62. The latter paradox would be a challenge to the Jewish notion that people have the freedom to choose between their drives (see, e.g., *T. Ash.* 1:5-7; *Pss. Sol.* 9:4; 4 Macc 1:35; see Shogren, "'Wretched Man,'" 121-24; Becker, *Paul*, 396) and to traditions that the knowledge of the Torah provides an antidote against the evil impulse (see, e.g., 4 Macc 1:14-17, 35; 2:2-6, 21-23; *b. Ber.* 5a; *b. Ned.* 32b; *b. Qidd.* 30b; *B. Bat.* 16a, 26; *b. Tem.* 16a; *b. Sukka* 52b; *Gen. Rab.* 22 [15a]; 70 [45a, 31; 45b, 12]; *Lev. Rab.* 35 [132c]; *Sifr. Deut.* 11:16, 18; *Mekh. Exod.* 18:27 [68b]; *Midr. Pss.* 119:64; *Midr. Song* 6:11; *ʾAbot R. Nat.* 16 [6a]; see also Str-B 3:237; Morissette, "Midrash," 181-82; Moore, *Judaism*, 1:491; Urbach, *Sages*, 1:425-428). Among other references Urbach cites R. Joḥanan, who interpreted the serpent in the wilderness account as *lust*, against which those who received the Torah at Sinai were inoculated. Urbach remarks in passing that this notion is "contrary to Paul's teaching" in Romans 7 (ibid., 1:428).

63. We use *unheilsgeschichtlich* to refer to the way that divinely sanctioned law functions historically in a non-salvific and even *disastrous* manner in regard to sin and life: rather than curtailing sin, it exacerbates it, and rather than fostering life, it becomes an ingredient in the potion that causes death (see Dietzfelbinger, *Heilsgeschichte*, 26-31; Bornkamm, *Das Ende*, 88-89). See n. 66, below.

64. Alletti appropriately points out the paradigmatic nature of divine law: "If being divine it results in death, then no merely human law (or *entole*) could possibly have better effects" ("Rhetorical Criticism," 81).

65. Schnackenburg nuances it thus: "Eine Unheils*geschichte* wird geschildert, das sollte man nicht übersehen. Gewiß geht es letzlich um bleibende Erfahrungen mit dem Gesetz; aber sie werden an der geschichtlichen Konstellation von Gesetz, Sünde und Tod erläutert und einsichtig gemacht" ("Römer 7," 292; see also Hoppe, *Heilsgeschichte*, 142; Garlington, "Creation Theology," 208. Dietzfelbinger, *Heilsgeschichte*, 26-31; Dodd,

even though the law's negative role, according to Paul, serves a purpose in God's plan of salvation by showing sin to be "sinful beyond measure" (Rom 7:13).[66] By placing it within the unsalvific economy of sin, of which it is an instrument, Paul, "with bold strokes of the pen," would be relegating "the law to the era of man's fall and its consequent ills."[67] And this brings us back to the triad of ὁ νόμος, ἡ ἁμαρτία, and ὁ θάνατος in 1 Cor 15:56. By its startling association there with ὁ θάνατος, the trenchant enemy of the eschaton, and with ἡ ἁμαρτία, the entity which imparts ὁ θάνατος with its venom, ὁ νόμος would not only appear to be a reality of the present age,[68] but as the instrument that empowers ἡ ἁμαρτία, i.e., as "der auslösende Faktor der Unheilsgeschichte,"[69] it would experience the same end as the entities spoken of in 15:25; it will be vanquished along with ἡ ἁμαρτία and ὁ θάνατος by Christ at his coming.[70] For since there

---

*Paradigmatic*, 234; Aletti, "Rhetorical Criticism," 81).

66. Based on 7:13 and the two ἵνα clauses there, one can perhaps say that the law plays an "*ultimately* positive salvation-historical role" (Moo, *Romans*, 348; see also Müller, *Gerechtigkeit*, 56). It may be more accurate, however, to say that the law, along with sin, plays a part in God's plan of salvation, but the role it plays is a negative one. Dietzfelbinger addresses this issue: "Der Einwurf, daß die Epoche des Unheils der des Heils vorausgehe und daß die Zeit des Gesetzes darum notwendige Voraussetzung für die Christuszeit sei, daß also doch das Gesetz die Gnade vorbereite, dieser Einwurf kann keinesfalls die Bezeichnung 'Heilsgeschichte' für die Zeit des Nomos rechtfertigen. Wenn auf die Epoche des Gesetzes die der Gnade folgt, dann geschieht das kraft des göttlichen Heilswillens, nicht kraft der Qualität der Gesetzesepoche" (*Heilsgeschichte*, 31 n. 66).

67. Garlington, "Creation Theology," 208-9. Similarly Jülicher: "Das Gesetz, dies hauptstück der wahrhaft göttlichen Offerbarung, kann mit der Sünde nichts gemein haben. Und dennoch gehört es ausschließlich in die Period hinein, die unter dem Zeichen der Sünde steht" ("Römer," 40) and Wright: "The law stands on the Adam side of the equation" ("Romans," 543). Moo is stronger still, "Against Jewish tendencies to attribute virtually salvific meaning to the law, Paul [in Rom 5:20] dethrones the law by ranging it on the side of Adam and sin" (*Romans*, 348; see also Sanday and Headlam, *Romans*, 153). Cranfield is repulsed at such "remarkably rash statements." It is not *law* itself, he argues, but legalism or abuse of the law that is deserving of negative characterizations (*Romans*, 1:319-20 n. 3). Yet, in Paul's strongly law-critical statements in 1 Cor 15:56 and Rom 7.7-11, he is speaking of the law as God gave it, not a misunderstanding of it (see the discussion in Moo, *Romans*, 388-89).

68. See Gal 4:3 and Col 3:20.

69. Schnackenburg, "Römer 7," 292.

70. Allo sees in 1 Cor 15:56-57 an end time scene where the law follows the funeral procession of death and perishes along with it (*Corinthiens*, 437). Johnson writes: "Verse 56 serves a particular purpose in Paul's argument. It serves to incorporate realities the audience knows have a connection (albeit somewhat ambiguous) with ὁ θάνατος into his overall argument by assigning them a role in the warfare narrative as part of the plu-

became no positive role for the law, with its do-or-die sanctions, in Eden, "there will be no positive role of the law to reprise in the new creation."[71] Such a scenario, we believe, prepares for Paul's argument in Romans 6–7 concerning the believer's present freedom from the law's jurisdiction and sin's dominion, to which we next turn.[72]

---

rality of enemies that will be done away with along with death" ("Resurrection Rhetoric," 292; see also Fee, *First Corinthians*, 67; Schrage, *Korinther*, 4:383; Díaz Rodelas, *Pablo*, 30; Lang, *Korinther*, 241; Hollander, "Death," 291; Schlatter, *Paulus*, 446).

71. Pate, *Curse*, 427.

72. We will focus in our next chapter on Romans 6 and 7 not only because of the place that the catalytic operation of the law occupies in the latter chapter but because of its presence that we believe is overlooked in the former.

# 9

# Reflections: The Catalytic Operation of the Law and Freedom from Sin

WHILE MOST COMMENTATORS, TO greater or lesser degrees, recognize the place that the law occupies in the argument of Rom 6:1—7:6, a reading that is particularly alert to the seminal nature of the law problematic is especially able to perceive and account for the central role that *freedom from the law* seems to play in the Apostle's logic regarding *freedom from sin*. For if, as appears to be the case, Genesis 3 contains a scenario in which "the tempter plied his seductions vis-à-vis God's commandment,"[1] and if Paul, observing this, considered law to be an entity belonging to the epoch of the Fall, we would not be surprised to find that deliverance from the law is at the center of his teaching regarding deliverance from sin.

## THE ASSOCIATION OF LAW AND SIN IN ROMANS 6:1—7:6

The opening question in Rom 6:1, "Should we continue in sin in order that grace may abound?" and the closing cry in Rom 7:24, "Wretched man that I am! Who will rescue me from this body of death" frame what appears to be the overall subject of chapters 6–7, *freedom from the bondage to sin*.[2] Yet while freedom from sin is the primary subject, *freedom*

---

1. Sloan, "Paul and the Law," 51.
2. See Talbert, "Tracing," 56. Kaye detects a noticeable shift in Romans 6 "from objective and general to personal and individual" (*Argument*, 29). The clustering of the term ἁμαρτία in Romans 6–7 suggests that deliverance from sin is the concern of both chapters. While the term occurs forty-eight times in Romans, it appears thirty-one times in chapters 6–7 (i.e., 62% of its occurrences). The word is spread evenly between the two chapters (sixteen times in chapter 6, fifteen times in chapter 7).

*from the law* is an intertwining and corollary theme.[3] The topic of law, for example, propels the discussion in both chapters.[4] It is the negative situation depicted in Rom 5:20 that resulted from *the law being added that transgression might abound* that sets up the question about further sin and abundant grace in Rom 6:1,[5] which in turn launches the "ethical excursus."[6] It is the assertion regarding *no longer being under law* in 6:14

---

3. It may be misleading, though understandable, for commentators to designate the theme of Romans 6 as *freedom from sin* and Romans 7 as *freedom from the law*. Though the law provides the dominant category in chapter 7, a distinction between the chapters is not absolute. Freedom from the law is not only explicit in 6:14-15 but seems to be implicit in the use of δικαιόω in 6:7, which likely anticipates the argument regarding death and freedom from the law's jurisdiction in 7:1-6 (see below, n. 25). The argument regarding the law becomes more vigorous in chapter 7 since Paul elaborates there the relation between law and sin. Considering the merging of themes, Käsemann argues that "the logic of the context will not let us separate the themes of freedom from death, from sin, and from the law" (*Romans*, 158-59).

4. Tobin observes that the rhetorical structure of chapters 6-7 is determined by a series of five questions contained in 6:1, 15; 7:1, 7, 13 (*Rhetoric*, 191). The law is a concern in each question, though indirectly so in v. 1.

5. The terminological association is so close between 5:20 and 6:1 that it is difficult to deny that the latter arises from the former (see Kaye, *Argument*, 22; Wright, "Romans," 543). Both the negative (5:20a) and the positive (5:20b) formulations seem to provide the presupposition behind Paul's question; i.e., the law multiplied sin which in turn multiplied grace; shall we continue to sin in order to multiply grace? (see Hellholm, "Argumentation," 139-40, 147-48; Thielman, *Paul*, 193; Sloan, "Paul and the Law," 48). Moo suggests that Paul in Rom 6:1ff. may be responding in part to a Jewish interlocutor who, after reading 5:20, asks how grace could quell sin when the law did not do so (*Romans*, 356).

6. Byrne, *Romans*, 187. That chapters 6-7 form a parenthetical unit is suggested by the fact that they arise in response to the statement regarding law and sin made at the end of chapter 5, by the manner in which the discussion in both chapters is prompted by questions (i.e., 6:1, 15, 16, 21; 7:7, 13, 24), by the occurrence of terms in chapter 5 that virtually "skip over" chapters 6 and 7 and reappear in chapter 8 (note, e.g., κατάκριμα [5:16, 18; 8:1], ἐλπίς/ἐλπίζω [5:2, 4, 5; 8:20, 24, 24, 24, 24, 25], δόχα/δοχάζω [5:2; 6:4; 8:18, 21, 30], εἰρήνη [5:1; 8:6], σῴζω—5:9, 10; 8:24, ἀγάπη/ἀγαπάω—5:5, 8; 8:35, 37, 39, θλίψις [5:3, 3; 8:35], ὑπομονή [5:3, 4; 8:25], πνεῦμα [5:5, 7:6; 8:2, 4, 5, 5, 6, 9, 9, 9, 10, 11, 11, 13, 14, 15, 15, 16, 16, 23, 26, 26, 27]), and by the way in which chapter 8 resumes themes that resonated in chapter 5 (note, e.g., *no condemnation* [5:16, 18; 8:1, 33-34], *solidarity with Christ* [5:12-21; 8:1, 2]; *suffering* [5:3-4; 8:17b-25, 35-39], *present and future security* [5:9-10; 8:29-30]; see Lamarche and Le Dû, 15-16; Byrne, "Living Out," 562-63; Dahl, *Studies*, 82-91; idem, "Notes," 37-38). Though the two chapters appear to be *parenthetical* in nature, it would nevertheless be a mistake to conclude that they are incidental to the argument of chapters 5-8 (see Kaye, *Argument*, 23). The theme of hope that permeates the chapters appears also in chapters 6-7. Rather than leading to sin, freedom from the law delivers the believer from sin (see 6:2, 4, 22; 7:4, 6). Sanctification,

that evokes the similar question in 6:15, "What then? Should we sin because we are not under law but under grace?" It is the observation about *death ending all obligations to the law* in 7:1-4 that seamlessly connects the maxim regarding death and freedom in 6:7 to the discussion regarding law, sin, and death in chapter 7.[7] It is the description of *sinful passions being aroused by the law* in 7:5 that prods the question in 7:7, "What then should we say? That the law is sin?" And it is the narrative concerning *the law inciting covetousness* in 7:7-11 that provokes the query in 7:13, "Did what is good, then, bring death to me?", which in turn leads to Paul's depiction of his struggle with sin. Thus, while freedom from sin is the lead topic of chapters 6-7, *the law*, indeed, *freedom from the law*, virtually steals the show.[8] The law is the mainspring that drives the argument, and it is within the *law-free* context of grace that liberation from sin is discussed and ultimately affirmed.[9]

---

in other words, is as certain for the believer as is justification and glorification (see Moo, *Romans*, 293-94, 351; Schreiner, *Romans*, 247).

7. See pp. 242-45, below, especially n. 25.

8. In Romans 6-7 νόμος occurs twenty-five times. In addition, the term ἐντολή is found six times in chapter 7. Wright observes that Paul, like a composer, modulates his theme from slavery to sin to the role of the law ("Romans," 543). We would retain the metaphor as long as "modulation" is correctly understood as a change of pitch, tone, or intensity rather than a change in melody. While chapter 7 *amplifies* the relation of the law to sin, the overall theme of the two chapters remains freedom from sin via freedom from law.

9. See Byrne, "Living Out," 562. For the phrase "under grace" in 6:14 compare 7:6 and Gal 5:18:

**Rom 6:14:** οὐ γὰρ ἐστε ὑπὸ νόμον  ἀλλὰ ὑπὸ χάριν
**Rom 7:6:** κατηργήθημεν ἀπὸ τοῦ νόμου  ὥστε δουλεύειν ἡμᾶς ἐν καινότητι πνεύματος
**Gal 5:18:** οὐκ ἐστε ὑπὸ νόμον  εἰ πνεύματι ἄγεσθε

The contrasts appear to suggest that being *under the law* (defined above, p. 214 n. 71), a situation that marked the old regime, has been replaced by serving God under the guidance of the Spirit (see 2:27-29; 8:4-14; 2 Cor 3:6-17; Gal 5:16-25; Phil 3:3; etc.). Ethics, in other words, "are not defined by Torah" (Wright, *Fresh Perspective*, 124); the Spirit is the believer's moral guide (see Westerholm, "'Letter' and 'Spirit,'" 237-46; Byrne, "Interpreting Romans," 251; Thurén, *Derhetorizing*, 85, 134; Becker, *Paul*, 39). Paul elsewhere provides form to this freedom by placing love at the heart of his ethic (Rom 13:8-9; Gal 5:14). His occasional use of the Mosaic law in his exhortations (see, e.g., 1 Cor 7:19; 9:8-10), as well as his paraenesis in general, need not contradict a notion of no longer being answerable to the Mosaic law. The law may be occasionally cited by Paul, but it seems to make its appearance from the wings to give definition to the Spirit-directed love that occupies center stage (see Deidun, *Morality*, 183-86; Bläser, *Gesetz*, 42-43; Schreiner, "Law of Christ," 544). Likewise, any overlap between the moral norms

Moreover, the correlation of *law* and *sin* in chapters 6–7 is observed in the ways in which *bondage to sin* is a virtual equivalent of *bondage to the law*, *death to sin* is used interchangeably with *death to the law*, and *freedom from sin* is identified with *freedom from the law*.[10] Thus, as in chapter 6 believers "with Christ" (vv. 3–6) have "*died to sin*" (v. 2) and have been "set free" from it (vv. 18, 22), so that it no longer has "dominion" over them (v. 14a), so in chapter 7 "through the body of Christ" they have "*died to the law*" (v. 4) and are "discharged" from it (v. 6), so that it is no longer "binding" on them (v. 1).[11] Likewise, as in chapter 6 serving God and producing fruit are expected of those who experience *freedom from sin* (vv. 18–22), so in chapter 7 belonging to Christ and fruit bearing are the intended results of the believer's *freedom from the law* (vv.

---

of the Mosaic law and those espoused by Paul need not imply that the Sinai code is the basis of his ethic (see Deidun, *Morality*, 160). To the extent that the behavior summoned by sinaitic law mirrors the righteousness of God, the Spirit of God can be expected to lead the believer to reflect those norms (see Westerholm, "'Letter and Spirit,'" 244). Futhermore, while Paul speaks of believers "fulfilling" the Mosaic law (e.g., Rom 8:4; 13:8,10; Gal 5:14), such statements do not necessarily imply that Christian behavior is enforced by the Mosaic law. Paul may be using language of the Mosaic law to *describe* rather than *prescribe* Christian ethics (see Barclay, *Obeying*, 142; van Dulman, *Theologie*, 229–30), and his description of Christians *fulfilling* (πληρόω) the law in contrast to those "under the law," who are obligated to *do* (ποιέω) the law (e.g., Rom 10:5; Gal 3:10, 12; 5:3) is consistent with a view that Christian righteousness is a *result* of being led by the Spirit (See Gal 5:22–23) rather than a *requirement* imposed by the law (see Westerholm, "Fulfilling," 233–37; Barclay, *Ethics*, 135–42). The way Paul appeals to the Spirit and to the logic of his readers as he exercises his authority among them would also be consistent with such a view (see Rom 15:14–15; 1 Cor 4:17; 7:40; 10:15; 11:13; 14:37; 2 Cor 1:24; 8:8; Phil 3:15; 1 Thess 2:7; Phlm 8–9). Westerholm's insights here are cogent: "It is . . . striking (and has struck many) that Paul repeatedly refrains from citing prohibitions from the law even when dealing with basic issues related to idolatry or sexual immorality, opting instead to argue from Christian principles (e.g., 1 Cor 6:12–20; 10:14–22; 1 Thess 4:3–8). And when Paul speaks of the need for Christians to discern the will of God, he does not refer them to the law (though, according to Rom 2:18, the law provided Jews with guidance about God's will), but speaks rather of presenting themselves to God, of refusing to pattern their way of life after that of this age, of being 'transformed by the renewal of [their] mind[s]' (12:2). They 'approve what is excellent' (the same phrase as in 2:18 is used of Christians in Phil 1:9–10) when their love grows in knowledge and judgment. The fact that Jews had to discover the will of God in the statutes of Torah but Christians must discover it as their minds are 'renewed' and they grow in insight shows clearly that the will of God is no longer defined as an obligation to observe the statutes of the Mosaic law" (*Perspectives*, 432–33; see also Hays, "Role," 144–45; Furnish, *Ethics*, 33; Becker, *Paul*, 394).

10. See Wilckens, *Römer*, 2:63.

11. Thus described by Moo, *Romans*, 409.

4-6).¹² In short, what the Apostle says about sin in the one chapter he says about the law in the other.¹³ Such, for Paul, appears to be the association between the two powers of the old regime.¹⁴ And such, for Paul appears to be the central role that law plays in his discussion of sin.

## THE CATALYTIC OPERATION OF THE LAW AND ROMANS 6

It is hard to miss the paradox in Romans 6-7, and it is not a little surprising to some,¹⁵ that sin is said to spawn in a legal climate (7:5, 8a), whereas it is deemed *impotent* (6:14) and *lifeless* (7:8b) in a law-less environ-

---

12. "Befreiung von der Sündemacht (Kap 6)," Schnackenburg argues, "bedeudet auch Befreiung vom Gesetz, das mit jener verbündet war, und Befreiung vom Gesetz bedeutet die ermöglichung eines Gott-Dienens und Fruchtbringens, das zum ewigen Leben führti ("Römer 7," 290; see also Kuss, *Römerbrief*, 2:436-37).

13. The following terms used in reference to both *law* and *sin* underscore the continuity between the chapters and the relationship that these entities bear to one another: ἢ ἀγνοεῖτε (6:3; 7:1); θάνατος/θανατόω/ἀποθνῄσκω (6:2, 3, 4, 5, 7, 8, 9, 9, 10, 10, 16, 21, 23; 7:2, 3, 4, 5, 6, 10, 10, 13, 19, 24); ἐγείρω (6:4, 9; 7:4); παλαιότης/καινότης (6:4; 7:6); καταργέω (6:6; 7:2, 6); μέλος (6:13, 13, 19, 19; 7:5); κυριεύω (6:9, 14; 7:1); ἐλεύθερος/ἐλευθερόω (6:18, 20, 22; 7:3); δοῦλος/δουλεύω (6:16, 16, 17, 19, 20, 22; 7:6); καρπός/καρποφορέω (6:21, 22; 7:5, 6); ὅτε—νυνὶ δέ (6:20-22; 7:5-6) (see Little, "Analogy," 83; Gieniusz, "Imagination," 390; Hellholm, "Funktion," 386-90, 410-11; Lamarche and Le Dû, Structure *Littéraire*, 32-34; Michel, *Römer*, 166; Nygren, *Romans*, 268; Dunn, *Romans*, 1:358). In addition, Luz lists the following phrase and theme comparisons (Luz, "Aufbau," 170):

| | |
|---|---|
| 6:16: οὐκ οἴδατε ὅτι ᾧ παριστάνετε ἑαυτοὺς ... δοῦλοί ἐστε | 7:1: Ἢ ἀγνοεῖτε ... ὅτι ὁ νόμος κυριεύει τοῦ ἀνθρώπου ... |
| 6:20: ὅτε γὰρ δοῦλοι ἦτε τῆς ἁμαρτίας, ἐλεύθεροι ἦτε τῇ δικαιοσύνῃ. | 7:5: ὅτε γὰρ ἦμεν ἐν τῇ σαρκί, τὰ παθήματα τῶν ἁμαρτιῶν τὰ διὰ τοῦ νόμου |
| 6:21: Τίνα οὖν καρπὸν εἴχετε τότε ... τὸ γὰρ τέλος ἐκείνων θάνατος. | ἐνηργεῖτο ... εἰς τὸ καρποφορῆσαι τῷ θανάτῳ |
| 6:22: νυνὶ δὲ ἐλευθερωθέντες ἀπὸ τῆς ἁμαρτίας ... ἔχετε τὸν καρπὸν ... εἰς ἁγιασμόν ... | 7:6: νυνὶ δὲ κατηργήθημεν ἀπὸ τοῦ νόμου ... ὥστε δουλεύειν ἡμᾶς ἐν καινότητι πνεύματος ... |

14. See Lichtenberger, *Das Ich*, 117-18. Not to leave out death, the third member in the triumvirate. More than half of the occurrences of θάνατος in the epistle (twelve of twenty-two occurrences) occur in chapters 6-7. While Paul depicts *death* as the payoff of sin in chapter 6 (vv. 16, 23), in chapter 7 he specifies the *law* as the means by which sin produces death (vv. 5, 10, 13).

15. Noted by Wright, "Romans," 543; Thielman, *Paul*, 193.

ment.[16] For Paul, the fact that the law with its obligations and sanctions has been displaced as a moral guide poses no problem to ethics. Indeed, the problem becomes the solution: "For sin will have no dominion over you, since you are not under law but under grace."[17] This conclusion is all the more ironic since Paul anticipates in 6:15 the charge that freedom from the law's jurisdiction inevitably leads to sin. Nevertheless, in light of the present study, for Paul to undergird his doctrine of sanctification with a statement concerning freedom from the law not only should come as no surprise, it should be expected. While his logic might initially appear disconnected,[18] Paul's rationale follows naturally and, indeed, axiomatically, since, in his mind, the law is the *dynamo* in the process of sin.[19]

Yet, even apart from our familiarity with Paul's axiom in 1 Cor 15:56, the reference to the law and its relation to sin in 6:14 should not surprise the reader of Romans since, as we noted,[20] it was the abounding of sin *through the law* in 5:20a that led to the abundance of grace in 5:20b, which in turn provoked the question in 6:1 and the discussion that follows. Moreover, the problem that the catalytic operation of the law poses to sanctification is assumed, we believe, in Paul's argument in Romans 6 that freedom from sin's dominion is inevitably experienced in one's deliverance from the law's jurisdiction. This deliverance from the law and sin is not only explicitly stated in 6:14 but appears to underlie the logic of 6:7: "For whoever has died is freed (δεδικαίωται) from sin."

---

16. Note also the similarly abrupt introduction of the law in Gal 5:18.

17. Wright quips: "If one did live under the law, sin *would* indeed have dominion" ("Romans," 543).

18. Among commentators, Moo explains what appears to be an abrupt reference to the law in 6:14 by suggesting that the Apostle never moves far from the salvation-historical themes of Old Covenant and New, Jew and Gentile (see also Schreiner). Esler applies the statement to social psychology and group identity (see also Dunn). Fitzmyer considers the logic to be that the *kyrios* of the Christian life is not legalism, but the prompting of the Spirit (see also Barrett, Witherington). Stuhlmacher relates the phrase "under the law" to condemnation, under which one experiences death, not sanctification (see also Calvin, Cranfield). Luther, facing the similarly abrupt reference to being *under the law* in Gal 5:18, argues that "Paul cannot forget about his doctrine of faith; but he keeps on repeating and emphasizing it, even when he is dealing with good works" ("Galatians," 27:77). None of these writers appear to entertain the relevance of the *catalytic operation of the law* to the rationale underlying Paul's assertion in 6:14.

19. Haacker makes a b-line from 6:14 to 1 Cor 15:56 (*Römer*, 130 n. 34).

20. See above, n. 5.

This verse, it would seem,²¹ provides the basis for Paul's statement in 6:6 that "our old self was crucified with him so that the body of sin might be destroyed, and we might no longer be enslaved to sin."²² While the explanation of how it does so is debated,²³ if we assume for δικαιόω Paul's normal forensic meaning of the term,²⁴ and if we connect the maxim in 6:7 to the argument in Rom 7:1-4,²⁵ it would appear that Paul is asserting that being *justified* from sin, i.e., being no longer *legally* answerable for sin,²⁶ is the basis of the co-crucified's freedom from sin.²⁷ In other words,

21. Note the γάρ.

22. Not an illustration (contra Moo, *Romans*, 377) but the ground of the assertion in v. 6. See below, n. 28.

23. See Schreiner's discussion of the options (*Romans*, 318-19).

24. While it is not *a priori* impossible that the verb here means "to free" (so most English translations; BDAG 249.3 cites Ps 72:13; Sir 26:29; Acts 13:38), it is hard to imagine that Paul would use the term without having in mind the doctrine to which the term refers everywhere else in his writings (see Scroggs, "Romans VI.7," 104-5; Thielman, *Theology*, 360-61; Martin, *Christ and the Law*, 70-71; Barth, *Romans*, 200; Cranfield, *Romans*, 1:311 n. 1, Dunn, *Romans*, 1:320; Ziesler, *Romans*, 160-61; Morris, *Romans*, 253 n. 44; Shedd, *Romans*, 155-56). In view of the parallelism between 6:7 and 7:2 (see next note), we would suggest that δεδικαίωται ἀπὸ τῆς ἁμαρτίας is virtually synonymous with the phrase κατήργηται ἀπὸ τοῦ νόμου (7:2). The latter phrase conveys the notion of being *discharged* from the obligations and sanctions of the law (cf. 7:3; for a survey of meanings of the verb, see Dunn, *Romans*, 1:319). The former phrase, we believe, conveys the same idea (see further, n. 26). For δικαιοῦσθαι ἀπό in the New Testament, see Acts 13:38, where it appears to bear its normal Pauline sense. Similarly, see also Sir 26:29, where a peddlar is deemed never "innocent of sin": οὐ δικαιωθήσεται κάπηλος ἀπὸ ἁμαρτίας.

25. The relationship between the maxim in 6:7, ὁ γὰρ ἀποθανὼν δεδικαίωται ἀπὸ τῆς ἁμαρτίας, and the forensic thesis in 7:1, ὁ νόμος κυριεύει τοῦ ἀνθρώπου ἐφ' ὅσον χρόνον ζῇ, has been duly noted (see, e.g., Earnshaw, "Reconsidering," 81-82; Robinson, *Wrestling*, 77; Tannehill, *Dying and Rising*, 44; also, Wilckens, *Römer*, 2:64; Stuhlmacher, *Romans*, 102; Legasse, *Romains*, 434-44; Michel, *Römer*, 166; Nygren, *Romans*, 244, 272). Note also the parallelism between 6:7 and 7:2-3:

| 6:7: | ὁ γὰρ | ἀποθανὼν | δεδικαίωται | ἀπὸ τῆς ἁμαρτίας. |
| 7:2: | ἐὰν δὲ | ἀποθάνῃ ὁ ἀνήρ, | κατήργηται | ἀπὸ τοῦ νόμου. |
| 7:3: | ἐὰν δὲ | ἀποθάνῃ ὁ ἀνήρ, | ἐλευθέρα ἐστὶν | ἀπὸ τοῦ νόμου. |

26. See NJB, NEB, NAB. Black interprets the phrase juridically: "the old self has died and has been destroyed (6:6) and thus is acquitted, because the once-deserved guilty verdict cannot now be passed" ("Perspectives," 423). Among commentators, Dunn suggests the rendering "declared free from (responsibility in relation to) sin." Sanday and Headlam propose "acquitted from guilt." Stuhlmacher presents the similar translation "absolved from sin." Schlatter paraphrases the thought, "every legal demand has been settled." See also Moule, *Studies*, 115; Meyer, *Romans*, 1:290-91.

27. So, e.g., Cranfield, *Romans*, 1:311 n. 1; Murray, *Romans*, 1:222; Morris, *Romans*,

what is explicitly stated in 7:4 ("you have died to the law through the body of Christ . . . that we may bear fruit for God") would seem to lie implicit in the argument of 6:6–7.[28] In each case, liberation from sin is the result of being severed from the jurisdiction of the law through participation in the crucifixion of Christ.[29] And though the rationale regarding

---

253. Wright argues that "Paul is able to keep the law court metaphor still running in his mind even while expounding baptism and the Christian's solidarity in Christ. The Christian's freedom from sin comes through God's judicial decision" ("Romans," 540). The symmetry between 6:6, 7 and 6:14a,b would seem to suggest that freedom from sin is linked in 6:6–7, as well as in 6:14, to the believer's *acquittal*:

τοῦ μηκέτι δουλεύειν ἡμᾶς τῇ ἁμαρτίᾳ (6:6)
   ὁ γὰρ ἀποθανὼν δεδικαίωται ἀπὸ τῆ ἁμαρτίας (6:7)
ἁμαρτία γὰρ ὑμῶν οὐ κυριεύσει (6:14a)
   οὐ γάρ ἐστε ὑπὸ νόμον ἀλλὰ ὑπὸ χάριν (6:14b)

28. Kearns proposes that the phrase ὁ ἀποθανὼν (in accord with 8:34; 2 Cor 5:15; 1 Thess 5:9–10) refers to Christ ("Romans 6,7," 1:301–7). This, however, introduces an unexpected shift in subject and would make v. 10 tautologous (see Moo, *Romans*, 377; Dunn, *Romans*, 1:321). Though it may seem tautologous in light of 6:6, it seems to us more likely that Paul is speaking theologically in 6:7 of the one who died with Christ (see, e.g., Tobin, *Rhetoric*, 196; Kaye, *Argument*, 52; Cranfield, *Romans*, 1:310–11; Wright, "Romans," 540; Lyonnet, "Qui enim mortuus est," 17–21; Klaar, "Rm 6,7," 131–34) than that he is merely citing a general maxim (see, e.g., Moo, *Romans*, 376–77; Dunn, *Romans*, 376–77; 1:320–21; Käsemann, *Romans*, 170). The verse is loaded with theological terms, and Paul nowhere else suggests that physical death settles eschatological accounts in God's sight (see Scroggs, "Romans VI.7," 105; Schreiner, *Romans*, 318). Hence, while the Apostle may be conscious of rabbinic legal principles regarding death and obligations to the law (e.g., "Once a man is dead he is free from religious duties" [*b. Šabb.* 151b (*BTal.* 8:772), see further, Str-B, 3:232; Lichtenberger, *Das Ich*, 113–116; *TDNT* 2:218], he is likely using the notion in his own sense (see Cranfield, *Romans*, 1:311). Kuhn's proposal that Paul is alluding to the Jewish maxim in *Sifr. Num.* 15:31: "All who die receive atonement through their death" ("Rm 6,7," 305–10; see also *TDNT* 2:218) is unlikely. Kuhn offers no convincing evidence that death was widely considered in Judaism to be a means of atonement, and, more importantly, as Scroggs notes, it is almost preposterous to think that Paul, who embraced the cross as the only means of atonement, would accept such a view, even assuming that he knew it (see "Romans VI.7," 105). Nevertheless, (an identification with) *Christ's* atoning death is almost certainly implicit in the verse (see next note).

29. Moo objects that Paul could not mean that justification through participation in Christ's death is the basis for freedom from sin because Paul, he argues, never connects the believer's death with justification (*Romans*, 376). Yet, Paul indeed appears to do so in 7:4, 6 where he speaks of believers as having *died to the law*. While *death to the law* there means more than freedom from *condemnation*, the phrase (as Moo himself argues [ibid., 415]) includes the notion, which in turn would entail the idea of justification (for δικαιόω/δικαίωσις as the opposite of κατακρίνω/κατάκριμα, see, e.g., 5:18; 8:33–34). Paul is perhaps arguing in 6:7 that those who have been crucified with Christ enter into

the need to be delivered from the law in order to be free from sin only becomes explicit in 7:5—viz., our sinful passions were "aroused by the law"[30]—the law's catalytic operation can be easily read back into 6:6–7 and 6:14.[31] It explains the connection in each passage between law and sin as well as provides the reason why deliverance from the law inevitably short-circuits the workings of sin.[32]

## THE DEATH OF THE ADAMIC SELF TO THE LAW

The catalytic operation of the law seems to lie implicit, then, in the logic of chapter 6. Freedom from the law, Paul states, delivers the believer from slavery to sin, because the law, he asserts, plays a fundamental role in the

---

Christ's atonement and are thereby justified from their sin (see Morris, *Romans*, 253).

30. "[For] while we were living in the flesh, our sinful passions, aroused by the law, were at work in our members to bear fruit for death."

31. In light of the unity and parallels between chapters 6–7, it would seem reasonable to interpret each chapter in light of the other (see Nygren, *Romans*, 268; Wright, "Romans," 559). Yet Witherington scolds those who read chapter 7 back into chapter 6 since the original readers would not have known what Paul was going to say in chapter 7 as they were hearing chapter 6. Thus, he argues, chapter 6 should only be interpreted by what comes *before* rather than from what comes *afterwards* (*Romans*, 156 n. 5). While it is true that the first-time readers of Romans did not know the end from the beginning, second-time readers do. It would be only natural for the latter to take advantage of explanations and amplifications in later passages to better understand earlier statements. Witherington, in fact, does so himself when commenting on Rom 3:3. Whom, he asks, did Paul have in mind when he said that "some Jews" had been unfaithful? Having, and utilizing, the advantage of having read ahead, he answers, "Perhaps 15.31 provides a clue: Paul speaks there of the 'disobedient ones in Judea'" (ibid., 93). Witherington's use here of a later text to illuminate an earlier text is, we believe, appropriate, even though by doing so he appears to be inconsistent with his own methodology.

32. Cranfield's conclusion that "justification" provides the basis from which to resist sin is correct (*Romans*, 1:311), but it misses, we believe, the pith of Paul's argument since he fails to specify the role that deliverance from the law plays in the equation. Better: it is the deliverance from the (catalytic operation of the) law afforded by justification that short-circuits sin's power to enslave. Gieniusz similarly overlooks the significance (presence?) of the catalytic operation of the law in Paul's argument: "Because the term νόμος abounds in the passage (7:1–6) and in Romans 6 occurs only twice, this does not mean a radical change of perspective. We have seen that it is not the law as such nor freedom from it that is the real point of unity, but the revindication of an ethic for that time when the law no longer governs (κυριεύει)" ("Imagination," 395). To the contrary, it is not that Paul is "revindicating" an ethic apart from the jurisdiction of the law; the Apostle, we believe, is asserting that an ethic is *only possible* apart from the jusrisdiction of the law.

process of sin.³³ What seems to be latent in chapter 6 (viz., the catalytic operation of the law) becomes overt, however, in chapter 7,³⁴ and what is maintained in chapter 6 (viz., freedom from the law ends the reign of sin) is illustrated in chapter 7.³⁵ Indeed, 6:14-15 and its statements regarding freedom from the law can almost be considered the "preaching text" of Romans 7.³⁶ Thus, as we just noted, 7:5 and its portrayal of the law's

---

33. In light of the lack of elaboration by Paul, this, perhaps, is as far as we can safely go in explaining *why* Paul assumes that the power of sin is disengaged in a law-less setting. Sin becomes impotent in a law-free environment because the law is the source of its power (1 Cor 15:56). Nevertheless, though we argue that deliverance from the *catalytic* operation of the law plays a lead role in the process of sanctification, some commentators consider *the motivation drawn from unmerited favor* to be the factor that sacks sin of it power. Thus Barclay contends: "not law, but love, is the motive of his life, and the inspiration of love can make him able to do what the restraint of law was powerless to help him do" (*Romans*, 94). Perhaps Barclay was consciously echoing Augustine: "We are not under the Law, which indeed commandeth what is good yet giveth it not: but we are under Grace, which, making us to love that which the Law commands, is able to rule over the free" (*Cont.* 8 [*NPNF¹* 3:382]). Similar thoughts are expressed by Hodge: "So long as we are under the influence of a self-righteous or legal spirit, the motive and aim of all good works, are wrong or defective. The motive is fear, or some merely natural affection, and the aim, to merit the bestowment of good. But when we accept of the gracious offers of the gospel, and feel that our sins are gratuitously pardoned, a sense of the divine love, shed abroad in the heart of the Holy Spirit, awakens all holy affections. The motive to obedience is now love, and its aim the glory of God" (*Romans*, 211-12). Likewise, though more succinct, is Denney's observation: "It is not restraint, but inspiration, which liberates from sin: not Mount Sinai but Mount Calvary which makes saints" ("Romans," 2:635; see also Haldane, *Romans*, 251; Moule, *Studies*, 115; Cranfield, 1:320; Stott, *Romans*, 181). Yet, while Paul elsewhere appears to allude to the motivation of love (e.g., 2 Cor 5:14), he does not do so in Romans 6-7. Furthermore, the emphasis in Romans 6-7 is on the role that deliverance from the *catalytic operation of the law* plays in setting believers free from the throes of sin, not on any ethical motivation that they draw from pondering God's unconditional love. Nevertheless, though Paul, we believe, argues that freedom from the law essentially deprives sin of its power, he does not state that freedom from the law *by itself* empowers righteousness. Rather, once set free from the law, the believer is transferred to the realm of grace (6:14), is joined to Christ (7:4), and serves in the "newness of the Spirit" (7:6). It is within *this* new positive setting and under *such* influences that life is produced (2 Cor 3:6) and fruit pleasing to God grows (Gal 5:22-23).

34. "The law," Kaye observes, "is at the centre of discussion in Rom. 7" (*Argument*, 106). All major commentators agree.

35. See Denney, "Romans," 2:637. The opening words in chapter 7, Ἡ ἀγνοεῖτε, ἀδελφοί, indicate that what follows provides an *explanation* of what precedes. The assertion of 6:14b (and that of 5:20a) virtually cries out for elaboration and Paul provides it here (see Moo, *Romans*, 411).

36. Noted by Sanday and Headlam, *Romans*, 171. Moo observes that 6:14-15 "is the

arousal of sinful passions not only explains 7:4,[37] but it elucidates 6:14 and why it is necessary for the believer to be rescued from the domain of the law in order to experience deliverance from the reign of sin.[38] Likewise, though the depiction of the catalytic operation of the law in 7:7-25 is immediately launched by the negative statement about the law in 7:5,[39] the fuse had already been burning.[40] The narrative portrays in dramatic form the law problematic that is implicit in 6:14.[41] The opening words in 7:1, ἢ ἀγνοεῖτε, thus appear to function as a backward reference, as a "reminding signal,"[42] that connects the two chapters.[43] Chapter 7 does not introduce a new subject.[44] The implication of the ἢ ἀγνοεῖτε ... ὅτι ὁ νόμος is that the conversation regarding *law*, which emerged explicitly

---

immediate occasion for the chapter, as Paul explains what it means to be no longer 'under the law,' how this transfer from the law's dominion has been accomplished, and why it was necessary" (*Romans*, 410; see also Little, "Analogy," 82).

37. The introductory γάρ indicates the relation of vv. 5-6 to v. 4.

38. Kuss argues that 7:4 "recapitulates" themes in chapter 6 while 7:5 explains 7:4 (*Römerbrief*, 2:437; see also Little, who links 7:5 directly to 6:14 ["Analogy," 82] and Moo, who finds 7:5 to be consonant with 6:14 [*Romans*, 448; see also Wright, "Romans," 560]). Besides the correspondence in 6:14 and 7:4 between law and sin, note the possible connection in 6:12 and 7:5 between παθήματα τῶν ἁμαρτιῶν (cf. 7:6-7) and ἐπιθυμίαι and ἐν τῇ σαρκί and τῷ θνητῷ ὑμῶν σώματι. A connection is likely since Paul already used the terms together in Gal 5:24 (see Wilckens, *Römer*, 2:67).

39. The questions that launch vv. 7-25 (τί οὖν ἐροῦμεν; ὁ νόμος ἁμαρτία;) are almost certainly precipitated by the phrase in 7:5, τὰ παθήματα τῶν ἁμαρτιῶν τὰ διὰ τοῦ νόμου. Dunn observes that 7:5, in fact, traces the course of discussion in vv. 7-25: v. 5a (vv. 14-25) and v. 5b (vv. 7-13). Byrne makes a similar observation. The verse, he maintains, outlines the depiction in vv. 7-25 of "life under law" (see also Garlington, *Faith*, 116; Michel, *Römer*, 167).

40. The fuse was, in fact, lit in 3:20b. The sparks were fanned, however, by the negative assertion in 5:20, which contributed to the discussion in chapter 6 (see Schnackenburg, "Römer 7," 290).

41. Hellholm argues that the question in 7:7 is not in response to 6:14 but to 7:1-6 "weil die Gesetzesproblematik noch nicht thematisiert worden war" ("Funktion," 388). This is perhaps correct, but the law problematic, in fact, appears in 5:20 and, as we have maintained, underlies the logic of 6:14. While immediately precipitated by 7:5-6, 7:7-25 elaborates on the law problematic implicit in 6:14.

42. Hellholm, "Argumentation," 150; see also 124-25 and idem, "Funktion," 387-88.

43. As this "Pauline bridge" does in 6:3; see also 11:2; 1 Cor 6:9, 16, 19 (see Engberg-Pedersen, "Galatians," 481). Tobin misses the *immediate* connection of chapters 6 and 7 by relating the latter to the cryptic and negative statements regarding law in 3:20; 4:15; 5:13, 20 (*Rhetoric*, 219-20).

44. Noted by Elliott, *Rhetoric*, 242 (see also Harrisville, *Romans*, 99).

in 6:14-15, continues, and the fluid hand off of the theme between the chapters suggests that freedom from the (catalytic operation of the) law has been a topic of discussion all along.[45] Indeed, the attention devoted to the theme in chapter 7 implies that it is a *pivotal* topic.[46]

Along with the theme of law and its relation to sin, integral to the argument of both chapters is the notion of *co-death with Christ*. While freedom from the law is, for Paul, the path to freedom from sin, death with Christ is the gateway through which one must pass to experience freedom from law.[47] This theme comprises the gist of the argument of chapter 6,[48] and the topic hits the ground running in the opening verses

---

45. Little argues that parallel constructions found in chapter 6 and 7:1-6 underscore the continuity that Paul wishes to establish between the two chapters (see "Analogy," 82; see also Schnackenburg, "Römer 7," 288-91).

46. This is the conclusion of Lamarche and Le Dû in their analysis of chapters 6-7: "Selon la section C (6, 1-14) il doit se conformer à la nouvelle vie qu'il a reçue. Mais cette nouvelle vie, selon la section C, (6, 15 à 7,6) est non seulement libérée du péche, mais encore libérée de la Loi. Sans minimiser le premier aspect, c'est sans doute le second qui constitue la pointe logique de cette double section" (*Structure Littéraire*, 48, see also 43). We would prod this conclusion further by suggesting that freedom from the law, in fact, drives the logic of chapters 6 and 7 in their entirety.

47. The preposition διά in 7:4 introduces the means by which the believer died to the law. The parallelism with 6:3-6 suggests that διὰ τοῦ σώματος τοῦ Χριστοῦ refers (as in Col 1:22) to the crucified Christ (see Wilckens, *Römer*, 2:65; Moo, *Romans*, 417-18; et al.). Some read the term "body" here in a corporate sense as in Rom 12:4-5; 1 Cor 12:12ff. (see, e.g., Dodd, *Romans*, 102; Byrne, *Romans*, 211; Best, *Romans*, 77). Whether or not Paul's term was meant to evoke such an association in 7:4, the idea of identification with Christ's crucifixion is likely carried over from Rom 6:3-6 (cf. Gal 2:19). If we apply this notion to the illustration in 7:1-3, the logic appears to be that the Mosaic law has a claim over people as long as they live; believers, however, died to the law through their union with Christ's death; therefore the law no longer has jurisdiction (κυριεύω) over them. It is possible, however, that the meaning runs deeper still. Paul (as in Gal 3:10, 13?) may be arguing that the believer, through participation in Christ's crucifixion, vicariously suffered the law's sentence of death and is *for this reason* out of reach of its obligations and sanctions. The term "death" here, then, would convey more than the idea of cessation of life (per the illustration in 7:1-3) but, as in 6:23 (cf. "crucifixion" in 6:6?), it would also convey a punitive sense. Thus, Murray writes that discharge from the law "occurs in our union with Christ in his death, because all the virtue of Christ's death in meeting the claims of the law becomes ours" (*Romans*, 1:243; see also Calvin, *Romans*, 139; Schlatter, *Romans*, 154; Cranfield, *Romans*, 1:336; Hodge, *Romans*, 216-17; Fitzmyer, *Romans*, 458; Moule, *Romans*, 159, 181; Sanday and Headlam, 174; Stott, *Romans*, 194; Westerholm, *Perspectives*, 432; Lloyd-Jones, *Romans*, 42-54).

48. E.g., "How can *we who died* to sin go on living in it?" (6:2); "We know that *our old self was crucified with him* so that the body of sin might be destroyed, and we might no longer be enslaved to sin." (6:6); "For *whoever has died* is freed from sin" (6:7). See also 6:3, 4, 5, 8, 11.

of chapter 7. What is described in chapter 6 as *death to sin*, however, is specified in chapter 7 as *death to the law*,⁴⁹ i.e., the cessation of existence in the realm of the law's jurisdiction.⁵⁰ While Paul's meaning might be that the former reality is achieved by the latter,⁵¹ it is possible that the latter is implicit in, if not identical with, the former.⁵² In either case, both realities go hand in hand, and when Paul arrives at his summary statements in 7:4 and 6,⁵³ the event, he argues, that disengages believers from

---

49. It may be worth noting that in other contexts where Paul expresses the idea of the believer's death with Christ, the notion of a consequent immunity to the rule of law is often present (see, e.g., Gal 2:19; Col 2:20–22).

50. Cf. 6:14: "You are no longer under law." The picture of *death* can hardly be more definitive; the believer has experienced a decisive separation from the Mosaic law (such a decisiveness may also be implicit in Paul's use of the perfect κατήργηται in 7:2 [see Moule, *Studies*, 123]). We suggested above that this entails more than freedom from condemnation (see n. 71); the law is no longer "the definitive criterion, the necessary and sufficient authority over life and behavior" (Ziesler, *Romans*, 178; see also Thielman, *Paul*, 295 n. 11). The believer, Paul seems to argue, is no more accountable to the regulations of the Mosaic law than a widow is to legislation regarding marriage (7:1–3). Regarding the ethical implications of this, see above, n. 9.

51. On this view, *death to sin* in 6:2 is a separation from the *rule* or *realm* of sin (see Dunn, *Romans*, 1:307; Moo, *Romans*, 357; Bruce, *Apostle*, 330; Ridderbos, *Paul*, 206–7; Murray, *Principles*, 204–5). See 5:21; 6:14a.

52. On this view, *death to sin* in 6:2 refers to a forensic deliverance from the *penalty* of sin. If Christ's "death to sin" in 6:10 bears, or includes, a *juridical* sense, i.e., "He bore for them the full penalty of their sin" (Cranfield, *Romans*, 1:314; see also Calvin, *Romans*, 127; Sanday and Headlam, *Romans*, 160; Moule, *Studies*, 116; Witherington, *Romans*, 161; Legasse, *Romains*, 403; Schlier, *Römerbrief*, 199–200; Kaye, *Argument*, 49–52; etc.; [contra Winandy ("La mort," 433–34), 6:10 is not a truism, but refers to Christ, the closest antecedent to the verse (cf. v. 9)]), it is possible that a *legal* notion is also implicit in the phrase "died to sin" in 6:2; i.e., believers (by participation with Christ's death) died to the *guilt* of sin and this in turn ends their relation to sin (argued famously by Haldane, *Romans*, 247–51; see also Cranfield, *Romans*, 1:299–300; Shedd, *Romans*, 156–57; Stott, *Romans*, 171–72; Moule, *Studies*, 112, 115; idem, *Epistle*, 159). We would argue that a forensic interpretation of 6:7 would lend support to this interpretation of 6:2 (see Shedd, *Romans*, 157; Haldane, *Romans*, 250), as would the parallel phrase "died to the law" in 7:4. Stott concludes: "If to die to sin means to bear its penalty, which is death, it is the law which prescribes this penalty. Therefore to die to sin and to die to the law are identical. Both signify that through participation in the death of Christ the law's curse or condemnation on sin has been taken away" (*Romans*, 194). If 6:2, in fact, is to be understood in a legal rather than a merely moral sense, what becomes explicit in 6:14 regarding freedom from the jurisdiction of the law and appears to be implicit in the δικαιόω of 6:7 may have begun to emerge as early as 6:2.

53. Hellholm refers to 7:4 as an "Inferenz" and 7:5 as an "Ethos-Argument" ("Funktion," 403, 406). Schreiner argues that v. 4 contains the central proposition of

the domain of sin, is the *death* to the law that they experienced through their union with Christ:⁵⁴

> In the same way, my friends, *you have died to the law* (ἐθανατώθητε τῷ νόμῳ) through the body of Christ, so that you may belong to another, to him who has been raised from the dead in order that we may bear fruit for God. (v. 4)

> But now we are discharged from the law, *dead to that which held us captive* (ἀποθανόντες ἐν ᾧ κατειχόμεθα), so that we are slaves not under the old written code but in the new life of the Spirit. (v. 6)

And what, Paul notes, is short-circuited by their death to the law is the *catalytic operation of the law*,⁵⁵ whose negative depiction acts as a foil to the positive assertions of vv. 4 and 6:⁵⁶

> For while we were living in the flesh, our sinful passions, aroused by the law, were at work in our members to bear fruit for death. (v. 5)⁵⁷

---

the unit, with vv. 5–6 serving to elucidate the proposition (*Romans*, 349). The conjunction ὥστε, which introduces v. 4, indicates the inferential nature of v. 4 (see Sanday and Headlam, *Romans*, 172; Wilckens, *Römer*, 2:64). Robinson argues that 7:4 could indeed "stand as a summary of the whole of Pauline theology" (Robinson, *Body*, 47).

54. Contra Tobin (*Rhetoric*, 224), Elliott (*Rhetoric*, 244 n. 2), and others, the relative pronoun ᾧ in v. 6 is almost certainly masculine and refers to the law, not to the sinful passions of v. 5. The verb ἐθανατώθητε in v. 4 parallels the participle ἀποθανόντες in v. 6, and since the former verb is followed by τῷ νόμῳ, we can assume that the τούτῳ or ἐκείνῳ to be supplied as the antecedent of ᾧ refers to the law (see Cranfield, 1:338–339; Wilckens, *Römer*, 2:69–70; Kümmel, *Römer* 7, 42).

55. There is little doubt among most commentators that v. 4 depicts the role that the law plays in the provocation of concrete acts of sin (see citations above, p. ### n. 71). Besides what appears to be the evident meaning in the text itself (see Moo, *Romans*, 419 n. 54), the response of v. 7 would make little sense otherwise. Wilckens finds the expression here to be even sharper than that of 5:20 (*Römer*, 2:69). In fact, the statement stands near the end of a string of negative declarations that Paul has expressed with ever increasing sharpness (3:20b; 4:15b; 5:13b, 20b). The culmination is reached in vv. 7–11.

56. On this *negative* (v. 4), *positive* (v. 5), *negative* (v. 6) pattern, see Lamarche and Le Dû, *Structure Littéraire*, 46; Kuss, *Römerbrief*, 2:437. Verse 6 actually comprises a positive, negative, positive structure within itself.

57. We have added the word "for" to the NRSV here to reflect the introductory γάρ. The conjunction introduces v. 5 as the explanation of v. 4. The NRSV, however, maintains the "then/while" (ὅτε) and "now" (νυνὶ δέ) contrast at the beginning of each verse (see the same contrast in 6:20, 22).

It is significant, we note as we conclude, that while Paul designates those who died (with Christ) to the law in 7:4 as "you," in 6:6, he specifies the deceased as "the old self": "We know that our old self was crucified with him so that the body of sin might be destroyed, and we might no longer be enslaved to sin." Although much discussion surrounds the phrase ὁ παλαιὸς ἡμῶν ἄνθρωπος,[58] most commentators find an allusion here to Adam: "ὁ παλαιὸς ἄνθρωπος is a man belonging to the age of Adam."[59] "The 'old man' is what we were 'in Adam'—the 'man' of the old age, who lives under tyranny and death."[60] "It is much more exact to say that the 'old man' is Adam—or rather, ourselves in union with Adam."[61] That Adamic images are present in Paul's designation is almost certain since 1) the term ἄνθρωπος most likely alludes back to the Adam side of Adam-Christ contrasts of Romans 5,[62] a passage whose conclusion (5:20) laid the foundation for the discussion in Romans 6;[63] 2) the term παλαιός is suggestive of the old created order;[64] and 3) the designation παλαιός ἄνθρωπος is used only twice elsewhere in the New Testament

---

58. There is the question, e.g., of whether the designation is ontological (Cranfield, Hodge, Godet) or positional (Byrne, Schreiner, Wilckens). If the phrase "body of sin" refers here to the physical body "ruled by sin" (TNIV), as we believe the context suggests (e.g. 6:12-13, 7:23-24; see Jewett, *Anthropological Terms*, 290-92; Gundry, "Sōma," 39, 57-59; Kaye, *Argument*, 77-78; Schreiner, *Romans*, 316; *NIDNTT* 1:73), the latter interpretation would appear more likely since the logic of Paul's argument seemingly assume a distinction between "the body of sin" from "the old self" (see Stott, *Romans*, 176 and n. 62, below).

59. Dunn, *Romans*, 1:318.

60. Moo, *Romans*, 373.

61. Barrett, *Romans*, 125. See also idem, *First Adam*, 98-99; Peterson, *Römer*, 1883.

62. Note, e.g., ἑνὸς ἀνθρώπου (vv. 12, 19; cf. ὁ πρῶτος ἄνθρωπος in 1 Cor 15:45, 49). See Schnackenburg, "Typologie," 45; Tannehill, *Dying and Rising*, 25; Wright, "Romans," 539; Käsemann, *Romans*, 169; Wilckens, *Römer*, 2:16; Ridderbos, *Paul*, 62-64. The term ἄνθρωπος in 6:6, Moo observes, designates the person as a whole "considered in relation to the corporate structure to which he or she belongs" (*Romans*, 373; see also Larsson, *Christus*, 197; Moule, *Colossians*, 119-20). The participation language in 6:3-8, which links the verses to the solidarity motif of 5:12-21, appears to support Moo's observation (see Dunn, *Paul*, 411; Ridderbos, *Paul*, 61-62; Schnackenburg, "Adam-Christus," 45).

63. See Tannehill, *Dying and Rising*, 24-27.

64. Note the counterpart term καινός in the *new* creation contexts of 2 Cor 5:17; Gal 6:16; Eph 4:24 (see O'Brien, *Colossians*, 189). It is possible that this new creation motif is also implicit in 6:4 and 7:6 by way of the καινο- terminology (see Grappe, "Qui me délivrera," 484-485; Wilckens, *Römer*, 2:16).

(Eph 4:22 and Col 3:9), and in both instances "Adam-categories" are present.[65]

If Paul's designation "old man" in 6:6 likely alludes to Adam, then this would bring our study of the catalytic operation of the law full circle. We would again discover edenic allusions occupying territory surrounding Paul's discussion of the catalytic notion of the law.[66] And, again, we should not be surprised. If, as we argued, the law problematic is primeval, we would expect Paul to discuss it in Adamic terms. And if, as seems likely, the "you" of 7:4 who was "put to death" to the law is to be identified with the "old [Adamic] man" of 6:6,[67] then this, like 1 Cor 15:56 and Rom

---

65. Ridderbos, *Paul*, 64. In contrast to the "old self," the "new self" in Col 3:10 is being "renewed in knowledge according to the image of its creator" and in Eph 4:24 is "created according to the likeness of God." The allusions to Gen 1:26–27 are unmistakable (see Brandenburger, "Adam-Anthropos," 196–98).

66. Besides the allusion in 6:6, Grappe detects a discreet allusion in 6:12: "Quant à la mention qui est faite, un peu plus loin, in 6:12, du 'corps mortel' qui caractérise l'humaine condition, elle peut être lue comme un nouveau rappel, discret, de le chute et de ses conséquences, au même titre d'ailleurs que l'évocation faite, dans le même verset, de nos 'désirs' ou de nos 'convoitises'" ("Qui me délivrera," 485).

67. Wright forcefully argues for this interpretation: "Who is it, then, that has 'died' [to the law]? The previous chapter gives a clear unambiguous answer, and indeed repeats it seven times: 'we died to sin' (6:2), we 'were baptized into Christ's death' (6:3), 'we were buried with him into death' (6:4), 'we were planted with him in the likeness of his death' (6:5), 'our old self was co-crucified' (6:6), 'we died with Christ" (6:8), 'reckon yourselves dead to sin' (6:11). It might seem tedious to list all these, were it not for the fact that chap. 6 is so little invoked to explain 7:4, and that commentators who have referred to 6:6 to do so are frequently waved away by those insist on treating chap. 7 as though it were an entirely separate discussion. Once we link law with sin, however (the point of 5:20, which Paul will address in 7:7), 'you died to the law' can only have one meaning. 'You' in the first half of 7:4 is the 'former husband'; 'you' in the second half is the 'wife.' Or, if we prefer [which *we* do], 'you' in the first half is the 'old human being of 6:6—the 'old Adam,' or perhaps better 'the person "in Adam"'. 'You' in the second half, at least when the re-marriage has occurred, is the person 'in Christ.' Just as later in the chapter the argument hinges on the double "I," so here it hinges on a double "you" ("Romans," 559; see also idem, *Climax*, 196; Sanday and Headlam, *Romans*, 173; Kuss, *Römerbrief*, 436; Leenhardt, *Romans*, 178; Byrne, *Romans*, 211; Ridderbos, *Paul*, 63; Luther, "Romans," 25:57; Gifford, *Romans*, 135). Other writers appear to assume an identification of the one in 7:4 who "died to the law" with the "old man" of 6:6 by the way they interpret the "death" of 7:4 in terms of 6:3–6. Thus Schlier writes: "Es ist ein und dasselbe Geschehen, welches der Sünde sterben und dem Gesetz getötet werden ließ" (*Römerbrief*, 216; see also Godet, *Romans*, 266; Denney, "Romans," 2:637; Dodd, *Romans*, 102; Ziesler, *Romans*, 175; Middendorf, *Storm*, 70; Stott, *Romans*, 194; Tannehill, *Dying and Rising*, 43–47). A number of factors argue for the identification of the "old man" of 6:6 with the "you" of 7:4: 1) the argumentative flow of 6:1–8 implies that the "old man" of 6:6 identical with

7:7-11, would not only appear to link edenic themes to the catalytic operation of the law, but would account for the means by which deliverance from the dominion of sin is achieved. Humans, Paul seems to imply, are not only bound through Adam to the nexus of sin and death (Romans 5; 1 Cor 15:56a), they, like their prototype, have become entangled in the nexus of law and sin (Romans 6–7; 1 Cor 15:56b). And since *law*, with its obligations and sanctions, is part and parcel of the Adamic world order,[68] nothing short of death, through participation in the atoning death of Christ, can release one from its jurisdiction. And because *the catalytic operation of the law* is a part of the primeval story, it is only by being transferred from the story of Eden to the story of Calvary that the nexus of law and sin can be left behind.

---

the "we"/"us" of 6:3-5, 8 (see Murray, *Principles*, 213); 2) as we have observed, there are strong conceptual parallels between 6:3-7 and 7:4-6 (see Stott, *Romans*, 194; Käsemann, *Romans*, 188; Tobin, *Rhetoric*, 222); 3) in both passages Paul depicts the experience of death in the passive (συνεσταυρώθη . . . ἐθανατώθητε); 4) each passage contains purpose clauses that depict similar outcomes; 5) there is a likely link between παλαιός in 6:6 and παλαιότης in 7:6 (see Hofius, "Mensch," 109 n. 18; Middendorf, *Storm*, 70); and 6) as we noted above, "death to the law" in chapter 7 may be implicit in, if not identified with, the "death to sin" in chapter 6 (see above, n. 52).

68. See above, pp. 234-36.

# Bibliography

Abel, F.-M. *Grammaire du Grec Biblique: suivie d'un choix de papyrus.* 2nd ed. Paris: Gabalda, 1927.
Achtemeier, Paul J. *Romans.* Interpretation. Atlanta: John Knox, 1985.
Adams, Edward. "Paul's Story of God and Creation: The Story of How God Fulfills His Purposes in Creation." In *Narrative Dynamics in Paul: A Critical Assessment*, edited by Bruce W. Longenecker, 19–43. Louisville: Westminster John Knox, 2002.
Aharoni, Yohanan, and Michael Avi-Jonah, editors. *The Macmillan Bible Atlas.* New York: Macmillan, 1983.
Aland, Barbara, et al. *Novum Testamentum Graece.* 27th rev. ed. Stuttgart: Deutsche Bibelgesellschaft, 2001.
Aland, Kurt, and Barbara Aland. *The Text of the New Testament: An Introduction to the Critical Editions and to the Theory and Practice of Modern Textual Criticism.* 2nd ed. Translated by Erroll F. Rhodes. Grand Rapids: Eerdmans, 1989.
Albertz, Rainer. "'Ihr werdet sein wie Gott' (Gen 3,5)." In *Was ist der Mensch . . . ? Beiträge zur Anthropologie des Alten Testaments: Hans Walter Wolff zum 80. Geburtstag*, edited by Frank Crüsemann et al., 11–27. Münich: Kaiser, 1992.
Aletti, Jean-Noël. "L'argumentation de Paul et la position des Corinthiens." In *Résurrection du Christ et des chrétiens (1 Co 15)*, edited by Lorenzo De Lorenzi, 63–81. SMBen 8. Rome: Abbey of St. Paul, 1985.
———. "La *dispositio* rhetorique dans les épîtres pauliniennes. Proposition de méthode." *NTS* 38 (1992) 385–401.
———. *Israël et la loi dans la lettre aux Romains.* LD 173. Paris: Cerf, 1998.
———. "Romans 7,7-25: Rhetorical Criticism and Its Usefulness." *SEÅ* 61 (1996) 77–95.
Alexander, Patrick H., et al., eds. *The SBL Handbook of Style: for Ancient Near Eastern, Biblical, and Early Christians Studies.* Peabody, MA: Hendrickson, 1999.
Allo, E.-B. *Saint Paul Première Épître aux Corinthiens.* 2nd ed. EBib. Paris: Gabalda, 1956.
Alonso-Schökel, Luis. "Sapiential and Covenant Themes in Genesis 3." In *Studies in Ancient Israelite Wisdom*, edited by James L. Crenshaw, 468–80. New York: Ktav, 1976.
Althaus, Paul. *Der Brief an die Römer.* 11th ed. NTD 6. Göttingen: Vandenhoeck & Ruprecht, 1970.
Ambrosiaster. *Ambrosiastri qui dicitur commentarius in epistulas Paulinas: Pars 1: In epistulam ad Romanos.* CSEL 81. Edited by Henricus Josephus Vogels. Vienna: Hölder-Pichler-Tempsky, 1966.

———. *Ambrosiastri qui dicitur commentarius in epistulas Paulinas: Pars 2: In epistulas ad Corinthios*. CSEL 81. Edited by Henricus Josephus Vogels. Vienna: Hölder-Pichler-Tempsky, 1968.

Andersen, Francis I., and David Noel Freedman. *Hosea: A New Translation with Introduction and Commentary*. AB 24. Garden City, NY: Doubleday, 1980.

Aquinas, Thomas. *Summa Theologiae: Latin Text and English Translation, Introductions, Notes, Appendices and Glossaries*. Edited by Thomas Gilbey. 61 vols. Blackfriars: London. 1964–1981.

Asher, Jeffrey R. *Polarity and Change in 1 Corinthians 15*. HUT 42. Tübingen: Mohr/Siebeck, 2000.

Attridge, Harold W. *First-century Cynicism in the Epistles of Heraclitus*. HTS 29. Missoula, MT: Scholars, 1976.

Augustine. *Against the Two Letters of the Pelagians*. In vol. 3 of *The Nicene and Post Nicene Fathers*, Series 1. 14 vols. Edited by Philip Schaff. Translated by Peter Holmes, et al. 1886–1890. Reprint, Peabody, MA: Hendrickson, 1994.

———. *The City of God*. In vol. 2 of *The Nicene and Post Nicene Fathers*, Series 1. Edited by Philip Schaff. Translated by Marcus Dods. 1886–1890. Reprint, Peabody, MA: Hendrickson, 1994.

———. *Eighty Three Different Questions*. In vol. 70 of *The Fathers of the Christian Church*. Edited by Ludwig Schopp, et al. 107 vols. Washington, DC: Catholic University of America Press, 1946–.

———. *Expositio Quarundam Propositionum ex Epistula ad Romanos*. Patrologia latina 35. Edited by J.-P. Migne. Paris: Migne, 1844–1864.

———. *On Continence*. In vol. 3 of *The Nicene and Post Nicene Fathers*, Series 1. Edited by Philip Schaff. Translated by C. L. Cornish. 1886–1890. Reprint, Peabody, MA: Hendrickson, 1994.

———. *On Grace and Free Will*. In vol. 5 of *The Nicene and Post Nicene Fathers*, Series 1. Edited by Philip Schaff. Translated by Peter Holmes, et al. 1886–1890. Reprint, Peabody, MA: Hendrickson, 1994.

———. *On the Morals of the Catholic Church*. In vol. 4 of *The Nicene and Post Nicene Fathers*, Series 1. Edited by Philip Schaff. Translated by Richard Stothert. 1886–1890. Reprint, Peabody, MA: Hendrickson, 1994.

———. *On the Spirit and the Letter*. In vol. 3 of *The Nicene and Post Nicene Fathers*, Series 1. Edited by Philip Schaff. Translated by Peter Holmes, et al. 1886–1890. 14 vols. Reprint, Peabody, MA: Hendrickson, 1994.

———. *To Simplician on Various Questions*. In vol. 6 of *The Library of Christian Classics*. Edited by John Baillie, et al. 26 vols. Philadelphia: Westminster, 1953–1966.

Aune, David E. "Aphorism." In *The Westminster Dictionary of New Testament and Early Christian Literature and Rhetoric*, 36–41. Louisville: Westminster John Knox, 2003.

Bachmann, Philipp. *Der erste Brief des Paulus an die Korinther*. KNT. Leipzig: Deichertsche, 1921.

Bailey, J. A. "Initiation and the Primal Woman in Gilgamesh and Genesis 2–3." *JBL* 89 (1970) 144–47.

Balz, Horst, and Gerhard Schneider, editors. *Exegetical Dictionary of the New Testament*. 3 vols. Grand Rapids: Eerdmans, 1990–1993.

Bandstra, A. J. *The Law and the Elements of the World*. Kampen: Kok, 1964.

Banks, Robert. "Romans 7.25a: An Eschatological Thanksgiving?" *ABR* 26 (1978) 34–42.

Barclay, John M. G. *Obeying the Truth: A Study of Paul's Ethics in Galatians*. SNTW. Minneapolis: Fortress, 1991.
Barclay, William. *The Letters to the Corinthians*. Translated with an Introduction and Interpretation. DBS. Philadelphia: Westminster, 1975.
———. *The Letter to the Romans*: Translated with an Introduction and Interpretation. DBS. Philadelphia: Westminster, 1975.
Barnes, Jonathan. "Aphorism and Argument." In *Language and Thought in Early Greek Philosophy*, edited by Kevin Robb, 91–109. LaSalle, IL: Hegeler, 1983.
Barrett, C. K. *The Epistle to the Romans*. Rev. ed. 1991. Reprint, Peabody, MA: Hendrickson, 1991.
———. *Essays on Paul*. Philadelphia: Westminster, 1982.
———. *The First Epistle to the Corinthians*. 1968. Reprint, Peabody, MA: Hendrickson, 1968.
———. *From First Adam to Last*. New York: Scribner, 1962.
———. "The Significance of the Adam-Christ Typology." In *Résurrection du Christ et des chrétiens (1 Co 15)*, edited by Lorenzo De Lorenzi, 99–122. SMBen 8. Rome: Abbey of St. Paul, 1985.
Barrosse, Thomas. "Death and Sin in St. Paul's Epistle to the Romans." *CBQ* 15 (1953) 438–59.
Barth, Gerhard. "Erwägungen zu 1. Korinther 15,20–28." *EvT* 30 (1970) 515–27.
Barth, Karl. *Christ and Adam: Man and Humanity in Romans 5*. Translated by T. A. Smail. New York: Macmillan, 1968.
———. *Church Dogmatics Volume 3: The Doctrine of Creation: Part One*. Edited by G. W. Bromiley and T. F. Torrance. Translated by J. M. Edwards, et al. Edinburgh: T. & T. Clark, 1958.
———. *The Epistle to the Romans*. Translated by Edwyn Hoskyns. Oxford: University Press, 1968.
———. *The Resurrection of the Dead*. Translated by H. J. Stenning. London: Hodder and Stoughton, 1933.
Bartlett, David Lyon. *Romans*. WBComp. Louisville: Westminster John Knox, 1995.
Baudissin, Wolf Wilhelm Grafen. *Studien zur Semitischen Religionsgeschichte*. 2 vols. Leipzig: Grunow, 1878.
Bauer, Walter. *A Greek-English Lexicon of the New Testament and Other Early Christian Literature*. 3rd ed. Revised and edited by Frederick W. Danker. Chicago: University of Chicago Press, 2000.
———. *Griechisch-deutsches Wörterbuch zu den Schriften des Neuen Testaments und der frühchristlichen Literatur*. 6th ed. Edited by Kurt Aland and Barbara Aland. Berlin: de Gruyter, 1988.
Bayes, Jonathan F. *The Weakness of the Law: God's Law and the Christian Perspective*. PBTM. Carlisle, UK: Paternoster, 2000.
Beale, Gregory K. "Eden, the Temple, and the Church's Mission in the New Creation." *JETS* 48 (2005) 5–31.
Beattie, D. R. G. "*Peshat* and *Derash* in the Garden of Eden." *IBS* 7 (1985) 62–75.
Beauchamp, Paul. *Création et séparation: Étude exégétique du chapitre premier de la Genèse*. Bsr. Paris: Aubier-Montaigne, 1969.
———. *La loi de Dieu: d'une montagne à l'autre*. Paris: Seuil, 1999.
Becker, Jürgen. *Paul: Apostle to the Gentiles*. Translated by O. C. Dean. Louisville: Westminster John Knox, 1993.

Beet, Joseph Agar. *A Commentary on St. Paul's Epistle to the Corinthians.* London: Hodder and Stoughton, 1882.

Beker, J. Christiaan. *Paul the Apostle: The Triumph of God in Life and Thought.* Philadelphia: Fortress, 1980.

———. "The Relationship Between Sin and Death in Romans." In *The Conversation Continues: Studies in Paul and John*, edited by Robert T. Fortna and Beverly R. Gaventa, 55–61. Nashville: Abingdon, 1990.

Ben Yasher, Menahem. "Zu Gen 4,7." *ZAW* 94 (1982) 635–37.

Bénétreau, Samuel. *L'Épître de Paul aux Romains.* 2 vols. CEB. Vaux-sur-Seine: Edifac, 1996–1997.

Bengelii, Joh. Alberti. *Gnomon Novi Testamenti: in quo ex nativa verborum VI: simplicitas, profunditas,concinnitas, salubritas sensuum coelestium indicatur.* 3rd ed. Stuttgart: Steinkopf, 1860.

Benoit, Pierre. "The Law and the Cross according to St. Paul: Rom 7:7–8:4." In *Jesus and the Gospel: Volume 2*, 11–39. Translated by Benet Weatherhead. New York: Seabury, 1974.

Berman, Samuel K. *Midrash Tanhuma-Yelammedenu: An English Translation of Genesis and Exodus from the Printed Version of Tanhuma-Yelammedenu with Introduction, Notes, and Indexes.* Hoboken, NJ: Ktav, 1996.

Bergmeier, Roland. "Das Gesetz im Römerbrief." In *Das Gesetz im Römerbrief und andere Studien zum Neuen Testament*, 31–102. WUNT 121. Tübingen: Mohr Siebeck, 2000.

———. "Röm 7,7–25a (8,2): Der Mensch–das Gesetz–Gott–Paulus—die Exegesis im Widerspruch?" *KD* 31 (1985) 162–72.

Best, Ernest. *The Letter of Paul to the Romans.* CBC. Cambridge: Cambridge University Press, 1967.

Betz, Hans Dieter. *Galatians: A Commentary on Paul's Letter to the Churches in Galatia.* Hermeneia. Philadelphia: Fortress, 1979.

Betz, Otto. "δυναμις." In *The New International Dictionary of New Testament Theology*, edited by Colin Brown, 2:601–6. Grand Rapids: Zondervan, 1975–1978.

Black, C. Clifton. "Pauline Perspectives on Death in Romans 5–8." *JBL* 103 (1984) 413–33.

Black, Matthew. *Romans.* 2nd ed. NCB. Grand Rapids: Eerdmans, 1989.

Bläser, P. *Das Gesetz bei Paulus.* NTAbh. 19. Münster: Aschendorff, 1941.

Blass, Friederich, and Albert Debrunner. *A Greek Grammar of the New Testament and Other Early Christian Literature.* Translated and revised by Robert W. Funk. Chicago: University of Chicago Press, 1961.

———. *Grammatik des neutestamentlichen Griechisch.* 15th ed. Edited by Friedrich Rehkopf. Göttingen: Vandenhoeck & Ruprecht, 1979.

Blenkinsopp, Joseph. *The Pentateuch: An Introduction to the First Five Books of the Bible.* ABRL. New York: Doubleday, 1992.

Blocher, Henri. *La doctrine du péché et de la rédemption.* 3rd ed. CD. Vaux-sur-Seine: Edifac, 2000.

———. *Evil and the Cross: Christian Thought and the Problem of Evil.* Translated by David G. Preston. Leicester, UK: Apollos, 1994.

———. *In the Beginning: The Opening Chapters of Genesis.* Translated by David G. Preston. Downers Grove, IL.: InterVarsity, 1984.

———. *Original Sin: Illuminating the Riddle.* NSBT 5. Leicester, UK: Apollos, 1997.

Bonhoeffer, Dietrich. *Creation and Fall*. Translated by John C. Fletcher. London: Collins, 1959.
Bonneau, Normand. "Stages of Salvation History in Romans 1:16–3:26." *EgT* 23 (1992) 177–94.
Bornkamm, Günther. *Das Ende des Gesetzes: Paulusstudien*. BEvT 16. Münich: Kaiser, 1952.
———. "Sin, Law and Death: An Exegetical Study of Romans 7." In *Early Christian Experience*, translated by Paul L. Hammer, 87–104. NTL. London: SCM, 1969.
Botterweck, Johannes, Helmer Ringgren, and Heinz-Josef Fabry, editors. *Theological Dictionary of the Old Testament*. Translated by John T. Willis, et al. 14 vols. Grand Rapids: Eermans, 1974–2004.
Bousset, Wilhelm. *Der erste Brief an die Korinther*. 3rd ed. SchNT 2. Göttingen: Vandenhoeck & Ruprecht, 1917.
Brandenburger, E. *Adam und Christus: Exegetisch-religionsgeschichtliche Untersuchung zu Röm. 5,12–21 (1 Kor 15)*. WMANT 7. Neukirchen-Vluyn: Neukirchener, 1962.
———. "Alter und neuer Mensch, erster und letzter Adam-Anthropos." In *Vom alten zum neuen Adam*, edited by Walter Strolz, 182–217. VSOD 13. Freiburg: Herder, 1986.
———. *Fleisch und Geist: Paulus und die dualistische Weisheit*. WMANT 29. Neukirchen-Vluyn: Neukirchener, 1968.
Brandscheidt, Renate. "Der Mensch und die Bedrohung durch die Macht des Bösen." *TTZ* 109 (2000) 1–23.
Branick, Victor P. "The Sinful Flesh of the Son of God (Rom 8:3): A Key Image of Pauline Theology." *CBQ* 47 (1985) 246–62.
Braude, William G., translator. *The Midrash on the Psalms*. 2 vols. New Haven: Yale University Press, 1992.
———, translator. *Pesikta Rabbati*. 2 vols. New Haven, CT: Yale University Press, 1968.
Bray, Gerald. "The Significance of God's Image in Man." *TB* 42 (1991) 195–225.
Brecht, Martin. "Martin Luther: Sing mir das Lied gegen den Tod." *Luther* 67 (1996) 52–58.
Brin, Gershon. *Studies in Biblical Law: From the Hebrew Bible to the Dead Sea Scrolls*. JSOTSup 176. Sheffield, UK: JSOT, 1994.
Brooks, James A., and Carlton L. Winbery. *Syntax of New Testament Greek*. Washington, D.C.: University Press of America, 1978.
Brown, Colin, editor. *The New International Dictionary of New Testament Theology*. 3 vols. Grand Rapids: Zondervan, 1975–1978.
Brown, Francis, S. R. Driver, Charles A. Briggs. *A Hebrew and English Lexicon of the Old Testament: with an Appendix Containing the Biblical Aramaic*. Oxford: Clarendon, 1977.
Brown, John. *The Resurrection of Life: An Exposition of First Corinthians XV with a Discourse on Our Lord's Resurrection*. Edinburgh: Oliphant, 1866.
Bruce, F. F. *1 and 2 Corinthians*. Grand Rapids: Eerdmans, 1971.
———. *The Letter of Paul to the Romans: An Introduction and Commentary*. 2nd ed. TNTC 6. Grand Rapids: Eerdmans, 1985.
———. *Paul: Apostle of the Heart Set Free*. Grand Rapids: Eerdmans, 1977.
———. "Paul and the Law of Moses." *BJRL* 57 (1974–1975) 259–79.
Bruckner, James K. "Boundary and Freedom: Blessings in the Garden of Eden." *CQ* 57 (1999) 15–35.

———. "The Creational Context of Law Before Sinai: Law and Liberty in Pre-Sinai Narratives and Romans 7." *ExAud* 11 (1995) 91–110.

Brueggemann, Walter. *Genesis*. Interpretation. Atlanta: John Knox, 1982.

Bruggen, Jakob van. *Paul: Pioneer for Israel's Messiah*. Translated by Ed M. Van der Maas. Phillipsburg, NJ: Presbyterian and Reformed, 2005.

Brunner, Emil. *The Letter to the Romans*. Translated by H. A. Kennedy. Philadelphia: Westminster, 1959.

Buber, Martin. *Good and Evil: Two Interpretations*. 2nd ed. Translated by Ronald Gregor Smith and Michael Bullock. New York: Scribner, 1953.

Buchanan, George Wesley. "OT Meaning of Knowledge of Good and Evil." *JBL* 75 (1956) 114–20.

Budde, Karl. "Der Baum des Lebens." In *Die biblische Urgeschichte (Gen. 1–12,5)*, 46–88. Giessen: Ricker, 1883.

———. *Die Biblische Paradiesesgeschichte*. BZAW 60. Giessen: Töpelmann, 1932.

Bultmann, Rudolph. "Romans 7 and the Anthropology of Paul." In *Existence and Faith: Shorter Writings of Rudolf Bultmann*, edited and translated by Schubert M. Ogden, 147–57. Cleveland, OH: World, 1960.

———. *Der Stil der paulinischen Predigt und die stoisch-kynische Diatribe*. FRLANT 13. Göttingen: Vandenhoeck & Ruprecht, 1910.

———. *Theology of the New Testament*. 2 vols. Translated by Kendrick Grobel. New York: Scribner, 1951.

Bünker, Michael. *Briefformular und rhetorische Disposition im 1. Kor*. GTA 28. Göttingen: Vandenhoeck & Ruprecht, 1983.

Burnett, Gary W. "The Individual and the Struggle with Sin and the Law." In *Paul and the Salvation of the Individual*, edited by R. Alan Culpepper and Rolf Rendtorff, 173–214. BIS 57. Leiden: Brill, 2001.

Burton, Ernest De Witt. *A Critical and Exegetical Commentary on the Epistle to the Galatians*. ICC. Edinburgh: T. & T. Clark, 1921.

———. *Syntax of the Moods and Tenses in New Testament Greek*. Edinburgh: T. & T. Clark, 1898.

Burton, Keith Augustus. *Rhetoric, Law, and the Mystery of Salvation in Romans 7:1–6*. SBEC 44. Lewiston: Mellen, 2001.

Busch, Austin. "The Figure of Eve in Romans 7:5–25." *BibInt* 12 (2004) 1–36.

Bussini, François. *L'homme pécheur devant Dieu: Théologie et anthropologie*. Paris: Cerf, 1978.

Byrne, Brendan. "Living Out the Righteousness of God: The Contribution of Rom 6:1–8:13 to an Understanding of Paul's Ethical Presuppositions." *CBQ* 43 (1981) 557–81.

———. *Romans*. SP 6. Collegeville, MN: Liturgical, 1996.

Caird, George B. "Everything to Everyone." *Int* 13 (1959) 387–99.

———. *Principalities and Powers*. Oxford: Oxford University Press, 1956.

———. "Towards a Lexicon of the Septuagint. II." *JTS* 20 (1969) 21–40.

Callender, Dexter E. *Adam in Myth and History: Ancient Israelite Perspectives on the Primal Human*. HSMP 48. Winona Lake, IN: Eisenbrauns, 2000.

Calvin, John. *Commentaries on the First Book of Moses, called Genesis*. Translated by John King. Grand Rapids: Eerdmans, 1948.

———. *The Epistles of Paul the Apostle to the Romans and to the Thessalonians*. Translated by Ross Mackenzie. Edinburgh: Oliver and Boyd, 1960.

———. *The First Epistle of Paul to the Corinthians*. Translated by John W. Fraser. Calvin's Commentaries. Edinburgh: Oliver and Boyd, 1960.

———. *Institutes of the Christian Religion*. Translated by John T. McNeill. LCC 20. 2 vols. Philadelphia: Westminster, 1960.

Cambier, Jules-Marie. "Le 'moi' dans Rom. 7." In *The Law and the Spirit in Rom 7 and 8*, edited by Lorenzo De Lorenzi, 13–72. SMBen 1. Rome: Abbey of St. Paul, 1976.

Campbell, D. H. "The Identity of ἐγώ in Romans 7:7–25." In *Studia Biblica 1978: Sixth International Congress on Biblical Studies, Oxford 3–7 April 1978: III. Papers on Paul and Other New Testament Authors*, edited by E. A. Livingstone, 57–64. JSNTSup 3. Sheffield: JSOT, 1980.

Carmichael, C. M. "The Paradise Myth: Interpreting without Jewish and Christian Spectacles." In *A Walk in the Garden*, edited by P. Morris and D. Sawyer, 47–63. JSOTSup 136. Sheffield: JSOT Press, 1992.

Carr, Wesley. *Angels and Principalities: The Background, Meaning, and Development of the Pauline Phrase hai archai kai exousiai*. SNTSMS 42. Cambridge: Cambridge University Press, 1981.

Carrez, Maurice. *La Deuxième Épître de Saint Paul aux Corinthiens*. CNT. Geneva: Labor et Fides, 1986.

Carson, D. A. "Adam in the Epistles of Paul." In *In The Beginning. . . . A Symposium on the Bible and Creation*, edited by N. M. de S. Cameron, 28–43. Glasgow: The Biblical Creation Society, 1980.

Carson, D. A., and Douglas J. Moo. *An Introduction to the New Testament*. 2nd ed. Grand Rapids: Zondervan, 2005.

Carson, D. A., et al., eds. *Justification and Variegated Nomism: Volume I: The Complexities of Second Temple Judaism*. WUNT 2/140. Tübingen: Mohr/Siebeck, 2001.

———. *Justification and Variegated Nomism: Volume II: The Paradoxes of Paul*. WUNT 2/181. Tübingen: Mohr/Siebeck, 2004.

Carter, T. L. *Paul and the Power of Sin: Redefining "Beyond the Pale."* SNTSMS 115. Cambridge: University Press, 2002.

Cassuto, Umberto. *A Commentary on the Book of Genesis: Part 1: From Adam to Noah: Genesis I–VI:8*. Translated by I. Abrahams. Jerusalem: Magnes, 1961.

Cathcart, Kevin, Michael Maher, and Martin McNamara, editors. *The Aramaic Bible: The Targums*. 19 vols. Collegeville, MN: Liturgical, 1987–2003.

Causse, J. D. "Le renversement diabolique du symbolique: Réflexions à partir de Romains 7." *ETR* 75 (2000) 363–72.

Charles, R. H., ed. *The Apocrypha and Pseudepigrapha of the Old Testament*. 2 vols. Oxford: Oxford University Press, 1913.

Charlesworth, James H., editor. *The Old Testament Pseudepigrapha*. 2 vols. New York: Doubleday, 1998.

Chester, Stephen J. *Conversion at Corinth*. SNTW. London: T. & T. Clark, 2003.

Childs, Brevard S. *Biblical Theology in Crisis*. Philadelphia: Westminster, 1970.

Chrysostom, John. *Homilies on the Epistles of Paul to the Corinthians*. In vol. 12 of *The Nicene and Post Nicene Fathers*, Series 1. Edited by Philip Schaff. Edinburgh: T. & T. Clark, 1887–1894. 14 vols. Reprint, Peabody, MA: Hendrickson, 1991.

Cicero. *De republica*. Translated by Clinton Walker Keyes. LCL. Cambridge: Harvard University Press, 1951.

———. *Rhetorica ad Herennium*. Translated by Harry Caplan. LCL. Cambridge: Harvard University Press, 1954.

Clark, Gordon H. *1 Corinthians: A Contemporary Commentary*. Nutley, NJ.: Presbyterian & Reformed, 1975.

Clark, W. Malcolm. "Law." In *Old Testament Form Criticism*, edited by John H. Hayes, 99–139. TUMSR. San Antonio: Trinity University Press, 1974.

———. "A Legal Background to the Yahwist's Use of 'Good and Evil' in Genesis 2–3." *JBL* 88 (1969) 266–68.

Clemen, Carl. *Die Einheitlichkeit der paulinischen Briefe an der Hand der bisher mit bezug auf sie aufgestellten Interpolations- und Compilationshypothesen*. Göttingen: Vandenhoeck & Ruprecht, 1894.

Clemens, David M. "The Law of Sin and Death: Ecclesiastes and Genesis 1–3." *Them* 19 (1994) 5–8.

Clines, D. J. A. "Themes in Genesis 1–11." *CBQ* 38 (1976) 483–507.

———. "The Tree of Knowledge and the Law of Yahweh." *VT* 24 (1974) 8–14.

Coats, George W. *Genesis: with an Introduction to Narrative Literature*. The Forms of the Old Testament Literature. Grand Rapids: Eerdmans, 1983.

Cohen, A. translator. *The Minor Tractates for the Talmud*. 2 vols. London: Soncino, 1965.

Collins, Raymond F. *First Corinthians*. SP 7. Collegeville, MN: Liturgical, 1999.

Conzelmann, Hans. *1 Corinthians: A Commentary on the First Epistle to the Corinthians*. Hermeneia. Translated by James W. Leitch. Philadelphia: Fortress, 1975.

———. "On the Analysis of the Confessional Formula in 1 Corinthians 15:3–5." *Int* 10 (1966) 15–25.

———. *An Outline of the Theology of the New Testament*. NTL. London: SCM, 1969.

Coppens, J. *La Connaissance du Bien et du Mal et le Péché du Paradis: Contribution à l'interprétation de Gen. II–III*. ALBO 2:3. Louvain: Nauwelaerts, 1948.

Craig, Kenneth M. "Misspeaking in Eden, or, Fielding Questions in the Garden (Genesis 2:16–3:13)." *PRSt* 27 (2000) 235–47.

Cranfield, C. E. B. "St. Paul and the Law." *SJT* 17 (1964) 43–68.

———. *A Critical and Exegetical Commentary on the Epistle to the Romans*. 2 vols. ICC. Edinburgh: T. & T. Clark, 1973, 1975.

———. *On Romans and Other New Testament Essays*. Edinburgh: T. & T. Clark, 1998.

Crespy, Georges. "Exégèse et psychanalyse: Considérations aventureuses sur Romains 7:7–25." In *L'évangile, hier et aujourd'hui: melanges offerts au Professeur Franz -J. Leenhardt*, 169–79. Geneva: Labor & Fides, 1968.

Culley, Robert. "Action Sequences in Genesis 2–3." *Semeia* 18 (1980) 25–33.

Dahl, M. E. *The Resurrection of the Body: A Study of 1 Corinthians 15*. SBT 1/36. London: SCM, 1962.

Dahl, Nils Alstrup. *Studies in Paul: Theology for the Early Christian Mission*. Minneapolis: Augsburg, 1977.

———. "Two Notes on Romans 5." *ST* 5 (1952) 37–48.

Dana, H. E., and Julius R. Mantey. *A Manual Grammar of the Greek New Testament*. New York: Macmillan, 1957.

Das, A. Andrew. *Paul and the Jews*. LPS. Peabody, MA: Hendrickson, 2003.

———. *Paul, the Law, and the Covenant*. Peabody, MA: Hendrickson, 2001.

———. *Solving the Romans Debate*. Minneapolis: Fortress, 2007.

Daube, David. *Studies in Biblical Law*. Cambridge: Cambridge University Press, 1947.

Davidson, Richard M. "The Theology of Sexuality in the Beginning: Genesis 3." *AUSS* 26 (1988) 121–31.

Davies, W. D. *Paul and Rabbinic Judaism: Some Rabbinic Elements in Pauline Theology.* Rev. ed. London: SPCK, 1955. Reprint, New York: Harper, 1967.

de Boer, Martinus C. *The Defeat of Death: Apocalyptic Eschatology in 1 Corinthians 15 and Romans 5.* JSNTSup 22. Sheffield, UK: Sheffield Academic, 1988.

de Boor, Werner. *Der erste Brief des Paulus an die Korinther.* Wuppertaler Studienbibel. Wuppertal: Brockhaus, 1974.

Deidun, T. J. *New Covenant Morality in Paul.* AnBib 89. Rome: Biblical Institute, 1981.

Deissmann, Gustav Adolph. *Light from the Ancient East: The New Testament Illustrated by Recently Discovered Texts of the Graeco-Roman World.* Translated by Lionel R. M. Strachan. London: Hodder and Stoughton, 1927.

Delitzsch, Franz. *A New Commentary on Genesis.* Translated by Sophia Taylor. Edinburgh: T. & T. Clark, 1888. 2 vols. Reprint, Minneapolis: Klock & Klock, 1978.

Deluz, Gaston. *A Companion to 1 Corinthians.* London: Darton, Longman & Todd, 1963.

Démann, Paul. "Moïse et la loi dans la pensée de saint Paul." In *Moïse, l'homme de l'alliance,* 189-242. Paris: Desclée, 1955.

De Moor, Johannes C. "'O Death, Where Is Thy Sting?'" In *Ascribe to the Lord: Biblical and Other Studies in Memory of Peter C. Craigie,* edited by Lyle Eslinger and Glen Taylor, 99-107. JSOTSup 67. Sheffield: Sheffield University Press, 1998.

Denis, Albert-Marie, ed. *Concordance Grecque de Pseudépigraphes: d'Ancien Testament,* Louvain-la-Neuve: Université Catholique de Louvain, Institut Orientaliste, 1987.

Denney, James. "St. Paul's Epistle to the Romans." In *The Expositor's Greek New Testament,* edited by W. R. Nicoll, 2:555-725. 1900. Reprint, Grand Rapids: Eerdmans, 1970.

Deurloo, Karel Adriaan. "תְּשׁוּקָה 'dependency', Gen 4,7." *ZAW* 99 (1987) 405-6.

de Wette, W. M. L. *Kurze Erklärung der Briefe an die Corinther.* KEHNT 2/2. Leipzig: Weidmannsche, 1841.

———. *Kurze Erklärung des Briefes an die Römer.* KEHNT 2/1. Leipzig: Weidmannsche, 1847.

Díaz Rodelas, Juan Miguel. *Pablo y la ley: la novedad de Rom 7,7-7,4 en el conjunto de la relexión Paulina sobre la ley.* Institucíon San Jerónimo. Estella, Spain: Editorial Verbo Divino, 1994.

Diels, Hermann, and Walther Kranz. *Die Fragmente der Vorsokratiker: griechisch und deutsch.* 6th ed. 3 vols. Berlin: Weidmann, 1951.

Dietzfelbinger, Christian. *Heilsgeschichte bei Paulus?: Eine exegetische Studie zum paulinischen Geschichtsdenken.* TEH 126. Munich: Kaiser, 1965.

Dillmann, A. *Genesis: Critically and Exegetically Expounded.* 2 vols. Translated by William B. Stevenson. Edinburgh: T. & T. Clark, 1897.

Diogenes Laertius. *Lives of Eminent Philosophers.* Translated by R. D. Hicks. 2 vols. LCL. Cambridge: Harvard University Press, 1925.

Dochhorn, Jan. *Die Apokalypse des Moses: Text, Übersetzung, Kommentar.* TSAJ 106. Tübingen: Mohr/Siebeck, 2005.

Dodd, Brian. *Paul's Paradigmatic "I": Personal Example as Literary Strategy.* JSNTSup 177. Sheffield: Sheffield Academic Press, 1999.

Dodd, C. H. *The Epistle of Paul to the Romans.* MNTC. London: Fontana, 1959.

Donaldson, Terrance L. "The 'Curse of the Law' and the Inclusion of the Gentiles: Galatians 3.13-14." *NTS* 32 (1986) 94-112.

———. "'The Gospel That I Proclaim among the Gentiles' (Gal. 2.2): Universalistic or Israel-Centered?" In *Gospel in Paul: Studies on Corinthians, Galatians and Romans for Richard N. Longenecker*, edited by L. Ann Jervis and Peter Richardson, 166–93. JSNTSup 108. Sheffield: Sheffield Academic, 1994. **[ED: check series]**

———. *Paul and the Gentiles: Remapping the Apostle's Convictional World*. Grand Rapids: Eerdmans, 1997.

Doriani, D. "History of the Interpretation of 1 Timothy 2." In *Women in the Church: A Fresh Analysis of 1 Timothy 2:9–15*, edited by Andreas J. Köstenberger, et al., 215–69. Grand Rapids: Baker, 1995.

Drane, J. W. *Paul: Libertine or Legalist? A Study in the Theology of the Major Pauline Epistles*. London: SPCK, 1975.

Drewermann, Eugen. *Strukturen des Bösen I: Die Jahwistic Urgeschichte in exegetischer Sicht*. Paderborn: Schöningh, 1982.

Driver, S. R. *The Book of Genesis: with Introduction and Notes*. 15th ed. London: Methuen, 1948.

Dubarle, A. M. *Le péché originel dans l'Écriture*. Paris: Cerf, 1967.

———. *Les sages d'Israël*. Paris: Cerf, 1946.

Duhm, Hans. *Die bösen Geister im Alten Testament*. Tübingen: Mohr/Siebeck, 1904.

Dülmen, Andrea van. *Die Theologie des Gesetzes bei Paulus*. SBM. Stuttgart: Katholisches Bibelwerk, 1968.

Dunn, James D. G. *1 Corinthians*. NTG. Sheffield: Sheffield Academic, 1995.

———. "1 Corinthians 15:45—Last Adam, Life-Giving Spirit." In *Christ and Spirit in the New Testament*, edited by Barnabas Lindars and Stephen S. Smalley, 127–41. Cambridge: Cambridge University Press, 1973.

———. "Christ, Adam, and Preexistence." In *Where Christology Began: Essays on Philippians 2*. edited by Ralph P. Martin and Brian J. Dodd, 74–83. Louisville: Westminster John Knox, 1998.

———. *Christology in the Making: A New Testament Inquiry into the Origins of the Doctrine of the Incarnation*. Grand Rapids: Eerdmans, 1989.

———. *Jesus, Paul, and the Law: Studies in Mark and Galatians*. Louisville: Westminster John Knox, 1990.

———. "The New Perspective on Paul." *BJRL* 65 (1983) 95–122.

———. "Paul: Apostate or Apostle of Israel?" *ZNW* 89 (1998) 256–71.

———. "Paul and 'Covenantal Nomism.'" In *The Partings of the Ways: Between Christianity and Judaism and Their Significance for the Character of Christianity*, 117–39. London: SCM, 1991.

———. editor. *Paul and the Mosaic Law*. TDTRSECJ. Grand Rapids: Eerdmans, 2001.

———. "Paul's Understanding of the Death of Jesus." In *Reconciliation and Hope: New Testament Essays on Atonement and Eschatology presented to L. L. Morris on his 60th Birthday*, edited by Robert Banks, 125–41. Grand Rapids: Eerdmans, 1974.

———. "Rom. 7:14–25 in the Theology of St. Paul." *TZ* 31 (1975) 257–73.

———. *Romans*. 2 vols. WBC 38A, 38B. Waco, TX: Word, 1988.

———. *The Theology of Paul the Apostle*. Grand Rapids: Eerdmans, 1998.

Earnshaw, John D. "Reconsidering Paul's Marriage Analogy." *NTS* 40 (1994) 60–68.

Ebeling, Gerhard. *Word and Faith*. Philadelphia: Fortress, 1963.

Edwards, James R. *Romans*. NIBCNT 6. Peabody, MA: Hendrickson, 1992.

Edwards, Thomas Charles. *A Commentary on the First Epistle to the Corinthians*. London: Hodder and Stoughton, 1903.

Eichrodt, Walther. *Die Hoffnung des ewigen Friedens im alten Israel: Ein Beitrag zu der Frage nach der israelitischen Eschatologie*. Beitrage zur Förderung christlicher Theologie. 25. Güttersloh: Bertelsmann, 1920.
Elias, J. J. *The First Epistle to the Corinthians with Notes, Map, Introduction and Appendices*. CGTSC. Cambridge: Cambridge University Press, 1899.
Ellicott, Charles J. *St. Paul's First Epistle to the Corinthians: With a Critical and Grammatical Commentary*. London: Longmans, 1887.
Elliger, Karl, and Wilhelm Rudolph, editors. *Biblia Hebraica Stuttgartensia*. Stuttgart: Deutsche Bibelstiftung, 1983.
Ellingworth, Paul, and Howard Hatton. *A Translator's Handbook on Paul's First Letter to the Corinthians*. Helps for Translators. London: United Bible Societies, 1985.
Elliott, Neil. *Liberating Paul: The Justice of God and the Politics of the Apostle*. Maryknoll, NY: Orbis, 1984.
———. *The Rhetoric of Romans: Argumentative Constraint and Strategy and Paul's Dialogue with Judaism*. JSNTSup 45. Sheffield: Sheffield Academic, 1990.
Ellis, E. Earle. "A Note on Pauline Hermeneutics." *NTS* 2 (1955–1956) 127–33.
———. *Paul's Use of the Old Testament*. Edinburgh: Oliver and Boyd, 1957.
Emmrich, Martin. "The Temptation Narrative of Gen 3:1–6: A Prelude to the Pentateuch and the History of Israel." *EQ* 73 (2001) 3–20.
Engberg-Pedersen, Troels. "Galatians in Romans 5–8 and Paul's Construction of the Identity of Christ Believers." In *Texts and Contexts: Biblical Texts in Their Textual and Structural Contexts: Essays in Honor of Lars Hartman*, edited by Tord Fornberg and David Hellholm, 477–505. Oslo: Scandinavian University Press, 1995.
Engnell, I. "'Knowledge' and 'Life,' in the Creation Story." In *Wisdom in Israel and the Ancient Near East*, edited by M. Noth and D. Winston Thomas, 103–19. VTSup 3. Leiden: Brill, 1955.
Epictetus. *Discourses*. Translated by W. A. Oldfather. LCL. Cambridge: Harvard University Press, 1925.
Epstein, I., editor and translator. *The Babylonian Talmud*. 35 vols. London: Soncino, 1935–1952.
Erickson, Millard J. *Christian Theology*. 2nd ed. Grand Rapids: Baker, 1998.
Eriksson, Anders. *Traditions as Rhetorical Proof: Pauline Argumentation in 1 Corinthians 7*. Stockholm: Almqvist & Wiksell, 1998.
Esler, Philip F. *Conflict and Identity in Romans: The Social Setting of Paul's Letters*. Philadelphia: Fortress, 2003.
———. *Galatians*. NTR. London: Routledge, 1998.
Espy, John. "Paul's Robust Conscience Re-Examined." *NTS* 31 (1985) 161–87.
Evans, J. M. *Paradise Lost and the Genesis Tradition*. Oxford: Oxford University Press, 1968.
Ewald, Heinrich. *Die Sendschreiben des Apostels Paulus*. Göttingen: Dieterich, 1857.
Ezra, Ibn. *Ibn Ezra's Commentary on the Pentateuch: Genesis (Bereshit)*. Translated by H. Norman Strickman and Arthur M. Silver. New York: Menorah, 1988.
Fanning, Buist M. *Verbal Aspect in New Testament Greek*. OTD. Oxford: Clarendon, 1990.
Farina, Claudio. *Die Leiblichkeit der Auferstandenen: Ein Beitrag zur Analyse des paulinschen Gedankenganges in 1 Kor 15,35–58*. Würzburg: University of Würzburg, 1971.
Fee, Gordon D. *The First Epistle to the Corinthians*. Grand Rapids: Eerdmans, 1987.

———. *God's Empowering Presence: The Holy Spirit in the Letters of Paul.* Peabody, MA: Hendrickson, 1994.

Fernández Marcos, Natalio. *The Septuagint in Context: An Introduction to the Greek Version of the Bible.* Translated by Wilfred G. E. Watson. Leiden: Brill, 2000.

Feuillet, André. "Loi de Dieu, loi du Christ et loi de l'Esprit d'après les épîtres pauliniennes: Les rapports de ces trois lois avec la loi mosaique." *NovT* 22 (1980) 29–63.

———. "Le plan salvifique de Dieu d'après l'Épître aux Romains: essai sur la structure littéraire de l'épître." *RB* 57 (1950) 489–529.

Fiensy, David A. "The Roman Empire and Asia Minor." In *The Face of New Testament Studies: A Survey of Recent Research*, edited by Scot McKnight and Grant R. Osborne, 36–56.

Findlay, G. G. "St. Paul's First Epistle to the Corinthians." In *The Expositor's Greek New Testament*, edited by W. R. Nicoll, 2:727–953. 1900. Reprinted, Grand Rapids: Eerdmans, 1970.

Finsterbusch, Karin. *Die Thora als Lebensweisung für Heidenchristen.* SBTE 20. Göttingen: Vandenhoeck & Ruprecht, 1996.

Fiore, Benjamin, translator. "Diogenes." In *The Cynic Epistles: A Study Edition*, edited by Abraham J. Malherbe, 91–183. SBLSBS 12. Missoula, MT: Scholars, 1977.

Fischer, H. *Gespaltener christlicher Glaube: eine psychoanalytische orientierte Religionskritik.* Hamburg: Reich, 1974.

Fishbane, Michael. *Text and Texture: Close Readings of Selected Biblical Texts.* New York: Schocken, 1979.

Fitzmyer, Joseph A. *Romans: A New Translation with Introduction and Commentary.* AB 33. New York: Doubleday, 1993.

Forsyth, James J. "Faith and Eros: Paul's Answer to Freud." *RL* 46 (1977) 476–87.

Franzmann, Martin H. *Romans.* ConC. St. Louis: Concordia, 1968.

Freedman, David Noel, editor. *The Anchor Bible Dictionary.* 6 vols. Doubleday: New York, 1992.

Freedman, H., and Maurice Simon. *Midrash Rabbah.* 10 vols. London: Soncino, 1939.

Fretheim, Terence E. "The Book of Genesis: Introduction, Commentary, and Reflections." In *The New Interpreter's Bible: General Articles and Introduction, Commentary, and Reflections for Each Book of the Bible, Including the Apocryphal/Deuterocanonical Books*, edited by Leander E. Keck, et al., 1:319–674. Nashville: Abingdon, 1994.

———. "ידע." In *The New International Dictionary of Old Testament Theology and Exegesis*, edited by William VanGemeren, 2:409–14. Grand Rapids: Zondervan, 1997.

Friedlander, Gerald, editor and translator. *Pirkê de Rabbi Eliezer: (The Chapters of Rabbi Eliezer the Great) according to the Text of the Manuscript belonging to Abraham Epstein of Vienna.* 4th ed. New York: Sepher-Hermon, 1981.

Frye, Northrop. *The Great Code: The Bible and Literature.* Toronto: Acadamic, 1981.

Fuller, D. F. *Gospel and Law: Contrast or Continuum? The Hermeneutics of Dispensationalism and Covenant Theology.* Grand Rapids: Eerdmans, 1980.

Furnish, Victor Paul. *2 Corinthians: A New Translation with Introduction and Commentary.* AB 32A. Garden City, NY: Doubleday, 1984.

———. "Theology in 1 Corinthians." In *Pauline Theology: Volume II: 1 and 2 Corinthians*, eedited by David M. Hay. SBLSympS 22, 59–89. Atlanta: Society of Biblical Literature, 2002.

———. *Theology and Ethics in Paul.* Nashville: Abingdon, 1968.

———. *The Theology of the First Letter to the Corinthians.* NTTh. Cambridge: Cambridge University Press, 1999.
Gager, John G. *The Origins of Anti-Semitism: Attitudes Towards Judaism in Pagan and Christian Antiquity.* New York: Oxford University Press, 1985.
García Pérez, J. M. "1 Co 15,56: ¿Una Polemica contra la Ley Judía?" *Estudios Biblicos* 60 (2002) 405–14.
Garland, David E. *1 Corinthians.* ECNT. Grand Rapids: Baker, 1998.
Garlington, Donald B. *Faith, Obedience, and Perseverance.* WUNT 79. Tübingen: Mohr Siebeck, 1994.
———. "The Obedience of Faith": A Pauline Phrase in Historical Context. Tübingen: Mohr Siebeck, 1991.
———. "Romans 7:14–25 and the Creation Theology of Paul." *TJ* 11 (1990) 197–235.
Garvie, Alfred E. *Romans: Introduction, Authorized Revised Version with Notes, Index, and Map.* CB. Edinburgh: Jack, n.d.
Gaston, Lloyd. *Paul and the Torah.* Vancouver: University of British Columbia Press, 1987.
Gathercole, Simon J. "Justified by Faith, Justified by His Blood: The Evidence of Romans 3:21–4:5." In *Justification and Variegated Nomism: Volume II: The Paradoxes of Paul*, edited by D. A. Carson, et al., 147–84. WUNT 2/181. Tübingen: Mohr/Siebeck, 2004.
———. *Where Is Boasting?: Early Jewish Soteriology and Paul's Response in Romans 1–5.* Grand Rapids: Eerdmans, 2002.
Gaugler, E. *Der Römerbrief.* 2 vols. Prophezei. Zurich: Zwingli, 1952, 1958.
Gaventa, Beverly R. "The Cosmic Power of Sin in Paul's Letter to the Romans." *Int* 58 (2004) 229–40.
Gemser, B. "The Importance of the Motive Clause in Old Testament Law." In *Congress Volume: Copenhagen, 1953*, 50–66. VTSup 1. Leiden: Brill, 1953.
Gemünden, Petra von. "Der Affekt der ἐπιθυμία und der νόμος: Affektkontrolle und sozialle Identitätsbildung im 4. Makkabäerbuch mit einem Ausblick auf den Römerbrief." In *Das Gesetz im frühen Judentum und im Neuen Testament: Festschrift für Christoph Burchard zum 75. Geburtstag*, edited by Dieter Sänger and Matthias Konradt. NTOA, 55–74. Göttingen: Vandenhoeck & Ruprecht, 2006.
Gerstenberger, Erhard S. "'. . . (He/They) Shall be Put to Death': Life-Preserving Divine Threats in Old Testament Law." *ExAud* 10 (1994) 43–61.
———. *Wesen und Herkunft des "apodiktischen Rechts."* WMANT 20. Neukirchen-Vluyn: Neukirchener, 1965.
Gertner, M. "Midrashim in the New Testament." *JSS* 7 (1962) 267–92.
Gese, Hartmut. "The Law." In *Essays on Biblical Theology*, 60–92. Translated by Keith Crim. Minneapolis: Fortress, 1981.
Gesenius, Wilhelm, E. Kautzsch, and A. E. Cowley. *Gesenius' Hebrew Grammar.* Edited by E. Kautzsch. Oxford: Clarendon, 1910.
Gieniusz, Andrzej. "Rom 7,1–6: Lack of Imagination? Function of the Passage in the Argumentation of Rom 6, 1–7,6." *Bib* 74 (1993) 389–400.
Gifford, E. H. *The Epistle of St. Paul to the Romans.* London: Murray, 1886.
Gillespie, Thomas W. *The First Theologians: A Study in Early Christian Prophecy.* Grand Rapids: Eerdmans, 1994.
Gillman, John. "A Thematic Comparison: 1 Cor 15:50–57 and 2 Cor 5:1–5." *JBL* 107 (1988) 439–54.

———. "Transformation in 1 Cor 15,50-53." *ETL* 58 (1982) 309-33.
Ginzberg, Louis. *Die Haggada bei den Kirchenvätern und in der apokryphischen Litteratur*. Berlin: Calvary, 1900.
———. *The Legends of the Jews*. 7 vols. Philadelphia: Jewish Publication Society, 1909-1938.
Gispen, W. H. *Schepping en Paradijs*. Kampen: Kok, 1966.
Godet, F. *Commentary on St. Paul's Epistle to the Romans*. Translated by A. Cusin and Talbot W. Chambers. New York: Funk & Wagnalls, 1883.
———. *Commentary on St. Paul's First Epistle to the Corinthians*. Translated by A. Cusin. CFTL. Edinburgh: T. & T. Clark, 1887.
Goldingay, John. *Old Testament Theology*. Downers Grove, IL: InterVarsity, 2003.
Goldsworthy, Graeme. "Biblical Theology and the Shape of Paul's Mission." In *The Gospel to the Nations: Perspectives on Paul's Mission*, edited by Peter Bolt and Mark Thompson, 7-18. Leicester, UK: Apollos, 2000.
Goodwin, William Watson. *Syntax of the Moods and Tenses of the Greek Verb*. London: Macmillan, 1889.
Goossens, W. "Immortalité Corporelle." In *Dictionaire de la Bible: Supplément*, edited by Louis Pirot and A. Robert, 298-51. Paris: Letouzey et Ané, 1949.
Gordis, Robert. "The Knowledge of Good and Evil in the Old Testament and the Qumran Scrolls." *JBL* 76 (1957) 123-38.
Gorman, Michael J. *Apostle of the Crucified Lord: A Theological Introduction to Paul and His Letters*. Grand Rapids: Eerdmans, 2004.
Goudge, H. L. *The First Epistle to the Corinthians: with Introduction and Notes*. 3rd. WC. London: Methuen, 1911.
Goulder, Michael D. *Paul and the Competing Mission in Corinth*. Peabody, MA: Hendrickson, 2001.
Gowan, Donald E. *Genesis 1-11: From Eden to Babel*. ITC. Grand Rapids: Eerdmans, 1988.
Grappe, Christian. "Qui me délivrera de ce corps de mort? L'Esprit de vie! Romains 7,24 et 8,2 comme éléments de typologie adamique." *Bib* 83 (2002) 472-92.
Greidanus, Sidney. "The Universal Dimension of Law in the Hebrew Scriptures." *SR* 14 (1985) 39-51.
Grelot, Pierre. *Péché originel et rédemption examinés à partir de l'épî[note diacrtical]tre aux Romains: Essai théologique*. Paris: Desclée, 1973.
Grosheide, F. W. *Commentary on the First Epistle to the Corinthians*. Grand Rapids: Eerdmans, 1953.
Gross, John, ed. *The Oxford Book of Aphorisms*. Oxford: Oxford University Press, 1983.
Gruenthaner, Michael. "The Demonology of the Old Testament." *QBC* 6 (1944) 6-11.
Grundmann, Walter. *Der Begriff der Kraft in der neutestamentlicher Gedankenwelt*. BWANT 8. Stuttgart: Kohlhammer, 1932.
———. "Gesetz, Rechtfertigung, und Mystik bei Paulus. Zum Problem der Einheitlichkeit der paulinischen Verkündigung." *ZNW* 32 (1933) 52-65.
Gundry, Robert H. "The Moral Frustration of Paul Before His Conversion: Sexual Lust in Romans 7:7-25." In *Pauline Studies: Essays Presented to Professor F. F. Bruce on His 70th Birthday*, edited by D. A. Hagner and M. J. Harris, 228-45. Grand Rapids: Eerdmans, 1980.
———. *"Sōma" in Biblical Theology: With Emphasis on Pauline Anthropology*. SNTSMS 29. Cambridge: Cambridge University Press, 1976.

Gunkel, Hermann. *Genesis*. Translated by Mark E. Biddle and Ernest W. Nicholson. Macon, GA: Mercer University Press, 1997.
Haacker, Klaus. *Der Brief des Paulus an die Römer*. THKNT 6. Leipzig: Evangelische Verlagsanstalt, 1999.
———. *The Theology of Paul's Letter to the Romans*. NTTh. Cambridge: Cambridge University Press, 2003.
Haering, Th. *Der Römerbrief des Apostels Paulus*. Stuttgart: Calwer, 1926.
Hafemann, Scott J. *Paul, Moses, and the History of Israel: The Letter/Spirit Contrast and the Argument from Scripture in 2 Corinthians 3*. Peabody, MA: Hendrickson, 1996.
Haldane, Robert. *Commentary on Romans*. 1853. Reprinted, Grand Rapids: Kregal, 1988.
Hall, David R. *The Unity of the Corinthian Correspondence*. JSNTSup 251. London: T. & T. Clark, 2003.
Hamerton-Kelly, Robert J. *Sacred Violence: Paul's Hermeneutic of the Cross*. Minneapolis: Sigler, 1992.
———. "Sacred Violence and Sinful Desire: Paul's Interpretation of Adam's Sin in the Letter to the Romans." In *The Conversation Continues: Studies in Paul and John*, edited by Robert T. Fortna and Beverly R. Gaventa, 35–54. Nashville: Abingdon, 1990.
Hamilton, Victor P. *The Book of Genesis*. 2 vols. NICOT. Grand Rapids: Eerdmans, 1990, 1995.
Hammer, Reuvan. *Sifra on Deuteronomy*. New Haven: Yale University Press, 1986.
Harrelson, Walter. "Death and Victory in 1 Corinthians 15:51–57: The Transformation of a Prophetic Theme." In *Faith and History: Essays in Honor of Paul W. Meyer*, edited by John T. Carroll, et al., 149–59. Atlanta: Scholars, 1990.
Harris, Murray J. *The Second Epistle to the Corinthians: A Commentary on the Greek Text*. NIGTC. Grand Rapids: Eerdmans, 2005.
Harrison, Everett F. "Romans." In *The Expositor's Bible Commentary*, edited by Frank E. Gaebelein, 10:3–171. Grand Rapids: Zondervan, 1976.
Harrison, R. K. *Introduction to the Old Testament*. Grand Rapids: Eerdmans, 1969.
Harrisville, Roy A. *Romans*. ACNT. Minneapolis: Augsburg, 1980.
Hartman, Louis F. "Sin in Paradise." *CBQ* 20 (1958) 26–40.
Hauser, A. J. "Linguistic and Thematic Links between Genesis 4:1–16 and Genesis 2–3." *JETS* 23 (1980) 297–305.
Hay, David M., editor. *Pauline Theology: Volume III: 1 and 2 Corinthians*. SBLSympS 22. Atlanta: Society of Biblical Literature, 2002.
Hays, Richard B. *Echoes of Scripture in the Letters of Paul*. New Haven: Yale University Press, 1989.
———. *The Faith of Jesus Christ: The Narrative Substructure of Galatians 3:1—4:11*. 2nd ed. BRS. Grand Rapids: Eerdmans, 2002.
———. *First Corinthians*. Interpretation. Louisville: Westminster John Knox, 1997.
———. "The Role of Scripture in Paul's Ethics." In *The Conversion of the Imagination: Paul as Interpreter of Scripture*, 143–62. Grand Rapids: Eerdmans, 2005.
Healey, J. F. "Canaanite Mot in Prophecy and Apocalypse." In *New Heaven and New Earth Prophecy and the Millennium: Essays in Honor of Anthony Gelston*, edited by P. J. Harland and C. T. R. Hayward, 205–15. VTSup 77. Leiden: Brill, 1999. **[ED: series]**
Heil, John Paul. *Romans: Paul's Letter of Hope*. AnBib 112. Rome: Biblical Institute Press, 1987.
Heim, Karl. *Die Gemeinde des Auferstandenen: Tübinger Vorlesungen über den ersten Korintherbrief*. TVM. Basel: Brunnen, 1987.

Heinisch, Paul. *Das Buch Genesis*. HSAT 1.1. Bonn: Hanstein, 1930.
Heinrici, C. F. Georg. *Der erste Brief an die Korinther*. KEK. Göttingen: Vandenhoeck & Ruprecht, 1896.
Hellholm, David. "Die Argumentative Funktion von Römer 7.1–6." *NTS* 43 (1997) 385–411.
———. "Enthymemic Argumentation in Paul: The Case of Romans 6." In *Paul in His Hellenistic Context*, edited by Troels Engberg-Pedersen, 119–79. Minneapolis: Fortress, 1995.
Hengel, Martin, and Anna Maria Schwemer. *Paul between Damascus and Antioch: The Unknown Years*. Translated by John Bowden. Louisville: Westminster John Knox, 1997.
Henry, Marie-Louise. "'Tod' und 'Leben,' Unheil und Heil als Funktionen des richtenden und rettenden Gottes im Alten Testament." In *Leben angesichts des Todes: Beiträge zum theologischen Problem des Todes*, edited by Helmut Thielicke, 1–26. Tübingen: Mohr/Siebeck, 1968.
Heppe, Heinrich. *Reformed Dogmatics: Set Out and Illustrated from the Sources*. Edited by Ernst Bizer. Translated by G. T. Thompson. Grand Rapids: Baker, 1978.
Héring, Jean. *The First Epistle of Saint Paul to the Corinthians*. Translated by A. W. Heathcote and P. J. Allcock. London: Epworth, 1962.
———. *La seconde Épître de Saint Paul aux Corinthiens*. CNT. Paris: Delachaux & Niestlé, 1958.
Hesselink, I. John. *Calvin's Concept of the Law*. Princeton Theological Monograph Series 20. Allison Park, PA: Pickwick, 1992.
Hinschberger, R. "Une lecture synchronique de Gn 2–3." *Revue des sciences religieuses* 63 (1989) 1–16.
*Hippocrates*. Translated by W. H. S. Jones et al. 8 vols. LCL. Cambridge: Harvard University Press, 1923–1995.
Hodge, Charles. *A Commentary on Romans*. Carlisle, PA: Banner of Truth, 1972.
———. *An Exposition of the First Epistle to the Corinthians*. Grand Rapids: Eerdmans, 1956.
———. *Systematic Theology*. 3 vols. Grand Rapids: Eerdmans, 1982.
Hofius, Otfried. "Die Adam-Christus-Antithese und das Gesetz." In *Paul and the Mosaic Law*, edited by James D. G. Dunn, 165–206. Tübingen: Mohr/Siebeck, 1996.
———. "Das Gesetz des Mose und das Gesetz Christi." *ZTK* 80 (1983) 262–86.
———. "Der Mensch im Schatten Adams." In *Paulusstudien II*, 104–54. WUNT 143. Tübingen: Mohr/Siebeck, 2002.
Holland, Glenn S. "The Self Against the Self in Romans 7.7–25." In *The Rhetorical Interpretation of Scripture: Essays from the 1966 Malibu Conference*, edited by Stanley E. Porter and Dennis L. Stamps, 260–71. JSNTSup 180. Sheffield: Sheffield Academic, 1999.
Hollander, Harm W. "The Meaning of the Term 'Law' (ΝΟΜΟΣ) in 1 Corinthians." *NovT* 40 (1998) 117–35.
Hollander, H. W., and J. Holleman. "The Relationship of Death, Sin, and Law in 1 Cor 15:56." *NovT* 35 (1993) 270–91.
Hollander, John. *The Figure of Echo: A Mode of Allusion in Milton and After*. Berkeley: University of California Press, 1981.
Holleman, Joost. *Resurrection and Parousia: A Traditio-Historical Study of Paul's Eschatology in 1 Corinthians 15*. NovTSup 84. Leiden: Brill, 1996.

Honeyman, A. M. "*Merismus* in Biblical Hebrew." *JBL* 71 (1952) 11-18.
Hong, In-Gyu. *The Law in Galatians*. JSNTS 81. Sheffield, UK: Sheffield Academic, 1993.
Hooker, Morna D. "Adam in Romans 1." *NTS* 6 (1959-1960) 297-306.
———. "A Further Note on Romans 1." *NTS* 13 (1966-1967) 181-83.
———. "Interchange in Christ." *JTS* 22 (1971) 349-61.
———. "Paul and 'Covenantal Nomism': Essays in Honor of C. K. Barrett." In *Paul and Paulinism: Essays in Honor of C. K. Barrett*, edited by Morna D. Hooker and S. G. Wilson, 47-56. London: SPCK, 1982.
Hoppe, Theodor. *Die Idee der Heilsgeschichte bei Paulus*. Gütersloh: Bertelsmann, 1926.
Horn, Friederich Wilhelm. "1 Korinther 15,56—ein exegetischer Stachel." *ZNW* 82 (1991) 88-105.
Horovitz, H. S., ed. *Siphre d'be Rab. Fasciculus primus: Siphre ad Numeros adjecto Siphre zutta*. Jerusalem: Wahrmann, 1976.
Horrell, David G. *The Social Ethos of the Corinthian Correspondence*. SNTW. Edinburgh: T. & T. Clark, 1996.
Horsley, G. R. S, and S. Llewelyn. *New Documents Illustrating Early Christianity*. 9 vols. North Ryde, N.S.W.: Macquarie University: Ancient History Documentary Research Center, 1981-.
Horsley, Richard A. *1 Corinthians*, ANTC. Nashville: Abingdon, 1998.
House, Paul R. *Old Testament Theology*. Downers Grove, IL: InterVarsity, 1998.
Hübner, Hans. *Law in Paul's Thought*. Translated by James C. G. Greig. SNTW. Edinburgh: T. & T. Clark, 1984.
Hultgren, Arland J. *Paul's Gospel and Mission: The Outlook from His Letter to the Romans*. Philadelphia: Fortress, 1985.
Hultgren, Stephen. "The Origin of Paul's Doctrine of the Two Adams in 1 Corinthians 15.45-49." *JSNT* 25 (2003) 343-70.
Hunter, A. M. *The Epistle to the Romans: Introduction and Commentary*. TBC. London: SCM, 1961.
Hurd, John Coolidge, Jr. *The Origin of 1 Corinthians*. London: SPCK, 1965.
Jackson, Bernard S. *Studies in the Semiotics of Biblical Law*. JSOTSup 314. Sheffield: Sheffield Academic, 2000.
Jacob, B. *The First Book of Genesis*. Edited and translated by Ernest I. Jacob and Walter Jacob. New York: Ktav, 1974.
Janowski, Bernd. "Jenseits von Eden: Gen 4:1-16 und die nichtpriesterliche Urgeschichte." In *Die Dämonen Demons: Die Dämonologie der israelitisch-jüdischen und früchristlichen Literatur im Kontext ihrer Umwelt*, edited by Armin Lange, et al., 137-59. Tübingen: Mohr/Siebeck, 2003.
Jenni, Ernst, and Claus Westermann, editors. *Theological Lexicon of the Old Testament*. 3 vols. Translated by M. E. Biddle. Peabody, MA: Hendrickson, 1997.
Jens, Walter. *Der Römerbrief*. Stuttgart: Radius, 2000.
Jeremias, Joachim. *The Eucharistic Words of Jesus*. Translated by Norman Perrin. NTL. New York: Scribner, 1966.
———. "'Flesh and Blood Cannot Inherit the Kingdom of God' (1 Cor 15.50)." *NTS* 2 (1955-56) 151-59.
Jervell, Jacob. *Imago Dei: Gen. 1:26f in Spätjudentum, in der Gnosis und in den paulinischen Briefen*. FRLANT 76. Göttingen: Vandenhoeck & Ruprecht, 1960.
Jervis, L. Ann. "'The Commandment Which is for Life' (Romans 7.10): Sin's Use of the Obedience of Faith." *JSNT* 27 (2004) 193-216.

Jewett, Robert. "The Law and the Coexistence of Jews and Gentiles in Romans." *Int* 39 (1985) 341–56.

———. *Paul's Anthropological Terms: A Study of Their Use in Conflict Settings*. AGJU 10. Leiden: Brill, 1971.

———. *Romans*. Hermeneia. Minneapolis: Fortress, 2007.

Jobes, Karen H., and Moisés Silva. *Invitation to the Septuagint*. Grand Rapids: Zondervan, 2000.

Jobling, David. "Myth and Its Limits in Genesis 2:4b—3:24." In *The Sense of Biblical Narrative: Structural Analysis in the Hebrew Bible*, 17–43. JSOTSup 39. Sheffield: JSOT Press, 1986.

Johnson, Alan F. *1 Corinthians*. IVPNTCS. Downers Grove, IL: InterVarsity, 2004.

Johnson, Clinton Andrew. "Resurrection Rhetoric: A Rhetorical Analysis of 1 Corinthians 15." Th.D. diss., Luther Seminary, 1994.

Johnson, Luke Timothy. *The First and Second Letters to Timothy: A New Translation with Introduction and Commentary*. AB 35A. New York: Doubleday, 2001.

———. *Reading Romans: A Literary and Theological Commentary*. RNTS. New York: Crossroad, 1997.

Joines, Karen Randolph. *Serpent Symbolism in the Old Testament: A Linguistic, Archaeological, and Literary Study*. Haddonfield, NJ: Haddonfield, 1974.

Joüon, Paul, and T. Muraoka. *A Grammar of Biblical Hebrew: Part Three: Syntax*. Translated by T. Muraoka. SubBi 14. Roma: Editrice Pontificio Istituto Biblico, 1991.

*Josephus*. Translated by H. St. J. Thackeray, et al. 10 vols. LCL. Cambridge: Harvard University Press, 1930–1965.

Jülicher, Adolf. "Der Brief an die Römer." In *Die Schriften des neuen Testaments*, edited by Johannes Weiß, 2:217–327. Göttingen: Vandenhoeck & Ruprecht, 1907–1908.

Karlberg, Mark W. "Israel's History Personified: Romans 7:7–13 in Relation to Paul's Teaching on the 'Old Man.'" *TJ* 7 (1986) 65–74.

Käsemann, Ernst. *Commentary on Romans*. Translated and edited by Geoffrey Bromiley. Grand Rapids: Eerdmans, 1980.

———. *Essays on New Testament Themes*. Translated by W. J. Montague. SBT 1/41. Naperville, IL: Allenson, 1961.

———. *New Testament Questions of Today*. Translated by W. J. Montague and Wilfred F. Bunge. NTL. London: SCM, 1969.

Kay, W. *A Commentary on the Two Epistles of St. Paul to the Corinthians*. London: Macmillan, 1887.

Kaye, Bruce Norman. *The Argument of Romans: With Special Reference to Romans 6*. Austin: Scholar, 1979.

Kearns, Conleth. "The Interpretation of Rom 6,7." In *SPCIC 1961*, 1:301–7. 2 vols. AnBib 17–18. Chicago: Loyola University Press, 1963.

Keck, Leander E. *Romans*. ANTC. Nashville: Abingdon, 2005.

Keil C. F., and F. Delitzsch. *Commentary on the Old Testament: Vol. 1: The Pentateuch*. Translated by James Martin. 1878. Reprint, Grand Rapids: Eerdmans, 1976.

Kelly, J. N. D. *The Pastoral Epistles*. BNTC. Peabody, MA: Hendrickson, 1960.

Kendall, G. "The Sin of Oedipus." *CR* 25 (1911) 195–97.

Kenyon, Frederic G. *The Chester Beatty Biblical Papyri Descriptions and Texts of Twelve Manuscripts on Papyrus of the Greek Bible: Fasciculus III Supplement Pauline Epistles*. London: Emery Walker, 1936.

Kertelge, Karl. "Exegetische Überlegungen zum Verständnis der paulinischen Anthropologie nach Römer 7." *ZNW* 62 (1971) 105–14.

Kidner, Derek. *Genesis: An Introduction and Commentary.* TOTC 1. Downers Grove, IL: InterVarsity, 1967.

Kim, Seyoon. *The Origin of Paul's Gospel.* 2nd ed. WUNT 2/4. Tübingen: Mohr/Siebeck, 1984.

―――. *Paul and the New Perspective: Second Thoughts on the Origin of Paul's Gospel.* Grand Rapids: Eerdmans, 2002.

Kistemaker, Simon J. *Exposition of the First Epistle to the Corinthians.* NTC. Grand Rapids: Baker, 1993.

Kittel, Gerhard, and Gerhard Friedrich, editors. *Theological Dictionary of the New Testament.* Translated by Geoffrey W. Bromiley. 10 vols. Grand Rapids: Eerdmans, 1964–1976.

―――, editors. *Theologisches Wörterbuch zum Neuen Testament.* 10 vols. Stuttgart: Kohlhammer, 1932–1979.

Klaar, Erich. "Rm 6,7: Ο γαρ ἀποθανὼν δεδικαίωται ἀπὸ τῆς ἁμαρτίας." *ZNW* 59 (1968) 131–34.

Klauck, Hans-Josef. *1. Korintherbrief.* NEchtB 7. Würzburg: Echter, 1984.

Klein, Günter. "Gesetz III. Neues Testament." In *Theologische Realenzyklopädie*, edited by Gerhard Krause and Gerhard Müller, 13:58–75. 36 vols. Berlin: de Gruyter, 1976–2004.

―――. "Sündenverständnis und Theologia Crucis bei Paulus." In *Theologia Crucis-Signum Crucis: Festschrift für Erich Dinkler zum 70. Geburtstag*, edited by Carl Andresen and Günter Klein, 249–82. Tübingen: Mohr/Siebeck, 1979.

Kleinknecht, H. "νόμος, κτλ." In *TDNT* 4 (1967) 1022–35.

Kling, Christian Friedrich. *The First Epistle of Paul to the Corinthians.* Translated by Daniel W. Poor. New York: Scribner, 1869.

Kloppenborg, John. "An Analysis of the Pre-Pauline Formula 1 Corinthians 15:3b–5 in Light of Some Recent Literature." *CBQ* 40 (1978) 351–67.

Knight, George A. F. *Theology in Pictures: A Commentary on Genesis, Chapters One to Eleven.* Edinburgh: Handsel, 1981.

Knight, George W. *The Pastoral Epistles.* NIGTC. Grand Rapids: Eerdmans, 1994.

Knittel, Thomas. *Das griechisch "Leben Adams und Evas": Studien zu einer narrativen Anthropologie im frühen Judentum.* TSAJ 88. Tübingen: Mohr/Siebeck, 2002.

Koch, Dietrich-Alex. *Die Schrift als Zeuge des Evangeliums: Untersuchung zur Verwendung und zum Verständnis der Schrift bei Paulus.* Tübingen: Mohr Siebeck, 1986.

Köhler, Ludwig, et al. *The Hebrew and Aramaic Lexicon of the Old Testament.* Translated and edited by M. E. J. Richardson. 5 vols. Leiden: Brill, 1994–2000.

Köhler, Ludwig Hugo. *Old Testament Theology.* Translated by A. S. Todd. Philadelphia: Westminster, 1957.

Krašovec, Jože. *Der Merismus im Biblischen-Hebräischen und Nordwestsemitischen.* Rome: Biblical Institute Press, 1977.

Krimmer, Heiko. *Römerbrief.* BKNT 10. Neuhausen-Stuttgart: Hänssler, 1983.

Kruse, Colin G. *Paul, the Law, and Justification.* Peabody, MA: Hendrickson, 1996.

Kühl, Ernst. *Der Brief des Paulus an die Römer.* Leipzig: Quelle & Meyer, 1913.

Kuhn, Karl George. "New Light on Temptation, Sin and Flesh in the New Testament." In *The Scrolls and the New Testament*, edited by Krister Stendahl, 94–113. London: SCM, 1957.

———. "Rm 6,7: Ο γαρ ἀποθανὼν δεδικαίωται ἀπὸ τῆς ἁμαρτίας." ZNW 30 (1931) 305–10.
Kümmel, Werner Georg. *Introduction to the New Testament*. Rev. ed. Translated by Howard Clark Kee. Nashville: Abingdon, 1975.
———. *Römer 7 und das Bild des Menschen im Neuen Testament*. Munich: Kaiser, 1974.
———, and Hans Lietzmann. *An die Korinther I/II*. 4th ed. HNT 9. Tübingen: Mohr/Siebeck, 1969.
Kuss, Otto. *Paulus: Die Rolle des Apostels in der Theologischen Entwicklung der Urkirche*. 2nd ed. AusVerk 3. Regensburg: Pustet, 1976.
———. *Der Römerbrief*. 3 vols. Regensburg: Pustet, 1957–1978.
Kuula, Kari. *The Law, the Covenant and God's Plans*. PFES 72. Göttingen: Vandenhoeck & Ruprecht, 1999.
Laato, Timo. *Paul and Judaism: An Anthropological Approach*. Translated by T. McElwain. SFSHJ 115. Atlanta: Scholars, 1991.
———. "Paul's Anthropological Considerations: Two Problems." In *Justification and Variegated Nomism. Volume II: The Paradoxes of Paul*, edited by D. A. Carson, et al., 343–59. WUNT 2/181. Tübingen: Mohr/Siebeck, 2004.
Lagrange, M.-J. "L'innocence et le péché." *RB* 6 (1897) 341–79.
———. *Saint Paul Épître aux Romains*. Paris: Gabalda, 1950.
Lamarche, Paul, and Charles Le Dû. *Épître aux Romains V–VIII: structure littéraire et sens*. Paris: Centre National de la Recherche Scientifique, 1980.
Lambrecht, Jan. "Gesetzesverständnis bei Paulus." In *Das Gesetz im Neuen Testament*, edited by Karl Kertelge, 88–127. QD 108. Freiburg: Herder, 1986.
———. "Man Before and Without Christ: Rom. 7 and Pauline Anthropology." *LS* 5 (1974) 18–33.
———. *The Wretched 'I' and Its Liberation: Paul in Romans 7 and 8*. LTPM 14. Grand Rapids: Eerdmans, 1992.
Lang, Friedrich. *Die Briefe an die Korinther*. NTD 7. Göttingen: Vandenhoeck & Ruprecht, 1986.
Lanham, Richard A. *A Handlist of Rhetorical Terms*. 2nd ed. Berkeley: University of California Press, 1991.
Lapide, Pinchas. "Touching the Forbidden Fruit." *BRev* 4 (1988) 42-43.
Larsson, Edvin. *Christus als Vorbild: Eine Untersuchung zu den paulinischen Tauf- und Eikontexten*. Uppsala: Gleerup, 1962.
Lauer, Stewart. "Was the Tree of Life Always Off-Limits?: A Critique of Vos's Answer." *Kerux* 16 (2001) 42–50.
Lausberg, Heinrich. *Handbook of Literary Rhetoric: A Foundation for Inquiry*. Edited by David E. Orton and R. Dean Anderson. Translated by Matthew T. Bliss et al. Leiden: Brill, 1998.
Lauterbach, Jacob Z., translator. *Mekilta de-Rabbi Ishmael*. 3 vols. Philadelphia: Jewish Publication Society, 1933–1936.
Leenhardt, F. J. *The Epistle to the Romans*. Cleveland: World, 1961.
Légasse, Simon. *L'Épître de Paul aux Romains*. LD10. Paris: Cerf, 2002.
Lenormant, François. *The Beginnings of History according to the Bible and the Traditions of Oriental Peoples: From the Creation of Man to the Deluge*. Translated by Mary Lockwood. New York: Scribner, 1891.
Levenson, Jon D. "The Theologies of Commandment in Biblical Israel." *HTR* 73 (1980) 17–33.

Levertoff, Paul P., trans. *Midrash Sifre on Numbers: Selections from Early Rabbinic Scriptural Interpretations*. London: SPCK, 1926.

Levine, Baruch A. *Numbers: A New Translation with Introduction and Commentary*. 2 vols. AB 4, 4A. New York: Doubleday, 1993.

Levison, John R. *Portraits of Adam in Early Judaism: From Sirach to 2 Baruch*. JSPSup 1. Sheffield: JSOT Press, 1988.

———. *Texts in Transition: The Greek Life of Adam and Eve*. SBLEJL 16. Atlanta: Society of Biblical Literature, 2000.

Lichtenberger, Hermann. *Das Ich Adams und das Ich der Menscheit: Studien zum Menschenbild in Römer 7*. WUNT 164. Tübingen: Mohr/Siebeck, 2004.

Liddell, H. G., et al. *A Greek-English Lexicon*. Oxford: Oxford University Press, 1996.

Liedke, Gerhard. *Gestalt und Bezeichnung alttestamentlicher Rechtssätze: Eine formgeschichtlich-terminologische Studie*. WMANT 39. Neukirchen-Vluyn: Neukirchener, 1971.

Lietzmann, Hans. *An die Korinther I/II*. 2nd ed. HNT 9. Tübingen: Mohr/Siebeck, 1923.

———. *An die Römer*. HNT 8. Tübingen: Mohr/Siebeck, 1933.

Lindars, Barnabas. "Paul and the Law in Romans 5–8: An Actantial Analysis." In *Law and Religion: Essays on the Place of the Law in Israel and Early Christianity by Members of the Ehrhardt Seminar of Manchester University*, 126–40. Cambridge: Cambridge University Press, 1988.

Lindemann, Andreas. "Die biblischen Toragebote und die paulinsche Ethik." In *Paulus, Apostel und Lehrer der Kirche: Studien zu Paulus und zum frühen Paulusverständnis*. Tübingen: Mohr/Siebeck, 1999.

———. *Der erste Korintherbrief*. HNT 9/1. Tübingen: Mohr/Siebeck, 2000.

Little, Joyce A. "Paul's Use of Analogy: A Structural Analysis of Romans 7:1–6." *CBQ* 46 (1984) 82–90.

Livy. Translated by B. O. Foster et al. 14 vols. LCL. Cambridge: Harvard University Press, 1919–1959.

Lockwood, Gregory J. *1 Corinthians*. ConC. St. Louis: Concordia, 2000.

Lohse, Eduard. *Der Brief an die Römer*. KEK 4. Göttingen: Vandenhoeck & Ruprecht, 2003.

Longenecker, Bruce W. *Eschatology and the Covenant: A Comparison of 4 Ezra and Romans 1–11*. JSNTSup 57. Sheffield: Sheffield Academic, 1991.

Longenecker, Richard N. *Galatians*. WBC 41. Dallas: Word, 1990.

———. *Paul, Apostle of Liberty: The Origin and Nature of Paul's Christianity*. Grand Rapids: Baker, 1976.

Lloyd-Jones, D. Martyn. *Romans: An Exposition of Chapters 7.1—8.4: The Law: Its Functions and Limits*. Grand Rapids: Zondervan, 1973.

Lucian. Translated by A. M. Harmon et al. 7 vols. LCL. Cambridge: Harvard University Press, 1913–1961.

Luck, Ulrich. "Das Gute und das Böse in Römer 7." In *Neues Testament und Ethik: für Rudolph Schnackenburg*, edited by Helmut Merklein, 220–37. Freiburg: Herder, 1989.

Lüdemann, Gerd. *Opposition to Paul in Jewish Christianity*. Minneapolis: Fortress, 1989.

———. *Paul, Apostle to the Gentiles: Studies in Chronology*. Translated by F. Stanley Jones. Philadelphia: Fortress, 1984.

Lührmann, Dieter. *Galatians*. Translated by O. C. Dean Jr. CC. Minneapolis: Fortress, 1992.

Luther, Martin. "Commentary on 1 Corinthians 15." In *Luther's Works*, edited by Jaraslov Pelikan, translated by George Schick, et al., 57–213. Saint Louis: Concordia; Philadelphia: Fortress, 1955–1976.

———. "Lectures on Galatians, 1535: Chapters 5–6." In *Luther's Works*, edited by Jaraslov Pelikan, translated George Schick, et al., 1–149. Saint Louis: Concordia; Philadelphia: Fortress, 1955–1976.

———. "Lectures on Genesis: Chapters 1–5." In *Luther's Works*, edited by Jaraslov Pelikan, translated by George Schick, et al., 1–359. Saint Louis: Concordia; Philadelphia: Fortress, 1955–1976.

———. "Lectures on Romans: Glosses and Scholia." In *Luther's Works*, edited by Jaraslov Pelikan, translated by George Schick, et al., 1–523. Saint Louis: Concordia; Philadelphia: Fortress, 1955–1976. [AQ: vol?]

Luz, Ulrich. *Das Geschichtsverständnis des Paulus*. BEvT 49. Münich: Kaiser, 1968.

———. "Zum Aufbau von Röm 1–8." *TZ* 25 (1969) 161–81.

Lyonnet, Stanislas. *Les étapes de l'histoire du salut selon l'épître aux Romains*. Bibliothèque Œcuménique 8. Paris: Cerf, 1969.

———. "L'histoire de salut selon le chapitre VII de l'épître aux Romains." *Bib* 43 (1962) 117–51.

———. "Qui enim mortuus est, iustificatus est a peccato." *VD* 42 (1964) 17–21.

———. "'Tu ne convoiteras pas' (Rom Vii, 7)." In *Neotestamentica et Patristica: Eine Freundesgabe, Herrn Professor Dr. Oscar Cullmann zu seinem 60. Geburtstag überreicht*, edited by W. C. van Unnik, 157–65. NovTSup 6. Leiden: Brill, 1962.

Lyonnet, Stanislas, and Léopold Sabourin. *Sin, Redemption, and Sacrifice: A Biblical and Patristic Study*. AnBib 48. Rome: Editrice Pontificio Istituto Biblico, 1998.

Mack, Burton L. *Rhetoric and the New Testament*. Guides to Biblical Scholarship. Minneapolis: Fortress, 1990.

Maillot, Alphonse. *L'Epître aux Romains: épître de l'œcuménisme et théologie de l'histoire*. Paris: Le Centurion, 1984.

Maimonides, Moses. *The Code of Maimonides (Mishneh Torah)*. Translated by Jacob J. Rabinowitz et al. 14 vols. New Haven: Yale University Press, 1949.

Malina, Bruce J. "Some Observations on the Origin of Sin in Judaism and St. Paul." *CBQ* 31 (1969) 18–34.

Mangan, Edward. "A Discussion of Genesis 4:7." *CBQ* 6 (1964) 91–93.

Manson, T. W. *Studies in the Gospels and Epistles*. Philadelphia: Westminster, 1962.

Marcus, Joel. "The Evil Inclination in the Letters of Paul." *IBS* 8 (1986) 8–21.

Marrow, Stanley B. Review of Robert G. Hamerton-Kelly. *Sacred Violence: Paul's Hermeneutic of the Cross* in *CBQ* 56 (1994) 137–38.

Marshall, I. Howard. *A Critical and Exegetical Commentary on the Pastoral Epistles*. ICC. Edinburgh: T. & T. Clark, 1999.

Martin, Brice L. *Christ and the Law in Paul*. NovTSup 62. Leiden: Brill, 1989.

———. "Some Reflections on the Identity of ἐγώ in Rom. 7:14–25." *SJT* 34 (1981) 39–47.

Martin, Ralph P. *The Spirit and the Congregation: Studies in 1 Corinthians 12–15*. Grand Rapids: Eerdmans, 1984.

Martínez, Florentino García, and Eibert J. C. Tigchelaar, editors and translators. *The Dead Sea Scrolls Study Edition*. 2 vols. Leiden: Brill, 1997–1998.

Matand Bulembat, Jean-Bosco. *Noyau et enjeux de l'eschatologie paulinienne: De l'apocalyptique juive et de l'eschatologie hellénistique dans quelques argumentations de* l'apôtre Paul: Étude rhétorico-exégétique de 1 Co 15,35-38; 2 Co 5,1-10 et Rm 8,18-30. BZNW 84. Berlin: Walter de Gruyter, 1997.

Mathews, Kenneth A. *Genesis 1-11:26*. NAC 1A. Nashville: Broadman, 1996.

Mayes, Andrew. "The Nature of Sin and Its Origin in the Old Testament." *ITQ* 40 (1973) 250-63.

McRay, John. *Paul: His Life and Teaching*. Grand Rapids: Baker, 2003.

Ménard, Jacques-É. "L'évangile selon Philippe: Introduction Texte—Traduction Commentaire." Th.D. diss., University of Strasbourg, 1967.

Mendenhall, George E. "The Shady Side of Wisdom: The Date and Purpose of Genesis 3." In *A Light Unto My Path: Old Testament Studies in Honor of Jacob Meyers*, edited by H. N. Bream, et al., 319-34. Philadelphia: Temple University, 1974.

Metzger, Bruce M. *A Textual Commentary on the Greek New Testament*. 2nd ed. Stuttgart: Deutsche Bibelgesellschaft, 1994.

Meyer, Heinrich August Wilhelm. *Critical and Exegetical Handbook to the Epistles to the Corinthians*. 2 vols. Edited and translated by William P. Dickson and William Stewart. Edinburgh: T. & T. Clark, 1884.

———. *Critical and Exegetical Handbook to the Epistle to the Romans*. Edited by William Dickson. Translated by John C. Moore and Edwin Johnson. Edinburgh: T. & T. Clark, 1879.

Meyer, Paul W. "The Worm at the Core of the Apple." In *The Conversation Continues: Studies in Paul and John*, edited by Robert T. Fortna and Beverly R. Gaventa, 62-84. Nashville: Abingdon, 1990.

Michel, Diethelm. "Ihr werdet sein wie Gott: Gedanken zur Sündenfallgeschichte in Genesis 3." In *Menschwerdung Gottes-Vergöttlichung von Menschen*, edited by Dieter Zeller, 61-87. Göttingen: Vandenhoeck & Ruprecht, 1988.

Michel, Otto. *Der Brief an die Römer*. KEK 4. Göttingen: Vandenhoeck & Ruprecht, 1955.

Middendorf, Michael Paul. *The "I" in the Storm*. Saint Louis: Concordia, 1997.

Milgrom, Jacob. *Numbers = Ba-Midbar: The Traditional Hebrew Text with New JPS Translation*. JPSTC. Philadelphia: Jewish Publication Society, 1990.

———. *Studies in Levitical Terminology, 1: The Encroacher and the Levite: The Term 'Aboda*. University of California Publications: Near Eastern Studies 14. Berkeley: University of California, 1970.

Milne, D. J. W. "Genesis 3 in the Letter to the Romans." *RTR* 39 (1980) 10-18.

Mitchell, Margaret Mary. *Paul and the Rhetoric of Reconciliation: An Exegetical Examination of the Language and Composition of 1 Corinthians*. Louisville: Westminster John Knox, 1993.

Moberly, R. W. L. "Did the Serpent Get It Right?" *JTS* 39 (1988) 1-27.

Modalsli, O. "Gal 2, 19-21; 5, 16-18 und Röm 7, 7-25." *TZ* 21 (1965) 22-37.

Moffatt, James. *The First Epistle of Paul to the Corinthians*. MNTC. London: Hodder and Stoughton, 1947.

Moiser, Jeremy. "1 Corinthians 15." *IBS* 14 (1992) 10-30.

Montefiore, C. G., and H. Loewe, editors. *A Rabbinic Anthology: Selected and Arranged with Comments and Introductions*. London: Macmillan, 1938.

Moo, Douglas J. *The Epistle to the Romans*. NICNT. Grand Rapids: Eerdmans, 1996.

———. "Israel and the Law in Romans 5-11: Interaction with the New Perspective." In *Justification and Variegated Nomism: Volume 2: The Paradoxes of Paul*, edited by D. A. Carson et al., 185-216. WUNT 2/181. Tübingen: Mohr Siebeck, 2004.

———. "Israel and Paul in Romans 7:7–12." *NTS* 32 (1986) 122–35.
———. "'Law,' 'Works of the Law,' and Legalism in Paul." *WTJ* 45 (1983) 73–100.
———. "Paul and the Law in the Last Ten Years." *SJT* 40 (1987) 287–307.
———. "What Does It Mean Not to Teach or Have Authority Over Men?: 1 Timothy 2:11–15." In *Recovering Biblical Manhood and Womanhood: A Response to Evangelical Feminism*, edited by John Piper and Wayne Grudem, 179–93. Wheaton, IL: Crossway, 1991.
Moore, George Foot. *Judaism in the First Centuries of the Christian Era: The Age of Tannaim*. 3 vols. Cambridge: Cambridge University Press, 1927–1930.
Morgan, Robert. *Romans*. NTG. Sheffield: Sheffield Academic, 1997.
Morissette, Rodolphe. "Un Midrash sur La Mort: (1 Cor. 15, xv, 54c à 57)." *RB* 79 (1972) 161–88.
Morner, Kathleen, and Ralph Rausch. *NTC's Dictionary of Literary Terms*. Lincolnwood, IL: National Textbook Company, 1991.
Morris, Leon. *The Epistle to the Romans*. PNT. Grand Rapids: Eerdmans, 1988.
———. *The First Epistle of Paul to the Corinthians*. Rev. ed. TNTC 7. Grand Rapids: InterVarsity, 1985.
Morris, T. F. "Law and the Cause of Sin in the Epistle to the Romans." *HeyJ* 28 (1987) 285–91.
Moule, C. F. D. *The Epistles of Paul to the Colossians and to Philemon*. CGTC. Cambridge: Cambridge University Press, 1957.
———. *An Idiom Book of New Testament Greek*. Cambridge: Cambridge University Press, 1953.
———. "'Justification' in Its Relation to the Condition κατα πνευμα (Rom. 8:1–11)." In *Battesimo e Giustizia in Rom 6 e 8*, edited by Lorenzo Lorenzi, 177–201. SMBen 2. Rome: Abbey of St. Paul, 1974.
———. "Obligation in the Ethic of Paul." In *Christian History and Interpretation: Studies Presented to John Knox*, edited by William R. Farmer et al., 389–406. Cambridge: Cambridge University Press, 1967.
Moule, Handley C. G. *The Epistle to the Romans*. London: Pickering & Inglis, 1894.
———. *Studies in Romans*. 1892. Reprinted, Grand Rapids: Kregel, 1977.
Moulton, James Hope, and George Milligan. *The Vocabulary of the Greek Testament: Illustrated from the Papyri and Other Non-Literary Sources*. Grand Rapids: Eerdmans, 1982.
Müller, Christian. *Gottes Gerechtigkeit und Gottes Volk: Eine Untersuchung zu Römer 9–11*. FRLANT 86. Göttingen: Vandenhoeck & Ruprecht, 1964.
Müller, Hans-Peter. "Erkenntnis und Verfehlung: Prototypen und Antitypen zu Gen 2–3 in der altorientalischen Literatur." In *Mythos-Kerygma-Wahrheit: Gesammelte Aufsätze zum Alten Testament in seiner Umwelt, und zur Biblischen Theologie*, 68–87. BZAW 200. Berlin: de Gruyter, 1991.
Müller, Karlheinz. "Die Leiblichkeit des Heils 1 Kor 15,35–58." In *Résurrection du Christ et des Chrétiens (1 Co 15)*, edited by J.-N. Aletti, S. Agourides, et al. SMBen 8, 172–255. Rome: Abbey of St. Paul, 1985.
Murray, John. *The Epistle to the Romans: The English Text with Introduction, Exposition, and Notes*. 2 vols. NICNT. Grand Rapids: Eerdmans, 1959, 1965.
———. *Principles of Conduct: Aspects of Biblical Ethics*. Grand Rapids: Eerdmans, 1957.
Nanos, Mark D. *The Mystery of Romans: The Jewish Context of Paul's Letter*. Minneapolis: Fortress, 1996.

Napier, D. "Paul's Analysis of Sin and Torah in Romans 7:7-25." *ResQ* 44 (2002) 15-32.

Narrowe, Morton H. "Another Look at the Tree of Good and Evil." *JBQ* 26 (1998) 184-88.

Neusner, Jacob, ed. *The Talmud of the Land of Israel: A Preliminary Translation and Explanation*. Translated by Zahary Tzvee, et al. 35 vols. CSJH. Chicago: University of Chicago Press, 1982-1994.

Neusner, Jacob, and Richard S. Sarason, editors. *The Tosefta: Translated from the Hebrew*. 6 vols. Hoboken, NJ: Ktav, 1986.

Newman, Barclay M., and Eugene A. Nida. *A Handbook on Paul's Letter to the Romans*. UBSHS. New York: United Bible Societies, 1973.

Neyrey, Jerome H. *Paul in Other Words: A Cultural Reading of His Letters*. Louisville: Westminster John Knox, 1990.

Niehr, Herbert. "ערם; ערום; ערמה." In *Theological Dictionary of the Old Testament*. edited by Johannes Botterweck and Helmer Ringgren, 11:361-66. Translated by John T. Willis et al. Grand Rapids: Eerdmans, 2001.

Novak, David. *Natural Law in Judaism*. Cambridge: Cambridge University Press, 1998.

Nunn, H. P. V. *A Short Syntax of New Testament Greek*. Cambridge: Cambridge University Press, 1956.

Nygren, Anders. *Commentary on Romans*. Philadelphia: Fortress, 1983.

O'Brien, Peter T. *Colossians, Philemon*. WBC 44. Waco, TX: Word, 1982.

Olshausen, Hermann. *Biblical Commentary on St. Paul's First and Second Epistles to the Corinthians*. Translated by John Edmund. Clark's Foreign Theological Library. Edinburgh: T. & T. Clark, 1863.

Oltramare, Hugues. *L'Épître aux Romains*. 2 vols. Paris: Fischbacher, 1882.

Orbe, Antonio. "El dilema entre la vida y la muerte (Exegesis prenicena de Deut 30, 15.19)." *Greg* 51 (1970) 509-36.

Origen. *Commentary on the Epistle to the Romans: Books 6-10*. Translated by Thomas P. Scheck. FC. Washington, DC: Catholic University of America Press, 2002.

Ortkemper, Franz-Josef. *1. Korintherbrief*. SKKNT. Stuttgart: Katholisches Bibelwerk, 1993.

Orr, William F., and James Arthur Walther. *1 Corinthians: A New Translation. Introduction with a Study of the Life of Paul, Notes, and Commentary*. AB 32. Garden City, NY: Doubleday, 1976.

Osborne, Grant R. *Romans*. IVPNTCS. Downers Grove, IL: InterVarsity, 2004.

Osten-Sacken, P. von der. *Römer 8 als ein Beispiel paulinischer Soteriologie*. FRLANT 112. Tübingen: Mohr/Siebeck, 1975.

Ovid. *Heroides and Amores*. Translated by Grant Showerman. LCL. New York: Putnam. 1931.

———. *Metamorphoses*. Translated by Frank Justus Miller. 2 vols. LCL. Cambridge: Harvard University Press, 1916.

Pate, C. Marvin. *Adam Christology As the Exegetical and Theological Substructure of 2 Corinthians 4:7-5:21*. Lanham, MD: University Press of America, 1991.

———. *The Reverse of the Curse: Paul, Wisdom, and the Law*. WUNT 2/114. Tübingen: Mohr/Siebeck, 2000.

Patrick, Dale. *Old Testament Law*. Atlanta: John Knox, 1985.

Paulien, J. *Decoding Revelation's Trumpets: Literary Allusions and the Interpretation of Revelation 8:7-12*, AUSDDS 11. Berrien Springs, MI: Andrews University Press, 1987.

Pedersen, Sigfred. "Paul's Understanding of the Biblical Law." *NovT* 44 (2002) 1–34.
Perdue, Leo G. *Wisdom and Creation*. Nashville: Abingdon, 1994.
Perkins, Pheme. "Pauline Anthropology in Light of Nag Hammadi." *CBQ* 48 (1986) 512–22.
Perriman, A. C. "Paul and the Parousia." *NTS* 35 (1989) 512–21.
Pesch, Rudolph. *Römerbrief*. NEchtB 6. Würzburg: Echter, 1983.
Peterson, Erik. *Der Brief an die Römer*. AusSch. Würzburg: Echter, 1997.
Pfister, Otto. "Die Entwicklung des Apostels Paulus: Eine religionsgeschichtliche und psychologische Skizze." *Imago* 6 (1920) 243–90.
*Philo*. Translated by F. H. Colson, et al. 10 vols. (with two supplemental volumes). LCL. Cambridge: Harvard University Press, 1929–1962.
Plank, Karl A. "Resurrection Theology: The Corinthian Controversy Reexamined." *PRSt* 8 (1981) 41–54.
Plato. *Protagoras*. Translated by C. C. W. Taylor. CPS. Oxford: Clarendon, 1976.
*Plutarch*. Translated by Frank Cole Babbit, et al. 15 vols. LCL. Cambridge: Harvard University Press, 1927–1969.
Poirier, J. C. "Romans 5:13–14 and the Universality of Law." *NovT* 38 (1996) 244–58.
Pop, F. J. *De eerste brief van Paulus aan de Corinthiërs*. PNit. Nijkerk: Callenbach, 1965.
Porter, Frank Chamberlin. "The Yecer Hara: A Study in the Jewish Doctrine of Sin." In *Biblical and Semetic Studies*. New York: Scribner, 1901.
Porter, Stanley E. *Idioms of the Greek New Testament*. 2nd ed. Biblical Languages: Greek 2. Sheffield: Sheffield Academic, 1994.
———. "The Theoretical Justification for Application of Rhetorical Categories to Pauline Epistolary Literature." In *Rhetoric and the New Testament: Essays from the 1992 Heidelberg Conference*, edited by Stanley E. Porter and Thomas H. Olbricht, 100–122. Sheffield: JSOT Press, 1995.
Price, James L. *The New Testament: Its History and Theology*. New York: Macmillan, 1987.
Pritchard, J. B. *Ancient Near Eastern Text Relating to the Old Testament*. 3rd ed. Princeton: Princeton University Press, 1969.
Procksch, Otto. *Theologie des Alten Testaments*. Gütersloh: Bertelsmann, 1950.
Rad, Gerhard von. *Genesis: A Commentary*. OTL. Philadelphia: Westminster, 1972.
Rahlfs, Alfred, editor. *Septuaginta*. Stuttgart: Deutsche Bibelegesellschaft, 1979.
Räisänen, Heikki. *Paul and the Law*. 2nd ed. Philadelphia: Fortress, 1983.
Ramaroson, Léonard. "A propos de Gn 4,7." *Bib* 49 (1968) 233–37.
Ramban (Nachmanides). *Commentary on the Torah*. Translated by Charles B. Chavel. 5 vols. New York: Shilo, 1971.
Rashi. *"Rashi" on the Pentateuch: Genesis*. Trans. James H. Lowe. Tutorial Preparations for Rabbinics. London: Hebrew Compendium, 1928.
Reicke, Bo. "The Knowledge Hidden in the Tree of Paradise." *JSS* 1 (1956) 193–201.
———. *Re-examining Paul's Letters: The History of the Pauline Correspondence*. Edited by David Moessner and Ingalisa Reicke. Harrisburg, PA: Trinity, 2001.
Reinhardt, K. *Poseidonios über Ursprung und Entartung*. Heidelberg: Winter, 1928.
Reiser, Marius. "Sünde und Sündenbewusstsein in der Antike, bei Paulus und bei uns." *Erbe und Auftrag* 77 (2001) 455–69.
Renckens, Henricus. *Israel's Concept of the Beginning: The Theology of the Genesis 1–3*. New York: Herder and Herder, 1964.
Ridderbos, Herman. *Paul: An Outline of His Theology*. Grand Rapids: Eerdmans, 1975.

Robertson, A. T. *A Grammar of the Greek New Testament in the Light of Historical Research*. Nashville: Broadman, 1934.
Robertson, Archibald, and Alfred Plummer. *A Critical and Exegetical Commentary on the First Epistle of St. Paul to the Corinthians*. ICC. Edinburgh: T. & T. Clark, 1986.
Robinson, James M. editor. *The Nag Hammadi Library in English*. 3rd ed. Leiden: Brill, 1988.
Robinson, John A. T. *The Body: A Study in Pauline Theology*. SBT 1. London: SCM, 1952.
———. *Wrestling with Romans*. Philadelphia: Westminster, 1979.
Romanello, Stefano. "Rom 7:7-25 and the Impotence of the Law." *Bib* 49 (2003) 510-30.
Ross, Allen P. *Creation and Blessing: A Guide to the Study and Exposition of Genesis*. Grand Rapids: Eerdmans, 1996.
Roth, Cecil, editor. *Encyclopaedia Judaica*. 16 vols. Jerusalem: Keter, 1972.
Roth, Y. "The Intentional Double-Meaning Talk in Biblical Prose." *Tarbiz* 41 (1972) 245-54.
Ruppert, Lothar. *Genesis: Ein kritischer und theologischer Kommentar*. 3 vols. FB. 70, 98. Würzburg: Echter, 1992, 2002.
Sailhamer, John H. "Genesis." In *The Expositor's Bible Commentary*, edited by Frank E. Gaebelein, 2:1-284. Grand Rapids: Zondervan, 1990.
Sampley, J. Paul. "The First Letter to the Corinthians: Introduction, Commentary, and Reflections." In *The New Interpreter's Bible: General Articles and Introduction, Commentary, and Reflections for Each Book of the Bible, Including the Apocryphal/Deuterocanonical Books*, edited by Leander E. Keck, et al., 10:771-1003. Nashville: Abingdon, 2002.
Sand, Alexander. *Der Begriff 'Sarx' in den paulinischen Hauptbriefen*. BU 2. Regensburg: Pustet, 1967.
Sanday, William, and Arthur Headlam. *A Critical and Exegetical Commentary on the Epistle to the Romans*. ICC. Edinburgh: T. & T. Clark, 1902.
Sandelin, Karl-Gustav. *Die Auseinandersetzung mit der Weisheit in 1. Korinther 15*. Meddelanden från Stiftelsens för Åbo akademi forskningsinstitut. Åbo: Akademi, 1976.
Sanders, E. P. *Paul, the Law, and the Jewish People*. Philadelphia: Fortress, 1983.
———. *Paul and Palestinian Judaism*. Philadelphia: Fortress, 1977.
Sapp, Stephen. *Sexuality, the Bible, and Science*. Philadelphia: Fortress, 1977.
Sarna, Nahum M. *Genesis = Be-Reshit: The Traditional Hebrew Text with the New JPS Translation*. JPSTC. Philadelphia: The Jewish Publication Society, 1989.
Sasson, J. M. "*welo' yitbosasû* (Gen 2:25)." *Bib* 66 (1985) 418-21.
Savran, George W. *Telling and Retelling: Quotation in Biblical Narrative*. Indiana Studies in Biblical Literature. Bloomington: Indiana University Press, 1988.
Saw, Insawn. *Paul's Rhetoric in 1 Corinthians 15: An Analysis Utilizing the Theories of Classical Rhetoric*. Lewiston, NY: Mellen, 1993.
Schade, Hans-Heinrich. *Apokalyptische Christologie bei Paulus: Studien zum Zusammenhang von Christologie und Eschatologie in den Paulusbriefen*. GTA 18. Göttingen: Vandenhoeck & Ruprecht, 1981.
Schaeffer, Francis. *Genesis in Space and Time: The Flow of Biblical History*. Downers Grove, IL: InterVarsity, 1972.
Schäfer, Peter. "Adam in der jüdischen Überlieferung." In *Vom alten zum neuen Adam*, edited by Walter Strolz, 69-93. Veröffentlichungen der Stiftung Oratio Dominica 13. Freiburg: Herder, 1986.

Schelkle, Karl Hermann. *Paulus, Lehrer der Väter: Die altkirchlich Auslegung von Röm 1-11.* Düsseldorf: Patmos, 1956.

Schick, Eduard. *Allen Alles werden: Besinnliche Gedanken zum ersten Brief des Apostels Paulus an die Korinther.* Stuttgart: Katholisches Bibelwerk, 1984.

Schlatter, Adolph. *Paulus der Bote Jesu: eine Deutung seiner Briefe an die Korinther.* Stuttgart: Calwer, 1969.

———. *Romans: The Righteousness of God.* Translated by Siegfried S. Schatzmann. Peabody, MA: Hendrickson, 1995.

Schlier, Heinrich. *Der Römerbrief.* HTKNT 6. Freiburg: Herder, 1977.

Schmid, Lothar. "κεντρον." In *TDNT* 3 (1965) 663-68.

Schmidt, Hans Wilhelm, *Der Brief des Paulus an die Römer.* THKNT 6. Berlin: Evangelische Verlagsanstalt, 1966.

Schmiedel, Paul W. *Die Briefe an die Thessalonicher und an die Korinther.* 2 vols. HKNT 2. Freiburg: Mohr/Siebeck, 1891.

Schmithals, Walter. *Die Briefe des Paulus in ihrer ursprünglichen Form.* ZWB. Zürich: Theologischer Verlag, 1984.

———. *Gnosticism in Corinth: An Investigation of the Letters to the Corinthians.* Translated by John E. Steeley. Nashville: Abingdon, 1971.

———. *Der Römerbrief: Ein Kommentar.* Gütersloh: Gerd Mohn, 1988.

———. *The Theology of the Early Christians.* Translated by O. C. Dean. Louisville: Westminster John Knox, 1997.

Schnackenburg, Rudolf. "Die Adam-Christus-Typologie (Röm 5,12-21) Als Voraussetzung für das Taufverständnis in Röm 6,1-14." In *Battesimo e Giustizia in Rom 6 e 8,* Lorenzo Lorenzi. SMBen 2, 38-81. Rome: Abbey of St. Paul, 1974.

———. *Baptism in the Thought of St. Paul: A Study in Pauline Theology.* Translated by G. R. Beasley-Murray. New York: Herder and Herder, 1964.

———. "Römer 7 im Zusammenhang des Römerbriefes." In *Jesus und Paulus: Festschrift für Werner Georg Kümmel zum 70. Geburtstag,* edited by E. Earle Ellis and Erich Gräßer, 283-300. Göttingen: Vandenhoeck & Ruprecht, 1978.

Schneider, Johannes. "παραβαίνω κτλ." In *TDNT* 5 (1967) 736-44.

Schneider, Sebastian. *Vollendung des Auferstehens: Eine exegetische Untersuchung von 1 Kor 15,51-52 und 1 Thess 4,13-18.* FB 97. Würzburg: Echter, 2000.

Schnelle, Udo. *Apostle Paul: His Life and Theology.* Translated by M. Eugene Boring. Grand Rapids: Baker, 2005.

Schniewind, Julius. "Die Leugnung der Auferstehung in Korinth." In *Nachgelassene Reden und Aufsätze,* 110-39. Berlin: Töpelmann, 1952.

Schoeps, Hans Joachim. *Paul.* Translated by Harold Knight. Philadelphia: Westminster, 1961.

———. *The Theology of the Apostle in Light of Jewish Religious History.* Philadelphia: Westminster, 1959.

Schrage, Wolfgang. *Der erste Brief an die Korinther.* 4 vols. EKKNT 7/1-4. Neukirchen-Vluyn: Neukirchener, 2001.

Schreiner, Thomas R. "Law of Christ." In *Dictionary of Paul and His Letters,* edited by Gerald F. Hawthorne and Ralph P. Martin, 542-54. Downers Grove, IL: InterVarsity, 1933.

———. *The Law and Its Fulfillment: A Pauline Theology of Law.* Grand Rapids: Baker, 1993.

———. *Paul, Apostle of God's Glory: A Pauline Theology*. Downers Grove, IL: InterVarsity, 2001.

———. *Romans*. ECNT. Grand Rapids: Baker, 1998.

Schrenk, Gottlob, "ἐντέλλομαι, ἐντολή." In *TDNT* 2 (1964) 544–56.

Schweizer, Eduard. "ψυχικός." In *TDNT* 9 (1974) 661–63.

Schwyzer, Eduard. *Griechische Grammatik auf der Grundlage von Karl Brugmanns Griechischer Grammatik*. Vol. 2: *Syntax und syntaktische Stilistik*. 5th ed. Edited by Albert Debrunner. Munich: Beck, 1988.

Scott, Charles A. Anderson. *Christianity according to St. Paul*. Cambridge: Cambridge University Press, 1927.

Scroggs, Robin. *The Last Adam: A Study in Pauline Anthropology*. Philadelphia: Fortress, 1966.

———. "Romans VI.7: Ο ΓΑΡ ΑΠΟΘΑΝΩΝ ΔΕΔΙΚΑΙΩΤΑΙ ΑΠΟ ΤΗΣ ΑΜΑΡΤΙΑΣ." *NTS* 10 (1963–64) 104–8.

Segal, Alan F. *Paul the Convert: The Apostolate and Apostasy of Saul the Pharisee*. New Haven: Yale University Press, 1990.

———. "Romans 7 and Jewish Dietary Laws." *SR* 15 (1986) 361–74.

Seger, Joe D. "Gath." In *The Anchor Bible Dictionary*, edited by David Noel Freedman, 2:908–9. New York: Doubleday, 1992.

Sellin, Gerhard. *Der Streit um die Auferstehung der Toten: Eine religionsgeschichtliche und exegetische Untersuchung von 1 Korinther 15*. FRLANT 158. Göttingen: Vandenhoeck & Ruprecht, 1986.

Seneca. *Ad Lucilium Epistulae Morales*. Translated by Richard M. Gummere. 3 vols. LCL. London: Heinemann, 1920, 1925.

Senft, Christophe. "Paul et Jésus." *ETR* 84 (1985) 49–56.

———. *La Première Épître de Saint-Paul aux Corinthiens*. CNT. Neuchâtel: Delachaux & Niestlé, 1979.

Setzer, Claudia. *Resurrection of the Body in Early Judaism and Early Christianity: Doctrine, Community, and Self-Definition*. Leiden: Brill Academic, 2004.

Shakespeare, William. *Hamlet*. Edited by Harold Jenkins. Arden Shakespeare. London: Routledge, 1989.

Sharpe, John Lawrence. "Prolegomena to the Establishment of the Critical Text of the Greek Apocalypse of Moses." Ph.D. diss., Duke University, 1969.

———. "The Second Adam in the Apocalypse of Moses." *CBQ* 35 (1973) 35–46.

Shedd, William G. T. *A Critical and Doctrinal Commentary on the Epistle of St. Paul to the Romans*. 1879. Reprinted, Eugene, OR: Wipf & Stock, 2001.

*The Shepherd of Hermas*. In *The Apostolic Fathers*, 161–473. Translated by Bart D. Ehrman. 2 vols. LCL. Cambridge: Harvard University Press, 2003.

Shogren, Gary S. "The 'Wretched Man' of Romans 7:14–25 as *Reductio ad Absurdum*." *EQ* 72 (2000) 119–34.

Sibinga, Joost Smit. "1 Cor 15:8/9 and Other Divisions in 1 Cor. 15:1–11." *NovT* 49 (1997) 54–59.

Sider, Ronald J. "The Pauline Conception of the Resurrection Body in 1 Corinthians XV. 35–54." *NTS* 21 (1975) 428–39.

Simon, W. G. H. *The First Epistle to the Corinthians: Creed and Conduct*. TBC. London: SCM, 1959.

Skinner, John. *A Critical and Exegetical Commentary on Genesis*. ICC. Edinburgh: T. & T. Clark, 1930.

Sloan, Robert B. "Paul and the Law: Why the Law Cannot Save." *NovT* 33 (1991) 35–60.
Smend, Rudolph, and Ulrich Luz. *Gesetz*. Biblische Konfrontationen. Stuttgart: Kohlhammer, 1981.
Smyth, Herbert Weir. *Greek Grammar*. Cambridge: Harvard University Press, 1984.
Snodgrass, Klyne. "Spheres of Influence: A Possible Solution to the Problem of Paul and the Law." *JETS* 32 (1988) 93–113.
Soden, Hans von. "Sakrament und Ethik bei Paulus." *MTS* 1 (1931) 1–40.
Soden, Hermann von. "Rezension: Carl Clemen, *Die Einheitlichkeit der paulinischen Briefe an der Hand der bisher mit bezug auf sie aufgestellten Interpolations*" *ThLZ* 5 (1895) 128–30.
Söding, T. "'Die Kraft der Sünde is das Gesetz' (I Kor 15,56) Anmerkungen zum Hintergrund und zur Pointe einer gesetzeskritischen Sentenz des Apostels Paulus." *ZNW* 83 (1992) 74–84.
Soggin, J. Alberto. *Das Buch Genesis*. Translated by Thomas Frauenlob et al. Darmstadt: Wissenschaftliche Buchgesellschaft, 1997.
Somerville, Robert. *La première épître de Paul aux Corinthiens*. 2 vols. CEB. Vaux-sur-Seine, Fr.: Edifac, 2005.
Spanje, T. E. van. *Inconsistency in Paul? A Critique of the Work of Heikki Räisänen*. WUNT 2/110. Tübingen: Mohr/Siebeck, 1999.
Speiser, E. A. *Genesis: Introduction, Translation, and Notes*. AB 1. Garden City, NY: Doubleday, 1964.
Spencer, Aída Besançon. *Paul's Literary Style: A Stylistic and Historical Comparison of II Corinthians 11:16—12:13, Romans 8:9–39, and Philippians 3:2—4:13*. ETSM. Jackson, MS: Evangelical Theological Society, 1984.
Spicq, Ceslas. *Theological Lexicon of the New Testament*. Translated and edited by James D. Ernest. 3 vols. Peabody, MA: Hendrickson, 1994.
Spörlein, Bernhard. *Die Leugnung der Auferstehung: eine historisch-kritisch Untersuchung zu 1 Kor 15*. Biblische Untersuchungen 7. Regensburg: Pustet, 1971.
Staab, Karl. *Pauluskommentare aus der Griechischen Kirche: aus Katenenhandschriften gesammelt und herausgegeben*. NTAbh. Münster: Aschendorff, 1933.
Stählin, Gustav. "ἁμαρτάνω, ἁμάρτημα, κτλ." In *TDNT* 1 (1964) 293–96.
Stamps, Dennis L. "Rhetorical Criticism of the New Testament: Ancient and Modern Evaluations of Argumentation." In *Approaches to New Testament Studies*, edited by Stanley E. Porter and David Tombs, 129–69. JSNTSup 120. Sheffield: Sheffield Academic, 1995.
Stanley, Arthur Penrhyn. *The Epistles of St. Paul to the Corinthians: with Critical Notes and Dissertations*. 4th ed. London: John Murray, 1876.
Stanley, Christopher D. *Arguing with Scripture: The Rhetoric of Quotations in the Letters of Paul*. London: T. & T. Clark, 2004.
———. *Paul and the Language of Scripture: Citation Techniques in the Pauline Epistles and Contemporary Literature*. SNTSMS 74. Cambridge: Cambridge University Press, 1992.
Stanley, D. M. "Paul's Interest in the Early Chapters of Genesis." In *SPCIC 1961*, 1:241–52. AnBib 17–18. 2 vols. Chicago: Loyola University Press, 1963.
Starke, Robert. "The Tree of Life: Protological to Eschatological." *Kerux* 11 (1996) 15–31.
Steck, Odil Hannes. *Die Paradieserzählung: Eine Auslegung von Genesis 2,4b—3,24*. BibS(N) 60. Neukirchen-Vluyn: Neukirchener, 1970.

Stemberger, Günter. *Introduction to the Talmud and Midrash*. 2nd ed. Translated and edited by Markus Bockmuehl. Edinburgh: T. & T. Clark, 1996.

Stendahl, Krister. "The Apostle Paul and the Introspective Conscience of the West." In *Paul Among Jews and Gentiles and Other Essays*, 78–96. Philadelphia: Fortress, 1976.

———. *Final Account: Paul's Letter to the Romans*. Minneapolis: Fortress, 1995.

Stenger, W. "Beobachtungen zur Argumentationsstruktur von 1 Kor 15." *LB* 45 (1979) 71–128.

Stern, Herold S. "The Knowledge of Good and Evil." *VT* (1958) 405–18.

Stigers, Harold G. *A Commentary on Genesis*. Grand Rapids: Zondervan, 1976.

Stone, Michael E., ed. *Jewish Writings of the Second Temple Period: Apocrypha, Pseudepigrapha, Qumran Sectarian Writings, Philo, Josephus*. Philadelphia: Fortress, 1984.

Stordalen, T. *Echoes of Eden: Genesis 2–3 and Symbolism of the Eden Garden in Biblical Hebrew Literature*. BET 25. Leuven: Peeters, 2000.

Stott, John R. W. *Romans: God's Good News for the World*. Downers Grove, IL: InterVarsity, 1994.

Stowers, Stanley K. *The Diatribe and Paul's Letter to the Romans*. SBLDS 57. Chico, CA.: Scholars, 1981.

———. *A Rereading of Romans: Justice, Jews and Gentiles*. New Haven: Yale University Press, 1994.

Straatman, J. W. *Kritische Studiën over den 1en Brief van Paulus aan de Korintiërs*. Groningen: van Giffen, 1865.

Strabo. *Geographica*. Translated by Harold Leonard Jones and J. R. Sitlington Sterrett. 8 vols. LCL. Cambridge: Harvard University Press, 1917–1932.

Strack, H. L., and P. Billerbeck. *Kommentar zum Neuen Testament aus Talmud und Midrash*. 6 vols. Munich: Beck, 1922–1961.

Strelan, G. "A Note on the Old Testament Background of Romans 7:7." *Lutheran Theological Journal* 15 (1981) 23–25.

Strobel, August. *Der erste Brief an die Korinther*. ZBK. Zürich: Theologischer Verlag, 1989.

Stuart, Douglas. *Hosea–Jonah*. WBC 31. Waco, TX: Word, 1987.

Stuhlmacher, Peter. "The Law as a Topic of Biblical Theology." In *Reconciliation, Law, and Righteousness*, 110–33. Philadelphia: Fortress, 1986.

———. *Paul's Epistle to the Romans: A Commentary*. Translated by Scott J. Hafemann. Louisville: Westminster John Knox, 1994.

———. "Paul's Understanding of the Law in the Letter to the Romans." *SEÅ* 50 (1985) 87–104.

Suhl, Alfred. *Paulus und Seine Briefe ein Beitrag zur Paulinischen Chronologie*. SNT 11. Gütersloh: Gütersloher, 1975.

Talbert, Charles H. *Romans*. SHBC. Macon, GA: Smyth & Helwys, 2002.

———. "Tracing Paul's Train of Thought in Romans 6–8." *RevExp* 100 (2003) 53–63.

Tamez, Elsa. "Justification as Good News for Women: A Re-Reading of Romans 1–8." In *Celebrating Romans: Template for Pauline Theology" Essays in Honor of Robert Jewett*, edited by Sheila McGinn, 177–89. Grand Rapids: Eerdmans, 2004.

Tanna Debe Eliyyahu. *The Lord of the School of Elijah*. Translated by. William G. Braude and Israel J. Kapstein; Philadelphia: Jewish Publication Society, 1981.

Tannehill, R. C. *Dying and Rising with Christ*. BZNW 32. 1967. Reprinted, Eugene, OR: Wipf & Stock, 2006.

Theissen, Gerd. *Psychological Aspects of Pauline Theology.* Translated by John P. Galvin. Philadelphia: Fortress, 1987.
Theobald, Michael. *Römerbrief.* 2 vols. SKKNT 6. Stuttgart: Katholisches Bibelwerk, 1992.
———. *Studien Zum Römerbrief.* WUNT 136. Tübingen: Mohr/Siebeck, 2001.
Theodoret. *Interpretatio primae epistolae ad Corinthios.* In vol. 82 of *Patrologia graece.* Edited by J.-P. Migne. Paris: Migne, 1857–1886.
Thielman, Frank. "The Coherence of Paul's View of the Law: the Evidence of First Corinthians." NTS 38 (1992) 235–53.
———. *From Plight to Solution: A Jewish Framework for Understanding Paul's View of the Law in Galatians and Romans.* NovTSup 61. Leiden: Brill, 1989.
———. *Paul and the Law a Contextual Approach.* Downers Grove, IL: InterVarsity, 1994.
———. "The Story of Israel and the Theology of Romans 5–8." In *Pauline Theology: Volume III: Romans*, edited by David M. Hay and E. Elizabeth Johnson, 169–95. Minneapolis: Fortress, 1995.
———. *Theology of the New Testament: A Canonical and Synthetic Approach.* Grand Rapids: Zondervan, 2005.
Thiselton, Anthony C. *The First Epistle to the Corinthians: A Commentary on the Greek Text.* NIGTC. Grand Rapids: Eerdmans, 2000.
Thompson, J. A. "Genesis 1: Science? History? Theology?" TSF Bulletin 50 (1968) 12–23.
Thompson, Michael B. *The New Perspective on Paul.* GBS 26. Cambridge: Grove, 2005.
Thrall, Margaret E. Thrall, Margaret E. *A Critical and Exegetical Commentary on the Second Epistle to the Corinthians.* ICC. Edinburgh: T. & T. Clark, 1994.
———. *The First and Second Letters to the Corinthians.* CBC. Cambridge: Cambridge University Press, 1965.
Thurén, Lauri. *Derhetorizing Paul: A Dynamic Perspective on Pauline Theology and Law.* WUNT 124. Tübingen: Mohr/Siebeck, 2000.
Tobin, Thomas H. "The Jewish Context of Rom 5:12-14." SPhilo 13 (2001) 159–75.
———. *Paul's Rhetoric in Its Context: The Argument of Romans.* Peabody, MA: Hendrickson, 2004.
Toews, John E. *Romans.* BCBC. Scottsdale, AZ: Herald, 2004.
Toorn, Karel van der et al., editors. *Dictionary of Deities and Demons in the Bible.* 2nd ed. Leiden: Brill, 1999.
Townsend, John T. *Midrash Tanhuma (S. Buber Recension).* 2 vols. Hoboken, NJ: Ktav, 1997.
Townsend, P. Wayne. "Eve's Answer to the Serpent: An Alternative Paradigm for Sin and Some Implications in Theology." CTJ 33 (1998) 399–420.
Trail, Ronald L. *An Exegetical Summary of 1 Corinthians 10–16.* Dallas: SIL, 2001.
Trible, Phyllis. *God and the Rhetoric of Sexuality.* Overtures to Biblical Theology. Philadelphia: Fortress, 1978.
Tromp, Johannes. *The Life of Adam and Eve: A Critical Edition.* PVTG 16. Leiden: Brill, 2005.
Turner, Nigel. *Syntax.* Vol. 3: *A Grammar of New Testament Greek*, by J. H. Moulton. Edinburgh: T. & T. Clark, 1963.
Urbach, Efraim Elimelech. *The Sages: Their Concepts and Beliefs.* 2 vols. Jerusalem: Magnes, 1979.
Usami, Kôshi. "'How Are the Dead Raised?' (1 Cor 15:35–58)." Bib 57 (1976) 468–93.

VanGemeren. William A. ed. *The New International Dictionary of Old Testament Theology and Exegesis*. 5 vols. Grand Rapids: Zondervan, 1997.

———. "The Story of Cain and Abel: A Narrative Study." *JSOT* 52 (1991) 25–41.

Vawter, Bruce. *On Genesis: A New Reading*. Garden City, NY: Doubleday, 1977.

Verburg, Winfried. *Endzeit und Entschlafene: Syntaktisch-sigmatische, semantische und pragmatische Analyse von 1 Kor 15*. FB 78. Würzburg: Echter, 1996.

Vergote, Antoine. "Der Beitrag der Psychoanalyse zur Exegesis: Leben, Gesetz und Ich-Spaltung im 7. Kapitel des Römerbriefs." In *Exegese im Methodenkonflikt: Zwischen Geschichte und Struktur*, edited by Xavier Léon-Dufour, 73–116. Munich: Kösel, 1973.

Vermes, Geza, *Post Biblical Jewish Studies*. SJLA 8. Leiden: Brill, 1975.

Versteeg, J. P. *Is Adam a 'Teaching Model' in the New Testament?: An Examination of One of the Central Points in the Views of H. M. Kuitert and Others*. Translated by Richard B. Gaffin Jr. Philadelphia: Presbyterian & Reformed, 1977.

Vicuña, Maximo. "1 Corintios 15:54b–57, un canto anticipado de victoria sobre la muerte: un Midrashim en el NT." *TBib* 3 (1988) 4–19.

Visotzky, Burton L., translator. *The Midrash on the Proverbs*. New Haven: Yale University Press, 1992.

Vlachos, Chris Alex. "Law, Sin, and Death: An Edenic Triad? An Examination with Reference to 1 Corinthians 15:56." *JETS* 48 (2004) 277–98.

Vogels, Walter. "'Like one of us, knowing *tôb and ra*ʿ." *Semeia* 81 (1998) 145–57.

Vollenweider, Samuel. *Freiheit als neue Schöpfung: Eine Untersuchung zur Eleutheria bei Paulus und in seiner Umwelt*. FRLANT 147. Göttingen: Vandenhoeck & Ruprecht, 1989.

Vollmer, Hans. *Die Alttestamentlichen Citate bei Paulus: textkritisch und biblischtheologisch gewürdigt nebst einem Anhang ueber das Verhältnis des Apostels zu Philo*. Freiburg: Mohr/Siebeck, 1895.

Volter, Daniel. "Ein Votum zur Frage nach der Echtheit, Integrität und Composition der vier paulinischen Hauptbriefe." *ThT* (1889) 265–325.

Vos, Johan S. "Argumentation und Situation in 1Kor. 15." *NovT* 41 (1999) 313–33.

Vriezen, Th. C. *Onderzoek naar de paradijsvoorstelling bij de oude Semietische volken*. Wageningen: Veenman, 1937.

———. *An Outline of Old Testament Theology*. Translated by S. Neuijen. Newton, MA: Branford, 1970.

Wacholder, Ben Zion. "The Date of the Mekilta de-Rabbi Ishmael." *HUCA* 39 (1968) 117–44.

Wallace, Daniel B. *Greek Grammar Beyond the Basics: An Exegetical Syntax of the New Testament*. Grand Rapids: Zondervan, 1996.

Wallace, Howard N. *The Eden Narrative*. HSM 32. Atlanta: Scholars, 1985.

Walsh, J. T. "Gen 2:4b—3:24: A Synchronic Approach." *JBL* 96 (1977) 161–77.

Waltke, Bruce K. *Genesis: A Commentary*. Grand Rapids: Zondervan, 2001.

Waltke, Bruce K., and M. O'Connor. *An Introduction to Biblical Hebrew Syntax*. Winona Lake, IN: Eisenbrauns, 1990.

Walton, John. *Genesis: The NIV Application Bible: From Biblical Text to Contemporary Life*. The NIV Application Commentary Series. Grand Rapids: Zondervan, 2001.

Waters, Guy Prentiss. *Justification and the New Perspectives on Paul: A Review and Response*. Phillipsburg, NJ: Presbyterian & Reformed, 2004.

Watson, D. F. "Paul's Rhetorical Strategy in 1 Cor 15." In *Rhetoric and the New Testament: Essays from the 1992 Heidelberg Conference*, edited by Stanley E. Porter and Thomas H. Olbricht, 231–49. JSNTSup 90. Sheffield: Sheffield Academic, 1993.

Watson, Francis. *Paul and the Hermeneutics of Faith*. London: T. & T. Clark, 2005.

———. *Paul, Judaism and the Gentiles*. SNTSMS 56. Cambridge: Cambridge University Press, 1986.

Watson, N. M. "The Interpretation of Romans VII." *ABR* 21 (1973) 17–39.

Watson, Nigel. *The First Epistle to the Corinthians*. EC. London: Epworth, 1992.

Weber, Reinhard. "Die Geschichte des Gesetzes und des Ich in Römer 7,7—8,4: Einige Überlegungen zum Zusammenhang von Heilgeschichte und Anthropologie im Blick auf die theologische Grundstellung des paulinischen Denkens." *NZSTR* 29 (1987) 147–79.

Webber, Randall. "A Note on 1 Corinthians 15:3–5." *JETS* 26 (1983) 265–69.

Wedderburn, A. J. M. "Adam in Paul's Letter to the Romans." In *Studia Biblica 1978: Papers on Paul and Other New Testament Authors*, edited by Elizabeth A. Livingstone, 413–30. JSNTSup 3. Sheffield: JSOT Press, 1980.

———. "Philo's 'Heavenly Man.'" *NovT* 15 (1973) 301–26.

———. "The Problem of the Denial of the Resurrection in 1 Corinthians XV." *NovT* 23 (1981) 229–41.

———. "The Theological Structure of Romans V. 12." *NTS* 19 (1972–73) 339–54.

Weder, Hans. "Gesetz und Sünde: Gedanken zu einem qualitative Sprung im Denken des Paulus." *NTS* 31 (1985) 357–76.

Wegener, Mark I. "The Rhetorical Strategy of 1 Corinthians 15." *CurTM* 31 (2004) 438–55.

Weima, Jeffrey A. D. "The Function of the Law in Relation to Sin: An Evaluation of the View of H. Räisänen." *NovT* 32 (1990) 219–35.

———. "What Does Aristotle Have to Do with Paul? An Evaluation of Rhetorical Criticism." *CTJ* (1997) 458–68.

Weiß, Johannes. *Der erste Korintherbrief*. KEK 9. Göttingen: Vandenhoeck & Ruprecht, 1910.

Wellhausen, Julius. *Prolegomena zur Geschichte Israels*. 6th ed. Berlin: de Gruyter, 2001.

Wendland, Heinz Dietrich. *Die Briefe an die Korinther*. Göttingen: Vandenhoeck & Ruprecht, 1968.

Wenham, David. "Whatever Went Wrong in Corinth?" *ExpTim* 108 (1997) 137–41.

Wenham, Gordon J. *Genesis*. WBC 1, 2. Waco, TX: Word, 1987, 1994.

———. "Sanctuary Symbolism in the Garden of Eden Story." *PWCJS* 9 (1986) 19–25.

Wenin, A. "Adam et Eve: la jealousie de Caïn, 'semence' du serpent: Un aspect du récit mythique de Genèse 1–4." *RevScRel* 73 (1999) 3–16.

Westerholm, Stephen. *Israel's Law and the Church's Faith: Paul and His Recent Interpreters*. Grand Rapids: Eerdmans, 1988.

———. "Letter and Spirit: The Foundation of Pauline *Ethics*." *NTS* 30 (1984) 229–48.

———. "The 'New Perspective' at Twenty-Five." In *Justification and Variegated Nomism: Volume II: The Paradoxes of Paul*, edited by D. A. Carson et al., 1–38 WUNT 2/181. Tübingen: Mohr/Siebeck, 2004.

———. "On Fulfilling the Whole Law (Gal. 5:14)." *SEÅ* 51–52 (1986–87) 229–37.

———. *Perspectives Old and New on Paul: The "Lutheran" Paul and His Critics*. Grand Rapids: Eerdmans, 2004.

Westermann, Claus. *Creation*. Translated by John J. Scullion. Philadelphia: Fortress, 1974.

———. *Genesis: A Commentary*. 3 vols. Translated by John J. Scullion. CC. Minneapolis: Augsburg, 1984–1986.

———. *Genesis: A Practical Commentary*. Translated by David Green. TI. Grand Rapids: Eerdmans, 1987.

Wevers, John William. *Text History of the Greek Genesis*. Göttingen: Vandenhoeck & Ruprecht, 1974.

Whitely, D. E. H. *The Theology of St. Paul*. Oxford: Blackwell, 1964.

Wilckens, Ulrich. *Der Brief an die Römer*. 3 vols. EKKNT 6/1–3. Neukirchen-Vluyn: Neukirchener, 1980.

———. "Statements on the Development of the Law." In *Paul and Paulinism: Essays in Honor of C. K. Barrett*, edited by M. D. Hooker and S. G. Wilson, 17–26. London: SPCK, 1982.

———. "Was heißt bei Paulus: 'aus Werken des Gesetzes wird kein Mensch gerecht?'" In *Rechtfertigung als Freiheit*. Neukirchen-Vluyn: Neukirchener, 1974.

———. *Weisheit und Torheit: eine exegetisch-religions-geschichtliche Untersuchung zu 1. Kor. 1 und 2*. BHT 26. Tübingen: Mohr/Siebeck, 1959.

———. "Zur Entwicklung des paulinischen Gesetzesverständnisses." *NTS* 28 (1982) 154–90.

Williams, Jay. "Genesis 3." *Int* 35 (1981) 274–79.

Wills, Garry. *Lincoln at Gettysburg: The Words That Remade America*. New York: Simon & Schuster, 1992.

Wilson, Jack H. "The Corinthians Who Say There Is No Resurrection of the Dead." *ZNW* 58 (1968) 90–107.

Winandy, Jacques. "La mort de Jésus: une mort au péché?" *ETL* 76 (2000) 433–34.

Windisch, Hans. *Der zweite Korintherbrief*. KEK 6. Göttingen: Vandenhoeck & Ruprecht, 1924.

Winer, George Benedict. *A Grammar of the Idiom of the New Testament: Prepared As a Solid Basis for the Interpretation of the New Testament*. 7th ed. Edited by Gottlieb Lünemann. Andover: Draper, 1872.

Winger, Michael. *By What Law? The Meaning of Νόμος in the Letters of Paul*. SBLDS 128. Atlanta: Scholars, 1992.

Witherington, Ben III. *Conflict and Community in Corinth: A Socio-Rhetorical Commentary on 1 and 2 Corinthians*. Grand Rapids: Eerdmans, 1995.

———. *Paul's Letter to the Romans: A Socio-Rhetorical Commentary*. Grand Rapids: Eerdmans, 2004.

———. *Paul's Narrative Thought World*. Louisville: Westminster John Knox, 1994.

Wolde, Ellen J. van. *A Semiotic Analysis of Genesis 2–3: A Semiotic Theory and Method of Analysis Applied to the Story of the Garden of Eden*. SSN 25. Assen, The Netherlands: Van Gorcum, 1989.

Wolff, Christian. *Der erste Brief des Paulus an die Korinther*. THKNT 7. Leipzig: Evangelische Verlagsanstalt, 1996.

———. *Der zweite Brief des Paulus an die Korinther*. THKNT 8. Berlin: Evangelische Verlagsanstalt, 1989.

Wolff, Hans Walter. *Hosea*. Translated by Gary Stansell. Hermeneia. Philadelphia: Fortress, 1974.

Wöller, Ulrich. "Zu Gen 4,7." *ZAW* 91 (1979) 436.

———. "Zu Gen 4,7." *ZAW* 96 (1984) 271–72.

Wright, N. T. "Adam in Pauline Christology." In *SBLSP* 22, edited by Kent Harold Richards, 359–89. Chico, CA: Scholars, 1983.

———. *Climax of the Covenant: Christ and the Law in Pauline Theology*. Minneapolis: Fortress, 1992.

———. "The Letter to the Romans: Introduction, Commentary, and Reflections." In *The New Interpreter's Bible: General Articles and Introduction, Commentary, and Reflections for Each Book of the Bible, Including the Apocryphal/ Deuterocanonical Books*, edited by Leander E. Keck, 10:393–770. Nashville: Abingdon, 2002.

———. "The Messiah and the People of God." Ph.D. diss., Oxford University, 1980.

———. *Paul for Everyone: 1 Corinthians*. Louisville: Westminster John Knox, 2004.

———. *Paul: In Fresh Perspective*. Minneapolis: Fortress, 2005.

———. "The Paul of History and the Apostle of Faith." *TynBul* 29 (1978) 61–88.

———. *The Resurrection of the Son of God*. London: SPCK, 2003.

———. "Romans and the Theology of Paul." In *Pauline Theology: Volume III: Romans*, edited by David M. Hay and E. Elizabeth Johnson, 30–67. Minneapolis: Fortress, 1995.

Xenophon. *Memorabilia*. Translated by Amy L. Bonnette. Ithaca, NY: Cornell University Press, 1994.

Yarbrough, Robert. "Paul and Salvation History." In *Justification and Variegated Nomism: Volume II: The Paradoxes of Paul*, edited by D. A. Carson et al., 297–43. WUNT 2/181. Tübingen: Mohr/Siebeck, 2004.

Young, Edward J. *Genesis 3: A Devotional and Expository Study*. London: Banner of Truth, 1966.

Zahn, Theodor. *Der Brief des Paulus an die Römer*. KNT. Leipzig: Deicherterscher, 1910.

Zeller, Dieter. *Der Brief an die Römer*. Regensburg: Pustet, 1985.

———. "Der Zusammenhang von Gesetz und Sünde im Römerbrief: Kritischer Nachvollzug der Auslegung von Ulrich Wilckens." *TZ* 38 (1982) 193–212.

Ziesler, John. *Paul's Letter to the Romans*. TPINTC. London: SCM, 1989.

———. "The Role of the Tenth Commandment in Romans 7." *JSNT* 33 (1988) 41–56.

Zimmerli, Walther. *1. Mose*. 2 vols. ZBK. Zürich: Zwingli, 1967, 1976.

———. *The Law and the Prophets: A Study of the Meaning of the Old Testament*. Translated by R. E. Clements. Oxford: Blackwell, 1965.

Žižek, Slavoj. *The Puppet and the Dwarf: The Perverse Core of Christianity*. Short Circuits. Cambridge: MIT Press, 2003.

Zlotowitz, Meir, and Nosson Scherman. *Bereishis = Genesis: [Sefer Bereshit] A New Translation with a Commentary Anthologized from Talmudic, Midrashic and Rabbinic Sources*. ArtScroll Tanach Series. Brooklyn: Mesorah, 1986.

Zobel, H.-J. "Bileam-Lieder und Bileam-Erzählung." In *Die hebraische Bibel und ihre zweifache Nachgeschichte: Festschrift für Rolf Rendtorff zum 65. Geburtstag*, edited by E. Blum et al. 141–54. Neukirchen-Vluyn: Neukirchener, 1990.

www.ingramcontent.com/pod-product-compliance
Lightning Source LLC
Chambersburg PA
CBHW061430300426
44114CB00014B/1616